THE MESSIAEN COMPANION

in the same series

THE NEW MONTEVERDI COMPANION
Denis Arnold and Nigel Fortune

THE PURCELL COMPANION
Michael Burden

THE MOZART COMPANION
H. C. Robbins Landon and Donald Mitchell

THE BEETHOVEN COMPANION
Denis Arnold and Nigel Fortune

THE BARTÓK COMPANION
Malcolm Gillies

THE NIELSEN COMPANION
Mina Miller

THE MESSIAEN COMPANION

edited by

PETER HILL

faber and faber

LONDON · BOSTON

First published in 1995
by Faber and Faber Limited
3 Queen Square, London, WC1N 3AU

Phototypeset in Sabon by Intype, London
Music examples typeset by Linda Lancaster
Printed in England by Clays Ltd, St Ives Plc

A CIP record for this book is available from the British Library

ISBN 0-571-16651-2 (cased)
0-571-17033-1 (pbk)

2 4 6 8 10 9 7 5 3 1

in memoriam
OLIVIER MESSIAEN
1908–1992

Contents

Illustrations

Foreword

With Messiaen's death, on 28 April 1992, music lost a figure remarkable for this or any age. Almost alone among the supreme artists of the twentieth century Messiaen was an optimist, so that even his most radical ventures into new territory were never mere dabbling with the bizarre, but always embedded in a clear purpose and conviction. Indeed the key to his achievement – and to his paradoxical position in musical history – is that he combined in the highest degree the mind of an innovator, of an explorer, with skills and beliefs which were rooted in tradition. A musician's musician – organist, pianist, improviser, and with a musical ear of legendary acuteness – the musical heritage which he had at his fingertips seems never to have hampered his decisive originality (any more than did his lifelong, unquestioning commitment to Catholicism). In this respect, among his near contemporaries only Bartók was his equal; and, like Bartók, for all his uncompromising intelligence Messiaen had at his heart a simplicity which makes his music universal.

The Messiaen Companion is the first major study since Messiaen's death, the first to view his life as a completed whole. There is necessary catching-up to be done, with an account of the last works (including the posthumously premiered *Eclairs sur l'au-delà*), and a reappraisal of the masterpieces of the 1960s and 1970s. Where previous accounts of Messiaen have tended to view him as a vast but monolithic presence, the portrait that emerges here is complex and many-sided. In part this is a reflection of the talents and interests of my contributors; significantly, a number of these are practising musicians, and indeed, almost all bridge the worlds of scholarship and music as a living art. But the book's diversity is also a consequence of its design, which focuses not only on Messiaen's music but on other aspects of his achievement.

The *Companion* falls into two very unequal halves, dividing around 1950, a time of radical new departures after the climactic achievement of *Turangalîla*. In the Interlude, a series of essays consider the inspiration of nature, and birdsong in particular; Messiaen's highly idiosyncratic approach to colour; and his theological outlook is set in context, and examined in relation to the *Quatuor pour la fin du temps*. The section concludes with tributes to Messiaen as a teacher, and an interview with the composer's widow, Yvonne Loriod-Messiaen, which contains much previously unrecorded biographical detail.

Before expressing my thanks to the numerous individuals who have helped in the preparation of this book, I should first like to record my deep gratitude to Messiaen himself, who advised, encouraged and inspired me in the study and performance of his music, and gave me unstintingly of his time. My profound thanks also to Mme Loriod-Messiaen, not only for her contribution to the book, but for making available unpublished material, and for her kindness and hospitality over many years.

The generous provision of music examples has been made possible by the willing co-operation of Messiaen's publishers: Durand et Cie, Alphonse Leduc et Cie, Editions Salabert and Universal Edition. I am most grateful to the staff at Faber and Faber for help at every stage of the book's genesis, in particular Helen Sprott, Andrew Clements, Jane Feaver and David Watson; to Elizabeth Holloway and Virginia Messenger for secretarial help, and to Ruth Jordan who transcribed meticulously the interview with Yvonne Loriod. I also received invaluable assistance from Christopher Sayward (of United Music Publishers) and Timothy Day of the National Sound Archive. Among friends and family who advised and encouraged were Bob Auger (engineer of all my recordings of Messiaen), George Benjamin, Malcolm MacDonald, Anthony Pople, and last (though she should be first) my wife, Charlotte, who was a constructive critic of my first drafts, and gave me constant support and encouragement. My particular thanks go to Christopher Dingle, who not only supplied the invaluable Catalogue of Works and Discography but placed his encyclopaedic learning at the service of eliminating errors; and finally to Ingrid Grimes, my dedicated copy-editor, who rooted out inconsistency and infelicity from my far from immaculate typescript, and who, moreover, contributed countless positive suggestions which have been immeasurably to the book's benefit.

Sheffield
September 1994

PETER HILL

Introduction

PETER HILL

Olivier Messiaen's life is remarkable for its scale. With a composing career spanning seven decades, only Stravinsky, of the major figures of the twentieth century, is his equal. Unlike Stravinsky, however, and unlike either Tippett or Carter (both, like Messiaen, composers active in their eighties) Messiaen was astonishingly precocious, still only in his teens when he reached a first maturity, if by that one means the discovery of a voice uniquely and unmistakably his own. Indeed Messiaen's life is best described as a series of maturities, his achievements coming in waves, given impetus by periods of self-renewal, undertaken either in response to circumstance or as conscious experiment. By far the most significant occurred around 1950, a sea-change reflected in the design of this book, which divides the music before and after this date with an interlude, a group of essays exploring facets of Messiaen's work. But although it is possible to separate Messiaen's life into sections, to do so is, in his case, especially artificial; for perhaps Messiaen's most remarkable trait was the firmness with which he kept faith with a basic set of principles, so that the language (and to a very great degree the technique) of Messiaen's earliest music is still apparent in the music composed sixty or so years later.

This unity was important to Messiaen as the means by which he kept to his course through the artistic upheavals of his time; yet it was not bought at the price of sealing off the outside world. On the contrary, Messiaen's life (from his mid-thirties) was increasingly a public one: he was active as organist, teacher and performer (and for the last three decades in worldwide demand at concerts of his music), with only the precious summer break reserved for privacy and composing. More than this, one of Messiaen's most engaging qualities, remarked on by all his pupils, was his curiosity. He seemed constantly alert to new experiences, renewing his art through researches into a vast range of music – ancient, exotic and ultra-modern – besides the collecting of birdsongs, which in later years took him to ever more remote parts of the world (so much so that even Yvonne Loriod, his wife and devoted musical companion, could be driven to exasperation: see p. 297).

Although Messiaen cast his net widely, certain fundamentals were ever-present. The main sources of inspiration are reflected on the bookshelves of his study in Paris. Prominent are the volumes of Shakespeare in the translation by his father, Pierre. The lower shelves are occupied by musical scores, while above space is equally divided between books on birds (in Messiaen's own view he was as much ornithologist as musician) and works of theology. This modest room, left exactly as it was at the time of Messiaen's death, is symbolic of the anomaly which struck all who met him: that the composer of music so transcendent in ambition and scale should have lived life so simply. Quietly spoken, Messiaen explained himself with the calm lucidity of the practised teacher. He possessed exceptional clarity of mind, and applied the same methodical care to all aspects of his life. His attention to detail was legendary, and in the more mundane duties of a composer he led his pupils by example, prescribing in his scores every detail of fingering or registration, and taking immense pains to eliminate all trace of ambiguity, let alone error. His students were amazed that so eminent a musician should devote so much time to teaching; and he was similarly punctilious over his duties at La Trinité, where neither age nor infirmity would deter him from climbing the sixty or so steps to the organ loft in order to accompany Sunday services.

The image of Messiaen as in some way a reincarnation of the medieval artist–craftsman has contributed to a misconceived view of him as standing outside the main preoccupations of twentieth-century music. It is true that, in an age which has invented restrictions for itself as fast as it has knocked them down, Messiaen's imperviousness in the face of the artistic dogma of the moment frequently irritated his critics. Like all people who swim against the tide of sophisticated opinion he found himself classified as naive, too gifted to be ignored, but eccentric and peripheral. At a time when to do so was deeply unfashionable Messiaen retained an unshakable faith in music's power to describe or symbolize. Even to some of his pupils this seemed perverse, or perhaps endearingly quaint, although arguably it is this fearless lack of all inhibition which is the greatest contribution Messiaen made to the music of his era. Almost single-handedly he embodied a kind of musical counter-reformation, in revolt against austerity, engaging in his music with the central issue of existence at a time when many composers have confined themselves to the margins of experience.

Not that Messiaen was unaware of his isolated position; indeed he was abnormally sensitive to adverse criticism, and the same sensitivity made him fanatically secretive about work in progress (concerning which any enquiry would receive a polite but unmistakable snub). Rather he seems to have developed at an early age a quite exceptional independence of mind. Even the Catholicism which was central to his life seems not to have been acquired from his parents,[1] while his formative musical experiences came through exploring operatic scores at the piano by himself – all before the age of ten,[2] a testimony to the early development of his consummate musical skills. Nonetheless in childhood the artistic stimulus was as much literary as musical – from his mother, the poetess Cécile Sauvage, as well as from his father; and Messiaen retained a vast knowledge of poetry which he could quote freely and accurately, including the English Romantics, from whom came the inspiration for his first known composition, *La dame du Shalott*. Messiaen was fond, also, of recalling the performances of Shakespeare that he enacted with his younger brother, and the toy theatre he constructed with lighting improvised by means of transparent coloured sweet papers; no doubt it was the pageantry and the magical which appealed, though the evidence is that Messiaen's literary gifts were at least as precocious as his music.

Messiaen might have been a writer, not musician, had it not been for the decisive impact of a score of Debussy's *Pelléas*, a gift on his tenth birthday; even before this, if one gives credence to the story recounted by Yvonne Loriod (see p. 297)[3] came a discovery which appealed to the latent musician – the love of birds, and the beginnings of Messiaen's belief, adhered to with increasing conviction, that their song is neither twittering ornament nor merely signals of defence and recognition, but *music*. Another prophetic revelation, combining the architecture of the Middle Ages with the sensuous shock of colour, came when his father and mother took him to the Ste Chapelle; the marvel of this early experience remained so vivid that Messiaen repeatedly used the example of stained glass to explain his music, citing the ways in which the details of the multicoloured mosaic, when viewed from a distance, fuse into a single entity, whose purpose (again as in Messiaen's music) is not only to represent or instruct, but to 'dazzle'.

> Stained glass is one of the most wonderful creations of man. You are overwhelmed. And I think this is the beginning of Paradise, because in Paradise we are overwhelmed. We won't understand God, but we will begin to see Him a little . . . Real music, beautiful music – you can listen to it without understanding it: you don't need to have studied harmony or orchestration. You must *feel* it. And here, also, one is overwhelmed – by the shock of the sound.[4]

Faith, as Messiaen repeatedly emphasized, was his sole reason for composing; yet this side of Messiaen has in the past created difficulties – as much for Catholic as non-Catholic listeners, although today it may seem less of an obstacle to a generation which values the visionary and numinous in the music of Pärt, Tavener, Harvey or Górecki. One does not have to share an artist's beliefs in order to respond to his art. And the experience of Messiaen's music is so all-consuming, and so completely overrides mundane critical responses, that it is difficult to see how one can (as some claim) choose what appeals from Messiaen's menu and ignore the rest. Even the structure of the music seems permeated by his faith, with complexity of detail embracing truths of great simplicity (a combination which has traditionally given Catholicism its appeal to sophisticated minds, and which, similarly, may go some way to explain the potency of Messiaen's music).

Religion leads also to a central paradox whereby music, an art which exists in the here-and-now, in measured time, is used by Messiaen to convey mysteries which lie *beyond* time. This expression of what Paul Griffiths calls 'the eternal within the temporal'[5] causes Messiaen to stand apart from the Western tradition (since the Renaissance, at least) in which musical events are ordered into a directional sequence or 'narrative'. Messiaen's music accumulates, but it does not *develop* (in the accepted sense) or argue. In part this is because Messiaen's acceptance of his faith is so complete that he is simply not concerned with the strains and tensions which are the stuff of drama in music. Indeed Messiaen recognized (notwithstanding that many of his early discoveries were in drama or opera – Shakespeare, Gluck, Mozart, Wagner) that he himself was not naturally suited to the theatre, and it was to take a sustained campaign (see p. 299) to persuade him to change his mind.

This does not mean (as is often said) that Messiaen's music is completely static; indeed, as Griffith's phrase so perfectly suggests, the essence of time in Messiaen's music is that it is ambiguous. In the harmonies of Messiaen's early music, it is true that his characteristic chords blur the distinction between consonance and dissonance, and so neutralize the means (through the preparation of tension and its subsequent release) whereby harmony is harnessed to a rhythmic flow. On the other hand, the same characteristics seem also to search, as if for some elusive closure, and have a yearning quality or 'sweetness' which gives the music its peculiar intensity. Moreover Messiaen early developed a range of strategies for welding ideas into larger paragraphs. Indeed, if one of the apparently timeless contemplations is played rapidly the result is instructive, for what is revealed is a carefully engineered momentum. Played as it should be, at Messiaen's exceptionally slow tempo, the structure is perceptible, but only dimly so, like the vault of a darkened cathedral. Moreover the effect is not only calm but strangely filled with tension; in part this is because such pieces as 'Louange à l'éternité de Jésus' (the cello solo from *Quatuor pour la fin du temps*) require nerveless control to perform, as any cellist who has felt the bow begin to tremble can testify. More than this, they are also mysteriously dramatic: for one of Messiaen's supreme gifts, apparent from his earliest music, was his mastery of vast segments of time – the ability to release ideas at the precise moment and context which enables them to strike with the force of sudden revelation. The question of time is fundamental to any study of Messiaen, and it becomes a complex and subtle issue because of his ability to counterpoint 'floating' and directional time (as he does very simply, but very effectively, in the 'Amen de la création', first of the *Visions de l'Amen*). Indeed, from *Cantéyodjayâ* (1949) onward, this counterpoint becomes the principal driving force, the key to grasping music which is all too often categorized (rather helplessly) as 'block' structure.

Many of Messiaen's procedures are described in the personal textbook, *Technique de mon langage musical*, written in the early 1940s. As much as anything the book is important for what it reveals about Messiaen's mind, and in particular of his obsession for categories and catalogues. After a preliminary page of typically fulsome prose, the book guides the reader through the composer's workshop, with its rows of tools neatly labelled as to their use. In one way Messiaen's mania for order provided a means of self-defence: because his method of analysis involved taking a new stimulus and boiling it down to a basic set of principles, separating out its strands and treating these in isolation, he was able to absorb influence in details rather than in essence, and so without compromise to his personal voice. Although the impression the book gives is somewhat claustrophobic, seeming to describe a closed world, one of such certainty and completeness that further progress is excluded, for Messiaen it seems to have acted as a springboard. For at the time the book was being sketched Messiaen was in the middle of one of those periodic self-renewals which recurred at regular intervals throughout his life. In the 1930s Messiaen's world had been centred on La Trinité, to which he was appointed as organist in 1931, and where he continued to serve until the end of his life. Early photos reinforce the image of Messiaen as a specialist organist–composer, an earnest bespectacled figure immured in the vast reverberations of La Trinité. This would be to ignore evidence of wider ambition in the resplendent orchestral works of these years and the song cycles, to poems by Messiaen, which celebrate in specifically Catholic imagery the joys of marriage (to the violinist Claire Delbos) and the birth of their son. Nonetheless the events of 1940–1 were – as Malcolm Hayes argues (see pp. 80–1) – decisive. The chaos and horror of war, which Messiaen witnessed at first hand, brought unlooked-for blessings. In prison-camp he somehow found the inspiration, the will and the means to compose; later, after repatriation in 1941, the persecution of the Jews in occupied Paris indirectly gave him a new pupil (see pp. 288–9), a young pianist Yvonne Loriod, who was to have an immediate and decisive influence on the future course of his music.

Messiaen's name became known to a wider public during the 1940s, particularly following the close proximity of three first performances in 1945 – of the *Vingt regards*, *Trois petites liturgies* and *Harawi*. One indication of this was Messiaen's first important commission – from Koussevitsky and the Boston Philharmonic – for an orchestral work, on which Messiaen began work in 1946: *Turangalîla*'s premiere in 1949 was to crown the most productive decade in Messiaen's life, a time when, as he himself observed, his powers seemed invincible. (The achievements of these years seem all the more astounding when set against the difficult and tragic circumstances of Messiaen's personal life – the illness of his wife who was to die prematurely, in 1959, after years in a mental institution.) The decade was to end, strangely, in the only apparent crisis in his composing life, precipitated not by adverse criticism but as a result of his own teaching. Since his repatriation, Messiaen had been giving classes in analysis, at first unofficial, later (in 1947) incorporated into the Paris Conservatoire. Messiaen's ability to elucidate 'forbidden' modern scores (of Stravinsky, Berg and Schoenberg) together with revelatory forays into non-Western music, attracted the brightest, most adventurous students, a generation whose natural spokesman was the young Pierre Boulez (' "furious" . . . like a lion that had been flayed alive, he was terrible', Messiaen was to recall).[7] In this climate of iconoclasm Messiaen launched into a brief period (1949–51) of radical experiment. For the first and only time his music became a central influence on his younger contemporaries; yet for Messiaen the works of these years represented a cul-de-sac, a temporary aberration which he later came to dislike and disavow. Messiaen's gloom is recalled by Alexander Goehr, a member of his class in the mid-1950s:

> One of the class-members had been particularly argumentative. Messiaen sat in silence for what seemed an eternity, visibly upset. The bust of a disapproving Gounod (the class met in the Salle Gounod) reflected inwards from the already darkened window. He said: 'Gentlemen, there's no point in arguing, we are all in the dark nowadays. Nobody knows what they are doing.'[8]

But for Messiaen there was a way forward. In the same year (1951) that he recorded the *Quatre études de rythme* for solo piano (a project funded by UNESCO to illustrate the ultimate in modernism) Messiaen composed a slight but masterly test piece for a flute competition, *Le merle noir*. This, the first work entirely based on birdsong, heralds a decade during which birdsong became Messiaen's exclusive concern. Was birdsong a retreat – from a world of disintegrating tradition, in which Messiaen faced with some desperation classes of would-be avant gardists, not above making fun of their teacher's quirks? Or, as Malcolm Troup argues in the course of his chapter, was it Messiaen's way of bringing into his own music the concerns of the avant garde – the open-ended musical forms, the fluid structuring of time (with Stockhausen-like 'moments') and, above all, the incorporating into music of 'non-musical' sources of sound?

Nowhere are the contradictions in Messiaen more vividly illustrated than in his approach to birdsong. The birdsong choruses of *Oiseaux exotiques* and *Chronochromie* impress with a granite-like strength which excludes all false prettiness. They are translations of course, into a language which is Messiaen's; nonetheless they have an air of objectivity which reflects the thoroughness of Messiaen's research. He took immense pains over authenticity, studying and notating in the field, shadowed always by Yvonne Loriod with primitive tape recorder, and regularly seeking the advice of expert ornithologists, with again that obsessive regard for detail which is so characteristic. In this Messiaen is unique: the first and only composer literally to set up his canvas (in his case the manuscript paper and tape recorder) and draw nature from life.

On the other hand the motivation for this care was not science but love. Birds were from the first as important to Messiaen as the spiritual inspiration with which, in his case, they are inseparably linked. For Messiaen, moreover, they were a source of 'pure' music, undefiled by the modern world. Despite this view, it would be wrong to link Messiaen with those artists who see nature nostalgically, as a symbol of lost innocence. Messiaen portrayed birds unsentimentally, although – as he was the first to admit – anthropomorphically, for their 'character' as much as for the contours of their song.

The premiere of *Chronochromie* was to be the last occasion on which Messiaen's music raised a storm of protest, provoked by the 'Epode' with its tangled complex of song. In his last decades, increasing fame, and particularly the opportunity this gave to travel, acted as a spur to the constant process of self-renewal, as instanced by the visits to Japan (1962) and Utah (1972). Nor was there the slightest diminishing of creative ambition; indeed, from the mid-1960s, Messiaen's energies were focused in a succession of massive works, any one of which might have served as the *summa* of his life's work. His most ambitious, the opera on the life of St Francis, was a challenge which Messiaen accepted only after agonizing self-doubt, and on which he worked in conditions of rigorous secrecy. This, the boldest venture of his career, undertaken when he was approaching seventy, left him exhausted; but he was lured back to composing (see p. 347) and the result was a series of uncharacteristically brief works, in which again there was a renewal and refreshing of vision – in the acerbic high spirits of the birdsong sketches [*Esquisses*] for solo piano or the delectable homage to Mozart, *Un sourire* – preparatory to the prophetic *Eclairs sur l'au-delà*, at which he worked during his final illness with the indomitable stubbornness and tenacity so much a part of this remarkable man.

In old age Messiaen, like Stravinsky, became a sort of historic monument and, again like Stravinsky, found himself much interviewed (although these conversations, read carefully, show Messiaen remaining to the end essentially secretive about his art). In some ways the present uncritical acceptance of Messiaen's stature may do a disservice to our appreciation of his art, blunting the music's edge, its power to startle and amaze. To Messiaen himself, who could never put out of his mind the slights of former times, the universal adulation held a hollow ring, proud though he was of the honours and distinctions which came his way. Against this background *The Messiaen Companion* makes no claim to be definitive. Instead the hope is that the presence of many (not always compatible) viewpoints – normally the inevitable defect of any symposium – will in Messiaen's case open windows and shed fresh light and air on a discussion which latterly has become somewhat stereotyped. The obituaries have been written; Messiaen as cultural phenomenon has been studied enough. Strange as it may seem, we need for the moment to abandon the long view, to step closer to the shimmering colours of the stained glass, to explore its details afresh, and feel again how extraordinary they are.

Notes

1 Brigitte Massin: *Olivier Messiaen: une poétique du merveilleux* (Aix-en-Provence, Alinéa, 1989), p. 20.
2 Claude Samuel: *Entretiens avec Olivier Messiaen* (Paris, Belfond, 1967), p. 122.
3 See also Massin, op. cit., p. 24.
4 *Everyman*, BBC television, 1988.
5 Paul Griffiths: *Olivier Messiaen and the Music of Time* (London, Faber and Faber, 1985), p. 18.
6 Though Messiaen remembered having shocked the elderly ladies of the congregation (an assault on the contrived piety being one of Messiaen's great contributions to religious music), when I last heard him play (in 1989) his contributions to the service were models of self-effacing usefulness: modulating fugatos and brief meditations on the plainsong of the

day; and he was not too grand for the humbler duties of a church organist: the Christmas carol service, for example, which he accompanied with excerpts from *Messiah* – not, as one might expect, from *La Nativité*.

7 'Entretien avec Claude Samuel' (CD booklet, ECD 75505; English translation by Stuart Walters), p. 27.
8 Obituary, *The Independent*, Wednesday 29 April 1992.
9 Messiaen had already in 1952 dabbled in this area in a short (and, by his estimation, unsuccessful) piece of *musique concrète*, *Timbres-durées*, a collage based on the sounds of water droplets.

PART I

Messiaen's Musical Language: an Introduction

ANTHONY POPLE

Of all great composers, Messiaen's musical character is arguably one of the most clearly defined. The vast majority of his works deal with subjects drawn from nature or Christian theology; most of them are written for organ, piano or orchestra. His melodic invention ranges from the liveliness of ecstatic dance to the serene austerity of plainsong; his rhythms are infused with the freedom of Indian classical music; his harmonies have an abundant and joyous richness, though their place in his music is not calculated for the effect of the moment, as might be said of Wagner, Debussy or Strauss. Yet beside these broad brush-strokes, which depict Messiaen's musical world with remarkable fullness, stand a number of conundrums that make his position in the history of twentieth-century music considerably more difficult to assess. One may hear echoes or pre-echoes of his style in works by composers as different as Debussy, Skryabin, Ravel, Stravinsky, Gershwin, Jehan Alain, Ohana and Stockhausen, and he is frequently cited as a crucial influence in the establishment of 'total serialism' in Europe. Yet his stylistic roots are far from obvious, despite his thorough and conventional Conservatoire training and his long service as a church organist – that most established of musical offices – and he founded no school,[1] though he was a revered teacher numbering some great composers and many fine ones among his pupils.

Language

Music and language were strongly linked in Messiaen's life from the very beginning. As a boy, he wrote plays before turning to musical composition, and as a young but established composer he published a book entitled *Technique de mon langage musical* (1944).[2] This title nicely reflects a family background in which the techniques of language were continually in focus: his father was an English teacher and translator of Shakespeare, his mother a poet. Perhaps in keeping with this, Messiaen's music does not use its 'language' to narrate, to dramatize, nor even to express, but rather to *represent*. In some cases, this is because the subject matter is conceived as an eternal truth (as in *Couleurs de la cité céleste*) or as an archetypal natural scene (as in the *Catalogue d'oiseaux*). In many other pieces, the retreat from narrative comes through the presentation of stories such as those of the Nativity or the Resurrection, which have been told so often that their narrative aspect has been entirely dissipated through mythologization. Such stories stand transformed into icons: their language is that of reflection and contemplation; they may be viewed from different angles or aspects (as in the *Vingt regards sur l'Enfant-Jésus*). Messiaen chose not to disentangle their details in such a way as to be able to articulate them more clearly by means of a time-bound, left-to-right exposition. He preferred to reach inside them only so as the better to understand – and therefore to represent – their essence.

This obsession with the eternal was bound to be profoundly subversive in the context of the Western humanist tradition, and particularly so in a musician, since that art had since the Enlightenment, if not since the Renaissance, aspired more and more to the condition of discourse. As Messiaen's career proceeded, his subversiveness manifested itself through a number of musical techniques, defining his 'language' with increasing clarity through its contrast with that of his predecessors and contemporaries. True, many of these techniques may be seen to have palpable connections with the work of others – and indeed Messiaen did not hesitate to list his sources alongside the hundreds of examples from his own work which illustrate *Technique de mon langage musical*. But the rich brew he created from these ingredients, and the clarity with which it was used to project his view of the world, turned this master of synthesis into one of the twentieth century's great originals.

Mode

Among Messiaen's earliest works was an organ piece entitled *Esquisse modale* (1927), and though the composer never published it one may see from its title that the idea of modal writing was one of his first technical concerns. He was not alone in this: modality of one kind or another was commonplace in French music of the late nineteenth century, and was central to the technique of composers so apparently diverse in style and sensibility as Fauré, Satie and Debussy. The interest in modes among French musicians of this era had much to do with the revival of plainchant in the mid-nineteenth century, which engendered a familiarity with the ancient Greek diatonic modes.[3] The improvisation of modal accompaniment to plainsong melodies soon became part of a composer's training at the Paris Conservatoire, transforming theoretical knowledge into the ease and fluency of diatonic modal thought that is so characteristic of Fauré's music, and was also to be heard in Messiaen's organ improvisations at La Trinité.

For some composers, the use of modal melodies and harmonies remained associated with a Hellenistic sensibility and a generally classical outlook. This is the case with Satie's famous *Gymnopédies*, for example – their title referring to dances performed by Greek youths. But Messiaen's interest in the non-Western connotations of modes was less fanciful, more genuinely exploratory: he looked to India and the East, where modal improvisation remained the mainstay of traditional music. In his explorations of these cultures he benefited from the scholarship of Maurice Emmanuel, who was his history of music tutor at the Conservatoire – and also from Emmanuel's example as a composer, for it was his *30 chansons bourguignonnes* (1913) which, Messiaen later explained, 'converted [me] to modal music'.[4] Non-Western modes offered the composer a more varied melodic and harmonic palette than did the modes of plainchant. Messiaen also heard non-diatonic modes in the music of those composers whose harmonic techniques carved out a broad Franco-Russian axis – among them Debussy, Skryabin and Stravinsky.[5] Coincidences like this fascinated him.

One historically important thing that all these modal explorations had in common was that they offered an alternative to the predominant musical force of post-Wagnerian chromatic tonality. Escaping Wagnerism was something dear to the hearts of many French musicians both before and after the Franco-Prussian war of 1870, but there were also those who followed the example of César Franck in attempting to emulate the German master within the generic constraints of French musical culture. Conventional histories of French music in this period tend to overemphasize the distinction between those who taught or studied at the Conservatoire – who are said to have eschewed Wagnerism – and those who worked in the orbit of Vincent d'Indy at the Schola Cantorum – who are said to have followed the Wagnerian trail, albeit transmuted through Franck's distinctive contributions. In reality there was much traffic of individuals and ideas between the two camps: even Debussy was deeply influenced by Wagnerian models, as Robin Holloway has shown.[6] Maurice Emmanuel worked in both institutions, and Messiaen himself taught at the Schola Cantorum in the 1930s before returning to the Conservatoire after the Second World War. Messiaen knew much of Wagner's music as a child,[7] and the immense impact on him of Debussy's music came through the crypto-Wagnerian opera *Pelléas et Mélisande* – its score a treasured tenth-birthday gift from his boyhood harmony teacher.[8] To say that this work was a great influence on Messiaen would be something of an understatement: his writings and recorded conversations show that it remained a musical talisman for him throughout his life.

It is not surprising, then, that Messiaen's use of modes has none of the ascetic quality that distinguishes a piece like Satie's *Gymnopédies* from late-Romantic tonal music. Satie's piece exhibits many of the characteristic features of diatonically modal music: an avoidance of both chromatic dissonance and conventional harmonic progressions, for example, and a tendency towards wandering melodic lines that cadence in unusual ways. The typical features of non-diatonic modal music – and this applies as much to Bartók or Szymanowski as to Messiaen[9] – are by comparison more positively drawn. The melodies are sharply characterized by recurrent intervals, often those which are but rarely found in diatonic music, and there is a pervasive harmonic 'atmosphere', all of this tending to give an aura of exoticism. In both cases, however, the underlying technical reason is the same. Whereas the melodic and harmonic patterns that underlie Romantic tonal music – scale and arpeggio formulae in the melodic lines, 'functional' chord progressions in the harmony – have a quality of temporal articulation that contributes strongly to the sense of phrasing, the concept of mode implies far less of this kind. All that is necessary for music to be modal is that it should adhere to the notes of a mode, and, this being so, it is hardly surprising that the most telling characteristic of both diatonic and non-diatonic modal music is a sense of improvisation – whether contemplative or frenetic – within a static atmosphere.

This point is confirmed by the many references in *Technique de mon langage musical* to Marcel Dupré's *Traité d'improvisation.*[10] Indeed Messiaen's book, so far as it goes, is quite candid in every respect about the sources of his technique. This in itself seems deliberate, as if he were attempting to show that his music was legitimate and accessible. The factual tone serves to disguise a number of assumptions, however, such as a constant reliance on the overtone series to validate modal and harmonic formulae that might otherwise seem merely contrived. For example, one of his favoured devices of melodic cadence, the falling tritone, is introduced by the statement that 'a very fine ear clearly perceives an F# in the natural resonance of a low C' (Ex. 1.1a).[11] So far, so good: there is nothing substantive here with which a psychoacoustician would disagree. 'This F#', Messiaen however continues, 'is endowed with an attraction toward the C, *which*

EX. 1.1

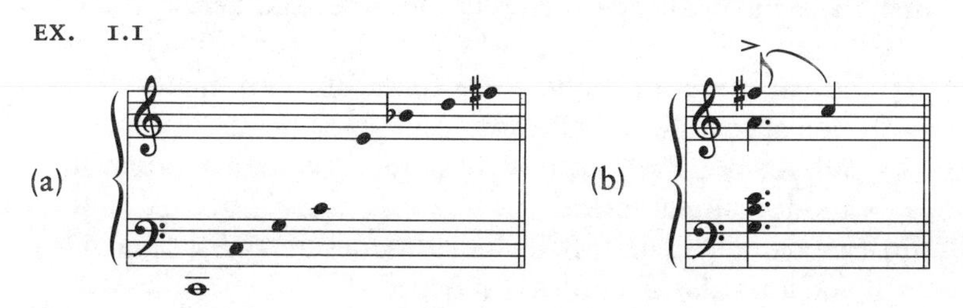

becomes its normal resolution' (Ex. 1.1b, my italics). This certainly does *not* follow from the acoustical premise, but it is more useful to examine the underlying reason for Messiaen's difficulty than to criticize his logic – since, plainly, a composer may use his materials however he chooses. One explanation for Messiaen's inability to come up with a sounder argument is that, in modal music, the very idea of a 'normal resolution' is itself difficult to maintain. This is not to say that modal music cannot proceed through melodic formulae – indeed, Messiaen's example serves to prove that it can – but rather that the duality of chord and scale, through which in tonal music the idea of 'resolution' is defined, is lacking. Whereas in tonal music it is thoroughly established that non-chordal notes normally 'resolve' to adjacent chordal notes by downward motion through the associated scale,[12] a mode has neither the linear force of a scale nor an associated set of harmonies. Thus no concept of 'normal resolution' within a harmonic context is strictly viable. But having decided to bring the idea of resolution back into his synthesis, Messiaen was of course at liberty to decide for himself just what was normal and what was not.

This sleight of hand is supplemented by a harmonic repertoire which similarly recalls tonal music. In *Technique de mon langage musical*, Messiaen himself explains at some length how his modes can simulate dominant-seventh chords and tonic triads – albeit with many foreign pitches brought into the orbit of these chords by the constitution of the modes themselves. This is as good a place as any, then, to list the seven 'modes of limited transposition' which were partially outlined by Messiaen in his preface to *La Nativité du Seigneur* (published in 1936) and more definitively treated in his later book.[13] They are shown in Ex. 1.2 in a way which indicates their relations to each other:

(i) all six notes of mode 1 are found in both mode 3 (nine notes) and mode 6 (eight notes)
(ii) all six notes of mode 5 are found in both mode 6 and mode 4 (eight notes)
(iii) mode 7 (ten notes) includes modes 6 and 4, and also includes all eight notes of mode 2

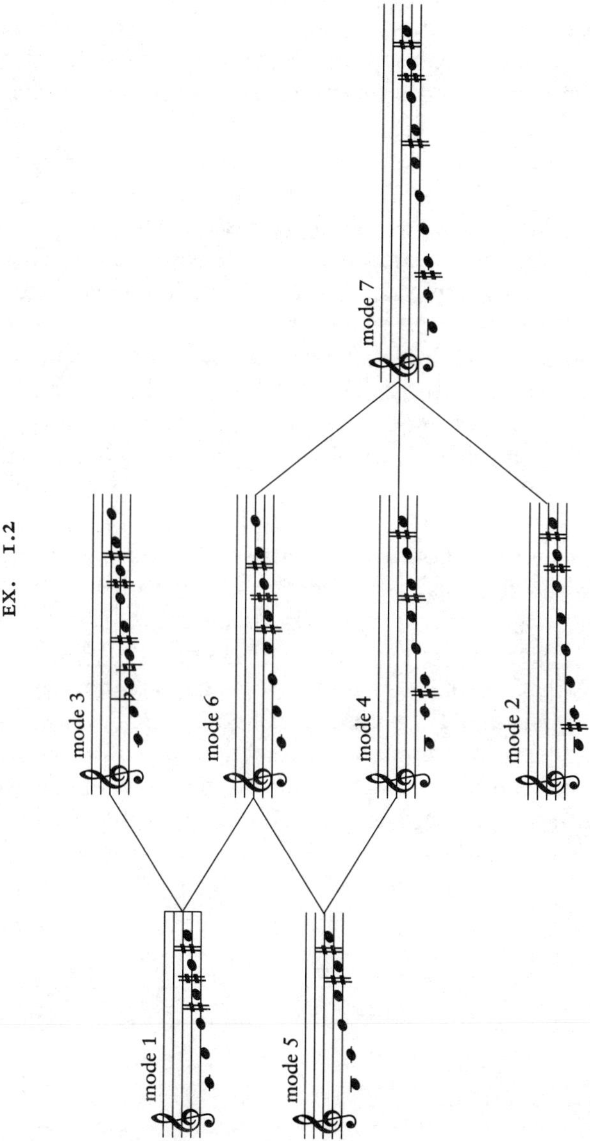

EX. I.2

These inclusion relations hold only in the case of certain transpositions of these modes, of course, as shown in Ex. 1.2. But since Messiaen explicitly avoids mode 1 (the whole-tone scale) – because 'Claude Debussy, in *Pelléas et Mélisande*, and Paul Dukas, in *Ariane et Barbe-bleue*, have made such remarkable use of it that there is nothing more to add',[14] – this table serves to show overall that the most distinctive of the modes he uses are numbers 3, 6, 4 and 2, none of which is closely related to another.[15] Each of the modes comprises a succession of a few intervals which is repeated at least once within the octave span. It is this feature, combined with the lack of inclusion relations between them, that gives each of these four modes the propensity to generate melodies with a characteristic vocabulary of leaps and scalar motions. The corollary, applicable to all seven modes, is that each mode may only be transposed a few times before repeating itself – as distinct from the diatonic scale, for example, which may appear on any of the twelve available pitch levels.

This is most economically shown with reference to mode 2, which in the Stravinsky literature has come to be known as the octatonic collection, or octatonic scale.[16] Ex. 1.3 shows this mode in successive transpositions beginning on C♮, C♯, D♮ and E♭. Allowing for the fact that the pitches are notated enharmonically (so that F♭ equals E♮, and so on), it is clear that the fourth transposition contains exactly the same notes as the first. This means that the next transposition (on E♮) would be synonymous with that on C♯, and so on. In other words, there is only a

EX. 1.3

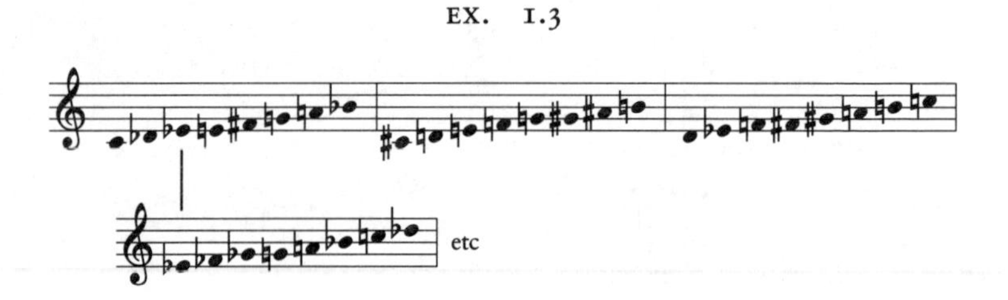

limited number of transpositions of this mode – three in all. This corresponds mathematically with the fact that the mode comprises a succession of intervals – semitone, then whole tone – which is repeated four times within the octave. Three (transpositions) multiplied by four (intervallic cells) gives twelve (notes in the octave). Like coincidences, such simple mathematical truths meant a great deal to Messiaen.

The example Messiaen uses to illustrate how these modes may be aligned with common tonal harmonies is summarized in Ex. 1.4a.[17] The chords on the upper stave within each bar use notes from only a single transposition of mode 2 – Ex. 1.4b shows the transposition used in bar 1, Ex. 1.4c shows that used in bar 2, with the notes of the central harmony highlighted in both cases. Perhaps the first thing that stands out here is the enormous extent to which the notes that embellish each chord depart from the F# major scale with which the central harmonic progression would be associated in tonal music. Messiaen lets this go by almost without comment, merely asserting that this 'modulation of the mode to itself' happens 'without the tonality's giving way'.[18] Secondly, one should recognize that the two transpositions of mode 2 that are heard here could have encompassed a further seven dominant-to-tonic cadences, as shown in Ex. 1.4d, not to mention a vast number of other harmonic progressions involving minor-seventh and half-diminished-seventh chords. And finally, one should consider the layout of the chords on the upper stave: the notes used here are of course in one sense arbitrary, being chosen only as representatives of the modes concerned, for the sake of explanation; but in another sense they are not arbitrary at all – they have been chosen according to Messiaen's musical sensibility, and are thus revealing of it. What emerges is that the chords on the upper stave are themselves common chords of tonal music – sometimes noted enharmonically – though none is synonymous with the chord it supposedly embellishes.

It is instructive to compare this schematic example, which is indeed typical of Messiaen, with a passage from Stravinsky's *The Rite of Spring* (1913) that shares so many common features one must be inclined to regard it as a close forebear of Messi-

EX. 1.4

(a)

(b)

(c)

(d)

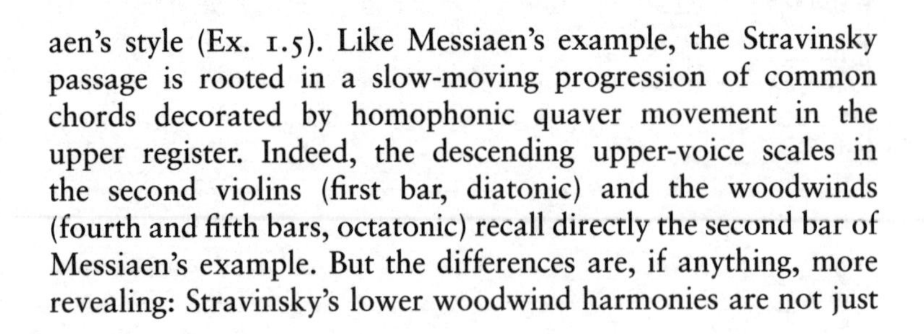

aen's style (Ex. 1.5). Like Messiaen's example, the Stravinsky passage is rooted in a slow-moving progression of common chords decorated by homophonic quaver movement in the upper register. Indeed, the descending upper-voice scales in the second violins (first bar, diatonic) and the woodwinds (fourth and fifth bars, octatonic) recall directly the second bar of Messiaen's example. But the differences are, if anything, more revealing: Stravinsky's lower woodwind harmonies are not just

EX. 1.5 Stravinsky: *The Rite of Spring*

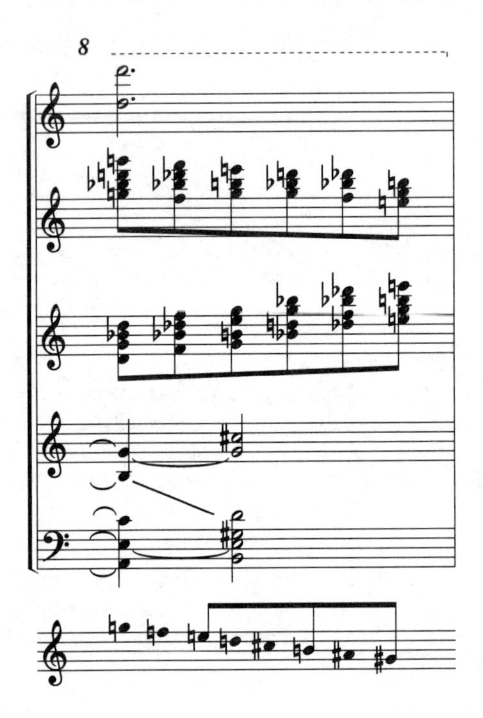

plain triads and seventh chords, but are themselves richly elaborated with modal notes; and the harmonies in the upper voices, while triadic as in Messiaen, proceed mainly through alternation – only in the last two bars of the passage is a semblance of Messiaen's parallel stepwise motion through the mode suggested.[19]

Both Messiaen's clarification of such modal thought and his tendency to place unadulterated tonal harmonies within the resultant embellishing frame may be seen even in his earliest compositions, such as the seventh of his *Préludes* for piano (1928, Ex. 1.6a). The first fourteen bars, and the last eight, of this 32-bar miniature are rooted to the spot, in a nine-note mode from which every pitch of the melodic and harmonic material is drawn (Ex. 1.6b).[20] This mode is actually a variant of mode 2 – it simply has a note added – and is not itself a mode of limited transposition. Like the Stravinsky example discussed above –

EX. 1.6 *Préludes* 7 'Plainte calme'

(b)

and indeed much octatonic music of Russian origin – Messiaen's prelude is dominated by the sound of the dominant-seventh chord, which occurs in mode 2 at four transpositional levels each a minor third apart.[21] In the prelude, the detail that confirms this sound as a musical priority occurs in bar 3, where the *additional* dominant-quality sonority afforded by its ninth modal note (E♮) is sounded. This is indeed the only harmonic appearance of this note, which is otherwise heard simply as a melodic passing note between E♭ and F♮.

While this gives an illustration of how Messiaen makes play with the sound of common tonal chords in non-diatonic modal surroundings, the next passage in the prelude (bars 15–16, Ex. 1.7a) shows him, conversely, using unusual harmonies in a diatonic modal context. Each bar in turn adheres to a single diatonic mode (Ex. 1.7b), but the harmonic sonority employed is determinedly unconventional. (Again, it is alternated at a number of transpositional levels, confirming its musical value as a sonority *per se*.) What is perhaps more surprising still is that the diatonic notes employed in each bar – six of the available seven – also lie within a transposition of the original nine-note mode (see Ex. 1.7c). The result is that the two passages together preserve the modal purity of the composition while affording contrast to the listener through exactly obverse references to tonal norms.

The superimposition of common chords that was observed in Ex. 1.4a relates Messiaen's early style to other music composed in France between the wars. He himself refers to Honegger and Milhaud in this regard.[22] This kind of writing was at one time called 'bitonal' – a term which has received short shrift from music theorists in recent decades because, it is argued, if 'tonality' is about considerably more than isolated chords, then 'bitonality' must be about more than the straightforward super-

EX. 1.7 *Préludes* 7 'Plainte calme'

imposition of chords. Messiaen, however, frequently writes such superimpositions in contexts which are undeniably 'bimodal', if still not bitonal. Ex. 1.8a shows the opening of 'Le collier', the eighth song of the cycle *Poèmes pour Mi.*[23] Here the upper stave of the piano part follows mode 3 (Ex. 1.8b) while the lower stave follows mode 2 (Ex. 1.8c); the bimodality is inverted in the continuation (Ex. 1.8d). Again, the music of the upper stave consists almost entirely of common triads, while that of the lower stave, despite the change of modality, is rooted to an E major triad in second inversion, alternating with whole-tone dominant-quality chords.

By extension, in more complex textures the various modal types are often applied as if with a broad brush, for the sake of clarity. Ex. 1.9, from the ninth movement of the *Turangalîla-symphonie*, is scored for solo strings in thirteen parts, with the players divided into five timbrally distinct groups (two first violins, four second violins, three violas, and two each of cellos and double basses), each of which also has its own rhythmic organization. The result is that, while the marvellous sonority of the thirteen players remains a striking feature of this passage,

EX. 1.8 *Poèmes pour Mi* 8 'Le collier'

(a)

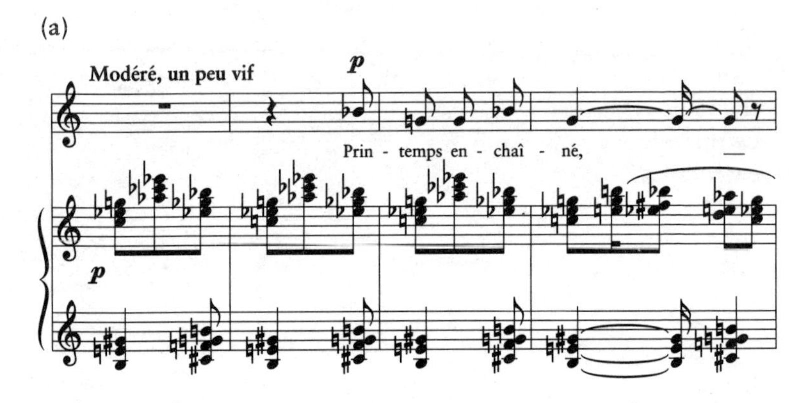

(b)

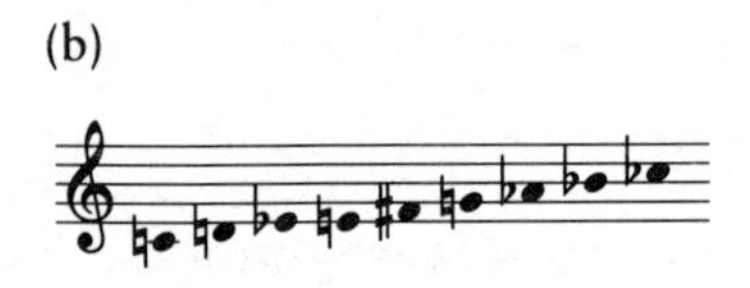

(c)

(d)

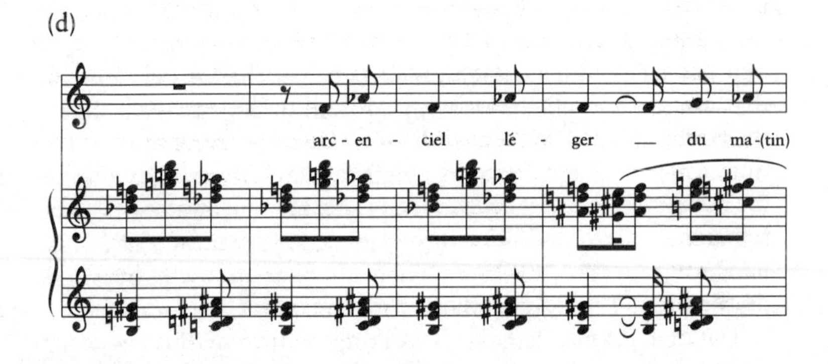

the potentially obscure counterpoint is reduced to an audible interaction among five layers of sound. Messiaen reinforces this by the polymodal organization of the overall harmony – the first violins being confined to mode 3, the second violins to mode 2, the violas to mode 6, the cellos to mode 4 and the basses to the comparatively rare whole-tone mode 1 – so that the notes within each layer revolve constantly through the corresponding mode, just as sub-atomic particles move incessantly within the most solid of objects.

Rhythm

Like his use of modes, Messiaen's rhythmic language was developed from a few simple ideas that could be related to Western practice in order to suggest a synthesis, but whose exoticism remained powerful, and importantly so. Messiaen regarded his rhythmic innovations as his most far-reaching contribution to Western music, which may well turn out to be the judgement of history also; but it was the mere separation of pitch and rhythm – and indeed other musical parameters – rather than any specific rhythmic practices, that was influential in his own time. To some extent, this separation of parameters was implied by the removal from his pitch materials of those factors that had traditionally accomplished the articulation of phrases, for it was then necessary to develop alternative means to deal with rhythm and phrasing. Messiaen found resonances of this approach in the separation of râga and tâla in Indian music, and also in medieval Western practices such as isorhythm. There is indeed much in Messiaen's music, both technical and otherwise, that confirms him as standing outside the humanist tradition that dates from the Renaissance in Western Europe – though in the twentieth century he could hardly do so without at the same time appearing determinedly individual. Whether he brought the components of his musical language into a genuine synthesis remains a matter for debate, but given his outlook it was perhaps not necessary for him to do so; it was sufficient merely to do the right things consistently and in quantity.

The most fundamental feature of Messiaen's rhythms – some-

EX. 1.9 *Turangalîla-symphonie* 9 'Turangalîla III'

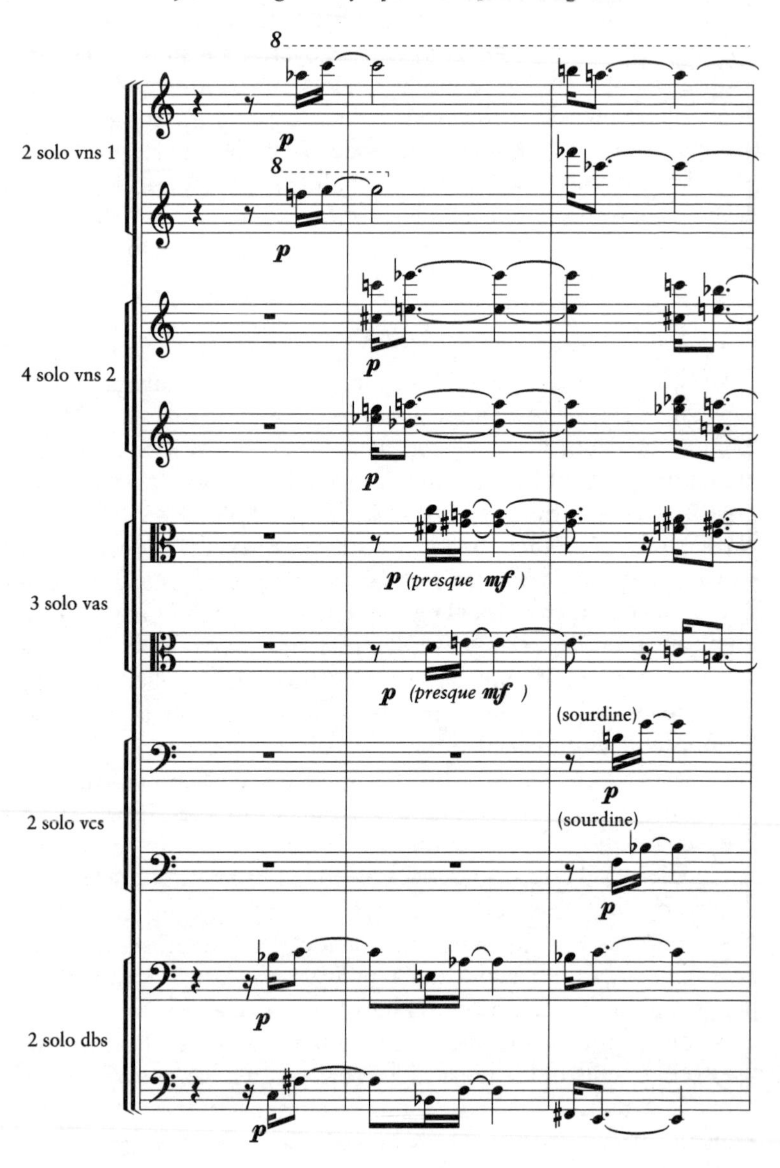

8

8
(sempre p)
(sempre p)
(sempre p.
presque mf)
(sempre p)
(sempre p)

thing which he found both in Stravinsky's *The Rite of Spring* and in classical Indian rhythms – is that they are *ametrical*.[24] This is not to say that there is no regular pulse. On the contrary, they are always built from multiples of a basic unit; but this basic unit is generally faster (by a factor of 2 or 3, say) than the succession of notes that we hear, whereas in most Western music the notes either move more or less with the pulse, or are at least clearly placed in relation to it. Ex. 1.10, from Messiaen's *Quatuor pour la fin du temps*, illustrates the opposite tendency, where the constant semiquaver pulse is comparatively obscure to the ear, although every note in the passage is a simple multiple of it. Instead, the ear hears a succession of pulses, varying in length between four and eight semiquavers (these are bracketed below the example), which alternate in a fluid succession. Furthermore, whereas classical Western music tends to fall not only into metres but into hypermetres – larger, but still regular periods[25] – Messiaen's phrase cannot do so, since it is irregular at even the most immediate level of rhythmic structure.

Rhythms of the kind exemplified by the extract from Messiaen's *Quatuor* are often described as additive: this refers principally to the manner in which small units are put together by the accretion of notes based on a common underlying unit, so that a group that is five semiquavers in length, for example, may be constructed as 2 + 2 + 1 (quaver–quaver–semiquaver). The first rhythmic technique that Messiaen identifies in *Technique de*

EX. 1.10 *Quatuor pour la fin du temps* 6 'Danse de la fureur, pour les sept trompettes'

mon langage musical makes this additive principle explicit. The 'added value' is conceived as a way of irregularizing regular patterns: it can be an extra note (Ex. 1.11a), an interpolated rest (Ex. 1.11b), or a lengthening of a single note within a pattern (Ex. 1.11c).[26] Of course, not just any extra note, rest, or lengthening will do. It is important to note that the added value in each case is calculated to knock the rhythmic pattern from the realm of Western (hyper-)metrical music into Messiaen's ametrical style. The way in which it is calculated is quite clearly shown in Ex. 1.11: the pulse in these examples starts out in the first two cases as a crotchet, in the third case as a dotted crotchet; the added value is a semiquaver, turning a four-semiquaver unit into one of five (Exx. 1.11a, 1.11b) or a six-semiquaver unit into one of seven (Ex. 1.11c). The resulting rhythms can no longer be assimilated into a metre.

It is no coincidence that the lengths of both these units – five and seven semiquavers – are measured by prime numbers. Although it is of course possible to write metrical and indeed hypermetrical music using such units, simply by repeating them (as Holst did in the relentless 5/4 of 'Mars' in *The Planets*), Messiaen's constant mixture of units makes a literally metrical perception impossible, as there can be no common divisor between a unit of prime length and its subdivisible – or other prime – neighbours. A group of five will never combine metrically with an adjacent group of three, four, six or seven, for example. Prime numbers, applied in this way, constitute another

EX. 1.11

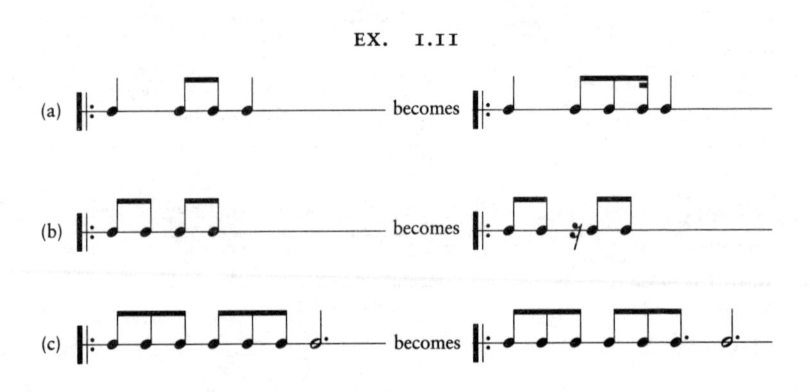

of those simple phenomena of nature that were especially prized by Messiaen.

Not all of Messiaen's rhythmic writing is as decidedly ametrical as the examples given above or in *Technique de mon langage musical* might seem to suggest. There is actually a good deal of genuinely metrical, and even hypermetrical, writing in his output – and not only in those otherwise quite characteristic works composed before 1935, when he came across the thirteenth-century treatise on rhythm by Çarngadeva, which contains a table of 120 small rhythmic formulae, called deçî-tâlas.[27] Before this, he had studied classical Greek rhythm, which is similarly based on formulaic conjunctions of short and long values, but this seems not to have fired his imagination in quite the same way: one may surmise that this may have been because Marcel Dupré and Maurice Emmanuel, who introduced the subject to him, did so in the context of a more generalized Atticism to which Messiaen was not entirely sympathetic. Nonetheless, as the example of the 'added value' and its explanation shows, the relationship between ametrical and metrical rhythmic perceptions was – like the accommodation between the modes of limited transposition and tonal harmony – a crucial and abiding concern for Messiaen.

As his discussions of phrase construction in *Technique de mon langage musical* make quite clear, Messiaen was aware that the tendency of Western listeners to perceive hypermetrical organization on the level of the musical phrase was not going to be subverted by the introduction of irregular rhythms at a more immediate level. Small groups, even of irregular size, would still tend to be rounded up and aligned with familiar patterns of 'upbeat–accent–termination'.[28] Indeed, having identified these underlying components of musical phraseology, he felt free to dispose them, too, in new combinations. Ex. 1.12, from *Poèmes pour Mi*, is analysed in *Technique de mon langage musical* as an upbeat preparation (A), and accent (B), followed by two terminations (C, D);[29] the use of added (and subtracted) semiquaver values to vary the rhythm of the 'terminations' from a regular quaver rhythm is also notable here. The consequence of constructing phrases in this way is to produce something

EX. 1.12 *Poèmes pour Mi* 8 'Le collier'

whose very amenability to conventional modes of musical perception focuses – and so preserves – its alien, exotic quality.

This usage also confirms Messiaen's tendency to work with formulae – in this case, tiny units which could be juxtaposed, varied, and played off against one another. In *Technique de mon langage musical*, he illustrates how such small units can be transformed by augmentation (lengthening all the note values) or diminution (shortening all the notes values);[30] by combining these methods with the use of added values he was able to generate transformations that were hardly amenable to analysis, such was the ambiguity of their derivation from the original patterns. Later in his career, however, he tended towards an increased clarity in this respect, making a distinction between some units which were repeated more or less verbatim and others whose variants were thus thrown into greater relief. This way of working dominates the *stile oiseau* of the 1950s, in which birdsong – transcribed into Messiaen's world – is the principal melodic basis, but it had already been given full expression in the decidedly abstract *Neumes rythmiques*, one of the *Quatre études de rythme* (1949–50) in which he set down markers for the expansion of his musical language beyond the elements of vocabulary and syntax he had earlier outlined in print.

An outline plan of *Neumes rythmiques* is shown in Fig. 1, with the three types of material labelled R, N and P in abbreviation of the composer's descriptions of them in the score. As Fig. 1 indicates, both R and P materials are deployed in the piece according to a strict scheme based on number sequences. The R material, presented twice on each appearance, is simply

FIG. 1: SEQUENCE OF MUSICAL MATERIALS IN NEUMES RYTHMIQUES

R	N	P
R (1–6–11)		
R (2–7–12)		
	N (9 bars)	
		P (41)
	N (9 bars)	
R (2–7–12)		
R (3–8–13)		
	N (9 bars)	
		P (43)
	N (11 bars)	
R (3–8–13)		
R (4–9–14)		
	N (17 bars)	
		P (47)
	N (9 bars)	
R (4–9–14)		
R (5–10–15)		
	N (22 bars)	
		P (53)

Key: R *rythme en ligne triple*
N *neumes rythmiques, avec résonances, et intensités fixes*
P *nombre premier en rythme non rétrogradable*

expanded as the piece proceeds by the regular addition of a semiquaver value to each of its three elements (see Ex. 1.13a). The P material is less rigorously handled from one appearance to the next, though it is characterized on each occasion by an insistent percussive beating at the extremes of the keyboard (Ex. 1.13b). Two features of its rhythmic organization stand out: firstly that the total length of each P block, measured in semiquavers, is a prime number, and secondly that the overall rhythm of each block is palindromic. Because they are the same backwards as forwards, such rhythms were termed 'non-retrogradable' by Messiaen – a terminology through which, as with the modes 'of limited transposition', the composer chose to emphasize a *restriction* inherent in the musical material.

Although the analogy between non-retrogradable rhythms and the modes of limited transposition can hardly be said to go beyond a certain abstract symmetry, this was sufficient for Messiaen to identify both as representatives of the 'charm of impossibilities'. Moreover, although it is the 'impossibility' that constitutes the link between these musical materials, it was quite clearly the *charm* that was more important to Messiaen:

> It is a glistening music we seek, giving to the aural sense voluptuously refined pleasures. At the same time, this music should be able to express some noble sentiments (and especially the most noble of all, . . . the truths of our Catholic faith). This charm, at once voluptuous and contemplative, resides particularly in certain mathematical impossibilities [in] the modal and rhythmic domains.[31]

Charming in a different way is the third type of material in the piece, comprising the 'rhythmic neumes' (N) after which it is named. A *neume* – exemplified in the medieval notation of plainchant – is an indivisible musical figure comprising very few notes: Messiaen's neumes in this work fit this description but are also highly characteristic (Ex. 1.13c). In the 'N' passages, the neumes are combined and recombined in fluid succession, as if to mimic the post-Beethovenian principle of motivic 'development' through the continual expansion, contraction and juxtaposition of fragments. But, like the suggestion of conventional tonalities through the modes of limited transposition, this is an illusion: the kaleidoscopic presentation and re-presentation of the musical material is simply an inevitable corollary of the temporal projection of this kind of formulaic material.

This is not to deny the historical importance of Messiaen's exploration of this device as a method of musical construction. It is no less characteristic of him than it is of Stravinsky, and provides a link with another giant of the twentieth century, Pierre Boulez. The organization of interlocking cycles in the latter's *Le marteau sans maître* owes much to the example of

EX. 1.13 *Neumes rythmiques*

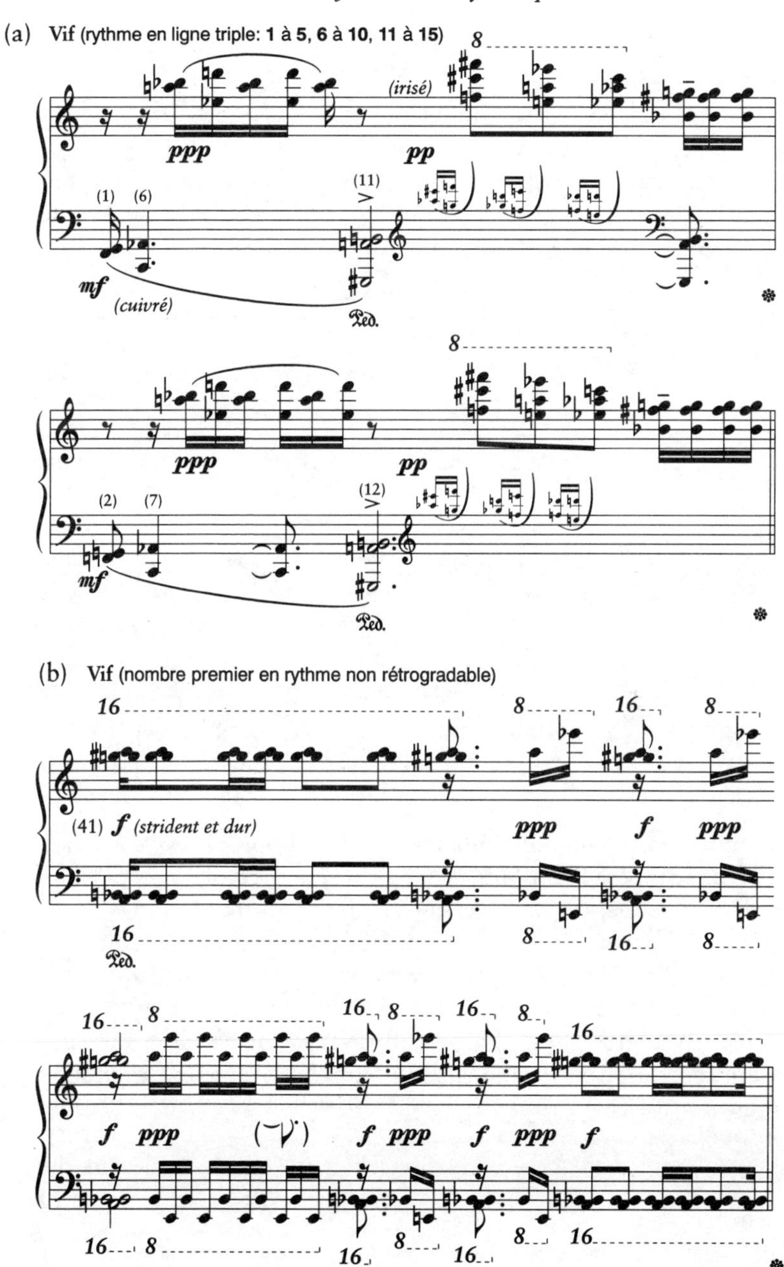

Turangalîla, while the 'commentaires' in Boulez's work are not too far removed from Messiaen's typical contemplations of transcendental images. But Messiaen's ability to make things seem what they are not marks him out from these and other composers who, in line with mid-century scientific rationalism, were content to let block structure 'speak for itself'. Rather, Messiaen's block structures, like virtually everything else in his music, were calculated to speak instead of 'noble sentiments' and theological truths.

Magic

The 'charm of impossibilities' indeed holds the key to Messiaen's sensibility. Conceived as a self-sufficient guarantee of musical value, it confirms his general fascination with things magical, which also lies behind his emphasis on the mystical and the miraculous in Christian epic. It is this quality of magic that links the further elements of Messiaen's music with the materials and methods discussed in *Technique de mon langage musical*, which do not, of course, tell the whole story, even in respect of the works composed up to that time. No less characteristic are his use of harmony, orchestration and resonance interchangeably to suggest visual colours,[32] his direct use of ciphers and number symbolism to encode theological ideas, his use of extremes of tempo, such as the desperately slow 𝅗𝅥 = 13 (notated as ♪ = 52) of *Le banquet céleste*, and his use of cyclic repetitions of pitch patterns or rhythmic units.

An example of the latter may be observed in *Harawi* (1945), one of Messiaen's most secular works. This is a cycle of love-songs, composed at a difficult period of the composer's life when his feelings for Yvonne Loriod were as yet unable to find legitimate expression outside the realm of music. The strain of exoticism, normally associated in Messiaen's works with religious mysticism, is here reduced to the ostensibly Peruvian setting – though the poetic texts are Messiaen's own work. The conjunction of tenderness and helpless mystery is nowhere clearer than in the final song, 'Dans le noir', which alternates two contrasting types of material before a *cri de cœur* ('Mon amour, mon souffle!') leads to a delicate evocation of a deep and latent love, confined at the very end to expression *à bouche fermée*. The two opening sections are shown in Ex. 1.14: the opening bars decorate major triads of E♭ and A by motion within mode 2, precisely in line with the pattern of Ex. 1.4a; the 'bien modéré' is organized rhythmically as a canon by augmentation, using repeating cycles of harmonic and rhythmic materials. The basic rhythmic pattern is ♪♪♪♩♩♪♩𝅗𝅥♩♩. 𝅗𝅥. (eleven durations – a prime number). This is used directly by the right-hand part, while the chords in the left hand follow the same sequence, but with each duration augmented by 25 per cent. Harmonically, the right hand cycles through six chords drawn from mode 6, while the left hand uses a repeating pattern of seven chords drawn from mode 4. The end of this ten-bar section of the song interrupts all these cycles in mid-rotation with a reprise of the opening material, after which the cycles begin again from square one, continuing this time for seventeen bars. After another interruption they are allowed twenty-five bars, permitting the right-hand part to complete its fourth rhythmic cycle but interrupting all the other concurrent cycles at arbitrary points as before.

Within a few years of composing *Harawi* and a few months of composing *Neumes rythmiques*, Messiaen had expanded the scope of his cyclically repeating materials to include twelve-note configurations that might technically be called serial, in the sense established by Schoenberg and his pupils. During the 1950s and 1960s, a number of successful composers who had hitherto eschewed serial techniques were to turn to them in one way or another: Stravinsky, Shostakovich, Copland and Britten, for example. While all of these composers found ways of accommodating serialism on their own terms, Messiaen's usage was perhaps the most subversive of classical serial principles, despite being located in a musical language whose separate treatment of pitch, rhythm and the other elements of music appeared to some of his pupils to lead inexorably towards the serialization of all of these aspects of musical construction. Messiaen defused the serial principle by undermining its central concept of ordering through the technique of 'interversion'. In its most characteristic form, this involves reordering the elements of a series from the centre, working outwards by alternation between the two halves, so that the sequence 12–11–10–9–8–7–6–5–4–3–2–1, for example, would be transformed into 6–7–5–8–4–9–3–10–2–11–1–12, as it is in the episodes of *Ile de feu 2*. This process, which can in fact be applied to a sequence of any length and consisting of pitches, durations or other elements, can itself be repeated cyclically.[33] Its principal effect is to prevent any one ordering from acquiring the central role allotted to the series in classical Schoenbergian usage, just as classical serialism had

EX. 1.14 *Harawi* 12 'Dans le noir'

sought to prevent a central tonic-like role accruing to any of the twelve chromatic pitches.

The encounter with serialism seems to have provoked, or at least coincided with, something of an aesthetic crisis for Messiaen. He was clearly fascinated by the 'charm of impossibilities' that was to be found in the basic mathematical properties of his musical material. Nonetheless, beyond certain basic manipulations, he refused to 'play God' in the way that Boulez was to attempt through 'total' or 'integral' serialism – by means of which all parameters of the musical elements were, in principle at least, subjected to strict control. This turn of events in European music was presented as a historical necessity by its advocates, however, and may well have left Messiaen for the first time feeling his age.

Given his faith, one can understand Messiaen's refusal to 'play God'. His chosen alternative was to turn to 'God's musicians' – the birds – whose songs and cries began to dominate his works from the early 1950s. It was of course necessary that these birdsongs should be transcribed into musical notation, which meant that Messiaen had to act as intercessor for them. And indeed they end up singing very much in his own style, though they are clearly recognizable as birds – and to ornithologists might in many cases be recognizable as distinct species. If the use of birdsong was after all intended to answer a need on Messiaen's part for spiritual purity and humility, then the necessity for transcription was unfortunate – it could perhaps at best be explained away as an inevitable consequence of the human condition, as dramatized by Schoenberg in his opera *Moses und Aron*.

But was there really a problem? Was not this Olivier Messiaen, after all, the man who had published a book about 'my musical language' at the ripe old age of thirty-five or so? True, Messiaen's art shows a delight in systems, and in their explanation, which to modern eyes would make him appear to be a scientist of sorts, but it combines this with a belief that music undeniably should, and undeniably can, bring its listeners into profound contact with the divine – which would make him, rather, a magician in the medieval mould. It is the latter which is surely nearer the mark: the bewitching effect of his music, as it leads us from the one perspective to the other, comes not through calculated complexity but through the constant accretion of magic ingredients, which he adds one after another, unshakeable in his faith that they will make their effect by sheer weight of numbers:

> Let us now think of the hearer of our modal and rhythmic music; he will not have time at the concert [i.e. while listening] to inspect the nontranspositions and the nonretrogradations, and, at that moment, these questions will not interest him further; *to be charmed will be his only desire* [my italics]. And that is precisely what will happen; in spite of himself he will submit to the strange charm of impossibilities . . . which will lead him progressively to that sort of *theological rainbow* which the musical language . . . attempts to be.[34]

Was Messiaen also taken in, 'in spite of himself'? Certainly his naivety can be breathtaking – such as when, throughout *Technique de mon langage musical*, the appearance of repeated notes in melodic fragments are said to recall 'Hindu melody'.[35] But to many of his admirers, this naivety is an endearing quality, which makes it out of the question to regard his glistening added-sixth chords as kitschy, for example. The deeply religious subject matter of many of his works is another factor that convinces one of his overwhelming sincerity. From such a man one can accept a great deal in the name of faith, and art. The paradox here is that it is the acceptance of the man that allows one to be drawn into his world of magic, and so to experience his works as representations of the transcendental forces beside which he, along with the rest of us, is reduced to insignificance. Not for nothing does the myth of Tristan and Isolde feature as his greatest secular inspiration. Those lovers, too, were drawn in by a potent brew of magic ingredients, ill-defined perhaps but nonetheless of fateful power, and through it were transfigured into a world beyond personal identity, even as their names were preserved for the temporal world in the telling and re-telling of their story.

Similarly, so long as they are played, Messiaen's identity as the composer of *La Nativité*, of the *Quatuor pour la fin du temps*, the *Vingt regards*, *Turangalîla*, the *Catalogue d'oiseaux*, *La Transfiguration*, *Saint François d'Assise*, and the many other marvellous works that came from his sixty-five-year career, is not likely to be overlooked in a modern world which emphasizes property and personality. But in the pre-humanist terms that seem more appropriate to his view of the world, he was also successful. Undoubtedly a master craftsman, he was at the same time a master of magic, 'in the best sense of the term: in the sense of a hidden ritual the signs of which are only revealed to the initiated. I don't think that this is forbidden by the Church and by religion; it's an admirable thing.'[36]

Notes

1 This is not to overlook Messiaen's membership of the group La Jeune France, established in 1936. However, theirs was a loose association which was barely established before the Second World War interrupted French musical life. The composers involved – Messiaen, André Jolivet, Daniel-Lesur and Yves Baudrier – had little in common stylistically, though a

number of Daniel-Lesur's pupils went on to compose music which recalls Messiaen's harmonic and coloristic sensibility.

2 Olivier Messiaen: *Technique de mon langage musical*, 2 volumes (Paris, Leduc, 1944). Volume 1, translated by John Satterfield as *The Technique of My Musical Language* (Paris, Leduc, 1956). Volume 2 consists of music examples, drawn principally from Messiaen's own compositions.

3 It was symptomatic that the revival of religious music was the express aim of those who founded the Schola Cantorum in Paris in 1894.

4 Messiaen: 'Maurice Emmanuel: ses "trente chansons bourguignonnes" ', *Revue musicale*, 206 (1947), p. 108, cited in P. Griffiths: *Olivier Messiaen and the Music of Time* (London, Faber and Faber 1985), pp. 26–7.

5 See Richard S. Parks: *The Music of Claude Debussy* (New Haven, Yale University Press, 1989); Manfred Kelkel: *Alexandre Scriabine: sa vie, l'ésotérisme et le langage musical dans son œuvre* (Paris, Champion, 1978); Pieter C. van den Toorn: *The Music of Igor Stravinsky* (New Haven, Yale University Press, 1983).

6 Robin Holloway: *Debussy and Wagner* (London, Eulenburg, 1979).

7 Claude Samuel: *Entretiens avec Olivier Messiaen* (Paris, Belfond, 1967); translated by Felix Aprahamian as *Conversations with Oliver Messiaen* (London, Stainer & Bell, 1976), pp. 67–8.

8 Ibid., p. 69.

9 See Malcolm Gillies: *Notation and Tonal Structure in Bartók's Later Works* (New York, Garland, 1989); Ann K. McNamee: 'Bitonality, Mode, and Interval in the Music of Karol Szymanowski', *Journal of Music Theory*, 29/i (1985), pp. 61–84.

10 Marcel Dupré: *Traité d'improvisation* [vol. 2 of *Cours complet d'improvisation à l'orgue*] (Paris, Leduc, 1926).

11 Messiaen, *The Technique of My Musical Language*, vol. 1, p. 31; vol. 2, Exx. 70–1.

12 A distinction is normally observed between 'diatonic' dissonances, which resolve by motion through a diatonic scale, and 'chromatic' dissonances, which resolve by chromatic motion.

13 Messiaen, *The Technique of My Musical Language*, vol. 1, pp. 58–62; vol. 2, Exx. 312–57.

14 Ibid., vol. 1, p. 59.

15 This point is also made by Rosemary Walker ('Modes and Pitch-Class Sets in Messiaen: A Brief Discussion of "Première communion de la Vierge" ', *Music Analysis*, 8 (1989), pp. 159–68). Messiaen himself makes it clear that mode 5 is of little consequence. (*The Technique of My Musical Language*, vol. 1, p. 62).

16 See especially Arthur Berger: 'Problems of Pitch Organization in Stravinsky', in Benjamin Boretz and Edward T. Cone (eds), *Perspectives on Schoenberg and Stravinsky* (New York, Norton, 1972), pp. 123–54; P. C. van den Toorn, op. cit.

17 Messiaen, *The Technique of My Musical Language*, vol. 2, Ex. 366.

18 Ibid., vol. 1, p. 65.

19 On a broader level, one ought not to overlook how both the slow descent

in the first violins and the ascending motion in the bass follow the scale of D major – this ordered diatonic mode interacting differently from bar to bar with the local diatonic and other modes that fall within the scope of the phrase.

20 Modes illustrated schematically in this chapter are set out on the page as if they were ascending scales. This is merely a convenience, however, and it is important to bear in mind that the sense of melodic progression inherent in a modal conception is far less fixed than the scalar presentation might seem to imply. The fluid melodic contour of Messiaen's prelude affords a good illustration of this point.

21 See P. C. van den Toorn, op. cit., pp. 13–15 *et passim.*

22 Messiaen, *The Technique of My Musical Language*, vol. 1, pp. 52, 53.

23 Ibid., vol. 1, pp. 69–70; vol. 2, Ex. 380.

24 Ibid., vol. 1, p. 14.

25 An influential treatment of this phenomenon may be found in Fred Lerdahl and Ray Jackendoff: *A Generative Theory of Tonal Music* (Cambridge, MA, MIT Press, 1983), pp. 12–30.

26 Messiaen, *The Technique of My Musical Language*, vol. 1, p. 16; vol. 2, Exx. 6–9.

27 According to John Satterfield, Messiaen's source was A. Lavignac and L. de la Laurencie (eds): *Encyclopédie de la musique et dictionnaire du conservatoire* (Paris, Delagrave, 1913–31), cited in Messiaen, *The Technique of My Musical Language*, vol. 1, p. 14, n. 2. The list is reproduced in Robert Sherlaw Johnson: *Messiaen* (London, Dent, 2/1989), pp. 206–10. Some of the deçî-tâlas take more than one form, so that there are actually more than 120 rhythms altogether.

28 Messiaen, *The Technique of My Musical Language*, vol. 1, p. 17.

29 Ibid., vol. 1, p. 17; vol. 2, Ex. 17.

30 Ibid., vol. 1, pp. 18–19; vol. 2, Exx. 20–7.

31 Ibid., vol. 1, p. 13.

32 See Jonathan Bernard's contribution to this volume, pp. 203–19.

33 See the tabulation of interversions in *Ile de feu* 2, in Sherlaw Johnson, op. cit., p. 109.

34 Messiaen, *The Technique of My Musical Language*, vol. 1, p. 21. Messiaen later repeats this passage for emphasis (vol. 1, p. 63).

35 For example, ibid., vol. 1, p. 39.

36 Samuel, op. cit., p. 46.

Organ Music I

JOHN MILSOM

Verily it is well for the world that it sees only the beauty of the completed work and not its origins nor the conditions whence it sprang; since knowledge of the artist's inspiration might often but confuse and alarm and so prevent the full effect of its excellence.

Thomas Mann, *Death in Venice*[1]

Few composers in history have more fully documented the ideas that lie behind their music – or, more accurately, the extra-musical ideas they regard as relevant to the audience of their works – than did Olivier Messiaen. A piece for organ bears the title 'Les eaux de la grâce'. At its head are the words of Revelation 7:17: 'L'Agneau, qui est au milieu du trône, conduira les élus aux sources des eaux de la vie'. It is the second movement of a cycle called *Les corps glorieux*, subtitled 'Sept visions brèves de la vie des ressuscités'. All this is in the score. Elsewhere Messiaen says of the work that 'The life of the resurrected is free, pure, luminous, colourful. The timbres of the organ will reflect these characteristics.' He also tells us that the cycle was composed 'in sight of the Lac de Laffrey and the mountain of the Grand Serre', as if landscape too helped to shape his conception of the music, and the idea of that landscape might be useful to his audience.[2] This is a great deal for us to address when confronting 'Les eaux de la grâce'. Well might the listener be confused and alarmed.

The copious annotation of 'Les eaux de la grâce', the rich documentation of what Messiaen regarded as essential to its conception and its interpretation, is characteristic of the composer. Where Thomas Mann's Aschenbach fashions his page and a half of choicest prose after the model of Tadzio's beauty confident in the knowledge that the 'strangely fruitful intercourse' between external stimulus and the creator's mind will be understood by the author alone and is irrelevant to the reader of the finished work, in 'Les eaux de la grâce' it was always Messiaen's aim that his choice of musical sounds, inspired by a contemplation of the divine, would in turn be associated in the listener's mind with the same extra-musical ideas. As a symbol of those ideas the music on its own is ambiguous, if comprehensible at all. To function in what might loosely be called a semantic fashion it must first be explained. All Messiaen's organ works are surrounded by words. Titles, subtitles, quotations from the Bible and the Missal, references to the place of composition, analyses of the technical resources used in the piece and their intended symbolic meaning and psychological effect: these are the agents of exegesis, chosen to guide the listener through the music towards a deeper communion with the divine. There is no doubting the end that Messiaen had in mind:

> a *true* music, that is to say, spiritual, a music which may be an act of faith; a music which may touch upon all subjects without ceasing to touch upon God; an original music, in short, whose language may open a few doors, take down some yet distant stars . . . To express with a lasting power our darkness struggling with the Holy Spirit, to raise upon the mountain the doors of our prison of flesh, to give to our century the spring water for which it thirsts, there shall have to be a great artist who will have to be both a great artisan and a great Christian.[3]

Messiaen's organ music is so closely identified with the spiritual that it would be churlish to turn our backs entirely on that subject. Even if we pay no attention to the titles, to the attendant texts or to the composer's explanations of his technical procedures and their symbolic function, it is hard to ignore the traditions of religious music on which the music so audibly draws, and even harder to disregard the knowledge that organs and the buildings in which many of them live are associated with the worship of God. But there is a point at which a discussion of Messiaen's organ music in terms of the theology with which the composer allied it passes beyond the threshold of common experience of all listeners. Certainly it is possible to have some kind of rich communion with a piece such as 'Les eaux de la grâce' without knowing anything about the specific extra-musical ideas to which Messiaen draws our attention. The literature on Messiaen's organ music abounds in studies that seek to evaluate it in the composer's own terms, but we must face the fact that for many listeners the concepts used in those discussions will be incomprehensible and irrelevant.

How else can we try to understand the effect it works upon us? Messiaen's own writings offer another route of entry, one that has also been followed by many of his commentators. So methodically formulated and rigidly followed are the technical procedures of his 'musical language' that they can be described and evaluated in reassuringly concrete terms, at least in relation to the notated score. In the case of 'Les eaux de la grâce' it is relatively easy to discuss the materials out of which it is made, the way in which they have been assembled into what seems to be a well-ordered piece, even to talk about the effects those materials and their morphology might have upon listeners reared in the tradition of Western tonal music.

Ex. 2.1 shows the first eight bars of the score. The eye will immediately notice three discrete layers of music. In the right hand there are phrases of three-note chords, the uppermost notes of which connect to form a melody. According to Messiaen's own terminology, all the pitches in these right-hand chords belong to the second mode of limited transposition. Although the chords themselves are conventional triads, the building-blocks of all tonal music, they do not progress from one to another in the manner of traditional tonal harmony. Indeed it is difficult to relate them to any specific tonal centre; even the G major chords that regularly bring phrases to a close are relatively arbitrary points of repose, one possibility among several. The lowest layer of the score, the melodic line given to the pedals, is notated in the bass clef but assigned a registration that makes the notes sound an octave higher than written. It contains only the notes of the whole-tone scale, which too defies the gravitational pull of tonal functional harmony. Played together, the right-hand chords and the pedal melody allude to several tonal centres but never firmly settle on any one. Even the latent G major of the chordal phrases is regularly undermined by the whole-tone motion of the pedals.

From the score alone it is hard to imagine the sound of the semiquaver flow that the left hand plays, let alone the relation-

EX. 2.1 *Les corps glorieux* 2 'Les eaux de la grâce'

ship it has with the other two layers. Although notated in the bass clef, this line sounds simultaneously in three registers: at written pitch, functioning as the true bass of the texture, and as two treble sonorities. In those upper registers the pitches that the listener hears are not those that are written in the score. Messiaen's registration, 'Nazard et Tierce', will not produce quite the same effect on any two organs, but the general quality is of a bright triadic halo hovering over each notated pitch. In particular the Tierce will be audible, sounding at the interval of a major seventeenth above notated pitch; the opening note E, for example, will have a G♯ sounding two octaves and a third above it. This is what the ear hears. In terms of what the eye sees, however, the line largely consists of notes that are also used in the other two layers. Initially its pitch-classes are those of the right hand's mode 2. In the second bar, a moment before figure B1, the left hand brings into play the pitches of A♮ and D♯, which are foreign to the right hand's mode but present in the pedal part's whole-tone scale. Thus far, the pitches played by the left hand have a modal status of their own: this is Messiaen's seventh mode of limited transposition, a ten-note mode which in this transposition contains all the notes of the chromatic scale other than F♯ and C♮. Messiaen subsequently allowed himself a few F♯s; the fourth notes of figures C1 and C2, and note 26 of figure A2, strictly fall outside the mode. But (notated) C♮ is entirely absent from Ex. 2.1.

Judged from the score, there are places where the left-hand semiquavers consolidate the G major polarity of the right-hand chords (figures B1 and B2), and also places where they join with the pedals in obfuscating it (figures C1 and C2). But this is reckoning without the halo produced by the Tierce. In fact the upper resonances of the left-hand part are more likely to confuse the tonal focus than to clarify it, as Ex. 2.2 shows. At figures B1 and B2 the Tierce emphasizes not G major but rather the key a major third higher, B major; and the pitches it plays at those two points – F♮, A♮, E♭ and B♮ – all belong to the whole-tone scale played by the pedals. The left-hand thus produces a double focus, towards G major (in association with the right hand), and into the tonal no-man's-land of the whole-tone scale (in association with the pedals). If there is any tonal gravitation to be felt from all this, then it is as much towards B as it is towards G. But even those attractions are weak, ambiguous ones. It is a characteristic outcome of what Messiaen called 'polymodality':

EX. 2.2 *Les corps glorieux* 2 'Les eaux de la grâce'

a tonal stalemate in which the elements of traditional harmony largely float free of the forces that conventionally bond them together.

Returning to Ex. 2.1, it is clear that in relation to the music that surrounds it, figure B1 is a point of congruence, even of arrival; Messiaen re-used this material to bring 'Les eaux de la grâce' to a close. By comparison the right-hand music of A1 has the quality of a prolonged ornamental appoggiatura that achieves its resolution only with the G major triads of B1. Figure C1 consolidates that cadence, but is now accompanied by a rising chromatic line in the left hand that has a distinctive upbeat function. It leads into A2, a repeat of A1 with an additional flourish. B2 is its resolution; C2, a more extended upbeat than C1, serves as a transition into the middle section of 'Les eaux de la grâce'. From the rest of the score we can see that this middle section of the work effectively flushes the modes of Ex. 2.1 out of the system, and brings prominently into play the one note that has been missing so far: C♮. Like the opening section it is made up of discrete phrases, some of them upbeat-like, some that are expanded by addition. The largest expansion of all exhausts the process, and at bar 19 the opening music returns, again with additions. Throughout his life Messiaen found satisfaction in simple ternary forms; 'Les eaux de la grâce' is a classic example. Three final observations should be made: the semiquaver flow of the left hand is relentless throughout the piece; the score contains no tempo markings other than the opening 'Rêveur, bien modéré' and the rallentando in the last bar; and the only adjustment to the dynamic markings of the opening is the decrescendo that accompanies the closing rallentando.

Any one of Messiaen's organ compositions could sustain a technical description as detailed as the one given above, and indeed many of them have been dissected in this way, some by Messiaen himself, others by those who have been beguiled by Messiaen's world of self-discipline and the often paradoxically recondite sound-products thrown up by his technical procedures. Many fascinating hours can be had from the study of the scores. But there remain two questions. First, what relevance does a knowledge of the technical procedures used to generate the score have to the aural experience of the music? Second, how does a knowledge of the score, or the experience of hearing the music – or indeed both of these – tie in with Messiaen's verbal glosses to the work: its title, its biblical head-quotation, and all the other information he provided both about 'Les eaux de la grâce' and the cycle of pieces to which it belongs?

To speak of 'the aural experience' of the work immediately raises formidable questions. We have already seen that the notated score is a form of tablature, a set of instructions to the player's hands and feet, that only imprecisely represents the actual sound of the music. But clearly the sound of the music itself will depend upon the organ that is being used, and the organist's choice of registrations. Play two different recordings of 'Les eaux de la grâce' side by side and you will quickly understand why we are treading on slippery ground. Messiaen himself conceived and recorded the piece on a large nineteenth-century French organ, producing a sharply characterized result that we will have to consider in some detail. Other players have used similar organs, but with quite different outcomes, sometimes remote from Messiaen's own. On organs built according to different national or technical traditions the piece takes on a multiplicity of appearances. There is not one 'aural experience' of 'Les eaux de la grâce', but many.

At first sight 'Les eaux de la grâce' seems to be scrupulously notated. As in everything Messiaen wrote, durations are specified down to the last demisemiquaver, and the organist is given detailed information about registration. It is those two components of the work, its rhythm and its timbre, that will give listeners their greatest shock when confronted with Messiaen's own recorded performance, made on the organ at La Trinité in 1956. What appears from the page to be a steady stream of undifferentiated semiquavers played in a constant pulse is, in Messiaen's own mind, nothing of the sort. He speeds up; he slows down; he compresses; he lingers; there are agogic accents and tiny moments of suspended motion all over the place; it is music of far greater rhythmic variety and life than one could possibly have imagined from the notation. The word 'rubato', so conspicuously missing from most of Messiaen's scores, is clearly taken for granted by the composer. As for the sonority, it is utterly unexpected. Possibly the age and the engineering of the recording have something to answer for, but even so the result must at least partially reflect the reality. Of the three layers notated in the score, it is the left-hand music that immediately attracts the ear, not in its notated bass range (which is well nigh inaudible), nor in its Nazard register (which is largely submerged by the right-hand chords), but through the shrill presence of the Tierce. Since this is the line notated in constant semiquavers, its dizzy, drunken gait is all the more arresting. Around it there is a thick tangle of sound, discernible as right-hand chords and a whole-tone melody in the pedal when either one of them stands still or goes into a register unoccupied by the other, but otherwise densely matted together. A sense of polyphony, so clearly visible in the notation, certainly registers, but the overwhelming sensation is of the utter strangeness of the composite sound and its equally strange morphology as the piece progresses. It also becomes abundantly clear that the music of 'Les eaux de la grâce' bears a close relationship to at least part of its title. In Messiaen's hands and on Messiaen's favourite instrument, 'Les eaux de la grâce' simulates the giddy sensation of drowning. A watery gurgle haloed in phantom squeaks and groans, it must surely rank as one of the oddest noises ever heard coming out of an organ.

This excursion into Messiaen's performance of his own music might at first seem to have cleared the path towards addressing one of the questions posed earlier – what relevant information the listener can hope to gain from studying or knowing about the technical procedures used to generate the score. Again, however, we must pause before answering. Does Messiaen's 1956 recording, made on the organ whose registrations he specified in the notated score, possess any authority in determining the sonorous nature of the work? Might it have sounded different in 1939, when the organ at La Trinité was in a less precarious state of repair and the score of *Les corps glorieux* was still fresh from his pen? Might he have played it differently again in old age, on the renovated and enlarged organ? Would he have regarded as inferior any performance made on an instrument other than his own? Could anyone else play the music with equal or greater authority? What status does Messiaen's 1956 recording have in defining the identity of 'Les eaux de la grâce'?

At this point fact gives way to opinion. Jennifer Bate recalls her first experience of playing Messiaen's music to the composer, on a Harrison and Harrison organ in a north London church:

> Messiaen's initial reaction to my performance was not encouraging. 'Well, I suppose you have my records?' Embarrassed, I had to confess otherwise. The point was pursued inexorably until, in desperation, I promised next day to buy everything he had ever recorded. This brought a shout of laughter – 'But that is how I play it on my records, and no one plays Messiaen like that.'[4]

It is a splendid anecdote, and it will give organists much to ponder. Many recordings of Messiaen's organ music have been made partially or substantially under Messiaen's artistic supervision, on instruments that are generically related to the organ at La Trinité. In general they come much closer to his own interpretations than do the performances made from the score alone, using organs built according to different traditions. They do not replicate Messiaen's own solutions, but they do broadly adhere to what we might call his manner of realization. The scores do not say so, but Messiaen seems to have taken a certain style of performance practice and range of sonorities for granted, and when asked for advice by other organists would guide them towards those solutions. As far as the sonic realization of 'Les eaux de la grâce' is concerned, this is as close as we can come to evaluating the status of Messiaen's 1956 recording. It will be interesting to see what influence it and other Messiaen recordings have on his music's interpretation in the future.

With those thoughts in mind, we can begin to compare the experience of the analyst's eye with that of the hearer's ear. The clear separation of the score into three layers, each with a discrete modality, is interesting in theory but less obviously relevant to the listener, who hears largely an amalgam of sounds, and by no means all the pitches that the score would lead us to expect. Only the whole-tone scale of the pedals emerges with clear integrity, largely because of the prevailing stepwise motion. The left-hand semiquavers, sounding predominantly in their Tierce registration a seventeenth above the notated line, do nothing to reinforce the latent G major tonal centre of the right-hand chords, and if anything they side more with the whole-tone scale of the pedal, with which they share so many notes. Moments when the whole-tone scale is heavy in the air, such as at figures B1 and B2 of Ex. 2.1, do indeed seem to be moments of repose, precisely because the number of pitch-classes is relatively restricted. When the modes change in the middle of the piece, the whole character of the music changes with them, but it would take both a sharp ear to work out which new modes have come into play, and an eloquent argument to convince most listeners that it is strictly necessary to know by name the modes that are being used in each layer. What the listener will discover, however, are the following points. First, the whole-tone scale, so securely present in the outer sections of the piece, all but disappears in the middle section. Second, in the outer sections the whole-tone scale, in partnership with the predominantly major triads that the right hand plays, lays particular stress on the interval of the major third (or its inversion, the minor sixth), certainly more than do the modes of the more densely chromatic middle section. Third, the hierarchical relationship that exists between the three layers, seemingly so stable in the score, is in fact materially affected by the movement of those three layers through their available registers. In particular the penetrating shrillness of the Tierce increasingly demands attention the higher it ventures into its upper regions. In sum, not everything the reader sees in the score will matter to the listener, and not everything that attracts the listener's attention will stand out to the analyst of the score.

What of the title and the attendant texts? Clearly the word 'eaux' is hard to ignore, but nothing else is so obviously invoked. As we listen to 'Les eaux de la grâce' we may, if we so choose, keep in our minds the idea of the Lamb in the midst of the throne leading the chosen ones to the living fountains of water, or the idea that 'the life of the resurrected is free, pure, luminous, colourful' and the possibility that 'the timbres of the organ will reflect these characteristics'. We might even construct a mental image of the Lac de Laffrey and the mountain of the Grand Serre. We can bring all those ideas to the music, but it would be difficult to argue that they actually reside within it or could have been deduced from it, any more than the reader of Aschenbach's page and a half of choicest prose would have sensed Tadzio's presence in them. We might agree that the music could just as appropriately have been attended by a different title and prefatory text, or that title and text might have engendered completely different music. Relatively easy as it is to define and describe the technique of Messiaen's 'musical language', the extent to which it genuinely operates as a musical 'language', expressive both of the concrete and the spiritual, and independent of the verbal exegeses that Messiaen provided, remains a moot point.

What Messiaen's organ music can achieve, and indeed does achieve with astonishing success, is a sense of the bizarre, the irrational, the unexplained, the surreal, the mysterious, the erotic, even the sublime. That it can achieve those effects by using compositional techniques that are orderly and systematic is one of its central paradoxes. But it must be said that those techniques are not wholly or principally responsible for the effect the music has upon the listener. Repetition and invariance are two of the more potent agents through which Messiaen evokes the spiritual. This is true of all his music, for whatever medium. Specific to his organ works are slow motion, easily achieved by the instrument's inexhaustable lungs, strangeness of timbre and, where necessary, awesome intensity of sound. From his earliest organ composition, *Le banquet céleste* (1928), right up to the *Livre du Saint Sacrement*, completed in 1984, Messiaen was aware of those special qualities the organ had to offer, and he never tired of exploring them. Tempting as it might be to survey the organ works with reference to their titles and attendant texts, or to the specific technical procedures used in them, there is in fact a good deal to be gained by simply listening to the sounds themselves, and paying close attention to their most obvious outward qualities: their virtuosity or their stillness; their density or their simplicity; their noise or their silence; and often the strangeness of their timbres.

In no organist's hands have these works sounded stranger than they do in Messiaen's own. Others have learnt to match his famously long-drawn-out playing of the slow, soft movements, and in the loud works it takes little imagination to discover how to strike awe into the minds of an audience. But even in those extreme pieces, and more obviously still in ones that border neither on the ethereal nor the terrible, there are more brilliant colours on Messiaen's palette than those of his followers, and he makes ingenious use of them. His choice of timbre is fascinating even in *Le banquet céleste*, a piece that all too easily sounds like improvisatory time-killing before a church service. In his 1956 recording, Messiaen's registration has a thick, throaty texture that energizes those long-held chords, so pregnant with potential harmonic movement yet so frozen in time. This audacious early work also introduces his most baffling organ sonority, the 'staccato bref, à la goutte d'eau', an uncanny dripping sound that turns up in several later organ scores. What this texture is meant to signify in a piece called *Le banquet céleste* Messiaen never explained, yet its oddness somehow seems justified in music that asks us to ponder the unfathomable.

Not even Messiaen's own performance can make the *Diptyque* of 1930 seem an interesting piece, and his later imaginative rescoring of its second panel as the violin–piano duet at the end of the *Quatuor pour la fin du temps* suggests that even the composer questioned its effectiveness as organ music. Its successor, however, shows no such hesitancy in exploring the unique properties of the medium. Anyone who doubts the significance of *Apparition de l'église éternelle* of 1932 – and it has always been overshadowed by the more popular *Le banquet céleste* – will have them dispelled by the sound of Messiaen playing the piece. It represents a major step forward. Where *Le banquet céleste* and the *Diptyque* might effectively have been orchestrated, and the next organ work, *L'Ascension*, actually began life in an orchestral version, *Apparition* is unimaginable in any other instrumental state, and unforgettable in the rasping throat of the machine at La Trinité. Rarely before had the timbre of an organ been used in such a sculptural fashion. Messiaen's himself spoke of the work in physical terms – 'monolithic' on one occasion,[5] 'granite-like' on another[6] – and clearly he calculated his choice of menacing harmonies and heavy-treading rhythm in conjunction with the relentlessly sustained growl of the organ. Few of Messiaen's early titles refer to concrete, inanimate objects, or dreamlike images of them. In this weird attempt to evoke the sense of imagined vision, Messiaen gave music one of its most startlingly surreal works. Later in life he developed the concept more extensively; 'Les langues de feu' from the *Messe de la Pentecôte* and 'Les mains de l'abîme' from the *Livre d'orgue* come to mind as startlingly vivid 'sound-images'.

Its third movement excepted, *L'Ascension* (1933–4) is a transcription of orchestrally conceived music, and for that reason its use of the organ locks less tightly with the musical argument than does *Apparition de l'église éternelle*. In particular Messiaen took pains to replicate the instrumental sonorities of the second movement, 'Alléluias sereins'; his 1956 recording occasionally goes against the letter of the organ score in its attempt to simulate the original orchestral sound. The two outer movements gain more from the adaptation. Magnificent though it is on brass and woodwind, the opening 'Majesté du Christ' benefits from the elasticity of the long-breathed organ; and the rapt fourth movement, originally for string orchestra, sheds at least some of its gratuitous sentimentality in its arranged form. 'Transports de joie', the celebrated new third movement, is pure organ music, but of a kind that Messiaen had learnt from generations of organ-composers before him. It is a startling work, but not a telling indicator of the direction Messiaen was about to take. In his two major organ cycles of the later 1930s, *La Nativité du Seigneur* and *Les corps glorieux*, the dazzling rhetoric and virtuosic bravura of 'Transports de joie' is only rarely to be heard.

Messiaen regarded *La Nativité du Seigneur* (1935) as something of a breakthrough. Later in life he was more modest about its achievement,[7] but to judge from the long preface to the score and the cycle's frequent citation in *Technique de mon langage musical*, at the time it was the work in which Messiaen reckoned himself to have come of age. Although the extended preface opens with theological exegesis and soon turns to a detailed discussion of technical procedures, it also includes an important paragraph in which the medium of the organ itself comes under scrutiny:

> Chaque pièce traitée en larges plans. Economie des timbres par des tutti de couleur et de densité differentes: anches avec peu de fonds, fonds sans gambes ni flûtes, etc. La pédale sort de son rôle de basse. Rarement registrée 16, 8, souvent 4 pieds et mixtures sans 8, elle chante en soprano (8e pièce) ou enguirlande les mains de légers carillons (1re piéce). Quelques effets d'exception: flûte 4 et nazard seuls (2e pièce), basson 16 seul (7e pièce), gambe et voix céleste opposées aux mixtures (1re et 8e pièces): opposer n'est pas mélanger.[8]

Timbre has now become a matter of central concern. With the rich resources of the Trinité organ at his fingertips, Messiaen could manipulate sounds such as no orchestra could produce. There is only one movement of *La Nativité* that reworks an existing orchestral piece, and significantly it does so not by mimicking the sound-world of its prototype but by rejecting it. The model in question is the finale of *Les offrandes oubliées*, a slow movement delicately scored for high violins and violas. For its reincarnation as 'Desseins éternels' Messiaen retained the opening chord-sequence and generously expanded the melodic line; Ex. 2.3 shows how the rewriting was done. The radiant warmth of its shimmering string sonority, however, is abandoned. Instead Messiaen substituted a throbbing fog of low sound, dominated by 16′ registrations that explore the lower half of the organ's voice. It is a dense, subdued and inscrutable sound, inconceivable in orchestral terms. This is Messiaen's new sonorous metaphor for the mystery of the divine.

La Nativité is full of such surprises. Led by the eye, most discussions of the work concentrate on melody, rhythm and

EX. 2.3 (a) *Les offrandes oubliées*

(b) *La Nativité du Seigneur* 3 'Desseins eternels'

harmony, but in Messiaen's own recorded performance it is often timbre that commands the attention and lingers in the mind as a startling and memorable attribute of the music. On paper, the two-part counterpoint of 'Les anges' can be read as a study in ametrical rhythms and cellular expansions and contractions, fleshed out with pitches generated by the modes of limited transposition. In Messiaen's impulsive performance, most of that detail is subsumed into flashes of colour and light; the notated score becomes in effect a set of instructions designed to kindle the organ's shrillest pipework into an astonishing display of fireworks. 'Les mages', realized by some organists as a dutiful plod of a piece, proves to be made from ghostly, disembodied sounds; it is a forerunner of 'Les eaux de la grâce', with which it shares much of its registration. In 'Jésus accepte la souffrance' we get an early foretaste of the cavernous staccatos and the snarling solo Basson that haunt the organ pieces of the 1950s, most obviously the Offertoire of the *Messe de la Pentecôte*. In 'Desseins éternels' Messiaen specifies for the first time the 32′ Bourdon, a stop which speaks with truly sepulchral hush on the organ at La Trinité. It is a tentative first step; by *Les corps glorieux* its solo status has become fully established, most spectacularly in the concluding 'Le mystère de la Sainte Trinité'.

It would be easy to extend this catalogue of innovations. Admittedly not everything in *La Nativité de Seigneur* is remarkable for its novel choice of registration. 'Dieu parmi nous', for example, is more a study in velocity and mass of sound than in special effects; it brings the cycle to a close in a traditionally upbeat, affirmatory manner. Neither the gentle opening cameo, 'La Vierge et l'Enfant', nor its good-humoured successor, 'Les bergers', aims to perplex the ear with strangeness of sound; the deliberate naivety of these pieces is calculated to underscore the human aspect of the Nativity rather than the mystical. A few years later Messiaen might have aimed for something less sweet and conventionally euphonious for the long, hushed ending of 'Le Verbe'; its successor in 'Combat de la mort et de la vie', the central movement of *Les corps glorieux*, shows far greater sophistication in the handling of timbre as well as of melody and harmony. Arguably the popular success of *La Nativité du*

Seigneur owes more to these accessible movements than to their less orthodox, oddly textured and obscurely titled counterparts, of which 'Desseins éternels' is the most extreme. For Messiaen, however, it was the bizarre rather than the traditional in *La Nativité* that suggested the way forward. His next cycle, *Les corps glorieux* of 1939, is noticeably more ruthless in its pursuit of the arcane. From here it would be a small step to the esoteric sound-worlds of the *Messe de la Pentecôte* (1949–50) and the *Livre d'orgue* (1951).

Its overtly programmatic central movement apart, *Les corps glorieux* is unremittingly cryptic. For all that Messiaen insisted on the word 'theological' to describe his music, 'mystical' seems altogether more suited to this particular cycle. Its opening movement, 'Subtilité des corps glorieux', sets the tone: what are we to make of this uncompromising monody, with its echoes of plainchant, ample motivic development and shawm-like cornet registrations, music that unfolds with self-controlled moderation only to coil back at the end into its inscrutable shell? It is followed by another enigma, 'Les eaux de la grâce'. The third movement, 'L'ange aux parfums', audaciously begins as another unaccompanied melody, this time of a more assertive and oriental character. When the melody repeats a little later, it has acquired an accompaniment of quietly juddering chords. Two other ideas are introduced into the piece. One is a three-layered counterpoint (*Bien modéré*) of imiscible components and sonorities, whose labyrinthine musical argument denies it the chance of making any actual progress. The second, a curious bubbling sound (*Presque très vif*), is technically a two-part canonic development of the opening melody, but it would take a sharp ear to hear it as such; its most striking quality is its liquid sonority, more of a gush than the wallowing of 'Les eaux de la grâce'. For all that the music beguiles and delights, it is also music calculated to confuse, beckoning us as it does into a world peopled by ghostly presences and disconcerting unfamiliarity.

The curtains part on 'Combat de la mort et de la vie', and suddenly we are plunged into drama. Where the first three movements of *Les corps glorieux* play upon circularity of motion and invariance of idea, in this piece we know from the start that such mighty turmoil must reach some kind of denouement. Its toccata-like opening, more awesome than anything in 'Transports de joie' or 'Dieu parmi nous', at first uses the resources of the organ with masterful economy, the weight of sound achieved more by the density and dissonance of the chording than by volume alone. As the texture thickens and the register rises, so more stops come into play. The climax is terrifying. To analyse such music only in terms of the technical resources it uses – its modes and rhythms, for example – is to risk underestimating the sheer physical impact of its accumulating noise and confusion. In the vast span of slow music that follows, Messiaen builds wisely upon earlier experience: compared with equivalent sections of the *Diptyque* and 'Le Verbe', the melody here is strangely angular and resistant to resolution; its accompanying harmonies deftly side-step any expected motion, at least until the closing stages; and its bass-line lures the ear downwards towards the threshold of inaudibility.

Just as three pieces precede 'Combat de la mort et de la vie', so a further three follow it. Messiaen returned to the medium of pure melody in 'Force et agilité des corps glorieux', but this time it is monody of a newly athletic and garrulous kind. By scoring the melodic line for the two hands playing in octaves, a new and special depth of sonority is achieved. (Messiaen subsequently developed the effect to even more spectacular ends in the unison 'Danse de la fureur, pour les sept trompettes' from the *Quatuor pour la fin du temps*.) 'Joie et clarté des corps glorieux', the sixth movement, is the only piece in *Les corps glorieux* that might just as easily have been part of *La Nativité du Seigneur*. With its bright fanfares, solid tonality and uncomplicated developmental structure, it seems the stuff of a triumphant finale, a role Messiaen might have assigned it earlier in his career. Instead it serves to clear the air in preparation for the true close, a movement that ends the cycle as inscrutably as it began.

It is hard to ignore the presence of symbolism in 'Le mystère de la Sainte Trinité'. Most analyses of the piece follow Messiaen's lead by focusing upon the identity and interpretation of those symbols – not only the trinity of melodic strands, one ninefold in its phrase-structure, the second sevenfold, the third fivefold, but also the melodic cross-references to earlier movements, the oblique citation of plainchant melody, and the three literally-quoted Hindu rhythms that control the motion of the bass line. Never before had Messiaen conceived anything so tightly rational and meaning-laden as this, more amply stocked with extra-musical ideas for us to hold in the mind and use to enrich the aural experience of the work. Yet even without their aid 'Le mystère de la Sainte Trinité' performs its magic on us. More fundamentally communicative than its symbolic content is the music's fantastical serenity, achieved through a breathtaking selection of organ timbres, the most audacious Messiaen had devised up to this date. The left-hand melody, placed in the foreground with a dynamic marking of *piano*, is assigned a simple 8′ Flûte registration. In the right hand, marked *ppp*, a quiet 16′ registration is coupled with the tiny 2′ Octavin, producing parallel motion separated by three octaves, a truly uncanny effect. The pedal line latches on to the right-hand registration, and adds to it the 32′ Bourdon, a rank so low that its bottom register is barely audible, rather felt by the body as vibration. As the pedal line sinks into its depths, so the right hand's Octavin ascends to giddy heights at which specific pitch gives way to unquantifiable sibilation. Each of the three melodic strands proceeds according to its own logic, following a course of strict or modified repetition. Variation is achieved only by their changing alignment. There is no direction, no climax, no resolution. At the end the music simply loses its breath and becomes silence.

In Messiaen's music there is a fascination with timbre and sonority that places it firmly within a French tradition of innovation. Although the composer's own writings lay greater stress on his music's theological mission and on technical aspects of its construction, we should not lose sight of the fact that in purely sonorous terms it breaks new ground, and that Messiaen was fully aware of the fact. No less than Debussy and Varèse, Messiaen's exploration of new sound-worlds profoundly influenced a younger generation of composers, not least among them the pioneers of *musique concrète* and electronic music. It is arguable that, in his organ works, the path along which Messiaen proceeded was not essentially different from the one that was followed by composers whose medium was magnetic tape. In both there is an urge to escape from conventions of instrumental and orchestral colour, to discover sounds that had never been heard before, to investigate registral extremities, to suspend time through musical motionlessness; above all, to dislocate the listener through unfamiliarity, and evoke the unknown or unknowable. In his early organ works, Messiaen progressed only so far along this path. For his most radical experiments we have to turn to his two great cycles of the early 1950s: the *Messe de la Pentecôte* and, above all, the *Livre d'orgue*. It comes as no surprise to find that Messiaen's single contribution to the field of *musique concrète* – a piece that the composer promptly withdrew, but which has recently resurfaced in notated form – is contemporary with the *Livre d'orgue*, and in many ways turns out to be its spiritual heir.[9]

Notes

1 Translated by H. T. Lowe-Porter (London, 1928).
2 Insert booklet to EMI CZS 7 67400 2, pp. 14–15.
3 Olivier Messiaen: *Technique de mon langage musical*, 2 volumes (Paris, Leduc, 1944); volume 1 translated by John Satterfield as *The Technique of My Musical Language*, (Paris, 1956), p. 8.
4 Obituary, *The Independent* (29 April 1992).
5 Claude Samuel: *Entretiens avec Olivier Messiaen* (Paris, Belfond, 1967); translated by Felix Aprahamian as *Conversations with Olivier Messiaen* (London, 1976), p. 77.
6 Note for EMI 2C 153 16291/6.
7 Samuel, op. cit., p. 77.
8 Messiaen, Author's Note, *La Nativité du Seigneur* (Paris, 1936).
9 The pencil autograph score of *Timbres-durées* is now in private possession in England. For an extract of the score, edited for realization on four-track tape by Pierre Henry, see Erhard Karkoschka: *Das Schriftbild der neuen Musik* (Celle, 1966), p. 166.

Piano Music I

PETER HILL

Messiaen began his career as an organist,[1] yet circumstances led him (from the 1940s) to make the piano his principal medium, with his eventual contribution to its literature the equal of any twentieth-century composer in scale[2] and scope, and arguably without parallel in the originality of its technique. Messiaen's very first composition, *La dame du Shalott*, was for piano, though only because (as he remembered) at the age of nine any other instrument was beyond him. The music was a childish 'stammering',[3] though Messiaen also recalled a fondness for a piece which was 'not altogether stupid and not entirely without sense'.[4] Another early piece, written when Messiaen was thirteen, was *La tristesse d'un grand ciel blanc*, suggested by a pallid sky hanging oppressively over Paris, and sounding 'almost like Stravinsky'.[5] This vein of self-conscious pessimism continues in the titles of the *Préludes*, Messiaen's first major piano work, and the first of his music to appear in print (published in 1930 by Durand on the insistent recommendation of Dukas). The music is anything but cloying, however, having a transparent simplicity and directness; also remarkable is how little it owes to Debussy, bearing out Messiaen's remark (made during one of our conversations) that he had never considered himself an 'impressionist' in the French tradition. Significantly the one passage which does attempt a Debussian virtuosity (in the final piece, 'Un reflet dans le vent . . .') sounds uncharacteristically insipid. Elsewhere the writing appears modest, at times like organ music transferred to the piano (as in the opening to the fifth piece, 'Les sons impalpables du rêve'). Again appearances are deceptive, since Messiaen's deep sensitivity to the piano is expressed in the precision with which he calculates the effects of fading piano tone – so that the fascination for the performer lies in experimenting with minute adjustments of balance. Though predominantly inward-looking, the spiritual grandeur of Messiaen's music is already present, but restrained, so that the prevailing tone (which gives the *Préludes* a unique place in Messiaen's output) is one of great tenderness. There is more interest in harmonic nuance, in the exquisite moment, than in later Messiaen; nonetheless the strength of the architecture is characteristic, for here, as later, Messiaen shows little interest in bevelling the right angles of his forms. Indeed the fascination of these pieces, out of all proportion with their surface simplicity, arises perhaps from the way this 'squareness' combines with a sound and mood which is veiled and mysterious.

All these characteristics are perfectly in focus in the opening piece, 'La colombe', which is worth quoting in full (Ex. 3.1). What impresses immediately is its perfect articulation of musical space. The shape is binary, with an unbroken melodic line which curves down, then up to a point of balance (a complex dominant chord); from here (bar 11) the music restarts, with the complementary second circuit swinging to the tonic. The discretion with which Messiaen confirms this arrival (touched in by soft bass octaves) is typically sensitive, as is the way the chromatic slip F♯ to F♮ at the mid-point is balanced by the push from minor to major, from C♮ to C♯, at the broadening of the final cadence (another complex harmony which combines dominant and subdominant into a cadence which is both plagal and perfect). Also characteristic is the merging of tonality (E major) with the octatonic mode (Messiaen's mode 2). The whole melody is coloured by this relationship: in its descending spirals the principal notes, from the triad of E major, are tinged chromatically by ancillary notes from the mode (A♯, F♮, etc). Similarly, while the basic moves are clearly within the key of E, the modal flavour is discreetly underlined by the fluttering descant, so that the melody is as much coloured by resonances above as by harmonies below. The reminiscence of the closing bars is made especially exquisite by the parallel descant being almost, but not quite, two octaves away. (Incidentally, I once asked Messiaen about his formidably accurate ear, and whether he had perfect

EX. 3.1 *Préludes* I 'La colombe'

A tempo
Rall.
ppp
pp
p
rubato
expressif
cresc.

pitch. He said not, but that he believed he had an abnormally fine sense of pitch in the extreme treble or bass registers.)

The acute sensitivity to harmony is also apparent in the other quiet miniatures. 'Plainte calme' is built round one of those musical paradoxes which hold such a fascination for Messiaen; in this case he creates a tiny mirror form which hovers between chords a tritone apart (on D⁷ and A♭⁷): harmonically at opposite poles, their connection is through the notes which they have in common (C and F♯/G♭). This tiny self-contained binary statement, enclosed by a pair of balancing cadences, is similar in principle to that in 'La colombe'; once complete, it is then gently prised open, first with a prim little canon, then in a more passionate sequence, turning the corner with exquisite finesse as the music elides back into a reprise of the opening. In 'Instants défunts' Messiaen's attempts to reconcile his material are more complex, reflecting a troubled, darker mood. The form is of the type described by Messiaen as 'strophe–antistrophe–epode'; again the statements within the form are binary, with the first idea clearly tonal (enclosed by cadences on A and D), the second, more ambiguous, hinging around a tritone (D–G#). Again Messiaen turns to canon, this time as a way of blurring the edges of the design, and again the transition to the closing section is paced with marvellous discretion: in this case Messiaen feints as if to restart, before lifting the music on to a serene plateau (the epode) in which the previous confrontation is not so much resolved as transcended.

Of the longer slow movements, 'Chant d'extase dans un paysage triste' (placed second in the set) has a hypnotic pacing measured by recurrences of a refrain. At the opening this theme is accompanied by a single line, in an austere but expressive sonority reminiscent of the later stages of Debussy's *Pelléas*, and, less predictably, of the haunting duet for clarinet and bassoon from Stravinsky's *Histoire du soldat*, subsequently, however, acquiring a most un-Stravinskian lushness of harmony which culminates at the apex of the formal pyramid in a lovely running inner voice. The sincerity of the poetic feeling makes one accept the slightly cloying sweetness of the second section, and the peppery development section which seems to have dropped in from another piece. The fifth *Prélude*, 'Les sons impalpables du rêve' (which curiously Messiaen cited to Samuel[6] as a favourite), is less convincing: the opening texture, with its theme inflected by chains of chords in the upper register, has a radiant sonority, but the theme as a whole seems aimless, as also do the ruminations of the central section (another canon), while the secondary idea is unconvincingly cheerful. Altogether, indeed, the dearth of fast music in the *Préludes* reflects Messiaen's unease with extrovert moods. The short third *Prélude*, 'Le nombre léger', is really a slow movement played quickly, a sort of lyrical *étude*, with a pattern of broken chords weaving around a wonderfully long-breathed melody, in a key (E major) which underlines its similarity of mood to 'La colombe'. Again Messiaen relies on canon as the means of stepping up the impetus, but here, in the coda, the effect really is exhilarating, in an ecstatic entwining, impelled by marvellous shifts of harmonic colour towards a final fizz of virtuosity.

Quite unlike all these – and one of the most extraordinary compositions of Messiaen's early years – is the sixth *Prélude*, 'Cloches d'angoisse et larmes d'adieu'. Here with a vengeance is an indication of Messiaen's future path: the vision is Apocalyptic, the religious inspiration (though unstated) clear. And with this power, inevitably, there comes a cruder form of expression, the interest in subtle shadings replaced by a frightening intensity. It is perhaps significant that the music is more literal, more programmatic, corresponding exactly to the two halves of Messiaen's title. The tolling bell-sounds and harsh, bunched chords of the opening rise in a sequence, the pacing calculated so that the second tonal plateau is abbreviated, the third stretched out into a screaming impasse of circling harmonies. Abruptly this tension evaporates, into an arching melody bathed in gently broken harmonies. Despite the hushed dynamic, this is the grandest of slow movements. Only at the very end does the music return to the inwardness of the other *Préludes* as, in a superb final page, Messiaen meditates on the final notes of the melody (B–E♯–B) in textures which dissolve the pedal notes and anguished harmonies of the opening.

The period of fourteen years between the publication of the *Préludes* and the composition of the two-piano *Visions de l'Amen* contains only three pieces for piano. Of the two from the 1930s, much the better is the *Pièce pour le tombeau de Paul Dukas*, which can be found in a memorial tribute (or 'tombeau') for Messiaen's teacher published in the *Revue musicale* of May/June 1936. Here, among graceful contributions by Falla, Rodrigo, and Florent Schmidt and others, Messiaen's sits uncompromisingly, raging at the dying of the light. The other piece, the *Fantaisie burlesque*, sounds as though Messiaen had attempted to compose a test piece for admission to Les Six. Amusingly, on her complete recording, neither Loriod (nor presumably Messiaen) could stomach the final banal flourish, which was simply omitted. But composers' failures are still fascinating – and the weird effect produced when Messiaen's tritone-heavy harmonies collide with the rhythms of ragtime was in the very long term to bear fruit in the zany clowning of 'La rousserolle effarvatte' from the *Catalogue d'oiseaux*.

The nimble and light-hearted *Rondeau* was a test piece for the Paris Conservatoire. Incredibly, given its rather pallid virtuosity, this dates from the same year (1943) as the *Visions de l'Amen*: comparing the two serves to underline the key importance of *Visions* in Messiaen's career, above all as the first work directly inspired by the talent of Yvonne Loriod, who had joined Messiaen's class in harmony at the Conservatoire, to which he had been appointed in 1941, not long after his repatriation from prison camp. Conceived as a virtuoso vehicle for Messiaen and his brilliant young pupil, the music exploits their very different temperaments and techniques by assigning entirely separate roles to the two pianos. The first (given to Loriod) has the tigerish pianism, the bells, birdsongs and swirls of decorative figuration, while Messiaen's more sonorous part carries the themes and underlying harmonies.

Visions ushers in a new era in which the piano becomes the central focus of Messiaen's compositions. Not only that, the use of piano rather than organ means that in *Visions* religious-inspired music comes out of church and into the concert hall, as it also does in the subsequent works of the war years, the *Trois petites liturgies* and the *Vingt regards*. The step is symbolic of the change in Messiaen's music in the 1930s, in which inward, 'private' experience is increasingly given universal expression. As it happens, the works of the 1930s which gave Messiaen most opportunity to develop his piano writing are also those which most underline this development: the song cycles, *Poèmes pour Mi* and *Chants de terre et de ciel*, in which the human experiences of love, marriage and parenthood are projected on to a cosmic dimension.

Visions was also a new departure in that its central inspiration, the idea of Amen, comes not from a biblical source, but from a work of theology – by Ernest Hello, whose writings exerted a profound fascination on Messiaen. Nonetheless *Visions* does contain a scene derived directly from the Bible, Christ's agony in the garden of Gethsemane. In this the sense of Amen is that of acceptance – Thy Will be done – to which Messiaen adds three more: 'Let it be' – the act of creation; the thirst of creation for divine love; and finally the fixing of creation in eternity, consumed in Paradise. Musically these additional meanings give the work a symmetry: the cyclic 'theme of creation' heard at the outset returns to dominate the final 'Amen de la consommation', with its wave-upon-wave of ecstatic developments, while the central 'Amen du désir' acts as the pivot between these two extremes, representing as it does the convulsive energy with which creation strives to be united with its creator. Moreover this fourth Amen stands in marked contrast to the unwavering discipline which characterizes the early stages of *Visions*, first in the repose and ineffable calm of its opening page, then in the stunning energy and freedom of the colossal solo for the second pianist. Meanwhile the sense of symmetry is reinforced by the satisfying balance between the Amens on either side: the 'Amen de l'agonie de Jésus' (No. 3) has its counterpart in the implacable rituals of the 'Amen du jugement' (No. 6), while the grim, obsessive 'Amen des étoiles, de la planète à l'anneau' (concerned with the inanimate aspect of creation) is balanced by the scherzo of the set, the 'Amen des anges, des saints, du chant des oiseaux', in which the dancing medleys of song have a virtuosity which is relaxed and genial.

From the perspective of the *Préludes* the step to *Visions* is a giant one, from scrupulous sensitivity of detail to music which is epic in its scale and ambition. This is, so to speak, 'Hollywood' Messiaen, a shout of joy, as George Benjamin has put it, and (remembering the date of its composition) a defiant affirmation of faith in the face of man's inhumanity. *Visions* is a work which divides listeners. While most are caught up in Messiaen's paeans of ecstasy, a few find the heady cocktail hard to stomach. The comparative crudeness of *Visions*, certainly when compared with the *Vingt regards* (which it anticipates in so many respects and where by contrast Messiaen was able, miraculously, to combine scale with refinement), calls for a digression. While one cannot argue with personal preferences, it is worth noting that Messiaen was accustomed to suffering abuse equally from conservative minded critics and from the younger avant garde. The charge of 'vulgarity' which came from both quarters can be countered by pointing to Messiaen's place in the tradition of Catholic art, in which examples – such as Bernini's swooning St Teresa or the rococo churches of Bavaria and Austria – can still seem faintly shocking to the prim Protestant mind. More than that, one of Messiaen's great achievements was to recognize and reject the fake piety which accounted for the virtual extinction of great religious art in the nineteenth century, and which extended its deadening inhibition to our own time. Indeed in the twentieth century masterpieces of religious art are rare, and are often isolated, unique productions which – like Henry Moore's Madonna in Northampton or Matisse's Chapel at Vence – express the artist's sense of reverence in a moving simplicity.

Messiaen's ambition is of course of quite a different order, and leads in *Visions* to an inclusiveness of expression in which there is an unblushing acceptance of the musically tawdry. Personally I find this refusal to 'censor' his material, this contempt for normal canons of good taste, magnificent and exhilarating. What reservations I do have concern musical matters: whether Messiaen's material, and in particular his rather ponderous structures, can bear the emotional weight placed on them. Part of the problem is the entirely separate functions assigned to the two pianos: the second (Messiaen's part) has the main thematic and harmonic ideas, while the first piano exploits Loriod's virtuosity. One consequence of this is that, though the piece is a vehicle for Loriod, her part is essentially decorative and only rarely takes the musical initiative. Several of the pieces rely on a formal stereotype, with typically an exposition given largely, or wholly to piano 2, later repeated literally with additional commentary on piano 1. In the recapitulation to the second piece, for example ('Amen des étoiles, de la planète à l'anneau'), the piano 1 part seems largely redundant, doing little more than add accentuations to what is already emphatic.

Experiencing the work in the heat of performance, however, is quite another thing from considering it in cold blood, and no other work of Messiaen demonstrates so completely the inspiration derived from what on paper may appear contrived. In this second piece the formal frame, prosaic and obstinate, is just what the piece needs; meanwhile the sequence of developments which occupy the centre of the piece, while never losing the overall sense of stubborn grandeur, twist the initial five-note motif to exciting effect, impelled by the streams of bunched

EX. 3.2 *Visions de l'Amen* 2 'Amen des étoiles, de la planète à l'anneau'

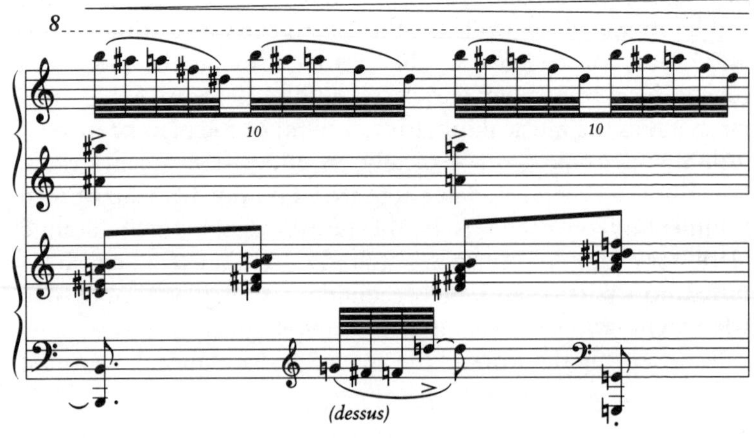

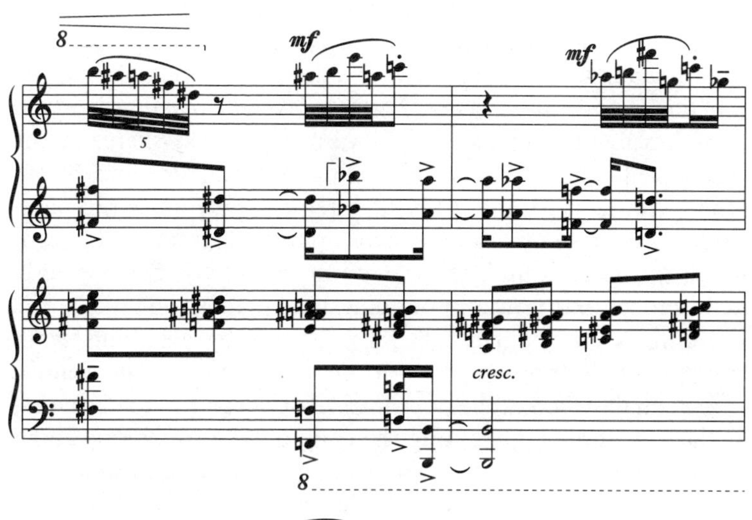

chords on piano 1. And where the pianos do, rarely, achieve parity the effect is electrifying: in Ex. 3.2 the third of these developments, a vast turbine of four orbiting strands, is actually controlled by the first piano, with the five-note motif (in the left hand) allied to a seventeen-note rhythm, the passage ending when melodic and rhythmic patterns have run their course.

This rhythmic complex derives from the core of ideas set out in the first Amen ('Amen de la création'), in particular the interweaving mirror patterns which float above the unfolding of the 'theme of creation' itself. Though developed primarily in the final Amen, both recur at significant points elsewhere. In the 'Amen de l'agonie de Jésus', the culmination again comes about when Messiaen permits genuine interaction between the pianists, in a passage of sonorous heterophony. This stylized 'weeping' is disrupted brutally by the seventeen-note rhythm,[7] exactly as in No. 2, but now in pounding bass percussions, while the profound silence which follows is broken by a halting, fragmented recollection of the 'theme of creation'. The central 'Amen du désir' takes the polarization of the pianos to extremes, at the same time highlighting the consequence of the prevailing formal scheme. This works wonderfully in the return of the slow introduction, where the majestic harmonic shifts are genuinely illuminated by the crystalline descant of piano 1 which manages to be expressive as well as decorative, and again, especially, in the peaceful coda, a foretaste of Paradise symbolized in the descending chains of the bell-chords (in mode 3) which anticipate the closing stages of No. 7. In the reprise of the jazzy second section (a passage of stupendous big-boned virtuosity which, on his recording with Loriod, Messiaen plays with the freedom of an improvisation) the first piano, again employing the seventeen-note rhythm, adds a turbulent, subversive layer of bass percussions to create an Ivesian free-for-all.

In No. 5 we again encounter the 'theme of creation' in a fluid, tender and slightly improvisatory version alongside exquisitely shaded meditations on the unison chanting with which the piece opens. In the recapitulation the theme is again (as in No. 3) presented in partnership with material which recalls the first piano part in the 'Amen de la création', with rhythmic canons below and in the treble a descant of glacial rippling dissonances. At the same time these upper decorations refer back to the central scherzando section of the piece, in which skipping rhythms on piano 2 accompany a miscellany of birdsong. These are the first virtuoso representations of birdsong in Messiaen's music, although in terms of truth to nature they are scarcely more advanced than the instances in the *Quatuor pour la fin du temps*. Messiaen specifies particular birds in his Preface, but not (as he always did later) in the score itself. Certainly the effect is generalized, and rather primitive – the left hand repetitive and incantatory, the right hand chirpy and freer – so, one feels, birdsong symbolized rather than described (see Ex. 3.3).

Another virtue of the formulae which I have described, is that the music's rhetoric remains firmly disciplined. The tone of the

EX. 3.3 *Visions de l'Amen* 5 'Amen des anges, des saints, du chant des oiseaux'

work as a whole is set in the first Amen, which on the face of it is one of Messiaen's most breathtaking naive conceptions, simply a hugely protracted crescendo in which the 'theme of creation' rises in four-square phrases from the depths of the keyboard. The necessary complexity comes from the first piano part, minutely calculated by Messiaen as a dispassionate, objective foil to the warmth and passion of the theme. In its superimposed rhythms, which seem to float beyond time, there is the paradox so often encountered in Messiaen of apparent randomness produced by extreme rigour. Another contradiction is that though initially virtually inaudible, the timbre is from the outset incisive, with later randomly placed accents causing sudden shafts of illumination, as when the face of a gem suddenly catches the light. The upper part responds to the theme, yet remains distant from it, with its crescendo lagging behind: this separation is emphasized in the closing stages as piano I continues with unflinching rigour, while the theme is decorated by broken chords (as Messiaen asks for a freer, more rhetorical style of playing). Harmonically the piece is left open-ended, with the cadence on the dominant (E), so that the reprises of the theme in the intervening pieces have the effect of reminding us of unfinished business. The resolution of this giant upbeat in the musical and theological 'consummation' of the seventh Amen is again audaciously simple, the theme in brisk march tempo storming the heavens, while the rhythmic patterns on piano 1 are heard in the bass (as they were in No. 3 for example) as well as treble. Increasingly they become bell-like, first as the rhythmic canons between the hands simplify to converging scales, subsequently as these pass from Messiaen's third mode (as in the coda to No. 4), settling finally on quiet superimposed scales of A major. The pianos unite in this moment of stillness which serves to clarify the tonality, hitherto obscured by the dissonant tumult on piano 1, as the music regains the dominant harmony left at the end of the first Amen. This is the hushed preliminary to a peroration made the more overwhelming by the way it sweeps beyond previous constraints. Piano 1 seizes the initiative, in streams of circling bell-chords, even taking over the theme (in broken arpeggios) before, finally, spirals and more chains of bells overlay thunderous developments on piano 2. These at last take wing as they burst with thrilling spontaneity through the theme's rigid frame.

The progress of Messiaen's music in 1944 seems to mirror the momentous events of the external world. With the completion of *Visions de l'Amen*, the first fruits of his partnership with Yvonne Loriod, subsequent works again centred on her playing: first the *Trois petites liturgies* with their important concertante piano part, quickly followed by the great cycle of the *Vingt regards*. This, the last of the great religious cycles until the organ *Méditations* of the 1960s, is also by far the most ambitious to date, both in its scale, and, as we shall see, in its dense plotting. While on the one hand it sets a seal on one phase of Messiaen's life – just as in the same year did the publication of his musical 'autobiography', *Technique de mon langage musical* – on the other it proclaims Messiaen's excitement in charting new territory, an excitement underlined by the extraordinary rapidity of its composition, in just six months (March to September 1944).

In *Vingt regards* the interweaving of cyclic ideas, whether themes or motifs, is one sense in which the work builds on the comparatively primitive example of *Visions*; another is the regaining of an inwardness of expression, with at times the tenderness so manifest in the *Préludes*. Allowing for a pianist's bias, I have to say that nothing in earlier Messiaen, and very little in later, quite touches the sublimity so consistently attained in the slow movements of the *Vingt regards*, which impress even more than the work's epic feats of virtuosity, staggering though these are. In all this one sees the inspiring influence of Loriod, whose unquenchable powers enabled new complexities of thought, and liberated Messiaen's imagination (as he many times testified) from practical limitations: of this, one striking instance is the increasing transformation of birdsong from a decorative to a soloistic role.

'Regard' is untranslatable by a single English word. Literally a 'look', it carries also its English connotations of 'aspect' and 'reverence'. From this one might have expected of Messiaen a series of devotional images, an expectation apparently confirmed by the opening 'Regard du Père' in which five pages of music stretch, in the extraordinarily slow tempo, to over nine minutes of playing time.[8] The impression continues with the subsequent four *regards*, all slow, and culminating in a paraphrase of the first piece in only marginally more flowing tempo. This calm, sustained over some twenty-five minutes, is part of Messiaen's design, for it enables him to spring the ambush in No. 6 – 'Par Lui tout a été fait', the 'big bang' (as Messiaen described it to me) of creation, and the first of the set-pieces whose stupendous difficulties make the *Vingt regards* an Everest among pianistic challenges.

Such virtuosity reflects Messiaen's antipathy to the 'insipid'[9] in sacred music. To Samuel he justified the opposite point of view in terms which perfectly describe the scale of the *Vingt regards*.[10] In a detailed and illuminating Preface to the work itself Messiaen described some of the factors which govern the work's architecture. The order of the movements is partly a matter of numerological significance:

> the 'Regard de la Croix' bears the number 7 (a perfect number) because the sufferings of Christ on the Cross restored the order that was disturbed by sin, and the angels are confirmed in grace in No. 14 (two times 7). The 'Regard du temps' bears the number 9 [representing] the nine months of maternity common to all children, and the 'Regard de l'onction terrible' has the number 18 (two times 9) – here, divinity is poured out over the humanity of Christ in the one person who is the Son of God. The two pieces which speak of creation and the divine government of creation are No. 6 (because 6 is the number of [days of] creation) and No. 12 (two times 6).

Musically the feature of Messiaen's numerological scheme most apparent is the recurrence of the principal cyclic theme, the 'theme of God'. This is heard at the outset and thereafter in every fifth piece, the *regards* concerned with the divinity. Together with important appearances of the theme in Nos. 6 and 11 the spacing of these repetitions suggests a ground plan with pieces grouped in fives. The design of the first section is especially clearly marked, since the fifth piece ('Regard du Fils sur le Fils') is an exact paraphrase of the opening 'Regard du Père', and thus seals the predominantly reflective tone of the work to this point. Another aspect of the scheme is that the outer movements are the longest: so in the second quarter, three short pieces of the type which Messiaen classifies as 'immaterial or symbolic' – the Cross, heights and time – are framed by outpourings of storming virtuosity, the fugal No. 6 and the 'Regard de l'Esprit de joie' which closes the first half. In the second half, although the pieces are still grouped in fives, the symmetries are less clear-cut. Instead the music is dominated by great slow movements; again their significance is marked by even spacing (they are Nos. 11, 15 and 19) and by the fact that thematically all refer back in some way to the 'theme of God' (subliminally so in the case of No. 19), their ultimate goal being its final ecstatic transformation in the closing pages of No. 20. One consequence is that the second half plays some twenty minutes longer than the first; yet despite this the sense of an unfolding core of ideas results in a marked gathering in momentum. This is paralleled in Messiaen's programme as it crystallizes around events of the Christmas story, symbolized musically by a quotation from *La Nativité du Seigneur* (the theme of 'La Vierge et l'Enfant) heard in No. 11 – the 'Première communion de la Vierge' – and again in No. 13 ('Noël'), and in mood carried forward in the rapt 'berceuse' which opens No. 15 ('Le baiser de l'Enfant-Jésus'). Another factor is that the intervening trios of shorter *regards* are arranged so that they contribute to the impetus: Nos. 12 to 14 in particular form a compact, powerful unit, and act in any complete performance as the engine room, climaxing in the closing pages of No. 14 (the 'Regard des anges') as the music of the angels collides with and is symbolically routed by the torrential virtuosity of the birds. Similarly the final trio, Nos. 16 to 18, reaches another culmination in the 'Regard de l'onction terrible' (whose title refers to Christ's coronation), the most massive of the 'independent' *regards*, those that are not based on the 'theme of God'.

The outer symmetry, whereby the principal theme is transformed and 'consummated', recalls *Visions*; so too does the marking of the work's mid point with a peak of virtuosity. Here, above all, in the 'Regard de l'Esprit de joie', Messiaen pays tribute to Loriod's powers, especially in the piece's central development, which Messiaen describes as like a hunting-song, scored for the 'intoxicated' tone-colour of a quartet of horns. The tumultuous pianism which results from this almost orchestral conception demands not only agility and power, but the ability to despatch at speed and with complete abandon complex patterns, notably in the descending scales of bell-chords (very reminiscent, incidentally, of the final Amen of *Visions*) which punctuate each line of Messiaen's tune, a version of another cyclic theme, the 'theme of love'. Still more daunting is the transition which precedes this central section, because here the pattern – a process of irregular, but logical, expansions which Messiaen terms 'agrandissements asymétrique' – makes no concessions to the lie of the notes under the hand (see Ex. 3.4a). The frequency with which Messiaen resorts to such

EX. 3.4 (a) *Vingt regards sur l'Enfant-Jésus* 6 'Par Lui tout à été fait'

(b) *Vingt regards sur l'Enfant-Jésus* 20 'Regard de l'église d'amour'

organized techniques of development and propulsion is a principal reason for the heroic demands *Vingt regards* makes on a pianist's mental and physical stamina. Not surprisingly, the huge build-up in the first part of the final *regard* is also driven by another similar process; in this instance the asymmetrical enlargement in bass octaves is overlaid with glittering figurations which are a series of 'interversions' (permutations) of a twelve-note row (the first such instance of 'serial' writing in Messiaen's music; see Ex. 3.4b).

The technique is still more fundamental to the fugue, No. 6, and is the main reason why pianists see this piece as the most difficult. Again it is characteristic of Messiaen that supreme energy should find expression in implacable discipline. So here the building-blocks of fugue, subject and countersubject are from the outset continuously deformed, but always in ways which are logically rigorous.[11] On top of this, the fugue is infiltrated by another idea used cyclically throughout the work, the so-called 'theme of chords'. This too is fragmented, finally into a cloud of two-part chords, played in canon between the hands, itself infiltrated by the re-emerging of the countersubject (see Ex. 3.5). This extraordinary passage, which stretches to the limits of pianistic feasibility, is the 'eye' in Messiaen's hurricane; not only that, it crucially foreshadows (as we shall see) the impasse with which the piece ends, at the same time being the hinge between the two halves of the fugue. For beyond this (another horror for the pianist) is the fearful symmetry in which the whole fugal edifice is replayed literally, note-for-note, backwards. The effect is curious: a sort of controlled *anti*climax, in which the fugue is dismantled, so that the subject re-emerges (like a film of an explosion played in reverse), as a preliminary to yet further asymmetrical enlargements, in agonizingly protracted strettos.

Beyond the inexorable rotations of these juggernauts the *Vingt regards* makes a notable advance in brilliance of writing and in real pace, an elusive quality in Messiaen's early music. By comparison, for example, with the unison drummings in the outer sections of No. 10, earlier tours de force, such as the 'Danse de la fureur, pour les sept trompettes' sound laboured

EX. 3.5 *Vingt regards sur l'Enfant-Jésus* 6 Par Lui tout à été fait'

and somewhat pedantic. In No. 10 the energy is real, not contrived, its fuel the continuous fluid interplay and collision of tiny motifs. Again the ferocity is sustained by implacable discipline, and is coloured by the percussive use of the bass of the piano, a foretaste of *Harawi* and, especially, the *Quatre études de rythme*. In *Vingt regards* this hard-edged piano writing continues in the *regards* which celebrate the birth of Christ – No. 14 ('Noël') and especially the extraordinary 'vast and reedy consort' of No. 16 ('Regard des prophètes, des bergers et des mages'). The most exhilarating conjunction of speed and sonority is in No. 12 ('La parole toute puissante') in which the winding melody is constructed out of two scales which meet in the constantly reiterated central D, with a collision of metric units to which the accompaniments of brusque grace-note arpeggios and thudding bass clusters add jolting syncopations.

This sort of writing reminds us that Stravinsky's *Rite of Spring*, and especially the 'Danse sacrale', was a cornerstone of Messiaen's analytical teaching. Stravinsky is evoked again in the 'Regard des hauteurs', where tiny melodic molecules twist and are deftly and wittily reformed. The sonority is equally exhilarating, a two-part invention with an uncharacteristically lean and 'woody' timbre, Messiaen's lark (the symbol for the heights) beating against a top note in the piccolo register, above the more sinewy curves of a bass clarinet. The élan is matched by a feeling (especially in the headlong unison sweep of the coda) that the birdsong is moving from stylization to a closer approximation to reality. Curiously this is less true of the triumphant birds of No. 14 ('Regard des anges'): these chirrup in the manner of the 'Amen des anges, des saints, du chant des oiseaux'; the 2/4 metre is a regularity necessitated perhaps by their tussle with the metric canons of the angels, but would be unthinkable in Messiaen's later birdsong music.

At the other end of the spectrum, and at least as difficult to play, are the great slow movements. As the first of these, the 'Regard du Père', slips majestically from harbour, the work's time-scale is measured by the ticking pulsations of the semiquavers; even and calm, these must be felt as a descant, folded into the dynamic of the bass harmonies, with miraculous control

EX. 3.6 *Vingt regards sur l'Enfant-Jésus* I 'Regard du Père'

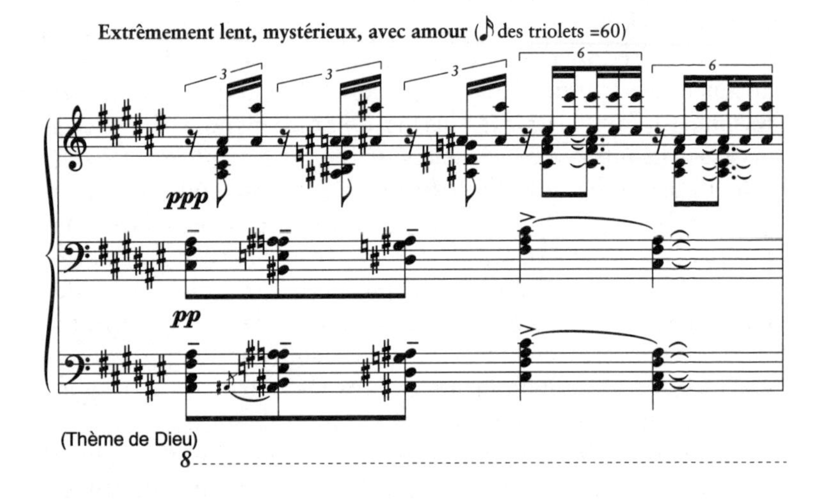

demanded for the final diminuendo, from *pianissimo* to inaudibility, graded over some twenty seconds. The opening five chords, the 'theme of God' itself, remind us of Messiaen's fascination with sequences of chords bound by a common pedal note. The second harmony slips chromatically, its push against the framing A♯s enhanced by the acciaccatura, before being balanced by the spacious cadence of the fourth and fifth chords. This enclosed geometry is twice pushed back but never broken. In both instances the beginning of each expansion is identical: first the three opening chords are answered on the dominant (C♯) – with a discreet colouring by a minor ninth of which more will be made later in the work; subsequently this dominant harmony launches a rising sequence, the first time re-establishing contact with the 'theme of God' by arriving on a transposition of its second harmony. At the parallel place in the second half the symmetry is completed, but in a way that strikes as a decisive new departure. What we hear has an arresting minor colouring: as the phrase sinks back, however, this reveals itself as no more than an inversion (with added sixths) of our tonic chord, of F♯ major. (The ambiguity which gives rise to this deception is one to which Messiaen will return again and again in the course of the work.) The magnificent shape of this first *regard* goes far beyond the cliché of inert meditation so often applied to Messiaen's slow movements. True, both the theme and the piece as a whole end as they begin, but the journey around the curve has a continuous sense of unfolding revelation, the more powerful for its implacable discipline. This tension between stillness and an expressive forward impulse, between (one might say) eternity and time, underlies all the subsequent slow movements. More than that, the 'Regard du Père' is a prologue to the whole journey, as Messiaen's musical expression of 'the inexpressible' is brought within the sphere of passionate human utterance.

This prophetic aspect of the 'Regard du Père' continues to be explored, in different ways, in the remainder of the first quarter of the work. The aphoristic second *regard* establishes the 'theme of the Star and the Cross' (symbols of Christ's earthly life), a sort of chromatic plainsong heard first in glacial unison, the hands four octaves apart. Again the form is binary, enabling the theme to be 'humanized' with an expressive commentary. In particular, the dragging slurs of this descant foreshadow the fulfilment of this *regard* in No. 7, the 'Regard de la Croix', in which the theme, in long notes, acts as a *cantus firmus* to upper layers of circling, plangent harmonies. In No. 3 the idea is formalized, Messiaen's theological inspiration being the 'terrible commerce' between God and mankind. Once the musical process is established the piece unfolds automatically in two-bar units, accompanied by the continuous crescendo which Messiaen seems to associate with creation. The piece ends as the figure in octaves (in the left hand) runs its course, arriving at the notes with which it began, albeit displaced in register. The other figures in the odd-numbered bars, representing as they do the divine, remain unchanging; whereas in the second bar of each pair we encounter the first instances of asymmetrical enlargement: in these, certain pitches rise, others fall or, exceptionally, remain static, so that the effect is of shapes which uncoil and reform.

To this rigour No. 4 – the 'Regard de la Vierge' – is the exception: the formality is still there, but looser, more supple (the opening rocking motif is almost, but not quite, a rhythmic symmetry), with exquisitely nuanced, slightly hesitant cadences, and a celebratory middle section which hints at the bells and birdsong to come. From this Messiaen derives a winding descant which has the effect of pushing the reprise into a profound interior calm: again this will prove to be prophetic, finding fulfilment in the rapt 'Première communion' which opens the work's second half.

In the 'Regard du Fils sur le Fils' the expressive focus is again in the descant. The 'theme of God', transposed to the middle register of the piano, is no longer mysterious but clear and luminous (a transformation anticipated in the visionary coda to No. 1). Against this the pair of upper lines is initially secretive and impenetrable: their sonority, using the more complex higher modes (4 and 6), is oddly muffled, and the rhythmic canons – augmented by a dot – are further confused by constant interweaving. Anthony Pople has even suggested that this musical obscurity is designed to parallel the inscrutable theological inspiration; be that as it may, Messiaen was certainly keen, from his comments to me, that the strands should be as clear as the hushed dynamics permits. Again the ritual is 'humanized'; this time, as the music of the 'Regard du Père' unfolds, the expressive pressure breaks through the rigid frame and releases in the heights the idealized acrobatics of a skylark, in a shower of gentle virtuosity. The effect is similar to the first of the *Trois petites liturgies*, but here the song is more jubilant, more urgent, though remote in dynamic. (Here I diverge from the composer: Messiaen – to me incomprehensibly – was insistent that this song should be 'très, très fort', the only instance I remember where his advice contradicted the letter of his text and, more importantly, its spirit.)

The step from this ethereal, spiritualized plane to the turmoil of No. 6 is the first dramatic juxtaposition of the *Vingt regards* (later matched by that between Nos. 18 and 19), and the plunge into the seething instabilities of the fugue underlines the sense of exposition in the calm, contained certainties of Nos. 1 to 5. As we have seen, this fugue is incapable of resolution: all it can do is consume itself. What follows from this mid-point confirms No.

6 as a key piece. The fugal subject reassembles in mountainous strettos, the labour which precedes the rebirth of the 'theme of God'; now, however, this is hugely transformed, interleaved with the new 'theme of love' and all but engulfed in rampant virtuosity. The final stages underline this sense of impasse, with the two themes confronted by elements from the fugue: the 'theme of God' shouted in canon, blocked by the 'theme of chords', then a counterpoint of descending chromaticism as the 'theme of love' circles in the left hand. The culmination is a passage which paraphrases the central 'eye' of the fugue. Here, instead of the countersubject, it is the 'theme of God' which struggles to assert itself – in a cannonade of *fortissimo* chords – while Messiaen's 'macrocosm' is a single harmony (again from the 'theme of chords') which quietly pulsates in the heights. So, at the end, all the elements which open the 'Regard du Père' resurface, now grotesquely deformed.

The other virtuoso peak of the first half, the 'Regard de l'Esprit de joie', is similarly inconclusive. In the final stages its energy is crystallized in versions of the 'theme of joy', each more tremendous than its predecessor. The intervening episodes heighten this tension, first in a scherzando treatment of the 'theme of God', then in the return of the opening 'drumming', now glittering in the high treble (in fourths) with surging patterns pounded in the bass. The final statement is on C♯, which continues on a pedal under spiralling figuration (a Messiaen invention, in which the flat of the hand swings to and fro across the pivoting thumb), but the final cascade, emphatic though it is, side-steps the signalled cadence on F♯.

The second half is a new beginning, the 'theme of God' for the first time transposed in key (to B♭) as well as register. The 'Première communion' reminds us how beautifully Messiaen can be simple – as in the ravishing recall of *La Nativité*, with at its cadence the heights and depths touched in with exquisite discretion. The upper pulsations of the 'theme of God' are missing, replaced with more idealized birdsong, but they reappear in the bass of the piano (as the Virgin contemplates the heartbeats of the unborn infant) – when playing to Messiaen, I remember attacking these low Fs with gusto, only to be implored to be more discreet! In the opening to No. 15 the tenderness of No. 11 merges with the lilting character of No. 4, the other Marian *regard*. The 'theme of God' is back in the key (F#) and register of No. 5, and this sense of gathering allusion is marked by the fullest reference yet back to the 'Regard du Père', telescoping its opening three chords with a subsequent move to the dominant harmony. The calm of this 'berceuse' is deceptive however: its music is quickly given a new intensity with a development (on the subdominant), coloured by meditations on the F#/D# ambiguity. No. 15 in fact is to be another crucial piece: the longest of the slow movements (and the longest piece apart from No. 20), its role is as significant as that of No. 6, which it balances symmetrically, with the difference that here a transformation for the first time attains resolution. As with No. 6 the piece is in two halves, with the position occupied by the fugal strettos here taken by a giant fulcrum, a sort of dramatic 'scena' inspired, Messiaen tells us, by a picture of 'the Christ-child leaving his mother's arms to embrace St Thérèse of Lisieux . . . as symbol of the communion, of divine love'. This harmonic build-up, culminating in screaming clusters at the top of the piano, is in effect a huge dominant pedal, underpinned by C# in a way that strikingly anticipates the central crisis of No. 20. So too does the sense of integration in what follows. The music of the 'kiss' has a resemblance to the 'theme of love' (in the falling fourth), and its profile is melodically (and rhythmically) an inversion of 'joy'. This, the first moment of arrival, of unfettered ecstasy, is pushed forward through a huge intensification (the subdominant again), then through a peroration on alternating harmonies of tonic and dominant, and a cadence in which again the D#/F# harmony is emphasized – all features which foreshadow the closing pages of No. 20. The sense of completion and fulfilment is underlined in the beautiful coda; the theme of the 'berceuse' now in even rhythm supports Chopinesque figurations, a graceful transformation of earlier descants which is difficult to play since it must sing, not glitter.

The next stage in this journey is one of distillation and concentration (No. 19). But before this comes the climax of the jubilatory *regards*, in No. 16 ('Regard des prophètes, des bergers et des mages') and in the yet more monolithic 'Regard de l'onction terrible' (No. 18). Both are framed by ascending and descending scales of duration, inspired by the example of Balinese music. Between these, the 'Regard du silence' expresses its paradox first in stillness, in rhythmic canons which float beyond measured time (using, incidentally, the same note-values and augmentation as No. 5) and then through colour, in iridescent, flickering figurations which culminate in the 'inverted rainbow' variant of the 'theme of chords'. The remarkable coda fuses rhythmic stillness with these glinting colours as the harmonies of the earlier canon circle in even semiquavers, with a long diminuendo to the edge of silence.

The opening of No. 19 is equally extraordinary: a motionless reverie, at the extremely slow tempo lasting more than a minute and a half, with a single underlying harmony held in suspension. But this is *the* chord, F# major in first inversion – by now sufficient on its own to suggest the presence of the 'theme of God' – in the register associated (since Nos. 5 and 15) with Christ. Similarly oblique reference is made to the theme from *La Nativité* before an impassioned development of the 'theme of love', checked only by a phrase marked 'berceuse', and launched by the D# minor colouring one remembers from No. 15. At the centre is a passage of supreme calm (see Ex. 3.7), with the 'theme of love' turned inside out, so that it *begins* with the falling fourth (F#–C#), cadencing on the exquisite C# minor-ninth harmony, which by now has acquired the status of a motif in its own right. Melodically, the falling fourths[12] connect back to the bass octaves which softly underpin the melismas of the opening, a link made yet more marked as they return, fragmented at the end with references back to the 'theme of love' (a ninth on C# again).

The concentration of motifs in No. 19 is a foretaste of the final piece, where everything (with the exception of the initial flourishes) is a fulfilment. The engine driving the music is the asymmetrical enlargement (described earlier) treated in relentless sequences, as are the developments of the themes of 'God' and 'love', so that the whole effect is of inexorable steps rising through a series of plateaux. After the largest of the 'agrandisse-

EX. 3.7 *Vingt regards sur l'Enfant-Jésus* 19 'Je dors, mais mon cœur veille'

ments' the music hacks its way into the open, hanging grimly on to the pedal C#. Once this is established, Messiaen launches the last transition, comparable to the 'fulcrum' of No. 15; above the hammered C#s we hear the bells of No. 2 and the 'theme of chords' in the 'inverted rainbow' of No. 17, the music finally crystallizing on C# via expanding rhythmic scales which recall Nos. 16 and 18.

The supreme inspiration of the closing pages makes comment unnecessary. Yet I cannot resist describing the details through which the circle is finally completed and transfigured. In the 'theme of God', triumphant, the shadowing pulsations are now absorbed, becoming the reiterations which launch each phrase. As in No. 5, it is the 'Regard du Père' in its entirety which is paraphrased (up to its coda), its cadences filled by shimmering birdsong derived from No. 4. The music follows the 'Regard du Père' up until its second climax – on the D#/F# harmony, now exultantly reiterated. From here Messiaen releases two further inspirations: the way forward is in the apotheosis of the subdominant intensification so important to No. 15, and from this flow Messiaen's 'tears of joy'. As these recede we hear again the alternating tonic–dominant harmonies (No. 15), before a last rising curve which dwells on the F# added-sixth harmony, coloured again, at its apex, by D# minor. Melodically there is the A#–C# rise of the 'theme of God', and in the imitation between the hands (which Messiaen made a point of asking me to emphasize) a calm recollection of the struggling canons at the end of No. 6. Finally its harmonies merge, so the theme forms a single indivisible gesture, chiming this last time in the bright treble register, and ringing on as if defying the inevitable fading of piano tone. Words cannot evoke these superb pages, and the attempt would in any case be superfluous. All they can do is, in some small way, to suggest reasons for their power. The proof is in the experience: in isolation the passage is a marvel in itself, but heard as a culmination and completion of the whole, it is inexpressibly overwhelming.

Notes

1 However it is not generally appreciated that, as Martin Neary points out 'he took up the organ only after Jean Gallon, his piano teacher at the Paris Conservatoire, on discovering Messiaen's phenomenal skills as an improviser, introduced his teenage prodigy to . . . Marcel Dupré ('An Organ Composer of Genius and Rocklike Faith', *Church Times*, 8 May 1992, p. 20).

2 Messiaen's music for solo piano, together with *Visions de l'Amen* for two pianos, has a total playing time of around eight hours.

3 Brigitte Massin: *Olivier Messiaen: une poetique du merveilleux* (Aix-en-Provence, Alinéa, 1989), pp. 32–3.

4 Claude Samuel: *Entretiens avec Olivier Messiaen* (Paris, Belfond, 1967), p. 122.

5 'Entretien avec Claude Samuel' (CD booklet, ECD 75505), p. 18.

6 Samuel, *Entretiens avec Olivier Messiaen*, p. 125.

7 Identical, incidentally, to the rhythm of the piano part in the 'Liturgie de cristal' from the *Quatuor pour la fin du temps*, and before that, heard in

'Arc-en-ciel d'innocence' from *Chants de terre et de ciel*, and 'Le mystère de la Sainte Trinité' from *Les corps glorieux*.

8 Though startling, the metronome mark here as elsewhere in the work, was calculated much more precisely than, for example, in the *Catalogue d'oiseaux*, and deserves careful consideration by the pianist. The exceptions to this are the rapid movements Nos. 6 and 10, where Messiaen conceded that his original tempos erred on the side of caution.

9 '. . . cette musique un peu fade . . . est le résultat de conventions et d'erreurs malheureusement trop répandues' (Samuel, op. cit., p. 20).

10 '. . . les Vérites de la Foi . . . sont terribles; ce sont des contes de fées, tour à tour mystérieux, déchirants, glorieux, terrifiants, reposant toujours sur une Réalité lumineuse et immuable' (ibid., p. 17).

11 This fundamental and perpetual instability caused Paul Griffiths to term this an 'anti-fugue' (*Olivier Messiaen and the Music of Time*, London, Faber and Faber, 1985, p. 119).

12 By imposing F# major in its second inversion, these also contribute to the sense of something incomplete, awaiting resolution.

The Songs and Song Cycles

JANE MANNING

Introduction

While Messiaen's superb command and creative use of keyboard techniques is rightly acclaimed, his understanding of the finer points of the singer's art is less often discussed. Messiaen's music for voice and piano includes a trio of substantial and enduringly rewarding contemporary classics, *Poèmes pour Mi* (1936), *Chants de terre et de ciel* (1938) and *Harawi* (1945), that must be considered essential repertoire for soprano voice (all were written for the dramatic soprano, Marcelle Bunlet). Messiaen's endearing long-standing fascination and affinity with birds and their song may perhaps provide the key to what seems an astonishing grasp of the mechanics of the female voice, including importantly, awareness of the physical feeling of freedom that results from properly energized and supported vocal tone. Messiaen's touching delight in birdsong, which by him is used to express joy, strikes a poignant personal chord – a keen amateur ornithologist, I was brought up among birds, and my father's pigeon-loft provided a tranquil escape from more mundane duties. In adult years it is easier to perceive symbolic and spiritual connections – doves represent peace and also purity, flying affords freedom from earthbound worries. Scholarly research has tended to concentrate on the undoubtedly fascinating rhythmic intricacies of notated birdsong, without much reference to philosophical and psychological aspects. Perhaps those who work with a living organic instrument have a special responsiveness to such an intimate connection between physique and psyche. And one cannot possibly ignore the larynx's crucial role in glandular activity and change – although less obvious in the female than the male voice, of course, physical and mental changes can quite noticeably affect the delicate vocal mechanism, and to the sensitive singer even the most minute responses are reflected in the larynx.

Birdsong must surely count as one of nature's purest and most delightful musical utterances, and we can also learn much from it of dynamic, pitch, articulation and resonance. Singers who push and strain to attain power must wonder at the torrents of perfectly aimed and penetrating sound that issue so effortlessly from such tiny throats. We should all be able to project much more effectively if only we could achieve such unfettered warbling. Teachers often talk of 'unlocking' the voice – too much conscious control, effort and tension can suppress the voice's natural functioning. But Messiaen does not fall into the trap of avoiding the singer's palpably human qualities, and elevating her merely to the world of birds, despite many specific verbal references, such as the 'colombe verte' of *Harawi*, as we shall see.

As a singer of Messiaen's vocal music, it is impossible not to identify closely with its wonderfully seductive blend of the physical and the spiritual. Thankfully, and most felicitously, the soprano voice, is for Messiaen an expression of womanliness in the fullest sense. He does not, unlike some composers, shrink from the female sexuality inherent in the trained soprano voice, and seek to impose a vocally inhibiting non-vibrato or childish timbre. Feminists may well take exception to the composer's idealization of the roles of wife and mother, most explicitly found in *Poèmes pour Mi* and *Chants de terre et de ciel* respectively (though not nearly as sentimentally as in Schumann's *Frauenliebe und Leben*), yet the singer of this music cannot fail to respond to such genuine warmth of affection and appreciation. His insight seems extraordinary. Deftly mingling eroticism with spiritual radiance, he creates an entrancing vocal language, which uses the voice to its fullest and most satisfying capacity. There is nothing better than being allowed to sing properly! The composer Brian Ferneyhough is often quoted as saying that his transcendentally difficult music, seemingly just beyond the bounds of capability, has an inbuilt expectation of stress, and that this element of striving against the odds contributes to the desired result: heightened excitement in performance. Messiaen has perhaps found a kinder approach to this aspect, although undoubtedly the major cycles require considerable stamina. *Harawi*'s fifty minutes or more can be compared to a mountain climb – 'second wind' tends to occur half-way through, and the performers emerge triumphant, having exercised themselves to their fullest powers. Messiaen has an innate grasp of the natural span of a singer's breath. Phrases are perfectly judged so that they can be sung without interruption, assuming the singer has a good standard of technical competence – amateurishness would be quickly exposed in these monumental masterpieces, but serious students and professionals can learn much of their own capacity and potential by singing Messiaen's music. I have always felt that almost any phrase could be isolated as a perfect exercise in vocal control – timing, intonation, tonal graduation and legato, and of course, articulation.

One ought not to go further without mentioning the texts. All except the middle poem of *Trois mélodies* (by Messiaen's mother Cécile Sauvage) are by the composer himself. With such a strong literary background (his mother a poetess, and his father, Pierre Messiaen, a famed translater of Shakespeare) it is not at all surprising that Messiaen displays a gift for words, with a specially acute ear for the distinctive nuances of the French language. Custom-made, and entirely at one with his musical visions, the texts provide startling and powerful images of religious and mystic symbolism. It would be perhaps inconceivable for Messiaen to set a language other than French. The syllables themselves create a glittering mosaic of sonorities and subtle resonances, in addition to their actual meaning (many of the poems do not translate at all satisfactorily). The composer's awareness of the minutiae of verbal enunciations and articulations is miraculous. Each vocal sound can be precisely placed as intended, all dynamics are scrupulously plotted, and the performer's involvement and intimate connection to the music is enhanced by the sensual nature of word projection: lips, tongue, teeth and palate are all involved, as each sound is savoured and poised for perfect precision of attack and control of timbre. Messiaen even takes account of the problem of exact co-ordination between singer and pianist at important cadences, by preceding final chords with his characteristic upbeat acciaccaturas which allow the singer to breathe during them and arrive securely and comfortably on target, without interrupting the music's natural flow. Messiaen's awareness of natural body-rhythms is satisfying for singer and listener. In an ideal performance, the audience may find themselves breathing with the singer, thus increasing contact and involvement.

Although Messiaen's music is undoubtedly challenging, both vocally and musically, it is eminently practical. Pitch orientation is hardly a problem for the singer, as favourite progressions and chords recur frequently, and harmonies and rhythms soon become comfortingly familiar with practice. The voice is used, above all, in a naturally lyrical and expressive way. Evenness and controlled legato are required, as in all classic 'art song' (and it must be stressed that Messiaen continues the unbroken line of the great writers of French *mélodies*, in particular showing the influence of Debussy in his use of the natural inflections of the language). Dramatic bursts of percussive declamation are always impelled by syllables which invite such treatment. Perfect intonation is imperative, and any sensitive artist will come to an increased awareness of the possibilities of vocal coloration and variety of timbre, according to mood, dynamic and register. A 'functional voice lesson' is offered in the course of negotiating the larger paragraphs.

For the interpreters of his music, Messiaen demands and effortlessly inspires complete commitment. In the voice and piano works, both performers are equal partners, not only because of the virtuosity of each part, but because it is essential that genuine rapport exists between them. The major cycles can be viewed as a dual act of faith, requiring the utmost mutual trust and sensitivity. By stretching the performers to a peak of intensity and concentration, Messiaen is fully aware of the sense of well-being and comfort engendered by the shared experience. With all masterpieces performers undergo a process of transformation, and technical rigours are eclipsed by higher thoughts. Messiaen's deep religious faith is so fundamental to his music, that it cannot be glossed over. Such shining inner conviction must invoke love and respect in the performer even if he or she does not share his specific beliefs.

Trois mélodies

Apart from some early unpublished efforts in the field, withdrawn by the composer, Messiaen's first recognized work for the voice/piano medium is the miniature cycle *Trois mélodies* of 1930.

One is at a loss to explain why this charming work is not in the standard repertoire; although not typical of the composer's later, full-blooded style, and modest in scope, lasting about six minutes, it would be an ideal recital item for a young singer and must be warmly recommended for this purpose. The piano figurations of the first and second songs in particular are redolent of late Fauré and Duparc, and demand no specialist expertise to perform them effectively. The vocal tessitura is perfectly judged so that the texts can be projected easily and clearly, with an automatic response to colour shadings suggested by the poems. The three movements are nicely balanced and contrasted. Family influences are easy to recognize in the touching warmth and delicacy of the words, and the mutual preoccupation with nature imagery linked to the miracle of creation.

'POURQUOI'

Messiaen's poem reiterates the title word to introduce a short catalogue of nature's gentlest and purest pleasures – birdsong, reflections in water, the seasons unfolding. The mood becomes more poignant, with the revelation that these no longer bring joy, but the reason remains a mystery, as the 'Whys' rings out and gradually fade.

Singers will inevitably be cheered and comforted by Messiaen's constant use of melodic unisons, just as they are by Puccini's. Problems of pitching of intervals are solved and the singer can relish blending tone and colour with the piano. This song is in one of Messiaen's favourite keys, F# major, one that for him always depicts rapt wonderment (see also the 'alleluia' section of the first song of *Poèmes pour Mi*). The word 'Pourquoi' gives the singer time to place the diphthong – 'quoi' – with the utmost care, and a sinewy legato through the phrases is helped by the smoothness of the syllables. The music rises and falls with complete naturalness. The piano writing does not yet have Messiaen's distinctive stamp, but already, on the upmost of the piano's three staves, we find the characteristic grace notes preceding single 'bell-chimes' which help further to centre pitches. The pianist mirrors and supports the voice for the duration of the poem and then bursts out into climactic chordal solos, while the voice reiterates the word 'Pourquoi' in a coda which, after some more intricate passagework on the piano, gradually dies away and eases firmly back on to the home ground of F# major.

'LE SOURIRE'

This enigmatic, yet subtly telling second song is the briefest of the three. The evocative words encapsulate a deeply private moment of spiritual empathy between two people. A tender word touches the soul and brings the response of a tremulous smile. This song presages the highly concentrated smaller songs of *Poèmes pour Mi* in its delicate placing of natural word stresses in quasi-recitative style. Its extreme economy and intimacy (it never rises above *pianissimo*) even reminds one of Webern (the op. 3 and op. 4 songs, for instance). It is a beautifully gauged exercise in control, yet, as ever, the syllables are a help – note the gentle rise followed by a *subito ppp* on 'l'âme', where it is easily possible for the singer to delay the release from the 'l' and, holding the tip of the tongue in position, float smoothly into the vowel in an unbroken line (see Ex. 4.1).

EX. 4.1 *Trois mélodies* 2 'Le sourire'

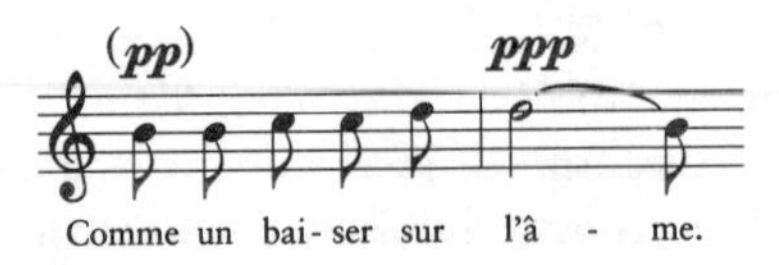

'LA FIANCÉE PERDUE'

The most extended song of the three begins with high cascading repeated figures in the piano, while the voice moves in plain crotchets, securely supported by pitch references contained in the piano's chords – a traditional songwriting device. There is a strong thematic connection between this poem and 'Pourquoi?' Nature's joys are again expounded, this time as metaphors for the qualities of the remembered sweetheart. The 'sourire' of the second song also makes a fleeting appearance ('pure as a child's heart'). The characteristics of this piece are found in different order and guise in the final song of *Poèmes pour Mi*. The chordal textures of the passage beginning 'Carillon' in *Poèmes*, for instance, have the same relationship and exuberant impetus as the opening of 'La fiancée perdue'. Irregular phrase-lengths and variety of metre already show Messiaen's fascination with rhythm, which was to prove so richly rewarding in his mature work. Deep-seated faith in man's relationship and connection to a higher authority is raptly affirmed. Idealized images of the beloved are halted by a slow piano line linking to the beatific 'Modéré' which ends the work. The piano has continuous *pianissimo* triplets while the voice intones a fervent prayer for divine blessing on the soul of the 'fiancée' of the title. Such exalted incantations recur frequently in Messiaen's vocal works, and it is interesting that the words 'Donnez-lui votre grâce' are very close to more emphatically declaimed phrases in the last of the *Poèmes*. This song affords a brief glimpse at the visionary rewards of the later cycle, although the language is at present limited to relatively conventional gestures.

La mort du nombre

This rarely heard piece of vocal chamber music, written in 1930 for soprano, tenor, violin and piano, gives a revealing foretaste of Messiaen's references and predilections in the casting of the solo roles. The text is Messiaen's own. Each voice represents a 'spirit': the soprano, Ame I, is the spirit of joy and optimism, and the tenor, Ame II, the soul in fear and torment at the point of death. The violin belongs with the soprano spirit, complementing the voice's ecstatic upward soaring. Imagery is already much richer than in the *Trois mélodies*, and language more elaborate, with more than a hint of the surrealism to come. A highly emotional and dramatic tenor role, evoking wild fantasies of the disintegration of the universe, is in sharp contrast to the soprano's comforting depictions of escape from earthly burdens, soaring, birdlike to higher planes in 'perpetual springtime'.

A 'plainchant' melody on the muted solo violin precedes the tenor's opening modal 'recitative' and recurs to divide this from more turbulent declamations, which gradually build in intensity to a passionate 'Je souffre!' The keys chosen for the tenor, mainly 'flat' ones, are in significant contrast to the radiant, shimmering 'sharper' tonalities of the soprano's music. At first her contribution takes the form of serenely angelic legato phrases of reassurance, which punctuate the tenor's troubled outbursts, the keys continually changing with the characters. At the soprano's exhortation, 'Attends, espère!', the violin soloist introducers the long rapturous B major section which completes the work. Soprano and violin are in glowing partnership, rising to an exultant climax, while the piano's figures become ever denser, gradually turning into rapid, harp-like arpeggios. After the soprano's triumphant high B, violin and piano together bring the work to a close, gradually calming to an ethereal *pianissimo*, the violin rising to the stratosphere. Interestingly, the piano part is constantly high, frequently in the same range as, or above, the violin, contributing to the luminous effect. The violinist is, perhaps, the deity, conferring benediction and calm assurance.

La mort du nombre anticipates elements of Messiaen's dramatic vocal masterpieces to come. Indeed the general love/death theme of *Harawi* in which the lovers aspire towards spiritual union after death, seems to be foreshadowed here, and there is a direct parallel with the dialogue between male and female and their contrasting key orientations and moods, in 'L'amour de Piroutcha' (the fifth song of *Harawi*). The rich, sensual harmonies might even evoke hints of Wagner's *Tristan*, combined with the more obvious influences of French impressionism.

Vocalise

This modestly scaled piece, dating from 1935, is unique in its lack of text, but it nonetheless exhibits features which belong with the later, more substantial cycles. Perhaps it can be seen as a preliminary study for the beautiful, soothing 'alleluia' section of *Poèmes* already mentioned. Certainly the piano part, and the pitch centre in particular, are strikingly similar. (See also the second song of *Chants de terre et de ciel*, 'Antienne du silence'.) Messiaen of course resorts to a very different kind of 'alleluia' for the last movement of *Chants*, but sharper keys consistently represent him at his most serene and affirmative.

This delightful piece would go particularly well in a church concert. Although it is written for piano, one wonders if the timbre of the organ might not be equally suitable. However the keyboard part is fairly demanding and relentless in its motion, supporting the voice and impelling it along. As a singer, one knows how difficult it can be to float with apparent ease through the whole vocal range, deprived of helpful explosive consonants to give impetus, and of the smoother liquid sounds ('n' 'm' 'l' and so on) which elide and blend across awkward transitions. There is also the question of stamina if the music is virtually seamless. The final section of the first song of *Poèmes*, with its long melismas on 'alleluia', gives similar challenges, but Messiaen always judges breathing spaces perfectly so that the singer does not tire, and *Vocalise*, too, is measured out expertly. Changes of key and cadences are enhanced by the voice's swooping lines, giving room for the subtlest rubato. Although rhythm is so crucial in Messiaen's music, repetitious passages, as found here, never become mechanical. Time-signatures change often, giving further flexibility to the fluid vocal lines. Just when the singer is in need of a rest, phrases become fragmented, granting recovery space (and a chance to 'run in' the demisemiquaver patterns in preparation for what is to come). The final section returns to the sustained opening phrases, and rises to a glorious high A♭, which unwinds in a descending coloratura cadenza, dying away and resolving calmly on to the home 'twin' keys of A major and F♯ minor (see Ex. 4.2).

EX. 4.2 *Vocalise*

dim.
dim.
rall.
au Mouvt
p
pp
p

Poèmes pour Mi

Messiaen himself said that anyone wishing to understand his music would do well to study first the two early cycles *Poèmes pour Mi* and *Chants de terre et de ciel*, because they are ' "true" in sentiment, and typical of my manner'.[1] The cycle is infinitely more complex rhythmically than the songs which precede it, yet Messiaen has already reached a wonderful purity of expression, and a refined and personal language, easily recognizable by even a single chord.

Poèmes pour Mi is dedicated to Messiaen's first wife, the composer and violinist Claire Delbos, and is a radiant affirmation of the joy and sanctity of marriage. It belongs to the early group of his works which concentrate on theological subjects, and immediately follows the organ work *La Nativité du Seigneur*, with which it shares some musical features.

Since the text is the composer's own, some interpreters may feel uncomfortable at what could seem a strongly traditionalist attitude to the woman's role in marriage. However, Messiaen's devout Catholicism is central to his vision. Throughout the cycle, all aspects of the loving partnership are put into perspective with their higher relationship with God. Nature images provide philosophical parallels with the spiritual life. It is impossible for a sensitive performer, of whatever creed, not to enter into heightened awareness of the world that lies beyond the notes.

The cycle's nine songs are divided into two books, containing four and five movements respectively. The more fervently dramatic declamations, some quite violent, are punctuated by brief, intimate pictures of the natural world. After undergoing trials and terrors, the lovers reach their heavenly goal, in a triumphant climax of joy and rebirth.

'ACTION DE GRÂCES'

The opening and closing movements of Book I are the most technically demanding of the cycle. The work begins with bell-like chord progressions on the piano, which impart a liturgical atmosphere. The soprano's psalm-like chants enumerate the wonders of the universe: first the natural elements of earth, sea and sky, and then the human form itself, inseparably connected to God, who watches, follows and mirrors even the subtlest movement ('comme la vague à la vague est unie'). Each sentence ends with a melisma of cumulative complexity on the final word: a testing exercise in breath control and evenness of tone thus early in the piece. The statements become more intense as they rise in pitch. Messiaen subtly helps to focus the voice as the song progresses – pitches are repeated so that sounds can be carefully matched. Vocal phrases are alternated with more elaborate chordal passages on the piano. Rhythms move in canon, a crotchet apart, between left and right hand, and between voice and piano. These sections already give the less experienced singer a chance to slip naturally into Messiaen's rhythmic idiom, free from the imprisonment of bar-lines and set metric patterns, listening and responding naturally to the piano without being fettered by regular beats. A peak is reached at a tempo change to 'Modéré', and the piano's music becomes more sustained. Chords in contrary motion lead up to the voice's luminous 'Tout cela, vous me l'avez donné' and thereafter her statements become briefer and more exultant, accelerating to a thrilling melisma on 'étoile'. (Messiaen's characteristic commas are placed with care, allowing for long breath spans. Here, the piano does not breathe with the singer, as happens elsewhere, so the singer should slightly shorten the note values before the commas. Messiaen is a master of punctuation, and his paragraphs are beautifully organized.)

At the unison cadence 'Mon Dieu', the final, seraphic 'alleluia' section, in the glowing key of F$^{\sharp}$ major, draws the movement to a close most memorably in a mood of serene adoration. This is Messiaen at his most simple and moving. In the soprano's long melismas, the flow of the music is again highlighted, rather than interrupted, by perfectly placed commas, to avoid vocal tension, and to manage register changes comfortably. The final lift from high A$^{\natural}$ to the long-held A$^{\sharp}$ is helped by the rocking syncopations that precede it. The voice remains in gentle perpetual motion until the very end. The composer knows instinctively that a succession of long notes at that register would have been more tiring. The final A# glows the more effectively for this grateful approach. Such rhythmic vitality is one of Messiaen's hallmarks, even in music which is slow and repetitive.

'PAYSAGE'

This miniature scena provides an immediate contrast in scope and content yet retains elements of divine mystery in its symbolic imagery. Despite the song's brevity a lot of ground is covered in constant changes of mood and emphasis. The pace of ordinary life is contrasted with the calm of the lake, and an idealized vision of the beloved is perceived in the distance, her enigmatic smile bringing comfort.

Vocally it is relatively simple and direct. The soprano begins with a gently gliding downward tritone on 'Le lac' (marked 'gracieux'). A slight portamento is surely permissible here. The composer's love of the ondes martenot has always encouraged one to feel that he desires as smooth a legato as possible wherever the phrase invites. (During the passage marked 'Un peu plus vif', the piano's left-hand triplets dictate the pulse, and the singer must take care to fit with them – she is momentarily the accompanist here.)

'LA MAISON'

The third song is even briefer: fluent and fast-moving at first, calming quite suddenly towards the close. The text condenses the message of *La mort du nombre*, in which morbid thoughts are soothed by the promise of lasting spiritual joy and enlightenment. The soprano's nervous phrases, expressing fear and impending loss, are accompanied by piano ostinatos. A rapid chant, rising to a pitch of excitement, dissolves suddenly into sustained phrases in unison with the piano's chords. These anticipate the vocal expansiveness found in *Harawi*, and a lighter voice may experience some difficulty in commanding such broad spans in the middle register. The last phrase in particular, with its abrupt diminuendo, needs iron control if the final E is to remain even.

'ÉPOUVANTE'

This is a searing outburst of anguish and terror. The text's nightmare images of hell are matched by the soprano's howls and monosyllabic ritual incantations. These reach a frenzy of horror, while the piano thunders, clashes and rumbles. Unisons between voice and piano help to give weight and security to the vocal declamation. The strength and steadiness of the soprano's occasionally vulnerable middle register is now put to the test. The refrain 'ha, ha' on the semitone A to G♯ constitutes a useful technical exercise in itself. Another challenge is the low-lying unaccompanied chant which immediately follows. Proliferating syllables contain percussive elements that could, under duress, bounce the sound out of place. However, as always, Messiaen gives just enough space round the notes for each one to be firmly centred, maintaining the line, and avoiding the gustiness that can come from forcing. It is important not to take large breaths in between these shorter phrases. Messiaen shows his understanding of the need to conserve air and increase resonance by muscular control; this is an example of the composer at his most physically aware. Security comes from the support and involvement of the whole body. As singers will know, using the body's muscular strength helps save the throat from pressure at moments of extreme tension. The final paragraph of wild cries descending from a high A♭ is rewarding to sing, but contains one of the very few problems of ensemble in the work: how to leave the high tied note together (see Ex. 4.3). Pianists have to be at their most intuitive, unless a signal can be given, perhaps by the tilt of the pianist's head.

The vocal fragments in the last line of the song should sound spent and exhausted, without actually being so! It is safer not to breathe in the rests, but to use the glottis for an unforced re-attack. The low tessitura is helpful in this respect. Many singers have problems with passages that would be quite comfortable if they merely spoke the lines at a natural pitch. There is a tend-

EX. 4.3 *Poèmes pour Mi* 4 'Epouvante'

ency not to make this connection. Those with high voices sometimes accept a breathy quality on low notes, when their own speaking voices give a much clearer indication of potential quality at this range. One can forget that singing is a natural function, and it is not necessary to overreach and push on beyond the pure kernel of resonance that springs instantly from a perfectly timed attack.

'L'ÉPOUSE'

This serenely beautiful song, the first of Book II, is the heart of the cycle. It represents the moment of marital union, when the bonds of earth and heaven are inseparable. A rapt refrain to the words 'Va, où l'esprit te mène' (Go where the spirit leads you) lies in the most flattering part of the voice. This time it is a rising tritone which conveys the feeling of beatitude (cf. 'Paysage'). A series of shimmering lyrical phrases test the singer's breath control. Ideally, they should not be broken up, since the message of the text concerns the continuous thread that binds wife to husband, and both to Christ. This sublimely uncompromising statement of faith is set in simple yet delicately sensuous harmonies. The pitches revolve around the crucial tritone, including minor thirds on either side, and the piano gently supports, mirrors and, in some cases, anticipates the vocal lines, further emphasizing the subtle interplay within the marital power structure. The last phrase, 'Comme l'Eglise est le prolongement du Christ', is exceptionally slow and intimate. The control needed to maintain a hushed intensity in the lower range anticipates the first song of *Harawi* which tests this skill even more extensively.

'TA VOIX'

A heart-warming picture of a spring afternoon employs the shining resonances of the soprano's higher range. The symbol of the open window, which allows both fresh air and birdsong to flood into the room, is extended to a vision of limitless space, in which the bird is transfigured and joins the heavenly choir of angels, secure and radiant in God's love. It is a joy to sing, and its buoyancy of spirit is reflected in bright soaring phrases, within a relatively gentle dynamic. The atmosphere of calm happiness is winningly sustained, as the soprano floats happily above the piano's successive semiquaver chords. Near the end comes a sudden interruption: a rapid passage of exuberantly repeated rhythmic fragments on the piano – perhaps a spontaneous song of praise from the bird in its new guise. The final tritone lift (on the same pitches as at the song's beginning) to a held *pianissimo* F#, leaves the singer exposed – one of only two or three such moments in his major song cycles where there is an element of risk if the quality is not entirely free and flawless.

'LES DEUX GUERRIERS'

This is an exciting and highly emotional 'aria', full of bravura and colourful imagery. The drama is shared equally between both performers, and the bizarre symbolism of the text ('les écroulements de sulfureuses géométriques') reaches a climax in an anguished plea for God's support, as the lovers – divine warriors – march towards their heavenly goal (see Ex. 4.4). Marriage as a battleground is a familiar concept, but in Messiaen's fervent vision, the battle is fought on a united front! The punched-out notes that begin and end it are very difficult for a soprano, but from experience I can say that it is much easier to keep the tone clear if one conserves air. As in so many cases over-eagerness can produce a clouded quality which is less penetrating than desired.

'LE COLLIER'

The violently extrovert mood of the previous song is at once dispelled by this intimate picture of married life. The wife's arms twined around her husband in the early morning, are described as an exotic necklace. Sensual and spiritual images are evoked, and mingle with poetic references to the colour and texture of jewels. One cannot help thinking of the mystical properties of crystals and prisms. Art and science are perfectly blended

EX. 4.4 *Poèmes pour Mi* 7 'Les deux guerriers'

in Messiaen's personal vision of the natural world. The gently rocking rhythm of the piano's bi-modal chords supports the voice's simple tune, irregular note values giving a lilting flexibility. A characteristically warm lyrical phrase in rhythmic unison with the piano gives the voice room to expand, although this requires considerable capacity to negotiate in one span. The melismas on repeated dancing rhythms are also a challenge of breath control. The second verse repeats the material of the first, and there then follows a coda of utmost tenderness and simplicity, the voice suspended in the middle register, unaccompanied and *pianissimo*. The piano's rocking chords return beneath the singer's final note.

'PRIÈRE EXAUCÉE'

The cycle's last movement is by far the most taxing vocally, bearing many similarities to the work's opening declamatory recitatives. The repeated hieratic exhortations of the soprano are punctuated by piano chords. Then comes a typical athletic melisma with voice and piano at the unison. This passage is rhythmically rigorous, leaving no room for manoeuvre if attacks are not precise. The repeat of the opening phrases breaks out into impassioned cries of 'Donnez-moi votre grâce!' The work's jubilant finale is almost unbearable in its intensity. A 'Très vif' marking introduces pulsating semiquavers representing jangling bells in the piano part, and the voice crescendos from *pianissimo* repeated fifths to jagged attacks together with the piano – 'Frappe, tape, choque' – the onomatopoeic character of the words enhancing the effect. From here onwards, balance must be carefully gauged so that the voice is not overwhelmed. Ascending vocal phrases burst into uninhibitedly joyful high notes celebrating 'glory' and 'resurrection'. The voice's final melisma on the word 'joie' (see Ex. 4.5) is the work's only major vocal problem: in the middle register, and relentlessly continuous, this paragraph is well-nigh impossible to encompass in one breath without cutting volume drastically. It is perhaps a little disappointing that the work ends with what seems to be a slight miscalculation. Unfortunately, the singer will invariably be blamed for not being strong enough, but she has to compete with striking chords in her own register, plus scintillating high semiquavers above. A heroic effort is required and the result is almost inevitably a little unsatisfactory. Thereafter the work cadences triumphantly, the piano's chromatic scales hurtling to the bottom register.

A year later, in 1937, Messiaen made an orchestral version of *Poèmes pour Mi*, in which there are some major tempo changes that subtly alter the dramatic emphasis and, for the most part,

EX. 4.5 *Poèmes pour Mi* 9 'Prière exaucée'

allow time for more expansive resonances. As might be expected there is a rethinking of the more specifically pianistic figurations, and orchestral colours are bright and glittering. Bell-chimes feature prominently in the more ritualized movements, especially at the work's end, where Messiaen allows for the change of ambience by adding a huge rallentando. Tempos of the smaller songs, especially 'La maison' and, even more crucially, 'Le collier', are quite considerably slower, although in the last-named, there is an accelerando through the most concentrated passage of melismas. The alleluia at the end of the first song, and the long hushed *pianissimo* at the close of 'L'épouse' are even more expansive (the latter enhanced by ethereal string harmonics) and demand the raptest treatment. Rhythms are generally made more flexible by additional accelerandos and ritenutos. Difficulties of rhythmic ensemble are simplified by re-barrings and re-divisions of beats, while some of the more strenuous passages in the original version move more swiftly, alleviating vocal wear and tear: for example, in the 'journey to hell' of the fourth song, and parts of 'Les deux guerriers'. In 'Epouvante', the reprise of the anguished cries is much easier to negotiate with a conductor in charge, and more intricate part-writing, including a syncopated countermelody, is added to the 'moto perpetuo' that immediately precedes the voice's re-entry. The coda to the final song is given additional embellishments, especially in the section beginning 'Carillon'. This time there are real bells, of course, and triplet figures for strings and woodwind are added to the running semiquavers. Fast grace-note swirls on strings provide cues immediately preceding the entries of 'Donnez-moi', and loud percussive attacks are frequently reinforced by brass. Perhaps it is the composer's intention that the singer should be almost engulfed by the torrent of jangling resonances in the problematic final passages, for to remain audible one would need a voice of phenomenal power. Messiaen specifies 'grand soprano dramatique', and the comparative rarity of the work's performance in this version may perhaps be explained by the dilemma of casting the vocal role. The weightier voices sometimes lack flexibility and tonal variety, and today's Wagner singers are rarely happy floating in *pianissimo*. A lyrical soprano with a strong lower range may perhaps represent the best compromise.

Chants de terre et de ciel

If *Poèmes pour Mi* is a deeply-felt tribute to the joy of commitment in the marital relationship, *Chants de terre et de ciel* is an equally intimate yet touchingly open-hearted picture of family life at its happiest and most unclouded. Once again, Messiaen uses familiar names with endearing eagerness to share with us his domestic bliss. The two middle songs of this six-movement cycle are dedicated to his infant son Pascal, known to the family as 'bébé-Pilule', and are a touchingly open expression of joy in the fresh innocence of childhood and the need to draw inspiration from it. Even here, though, the composer manages to avoid becoming saccharine, and steers carefully on the right side of the taste barrier, in music of the most disciplined and refined technique and vision. His musical language has become even more assured and, most notably, the piano writing has developed considerably. The pianist's role is now a highly individual and virtuoso one, the material in striking and dynamic contrast to the vocal lines.

Although the basic theme is fatherhood, there is of course a spiritual thread throughout. Even the most homely domestic scenes are seen as metaphors of loftier ideals. The first song is for and about his wife ('Mi' of *Poèmes*) and the second celebrates the Feast of Guardian Angels (2 October). Earthly and heavenly references are meaningfully juxtaposed. Then follow the two pictures of childhood, one direct and playful, the other more reflective. No. 5, dedicated to death, has a sense of foreboding, swiftly dispelled by the glorious Easter Hymn of Resurrection that ends the cycle in exultant vein.

'BAIL AVEC MI'

This song is a tender evocation of the earthly, yet spiritual qualities of the beloved, and the mutual joy of partnership. The choice of the word 'Bail' for the title (literally meaning 'lease') is both intriguing and meaningful. It emphasizes that the married state is loaned on trust from God, and is not an excuse for immodest exhibitions of self-congratulation. One must always be aware that husband and wife share in life's riches by the grace of the Almighty. Messiaen's text is full of memorable images connecting earth and heaven ('nos mains de terre, pour tisser l'atmosphère') and parallels human features with those in the firmament. The singer's ability to set a contemplative atmosphere and float the opening pitches with poised accuracy is put thoroughly to the test. (A more severe test is to be posed by the opening song of *Harawi*.) The piano part consists of chords, punctuated by single high C♯s introduced by grace-note groups. The tessitura is modest at first, widening later into rangy melismas with characteristic additive rhythms. Sudden *pianissimos* on high F♯s require technical expertise if they are not to sound cloudy or unsteady. Messiaen's dynamics are always practical but they do presume a high degree of professional skill. The 'Plus lent' middle section is followed by a return to the opening material. The very slow, rapt coda, to the words 'doux compagnon de mon épaule amère' (a poignant image), can be directly compared to the close of 'L'épouse' in *Poèmes*, especially in view of the subject matter.

'ANTIENNE DE SILENCE'

This is the section which is so reminiscent of the *Vocalise*, but is rather more demanding. The piano part is written on three treble staves, the top providing continuous semiquavers while the other two have elaborate counterpoint, matching the soprano's melismatic lines. The sibilant sounds of Messiaen's few words heighten the ethereal effect. Two rapt fragments of prayer invoke the 'silent angel' who binds earth to heaven. The rest of the text consists of repeated 'alleluias', and the quality of singing required is similar to that of the final 'alleluia' passage in the first of the *Poèmes*, but the tessitura climbs more slowly, and lingers around F#, G# and A almost too long for comfort. The centre of the song is potentially tiring and should not be over-practised at pitch, as it would be a great pity to sacrifice the finer edges of the sound. *Pianissimo* floating is a specific soprano skill, and tuning has to be scrupulous, despite other challenges of breath capacity and rhythm. The soprano must keep an unwavering legato and hypnotic concentration throughout, being especially careful to avoid a spreading of tone during the slow downward climb at the end. Any vulnerability in the middle range will be exposed. Holding the final low F is perhaps the hardest test of all. Apart from all this, co-ordination between voice and piano is by no means easy, and breaths must be perfectly timed to avoid disturbing the seamless lines. As the song ends, the piano's semiquavers trail upwards and disappear.

'DANSE DU BÉBÉ-PILULE'

Messiaen here paints a charming picture of playtime with his infant son, using the child's pet name. The little boy is encouraged to dance and play games. Surreal images of nature abound, and physical features, especially hands with their mercurial variations of gesture and emphasis, assume symbolic significance. The song almost bubbles over in its ebullience, a chanting 'non-sense' refrain punctuating each new strand. Throughout, the child's imaginative responses are monitored by the benevolent vigilance of the parents ('l'œil de ta maman' is ever present).

This is the longest song in the cycle. After the rigour of the preceding movement, Messiaen gives the singer a chance to recover a little, in bright straightforward writing, full of bouncing rhythms and naturally undulating phrases, which, though often shorter than in the preceding movement, should not be cut up unnecessarily by breaths. Four-bar, rather than two-bar phrases should be aimed at, so that the 'refrain' 'Ma-lon-lan-laine, ma' does not have to begin with a gusty re-attack. By now, the singer should feel quite at home with the uneven rhythmic groupings so that they swing along naturally. As any performer will know, spectacular, leaping lines are much easier to sing than they appear, and quite comfortable. The mood of happy childlike wonder and freshness is sustained through constant changes of tempo and dynamic, the piano an equal partner throughout. Excitement mounts, as fast-running semiquavers on the piano herald a middle episode which is more melismatic, using the 'nonsense syllables' of the refrain in ecstatic long phrases. Then the 'Vif' tempo returns with irrepressible verve, as descriptions of the wonders of nature culminate in a joyful 'Chanter, chanter-ah!' The next passage is very similar to the end of 'Ta voix' in *Poèmes*. A loud, intense rhythmic pattern on solo piano in treble octaves again seems to suggest a bird in full throttle. Then comes a more reflective moment, with piano in the foreground and voice gently commenting, before all surges ahead once more and the opening themes return. Tremendous energy is generated, and the voice descends in a cascade of boisterous laughter – difficult to place accurately without allowing the 'h's' to obtrude, but helped by the piano's chords in unison support. The song finishes with lusty, uninhibited cries of 'Io'! – a foretaste of some of *Harawi*'s wilder moments – as in, for example, 'Répétition planétaire' (No. 6).

'ARC-EN-CIEL D'INNOCENCE'

Messiaen here draws inspiration from the calm innocence of his sleeping son, with music of ravishing warmth and tenderness. The opening text describes the little boy's posture curled in repose 'comme une majuscule de vieux missel' (like a capital letter in an ancient missal). The syllables can be placed precisely in natural speech rhythms, enabling enunciation and intonation to be perfectly poised. The piano complements the voice with chordal patterns, or punctuates it with rippling flourishes. This song is an excellent example of Messiaen's awareness of the singer's need to exercise the voice in lines of varying length, building gradually through fragmented phrases to more expansive cantilena passages which are all the more effective thereby. The first of these comes at the words 'le soleil t'écrira' with typical soaring radiance. The more intimate, playful short phrases return for a while before the 'Plus lent' cantilena is repeated for the charming image of 'rainbows of innocence'. As always, the nuances of the text aid the singer in achieving a suitable vocal timbre – it would, I think, be difficult to avoid sounding idiomatic in the French language, provided with such a perfect succession of accurately moulded syllables, heard with pinpoint accuracy, the sibilant sounds further enhancing the effect (see Ex. 4.6). At the reference to the child's simple cup-and-ball toy, the pace quickens in anticipation of his morning awakening, as he begins to stir ('comme un battant de cloche pascale'). The final expansive cantabile phrase is left unaccompanied, unwinding from a glowing high G#, and the singer is left to gauge her own careful descent and diminuendo. The final two bars are a hushed, deeply affectionate greeting from father to son, requiring much vocal care and control.

'MINUIT PILE ET FACE'

This movement is the only one in the cycle to disrupt the prevailing mood of bliss and harmony. Its pounding catalogue of fearful images bring a harsher test of faith. It is in marked contrast to the infallibly angelic, unscathed innocence of the preceding song. In this dramatically charged scena, the highly demanding piano part is written on three staves. The security of the soprano's middle range is repeatedly tested, in the opening and closing sections in particular, with chanting monotones which do not rise to the top of the stave until increasingly climactic cadences are reached.

EX. 4.6 *Chants de terre et de ciel* 4 'Arc-en-ciel d'innocence'

Dark and terrifying evocations of death and destruction are interspersed with cries to the Lamb of God. A diabolical rhythmic dance, begun on the piano, needs scrupulous attention to attack and co-ordination. The singer will find that the tone remains clearer if breaths are taken only at the ends of sentences, despite the fragmented nature of the phrases. Messiaen again shows his flair for building on the fabric of the voice's natural resonance, but this is perhaps one place in the cycle where special skill may be needed. The mood becomes more frenzied and the text's symbols more violent ('Bête inouie qui mange, qui bave dans ma poitrine'). A heavily accented passage, with voice and piano hammering out their notes together, prepares the way for the grand climax – a paragraph of desperate long-drawn-out cries to God for consolation. All the singer's power and stamina are needed here to sustain the high tessitura at full strength, and yet not lose penetration as the pitch descends. After this exertion, the piano takes over in an expressive solo passage. The movement ends with a more intense version of the opening material, in which the piano's part is inverted, while the voice declaims strongly in the middle range. The 'coda' is rapt and magical (the piano's continuous right-hand *pianissimo* chords reminiscent of the sixth of the *Poèmes*). The voice wistfully compares man's weight of sin and nightly dread to the child's uncomplicated, unruffled sleep of innocence. The singer's final soft 'parlando' phrase is one of those highly original and spontaneous touches that make the composer so endearing, and dispel any suspicions of excessive emotionalism. This tiny 'throwaway' line breaks the atmosphere of doom and returns us to domestic reality. It can be compared with the last line of Ravel's *Chansons madécasses* ('Allez, et préparez le repas') which similarly breaks a spell, and requires deft handling.

'RÉSURRECTION'

The cycle ends magnificently in a paean of joy at the birth and resurrection of Christ, and with it the illumination and renewal of the whole universe. This movement is enormously rewarding to sing. Successions of spectacular melismas lie happily in the most flattering vocal register, although tuning requires constant care. The piano's rhetorical gestures respond excitedly to the voice, and tremendous momentum is generated. Here the two performers, instead of acting in tandem, have individual roles, with the voice for once predominating. This is perhaps the nearest thing to a vocal showpiece in any of the cycles, and is a stunning example of virtuoso writing (see Ex. 4.7). The piano's rapid flourishes and bursts of jangling chords seem to spring directly out of the vocal lines. The contrasting 'Bien modéré' sections at the end of each of the two verses, are perfectly timed protracted cadences of white-hot emotional intensity. There should be no trouble in negotiating the final leap to the glorious high note at the end – the run-up to it could hardly be more ideal. There is no time for hesitancy. In fact, the only potentially awkward phrase is the semiquaver run up from low C# in each verse, on the words 'Sept étoiles' and 'Un seul fleuve'. It is important not to hit the bottom note too hard, but to keep the semiquavers light and springy, so that they are not disconnected from the upper range.

Harawi

A series of overwhelming experiences preceded *Harawi*, Messiaen's last and biggest work for voice and piano, written in 1945. These included his time spent as a prisoner of war, and his meeting with the pianist Yvonne Loriod, who was to become an artistic soulmate, and (in 1961) his second wife. At this time too Claire Delbos was confined to hospital with a serious mental condition, and one suspects that the composer may have been facing a particularly poignant inner dilemma.

Harawi, a crucially demanding tour-de-force, comprises twelve settings of surrealist poems by the composer himself, many of which are extremely ambitious in scope. It belongs to his 'Tristan' trilogy – the three works based on the theme of love and death, which also include *Turangalîla-symphonie* and the *Cinq rechants*. The title is a Quechua (Peruvian dialect) word for a love song in which the lovers are united in death, hence the works subtitle: 'Chant d'amour et de mort'. Words and symbols

EX. 4.7 *Chants de terre et de ciel* 6 'Résurrection'

from Peruvian folklore enrich the text, emphasizing the sultry eroticism which surfaces more overtly here than in the previous cycles.

Given Messiaen's touching idealism concerning marriage and family life, displayed in the previous vocal works, it is impossible not to identify with his heart-rending personal crisis. It is hardly surprising under the circumstances that he is no longer able to refer to love and passion in specifically Christian terms. After the idyllic pictures of *Poèmes* and *Chants* a radical change of emphasis is evident. The Catholic view of the indissolubility of marriage was of course inescapable. Although this must remain conjecture, it could have been a relief to be able to express some of his feelings in musical and dramatic form. Messiaen's music is extremely sensuous even when contained within the framework of Catholic ritual (people of stricter Protestant background may occasionally feel uncomfortable with the way sensuality is embraced in such a natural and unselfconscious way). In *Harawi* he finds an increasingly penetrating vein of intensity. The references from Peruvian folklore in the text add new colours and onomatopoeic sounds, yet the musical language is still unmistakably the composer's own.

Piano and voice together undertake an epic adventure and emerge nobly transfigured. There are few truly intimate moments here; everything is on a grander scale than in the domestic portraits that came before. Proportions are naturally more spacious, given the cycle's fifty-minute length – the piano often has extensive solo passages, alternately weighty and dramatic, or hypnotically ethereal. The vocal part is as rich in variety as could be wished for, switching from primitive ritual chants and cries, to flights of sustained lyricism, either floating beatifically or soaring to heights of passionate declamation. The singer has a wonderful opportunity for vocal characterization. As before in *Poèmes*, 'grand soprano dramatique' is specified, but the tessitura is rather lower than in the previous cycles, so a darker-hued voice, even a flexible mezzo, could be appropriate here. Certainly, considerable strength is needed on the lower pitches. However, it is the crucial middle register of the voice which is most fully exploited in *Harawi*. Firmness on middle-register G in particular is essential. On a personal note, I now habitually use the central song 'Adieu' as an exercise for steadiness in this range. Once again Messiaen expects a generous breath capacity – spans are long and relentless, and, as ever, he employs commas for 'official' punctuation to let the music breathe too.

Above all, this towering work has a formal unity which is unique in the song cycles. Musical themes and verbal phrases are repeated, so that the structure is clear and coherent, and the moment of 'coming home' at the end (in the key of the main cyclic, hymn-like theme, E♭) is especially satisfying.

After many years of singing the work, one relishes the challenge of it more and more. It requires an effort of faith to launch into the piece for the first time, trusting that stamina and concentration will hold. At the half-way point, or even before, comes the happy realization that the composer has allowed for a gradual warming of the voice in the course of singing it, and that muscular co-ordination is inevitably continuing to improve, as in distance swimming. Only the delicate, floated opening of the cycle may give cause for apprehension, but psychologically, most performers would prefer to have to cope with this early on in the proceedings, rather than to have a potential hazard looming near the end, ready to spoil the overall effect.

At first the singer's role is fragmented, often confined to blocks of rhythmic 'parlando' repetitions. Messiaen always chooses the right moment to allow the voice free rein, and then, following a strenuous outburst, to rest again in a different tessitura, keeping the whole instrument in good condition. This means that at the very end, the strong low B♭ on 'tout' (the lowest note in the piece) should prove no problem. After the slow processional 'Adieu' (No. 7), more strenuous movements follow in rapidly accumulating tension and rate of activity. It is exhilarating to plunge into these movements with new-found energy and boldness, knowing that by now the audience is hanging on to every note, and is living the experience with the performers. I have often been told by listeners that they begin to breathe with the singer and feel great empathy with the physical aspect of the work as well as with its powerful psychology.

Contrary to what may be feared, the very slow, fine-spun lines of 'Amour, oiseau d'étoile' (No. 10) work better in context than if one were to isolate this as a single song. Voice and body respond automatically to the sudden change of pace, with support muscles the firmer for being properly used in the preceding song.

'LA VILLE QUI DORMAIT, TOI'

The opening song requires the singer to enter a dreamlike mood of deep contemplation. The text reflects the calm of the sleeping town (inviting comparison with the first movement of *Chants*, in linking the physical features of the scene with the lovers themselves). Here the symbols are confined to the female partner, who is portrayed in highly idealized terms. She carries the delicate modesty of the double violet – a symbol that is to recur. Her steady gaze brings calm and security. Most significantly, she symbolizes the bank on which the lovers lie in Act 2 scene ii of Wagner's *Tristan*.[2] The vocal writing repays close examination. Happily, the lingering, wide diphthong on the repeated 'moi' and 'toi' allows the singer to time the release carefully, so it can be left to reverberate naturally. The tempo must be as slow as possible; dynamics have to be graded with extreme sensitivity. The effectiveness of the opening depends on how softly the singer may dare to begin. The *mezzo forte* near the end should therefore seem comparatively strong, the line 'l'œil immobile' full of incident in the surrounding stillness. (The comma after 'l'œil' is not a breath mark, and there should not be a hard glottal attack on the re-entry, but the double 'm' of 'immobile' is useful in making a warm crescendo and maintaining legato.)

In the second half of the song, grace-note chords on the piano directly precede the most crucial unisons with the voice – a device used often by Messiaen, and one found in abundance in this cycle. The piano's 'upbeat' provides the singer with the ideal place to breathe if necessary and, better still, secures perfect ensemble at key moments. However, in this particular movement I have personally found it better not to breathe before the single sustained notes on 'moi' and 'toi', although the sound should be stopped and re-started. Thinking through the gap encourages proper use of breath capacity, a steadier line and a smoother arrival on the final note. The exposed high G on 'ton', marked *ppp*, at the end, is perhaps the most potentially worrying moment in the whole work. But even here there is a chance to relax and loosen up a little on the low Ds, which swing up an octave as the quaver movement is propelled along by the piano's acciaccaturas (see Ex. 4.8). It is important not to hesitate before the high note. The explosive 't' helps too – consonants must always be projected strongly, whatever the dynamic. The nasal 'on' should not be pinched too exaggeratedly at such a high pitch. The very last note is to be held as long as possible – well

EX. 4.8 *Harawi* I 'La ville qui dormait, toi'

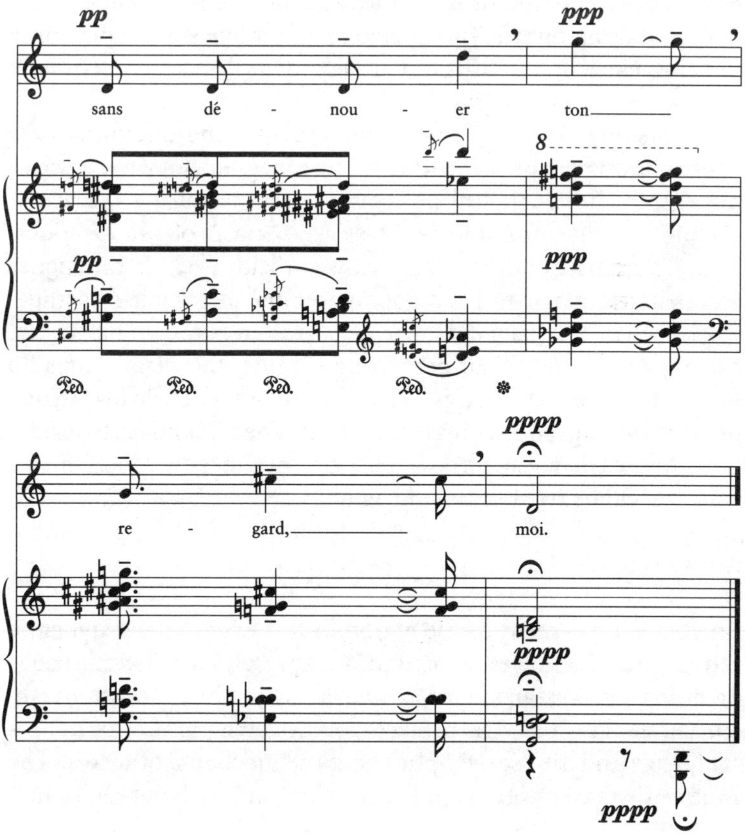
pp
ppp
sans
dé
-
nou
-
er
ton
8
pp
ppp
pppp
re
-
gard,
moi.
pppp
pppp

past the piano's final chord. The *pppp* can be achieved by a quasi-'bocca chiusa' effect – a vibrant thread of muted sound that can be sustained virtually at will.

'BONJOUR TOI, COLOMBE VERTE'

The colourful image of the mythical green dove, the beloved in Mayan folklore, now makes her first appearance, hailed in a series of elaborate images of 'flower, fruit, sky and water', all of which are to appear later in the cycle. She represents the 'limpid pearl', 'interlocking stars' and 'parted clouds' and, inevitably, birdsong. This marks the introduction of the work's recurring hymn-like cyclic theme, in the key of E♭. The soprano has her first opportunity to 'test the water', at a conveniently brisk tempo, staking out the full octave on the treble stave, and firmly centring each note and interval. The piano's highly decorative part is most helpful: the left hand moves chordally with the vocal melody, and the right hand provides the discipline of a definable quaver pulse within rapid arpeggio flourishes above the voice. These can still be registered easily during the act of singing – a fine example of Messiaen's grasp of practicalities. Many composers fail to realize how difficult it is for the higher voices in particular to keep good ensemble in complex passage-work, when the singer's own head resonance can block out accompanying detail. In between each line, the piano has solo interludes at a faster tempo, based on tropical birdcalls, which provide the soprano with time to relax. The vital middle-register G ending each vocal phrase must be rock-steady. Later on, its security will be tried again and again.

'MONTAGNES'

The pianist has most of the action in this exciting and dynamic setting, but the voice's contribution, sparsely distributed, needs precision of fast articulation and a distinctive, almost harsh, cutting quality. The text projects rough-hewn pictures of mountain crags and abysses, emphasizing the blackness of death. The sung phrases consist of rapid successions of low-lying semiquavers, at natural speech level, punched out *mezzo forte* with equal stress. Tuning needs to be meticulous, with the minor third from low C♯ to E♮ proving most crucial. The piano has two well-differentiated blocks of material: loud high clashing chords in contrary motion, marked 'Très vif', and gentler bell-like chordal progressions, the hands often moving in close canon. This material will be found again, transformed and extended into spell-binding *pianissimo* solos during the timeless final pages of the last song. As with the last few notes of 'Les deux guerriers' in *Poèmes*, the final 'Noir sur noir' will be clearer if the singer avoids taking a large breath before it.

'DOUNDOU TCHIL'

The title of this movement is an onomatopoeic representation of the jingling of the anklets worn by traditional Peruvian dancers and conjures up an exotic 'non-Western' atmosphere. In projecting the cumulatively louder repetitions (twenty each at the beginning and end) of 'Doundou tchil', there is a danger of discomfort if the explosive consonants are hissed out too fiercely, yet their sibilance aids audibility. As the music has to build over such a long span it is unwise to crescendo too quickly, otherwise the last few repetitions risk becoming very strained, and may even lose focus. Timing between release of consonant and arrival of vowel tone is absolutely vital, and each one has to be monitored individually. A breathy quality may enhance the mysterious atmosphere early on, but has to be controlled and later eliminated. As always, the secret is to avoid the habit of breathing in every rest. The sibilant 'tch' can be lengthened for the quiet entries, but the final group of three repetitions should be sung 'molto legato', deliberately extending the vowels to achieve the maximum crescendo. Even for singers with many years' experience of performing this work, the projection of this movement can still present a real danger of forcing through over-zealousness.

Here Messiaen is employing vocal devices of a 'non-traditional' kind, the sort of gestures that were to form the core of major vocal works of the sixties, pioneered by Berio and others.

During all the 'doundou tchils' the pianist has exceptionally demanding and complex passagework, played with the left hand only at first, and then expanding into the most intricate filigree counterpoint for the second verse. Both performers are stretched in different ways, and co-ordination may require considerable practice. Since the piano part is continuous, it is up to the soprano to listen carefully to the left hand, and fit exactly – she has the accompanying role here.

It is some relief to reach the comfortingly familiar territory of the song's refrain, in E♭. Both performers move in close harmony, the soprano projecting sturdily in mid-voice while the piano provides continuous motor rhythms. The 'Piroutcha' referred to is the Peruvian equivalent of Isolde, the beloved. After the elaborated repeat of the opening material, there is another of Messiaen's characteristic 'tag' endings, to be hammered out *fortissimo*, the voice on accented low B♭s. Even the strongest voice may have difficulty in achieving a well-defined and truly audible pitch centre, especially when the piano's thudding left hand is in precise synchrony. It is more productive to concentrate on exploiting the penetrative power of the percussive consonants, separating the notes clearly.

'L'AMOUR DE PIROUTCHA'

Now follows a charming and lyrical duet for the two young lovers, in two verses in binary form, each character clearly defined. The soprano should be able to differentiate tone quality accordingly, helped by Messiaen's impeccable word setting. The vocal role of 'La jeune fille' has a special sweetness (marked 'Lent, tendre et berceur') suffused with languor and nostalgia, especially expressive in dipping minor thirds and tritones (see Ex. 4.9). In contrast, the music for the male protagonist seems to invite a clear and bold tone, almost detached, allowing the text's luridly coloured images ('nos souffles, bleu et or. Chaînes rouges, noires, mauves') to make their point without embellishment, and concentrating on absolute accuracy in gauging chromatic intervals. It is left to the young man to refer directly to the prospect of death as the culmination of their love idyll.

EX. 4.9 *Harawi* 5 'L'amour de Piroutcha'

(Decapitation is even suggested as a means of release from their plight.) The final very soft note on 'mort' (that crucial middle-register G again) which comes at the end of each verse is preceded by a grace note. It has to be placed perfectly in order to float on unhindered.

'RÉPÉTITION PLANÉTAIRE'

The sixth song forms a colourful interlude in the proceedings. Alternately hypnotic and explosive syllabic repetitions eventually give way to a giddy parade of kaleidoscopic colours, as the planet spins and consumes all in its path. Primitive shrieks alternate with precipitous whirling figures on the piano, making this an extremely challenging piece for both performers, extending their resources and putting them firmly into gear for further tests to come. Anyone who sings this work will know that this is the movement where rhythmic discipline is paramount. The soprano must pounce on the end of each piano flourish so that the effect is spontaneous and unflagging. For the first section of this substantial movement, successions of 'jungle cries' alternate with long drawn-out 'mystérieux' passages, almost mesmerically static vocally, the singer intoning rounded syllables, complemented by a dark-toned piano part. The soprano must pay careful attention to the pianist's left hand: its decorative monody marks the pulse but grace notes obscure the outline. The composer reveals his acute ear for colour here, stipulating 'timbre noir et profond, comme une clarinette basse'.

In sharpest contrast to the wilder passages, these almost motionless sections confine the voice to a monotone. As this long paragraph is repeated almost identically, it is a good idea to choose a different tone-colour for each. My own preference is for a breathy, 'covered' tone first time, then a rather more sinister 'ghostly' quality. As for the increasing exuberance of the wild cries, the rapid chromatic flourishes can be practised slowly but, in the end, the voice must be allowed to run freely in one legato span, with the glottal flexibility required for yodelling or wide-interval trilling.

All these potently atmospheric sections serve to prepare for the introduction of the central theme in a long piano solo. This is built on a tritone, and undergoes a series of repetitions, each an octave higher. Beginning at the very bottom of the instrument, it eventually passes to the soprano on her re-entry, as surrealist textual images are added to the ritual syllabic chants heard earlier (see Ex. 4.10). The voice's repeated As involve complex rhythms, and breaths must be taken quickly at the ends of phrases to co-ordinate exactly with the piano. Messiaen's marked rests and commas are sufficient for the singer's needs, although support muscles have to be in good order. The slow build-up propels us into one of the work's most frenetic sequences. It is especially important not to force, and waste much-needed air, but to encompass as much as possible in one breath. The vulnerable middle range of the voice again comes under scrutiny, but by now there should be a reserve of stamina to bolster confidence. Both partners race towards the finish, almost, but not quite, throwing caution to the winds. Ideally the soprano's last seven hurled repetitions of 'mange en tournant' should be taken in one breath. The movement ends with a cataclysmic, condensed version of the opening cries.

EX. 4.10 *Harawi* 6 'Répétition planétaire'

'ADIEU'

Now we come to the very heart of the cycle. The slow hymn-like melody of the 'colombe verte', the beloved Piroutcha, rings out with fullest sonority. However this is no longer a cheerful greeting but a deeply emotional farewell tribute. The images of the second song are recalled, and new ones are added, as brightness fades, and 'heaven on earth', and 'the breath of love' recede for ever. Each vocal phrase covers a broad span and there can be no letting up until the very last beat has been counted out (see Ex. 4.11). Fortunately, after each line, the voice is given welcome respite by a loud piano solo of gong-like resonance. In performance, the singer will be at full stretch, retaining just enough strength to launch the first phrase, and then make the most of the following rest period. There is just enough time to recover poise and energy, which exemplifies once more the

EX. 4.11 *Harawi* 7 'Adieu'

composer's acute sensitivity to the act of performance. The singer should now be able to enjoy the sensation of securely focused resonance and ever-increasing power in one of the thrilling high points of the work: the exultant arch upwards to the cycle's top note, high B. This is marvellously prepared by a wide interval to relax the voice, and propelled by the helpful 'pl' of 'pleure'. The 'l' gives the opportunity for a carefully plotted release on to the high note which must be spacious and resonant, sinking down comfortably without constriction as the phrase descends. Only at the end of her final phrase is the soprano allowed a diminuendo on the vital middle-register G around which the whole movement is centred, and which must never show a trace of insecurity.

The grandeur of 'Adieu' can be compared to the calm progress of a stately ship sailing into harbour. Although it is a farewell lament on the death of Piroutcha, there is an underlying sense of fateful acceptance, and impending release from earthly passion.

'SYLLABES'

After spinning the relentlessly long lines of 'Adieu', the voice is now thoroughly warmed-up. Now is the perfect time to plunge into this extraordinary and colourful blend of exotic jungle sounds and driving repeated rhythms, separated by verses to be sung with lyrical poise. Even *in extremis* the singer has to have a firm hold on the reins to be able to switch moods and tempos in a split second. This is probably the most straightforwardly enjoyable movement for performers and audience. The beloved green dove, now transported to the world of the spirit, is addressed affectionately in floral and numerical symbols. The

EX. 4.12 *Harawi* 8 'Syllabes'

charmingly unaffected melody of the refrain is supported by piano chords which move with the singer (Messiaen instructs the pianist to give special emphasis to the bass line and the uppermost notes, both of which also carry the tune). The second part of the refrain is faster and more excited. The energetically reiterated chants include the familiar 'Doundou tchil', now combined, in ever more complex and varied patterns, with manic repetitions of 'Pia, pia, pia, pia' (see Ex. 4.12). These represent the alarm cries of apes, featured in both Peruvian and Indonesian legends, whose warning is reputed to have saved a prince's life.

The last huge sequence of 'pia, pia' should ideally be sung in one breath, but the singer must take care to reserve a balanced, delicate touch for the final, exposed *pianissimo* 'tout bas'. This has to be sung sweetly and steadily, 'molto semplice', as if quite detached from the frenzied activity preceding it.

'Adieu' and 'Syllabes', so strikingly in contrast, together form the twin centres of the work. Within their generous proportions they contain and develop all the work's basic musical and textual ingredients. From now on the lovers' predicament is fully identifiable as a spiritual quest, as, with burdens eased, they leave the earthly sphere in an atmosphere of renewed anticipation of their eternal union in heaven.

'L'ESCALIER REDIT, GESTES DU SOLEIL'

Fired with new energy, the performers are more than ready for an intoxicating display of their full resources. The lovers joyfully mount the stairway in the sky, and celebrate their union beyond the stars. The 'escalier tournant' of the whirling figures at the climax of 'Répétition planétaire' is recalled, and the green of springtime and of the beloved dove are celebrated in joyful cries. The text's cosmic symbolism is enhanced by vocal lines that sparkle with sunlit brilliance. Explosive consonants and dancing rhythms whip up the tension to a state of feverish excitement, and the whole movement surges along at a tremendous pace. The piano defines the pulse with a percussive 'toccata' of insistent triplets. In 'Répétition planétaire' it was the soprano who had to pounce on to the end of the piano's phrases; here the positions are reversed. The pianist must react very quickly indeed to the voice's abandoned declamations. The ability to span large paragraphs will be exploited even more than in the preceding movement, so the acquired co-ordination will be indispensable. After two hectic verses of unrelieved intensity and vigour, the voice soars to a resplendent high B. The words are particularly pertinent and revealing. 'Inventons l'amour du monde': 'Let us invent (perhaps redefine?) worldly love.' It will be difficult for the singer to hear the piano's repeated triplets pulsing through her long-held note, and it may be necessary for the pianist to indicate with a nod the first beat of the new bar (see Ex. 4.13). The following lines allow the voice to descend very gradually in pitch and dynamic, but even here iron control is needed. The voice's sublimely hushed, extended 'Toi' on low E♭ must show no trace of tremulousness. The singer reaches a pinnacle of fulfilment in the *fortissimo* declaration of 'L'amour! La joie!' – one of the work's two peaks of ecstasy (the other is in the final movement). After this, voice and piano hurl themselves into an almost delirious final reprise of the main material, ending in a glorious cadence in E♭, which celebrates the renewal of their mutual joy. The soprano's last long note can be launched with exultant confidence.

EX. 4.13 *Harawi* 9 'L'escalier redit, gestes du soleil'

'AMOUR OISEAU D'ÉTOILE'

This is perhaps the most exquisite and touching song in the work and comes at the moment when audience as well as performers are ready for still deeper insights in a gentler mood. As the composer tells us, the poem was inspired by a painting by Sir Roland Penrose (the original now lost), entitled 'Seeing is believing'. It shows a hand reaching upwards to the heavens, where a woman's head hangs inverted in the night sky above the town. The composer has said that this picture symbolizes the whole of *Harawi*. Significantly, the key is F# major, Messiaen's habitual choice for spiritual love. The female voice seems to glow naturally in this key, and for anyone with an acute sense of pitch it would be quite different if transposed enharmonically. The combination of acoustic and psychological reasons for this would make an absorbing study, but Messiaen's prime gift to singers is his purity of instinct, which complements his formidable intellect, technique and cultural resources. At last the soprano has some respite from the perpetual activity of the previous song. Spinning the long and tenderly rapt lines of this piece is a challenge, but a benevolent one. Tone should now be beautifully focused, and a pure, serene quality still easily possible. It is only the length of the final notes of each phrase which may cause concern. Messiaen's demands are unrelenting: the singer is asked to hold final notes to the limit of her capacity in a variety of dynamics throughout her range – yet all are practicable in context. At the end of every phrase, the pianist begins a subtly blended series of birdsongs, enhancing the happier tone of the work, and providing the soprano with a clearly defined point on which to poise the last grain of sound. Messiaen knows the psychological advantage of being able to see ahead to the point of release, so that remaining resources can be measured out prudently. The two matching verses of this movement contain some of the work's most ravishing moments, and perhaps evoke memories of the quieter passages in the two earlier vocal cycles. Especially tender and beautiful are the short descending cadential phrases, united with the piano's chords, in familiar seraphic vein. The final hurdle is the last note of all, held to the very limit of possibility, on middle-register A#. But here, as ever, the word setting is felicitous. To poise 'le ciel', in perfect *pianissimo*, requires tongue and teeth to synchronize, and the economy of smaller lip and tongue movements means that the jaw can remain relaxed. Opening the mouth too wide would disturb the line. The inherently nasal resonance of the vowels is useful here too. The sibilance of 'c' can be dwelt upon in order to effect a careful transition via the brighter 'i' into the final vowel. As in previous instances, the placing should be as in humming, maintaining a position from which it is comfortable to re-engage lips and teeth for the closing 'l', which can be begun early. Throughout the cycle the glowing radiance of the slow diphthong of 'étoile' is to be savoured, and the rapt atmosphere of this movement is one of the work's unalloyed pleasures. Technical flaws cannot be allowed to spoil it.

'KATCHIKATCHI LES ÉTOILES'

A wildly energetic 'danse macabre', this is the last of the more hectically paced movements, and is perhaps the most taxing of all for the pianist. Grace-note clusters precede almost every attack, chords leap around from register to register with frightening speed, and a workable tempo must be found. The pianist should be given every consideration, even though the singer may be tempted to jettison caution in what, is, for her, predominantly an exercise in verbal fluency and rhythmic accuracy. Otherwise there is a danger of the ensemble falling apart quite disastrously. Now comes the moment when the stars and planets, so often referred to in the text, are hurled into the vortex to be splintered for all eternity, as the lovers find their final refuge beyond. They themselves are transformed into atoms which jump around like grasshoppers (the 'Katchikatchi' of the title). Some loud upward glissandos on the piano are particularly difficult for the soprano to catch, but she is less stressed here and must take the accompanying role. The last paragraph, with its manic repetitions culminating in an abandoned shriek, is easier to project with a minimum of breath (see Ex. 4.14). The unpitched scream must seem involuntary as if the singer were suddenly stabbed, so

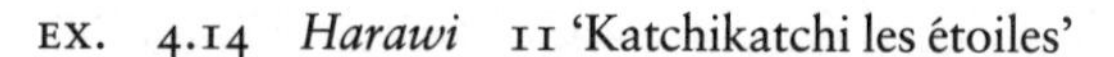
EX. 4.14 *Harawi* II 'Katchikatchi les étoiles'

that the attack has a clear edge and does not jar the larynx. The text's images become extremely gruesome near the end ('Coupez ma tête, son chiffre roule dans le sang'), even going so far as to suggest comparison with *Salome*. But just as decadence threatens, redemption comes in the form of the work's healing resolution.

'DANS LE NOIR'

Harawi ends with a profoundly moving and stately reaffirmation of the cyclic theme of the 'colombe verte'. Night's darkness has not after all obscured the green dove's lustre, and the 'breath of love' has proved triumphantly inextinguishable. The benevolent symbols of flowers and numbers found in 'Syllabes' again cast their spell on the sleeping town, and the work closes as it began, in hushed repose.

Each line is spaciously set between shimmering successions of high-lying chords in rhythmic canon. Time seems to stand still. The final return to the key of E♭ symbolizes majestic reassurance of the union of soul and body. The trials are over, and humanity and the universe are at one, as the lovers pass into infinity. The soprano may be near exhaustion here, as at the beginning of 'Adieu', but once again all she has to do is launch and control the first phrase, for there is then ample time to regain poise during the long piano interlude that follows. As before, the held middle-register Gs at the ends of phrases are a test of tonal security, and must remain reliable to the very end. The second of the two climactic peaks referred to earlier now occurs in an awesome declamation of 'Mon amour, mon souffle'. The piano carefully prompts and underpins the voice, its grace notes cuing in the most crucial attacks. One is reminded of the chorus's awed response to the earthquake at Golgotha, in Bach's *St Matthew Passion*. Even though *Harawi* is not a specifically religious work, it ends in an atmosphere of deep reverence. A vastly slower version of the main refrain of 'Syllabes' now follows, this time in the sonorously lower resonances of E♭ instead of the lighter, springier G major. It seems almost miraculous that the voice will still sound and feel fresh, relishing the opportunity to relax in the lower tessitura. The low B♭ has to undergo one last test of strength and steadiness. The repeated rising major sixth on 'tout bas' forms a gradual diminuendo, each one needing to be graded carefully. For the very last, marked *pianissimo*, it is a good idea to float both notes in 'head voice', to prepare for what lies immediately ahead. The almost unbearably hushed and poignant repeat of the cycle's opening bars has to be intoned as if time were suspended, making full use of facial resonance to keep even the finest thread of sound from faltering. The rising sixth ends the work in two hummed sighs of deep contentment, the last to be held until well after the piano's final chiming chord. A satisfied and prolonged silence will be the performers' reward for their exertion and commitment. There should be a corporate reluctance to break the spell.

Few works sustain their length so triumphantly. Despite the absence of liturgical references, the work's spiritual essence dominates throughout. The sacrificial act of the lovers, whose fantasies are symbolized, transformed and sublimely elevated during the course of the work, is mirrored by the dedication required by singer and pianist. An audience cannot help becoming involved in this overwhelming exploration of heart, mind and spirit.

After such a revelation of his personal attitudes and insights into the whole question of human and spiritual love, it is not at all surprising that *Harawi* marked the end of Messiaen's work for the special partnership of voice (that most intimately physical of instruments) and piano. One feels that he would have been the ideal person to write the major work for voice and organ which the repertoire still awaits. Yet if he had returned to the solo voice, it is perhaps more likely that the male singer would have been favoured. It is significant that his long-awaited opera has a masculine subject. He may well have felt that he had said as much as he could about womanliness in all its facets: his statement seems wonderfully complete, and will continue to speak to us across the generations with truth and sincerity.

Notes

1 Olivier Messiaen: *Technique de mon langage musical* (Paris, Leduc, 1944), 2 volumes; volume 1 translated by John Satterfield as *The Technique of My Musical Language* (Paris, Leduc, 1956), p. 71.

2 Antoine Goléa: *Rencontres avec Olivier Messiaen* (Paris, Julliard, 1960), p. 158.

Instrumental, Orchestral and Choral Works to 1948

MALCOLM HAYES

Most of the great composers have needed at least a little time to discover their own creative world. Some (notably Janáček) needed decades. The more usual syndrome is that of, say, the early piano sonatas of Brahms, where the young lion from dockside Hamburg has already found a personal voice, but is as yet using it to roar with a roughness which will quite soon mellow into maturity. Meanwhile there are a very few composers – one thinks of Britten, Walton and Shostakovich, along with Messiaen – who seem to have been born with a creative personality that matured with near-miraculous speed and completeness; each seems to have arrived fully-armed with a sequence of works of astonishing individuality and mastery, written in their late teens or early twenties.

For the most part the phenomenon of Messiaen's early achievement has been deservedly celebrated. His first acknowledged organ work, *Le banquet céleste* – composed by one among doubtless many earnest bespectacled nineteen-year-old students at the Paris Conservatoire – articulates an already unique spiritual territory with a completeness that reduces one to quiet wonderment. The *Préludes*, too, despite the attempts of commentators to disparage their occasional gauchenesses or their debt to Debussy's example, continue to dazzle the ear with their utterly individual approach to piano sonority. There is no *real* precedent in Debussy, Liszt, or anywhere else for the power and refracted beauty of the harmony in 'Cloches d'angoisse et larmes d'adieu'; let alone for the grandeur and sheer imaginative boldness of the piece's two-part design. (This is best described, rather helplessly, as AB. Messiaen was to develop the same structural idea even more spectacularly in the 'Combat de la mort et de la vie' in *Les corps glorieux*.)

Messiaen's first acknowledged orchestral work, while much less well known than either *Le banquet céleste* or the *Préludes*, is every inch their equal as an exceptional example of a composer laying out his shop with an artistic completeness that is absolute in all essentials. *Les offrandes oubliées* is not Messiaen's *very* first orchestral piece, in the sense that the catalogue lists a handful of earlier, unpublished, and withdrawn creations. A Fugue in D minor is on record as having been composed in Paris in 1928. The title of its immediate successor – *Le banquet eucharistique*, written later that year at the composer's aunt's home in Fuligny – is already more striking, and indicates that the piece shares the same subject matter as *Le banquet céleste*. A third 'pre-first' orchestral work, *Simple chant d'une âme*, was composed in Paris in 1930.

The unavailability of these early efforts means that a measure of guesswork is needed when it comes to trying to pin down just why the mastery of *Les offrandes oubliées* is already so comprehensive. Even a little experience of hearing one's own orchestral music goes a long way, and *Le banquet eucharistique* was performed by a student orchestra at the Conservatoire. For the rest, it is only possible to point to the young Messiaen's already extraordinarily complete awareness of the spiritual world he was to spend the next sixty-odd years exploring with such patience, love, and perfectly channelled abandon.

Les offrandes oubliées

Messiaen subtitles *Les offrandes oubliées* a 'méditation symphonique'. This neatly puts a finger on the intersection, here as in everything he wrote, between his own, extra-temporal musical syntax – dealing in precise spiritual eternities – and the quite different structural perspectives of the orchestral tradition he inherited, whose forms had developed from the goal-directed harmony that was the common currency of his nineteenth-century forebears. This convergence of tradition and singularity in the creativity of a young composer, however gifted, might have resulted in incoherence, due to garbled artistic objectives. That it does not do so is due above all to the perfection of the work's form, which achieves a deep and comprehensive orchestral statement within a single-movement structure lasting less than twelve minutes. Short as it is, there is nothing remotely preludial about *Les offrandes oubliées*. An utterance of startling spiritual density is achieved by the deployment of relatively simple material in an absolutely simple structure. The design looks to be straightforward ternary: slow opening, quick central section, reverting to a slow conclusion. But what in fact takes place in the course of the work is a subtle play between this apparent ABA form and a quite different, open-ended musical trajectory which charts a course somewhere between ABA and ABC. The idea relates back, structurally if not otherwise, to 'Cloches d'angoisse' in the *Préludes*. But it here integrates a much wider range of musical happenings: the savage, disjunct, surrealist contrasts typical of Messiaen's later and larger works are unleashed in *Les offrandes oubliées* for the first time at full force.

That the piece succeeds more truly than any of its instrumental successors before the *Quatuor pour la fin du temps* is also due to the inscrutable combination of factors that contributes to any fine work: intelligence, instinctive touch, and a necessary element of sheer luck. Artistic courage helps too. Messiaen was keen to absorb everything he could from the orchestral repertory he could get to know in late 1920s Paris, and his already burgeoning skill in writing for the orchestra goes some way to explaining why, from bar to bar, the music of *Les offrandes oubliées* works so well. As to why it also rings so true – a rather different issue – the singularity of the subject matter gives a clue. Printed on the score's title page is the first of that sequence of high-flown prefatory superscriptions which we now think of, with hindsight and familiarity, as quintessentially Messiaenic. But one wonders what the professors at the Conservatoire in 1930 must have made of this:

Les bras étendus, triste jusqu'à la mort,
sur l'arbre de la Croix vous répandez votre sang.
Vous nous aimez, doux Jésus, nous l'avions oublié.

Poussés par la folie et le dard du serpent,
dans une course haletante, effrénée, sans relâche,
nous descendions dans le péché comme dans un tombeau.

Voici la table pure, la source de charité,
le banquet du pauvre, voici la Pitié adorable offrant
le pain de la Vie et de l'Amour.
Vous nous aimez, doux Jésus, nous l'avions oublié.[1]

The interest is in not only in Messiaen's keenness, here as always, to spell out the forces at work in his music with the help of a poetically worded study in theological exactitude and/or precise spiritual imagery. For the preface also exactly images the work's structure. Since it is not certain whether the words or the music were written first, it is equally uncertain whether the words actually determined anything about the content, or form, of that music. What *is* clear is that from the very start of his creative life, the forms of Messiaen's works owed unusually little to pre-existing *musical* models.

Meanwhile in terms of its idiom, the issue of what *Les offrandes oubliées* does or does not owe to pre-existing models offers further food for thought. The assertion that the work's opening section proclaims the closest of affinities with Wagner might at first seem far-fetched. I am referring not to the Wagner of *Meistersinger* nor of *Lohengrin* – but to the mood of pain-shrouded spiritual anguish in which *Parsifal* is almost narcissistically embalmed, and to which the work's narrative sequence of events postulates a (necessarily sublimated) resolution. The precise musical chemistry of Wagner's study in opera-as-confessional, already presaging what was later to develop into the unstable extremes of Schoenbergian expressionism, was of course entirely foreign to the Messiaen of *Les offrandes oubliées*. The link between the two works is not there, but in a third that bridges the spiritual territory common to both. Debussy's earlier music in general, and that of *Pelléas et Mélisande* in particular, owes a debt to the Wagner of *Parsifal* that is as complex and refractory as it is enormous, and which is thrown into sharper relief by the radically different *psychological* territory charted by the two operas. Debussy's tirelessly and loudly voiced antipathy to Wagner is a fascinating case of how one composer's affinity with aspects of another's work can be illuminated all the more by that same composer's penchant for protesting too much. The listener's ear, meanwhile, refuses to be deflected from its awareness of the *Parsifal*-suffused sonorities that saturate Debussy's orchestral writing throughout the two decades from the twenty-two-year-old composer's *L'Enfant prodigue* onwards. *Pelléas* is still steeped in the sound-world that was opened up in *Parsifal*; and Messiaen, in turn, had steeped himself in Debussy's opera from childhood.

In his long and difficult creative dialogue with *Parsifal* Debussy was not, of course, concerned with evoking the Crucifixion of Christ: whereas Messiaen's response to Wagner, via Debussy, was to crystallize an idiom that evoked precisely that. The first section of *Les offrandes oubliées*, shown in Ex. 5.1, could hardly proclaim its genesis more clearly. The music looks simple to the point of naivety, but that is not how it sounds; indeed it is salutary to remember that the burgeoning surface complexity of Messiaen's later work springs from the same miraculously acute ear that conceived these few pages of score. In essence, the language is already in place. The indications as to tempo and expression (*douloureux, profondément triste*) are characteristically uninhibited; and where in the *Préludes* Messiaen has already probed the expressive possibilities of additive rhythms in very slow tempo, here the orchestral context extrapolates those possibilities still further. (It is intriguing to see how this always practically-minded composer felt the need to include some helpful indications for the conductor as to how to beat his music, even at a tempo of quaver equals 44.) The wind instruments' *Klangfarben*-like articulation of the opening bars' accompanying minor third looks on paper as if the effect might be too precious; in fact it lends an exactly judged touch of astringency to the potential blandness of the melody. The linear simplicity of the opening bars – is it too fanciful to sense a hint

EX. 5.1 *Les offrandes oubliées*

fls
obs
cls
bns
hns
tpts
vns 1
vns 2
vas
vcs
dbs
à 2
1°
ff
f
mf
p

fls
obs
cls
bns
hns
tpts
vns 1
vns 2
vas
vcs
dbs
à 2
1°
mf
ff
p

fls
obs
cls
bns
hns
tpts
vns 1
vns 2
vas
vcs
dbs
1° Solo
à 2
1°
mf
ff
pp

of long-distant, yet perhaps also longed-for medieval austerity in the plainsong-like suppleness of the melody itself? – is then beautifully offset by the sudden advent (bar 5) of the three-part chord-sequences converging in contrary motion.

This opening strophe duly articulated, the next four bars present a shortened counter-strophe which varies both the accompanying harmony and, in the seventh bar, the melody, where the thematic cell that dominates the work is introduced. At this first appearance it draws no attention to itself, sounding simply like an adjunct to the repetition of the work's initial phrase; then, in the bar before figure 1, it unexpectedly initiates what would seem to be about to unfold as a third strophe (the solo oboe's entry, marked with a stronger dynamic than the unison flutes and strings, is a touch as musically salient as it is beautiful). While at this early stage hardly able to realize its significance, already the ear has been introduced to and led further into a musical design of effortlessly widening spaciousness. The effect is out of all proportion to the means employed; much of the weight of utterance that is so striking in *Les offrandes oubliées* stems from the way that this opening section could easily have set up a structure much larger than it in fact turns out to be.

Just when the ear has been able to confirm to itself the significance of the work's 'real' theme by hearing it transferred to the basses and cellos in the bar after figure 1, the second section – 'Vif, féroce, désespéré, haletant' – explodes into violent anti-life at the double bar, setting in motion a torrent of orchestral convulsions whose fraught ferocity leaves no doubt as to Messiaen's command of the medium. Influences? Again, they are in themselves less striking than the desiccated fury of the result, which signifies the hideousness of sin in frighteningly explicit terms. Nor are they as obvious as they might seem. Messiaen knew Stravinsky's *Rite of Spring* by this time, and it has therefore been deduced that the rhythmic violence of this part of *Les offrandes oubliées* stems from that source. But the music does not sound like that – particularly not the swishy momentum of the string writing which, like the deployment of the orchestral sections in precipitate whirling blocks of sound, rather recalls

Ravel's similar method in the 'Bacchanale' of *Daphnis et Chloé*. The example of Messiaen's composition teacher at the Conservatoire, Paul Dukas, is also unmistakably evident. One device in particular – high, *fortissimo*, unison harmonics on both sets of violins, complete with shrill preceding grace notes shrieking out above the accompanying headlong cacophony on wind and brass – now sounds more typical of the avant-garde sonorities that an older Messiaen was to incorporate into his post-war works.

Spurred on by the solo trumpet's fierce repeated interjections of the main theme, the frenzied orchestral nightmare hurtles towards a climax that suddenly breaks off to leave the theme being played slowly and quietly again by the cellos and basses, as at the end of Ex. 5.1 but this time unaccompanied. This desolate orchestral 'question' is followed by a long pause. The answer comes with that same theme, now magically transformed (Ex. 5.2) in scoring, register, speed, key (from E minor to radiant E major), and – most tellingly of all – in its precise intervallic make-up within the same motivic outline. The theme and its exquisitely chorded accompaniment – chains of sixths, sevenths, and ninths floated on a nonet of muted solo strings – passes through a first statement and extension, returns for a second, and then, all *Parsifal*-like agony now long assuaged, soars slowly and rapturously heavenwards to alight on a final second-inversion chord (with added sixths) in harmonics. The gesture was to become one of the composer's fingerprints – *L'Ascension* and the *Quatuor pour la fin du temps* both end with a similar celestial ascent into a musical counterpart of the Empyrean in Dante's *Paradiso*. Yet Messiaen was not to surpass the beauty with which he here articulated the idea for the first time in this musical imaging of the Eucharist. In an ever more secular age, *Les offrandes oubliées* continues to speak to believers and unbelievers alike with a warmth and spiritual urgency that are each as rare as they are openly moving.

An achievement of this magnitude may have had an inhibiting effect on a composer who was still in his early twenties. Messiaen's progress in instrumental music over the next few years is indeed quite hesitant compared to the giant strides he continued

EX. 5.2 *Les offrandes oubliées*

to make in other areas – the song cycles with piano, and the organ works – where he was able to draw on a more personal involvement. Alongside this private side to his creativity, however, was his willingness in the earlier part of his career to appear as a public performer; he premiered most of his organ works himself, and also played the piano parts of *Poèmes pour Mi*, *Chants de terre et de ciel*, and the formidable *Harawi* at their first performances, although he appears not to have conducted any of his orchestral works.

Meanwhile his early awareness of the issue of the artist's public role is clear from the apparent enthusiasm with which he helped to found La Jeune France, a group of similarly young composers – the others were André Jolivet, Daniel-Lesur, and Yves Baudrier – who in 1936 joined intellectual forces with Messiaen; their aim was publicly to counter what they saw as the trivial musical posturings of Les Six with their own strong and unfashionable emphasis on the anti-ironic obligations of high art. As it turned out, however, La Jeune France was only able to organize a few concerts before its activities folded at the outbreak of the Second World War. By the time of its first concert, conducted by Roger Desormière in 1936, Messiaen had recently been busy with the composition of *La Nativité du Seigneur*, and was already beginning work on *Poèmes pour Mi*; he was therefore represented on the programme not by a new piece, but by repeat performances of *Les offrandes oubliées* and of the *Hymne au Saint Sacrement* of 1932.

Le tombeau resplendissant

Between these two works had already come another not played in that concert, and indeed included in very few anywhere since Pierre Monteux conducted its first performance in Paris in 1932 – the year after its completion, also at Fuligny. *Le tombeau resplendissant* is scored for the same orchestra as *Les offrandes oubliées*, and its layout is similarly short and concise. But while the quality of the earlier work makes its neglect inexplicable, it is rather more understandable why *Le tombeau resplendissant* has languished. Of course there is a sense in which Messiaen's less successful works tend to be more interesting than even the prime efforts of most of his contemporaries – including, in my experience, those of his colleagues in La Jeune France. Perhaps if *Les offrandes oubliées* had been withdrawn, lost, or both, the reader would at this point be in for a harangue regarding the astonishing creative originality of *Le tombeau resplendissant*. But in fact it offers very little that the earlier work does not. A harsh commentator could even make out a case that Messiaen here virtually wrote the same piece twice.

That this was not, at source, Messiaen's intention is clear from his choice of subject matter; perhaps conscious that the Eucharist had figured rather often in his pieces to date (as it was about to again in *Hymne au Saint Sacrement*), he here tried a different, more autobiographical idea. One commentator[2] has asserted that this score too was inscribed at first with a poem celebrating the Communion of Christ; but the published version is prefaced with a different one, corresponding to the new work's four sections as the superscription of *Les offrandes oubliées* corresponds to its three. The 'radiant tomb' of the title is revealed as the 'tomb of my youth'; his youth has died, says Messiaen, giving rise to paroxysms of 'despair and tears'; but consolation and understanding have been found in the acceptance of God.

The work's onward-moving, open-ended trajectory is similar to that of its predecessor, though the exact shape is different. A substantial and speedy opening section, replete with the hectic stridency of the central part of *Les offrandes oubliées* and making similar use of buffeting additive rhythms, gives way to a gentler interlude of attractive Debussian provenance: arabesques for solo oboe, flute, clarinet, and horn succeed each other gracefully beneath a tapestry of trills on muted and divided strings. The opening material then bursts in again and is developed and extended more violently. The response this time is a long, but not too long, melody for unison muted violas and cellos – the first fully-fledged manifestation in Messiaen of those rapt, ecstatic E major *louanges* which will so memorably dominate the *Quatuor pour la fin du temps*. This one too sings in E major, beneath a sustained triad of high string harmonics, eventually rising to absorb itself in a calm, similarly scored final chord. The effect *is* beautiful; it is also in several respects – the same key, same slow speed, same gesture, and not dissimilar scoring – a far too literal re-casting of the conclusion of *Les offrandes oubliées* to escape the direct comparison.

Hymne au Saint Sacrement

Less deserving of its neglect among Messiaen's early creations is the *Hymne au Saint Sacrement*. Whereas the subject is similar to that of *Les offrandes oubliées*, the form is now quite different, as is the tone of leaping joy which appealingly dominates its quick outer sections and which looks forward to the spectacular abandon of the *Turangalîla-symphonie*. The transition from anguished soulfulness to serene contemplation of the gift of the Eucharist, again featuring muted strings, here comes in a slow central section, to be succeeded by a passionate representation of the ensuing state of grace; a repeat of this musically enacted ritual of Communion then transposes its bright D major to a yet brighter B major. As in *Les offrandes oubliées*, the forces required are modest, the musical achievement is substantial, and the work's duration, at around thirteen minutes, is helpfully short. *Hymne au Saint Sacrement* has an unusual compositional history; the unpublished manuscript was lost during the war years, and Messiaen reconstructed the piece from memory for a performance by Leopold Stokowski in 1947. Since the composition of the *Turangalîla-symphonie* was by then in full swing, it is unlikely that that work's heady new technical discoveries left no trace on the rewritten version of a score first penned fifteen years previously. Hence, no doubt, the large advance in stylistic and technical precision that *Hymne au Saint Sacrement* demonstrates compared to the less sharply focused *Le tombeau resplendissant*.

L'Ascension

Far better known (and much more often played) than any of Messiaen's three earliest published orchestral works is *L'Ascen-*

sion, also composed in 1932, and again described as 'méditations symphoniques'. This time there are four movements, assembled into a thirty-minute structure that is much larger and more intricate than Messiaen had attempted before in an orchestral piece. It has therefore been all too readily assumed that *L'Ascension* must for that reason be artistically more important and substantial than any of the works that immediately preceded it – an assertion which can do with a healthy critical challenge (*vide* the opening pages of this chapter). The work certainly breaks spectacular new ground in its bold deployment of the orchestra. (No wonder conductors prefer *L'Ascension* to the earlier works.) The theological territory, too, is new. But precisely because of its larger scale, the work's unevenness is the more damaging to its total impact.

L'Ascension could hardly begin more impressively. In 'Majesté du Christ demandant sa gloire à son Père', the wind instruments' stark homophonic statements succeed each other in an unadorned, silence-punctuated procession, in the way that a colonnade of pillars in a cathedral interior leads the eye gradually onwards and upwards towards the lit spaces of the dome overhead. In its fusion of exalted tone and objective method, the movement remains a sound-object whose monumental power – again, something new for Messiaen, though hinted at in 'Cloches d'angoisse' of the *Préludes* – was not again to be equalled by its composer until *Et exspecto resurrectionem mortuorum* of 1964. 'Alléluias sereins d'une âme qui désire le ciel' offers a contrast of pace and mood in its swirling unaccompanied melismas for high unison woodwind, followed by gentler, orientally inflected solos for cor anglais, flute, clarinet, and oboe. These two ideas are extended by adding an accompaniment to the first, expanding that of the second, and then superimposing the two.

The work's disappointment is its third movement, 'Alléluia sur la trompette, alléluia sur la cymbale' – a banal dance of ostensible joy in quick compound time, culminating in a final fugato section whose academic provenance stifles its composer's voice with bemusing comprehensiveness. At least after this the impression made by the final 'Prière du Christ montant vers son

Père' is all the more remarkable. An extremely slow melody on the first violins, accompanied by seraphic chords on twelve solo strings, dips and soars in the rapt, suspended-in-time abandon that is uniquely Messiaen's. Technically the effect is achieved by taking the method of the exquisite closing section of *Les offrandes oubliées*, giving the scoring a subtle twist – whereas the melody-singing first violins are here muted, the accompanying solo strings are *un*muted, so lending the component notes of their closely massed chords an extra notch of penetration – and scoring the movement at a much stronger dynamic level, so that the strings' full bowing and vibrato kindle a sonority of saturated, full-throated radiance. The result is music that really does seem to blind the ear as light blinds the eye.

The more ambitious scale of *L'Ascension* compared to Messiaen's earlier instrumental works is matched by a parallel advance in a different and perhaps rather unexpected direction. Transcription was to be a relatively short-lived preoccupation for Messiaen, but it crops up often enough during the ensuing ten years, from the composition of the orchestral *L'Ascension* onwards, for it to amount to a central concern. With hindsight we can see now – as Messiaen himself evidently could not at the time – that the device of transcription was to do little to sort out his difficulties as an instrumental composer compared to his instinctive prowess in other genres. Indeed it may have compounded them. But it was also to engender some of his finest inspirations, whose achievement is not lessened by their second-time-around status.

The organ version of *L'Ascension* was finished one year after the completion of the orchestral original – a situation that raises the issue of whether or not Messiaen conceived the work in two versions from the start. After all, he had had the opportunity of working on the orchestral version at the organ console of La Trinité.[3] He may already have done the same with some of his earlier orchestral pieces too; but they do not explicitly sound like that, whereas on the contrary, in much of the material of *L'Ascension* the connection can clearly be sensed. The swirling octave melismas of 'Alléluias sereins d'une âme qui désire le ciel' if anything suit the organ rather better than the orchestra's woodwind; the music's steeply geared articulation bites more sharply. The scoring of the pastoral woodwind solos in this movement's second section, too, implies a spaciously layered perspective of sound-colours which turns out to suit the organ beautifully; it is hard to believe that Messiaen did not first hit on the idea in that context.

On the other hand the work's principal glory – the contrast across its entire span of the wind-and-brass-only scoring of the first movement with the strings-only fourth – is lost in the organ transcription, where the orchestral version's substandard third movement is also replaced by an entirely new one, the magnificent 'Transports de joie d'une âme devant la gloire du Christ qui est la sienne'. If this had been Messiaen's plan all along while working on the orchestral *L'Ascension*, it is arguably unlikely that he would have sanctioned the original third movement, or for that matter the entire work, for performance in that form. On the other hand, once the work *had* been performed and published in its orchestral incarnation, there could have been equally strong reasons why Messiaen would not have wished to withdraw it; indeed he never withdrew any of his published works after they had been released to make their own way in the world. The musical evidence remains as contradictory as it is intriguing.

The eight years after *L'Ascension*, though wonderfully productive for Messiaen in his (then) favourite genres of organ music and song cycles, show how unsure he must meanwhile have been of his direction as an instrumental composer. A job-lot of short and mostly unpublished pieces includes one that *was* published – the *Thème et variations* for violin and piano, composed in Paris in 1932 for Messiaen's first wife, the violinist and composer Claire Delbos. Both at this early stage of his career and subsequently, occasional pieces of this type were not his forte. Virtually everything about the *Thème et variations* sounds at odds with his true instincts as a composer – the chamber-music combination of violin and piano, which is handled in a traditional way that sits uncomfortably with Messiaen's already quite non-traditional harmonic world; the sense in which this dichotomy further emphasizes the always problematical relationship of the different temperament of the piano compared with stringed instruments; and the expectations of thematic development raised by the variation form which the music itself, while outwardly going through the motions, in fact neither confirms nor challenges but simply sidesteps. The theme's quiet initial statement proceeds through four increasingly quick variations towards a culminating restatement, now an octave higher (Delbos's upper E-string tone must have been good), with the piano's even accompanying chords much fuller, and with both elements extended into what is fairly described as a fifth variation in its own right. Yet the effect obstinately remains of something calculated from without, rather than springing from within.

Sundry items written during the next few years point to Messiaen's fitful progress in this kind of medium. A short *Fantaisie* composed in Paris in 1933, also for violin and piano, remains unpublished, as does the first evidence of Messiaen's interest in choral music – a Mass composed the same year at Neussargues, and scored for the bizarre combination of eight sopranos and four violins. Indeed Messiaen's only published liturgical work is the unaccompanied motet *O sacrum convivium!*; composed in Paris in 1937, this opens up a possible new direction in his music which one must regret he did not choose to pursue further. A sense of an inner stillness and simplicity, paradoxically articulated within musical dimensions of enormous length, elaboration, and decibel-level is a classic quality of Messiaen's later works in particular. For its part, *O sacrum convivium!* attains that same quality within just five minutes of almost entirely homophonic writing of unadorned beauty. Though the motet may be performed with an organ accompaniment, this appears to be suggested mainly for practical reasons; the tuning is in fact not difficult for a competent amateur choir, and the music is the more effective in its unaccompanied guise. In technical terms – precisely in respect of what is meant by harmonic progression, for instance – it is hard to think of a composer at a further remove from Messiaen than Bruckner. Yet it is Bruckner's spiritual world that is unmistakably suggested by this small, quiet masterpiece.

At the same time that he was exploring the purest musical medium of all – the sound of unaccompanied voices – Messiaen also began to take an interest in the sweetly swooping sonority of a newly invented electronic keyboard instrument, the ondes martenot,[4] which was from now on to be a regular presence in his music over the next ten years. His first essay in breaking this new ground was characteristically uninhibited: asked to compose something to accompany a *son-et-lumière*-style display of fireworks and illuminated fountains on the banks of the Seine during the 1937 Paris Exposition, Messiaen came up with the appropriately entitled *Fête des belles eaux* for a line-up of no fewer than six ondes martenot. Despite the element of the surreal in this scoring, it has to be said that the exoticism of the general idea is more alluring than the cloying sound of the music itself – which, detached from its original context, palls long before its thirty-odd minutes are up. Messiaen may have come to the same conclusion, because from now on he was to concentrate on using the ondes as a solo instrument in the context of the orchestra, in this way maximizing its impact as a disembodied voice apparently emanating from another musical planet.

One other early study by Messiaen for the instrument exists – the *Deux monodies en quarts de ton*, composed in Paris in 1938 and, like *Fête des belles eaux*, remaining unpublished. The supposedly brave new world of micro-intervals had already long been a twentieth-century obsession hampered by technical instrumental inadequacies, so it is natural that an ear as acute as Messiaen's should have momentarily been drawn to what the ondes could deliver in this field. It is also conspicuous that he was not to repeat the experiment.

A more significant project dating from these immediate pre-war years is not in fact an original work, but the transcription for voice and orchestra of the song cycle *Poèmes pour Mi*, whose piano version had been composed in 1936. Messiaen orchestrated it the next year in Paris, although this new incarnation was not performed until after the war, in Brussels in

1946. Orchestras of the time are reputed to have found the music's language of additive rhythms 'unplayable' – an accolade awarded to various works, from Schubert's Great C major Symphony onwards, which have duly gone on to hold a comfortable place in the repertory. Sure enough, the orchestral *Poèmes pour Mi* have established themselves as one of Messiaen's most attractive creations, whose technical demands are of the kind that modern orchestral players now take in their stride. As with *Les offrandes oubliées*, Messiaen added to much of the score a system of hieroglyphics intended to indicate the music's rhythmic language more succinctly than conventional time-signatures; a footnote states that the idea came from Roger Desormière.

As with Messiaen's earlier orchestral works, the forces required are quite modest, but the colours that he now conjures from them have a gilded beauty that is yet more vibrant and penetrating than before; this relates less to any sleight-of-hand of the instrumentation itself – expert as it is – and more to the enhanced vividness, pungency, and keyboard-conceived economy of the music's harmonic world. Messiaen was accordingly able to transcribe his music with little textural expansion beyond what the accompanying harmony already implies, and similarly little orchestration for orchestration's sake. The few examples of this that do occur are therefore all the more ear-catching, such as the 'dying fall' flute solo (pure *Pelléas*!) that is added to the concluding bars of the third song, 'La maison'. The closing sequence of the first song, 'Action de grâces', is the only extended passage in the score where Messiaen has seized on the obvious need to expand the original piano figuration. Ex. 5.3 shows the keyboard counterpart of what is transcribed orchestrally in Ex. 5.4, where the first two solo second violins and the two clarinets take the piano's left-hand pentatonic semiquavers, and the two flutes the right hand's second-mode ones; the other orchestral parts show how far Messiaen was prepared to go in decking out the musical implications of the original when he felt the context to be right.

EX. 5.3 *Poèmes pour Mi* (soprano and piano) 1 'Action de grâces'

Quatuor pour la fin du temps

Messiaen's next instrumental work was composed in rather different circumstances from those of his academic and domestic life in Paris. When the Second World War broke out in 1939, he was called up along with hundreds of thousands of his compatriots. Found unfit for active military service owing to his inadequate eyesight (just as well for the future of twentieth-century music, perhaps) he was made a medical auxiliary, and was captured by the invading German forces at Nancy in May 1940. He was then transported to Stalag 8A in Görlitz, in what was at that time Silesian Germany (now part of Poland). Conditions in the camp seem not to have been as harsh as they were for prisoners of war in some others; even so, it is difficult to imagine a more taxing contrast of surroundings compared to those with which Messiaen had so far been familiar.

EX. 5.4 *Poèmes pour Mi* (orchestral version) I 'Action de grâces'

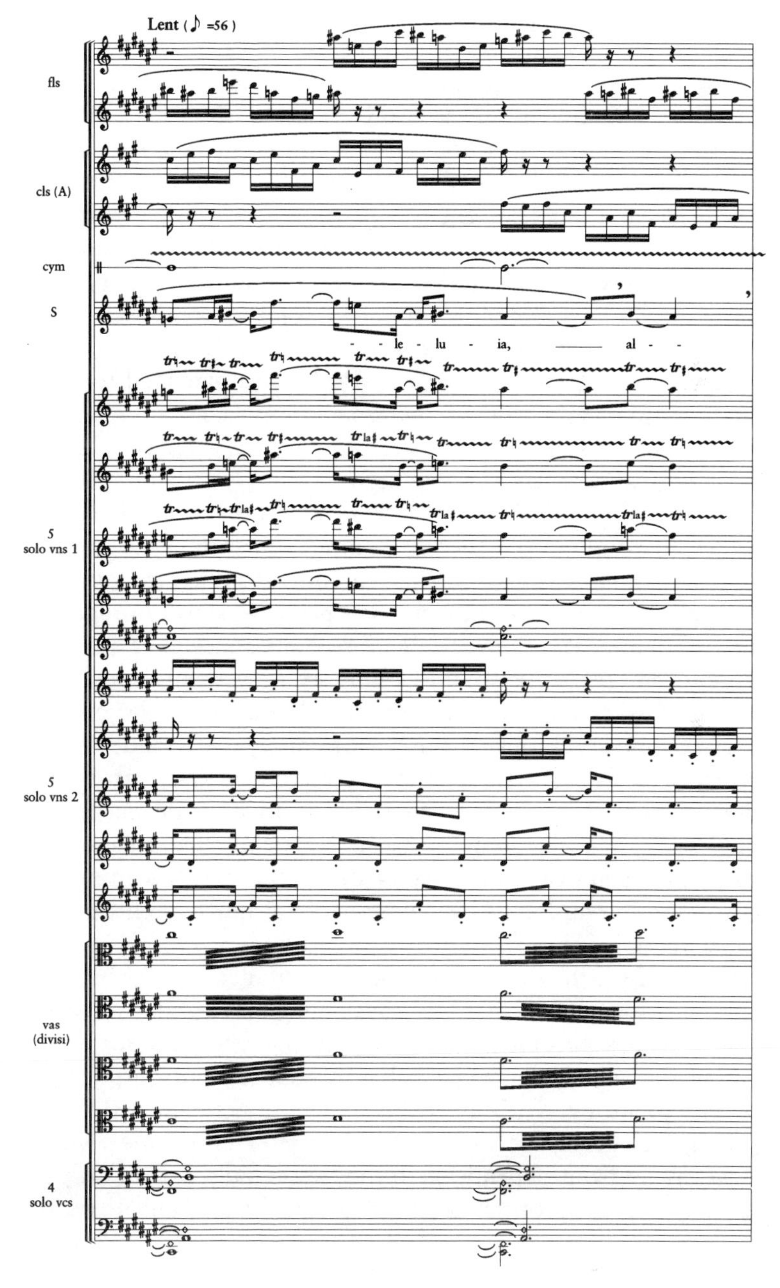

The story of the genesis of the *Quatuor pour la fin du temps* has passed into legend, to the extent that we present-day listeners, accustomed to the presence in our lives of what has become a celebrated work, may need to remind ourselves not to take for granted what an astonishing feat on Messiaen's part its creation actually was. Among his fellow-prisoners at Görlitz he got to know a violinist (Jean Le Boulaire), a cellist (Etienne Pasquier), and a clarinettist (Henri Akoka); to judge from the music that he was to write for them, all three were expert players. This stroke of fortune went hand in hand with others. The German camp commander obtained for the composer some manuscript paper, and for Pasquier a cello (with one of its strings missing); Le Boulaire and Akoka had managed to keep their instruments with them. Messiaen himself had no piano to start with, so he first wrote a short trio for his three colleagues. (This was apparently the prototype of the fourth movement, 'Intermède', of the *Quatuor.*) Still without a piano, he then proceeded to compose for this impromptu foursome a large-scale masterwork in eight movements, running to some fifty minutes. Eventually a worse-for-wear upright piano was also brought to the camp, and Messiaen and his three colleagues gave the new work its first performance on 15 January 1941 to an audience of 5000 fellow-prisoners. It was so cold that some of the piano's keys became stuck during the performance; one wonders how the players' fingers managed to negotiate any music at all, let alone Messiaen's virtuoso demands. As to how far the work truly succeeded in communicating to its shivering mass audience, Messiaen's own memory of the occasion is moving in its simplicity: 'Never have I been heard with as much attention and understanding.'[5]

So much for the cold facts which surrounded, in more senses than one, the birth of perhaps the single most significant work that Messiaen was ever to compose, in that the *Quatuor* is the technical source from which all of his subsequent output was directly to spring. With hindsight we can now perceive that the *Quatuor* is the hinge on which Messiaen's entire life's work turns, away from dependence on the essentially private inspiration of the early organ works and song cycles, and towards an unambiguous acceptance of the composer's public role. The circumstances in which he suddenly found himself, and the somewhat different audience he found himself addressing in the Stalag compared to that of the Parisian musical scene, between them triggered a process that might have happened in his music in any case, whether or not his life had taken this unexpected and (as we may surely surmise) traumatic turn. But we cannot be sure of this, any more than Messiaen can have been. Meanwhile the fact remains that for the only time in his creative life, external events did decisively impinge on the *technical* nature of his art to the extent that rather than simply developing it, they transformed it.

Times of trial throw each of us back on our innermost resources, and Messiaen's response to his imprisonment was to find solace and strength in the theological ideas and imagery of the Book of Revelation – hence his quartet's title and the exotic names he conjured for each of the work's eight movements, several of which are cyclically linked in their choice of material. This ingenious means of internally balancing a large instrumental structure has many precedents in earlier French music but was new for Messiaen. Also new, and even more striking, is the extreme inventiveness of the instrumentation, ranging from the third movement, 'Abîme des oiseaux' – written for clarinet alone – to the elaborate simultaneous deployment of all four players. But the work's most salient achievement is its liberation of Messiaen's interest in rhythm – a sudden and spectacular flowering of what is from now on to be a central technical resource in his music, and which is here engendered specifically by the disjunct instrumental forces for which he found himself writing.

The clearest instance of this is in 'Liturgie de cristal', the *Quatuor*'s first movement, whose preludial nature has it occupying a place outside the spiritual and musical agenda of the rest of the work (none of its material occurs in the other movements). A few years earlier, Messiaen's characteristic way of deploying the voice and its accompanying piano in *Poèmes pour Mi* had been to treat them rhythmically almost as a single instrument. Now, in 'Liturgie de cristal' (Ex. 5.5), we find the heterophonic superimposition of two independent rhythmic cycles – in the piano and the cello – with two independent birdsongs in the clarinet and violin (blackbird and nightingale respectively). The piano part itself consists of an unchanging sequence of twenty-nine different chords intersecting with a similarly unchanging sequence of seventeen rhythmic durations, which is already starting to repeat from the first beat of bar 6 of Ex. 5.5 (the

EX. 5.5 *Quatuor pour la fin du temps* I 'Liturgie de cristal'

gliss.
gliss.
gliss.

chords begin the first of *their* repeats from the last two semiquavers of bar 8). Meanwhile the cello's chain of harmonics outlines a rhythmic cycle of its own that is non-retrogradable – i.e. an image of eternity in its symmetry – both within its eighteen-unit sequence of durations and in the way that the last three units of each of those overlap with the first three of the next. It has been calculated that for the music to work its way through every possible heterophonic combination set up by these parallel processes, 'Liturgie de cristal' would last for about two hours. Messiaen, who has always preferred the dictates of the ear to those of mechanistic ideology, allows the movement's mere forty-three bars to speak for the rest of what could theoretically have followed.

Meanwhile his deployment of this technical symbolism – signifying the Angel of the Apocalypse who 'raises his hand heavenwards saying: "There shall be Time no longer" ' – intersects with a sensitivity that is purely musical. For instance the two beats' rest in the first bar of the piano part – the instrument's only moment of silence throughout 'Liturgie de cristal' – has nothing to do with predetermined rhythmic cycles; it is simply an instinctively judged touch in relation to the clarinet's entry that in an instant establishes the movement's mood of poised remoteness – an impression in turn confirmed by the placement of the cello's and violin's entries. The same is true of the harmonic spectrum explored in the piano's sequence of twenty-nine chords; each chord seems to not-quite-cadence into the next, so that the music's sense of forward motion (in one sense) intersects with its evocation of the stillness of eternity (in another) in flawlessly judged equipoise. As throughout the rest of the work, a vast and peaceful silence seems to hold its breath around the notes as they pursue their intricate foreground activity.

Two other manifestations of the exceptional musical imagination at work in the *Quatuor* should be mentioned particularly. The brilliance and originality of the sixth movement – 'Danse de la fureur, pour les sept trompettes', written entirely in unison – remain undimmed both by retrospective familiarity and by endless imitation of the idea by other composers. The movement also makes impressive use of a (then) very un-French technique at its climax, where the pitches of its opening bars (Ex. 5.6) reoccur in a vintage demonstration of the Schoenbergian device of octave displacement (Ex. 5.7). Given Messiaen's polite but comprehensive antipathy to the music of the leader of the

EX. 5.6 *Quatuor pour la fin du temps* 6 'Danse de la fureur, pour les sept trompettes'

EX. 5.7 *Quatuor pour la fin du temps* 6 'Danse de la fureur, pour les sept trompettes'

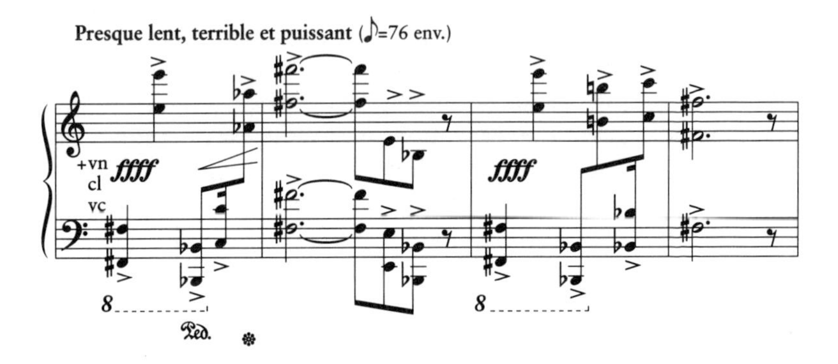

Second Viennese School,[6] it is interesting to recall that among the precious cargo of miniature scores that he took with him to the Stalag in his haversack was a copy of Berg's *Lyric Suite*. Perhaps the Schoenberg-related technical procedures and hyper-intense emotional climate of that work are the twin sources of Ex. 5.7's startling gesture.

The other technical aspect of the *Quatuor* which is artistically even more than usually significant is its transcription element. The fifth movement, 'Louange à l'éternite de Jésus' for cello and piano, has since become both loved and celebrated as one of the great songs of twentieth-century music, but it was not a new inspiration; the material had first appeared in *Fête des belles eaux* three years earlier. The *Quatuor*'s concluding 'Louange à l'immortalité de Jésus', too, is a transcription for violin and piano of the serene second half of the *Diptyque* for organ, composed in 1930. In each case, however, Messiaen came up with a masterstroke in the piano accompaniments for the new versions. The slow, imposing, bass-heavy, semiquaver-repeated accompanying chords for the piano in the cello's 'Louange' do not so much transcribe as transform the original idea – as surely as does the iambic, repeated-chord articulation of the accompaniment to the violin's celestial conclusion to the *Quatuor*. The exact psychological impulse that led Messiaen to transcribe these particular sections of two of his existing works has remained private; but he did later give a hint of the broader spiritual issues at stake while he was composing the *Quatuor*, in referring to the text from Revelation inscribed on the title-page of the score – 'There shall be Time no longer' – as having summed up 'all that I hope for, all that I loved, and continue to love'.[7] We know now that Messiaen was not to stay in captivity in a German prisoner-of-war camp for years to come, perhaps even to die there. He himself did not know that at the time.

In fact things turned out better for Messiaen than he surely could have hoped for while working on the *Quatuor pour la fin du temps*; in the spring of 1941, shortly after the work's premiere, he was repatriated to France. By May of that year he was already composing again, at Neussargues, and soon completed there two sections of what was to remain an unfinished and unperformed work, *Chœurs pour une Jeanne d'Arc* for large and small unaccompanied choirs. The first of the two existing parts is apparently a setting of the Te Deum; once again, what seems to have been intended as a liturgical work was destined not to see the light of day. At this time too Messiaen began his teaching career at the Paris Conservatoire, presiding over a harmony class through which many of the next forty years' most talented younger composers and performers were to pass. Among his first intake of pupils was a young pianist called Yvonne Loriod, with whom a deeply happy personal and professional relationship was soon to develop.

Trois petites liturgies

Initially his teaching commitments, combined with the first stages of work on his *Technique de mon langage musical*, seem to have got in the way of his composing; the only item dating from 1942 is an unpublished *Musique de scène pour un Œdipe* for ondes martenot. The floodgates of Messiaen's astonishing surge of creativity through the 1940s opened next year with *Visions de l'Amen* for two pianos, premiered in May 1943 by Loriod and Messiaen himself, and subsequently to be performed worldwide by them. Loriod's piano-playing was also a salient part of the inspiration behind Messiaen's next work, the *Trois petites liturgies de la Présence Divine* – composed in Paris in the winter of 1943 to 1944, and scored for the deliciously unusual combination of a choir of thirty-six women's voices, piano solo, ondes solo, celesta, vibraphone, three percussionists, and an orchestra of thirty-two strings.

Much of the sheer attractiveness of the *Trois petites liturgies* stems from this choice of instrumentation, which represents the first major example of the *ad hoc* assembling of forces that was to become Messiaen's standard practice in future decades. The work's crystalline, treble-orientated sound-spectrum is a coming-together of voices and instruments in joyful concatenation, as the composer's heterophonically enriched inspiration now dictates. The women's voices, apart from the odd excursion into ecstatic A major triads, sing in unison throughout – a device that encapsulates the work's fusion of technical sophistication with a tone of sweetly virginal innocence. Another musical layer is supplied by the deployment of the piano, celesta, and vibraphone in a kind of multiple gamelan obbligato; yet another by the disembodied melodic swooning of the ondes, dipping and soaring in its own obbligato relationship to the rest of the ensemble. Meanwhile the strings halo the voices in suffused celestial harmony in the (generally) slower outer *liturgies*, or surround them with cascading trills in the scherzo-like central one.

The music's winsome switchbacking between moods of rapt contemplation and dancing abandon is so beautifully judged that it needs an effort to remember that of all Messiaen's works, this was the one whose first performance – in Paris in 1945 under Roger Desormière – caused the biggest *scandale* of Messiaen's career. What mostly strikes our contemporary ears now is the music's loveliness; what struck those of its first audience was its assault on the received notion that a tone of piety was *de rigueur* in music whose inspiration was ostensibly sacred. Messiaen's young avant-garde colleagues and/or pupils meanwhile denounced his insistence on the validity of diatonic harmony, and above all his penchant for luscious added-sixth chords, as irretrievably vulgar. Much critical, professional, and public opprobrium was duly heaped on the work, and in particular on Messiaen's own text, whose language fuses images of the erotic and the divine after the manner of the biblical Song of Songs. The fact that the *Trois petites liturgies* set out quite unambiguously to convey divine joy in a *non*-liturgical, concert-hall context of course escaped most of the composer's detractors.

Turangalîla-symphonie

Given the work's forty-five-minute duration, the *Trois petites liturgies* are hardly *petites* in size; their title relates rather to the music's pointed lack of spiritual pretension. No such element of self-effacement applies to the orchestral monster that Messiaen was to unleash four years later on a startled musical public. The *Turangalîla-symphonie*[8] was commissioned by the Koussevitsky Foundation, which specified no limits as to the work's size or instrumentation. A delighted Messiaen worked for over two years on the composition of this ten-movement, seventy-five-minute symphony for large orchestra, complete with a tumultuously virtuoso solo piano part (written for Loriod), a solo ondes martenot as well, and an expanded, gamelan-like percussion section. He finished the work in November 1948, and the premiere was given in Boston's Symphony Hall in December 1949 by the Boston Symphony Orchestra under Leonard Bernstein.

Over forty years later, *Turangalîla* remains a gloriously controversial creation. For many it is one of the seminal orchestral masterpieces of the century. For others it is a noisy and overrated effusion whose now quite regular presence in concert schedules and recording catalogues owes more to its relatively convenient format than to its intrinsic artistic quality. For all its considerable size, *Turangalîla* remains the only large-scale work Messiaen was ever to compose which fits more or less comfortably into a standard concert programme. (The others, like *Chronochromie*, are either exceptionally difficult to play even by Messiaen's standards or, like *La Transfiguration de Notre-Seigneur Jésus-Christ*, call for vast rather than merely large forces, or like *Et exspecto resurrectionem mortuorum* use non-standard instrumental forces in similarly non-standard seating arrangements – a factor which still often jars with many orchestral administrations, as with the players themselves.) One consequence of this is that *Turangalîla* has become accepted far too readily as *the* typical Messiaen piece, when in fact its explicitly non-sacred subject matter renders it something of a maverick in his orchestral output. Another side-effect is that, as an inevitable consequence of being performed more often than its siblings, *Turangalîla* is also more often performed less well than it should be. I suspect that my own erstwhile resistance to the work – which used to be considerable – owed much to the too-frequent experience of hearing it being charged through by orchestras and conductors who did little more than cash in on the music's shock effect. A genuinely high-quality performance or recording of the *Turangalîla-symphonie* – one that does justice to the work's pronounced stylistic links with the French orchestral tradition along with the music's own shackle-breaking originality – remains rare.[9]

What is beyond serious dispute, however, is that *Turangalîla* has attained the status of a classic – a situation that can make it difficult for later generations to appreciate the force of the work's impact when it first appeared. Both the length of the piece and its instrumentation – triple woodwind, a D trumpet and cornet augmenting the brass section, vibraphone, glockenspiel, celesta, and not so very much other percussion along with the two soloists and the strings – are if anything quite modest compared to the size and scoring of most symphonies by Mahler. But Mahler's symphonies, though now staple concert-hall fare, were only rarely performed in the 1940s. *Turangalîla* must at the time have seemed gargantuan in its elaborate instrumental apparatus, hectic invention, flagrantly inflated rhetoric, and total lack of personal and artistic inhibition.

Turangalîla is the second of a group of three works inspired by the so-called 'Tristan myth' that tells of the fatal love of the medieval knight Tristan (or Sir Tristram, in his guise as one of the Knights of King Arthur's Round Table) and Yseult (or Isolda, or Isolde), the wife of King Mark of Cornwall. Messiaen always insisted that the three works – the first is the song cycle *Harawi* of 1945, and the last the *Cinq rechants* of 1948 – together constitute a 'cycle', but this is to use the term loosely; despite certain musical ideas and source material common to all three, the scoring and broad musical agenda of each could hardly be more different. Messiaen seems to have been drawn to the Tristan idea in a rather generalized sense – essentially to the 'love–death' element, and to the way that this mirrors his music's ceaseless preoccupation with the concepts of eternity and cosmic transcendence. In *Turangalîla* especially we are a long way from the world of Gottfried von Strasbourg's medieval poem which tells of the tale of Tristan, and almost as far from the mood of Schopenhauerian fatalism that dominates Wagner's operatic treatment of the subject. What does make all three components of Messiaen's 'Tristan trilogy' recognizable as a distinct group is their specifically non-sacred subject matter; even this, Messiaen seems to be proclaiming, exists and has its being under the cosmos-embracing *Vérité* of the Catholic faith. And these are also the first of Messiaen's large-scale works in which his love of the exotic, so far always implicit in his music, now became explicit.

As the world of Peruvian myth and folksong and its ancient Quechua language dominates the text of *Harawi*, so the *Turangalîla-symphonie* is (among much else) quite literally about the compound Sanskrit word enshrined in its title. *Turanga*, says Messiaen, denotes movement and rhythm – 'time that runs, like a galloping horse' and 'that flows, like sand in an hourglass'[10] – while *Lîla* signifies divine action on the cosmos, the play of creation and destruction, and also the spiritual–physical union of love.[11] These conceptually intersecting polarities are imaged both in the broad structure of the work – three rhythm-dominated 'Turangalîla' movements interleaved with four 'Amour' ones – and within the movements themselves, in which an exultantly elaborate superimposition of abstract rhythmic cycles[12] seethes together with the flaring rhetoric of the love-music in the same huge furnace of voracious and abandoned creativity. Both the *Turanga* and *Lîla* elements are presented and extended at the outset in the Introduction (itself a substantial

EX. 5.8 *Turangalîla-symphonie* 4 'Chant d'amour II'

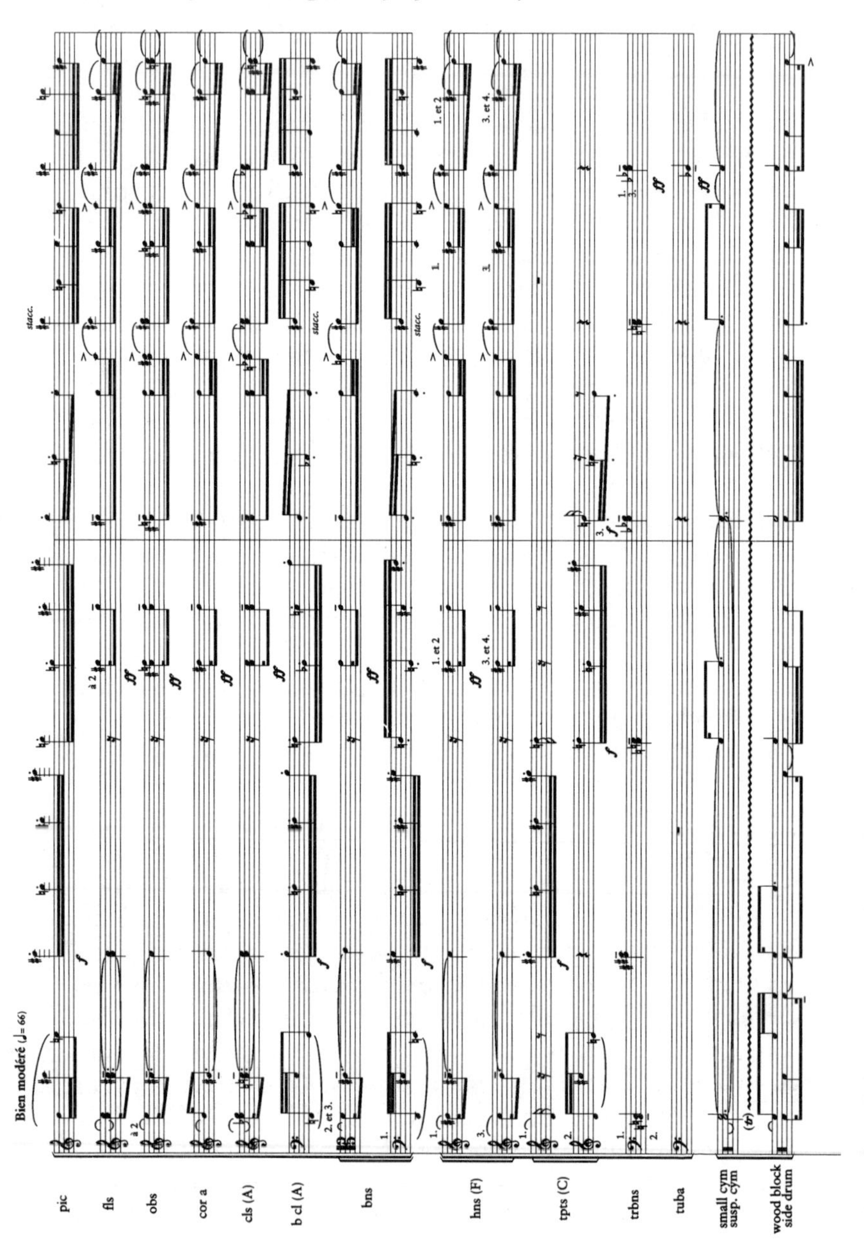

Bien modéré (♩= 66)
glock
celesta
vib
pf
onde
stacc.
3 solo vns 1
4 solo vns 2
3 solo vas
4 Altos Soli
pp
solo vc
vcs
dbs
(sempre pizz.)

and intricate structure); and the musically related fifth and tenth movements, 'Joie du sang des étoiles' and the Finale, simultaneously develop both components to a reckless and headlong pitch of frenetic intensity, while also delineating the work's two five-movement parts of roughly equal length.

The spectacular extent to which Messiaen was prepared to develop his newly unleashed heterophonic armoury in the *Turangalîla-symphonie* is illustrated in Ex. 5.8, which consists of two measures occurring during the course of the build-up towards the climax of the work's fourth movement, 'Chant d'amour II'. Both the ear and the eye can be forgiven for not immediately perceiving that the passage, which is by no means untypical of the work as a whole, is in fact a direct descendant of Ex. 5.5 – the quiet opening bars of the *Quatuor pour la fin du temps*'s 'Liturgie de cristal'. The principle of construction – the simultaneous multilayering of rhythmically, timbrally, and harmonically disjunct strands of material to assemble a kind of heterophonic 'mobile' – is identical. The difference between the two examples, apart from the obvious ones of the nature and volume-level of their individual components, is that whereas 'Liturgie de cristal' concerns itself with a mere four of these musical layers, 'Chant d'amour II' has by this stage built up more than twice as many as that. The dancing rhythmic material first heard at the start of the movement on the piccolo and first bassoon is here taken by the same instruments, doubled now on bass clarinet, trumpets, and ondes; meanwhile a complementary musical strand proceeds on pitched percussion (glockenspiel, celesta, vibraphone). The sensuous chorale-like 'chant d'amour' music, earlier heard in succession to this opening rhythmic material, meanwhile here proceeds simultaneously with it – on the violins, with *their* complementary component breaking in on cellos and horns and harmonically coloured by the woodwind. The unpitched percussion instruments – small (Turkish) cymbal, woodblock, and side drum – each also work through three self-contained rhythmic cycles of their own; the double basses pursue their quite independent chromatic bass line; the piano adds exotic decoration; and the trombones and tuba impose on all this cosmos-teeming activity their strident 'statue theme' (Messiaen's own term) which was first heard in the 'Introduction' as one of the symphony's several motto ideas. That makes a total of ten distinct musical layers in play at once – or eleven, if you count the purely coloristic trills of the violas and suspended cymbal.

The collective effect is of a quite unprecedented tumult of orchestral voices, which still has the power to disconcert and thrill that it must have had in 1949. The same is true of the *Turangalîla-symphonie*'s numerous other wonders – the curious depersonalized remorselessness of the three 'Turangalîla' movements themselves, with their brilliant, Varèse-connected rhythmic invention and their superlative control of structural trajectory; the singing tenderness of the muted strings, ondes, and accompanying piano-and-woodwind birdsongs in the drowsily harmonized sixth movement, 'Jardin du sommeil d'amour'; the unambiguously depictive eroticism of the love-music in general and of the eighth movement, 'Développement de l'amour', in particular ('avec passion – charnel et terrible' indicates Messiaen in the score, making things engagingly clear). And all this from a composer who less than twenty years beforehand had announced his creative arrival with a short, quiet, rapt meditation for organ on the nature of the Eucharist.

Cinq rechants

With *Turangalîla*'s mood of deliberate creative overload out of his system, Messiaen promptly completed his 'Tristan trilogy' with the *Cinq rechants*, which he finished in December 1948, less than one month after their gigantic predecessor. Yet again, as so often in this astonishingly fertile period in his life, the scoring of a new work breaks new ground: the *Cinq rechants* are written for an unaccompanied choir of twelve solo voices, a combination giving fresh scope to Messiaen's delight in intersecting sensuous harmony and technical virtuosity. The form is again idiosyncratic – a free adaptation of the strict verse-and-refrain forms explored by sixteenth-century French composers such as Claude Le Jeune. And the text is a gorgeously exotic concoction even by Messiaen's standards; passages of phonetic rhythmic chanting coexist with a whole constellation of references to the Tristan myth and to similar 'love–death' legends from Peru and Ecuador and elsewhere (e.g. that of Bluebeard[13]), all articulated in a free-falling blend of surrealist French, wordless phonemes, and the composer's personal brand of semi-invented Quechua–Sanskrit.

The form of each of the five movements varies in its treatment of the verse-and-refrain idea, but the alternation of the component strophes is always vividly clear; and compared to the joyful

EX. 5.9 *Cinq rechants* I 'Les amoureux s'envolent'

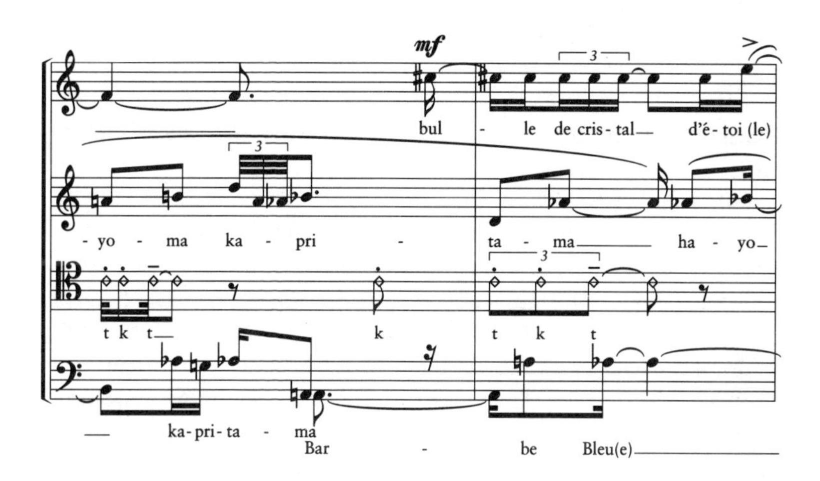

excesses of *Turangalîla*, the sonority of the *Cinq rechants* is at once more astringent and more seductively beautiful. The first movement is typical in this way, with its ecstatic unaccompanied introductory vocalise sung by the third soprano, then the ensuing straightforward alternation of speedy collective chorus refrain – *rechant*, three times, the third elaborated – and rapt, soloistic verse – couplet, twice, the second elaborated – leading to the unaltered return of the introductory vocalise as a coda. Ex. 5.9 shows six measures from the second couplet, which on its first appearance had consisted only of the two upper parts; the addition of the three tenors chanting in unison and of the bass part, which rotates between the three solo singers like its soprano and alto counterparts, sets up a suspended-in-time meditation whose beauty is as poised as its sonority is variegated. Again, the immediate ancestry of Ex. 5.5 – the heterophony of 'Liturgie de cristal' – is unmistakable. Other purple patches in the work include the third movement's virtuoso climax – a cascading wordless canon descending at whole-tone intervals and building to a whirl of twelve-part heterophony – and the exquisite final bars of the same movement. Here a tranced, *pianissimo* chord-sequence in six parts alights on a hummed chord of E major – second-inversion with an added sixth, and garlanded with a rapturous closing arabesque, *souple et caressant*, from the first soprano.

Messiaen has by now journeyed a long way from the E major chord – also second-inversion, as it happens, and also with an added sixth – which had concluded *Les offrandes oubliées* seventeen years previously. Yet even the *Cinq rechants*, for all their mastery, are also a work of transition; Messiaen was not to write for voices again until he began composing *La Transfiguration de Notre-Seigneur Jésus-Christ* in 1964, sixteen years later. Far from remaining content to disport himself in the hedonistic sound-world he had opened up in *Turangalîla*, he was already pressing on towards the new modes of musical thinking – altogether more hermetic, even austere – that were first to crystallize in the driving rhythmic inventiveness of *Cantéyodjayâ* and the *Quatre études de rythme* for piano, and then in the birdsong-saturated works of the 1950s. The soaring creative trajectory that was to continue from that point – via the monumental power of *Et exspecto resurrectionem mortuorum*, the vast musical synthesis of *La Transfiguration*, and the even vaster one of *Saint François d'Assise* – seems retrospectively a near-unimaginable achievement by a composer who, to judge from the idiom of his works written in the 1930s, had once seemed destined to spend his creative life within the narrow confines of the organ-loft. Is there such a thing as destiny in the life of an artist? Or is there just the occasional decisive convergence of a number of chance factors? It is food for quiet thought, as one considers what was set in motion when a medical orderly with a small collection of miniature scores in his haversack was taken prisoner by an invading army in a French provincial town, one day in May 1940.

Notes

1 Arms extended, sad unto death,
on the tree of the Cross you shed your blood.
You love us, sweet Jesus: that we have forgotten.

Impelled by folly or the serpent's tongue,
on a panting, frantic, unceasing course,
we went down into sin as into the tomb.

Here is the spotless table, the spring of charity,
the banquet of the poor, here the Pity to be adored,
offering the bread of Life and of Love.
You love us, sweet Jesus: that we have forgotten.

Paul Griffiths: *Olivier Messiaen and the Music of Time* (London, Faber and Faber, 1985, pp. 246–7).

2 Henri Martelli (Griffiths, op. cit., p. 48).

3 Messiaen had been appointed organist of the church of La Sainte-Trinité in Paris in 1931 – a post he was to hold for over fifty years.

4 The ondes martenot had been invented in 1928 by Maurice Martenot. It marked what was then the latest stage in the quest for a method of electronic musical sound-production that would work effectively in the concert hall – a quest that had been obsessively pursued by Varèse in particular since the early years of the century. The instrument works by means of a variable oscillator whose signal is amplified through a loudspeaker; pitch is controlled either by the keyboard, played by the right hand only, or by a device that can execute smooth glissandos throughout the instrument's range. The keys also allow a slight amount of lateral movement, making possible the variable degree of vibrato that is one of the ondes' most striking characteristics. Another is the range of electronic filters, controlled by the left hand, which change timbre and dynamics. Messiaen's use of the ondes in his works of the 1940s presupposes a relatively primitive specimen; his opera *Saint François d'Assise*, composed between 1975 and 1983, calls for three of the technically more advanced later models, and is also the first time that Messiaen had used the instrument at all since completing the *Turangalîla-symphonie* in 1948.

5 Antoine Goléa: *Rencontres avec Olivier Messiaen* (Paris, Julliard, 1960), p. 63.

6 Claude Samuel: *Entretiens avec Olivier Messiaen* (Paris, Belfond, 1967), p. 203: 'J'avoue que Schoenberg n'est pas un musicien que j'aime plus que d'autres'.

7 The following has been supplied by Charles Bodman Rae:

When I first went to live in Warsaw in the autumn of 1981, the Chopin Academy of Music arranged lodgings for me with a wonderful retired couple at 28 ul. Felinskiego in the district of Żoliborz on the northern side of the city (very near the Lutosławskis in ul. Śmiała). I stayed there for about six weeks while looking for my own flat. Aleksander Łyczewski and Janina Łyczewska were then (I suppose) in their early seventies. He is an architect (and very accomplished amateur painter) who spent much of his working life in the Far East.

During this period I was preparing for a performance of the *Quatuor pour la fin du temps* (as pianist). One day, I heard Aleksander Łyczewski rushing downstairs from his painting studio and he then burst into my room with a mixed expression of confusion and distress on his face. He said he recognised the piece I was playing and wanted to know who had composed it. He sat down and I explained about Messiaen and the circumstances under which the *Quatuor* had been written and first performed. He then recounted to me his experience as a prisoner of war in the same camp at Görlitz in Silesia. Aleksander was in a very emotional state while he was recalling these events. There were tears in his eyes and it took some time for him to regain his composure. He had been present at the first performance and vividly recalled the atmosphere in the large freezing hut where hundreds of prisoners (many Poles, other central Europeans, and some French) assembled to hear the piece. Apparently there were even wounded prisoners, brought from the hospital block, lying on stretchers at the front of the audience. He remembers his fellow-prisoners remaining in complete silence for the hour or so that it took to perform the piece. He himself had been deeply moved by the experience.

Some months later I wrote to Messiaen to tell him the story of Aleksander Łyczewski and how he had been affected by the *Quatuor.* I didn't expect to receive a reply, but in 1987 when I revisited the Łyczewskis, Aleksander showed me a charming letter he had received from Messiaen. As far as I know they may have corresponded occasionally until the composer's death.

8 A detailed description of the musical happenings in all ten movements of the *Turangalîla-symphonie* has been omitted here for two reasons. Firstly, rather than replicating material readily available elsewhere in book form, my main aim in this chapter has been to trace Messiaen's early *development* as a vocal and instrumental composer and the compositional connections (or otherwise) between the works concerned. Secondly, it seems reasonable to trust that a reader sufficiently interested to dip this far into a *Messiaen Companion* will either already have got hold of one of the several widely available recordings of *Turangalîla*, or will be on the point of doing so; and virtually all of these are accompanied by extensive documentation of the work's crucible of ideas and musical apparatus, often penned by the composer himself.

9 An outstanding example is the recording made by Yvonne Loriod, Jeanne Loriod, and the Orchestre de la Bastille conducted by Myung-Whun Chung, released in 1991 on DG 431 781–2. In particular, the presence of a French orchestra emphasizes how some of the work's woodwind scoring – the chorale-like material in 'Chant d'amour II', for instance – relates much more directly to the style of some of Messiaen's forebears (e.g. Debussy) than a non-French woodwind section will tend to reveal.

10 Messiaen, in the booklet accompanying DG 431 781–2.

11 *Passim.*

12 For a lucid, detailed, and by no means academically top-heavy exploration of this aspect of the work, see Robert Sherlaw Johnson: *Messiaen* (London, Dent, 1975, R/89), pp. 82–94.

13 See Ex. 5.9, bass part.

INTERLUDE

Colour

JONATHAN W. BERNARD

[One of the great dramas of my life] consists of my telling people that I see colours whenever I hear music, and they see nothing, nothing at all. That's terrible. And they don't even believe me.

When I hear music – and it was already like that when I was a child – I see colours. Chords are expressed in terms of colours for me – for example, a yellowish orange with a reddish tinge. I'm convinced that one can convey this to the listening public.

Messiaen[1]

It is clear that Messiaen regarded his faculty for colour hearing with a certain amount of ambivalence. On the one hand, he seemed resigned to the fact that most people are innocent of any gift for colour hearing and that those who can hear (or claim to hear) colours fail to hear the same ones he does; on the other, throughout his career he persisted in enumerating the colours of his compositions in the same way that he described their formal structure, their harmonic, contrapuntal and rhythmic components, and the species of birds whose song he has woven into the texture – exactly, that is, as if the colours were possessed of the same objective 'truth' as are the other aspects of his music. How does one reconcile these seemingly divergent attitudes? To what extent did Messiaen regard sound-colour as a true 'langage communicable'? And what implications does this have for the way we hear his music?

In later life, Messiaen's passion for colour became, if anything, even more intense; in an interview conducted in 1979 he placed the importance of sound–colour relationship 'above all else', even rhythm.[2] This represents a considerable revision of priorities when compared to such earlier pronouncements as

'Let us not forget that the first, essential element in music is Rhythm'.[3] It would be a grave mistake, then, for anyone seriously interested in Messiaen's music to dismiss out of hand the idea of colour as an attribute of sound, as if this were simply a delusion on Messiaen's part or evidence of an eccentric temperament. Indeed, it would be worth asking how one might follow Messiaen in his colour hearing – in however limited a fashion – towards a deeper understanding of his music. Some suggestions to that purpose will be supplied at the end of this chapter. Their meaningful interpretation will be possible, however, only in light of some of the technical background to the sound–colour relationship and some examples of its application.[4]

Investigators working with human perception as a frame of reference, using the methodologies of the social sciences, have found that in its more powerful manifestations – that is, beyond the simple associations that people often make between higher sounds and brighter or lighter colours, lower sounds and darker or more drab colours – *coloured-hearing synaesthesia*, as it is called, affects a relatively small percentage of the general population. For those individuals – either privileged, cursed, or just different, depending on one's point of view – the phenomenon is completely involuntary; likewise, the specific pairings of sounds and colours are beyond any conscious control on the part of the synaesthete. For this reason, there is an effectively infinite variety of possibilities, and the likelihood that the responses of any two synaesthetes would correspond in even a general way – to say nothing of the details – is vanishingly small. This is all the more true in view of the fact that the very basis for colour hearing varies greatly from individual to individual. Some synaesthetes, for instance, report associating colours with keys (in the tonal sense) or even with single tones. Messiaen rejected both of these bases, calling them 'naive' and 'childish'. For him, the complexity of colours linked them to 'sound-complexes' of greater intricacy than isolated tones or a conventionally tonal vocabulary.[5]

Messiaen's eminence as a composer, and the fact that he worked in an 'advanced', well-developed yet also highly personal harmonic idiom, sets his synaesthetic responses apart from those of others both in degree and in kind. Certainly we have far more detailed information about the sound–colour linkage in his case than we do even for Skryabin, Messiaen's most famous predecessor in this regard, whose responses were evidently tied firmly to keys. For Messiaen we know that it was harmony, specifically *chords*, that produced the response, and that other musical dimensions such as rhythm and timbre (the latter to be distinguished in French from 'couleur') affected it only peripherally.[6] It is also a measure of Messiaen's mastery of his art that he was subject to synaesthetic responses as much when he read a musical score as when he heard the music literally produced.[7] Messiaen's notion – shared of course by many other composers – that *real* musical hearing is internal accords very well with the fact that Messiaen, like most coloured-hearing synaesthetes, saw the colours only inwardly. This fact does not make the colours any less real, but they are clearly not to be confused with colours from the physical world.[8] For one thing, however intense their effect, their presence is only fleeting; this extreme evanescence is complicated by the simultaneous appearance of several colours in dizzying juxtapositions which endure scarcely long enough to be glimpsed before they give way to a new array. Thus even to describe what is seen is not a simple task for the synaesthete; one sometimes has the feeling, reading Messiaen's accounts of his visions, that some crucial flavour of the impression has been lost in transmission.[9]

There are, nevertheless, two reasons to believe that some understanding of Messiaen's synaesthetic responses could be gained without direct access on the part of the analyst to the sensory impressions themselves. One is that there was nothing whimsical or improvised about Messiaen's colour responses: they were absolutely fixed and consistent from hearing to hearing of a given passage. The other is that, despite the well-known tendency of synaesthetic pairing of senses to work in only one direction, and despite the fact that Messiaen apparently did not automatically hear particular sounds as the result of seeing particular colours in the objective, physical world, yet – partly because of the consistency of relationship – he was able to evoke colours consciously through his compositional choices. Messiaen was obviously no musical naif, simply reacting to whatever sounds happen to come along; the ability to control the colours plays an integral role in his compositional technique. There exists the very real possibility, then, that 'outsiders' may be able to infer the colour make-up of his sonorities through studying their structure, since as objective phenomena they *are* accessible to us.

It has been known for some time that Messiaen's employment of the modes of limited transposition is closely associated with his deliberate presentation of combinations of colours. Working from the available evidence – found in interviews that Messiaen has given, in the prefaces to published scores, and in the scores themselves – the definitive attributions of specific colours to specific modal passages can be tabulated. These attributions span most of Messiaen's career, from the eight *Préludes* to the *Livre du Saint Sacrement*, and including *Vingt regards sur l'Enfant-Jésus*, *Catalogue d'oiseaux*, *Couleurs de la cité céleste* and the massive *Des canyons aux étoiles. . .* . The results of this exercise, displayed in Table 1, show a high degree of correlation between the individual transpositions of modes 2, 3, 4 and 6 and certain colours and combinations of colours. (Ex. 6.1 presents these 'colour modes', each with all its possible transpositions.)[10]

The data of Table 1 can often be used to deduce the colour identities of modal passages for which Messiaen has provided relatively precise information about the colours present but no very exact indication of how these colours are matched with particular sonorities. For example, having ascertained that the opening of *Prélude* 1 comprises a primary texture in mode 3(2) and a secondary texture, in demisemiquavers in the upper register, in mode 2(2), we can quickly conclude that Messiaen's colours for this prelude – 'orangé, veiné de violet' – correspond to the primary and secondary material respectively.[11] Colours combined in this fashion can also sometimes exert subtle mutual influence. Such effects are impossible to predict exactly, but the modal identities are often useful in sorting them out. Toward the end of *La fauvette des jardins*, there is a passage marked 'bleu de ciel et vert doré de la montagne' (see Ex. 6.2).[12] Once

TABLE 1
MODALLY-BASED COLORATION IN MESSIAEN'S COMPOSITIONS

Mode	Composition, Movement	Colour(s)
2(1)	*Préludes*, V	violet-purple
	Vingt regards, V	blue-violet
	Catalogue, III	blue
	Catalogue, VII	rose and mauve
	Catalogue, VII	red and violet
	Couleurs (R75)	blue-violet
2(2)	*Préludes*, I	violet
	Vingt regards, V	blue-violet
	Vingt regards, XIII	gold and brown
	Vingt regards, XVII	gold and brown
	Vingt regards, XVII	rose and mauve
2(3)	*Canyons*, IV	green
3(1)	*Vingt regards*, XIII	orange, gold, milky white
	Catalogue, VII	orange
	Couleurs (after R75)	orange, gold, milky white
	Canyons, VII	orange and gold
	Canyons, VII	orange, gold, milky white
3(2)	*Préludes*, I	orange
	Vingt regards, XIII	grey and mauve
	Saint Sacrement, VIII	grey and mauve
	Canyons, IV	grey and gold
	Canyons, XII	grey and gold
3(3)	*Préludes*, V	blue-orange
	Préludes, VIII	blue-orange
	Vingt regards, XVII	blue and green
	Catalogue, IX	blue-green
	Canyons, VIII	blue
	Canyons, XII	blue and green
3(4)	*Préludes*, VIII	green-orange
	Vingt regards, XIII	orange, red, with a bit of blue
	Canyons, VII	orange striped with red
4(3)	*Canyons*, IV	yellow and violet
4(4)	*Vingt regards*, V	deep violet; white with violet design; purple violet
	Vingt regards, XVII	violet veined with white
4(5)	*Catalogue*, VII	mauve
	Catalogue, VII	violet; deep violet
	Couleurs (R76)	violet
	Canyons, IV	violet
4(6)	*Vingt regards*, VII	carmine red reflections; purplish blue; grey-mauve; grey-rose
	Canyons, VII	carmine red; purplish blue; mauve; grey-rose
6(1)	*Catalogue*, VII	golden
6(2)	*Canyons*, IV	brown, russet, orange, violet
	Canyons, VII	brown, russet, orange, violet
6(3)	*Vingt regards*, V	transparent sulphur yellow with mauve reflections and little patches of Prussian blue and brown purplish-blue
6(4)	*Vingt regards*, VII	vertical bands: yellow, violet, black

EX. 6.1 The colour modes

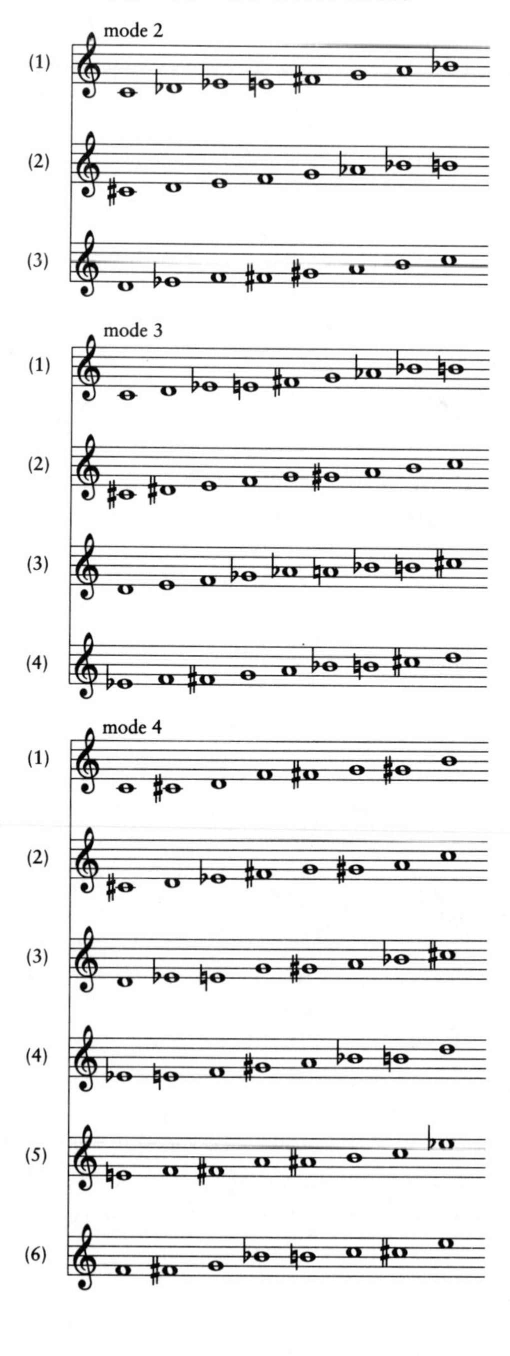

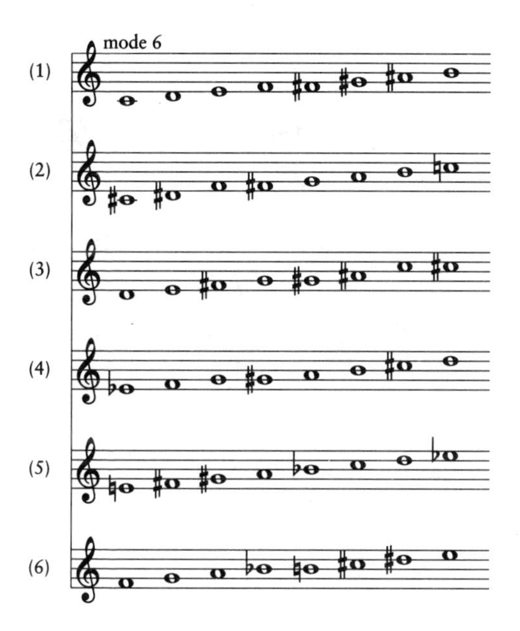

one has noticed that the chords on the middle staves are all written in mode 3(3), those of the uppermost staff in 2(2), the chords can easily be distinguished according to the identities of Table 1: 3(3) is basically blue but often tinged with green, while 2(2)'s brown and gold could be expected in this register to tend towards simple gold, since we know from Messiaen's own testimony that for him colours lighten and darken respectively with the rising and falling of pitch.[13]

This is not to say, however, that the data obtained always yield a perfect and unequivocal match between a particular colour and a particular modal transposition. Why, for instance, is mode 3(3) blue-green most of the time but occasionally blue-orange instead? And why is 3(2) sometimes orange, sometimes grey and mauve, sometimes grey and gold? Evidently, other

EX. 6.2 *La fauvette des jardins*

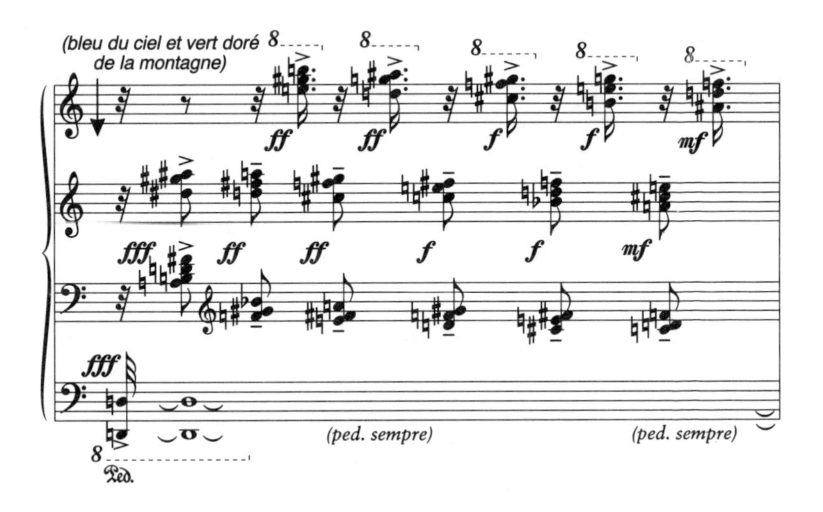

factors operate to influence these colour perceptions. But what are they?

The modes, of course, are hardly the sole basis of Messiaen's harmonic language. Although they were among the first components of his compositional practice to become firmly established,

EX. 6.3 *Quatuor pour la fin du temps* 2 'Vocalise pour l'ange qui annonce la fin du temps'

they were from the outset combined with other elements; already in the *Technique*, mention is made of the 'chord on the dominant', which evidently induces the impression of many colours at once in a manner akin to a rainbow or a stained-glass window, as well as the 'chord of resonance' and the chords of superior and inferior resonance. The modes also occasionally appeared, even early on, in 'impure' form, resulting in mixtures that Messiaen himself explained by means of 'borrowing'.[14] A series of chords played by the piano in the second movement of the *Quatuor pour la fin du temps* (Ex. 6.3), taken from a passage that Messiaen describes as 'cascades douces d'accords bleu et mauve, or et vert, violet-rouge, bleu-orange – le tout dominé par des gris d'acier',[15] presents initially some problems of interpretation, owing to the fact that the individual chords do not in general contain enough notes to establish one modal identity unambiguously. Once the decision is made, however, to divide the progression into five units defined by the shifts in pitch of the highest part, and once the available correspondences in Table 1 are consulted, the difficulties largely disappear, as follows:

1. 3(2) (borrowing D)
2. 4(4) (borrowing G♭)
3. 3(2) (borrowing D)
4. 4(5)
5. 3(2) (borrowing A♯)

The colours of this progression, then, appear to alternate between the gold and grey of 3(2) and the deep violets and mauves of 4(4) and 4(5).[16]

In certain works of the 1960s, Messiaen seems to have found the palette available to him through the modes to be too confining; most of the chords in the coloured strata of strophes I and II of *Chronochromie* and most of the labelled colour chords of *Couleurs de la cité céleste* and *Sept haïkaï* are non-modal.[17] Around this time we also begin to hear about 'turning chords', 'chords of contracted resonance' and 'chords of inverted transposition' as coloured phenomena. None of these is ever defined, either in terms of harmonic/pitch structure or in terms of the specific colours they evoke; all that is really clear about them is that they are non-modal.[18] Even outside the modal system, absolute pitch level appears to play a principal role, as the following quotation from the text of Messiaen's address *Conférence de Notre-Dame* makes abundantly clear:

> Take, for example, a complex of sounds which gives a group of colours: ash, pale green, mauve. If we move it higher by changing the octave, it will turn almost white, with some reflections of very pale green and violet. If we move it lower by changing the octave, it will turn almost black, with reflections of very deep green and violet. If, now, we transpose it up one semitone, it will become emerald green, amethyst violet and pale blue. If we transpose it up another semitone, it will give oblique bands of red and white, on a pink background with black patterns. In transposing it a semitone lower, it becomes white and gold; a tone lower we will have coloured crystals of burnt earth, amethyst violet, light Prussian blue, warm and reddish brown, with stars of gold.
>
> It then follows that there are, for each complex of sounds, twelve combinations of colours changing with each of the twelve semitones, but the combination of colours remains the same in a simple change of octave, lightening in a higher octave, darkening in a lower octave.[19]

One gathers that the 'complex of sounds' which Messiaen had in mind on this occasion is in fact non-modal, for two reasons: first, because none of the colour combinations mentioned bears even an approximate resemblance to the modal associations collected elsewhere; second, because Messiaen spoke of twelve transpositions, each with its distinctive array of colours – a result which could not be obtained with the modes, since their 'limited' nature ensures that the pitch content of a complex drawn from a particular transposition of such a mode would fall again within that transposition after only 3, 4 or 6 successive moves upward (or downward) by a semitone.[20] For some of the coloured but non-modal passages in *La fauvette des jardins*, this same radical shift in attributed colours accompanies changes in pitch level: for instance, the chordal succession labelled 'le lac rose à l'aurore' (score, p. 4) is transposed, note for note, down a semitone further on (pp. 18–19), where it becomes 'le lac vert et violet'.

Nevertheless, without a modal context, absolute pitch is not nearly so reliable an arbiter of colour associations – and not nearly so useful as a predictor in cases where Messiaen either has not matched colours precisely with harmonies or has not mentioned specific colours at all. It is under these circumstances that other factors come into play as indicators – and even, occasionally, determinants – of colour, notably chord *spacing* or vertical disposition of pitches. Even in a modal context, spacing is already of a certain subsidiary interest because, despite the fact that many spacings do occur in more than one mode, others seem to be the exclusive domain, not simply of one mode, but of one transposition in particular. In situations where the modal evidence is, to varying degrees, ambiguous, spacing can play a role ranging from confirmation of one's suspicions (formed on the basis of other evidence) to provision of a crucial correlation from non-modal sources. Two examples illustrating this range are presented below.

In the first of these (Ex. 6.4), the beginning of the passage titled 'le grand lac bleu' in *La fauvette*, the evocation of blue, combined with the A-major triad with added major sixth at the end of the excerpt, conjures up powerful associations with Mode 3(3). As his preface to the score makes clear, Messiaen meant to portray many different shades of blue: *paon* (peacock, a greenish blue) and *saphir* (sapphire, or purplish blue) are men-

EX. 6.4 *La fauvette des jardins*

(le grand lac bleu)
Très lent (♪=36) *(calme, extatique)*
mf
Ped. Ped. Ped. Ped. Ped.

tioned along with *azur* (sky blue). Indeed, as noted earlier, 3(3) often has a green tinge. The first and fourth chords can each be interpreted as 3(3) with a borrowed E♭, the second chord as 3(2) (mauve) with a borrowed D. An alternative reading, one which need not necessarily displace the first, would find a spacing match between the second chord (intervals, in semitones from bottom to top: 3, 2, 3, 2, 6, 5) and numerous harmonies in the passage labelled 'rouge, lilas, et pourpre violacé' in the fifth movement of *Sept haïkaï*. Since mauve is usually described as a strong shade of purple, this correspondence is surely plausible. The third chord is perhaps the most puzzling, since of all the transpositions of mode 3 it fits 3(4) the most closely, yet the red-accented orange of 3(4) is all wrong for this 'scene'. Conceivably, this chord must simply be heard consistently within the context of its neighbours – and here again, spacing criteria offer some support, for data gathered from other works suggest that the intervallic adjacencies 2, 4, 2, 3, 2, 2 correspond only to chords in 3(2).

Ex. 6.5 is taken from very near the end of the fifth movement (figure 22) of *La Transfiguration de Notre-Seigneur Jésus-*

EX. 6.5 *La Transfiguration de Notre-Seigneur Jésus-Christ*
'Quam dilecta tabernacula tua'

str; vv *(bouches fermées)*

22

3(1)	3(4) borr. C	3(4) borr. C	3(1) borr. F
4		2	2
4		5	5
2		6	4
4		4	6
3		6	4
8		4	4
			5

EX. 6.6 *Couleurs de la cité céleste*

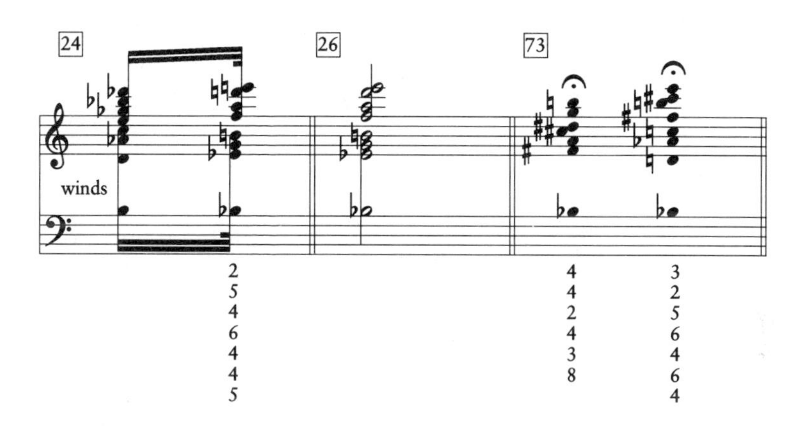

Christ. The four chords here are explicitly designated 'rouge et or' by Messiaen in his preface to the score. If modal characteristics are still somewhat in evidence – as the legends below each chord show – the absence of any mention of orange is difficult to explain. The analytical problem is solved, however, by the discovery that three of these chords (indicated by asterisks in Ex. 6.5) correspond exactly in their spacings to chords at various points in *Couleurs* labelled 'sardoine rouge', a deep red of somewhat orange hue (see Ex. 6.6). Interestingly, and significantly, none of these chords appears at the same pitch level as its correspondent in *La Transfiguration*; they are all a semitone higher in this later piece. What can be learned from this bit of detective work is, first, that Messiaen's colour designations may often be only approximate (one must bear in mind that the colours have no objective status as physical phenomena), and second, that spacing criteria may actually override absolute pitch for certain purposes, even if they never entirely supplant it.

Listeners who would like to emulate Messiaen in his synaesthetic experiences have a difficult path ahead of them. They may derive some encouragement from the composer himself, who maintains a firm conviction that at least *something* of what he perceives can be transmitted to the willing ear:

> I do believe that perceptions would agree with each other in broad outlines. One couldn't see a yellow instead of a red, or a blue instead of a green. But there are small details – I, for example, see grey, mauve, and gold tones in the second transposition of the third mode, which I'm especially fond of. Other people see it a bit differently, but whatever happens, they'll see something grey and violet; it wouldn't be exactly mauve and gold perhaps, but it would be a similar colour, but most certainly not red.[21]

Is this a forlorn hope? Perhaps not, if the initiate is prepared to do some homework. If Messiaen was correct in his surmise that 'most people have a kind of sixth sense and feel the sound-colour relationship, except that they are not conscious of it nor is it comprehensible to them,'[22] then clearly the only way one might hope to draw it out would be to concentrate on making a *voluntary* association between colours and sounds. In order for this approach to succeed, though, a good deal of aural/manual training will be necessary. At the very least, the modes of limited transposition must be learned thoroughly. The development of facility with the modes at the keyboard, along with the development of sensitivity to absolute pitch for the sake of recognizing the different transpositions of each mode, is probably the *sine qua non* to such an undertaking, since Messiaen himself gained his first intimacy with them by learning to improvise 'according to the modes' as a young organ student.[23] It would be irresponsible to suggest that conversance with the modes could be gained merely from listening, however extensively, to Messiaen's music. Learning the modes at the keyboard would also enable the student to become familiar with the various differences between chord spacings and – in conjunction with hearing and playing Messiaen's actual harmonies – the spacings characteristic of each mode.

Finally, all devotees of Messiaen's music can look forward to the probable appearance, sometime in the near future, of a new treatise by the composer. Originally announced over forty years ago as a 'Traité de rythme' in preparation, its size and scope have since grown in reflection of Messiaen's evolving interests to the point that the title will be revised to *Traité de rythme, de couleur et d'ornithologie* (see p. 284). The book will include 'lists of chords with all transpositions and all the corresponding colours' and 'analyses of the way in which the colours are in motion with the music'.[24] Will this treatise serve to explain, at long last, exactly what controls the sound–colour relationship? Will its revelations encompass the diverse varieties of non-modal sonorities as well? Will we discover why it is that certain transpositions of the modes produce different colours in different contexts – and, conversely, why some colours seem to be held in common, not only between different transpositions of the same mode, but also between different modes altogether? And if the colours always apply to these modes, then what about all those passages in Messiaen's many works for which the composer has not previously seen fit to provide colour characterizations?

In the event that completely satisfactory answers to these questions do not emerge, we ought not be disappointed. Perhaps it is just as well that a truly 'scientific' explanation for Messiaen's colour responses is unlikely to turn up. Some mysteries, as any devout Catholic knows, are meant only to be contemplated, not penetrated.

Notes

1 Conversation with Olivier Messiaen, 16 December 1983, in Almut Rössler: *Contributions to the Spiritual World of Olivier Messiaen*, translated by Barbara Dagg and Nancy Poland (Duisburg, Gilles und Francke, 1986), p. 122; Messiaen, platform discussion following European premiere of *Méditations sur le Mystère de la Sainte Trinité*, 11 June 1972 (ibid., p. 54).

2 Conversation with Olivier Messiaen, 23 April 1979 (ibid., p. 76).

3 Messiaen: *Conférence de Bruxelles*, translation uncredited (Paris, Leduc, 1958), p. 11.

4 A much more extensive treatment of the subject is to be found in my article, 'Messiaen's Synaesthesia: The Correspondence between Colour and Sound Structure in His Music', *Music Perception* 4 (1986), pp. 41–68. Some of what follows is freely borrowed and adapted from this earlier study; the examples of application are all new, however, and show that many of the general principles enunciated in the earlier study are confirmed by the data generated from examination of additional compo-

sitions. *Superimposition*, however, has been omitted from the present discussion, since further work with and reflection upon the material has convinced me, provisionally, that the kind of approximation of chord structure that superimposition involves is probably less relevant than the similarities between overtone complexes. Such phenomena, unfortunately, still pose considerable difficulties of consistent treatment.

5 See Claude Samuel: *Entretiens avec Olivier Messiaen* (Paris, Belfond, 1967); translated by Felix Aprahamian as *Conversations with Olivier Messiaen* (London, Stainer & Bell, 1976), p. 19; Messiaen: *Conférence de Notre-Dame* (4 December 1977), in Rössler, op. cit., p. 62. Interestingly, however, some individual major triads do have definite colours: C is white, F♯ is either silvery or 'a sparkling of all possible colours', G is yellow, A♭ blue violet, A blue. Such chords can of course be construed within the modes of limited transposition (see below); some of the interrelations of mode and key are addressed in 'Messiaen's Synaesthesia', pp. 48–9.

6 Messiaen has noted that his musical studies were traditional in that he was trained to think in terms of 'harmony, colour and rhythm . . . independently of timbre' (1979 conversation, in Rössler, op. cit., p. 108).

7 Samuel, op. cit., p. 17.

8 Messiaen: 'Address Delivered at the Conferring of the Praemium Erasmianum' (Amsterdam, 25 June 1971), in Rössler, op. cit., pp. 42–3.

9 Some of Messiaen's later published evocations of his synaesthetic responses were far more detailed than anything he had previously revealed. Quite possibly, he thereby attempted to address this problem of description. For example, Messiaen characterized the second transposition of his third mode (see below) as follows: 'Stacked horizontal bands: from low to high, dark grey, mauve, light grey, and white with mauve and pale yellow reflections – with flamboyant gold letters in an unknown script, and a quantity of little red or blue arcs, very thin and fine, hardly visible. Dominant [colours]: grey and mauve' (Olivier Messiaen: *Musique et couleur: nouveaux entretiens avec Claude Samuel* (Paris, Belfond, 1986), p. 68).

10 Table 1 is almost identical to Table 2 (p. 47) in 'Messiaen's Synaesthesia'; a few more colour attributions have been added. See also a similar table in Aloyse Michaely: *Die Musik Oliver Messiaens: Untersuchungen zur Gesamtschaffen* (Hamburg, Karl Dieter Wagner, 1987), pp. 220–2. Michaely's table, arrived at independently from the one in 'Messiaen's Synaesthesia,' omits some of the attributions listed there but also includes certain information not to be found in that earlier compilation, such as Messiaen's general characterizations of individual modal transpositions, along with some colour attributions by Messiaen that specify the work but not the passage(s) in which modally based coloured material is located.

In the present table, the number in parentheses following the number denoting the mode refers in each case to a particular transposition of that mode. See 'Messiaen's Synaesthesia' (p. 46) for speculation as to why modes 5 and 7 are omitted from this scheme.

11 See the example and discussion in 'Messiaen's Synaesthesia', pp. 49–50.

12 The arrow in the score indicates that this effect begins at the downbeat of

the bar, but the first chord on the middle staves actually belongs to the previous progression.

13 See quotation (p. 212), from the *Conférence de Notre-Dame*.

14 See Chapter 17 of Messiaen: *Technique de mon langage musical*, 2 volumes; vol. 1 translated by John Satterfield as *The Technique of My Musical Language*, (Paris, Leduc, 1956), p. 62.

15 Messiaen: 'Olivier Messiaen analyse ses œuvres', in *Hommage à Olivier Messiaen: novembre-décembre 1978* (Paris, La recherche artistique, 1979), p. 40.

16 It is possible that 3(2) here evokes grey and mauve instead; however, throughout this passage – not only in the brief excerpt presented here – 3(2) would seem to be the only plausible source for gold, whereas mauve and/or closely related shades are produced by several of the transpositions of modes 2 and 4.

17 In his book *Olivier Messiaen and the Music of Time* (London, Faber and Faber, 1985), Paul Griffiths devotes considerable attention (pp. 203–6) to the special device of *Couleurs* and *Sept haïkaï*: the use of colour chords that are twelve-note complementary. He notes the antecedents for the idea of 'simultaneous contrast of colours' in the painting of Robert Delaunay (which Messiaen cited) but also the fact that the specific pairings used by Messiaen (as construed along the lines of twelve-note complementation) do not correspond to the complementary colours of classical colour theory. I would guess, for this reason as well as the fact that Messiaen did not to my knowledge use this device subsequently, that the complementary nature of Messiaen's colours is not precisely addressed by the twelve-note feature, or at least not exclusively. Griffith's idea that Messiaen, by using literal complementation to partition the twelve pitch classes into smaller groups, 'acquires for himself a modal passage through a totally chromatic universe' (p. 206) is interesting but valid only to the extent that these modes are still even remotely recognizable in this non-modal environment.

18 To a certain extent this profusion of forms must be ascribed to the same tendency toward the unsystematic evident in Messiaen's treatment of harmony in the *Technique*, by comparison with his highly developed work on rhythm.

19 Messiaen, *Conférence de Notre-Dame*, in Rössler, op. cit., pp. 62–3.

20 Messiaen himself has confirmed this fundamental difference between the colour modes and the non-modal chords in *Musique et couleur*, p. 69.

21 Messiaen, 1979 conversation, in Rössler, op. cit., p. 88.

22 Messiaen, 1983 conversation, (ibid., p. 129).

23 Antoine Goléa: *Rencontres avec Olivier Messiaen* (Paris, Julliard, 1960), pp. 28–9. Among his teachers, Messiaen mentions Maurice Emmanuel and Marcel Dupré as the two in particular who steered him towards 'exotic modalities'; however, just what relationship these modalities might have borne to Messiaen's own system, as outlined in the *Technique*, is uncertain.

24 Messiaen, 1979 conversation, in Rössler, op. cit., pp. 85–6.

Mysticism and Theology

WILFRID MELLERS

The first man did not see God in his essence as a matter of course in his original state of life; though perhaps you could say that he saw him so in rapture, when God *cast a deep silence upon Adam*, as it says in *Genesis* II 21. And the reason is that since the divine essence is simply bliss itself, the mind of someone who sees the divine essence has the same attitude towards God as anyone does towards bliss in general. Now it is obvious that no-one can wilfully and deliberately turn away from bliss as such; for man naturally and necessarily wants bliss and shuns unhappiness. Thus nobody who sees God in his essence can wilfully and deliberately turn away from God, which is what sin is. And for this reason all who see God in his essence are so solidly established in love that never can they sin. Since Adam did sin, it is obvious that he never used to see God in his essence.

St Thomas Aquinas: *Summa* 1, 94. 1

The eminence of Olivier Messiaen among twentieth-century composers is now incontestable. Before his death in 1992, he was often referred to as 'the greatest living composer', and although he had rivals to this accolade, he was always a seriously considered candidate. Superficially, this seems surprising, for Messiaen was a man of profound religious conviction, whereas we live in an age unstably based at best on scientific rationality, at worst on cynical materialism. On reflection, however, we may decide that precisely because we are faithless, we may recognize, if not faith's necessity, at least a need for some of the satisfactions it may offer. In the modern world, Messiaen may seem an oddball: who fascinates because he reminds us of 'other modes of experience that may be possible'. We may even think of his work as a whole as an ironic gloss on the contemporary world, though irony is far from being a conscious concomitant of his art.

It is to the point that although Messiaen is a man of the Old Faith and a son of one of the oldest of European cultures, his religious roots stretch tentacularly beneath and around specifically Christian tradition. For Christianity, in becoming the hub on which Europe revolved, became the religion of 'Faustian' man: the pioneer–pilgrim who, with God's help, became a Protestant who protested on behalf of individual conscience, as against the idolatry of frozen creeds. So many of the central conventions of European music – notably sonata and symphony – are aural incarnations of this 'Western', aspirational pilgrimage; and this was a concept that barely touched Messiaen's consciousness. Rather than asserting man's ego and will, he sought release from them at a primitively physiological rather than maturely theological level, for from his earliest days he sought, in his music, to release the sensory moment from before and after, carrying this to a more extreme point than did Debussy himself. In one of his earliest pieces, *Le banquet céleste*, the movement of the chromatic chords is so slow as to seem almost stationary, while the chords themselves are so submerged in 'added' notes that they have no defined tonal identity. Similarly, the relationships *between* the chords are as disturbingly without harmonic direction as are the comparable passages in the Rose-Croix pieces of Erik Satie, such as the *Messe des pauvres*. These early works of Satie, written in the 1890s, are indeed 'poor men's masses' in that they offer numinous experience pre-existent to, or independent of, faith. Although Messiaen, throughout his long life, never lacked that faith, it would seem that in his early music faith is almost *pre*-conscious. This may even be true of a major work of his early maturity, the piano suite *Vingt regards sur l'Enfant-Jésus*, in that each of the movements is a glimpse of the infant Jesus, each virtually without movement, being built on an alternation of two or three chords, an ostinato, a pedal point or a reiterated figuration. This is a vast expansion of the static techniques explored in tiny works of Satie, and implicit in the 'spatial' aspects of Debussy's music, though these have no overt theological, or more accurately, theosophical content. Since such music evades the concept of beginning, middle and end, and with it the European time-sense, one may, however, validly describe much of Debussy's music, most of early Satie, and all of Messiaen as 'mystical' in the dictionary sense: which tells us that mysticism is not only 'mysterious, occult and awe-inspiring' but that it more specifically seeks 'by contemplation and self-surrender to obtain union with or absorption into the deity'. It 'believes in spiritual apprehension of truths beyond the understanding'; and since rationality does not come into the matter, the derivation of the word from the Greek *mustikos* – involving an initiated person (*mustes*) with hermetically sealed eyes and lips (*muo*) – is unsurprisingly ambivalent. This is why in modern times pejorative overtones have accrued round words like 'mystique'.

There is no reason, however, why things unknown and perhaps unknowable should be assumed to be bogus; in Debussy, in early Satie, in all Messiaen the mystical is 'merely' an admission of ultimate mystery. It may be that what we cannot know we should not speak of, but sing of it we may. Indeed, this is the ultimate validification of the art of music – which may blissfully embrace Aquinas's 'divine essence'.

In his early days Messiaen's mystical proclivities do not necessarily deny the normal contexts of European music. We may for instance regard his fusion of spatial and ritualistic structures with sumptuous and nervously titillating harmony as an extension of the sublimated eroticism of another fervent Roman Catholic who was also an organist, at times drunk on the sensory power with which an organ, being a one-man band, may imbue its player. But Messiaen's sublimatory mysticism goes further than that of César Franck: for whereas Franck's chromatic harmonies, aspiring to resolution, revolve narcissistically around themselves, Messiaen's harmonies, making no pretence of growth, may proliferate into melodic arabesques relatable to medieval and oriental cantillation. Again, Messiaen plumbs depths below the surface of New Testament theology, for the cult of Mariolatry rampant in his work is directly related to the Mariolatry of the medieval troubadours, for whom the Eternal Beloved was at once the Virgin Mary and a pre-Christian

Earth Goddess. For the heretical Gnostics Jesus was a Holy Spirit (which was female in Hebrew) who 'moved on the face of the waters'; and Mary, the name of the mother in whom Christ was made flesh, means 'of the sea'. It would therefore seem probable that the Virgin Mary was not far removed from Aphrodite, 'the wise one of the sea', from whom descended Eleusis the Divine Child, and after whom the Eleusian Mysteries were named. The return to the 'waters' of the unconscious is thus latent in Messiaen's Christianity, and it is not surprising that, in intuitively uncovering the remote mythological roots of his religion, he should metamorphose Christian chastity into fecundity, in a riot of ornament both linear and harmonic.

This is why, in his mature work, medieval Christian become inseparable from oriental concepts. Not only does Messiaen call on Eastern melismatic decoration, he also employs Indian râgas and tâlas in both pure and modified forms. Sometimes chord-formations may be 'vertical' arrangements of a traditional or invented *rag*: sometimes, complementarily, linear motifs may be a 'horizontalized' version of a 'mystic' chord: a procedure close to that of Skryabin, a still more esoteric musical theosophist who, depriving sensual harmonies of progressive momentum, aimed to effect a mystery embracing all accredited, and a few previously unarticulated, creeds and dogmas. When ultimately performed in a hemispherical temple in India this mystery was to induce in the participants a supreme final ecstasy, after which the physical plane of consciousness would dissolve away, to be succeeded by a world cataclysm. It is not surprising that, in the Apocalyptic era we have lived through, Skryabin has again become fashionable.

Messiaen, belonging to an orthodox church however unconventionally interpreted, is less atomically literal. Even so, it is to the point that the work that sums up the first phase of his career should have been written in a prison camp, in 1940, the year in which a cataclysm was indeed unleashed. The *Quatuor pour la fin du temps*, for clarinet, violin, cello and piano, directly relates this prison experience to the Christian Apocalypse as recounted in the Revelation of St John. Seven magic movements parallel the six days of creation and the seventh day of rest, while a coda-like eighth movement wings us from time into eternity. The brief first movement, 'Liturgie de cristal', is preludial: its birds, chittering at first dawn, are annunciatory, heralding the 'mighty angel' from the Book of Revelation, with a face like the sun and a rainbow around his head. In the long second movement this angel at first appears in aweful violence; but sings his visionary 'vocalise' in plainsong-like incantation divided between violin and cello, accompanied by what Messiaen calls 'blue-orange' chords and carillons on piano, resonating atemporally. The end of time, and therefore of consciousness, is prophesied, though the consummation is not yet.

Prophecy does, however, release the bird of the spirit who sings alone, impersonated by solo clarinet, from the 'abyss' of time itself. Monody and Spirit are here identified; and the avian nature of the song links Messiaen's Catholicism to his Pantheism, his awareness of nature as an 'other', non-human reality. The bird-cantillation employs not only râga and tâla formations, preordained but in floating, 'additive' rhythms; it also uses microtonal pitches such as do not occur in traditionally 'Western' contexts. Messiaen's birds seem to be at once nature's voice and God's: these are not identical, though both mirror man's desire for a heaven or haven beyond consciousness.

Even so, this liberation of the voice of the bird cannot be an end for Messiaen, who has Europe's materially human past behind him. This seems to be indicated by the odd, brief, scherzo-like movement that follows: this *opposes* the bird to the abyss he had sung from, since the abyss is now manifest not in supernatural terrors or wonders, but in the terrestrial, trivial round of our everyday lives. The dancing, simple-textured music combines charm and grace with a faintly comic pathos. Unambiguously diatonic, it sounds very French, at times almost café-orientated, and its final dominant–tonic cadence comes near to sounding, in context, like irony. If it represents our all too human frailty, it leads to the Christian heart of the work: the moment when the Word, for our sake, becomes flesh, here audible in an 'endless' cantilena ('Infiniment lent') for solo cello, accompanied by slowly pulsing piano chords in an isochronous metrical pattern that goes nowhere, being preordained in a medieval, and perhaps oriental, sense. Although the chords themselves are richly chromatic and humanistically sensuous, the spiralling cello melody flows over and through them, identifying Christ with us, so that through him our (harmonic) sensuality, pain and consciousness of mortality may be lyrically assuaged. This is enacted, as the tones of the melody grow gradually more sustained, the pulse of time incrementally slower.

Only after Christ's Incarnation may the seven trumpets of the Apocalypse blazon forth. They, of course, are entirely monodic, since the divine voice, whether represented by nature's bird-surrogates or by God himself, cannot admit the intrusion of 'human' harmony. Played by a melody instrument – or by two or three melody instruments – usually doubled in octaves by the piano, they resound in a non-retrogradable metre, rotating in an eternal circle. When the angel of the Apocalypse effects time's destruction in the seventh movement, Word and Flesh become one. This is a long movement – the destruction of time takes time – wherein melismatic arabesques are absorbed into, and grow out of, ripely sensuous piano harmonies and jazzily corporeal rhythms. But this climactic movement is not as long as the epilogue after time has been abolished: in which Messiaen effects a miracle in that the music, moving in time as all music must, seems to obliterate it. Scored for solo violin and piano, based on the traditionally 'heavenly' key of E major, it has a pulse so slow as to seem immobile. The endless violin line floats higher and higher until, with 'oriental' melismata, it fades into the stellar spaces, barely audible as well as ultimately pulseless, while the piano still (just) pulsates, senses suspended, on high chords of the added sixth. That this (Debussian) chord became a cliché of cocktail lounge jazz may hint at how eroticism may, at several levels, be a gateway to paradise!

Messiaen's wondrous *Quatuor* lives in equilibrium between the human and the divine. So does most of his later music, in which organization tends to become less harmonically and tonally European, more dependent on magical–oriental types of serialism, both linear and metrical. By the time of *Cinq rechants* – another masterwork, written in 1948 for twelve unaccompanied voices – one might say that division between sacred and profane has ceased to exist. Described by Messiaen as a 'chant d'amour', it has two musical sources: the Harawi, a love-song from the pagan folklore of Ecuador and Peru; and the medieval 'Alba' or dawn-song that warns lovers of approaching day. The text, by Messiaen himself, is partly in surrealistic French (springing from beneath those unconscious waters), and partly in an invented pseudo-Hindu language that dissolves meaning into purely musical sounds, sometimes mutated into the cries of insects, birds and beasts. References to Tristan and Isolde, Vivian and Merlin, Orpheus and Eurydice and other legendary lovers surface alongside contemporary references – for instance to the flying lovers in the paintings of Chagall. Although the movement of the note-values is usually rapid, the structures are all non-evolutionary and often circular, while the harmonies are non-progressive. In the Middle Ages the tritone (which sundered the godly 'perfection' of the fifth and fourth) had been a symbol of the Devil: '*si contra fa diabolus est*'. In Messiaen the tritone is not devilish, only negative in its neutrality, its lack of commitment. In this Messiaen's tritones may be related to those that obsess the Epilogue to the Sixth Symphony of a very different composer, the 'Christian agnostic', Vaughan Williams.

If the forms of *Cinq rechants* have no relation to post-Renaissance tonal development, they have close affinities with medieval variation techniques, and with oriental serial permutation. The title, *Rechants*, is borrowed from a French Renaissance composer, Claude Le Jeune, who experimented in numerical proportions derived from verbal inflexion. In the beginning was the Word which – although in Le Jeune's case it is not necessarily sacred – provides a non-subjective frame wherein the lovers unfold their destinies. After a free, monodic incantation in the invented – and therefore magical? – language, the first *rechant* introduces the panoply of legendary lovers, either monophonically, with wildly whirling leaps controlled by the Indian deçîtâla pattern of 2 + 2 + 3/16 alternating with 2/8, or in brutal, somewhat Stravinskian homophony, in which several potentially 'progressive' chords are telescoped in a timeless moment. Interspersing reiterations or permutations of these brief motifs are more extended lyrical 'couplets' in two- or three-part polyphony. These linking couplets are, as a formal device, derived from late Renaissance and Baroque French music and, perhaps because of this, the quasi-medieval linear textures acquire a tender voluptuousness, stemming from a prevalence of thirds, and from the caressing grace-notes, oriental in origin, with which the lines are embellished. It is significant that the words to this section describe the crystal bubble in which Hieronymous Bosch enclosed his lovers. Medievally biased, Bosch saw the dawn of Renaissance will as imprisonment and nightmare; Messiaen, at the twilight of the Renaissance, inverts this process, relinquishing the tonal perspective that is analogous to the visual perspective that Bosch had become scarily aware of. Antecedence and consequence are dissolved into discontinuous Time and Space.

Each of the five *rechants* is constructed on this same principle: an introductory invocation; the *rechant* (derived from the refrain of troubadour song), alternating with couplets; and a coda that returns to the original invocation, and sometimes includes references to the *rechants* and couplets also. Since this form is basically circular there is no climax within the individual movements, though the central (third) *rechant* is an apex to the whole work. This begins, not in strict monody, but with an undulating tritonal cantilena accompanied by wordless, sensuously static, chords. From this sensuality it attains the highest degree of magical or 'doctrinal' impersonality, since the three verses are in reversible metre – augmentation balanced by diminution of the central values. In the climactic third verse the effect – as Messiaen puts it – is 'intensified by a long crescendo, which unfurls like a veil of sound in twelve-part canon, culminates in a collective cry, and falls back to a soft, supple and tender coda'. This seems to be a (very effective) aural image for the act of coition: which may be why those neutral, if not explicitly devilish, tritones increasingly dominate the melodic lines themselves. Indeed the basic *theme* of the fourth *rechant* starts from the medieval *si contra fa*, spelt out boldly, and the love-ululation of the couplets is in tritonal organum. This hints at Messiaen's crucial position in the story of Europe. The tritones from which Wagner's Tristan had yearned to be released have become, monodically, a positive, as the Flesh becomes Word, to complement the Word's becoming Flesh. In this sense Messiaen has created, in a triptych of works of which *Cinq rechants* is the last, a song of love and death which extends the Wagnerian cycle. Tristan no longer needs to die in order to attain the metamorphosis of flesh into spirit. Debussy, in depriving Wagnerian harmony of even the desire for resolution, had shown the way to a musical apotheosis of the flesh; Messiaen completes the process in transforming harmonic tension into unaccompanied melodic line.

It would be difficult to imagine a more complete reversal of the will-domination of post-Renaissance Europe than the gigantic *Turangalîla-symphonie* – the second member of the triptych of love and death. In this work – still probably Messiaen's best-known piece – the fast movements are allied to the new-old primitivism of jazz in the hypnotic repetitiousness of their riffs, and in the blatantly scored opulence of their harmonies. However fast, they are as time-obliterating as are the vast slow movements, which evoke the sensual haven of a Garden of Love wherein the birds – represented by a gamelan of piano, vibraphone, xylophone, celesta and ondes martinot – ecstatically twitter, both tonally and rhythmically independent of the almost motionless string homophony. Such a pantheistic identification of man, God and nature increasingly pervades Messiaen's later work, such as *Réveil des oiseaux* which, in 1953, inaugurated a series of compositions based on scrupulous imitation of the songs of birds. The writing here, as in *Cinq rechants*, tends to be monophonic, or at least heterophonic, in principle, even when the strings are divided into thirty-two parts! The fascinating sonorities are an ultimate expression of Debussy's desire to 'reproduce what I hear . . . the mysterious accord between nature and the human imagination'. Of the sensitivity of Messiaen's imagination there can no doubt: though there are times in the immense *Catalogue d'oiseaux* for solo piano when one wonders whether Messiaen has not carried 'l'atrophie du moi' a shade too far. Birds may be angel-voices that have something we have lost; nonetheless one cannot completely follow Debussy in saying that there is more to be gained by watching the sun rise than by listening to the *Pastoral Symphony*; for although rivalry between these experiences is neither desirable nor necessary, we may reflect that sunrises, like birds, have never lost something that Beethoven had, because they never had it to lose. Moreover birds, after all, do not sing in Messiaen's equal tempered chromatics, nor even in the pentatonic formulae whereby European composers have usually represented them, probably because pentatonic motifs are, for acoustical reasons, those that spring most spontaneously to human beings. In fact birds chirrup microtonally, their song being too fast and too high for normal notation. Even if they were notatable, we could never know what they are 'saying' in their songs, though one suspects that their territorial messages are often far from angelic. None of this invalidates Messiaen's stylizations of their song in relation to his mysticism and even, by inference, to his theology.

This becomes evident in one of Messiaen's masterworks, *Chronochromie* for large orchestra, written in 1960. One of those rare pieces that make history, *Chronochromie* completes Messiaen's 'magical' retreat from humanism, for its structure is based not on human awareness of progression in time, but unequivocally on rhythmic proportions inherent in nature, at once preordained and permutatory. In this Messiaen owes something to the great Edgard Varèse, the French disciple of Debussy who in 1916 became an American citizen and, mostly during the twenties, composed a small series of revolutionary works which rejected process and progression for structural principles derived from nature, such as crystal and rock formation and the uniquely mysterious symmetries of snowflakes. With Varèse 'natural' law merged into the 'science' of architecture and mechanical engineering, in which he had been trained: so that his monolithic music paid simultaneous homage to the nature he had loved and studied in his native France, and to the machine culture of New York, where he found his second home. Messiaen was never tempted to effect this tie-up between nature and the machine; but he did see and hear nature as a cosmos overriding human subjectivity – 'an inexhaustible treasure-house of sounds, colours, forms and rhythms, and the unequalled model for tonal development and perpetual variation'. The ego and the ticking of time's clock were extraneous to this concept; and the melodic material, derived from the stylized and categorized imitation of specific birds, has no more need of thematic 'development' than have the blithe carollers themselves. The astonishing dawn-chorus for a plethora of solo strings becomes a climax only in attaining a maximum of heterophonic freedom. Hermes was a winged messenger, Papageno a feathered child of nature, and Messiaen's birds are flying angels free of humanly imposed restraints, such as tonality, periodic metre, accepted musical timbres, and so on. They are manifestations of the flux, and perhaps of the female principle, as are the waterfall images potent in the work.

The return to nature as a release from human turmoil has a long history in European music. In modern times it begins with the bird that warbles to Siegfried from the depths of the dark forest, and is active in the nature-musics of Debussy, Delius and Sibelius, in Janáček's evocations of the Moravian forests, and in the night-musics of Bartók, dizzy with buzzing insects, babbling birds and barking beasts. In all these, however, nature's otherness is seen or heard as distinct from the human: the fragmented cor anglais phrase that meanders through Debussy's *Nuages* suggests man's disconsolate littleness against the vast sky, while the nocturnal middle section of Bartók's Music for Strings, Percussion and Celesta juxtaposes man's melodic–harmonic endeavour against a timeless aural continuum of the natural world. Apart from Varèse, Messiaen is the first composer to reassert man's validity not in juxtaposition with or opposition to, but as part of, the 'eternal' principles of Nature. More than any other composer of our time he represents modern man's weariness with a literate, will-dominated 'patriarchal' culture, and his desire to recover a 'matriarchy' that worships the White Goddess and respects the Terrible Mothers.

It is not fortuitous that Messiaen's sequence of 'anacrouse-accent-désinence' – powerfully manifest in *Chronochromie* – parallels the lunar calendar, nor that the processes of metrical and intervallic metamorphosis that he began to explore in the *Quatre études de rythme* and brought to fruition in *Chrono-*

chromie, have affinities with the transformation techniques of the old alchemists, whether medievally European or Arabian. The fact that alchemy has again become a respectable subject, explored in its psychological connotations by Jung, is part of our age's rediscovery of the irrational, our consciousness of the unconscious. We may recall that Varèse referred to Debussy as a 'fantastic chemist', and detected alchemical analogies in the compositional principles of Satie and, by inference, of himself. In a no less profound sense Messiaen is a sound-alchemist, obsessed with the 'material' of sound itself; with the possibility of changing sound-matter through understanding of and identity with its laws; and ultimately with the possibility of man himself being alchemically reborn. Messiaen is not embarrassed to talk in such grandiloquently metaphysical terms, though he must be aware that opening oneself to the chthonic forces that surround one is perilous, since evil may be released along with, or instead of, good: as happened, in living memory, in Nazi Germany. But Messiaen would seem to be justified in believing that, buttressed by his faith, he was strong enough to evoke white magic, releasing powers for good. In a very real sense he loses the self in order to find it: which may be why the man who suffers and rejoices is instantly recognizable in the idiom of the mind that creates. The strophic and antistrophic structure of *Chronochromie* is significantly analogous to the chorus of a classical Greek tragedy, and the work effects a (Greek) catharsis whereby the wellsprings of being are released in order to be renewed. Messiaen has healed the breaches that Christianity committed us to, reaffirming the validity of the sexual impulse and the identity of the creator with created nature. This is why his appeal has been widespread, even in societies that are not specifically Christian, let alone Roman Catholic.

Messiaen would hardly have been able to do this had not his Catholicism been a matter of spontaneous conviction, as is manifest in what we have called his 'mysticism'. To define the sense in which he might also claim to be a theological composer is trickier, though he is indubitably theosophical in the dictionary sense of having sought 'a knowledge of God by spiritual ecstasy, direct intuition, or special individual relations': the divine essence that, according to Aquinas, is 'bliss in itself'. But theosophy is not identical with theology, which is a '*system* of (especially Christian) religion', or a 'rational analysis of a religious faith'. The Greek origin of the word theology signifies the knowledge of (or word of) God, while the word religion implies a bond and an obligation reasonably adhered to. One doubts whether Messiaen would admit to a distinction between theosophy as intuition and theology as rationally religious law, for his ambiguity – which may be at the heart of his appeal – is more a matter of heart than of head. The words of Robert Graves, attendant spirit of the White Goddess, are relevant to him:

> Circling the Sun, at a respectful distance,
> Earth remains warmed, not roasted; but the Moon
> Circling the Earth, at a disdainful distance,
> Will drive men lunatic (should they defy her)
> With seeds of wintry love, not sown for spite.
>
> Mankind, so far, continues undecided
> On the Sun's gender – grammars disagree –
> As on the Moon's. Should Moon be god, or goddess:
> Drawing the tide, shepherding flocks of stars
> That never show themselves by broad daylight?
>
> Thus curious problems of propriety
> Challenge all ardent lovers of each sex:
> Which circles which at a respectful distance,
> Or which, instead, at a disdainful distance?
> And who controls the regal powers of night?

If Messiaen, unable or unwilling to answer that last question, would seem to be a theosophist rather than a theologian, he is presumably left in the heretical position of believing that an artist, as creator, is indistinguishable from God. St Thomas Aquinas, from whom we started, taught that art imitates nature, but only in so far as it is 'able to'; *ars imitatur naturam in quantum potest*. The soul (mind, spirit) which can com-pose in placing things together, cannot create *ex nihilo*, as can God: *Anima enim facit novas compositiones, licet non faciat novas res; materia artificialium est a natura, naturalium vero per creationem a Deo*. It seems probable that Messiaen steered a way through this theological crux much in the same way as did Jean de Meun, the poet of the *Romaunt de la rose*, written not long after Aquinas's *Summa Theologica*: for de Meun, in a long digression on the nature of art, equivocates by claiming that although art cannot create forms as God can, it can transmute substances alchemically, so that momentarily their illusion may seem to be truth. This pseudo-scientific claim of the new humanism was, by Messiaen's day, very old; and however short on rationality, it contains a profound psychological truth, which Aquinas had himself defended. *Ununquodque tendens in suam perfectionem, tendet in divinam similitudinem*, he stated; and in this sense – that everything that tends towards its own perfection aspires to likeness with the divine – the alchemist Messiaen, though not himself God, has striven to embrace 'the divine essence which is bliss itself'. Sometimes he has succeeded: notably in the three works discussed in this essay – *Quatuor pour la fin du temps*, *Cinq rechants*, and *Chronochromie* – and consummately in two of the massive works of his 'late' years, his operatic Mystery on St Francis, and the choral and orchestral *La Transfiguration de Notre-Seigneur Jésus-Christ*, the latter being the closest he has come to a theological testament, and an epiphany of his life's work.

The End of Time: a Biblical Theme in Messiaen's Quatuor[1]

IAIN G. MATHESON

Can music engage with the Bible in any way other than the mere setting of its texts and stories? Thousands of musical works are linked to the Bible by their text; Handel's *Messiah*, Walton's *Belshazzar's Feast*, Britten's *Noye's Fludde*, Stravinsky's *Symphony of Psalms* – however complex or simple the musical language, the connection with the Bible is a straightforward verbal or narrative one. At this level the Bible is nothing more (or less) than a word-book, a source of texts for the composer. It is used in the same way as any other literary source, including the sacred texts of other religious traditions. It is set by composers who may or may not profess a Judaeo-Christian faith: that they should happen to take their text from the Bible rather than any other source-book is a matter of cultural conditioning, having no intrinsic connection with any music which results. At this level the link of Bible and music is fortuitous and contingent.

Compared to the vast repository of music connected to the Bible at this superficial level, there are few works concerned to respond to the Bible in any deeper theological way, even by composers who might happily acknowledge the influence of the Bible and of faith in their lives. Such a lack might suggest that explicit musical engagement with the Bible in any other than a verbal way is difficult if not impossible; the examination of this suspicion is the subject of the present chapter.

Messiaen, more than any other contemporary composer, has attempted to address specific biblical and theological concerns in his music. Almost all of his works written with explicit theological interest are instrumental: no words appear except in title and prefaces. Of forty-eight works noted in the definitive catalogue prepared by Yvonne Loriod, twenty-four have titles expressive of biblical, theological or liturgical themes; only four of these involve any word-setting. By contrast there are ten pieces for organ, seven for orchestra, two for piano(s) and one for an ensemble of four instruments – the *Quatuor pour la fin du temps*, written in Stalag 8A prison camp in 1941.

The *Quatuor* is based on Revelation 10.1–7:

> I saw a mighty angel coming down from heaven, wrapped in cloud, with a rainbow round his head. His face was like the sun, his feet like pillars of fire. He planted his right foot on the sea, his left on the land and, standing on the sea and the earth, he raised his hand to heaven and swore by Him who lives for ever and ever, saying: There shall be no more time; but on the day the seventh angel sounds the trumpet, the hidden purpose of God will have been fulfilled.

Messiaen's interpretation of this text is twofold. First there is the literal (verbal or narrative) use, spelled out in *Quatuor*'s title and the titles of its movements, which roughly parallel the symbols in the text. After the introductory 'Liturgie de cristal' the 'mighty angel' sings a vocalise for the end of time. The third movement, 'Abîme des oiseaux' may refer forward to John's prophecy in Revelation 11:7, 'the beast that comes up from the abyss will wage war'. 'Intermède' introduces 'Louange à l'éternité de Jésus': this and the last movement are devoted respectively to the divine nature and the human nature of Jesus, the Son of God 'who lives for ever and ever'. The sixth movement is a dance 'pour les sept trompettes': Messiaen's biblical text is the last of a sequence of seven angels appearing, each with a trumpet. The seventh movement celebrates the rainbow round the angel's head. It is not too whimsical to suggest that Messiaen's decision to use this particular text rather than any other may well have been prompted by the prisoner-of-war conditions in which he found himself, in which time might indeed have seemed literally endless, and the Apocalypse close at hand.

However, if this were all, the *Quatuor* would be nothing more than a sound-picture, albeit non-verbal; a setting of a biblical narrative, of the kind discussed at the outset, unfolding in some programmatic way the events surrounding the announcement of the end of time; like a Strauss tone-poem whose form is to some extent determined by the unspoken narrative it intends to depict. It is his second interpretation which Messiaen himself emphasizes as more important; the text is the starting-point for a work which articulates his philosophical views regarding different sorts of musical time. Messiaen assures his audience that 'I did not in any sense want to comment upon the Apocalypse. My only wish was to articulate my desire for the dissolution of time.'[2]

The text on which the *Quatuor* is based is a culmination of the Bible's concern with time as a theological issue from its opening verse to its last book. The Bible presents humans made in the image of God as creatures who are aware of time, history and their own impending death (in this they are distinct from the animals). But the Bible's point is not that time is a pre-existent thing into which God places his creation; instead, time itself is created as part of the whole. God does not create in order to fill up time, but gives the creation time to be alive.

Language fails when it tries to express the unity of past–present–future in God. Plato puts it this way:

> 'was' and 'will be' are created species of time which we in our carelessness mistakenly apply to eternal being. For we say that it was, is and will be; but in truth 'is' applies to it, while 'was' and 'will be' are properly said of becoming in time.[3]

Traditionally the nearest theology approaches an expression of this is the doctrine of eternal life; adopted and baptized, people are invited and enabled to participate in the life of God, the unity of identity and change. Clearly eternal life involves a good deal more than time, but one aspect of it is 'the end of time' and the step into eternity towards which Messiaen's selected text points.

Music appears well placed to respond to the Bible's presentation of time as a theological issue. Music is the art form most obviously concerned with the passage of time; rhythm, tempo, time-signature, pulse. The movement and irreversibility of time is the specific 'subject' of all music, made explicit in Messiaen's title. Sound is essentially fleeting and elusive; the listener who passes out of earshot for a moment has lost something irretrievable (at least until the next performance, when, however, the music will be different in crucial ways). Unchanging sounds quickly become either unnoticeable or intolerable.

Traditional music time is a subjective measurement of pure duration, measured objectively by pulse. The underlying principle of musical time is change; memory is important in the perception of this. It is memory which tells how a thing was compared to how it is, and what it retains of its former state. Composers stress different proportions of 'objective' and 'subjective' time, so that not only the duration but the quality of sound become significant; a musical moment may be great or trivial as well as long or short, subjectively significant although (when measured by the clock) objectively brief.

(From the composer's standpoint, time has another, added importance. As well as anticipating the planned effect on the audience of objective and subjective time, the composer occupies a separate world of what may be called architectural time; that is, the composer may take hours to write music which, objectively, takes only minutes or seconds to perform – his time as much as God's is outside the time he creates. Like God, the composer constructs a different kind of time from that which he himself occupies, and until the work is finished (that is, performed and heard creatively) not even the composer can fully participate in its new musical time-world, since it does not yet exist. The roles of performer and audience are thus crucial in bringing musical time into being.)

The 'dissolution of time' which Messiaen seeks implies a new sort of rhythmic music, one which for Messiaen 'eschews repetition, bar-lines and equal divisions, and ultimately takes its inspiration from the movements of nature, movements which are free and unequal in length[4] – in other words the very opposite of what is traditionally understood as 'rhythm'. Messiaen develops various rhythmic techniques in the *Quatuor* to articulate this very particular understanding of musical time, and his vision of 'the end of time' clearing the way for the beginning of a new type of musical time. Surprisingly, Messiaen does not make any special use of silence as a particular type of musical time, even though this has been held to be a poetic quality of the end of time – the hymn-writer's 'silence of eternity'.

The work contains two rhythmic innovations which have been important in the history of twentieth-century music. Both occur right away in the first movement, as well as later. The cello and piano in 'Liturgie de cristal' each follow an isorhythmic pattern (that is, a rhythmic sequence overlaid on a melodic shape, each recurring continuously but independently of one another); the cello has a five-note melodic shape over a rhythmic ostinato of fifteen values, while the piano plays a twenty-nine chord sequence over a rhythm of seventeen values. Such use of 'talea' and 'color' is a common organizing principle in many medieval compositions, a fact which Messiaen acknowledges, although he claims not to have known any such works when he wrote the *Quatuor.* Messiaen's innovation is to combine two such isorhythms, multiplying enormously the complexity of patterns which will occur before the two instruments return to their starting-point. This results in a dissociation of rhythm from melody and harmony (which together had assumed increasing dominance throughout the eighteenth and nineteenth centuries), emphasizing the autonomy of music's time over other formal matters. By their nature isorhythms have an inevitability about them: they do not develop, but simply apply precompositional decisions about patterns. The effect of this in the audience's subjective–objective perception is to create a sense of stasis, even while knowing that clock-time must be passing at its usual rate: and thus a tension is created between two sound-worlds, one 'temporal', the other 'eternal'. Because of Messiaen's use of two isorhythms, it would take long hours for the patterns to resolve themselves completely (which Messiaen allows to happen in some other works); instead, the movement is brought to a quite arbitrary end by the violin which, with the clarinet, has been accompanying the intellectual rigour of cello and piano with relatively undisciplined bursts of birdsong. Right away, time is brought to an 'untimely' end by the birds – Messiaen's symbol of eternity and freedom (see below).

The second innovation here is the use of 'non-retrograde' rhythm; the rhythm of the cello part is non-retrogradable, that is to say palindromic. It consists of a three-note rhythm (a) and a longer twelve-note pattern (b), each reflected around their mid-point:

EX. 8.1a I 'Liturgie de cristal'

When this is combined with Messiaen's five-note melodic shape, the following pattern emerges:

EX. 8.1b I 'Liturgie de cristal'

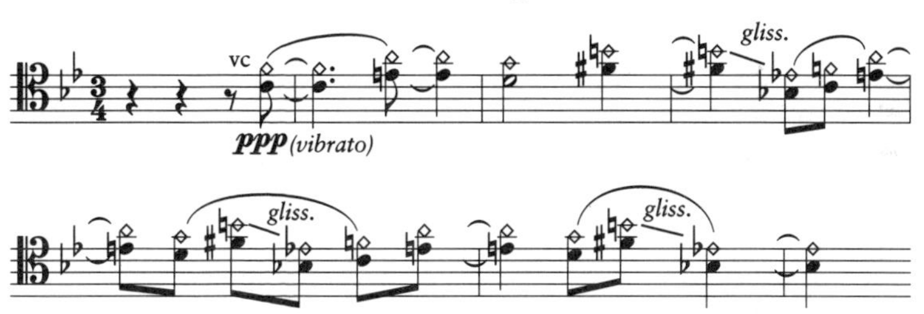

By the use of this technique at various points throughout the *Quatuor*, Messiaen aims to create rhythms which 'contribute to an elongation of time' – the direction of time is addressed, and its irreversibility questioned.

A rhythmic aspect of this movement (and later ones) which is perhaps more obvious to the performer than to the audience, is that Messiaen uses traditional notation to represent rhythms which have no correspondence to the given time-signature. He quotes in illustration a fragment 'as it was conceived by the composer':[5]

EX. 8.2a 1 'Liturgie de cristal'

and the same 'written in a false metre, with exact accentuation':[6]

EX. 8.2b 1 'Liturgie de cristal'

and comments: 'If the performers observe the indicated accents well, the listeners hears the *true* rhythm' (my italics). This shows the conflict between Messiaen's rhythmic ideas and traditional means of notating rhythm; and his belief that there is a 'true' rhythm which is heard rather than seen.

The third movement depicts 'the abyss of time, its sadness and weariness' contrasted with the birds who are 'the opposite of time; they are our desire for light, for the stars and for the things of heaven'. (Messiaen does not go into detail here – though he does elsewhere – as to the songs of which birds have been transcribed.) Contained within the birdsong are examples of note-lengths modified by adding and subtracting semiquavers, a technique which becomes important elsewhere in the *Quatuor*:

EX. 8.3 3 'Abîme des oiseaux'

and snippets of non-retrograde rhythm incorporated into the flow of music:

EX. 8.4 3 'Abîme des oiseaux'

In the fourth movement Messiaen deliberately contradicts his own revolutionary understanding of rhythm, by developing a very traditional rhythmic pattern for violin, clarinet and cello in unison. This roughly balances awareness of subjective and objective time: the audience's perception of the music advances at about the same rate as the clock (an example of 'chronometric time').

EX. 8.5 4 'Intermède'

The purpose of this vigorous and highly forward-moving 'Intermède' is to prepare the way for 'Louange à l'éternité de Jésus', the first of two melodic movements for stringed instrument and piano, marked 'Infiniment lent, extatique'. The two movements 5 and 8 are related by their texture, their tonal centre (E major – prior to this the *Quatuor* has established no clear tonality), their theological idea – first homage to Jesus the eternal Word, then homage to Jesus the man risen to immortality – and above all by their extreme slowness. Messiaen again questions the idea of musical progress by prescribing a tempo of 44 semiquavers per minute, so that the shortest note lasts 1.36 seconds. Subjectively the movement seems even slower; the audience is made aware that forward motion has been almost entirely removed.

It is worth noting at this point – it will become significant later – that both movements 5 and 8 had already appeared in other works by Messiaen; the fifth in *Fêtes des belles eaux* written for the Paris Exhibition of 1937; and the eighth as the second part of *Dyptique* (1930).

The sixth movement is another furious dance, this time for all four instruments in unison. It again makes use of non-retrograde rhythm; from letter F to H in the score each bar is a self-contained non-retrograde unit.

EX. 8.6 6 'Danse de la fureur, pour les sept trompettes'

In this movement Messiaen systematically uses the added value procedures begun in 'Abîme des oiseaux' to form groups of 5, 7, 11 and 13 semiquavers; saying laconically 'one recalls our predilection for these numbers'.

EX. 8.7 6 'Danse de la fureur, pour les sept trompettes'

The effect once again is to 'stretch' time (that is, to augment the more traditional note values of crotchet, dotted crotchet, minim and dotted minim – 4, 6, 8 and 12 semiquavers respectively) and slow it down.

The seventh movement has two themes, one new, the other derived from the second movement. One way in which Messiaen combines them is to present the pitches of one in the rhythm of the other, so that once again rhythm is declared to be independent of melody and harmony.

Messiaen succeeds in writing a work which focuses the audience's attention on time and rhythm, but whether he is equally successful in establishing the link which exists in his own mind between time as a musical concern and also as a theological one, is another matter. The Bible is quite clearly Messiaen's starting-point – his 'inspiration' – for the *Quatuor*, and he wants performers and audience to be aware of this; but the only means he has to guarantee this is the use of titles which create certain expectations for players and listeners. The titles of movements force their thoughts in a certain direction, and the title of the whole work is an unavoidable clue to the composer's intentions; any audience would have received the work quite differently if it had simply been called '*Quatuor*'. By composing a non-vocal piece, Messiaen *seems* to avoid the simplistic word-setting link between Bible and music; but in fact he is driven to use words to make his intentions clear, and they crucially influence the way the music is played and heard.

To be sure, the *Quatuor* is highly 'expressive' and 'evocative' in the way music is customarily presumed to be. But its expression and evocation captures the idea of timelessness *more* powerfully than words, not less, hinting at meanings beyond the expressive capacity of words. To surround music with words is to reduce it, not clarify it, as Schumann knew when, asked to explain his latest piano piece, he simply played it over again. In the preface to the score, Messiaen himself falls into the trap of using highly visual and descriptive language of the *Quatuor*, as though he thought it meant something: the language of the work, he says, is 'essentially ethereal; it is spiritual and universal. The modes harmonically and melodically realize ubiquitous tonality and they approach the listener from the eternity of outer space and infinity.' Elsewhere he describes his music as 'music which lulls to sleep and which sings, which is of new blood, speaking gestures, and unknown fragrance, an unsleeping bird, music of stained-glass church windows, a whirl of complementary colours, a theological rainbow'. The difficulty of finding words about music is equal to or greater than the difficulty of finding words about God, for in both cases words fail to express the unity of past–present–future. Again in the preface, Messiaen effectively admits that the biblical basis of the work, however crucial to himself as composer, is not important for others. 'Do not be preoccupied with all this [descriptive analysis] when you perform; simply play the score, the notes and the exact values, the marked nuances.'

Messiaen's use of the Bible here and elsewhere is intentional rather than fortuitous, to the extent that much of his music might well never have existed had he not been a Christian steeped in the Bible and theology. On the other hand, it is difficult for anyone except Messiaen (and perhaps for him also) to say that this is definitely the case: it may be that his music would have found some quite different starting-point. As has been said, the fifth and eighth movements of the *Quatuor* appeared in earlier works, though without such explicit theological connotations. It may be that the music nevertheless did have such a link, which Messiaen chose at that time to keep to himself. Given the evidence of these two movements, it is quite possible that Messiaen composed a series of independent movements on different occasions, and used the opportunity of his imprisonment to group them all under one heading which emphasized their common concern with musical time; given his theological background, it is not surprising that this should be expressed in a text from the Bible, though another text, such as Shakespeare's 'But wherefore do not you a mightier way/Make war upon this bloody tyrant Time?' (Sonnet 16), would have served equally well.

It is perfectly easy to impose extraneous programmes on music, especially tonal music with its inbuilt dramatic form of tension and resolution. Sonata form, for instance, corresponds neatly to an (Augustinian) outline of creation–fall–redemption:

Exposition	First subject – God creates the world
	Second subject (in related key) – Satan confounds the harmony of Eden
Development:	The cosmic struggle between God and Satan
Recapitulation:	First subject – God-in-Christ reconciles the world with God
	Second subject (now in tonic key) – Satan is overruled, and humanity is again able to live at peace with God

or almost any biblical narrative shape:

Exposition:	First subject – the loving father
	Second subject – the prodigal
Development:	Adventures of the prodigal
Recapitulation:	Reconciliation of father and son – the feast

Such programmes are entirely possible. Some are indeed sanctioned by the composer and are in that sense the 'real programme'. Nevertheless they are not intrinsic to the music, which can as well be listened to in purely musical terms without awareness of any extra-musical associations. (Western philosophical and religious traditions have encouraged people to seek meaning in everything, and it is not therefore surprising that Western listeners instinctively feel that music is – or should be – 'about' something. This is in sharp contrast to such Zen-inspired music as that of John Cage, who has commented 'I do not object to being engaged in a meaningless activity'.) Many composers have announced programmes for their works, and in some cases explained them in enormous detail – Berlioz's *Symphonie Fantastique*, for example – while others have acknowledged such precompositional programmes but chosen to keep them mysterious – Rakhmaninov's *Etudes-tableaux*; yet others have claimed religious or theosophic origins for their music – as in the work of Alexander Skryabin – in which the notional programme of the music is a positive hindrance to any listener who is aware of it, while to those who remain blissfully unaware of it, their appreciation of the music is unclouded. Finally, no doubt many works which are known only as 'abstract' music had connections in the minds of their composers with private events which have remained entirely private.

Messiaen's *Quatuor* can be considered as 'biblical' in a much more general way; not because it is linked in the composer's mind with a biblical text, or because biblical words are used in titles, but because all music (and all art) is intrinsically theological. It is concerned with the same matters as the Bible – space, time, transcendence, meaning – whether or not any given work has any verbal links with the Bible, whether or not it is the work of a Judaeo-Christian composer. Indeed, to the extent that both Bible and music relate to transcendent realities, music can be said to be more biblical than the Bible. The Bible points its audience towards transcendent reality – God – by depicting the Word in words; it is itself a secondary text. Music, on the other hand depicts *itself* – ontologically it is its own primary text and reality, pointing its audience towards nothing but itself; an absolute to which nothing can or need be added. Whether it is in fact possible to do what the Bible attempts, that is to represent God in an objective way, is a question beyond the scope of the present essay; it is certainly not possible to represent or describe music in any language other than music itself.

The ability to create is part of the image of God who creates. God's creative art may be broken down into four parts, each of which finds a human echo:

1. God's creation is a work of love, in which, through sharing himself, God prepares the way for the communion of creator and creature; and in which God places his purpose at risk (though his Being cannot be so placed) to be accepted or rejected. In the same way, music is a work of love; the composer enters a relationship with performers and audience, looking for a response, choosing to put him/herself at risk, for the sake of both audience and work.

2. God's creation is a work of freedom, brought about by nothing but God's decision to create. God is free-for-us, when he might otherwise have been free-from-us. In creation God brings something new into being, responsibly and intentionally. Music is similarly free; through the given categories of created existence it enables human choice for composer, performer and audience, exercised positively and responsibly; it makes freedom possible by bringing the new into being.

3. God's creation is open-ended; it is potential, and people as recipients of God's grace are invited to play a crucial part in its achievement. Music shares this open-endedness, leaving performer and audience a part to play in bringing the work to life and receiving it creatively. The composer is not isolated but depends on a response; his creation, so long as it remains with him, is incomplete.

4. God's creation is relational, just as God is in his Being. God the maker is freely immanent in his continuing involvement with all he has made. God is not content to remain within the community of the Trinity, but goes out to community with his creatures. In the same way, music is the basis of communication in the continuing chain of relationships between composer, performer and audience, to which a new link is added each time the work is performed. Music is thus a collective rather than an individual art.

These categories overlap in every direction; but they are helpful to clarify the nature of human creativity in the image of God.

Music, like God's actions seen in history, has its meaning in an unrepeatable cosmic event which is capable of recapitulation in the lives of those who participate in it by performing and hearing. In this it has a profoundly sacramental role, offering a revelation of the sublime. Music and faith are complementary aspects of transcendence, pointing to the deepest reality, 'that than which no greater can be thought' (Anselm). In an age of secularism and individualism, neither music nor faith can reach very great heights; and in an age which rejects overt expressions of faith, it is understandable that music can tend to become a substitute. Whether this is finally possible is a matter for debate. There can be no doubt, however, that in its power of revelation and of ecstasy, music often enters the realms of the holy; Messiaen's *Quatuor* itself is ample demonstration of this.

Notes

1 This article appeared in a slightly longer form in 'Text as Pretext : Essays in Honour of Robert Davidson', ed. R. P. Carroll (Sheffield University Press, 1992).

2 'Je n'ai voulu en aucune façon faire un commentaire de l'Apocalypse, mais seulement motiver mon désir de la cessation du temps' (Antoine Goléa: *Rencontres avec Olivier Messiaen*, Paris, Julliard, 1960, R/1984, p. 64).

3 Plato: *Timaeus* 37E6–38A6.

4 Claude Samuel: *Entretiens avec Olivier Messiaen* (Paris, Belfond, 1967), quoted by Roger Nichols in *Messiaen* (Oxford University Press, 1975, 2/1986), p. 21.

5 Olivier Messiaen: *Technique de mon langage musical* (Paris, Leduc, 1944), vol. 2, p. 11, Ex. 68.
6 Ibid., Ex. 69.

Birdsong

ROBERT SHERLAW JOHNSON

Although Messiaen began noting birdsong about 1923, when on holiday in the Aube district of France, it was not until the *Quatuor pour la fin du temps*, completed in 1941, that he made the first systematic compositional use of them in his music. He is not the first French composer, of course, to take an interest in birdsong, but he is the first composer of any nationality to take it seriously as an extensive source of musical material.

Until the 1960s, anyone wanting to gather birdsong in the field would have needed bulky recording equipment. Such equipment was not available to Messiaen, and although some commercial recordings became available, these were too few to have more than a limited use. Messiaen was therefore obliged to notate birdsong directly on to manuscript paper 'like an exercise in aural-training', as he himself has described it. The need to notate birdsong directly was an important factor in the compositional process. It led to an immediacy in the experience of nature, the perception of the song in its natural setting, which became crucial in forming the shape and character of *Catalogue d'oiseaux* (1956–8). For this work, and *La fauvette des jardins* (1970), it was not a question of using birdsong merely as a source of melody, as in many other compositions, but of painting a portrait of the bird of the title, representing it in its habitat, along with the more common birds found throughout France.

Messiaen's early sources of birdsong would have been those which he most commonly encountered in the regions of France where he lived or spent his holidays; as a result, those that have featured most frequently, and were the first to be named in his scores, were the blackbird and nightingale, as in the first movement of *Quatuor pour la fin du temps*. Both are prodigious songsters, the blackbird the more so because, unlike the nightingale, each individual has its own distinctive repertoire, and both are comparatively easy to capture in music. Messiaen's repertoire of European birds expanded dramatically in the fifties, but eventually, he could not be satisfied only with European birds. Although most of the birds of *Oiseaux exotiques* (for orchestra with piano, 1955–6) could be found at that time in the aviary at the Jardin des Plantes, in Paris, his trips abroad provided him with the opportunity to gather birdsongs from America, Japan and even extending to New Caledonia for birdsong for his opera *Saint François d'Assise*, completed in 1983.

The development of birdsong in Messiaen's composition

The first appearance of a melodic line bearing a resemblance to birdsong style was in *L'Ascension* (1932–3, for orchestra; arranged for organ, 1933–4). Although Messiaen refers to the passage as being freely based on style of a liturgical alleluia, without mentioning 'style oiseau', the melody which begins in the cor anglais at figure 1 in the score, continued in the clarinet and flute, has repetitive features, trills and arabesques which are a typical feature of later bird melodies (Ex. 9.1a). The title of the movement is 'Alléluias sereins d'une âme qui désire le ciel', with a quotation from the collect for the Feast of the Ascension: 'Nous vous supplions, ô Dieu . . . faites que nous habitions aux cieux en esprit.' ('We beseech thee, O God . . . make us to dwell in heaven in the spirit'). Its reference to heaven, and the desire for heaven, gives it an affinity with other contexts in which Messiaen makes symbolic use of birdsong. There is sufficient circumstantial evidence, in fact, to suggest an unconscious marriage of birdsong and plainsong style here.

There is a brief appearance of birdsong in 'Les bergers', the second movement of *La Nativité du Seigneur* (1935, for organ), and a more extended use, showing similar melodic features, in the last movement, 'Dieu parmi nous'. In *Technique de mon langage musical* (1944) Messiaen refers to the third main theme, as being 'a Magnificat, alleluiatic praise in bird style'. Here in the composer's own words is the suggestion of a combination of

EX. 9.1

(a) *L'Ascension*

(b) *La Nativité du Seigneur* 2 'Les bergers'

(i)

(ii)

'alleluia' melody and birdsong and a suggestion of Mary's joy at the birth of Jesus (Ex. 9.1b).

The first movement of the *Quatuor*, 'Liturgie de cristal', provides us with the first named use of birdsong in Messiaen's music on the violin and clarinet. The names are not given on the score itself, but in the preface to the work as blackbird and nightingale. The characteristics of the different melodies are sufficiently well defined to make it clear that it is the violin which has the nightingale's song and the clarinet the blackbird's throughout. Messiaen continues to label appearances of birdsong in his music simply as 'oiseau' for some time after this, with one or two exceptions. Occasionally he gives some clue in a preface to the work, which birds are being used, but even when he does, as in 'Amen des anges, des saints, du chant des oiseaux' from *Visions de l'Amen* (1943) he simply lists a number of species without specifying the derivation of specific phrases. He is slightly more explicit in 'Regard des hauteurs' from *Vingt regards sur l'Enfant-Jésus*, written the following year, where a nightingale is identified in the score, and the preface refers to the song of the skylark soaring above those of the blackbird, warbler (kind unspecified), chaffinch, goldfinch, Cetti's warbler and serin. The identification of particular birds by comparison with later versions of these songs in *Catalogue d'oiseaux* remains conjectural. Through comparison with the songs in 'Liturgie de cristal', however, it is possible to identify blackbirds in the second and third movement of the *Quatuor* and it is highly likely that this is also the bird of 'Amour oiseau d'étoile' from the song cycle *Harawi* (1945). The nightingale is always more clearly identifiable, forming the songs in the first movement of *Trois petites liturgies de la Présence Divine* (1943–4) and the sixth movement of the *Turangalîla-symphonie* (1946–8).

Hitherto, birdsong had either appeared together with other material, or for only brief spans on its own ('Regard des hauteurs' lasts only three minutes), so that it did not need to develop beyond a single monodic line, following the contour and broad rhythmic characteristics of the original birdsong. Messiaen did not aim for the meticulous accuracy which was the intended feature of his interpretation of birdsong in works from 1953 onwards. In Chapter 9 of *Technique de mon langage musical*, Messiaen wrote: 'Since they use untempered intervals smaller than the semitone, and as it is ridiculous servilely to copy nature, we are going to give some examples of melodies of the "bird" genre which will be transcription, transformation, and interpretation.'[1] But in his conversations with Claude Samuel, speaking of *Catalogue d'oiseaux*, he says: 'I tried to copy exactly the song of a bird typical of a region, surrounded by the neighbouring birds of its habitat . . . I am personally very proud of the accuracy of my work'.[2] As long as birdsong was used purely for symbolic purposes, Messiaen had no need to be meticulously accurate in its interpretation, or specific about which melodic phrase should be attributed to which bird. With *Réveil des oiseaux*, his work entered a realistic phase, demanding more precision in the treatment of the song. Ornithologists and others have criticized him strongly for this claim, maintaining that they cannot hear the resemblance to the original birdsong. The principles laid down in *Technique de mon langage musical*, however, still hold true in that compromises have to be made in transcribing birdsong for musical instruments. Messiaen goes on to elaborate on this point further with Claude Samuel when he talks about the need to slow up the extremely quick tempos of the original song, to transpose down the extremely high registers which are inaccessible to most instruments and especially to expand the interval structure of the song in order to accommodate small microtones in the equal tempered system:

> I am obliged to suppress the very small intervals which our instruments cannot play. I replace these intervals of the order of one or two commas by semitones, but I respect the scale of values between different intervals; that is to say, if several commas correspond to a semitone, then to the true semitone will correspond a whole tone or a third.[3]

So long as birdsong remained a subsidiary element in a composition, its monodic characteristics were not a serious limitation. It becomes clear, however, in *Réveil des oiseaux*, written for piano and orchestra, where everything is birdsong, that a purely monodic texture would not allow enough variation in the treatment of material to provide sufficient interest for the listener over an extended composition. In order to obtain contrast of texture, he is obliged to build up complex counterpoints of birdsong in the orchestra, representing choruses of birds, in particular the main central cadenza representing the dawn chorus. Contrasting with these choruses the piano has cadenzas devoted to different birds, presented singly, except in the last cadenza which recapitulates a number of different birdsongs. With some exceptions the piano tends to play in octaves during these cadenzas unless more than one bird is singing at a time. The exceptions are interesting in so far as they point the way towards a development of bird melody in future works – the representation of timbre by harmonic coloration.

A feature of Messiaen's harmony had always been its function to 'colour' a melodic line, rather than to 'harmonize' it in the traditional functional sense. This brought about a merging of the functions of harmony and timbres, so that a phrase such as that shown in Ex. 9.2 could be regarded as a 'thickened' or 'coloured' monody, rather than a harmonized melody. This conception of harmony led naturally to the coloration of birdsong to represent its timbre, and the first few examples of this occur in *Réveil des oiseaux*, for example in the case of the crow ('corneille noire'), to represent its harsh croak and the serin ('serin cini'), its high-pitched, tinkling song (Ex. 9.2).

The work following *Réveil des oiseaux* – *Oiseaux exotiques* – makes much more use of 'coloured' birdsong. As has previously been mentioned, most (if not all) of the birds used in this piece were present in the aviary of the Jardin des Plantes in Paris, and the work brings together birds of different continents, as distinct

EX. 9.2 Réveil des oiseaux

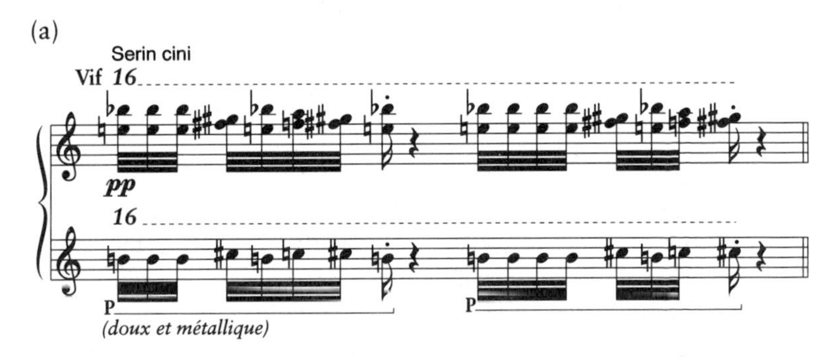

from its predecessor, which was based entirely on birds native to France. In addition to birdsong, the work makes use of rhythmic patterns underlying the orchestral tuttis in the percussion, indicating a need for more variety of material than could be provided by birdsong alone.

The harmonic expansion of birdsong was important for *Catalogue d'oiseaux* which was begun in the same year as the composition of *Oiseaux exotiques*. As the work is for solo piano, excluding the variety of orchestral timbre possible in *Réveil des oiseaux*, single birdsongs had to stand complete on their own, providing their onw contrast of harmonic timbre. The piano may seem, at first sign, an odd choice for a piece consisting mainly of birdsong, but from 1943 (the year of *Visions de l'Amen*), the piano was a favoured instrument for Messiaen, and one must remember that his intentions were for accuracy in the transcription of birdsong, not for literalness, 'the slavish copying of nature'. Ex. 9.3 illustrates the development of the nightingale's song from one of its earlier appearances in the *Turangalîla-symphonie* through to *Catalogue d'oiseaux* with an example from Ravel's *L'enfant et les sortilèges* for comparison. Ex. 9.3c illustrates what Messiaen calls the 'son lunaire': 'very distant and slow, which could be mistaken for a bird five hundred metres away, and which gradually draws nearer'.[4]

Messiaen has always indicated precisely the rhythms of birdsong, and up to the time when he wrote his opera, had always indicated their tempos and how they would interact with each other rhythmically when more than one birdsong was involved. In the opera, in the scene where St Francis preaches to the birds, he employs a more aleatory relationship between them. The conductor is directed to indicate the beginning of each successive entry of birdsong, but from that point, each instrumentalist follows an independent tempo until the end of the passage. The device features again in the later work for piano and orchestra *Un vitrail et des oiseaux* (1986).

EX. 9.3 Nightingales

(a) Ravel: *L'enfant et les sortilèges*

(b) Messiaen: *Turangalîla-symphonie* 6 'Jardin du sommeil d'amour'

(c) 'son lunaire'

(i) Ravel: *L'enfant et les sortilèges*

(ii) *Réveil des oiseaux*

(iii) *Catalogue d'oiseaux* 6 'L'alouette lulu'

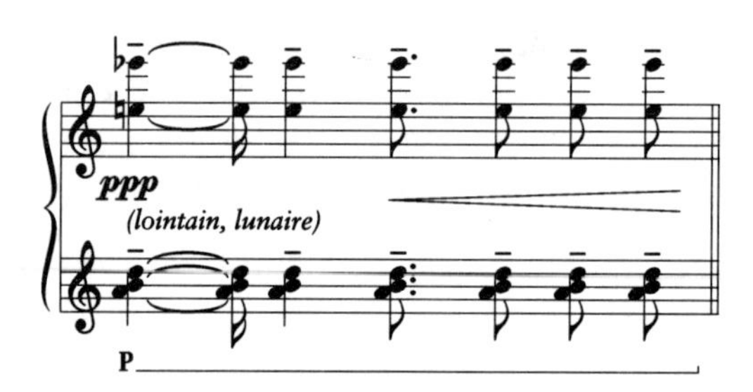

The symbolism of birdsong

'Our little servants of immaterial joy' is how Messiaen describes birds in *Technique de mon langage musical*,[5] and the symbolic implication of birdsong in this connection in Messiaen's early work has already been mentioned. After the composition of *Vingt regards sur l'Enfant-Jésus*, Messiaen turned away from Christian symbolism towards a symbolism derived partly from Hinduism, partly from Inca and Aztec sources and particularly from the myth of Tristan and Isolde and other sources of love and magic. For the song cycle *Harawi* he wrote a poem based on a Peruvian version of Tristan and Isolde: a love-poem which ends with the consummation of love in death, ritualistic in character, rather than narrative. The work was partly inspired by a painting by Sir Roland Penrose, 'Seeing is believing', described in the poem of the tenth movement, 'Amour oiseau d'étoiles', in which birdsong (blackbird – see above) pervades the whole movement (see p. 152). The movement is similar in idea and intention to 'Jardin du sommeil d'amour', the sixth movement of the *Turangalîla-symphonie*, where a nightingale in the piano part symbolizes the joy of the lovers sleeping in an exotic garden where, as described by Messiaen, 'The two lovers are immersed in the sleep of love. A garden has emanated from them. The garden which surrounds them is called "Tristan"; the garden which surrounds them is called "Isolde". This garden is full of light and shade, of plants and new flowers, of brightly coloured and melodious birds.'[6] In the early fifties Messiaen returned to Christian symbolism in *Messe de la Pentecôte* (1949–50) and *Livre d'orgue* (1951). In the former work birdsong is used in the 'Communion' which is headed by an extract from a canticle associated with Communion devotions: the canticle of the Three Young Men in the Fiery Furnace from the prophet Daniel. The extract which Messiaen quotes is 'Fountains of the Lord, bless the Lord, birds of heaven, bless the Lord', which gives the *raison d'être* for the use of birdsong in the movement. More extensive use is made in *Livre d'orgue*, in whose central movement, 'Chants d'oiseaux' (for Eastertide), four birds, blackbird, nightingale, song thrush and robin, sing of the joy of Easter. Most of the movements have similar dedications (for Holy Trinity Sunday, for Penitential seasons, etc), the last movement, entitled 'Soixante-quatre durées', has no dedication and uses a variety of unspecified birdsongs to colour the permutation of the sixty-four durations on which the movement is based.

In 'Liturgie de cristal' from the *Quatuor* Messiaen invokes the dawn, with the awakening of birds – blackbird and nightingale – to symbolize the 'harmonious silence of heaven'. The dawn was also the subject of *Réveil des oiseaux*, but devoid of the symbolism of earlier works. Like some of the pieces from *Catalogue d'oiseaux*, it has a narrative element, covering the period from before dawn (midnight in this case) through the awakening of the birds into the daytime. In both these works Messiaen presents a realistic, rather than a symbolic, world; they are essentially pictures of nature, of birds in their habitat. In *Catalogue* he uses additional material, not derived from birdsong, in order to create the sense of pictorial background to the principal bird – the crashing of waves on the seashore in 'Le merle bleu', the chords representing the quietly flowing river in 'La bouscarle', or the sound of frogs in 'La rousserolle effarvatte', for instance. Other works are more abstract in character, bringing together birds not normally found together in their natural habitat. *Oiseaux exotiques* draws from North America and Asia, *Chronochromie* for orchestra (1959–60) brings in birds from Japan and Mexico and after a visit to Japan in 1962 he wrote *Sept haïkaï* for piano and orchestra based exclusively on Japanese birds. In *Couleurs de la cité céleste*, for piano, wind and percussion (1963), he returns to Christian symbolism and expands the repertoire of birds to those of Australasia and South America. Further expansion of the repertoire continued in subsequent works with the inclusion of African birds in the large choral work *La Transfiguration de Notre-Seigneur Jésus-Christ* (1965–9) and in the opera *Saint François d'Assise*, for which he made a special journey to New Caledonia in order to be able to include birdsong from the furthest parts of the earth in the scene where St Francis preaches to the birds.

The choice of particular birds in the works from *Et exspecto resurrectionem mortuorum* (1964) onwards is sometimes one of association with a particular idea in the work itself. The third movement is preceded by a quotation from the Gospel of St John: 'The hour will come when the dead will hear the voice of the Son of God' (John 5:25). In this movement Messiaen uses the song of the uirapuru, a bird found in the region of the Amazon which, according to local legend, is heard only at the moment of death. In *Saint François d'Assise*, St Francis himself is represented by the blackcap ('fauvette à tête noire') which, although prevalent throughout most of Europe, is especially associated with Carceri at Assisi. In addition to the appropriate choice of birds, the treatment of their song also invokes atmosphere as in 'Le désert', the first movement of *Des canyons aux étoiles . . .* (1971–4), where the sparse treatment of the song of the hoopoe lark ('sirli du désert') with high notes on the piccolo, violin harmonics and crotale (played with a double bass bow), suggests the barrenness and loneliness of the desert regions of Colorado. Desert birds are used again in *Livre du Saint Sacrement* for organ (1984), this time from Palestine, in the movement which portrays the feeding of the Israelites in the desert with manna.

The pitch-structure of birdsong

In *Technique de mon langage musical* Messiaen discusses some aspects of pitch-structure in his music: intervals, chords of resonance, chords on the dominant, and modes of limited transposition are the main topics of discussion under this heading. None of these is of much use in discussing the pitch-structure of birdsong, except for isolated instances where he uses 'chords on the dominant' or 'chords of resonance'[7] for harmonic colour. The example of birdsong from the *Quatuor*, which he cites in Chapter 9, shows a melodic splitting of the 'chord on the dominant' at the end (Ex. 9.4) and the rock thrush in 'Le merle de roche' from *Catalogue d'oiseaux* provides an example of the harmonic use of the same chord and its derivations (Ex. 9.5). These, and other isolated examples, are not enough to indicate much about the general pitch-structure of Messiaen's birdsong. In style it

EX. 9.4

(a) *Quatuor pour la fin du temps* 3 'Abîme des oiseaux'

(b) Chord on the dominant with appoggiaturas

EX. 9.5 *Catalogue d'oiseaux* 10 'Le merle de roche'

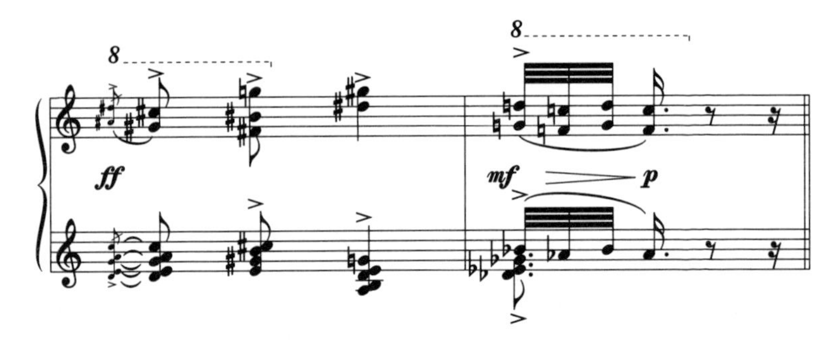

ranges from the tonal to atonal, with more of it coming in the latter category than the former. Set theory as a method of analysis is of no use in this context either, as it quickly becomes obvious that it cannot account for the features which give much of Messiaen's birdsong its particular character. Set theory deals with pitch in the general sense of 'pitch class', assuming that the register at which a pitch occurs is unimportant. In addition, intervals are considered to be equivalent to their inversions and compound forms. It quickly becomes obvious to the listener in listening to the blackbird melody in 'Liturgie de cristal' that, although it makes use of the total chromatic scale, certain fixed pitches and intervals have a pivotal function in providing

EX. 9.6 *Quatuor pour la fin du temps* I 'Liturgie de cristal'

'anchor' points for the transposition of figures and their development, and a displacement of a minor ninth, or major seventh, for instance, cannot be considered the equivalent of a minor second. Ex. 9.6 analyses the beginning of the blackbird melody in 'Liturgie de cristal'. The F forms a centre-point for the first phase, with its inflection G♭, and gives rise to the note-group G♭, F, D, D♭, marked 'a'. This appears first in a compressed form marked '(a)', focusing on B♭ with its inflection C♭. When the 'a' group is transposed up in bar 4, it becomes distorted by the structural framework set up these notes. Taking off from C♭ and B♭, instead of proceeding to G♮ and upper F♯, which would create an exact transposition, the G♭ from the beginning of the line is preferred, with the following note F to preserve the major-seventh leap. The 'a' group is not characterized, therefore, by its total interval structure, as set theory would demand, but only by the interval pairs of a semitone and a major seventh, which shift by a semitone in relation to each other on transposition. The same thing happens at the next transposition of the group in bar 5. The major seventh now moves up to A–A♭, while the semitone moves up a further semitone in relation to the major seventh (to D–E♭), the notes now being permutated to form a descending phrase. A subsidiary interval – the tritone – is used in this passage, mainly between pitches of the main structure and 'foreign' notes. The concluding phrase of the first statement highlights the tritone relationship between the first and last notes of the 'a' group. These pitches appear together as the third and fourth notes of this phrase and at the end of this phrase they again recur, but with the intervening B♭ removed to an earlier point and G♭ weakened to a grace-note. The C♭ is emphasized by the leading-up to it as an anacrusis from the low C and D. The notation is designed to show the main structural framework (open notes), which can be divided into two groups of four notes each (one – G♭ – common to both groups). Pitches lying outside the framework are black notes. The beaming indicates the emergence of the second group to take over from the first. This framework forms a reference-point for the clarinet part in the rest of the movement, although the development becomes more complex than the opening statement, and departs further from the strict framework. In spite of the fact that Messiaen establishes a sense of tonality in the clarinet part with an insistance a B♭/F axis immediately above middle C, the orientation is more of a modal than a tonal one because of the fixed nature of the B♭ as a 'final' rather than a tonic, and the predominance of the major third (D) in the lower octave as distinct from the minor third (D♭) in the upper octave.

'Le merle bleu' from *Catalogue d'oiseaux* provides a similar

EX. 9.7 *Catalogue d'oiseaux* 3 'Le merle bleu'

(a) basic structure
(b) first 3-note group
(c) first transposition with C♯ instead of C
(d) transposition of (c) with extra note – A♭ = G♯ of (a)
(e) second transposition of (b) with E instead of E♭ and repetition of (c)

example, but one which is not tonally orientated. The Thekla lark, at its first appearance on p. 10 of the score, establishes a framework of A, D♯, C♯, G♯, F♯ (in descending order), which causes distortions in a three-note figure each time it is transposed (Ex. 9.7).[8]

A thorough analytical discussion of the pitch-structure of Messiaen's birdsong would require a whole chapter to itself, but these examples should give some explanation of the sense of its audible coherence. The principles, of course, are not confined specifically to birdsong but extend to other melodic situations in his music.

Other characteristics of birdsong

With a musical material in which little or no motivic repetition takes place, it is necessary to find other criteria which account for the form of these pieces. Four basic categories are discernible: I 'calls' (as distinct from songs), usually dissonant and either (a) short and mostly repetitive, or (b) longer and varied; II short repetitive song patterns; III varied song patterns, usually with comparatively slower tempo than group IV, either (a) melodic in style, often with tonal implications (e.g. blackbird), or (b) more declamatory in style (e.g. nightingale, song thrush); IV long streams of rapid 'chattering' song which may be broken into shorter phrases and either (a) gravitating strongly towards a structural pitch centre or centres (roughly equivalent to a modal dominant), or (b) with no pronounced pitch centre.[9] The requirements of form demanded by recall (whether literal or transformed) and contrast of musical ideas are fulfilled by means of the similarities of, and contrasts between, these various types. For example: in spite of the fact that, in the case of the woodlark and the nightingale (the two birds which feature in 'L'alouette lulu', *Catalogue d'oiseaux* No. 5, most of their melodic material is not repeated literally, their characteristics are sufficiently recognizable on successive appearances to render the form of the piece clear. The eponymous woodlark uses figures which are more stereotyped than the nightingale, and so forms a point of stability or refrain in its dialogue with the nightingale. Even when a characteristic nightingale figure is repeated (such as the one shown in Ex. 9.3b, which makes five varied appearances at different points in the piece), this contributes nothing to the formal structure, as would be the case in a more 'classically orientated' work. The overall form of the piece is tripartite: an introduction defined by the alternation of chords representing night and couplets consisting of the woodlark's song; a central section with the woodlark forming a refrain to the nightingale's couplets; and a coda which resumes the dialogue of the introduction. 'L'alouette lulu' is one of the simpler forms in *Catalogue d'oiseaux*; most other pieces have more complex interaction of birdsong material, but based on the same principles.

With the improvement of tape recorders since the 1950s it has been possible to slow up birdsong to a considerable degree in order to note down detail which is totally inaudible in some cases at normal speed. Although Messiaen could have achieved greater accuracy by doing this, paradoxically he would have ended up with a result which would have been divorced from the reality he was trying to achieve. Only the approximations of birdsong, as perceived by his ear, would serve his purpose, whether for the portrayal of the reality of nature as in *Catalogue d'oiseaux*, or of the more symbolic usages of birdsong elsewhere.

Notes

1 Olivier Messiaen: *Technique de mon langage musical*, 2 volumes (Paris, Leduc, 1944); volume 1 translated by John Satterfield as *The Technique of My Musical Language* (Paris, Leduc, 1957), p. 34.
2 Claude Samuel: *Entretiens avec Olivier Messiaen* (Paris, Belfond, 1967), p. 111.
3 Ibid., pp. 113–4.
4 Ibid., p. 102.
5 Messiaen, op. cit., p. 34.
6 Messiaen: '*Turangalîla-symphonie*' (CD booklet, DG 431 781–2, p. 7).
7 Messiaen, *Technique*, vol. 2, p. 37, Exx. 201–12.
8 A further example is provided in the discussion of the black-eared wheatear's song in 'Le traquet stapazin' from *Catalogue d'oiseaux* in the reprinted version of Robert Sherlaw Johnson: *Messiaen* (London, Dent, 1975, R/1989), pp. 139–41.
9 Ibid., pp. 134–5, for a table of birds from *Catalogue d'oiseaux* classified in this way.

Messiaen as Teacher

The Power of Example[1]

PIERRE BOULEZ

My own link with Messiaen, with all its memories, goes back to that spring of 1944 when I presented myself at his house to become his pupil. At the Conservatoire he was just another member of the staff – the most recent member in fact – a professor of harmony with the reputation of being something of a revolutionary and of standing apart from the reigning orthodoxy of the day. That reputation was based on his works, which were not often performed though an almost chance hearing of one of his earliest – *Thème et variations* for violin and piano – was enough to inspire me with an immediate wish to study with him. I felt the force of his attraction immediately, as I say, at a single hearing.

I do not much care for veterans' reminiscences, but I should like to recall an experience that must have been shared by many others, both before and after me – that sudden feeling of attraction to a master of whom one knows, with an inexplicable sense of certainty, that it is he, and only he, that is going to reveal you to yourself. This is a kind of magic exercised partly by his music, but also by the power of his personality, by his immediate appeal and by the overwhelming force of his example. This chosen master acts as a stimulus by his very presence, his behaviour, his very existence and the glimpses that he gives of what he demands of himself. He sees and listens, understands the clashes in the pupil's personality as he tries to discover himself in a fog of contradictions and resentments. The master is prepared to accept ingratitude and injustice, rebuffs and rebelliousness, if these reactions mean the momentary loss of the pupil in order to establish him firmly as an original, independent personality. Attention and detachment are needed for this, and a sense of the adventure of preparing all the details of a long voyage without knowing its destination, a desire to set out for goals that are never clearly defined. Giving an example is as necessary as learning to forget it: 'Throw away the book I have taught you to read and add a new, wholly unexpected page!'

The miracle lies in the teacher combining this generous giving with the ability to preserve intact his fundamental egoism as a creative artist, which is the sole guarantee of his generosity. For how can one be generous without having anything to give? This is a problem that Messiaen has shown an enviable determination in solving: he has enriched himself by enriching us. The evidence for this is to be found in the present series of retrospective concerts, which enables us to sum up his work in all its profusion and variety, covering a very wide range that includes not only the composer's own instruments, piano and organ, but the most varied groupings, with a marked preference for the unfamiliar.

Today is not the occasion for drawing up a detailed balance sheet, but we can still pick out a number of the more specific characteristics that have made Messiaen the outstanding figure that he is at the present time. In the first place I should like to say that he has the great merit of having freed French music from that narrow and nervous 'good taste' inherited from illustrious forebears whose greatness has been reduced to the dimensions of their panting followers. Then I should like to point to his boldness and calm courage in treating music as a worldwide, universal phenomenon and his refusal of any obligation to retain any characteristics simply because they were considered the property of some national group. He has opened windows not only on Europe, but on the whole world, on civilizations as remote in space as in time. He has thought of the distinguishing marks of any civilization not as barriers but as possible links. Living in a world so much inclined to exclusive nationalism that neighbours, by their very existence, were thought of primarily as enemies and aggressors, Messiaen has been willing to accept freely everything that could enrich him, broaden his vision or increase his potential strength. Instead of harping on the genealogy of French music he pointed out that a 'tradition' is nothing if it does no more than preserve its own prerogatives – in fact he was 'ecumenical' before that word became popular in other contexts.

In fact there must be a predator in every creative artist; he gives, no doubt, but he also takes. Before he can give *his* vision of the world he must grasp that world in its entirety; if his adventure is at first an interior one, there is still no reason why it should not come from without. Messiaen's openness to all the musics of the world has greatly enriched his powers of expression, both in the matter of sonorities and actual instruments and in the theoretical field of rhythmic concepts and musical time. In this field specifically his originality and his contribution have been enormous and his influence unparalleled, the more so for his being the first to venture into these hitherto unexplored regions.

Finally, we should not forget the characteristic that makes him absolutely unique – his deep love of nature expressed in forms virtually unknown to the more artificial world of music. That love is so demanding that it can transpose in detail not so much what birds, rocks, colours, landscapes and mountains inspire in him, but what they actually dictate to him.

Were it not for the fear of being taken for a bad punster I would add that 'composer' is exactly the right word for Messiaen, in that it suggests the word 'composite'. His personality resembles some great baroque building: he fascinates us by the diversity of his options and the elaborate simplicity of his choices. Beneath the very real complexities of his intellectual world he has remained simple and capable of wonder – and that alone is enough to win our hearts.

The Master of Harmony

GEORGE BENJAMIN

When I was thirteen I saw a picture of Messiaen in the *Larousse Encyclopedia of Music*. Virtually the last item in the book, it showed the illustrious master surrounded by his pupils. One of these days, I thought, maybe I could find a full-time composition teacher, and the idea of going to Messiaen stuck in my mind.

Then when I was fifteen, Peter Gellhorn, a marvellous musician who was teaching me piano as well as composition, wrote to Messiaen about me. Some months later he took me to Paris to meet the great man and his wife, so that I could play my pieces to them. Messiaen was encouraging about my work from the very start and invited me to join his class at the Paris Conservatoire immediately. I was overwhelmed by this meeting – indeed, in many ways it was the decisive day of my life.

And so, while still at school doing A levels, I went to Paris once a month for two or three days. Messiaen's classes lasted more than four hours and took place on three mornings a week. I had to speak French – very badly at first – for he didn't speak a word of English, even though his father taught English and translated Shakespeare into French.

I then sat the appalling Conservatoire exams, passed and studied full time with him for a year. After forty years' teaching, it was his last year on the staff there. Unfortunately, the retirement age (even for a figure of his stature) was seventy, and in any case he wanted to devote himself entirely to his vast opera, *Saint François d'Assise*.

With Schoenberg, he must be the central teacher of this century. Most of the famous composers of the fifties and sixties went to him: Stockhausen, Xenakis, Boulez, nearly all French composers for over two generations (including Murail and Grisey), from this country people like Alexander Goehr, and a multitude of students from all round the world. His classes in the fifties were a central place for the avant garde.

He did not teach with rigid principles. That's the marvellous thing. Schoenberg was severe and demanding. Messiaen was benign, gentle, encouraging. He wanted to guide you to find your own voice, and to strengthen your gifts. He never imposed his ideas. He would be horrified if you copied anything of his. In fact he would only be stylistically censorious (although that is too strong a word) if he saw you were over-influenced by his musical world.

I was never told to do anything. It was never 'Benjamin, will you please bring me this study by next week.' But having him enthuse about my harmony was more than enough to make me work incessantly.

Boulez says that what Messiaen gave him was the power to reflect, to think really deeply about music. He was indeed a master of thought, not only a teacher of specific techniques. Above all he created an environment where there was much love, enthusiasm, human generosity, and great richness of resource. He perhaps spoilt me as I was his youngest pupil, but most of his pupils feel the deepest gratitude to him for having helped them realize their own voices.

Look at what he did for Xenakis. As a student in Paris after the war, Xenakis was in a quandary. He went to Messiaen and said: 'Other music teachers say I can't possibly write these mathematically based pieces without knowing about harmony and counterpoint. What should I do?' Now Messiaen was a product of the Conservatoire system in Paris. There every musician – not just composers – had learnt harmony and counterpoint as essentials from time immemorial. Messiaen himself had done so for over a decade and was a teacher of those very skills there at the time.

After reflection, he told Xenakis: 'Don't. Don't do harmony or counterpoint. Your gift is elsewhere. Follow your own voice.' To say that then was extraordinary. And he was right. His attitude was totally different from the other great French teacher at that time, Nadia Boulanger.

I had always been fascinated by harmony. The pieces I wrote at thirteen or fourteen may have been childish and incompetent, but they made harmonic sense. That was what drew the very first comments I had from Messiaen. He said I had a good ear, and my harmonies worked, and that was the greatest encouragement I had had.

His detailed harmonic analysis was fascinating. He would describe the growth and development of specific chord types and their changing function through musical history. The analyses were free from all forms of stifling academism, and were presented with great passion.

However, many harmonic concepts – background harmonic motion, tension and, above all, polyphony – were foreign to his thought, and I found myself growing away from certain aesthetic areas about which he felt strongly.

At first he reacted badly to my piece written for the London Sinfonietta, *At First Light*, though after repeated hearings he grew to admire it. I remember he looked in horror at one of the chordal sequences in it.

I asked: 'Don't you like the harmony?' He said: 'I can't see much harmony.' I said: 'But look, the harmony's everywhere.' He replied: 'Yes, but the harmony's diffused in the music.' It was a very strange thing to say. For me the harmony *must* be lost inside the form, inside the argument and texture of the music.

I also studied rhythm with him – because he said the rhythm in my early pieces was unadventurous and stiff. He would analyse his own music, and much music both from the past and present. Six weeks spent on Debussy's *Pelléas* was, I remember, the highlight, chord by chord, bar by bar, texture by texture, line by line.

But he was always saying: 'For goodness sake write melodies. After all, music is meant to be sung. Nowadays we don't write enough melodies.'

He never took our work away to study. Scores would be presented, and if there was a tape it would be played. If there was a concert performance (however modest the venue) and he was in Paris, he would always attend.

He would go through the score in class, obviously hearing what he saw perfectly, and he would point out faults in écriture or orchestration. Then perhaps he would comment on form and structure. For a sixteen-year-old it was sheer magic, and I kept notes on much he said to me then. His comments always seemed totally spontaneous, yet thoughtful.

I was getting even more attention than I realized. My piano teacher, his wife Yvonne Loriod, would let fall sometimes: 'While he was shaving this morning Messiaen said you should do . . .'. It was like studying with a friend, an uncle, a wiser and better companion – not a great master to whom I was but a pupil. I was almost unaware of being taught.

Of course he had prejudices or preferences in music, but he wanted you to find your own aesthetic. None of his pupils repeat his style – Boulez, Xenakis, Stockhausen could scarcely be more different. They are massively apart, though all were pupils at about the same time. He was there to show the wealth of possibilities, through nature or music or poetry or painting, even food!

It was a very open class. He would introduce a tuba player to explain new fingerings or flutter-tongue techniques. He would make us walk half-way across Paris in the snow to look at the newest cymbals.

For me it is not possible to deduce my musical language as methodically as he did: birdsong, plainchant, rhythmic cells, chords . . . But he made me organize what I want to do. In the past there were many common musical rules between composers' styles. Nowadays, in our present musical turmoil, no one composer's musical language can serve for another: one must do a huge amount of soul-searching and attempt to find one's own voice in isolation.

There was a crucial moment in my study with him. I was obsessed by chords, and to the chagrin of the class I would show him pages and pages of chords of all shapes and sizes, to play to him. For six months that was all I did: I didn't compose at all. And it proved a marvellous means for him to teach me harmony.

I became depressed because I didn't feel I was finding my own voice. He just said that subconsciously I was making progress. In desperation I said: 'Look, I can't find my harmonic language. I don't know where to search. I am finding nothing interesting. Show me something to help me find the route of my progress.' And he said he would, but in a minute. Having reassured me, he just went on with the class, and of course it got forgotten.

But he had intentionally defused that critical moment. If he had done what I asked, it would have been disastrous. I might have pursued his aesthetic, or some aspect of it, for the rest of my life. Yet he didn't simply say no to me either. He just gently let the request pass and fade away, which was an immensely subtle thing to have done, and which again I was totally unaware of at the time.

It was spontaneous on his part, it seemed. But it sprang from the most intensely careful thinking about how to approach me as a pupil. Messiaen's teaching was a foundation for my whole life. He gave me something I will never forget – confidence, technique; it opened my ears, opened my mind, made me think and try to understand. It was the greatest luck of my life to have met him and to have had that.

Messiaen on his own music

PETER HILL

My first visit to Messiaen began on a note of farce, when I was ushered to an improbable folding armchair which promptly collapsed me on to the floor (thickly carpeted, fortunately, as part of the rigorous sound-proofing with which Messiaen sought obsessively to exclude the noise of Paris). Another shock was the discovery that we were to converse exclusively in French. Messiaen apologized for his lack of languages, for which he wrily admitted he had little excuse in view of his father's mastery of English; fortunately he spoke with such unaffected clarity that not only could I follow him with ease, but (more surprisingly) my rusty French began to acquire an unexpected fluency.

In public Messiaen could seem forbidding, with a fixed, somewhat obstinate expression (the despair of photographers); in person he could not have been more different. He had a natural courtesy, with a sweetness and charm which came as a surprise; nonetheless the intensity with which he listened made playing to him a formidable experience. I had wondered what his attitude would be to music which he had composed so long ago (in the case of the *Catalogue d'oiseaux*, for example, thirty years earlier) but his knowledge was complete, and he showed little inclination to improve on what he had written (any revisions were not so much of intention but of details of notation which had proved misleading). Such confidence is rare, in my experience, among composers, a sign of the essential unity of purpose and technique which runs the whole course of Messiaen's exceptionally long career.

The room in which we worked was small, an austere space heated to sub-tropical temperatures and almost filled by a Steinway, so dry in tone that one pounded away, perspiring freely. There could be no let-up, since Messiaen was quick to pounce on any phrase remotely under-characterized. We began, I remember, with 'Le merle bleu' and it was at once apparent that for Messiaen the intensity and vividness of feeling were paramount; the competing sounds of sea and seabirds, which act as a frame to the secretive charm of the blue rock thrush itself, were to be played with absolute ferocity.

I was astounded and touched to discover that Messiaen placed no limit on the duration of our sessions: each continued until the work was done, often late into the evening. Messiaen's concentration appeared never to flag, though I was repeatedly urged to pause for refreshment (the tea or whisky suitable for British visitors). Messiaen was quick to encourage, and in passages where he was satisfied it was thrilling for me to feel he was moved by my playing. I think we really became friends when I (rather gauchely) admitted that 'Le traquet stapazin' was my favourite from the *Catalogue d'oiseaux* – it was his too, and he recalled how overwhelmed he had been when first visiting the Mediterranean scene which had inspired the piece.[3]

The curiosity and enthusiasm to which Messiaen's pupils testify was constantly in evidence. I remember being questioned closely about Durham Cathedral, which he had never visited and whose glories I found myself describing in halting French. He had an extensive knowledge of English poetry, not only Shakespeare's tragedies (which he knew from his father's translations) but Shelley and Keats, whose *Ode on a Grecian Urn* he recited (in French) sublimely. Nature was his great passion: he would vocalize birdsong imitations, his expression suffused with enchantment as he recalled the settings in which he had collected their song, and would fetch out ornithological reference books so that I could see illustrations of plumage.[4]

The decline in Messiaen's health was marked by loss of physical mobility, though he remained as clear and energetic as ever, and his extraordinary musical ear was unimpaired. On my early visits (which began in 1987) he would occasionally come to the piano; he had a beautiful touch, and those who regard Messiaen's music as lacking in subtlety should have heard the care with which he discussed the colours which could be obtained by slight adjustments of balance. One general point is the balance to be struck between a principal line and the 'resonant' line which accompanies it, often in parallel motion, and which inflects its colour. In many cases a quite fresh meaning is added, as in the song of the short-toed lark (from 'L'alouette calandrelle') which would be innocuous without the acid timbre contributed by the upper line. The opening to 'L'alouette lulu' is a particularly difficult example (we spent longer on this apparently simple passage than on any other in the *Catalogue*). The right hand chords have to be balanced with the left most precisely: soft enough to shadow the bass octaves, but not so quiet as to be entirely submerged (see Ex. 10.1).

Messiaen detested the gratuitous bringing-out of the top note, which he regarded as a persistent vice of pianists. What interested him were the effects produced by experimenting with the balance *within* the harmony. He made this point first when demonstrating at the piano the majestic E major harmony at the centre of 'Le loriot' (the golden oriole). This represents 'gold' (the sun at midday) and in the score is marked 'cuivré' (brassy). Messiaen suggested I achieve this by slight emphasis on the major third (G♯) in the left hand, so that the chord glows from within – 'like trombones', he said. (I was struck by Messiaen's evident concern to reinforce the sense of harmony as colour, and so to share something at least of the connection which he himself felt so intensely.) Another example was from 'La rousserolle effarvatte', in which the listener should be able to 'feel' the different colours of sunset, not only in the change in harmony but in the emotional character, from glowing 'rose-pink' to the more ominous chords based on mode 5 which represent the darker hues of twilight (Messiaen asked me to imagine these in a sombre orchestration for low reed instruments).[5]

Messiaen also pointed out that adjusting the internal balance of chords could be a way of discreetly emphasizing their tonality. So, returning to 'L'alouette lulu', he asked that I give a very slight preference to each D♮, since this is the pitch which of

EX. 10.1 *Catalogue d'oiseaux* 6 'L'alouette lulu'

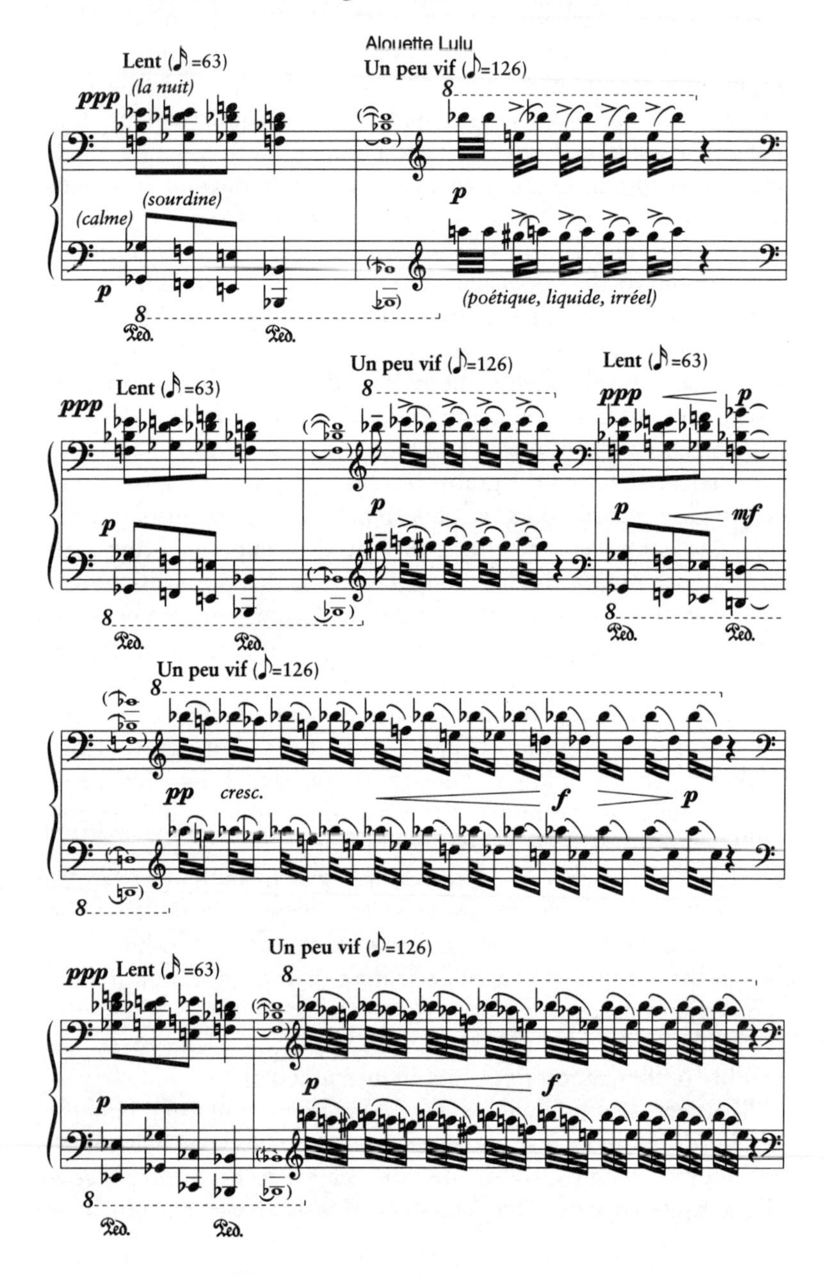

course gives the 'major', character (of B♭). Similarly in the depiction of sunset from 'La rousserolle effarvatte' he asked me to stress the thirds *inside* the minor harmonies of the cadences (the notes played by the thumb of the right hand). Yet another example comes from 'La bouscarle', the chorale of the 'river', where again it was the lower or inner C♯s (in A major) which were important (the chords are made yet more 'major' by the enriching added sixth). 'La bouscarle' was an example of Messiaen's tonal thinking: in our discussion of the middle section he described the music as swinging to the 'dominant', then to the 'dominant of the dominant'.

In virtuoso passages Messiaen was a stickler for clarity, yet even the most complex torrents of birdsong were to be shaped poetically – 'never like an *étude*', he frequently insisted. This shaping was often to be more fluid than the score suggests. In the passage from 'L'alouette lulu' (already quoted) the relationship between the chorale of chords (night) and the pairs of woodlark (which hover overhead, peeling off, we are told, two by two from the flock) is of particular interest as being almost the only instance in the *Catalogue* where Messiaen 'harmonizes' the tempos of two ideas. (In this instance the demisemiquavers of 'night' are equal to the quavers of the woodlark.) The intention is not only a hypnotic mood, but the sense that the birds are a descant to the chorale. (This is then a prelude to the main line of development, in which the song of the woodlark moves imperceptibly centre-stage, so provoking the sharp dialogue of birdsong which occupies the middle of the piece.) However, diligently counting out demisemiquavers and quavers as a means to mastering the rhythm is misleading, since part of the woodlark's character is that it floats free from the tread of night, and, as each phrase proceeds, increasingly comes to be heard as a triple rhythm. The effect is comparable to the famous passage from Beethoven's Sonata op. 101 (first movement) in which a line of chords which begin as syncopations gradually establishes a new pulse. In 'L'alouette lulu' Messiaen exploits a similar ambiguity, which properly played gives a certain looseness or 'swing' to the rhythms. In addition, the phrasing counterbalances the tendency of the ear to locate the pulse in the notes of the descending chromatic line.

This counterpart between inexorable chords and the freedom and fantasy of birdsong arises from Messiaen's view of birds as uniquely blessed; but it points also to his aim to free his music from rhythmic constraint through avoiding regular metre or pulse – this sense of a musical 'end of time' is discussed elsewhere by Iain Matheson (see p. 237–8). The example from 'L'alouette lulu' was one of many instances where Messiaen encouraged me not to be over-literal, for if too pedantic the pianist may miss the overall sense. Moreover I was constantly impressed by the latitude of tempo which (despite his very definite metronome markings) Messiaen would allow. He urged me always to phrase with flexibility, to allow the music to breathe. This is particularly true of some of the most difficult passages: the 'nuptial flight' of the kingfisher (from 'La bouscarle') where a Chopin-like grace is appropriate, and still more throughout the supremely taxing *La fauvette des jardins*, where the flood of song, however transcendent the virtuosity (extended page after page), must remain cheerful and good natured – 'always relaxed' Messiaen wrote at several points in my score. There were exceptions of course. I remember particularly the cruelly awkward first solo of 'La rousserolle effarvatte', in which Messiaen was absolutely insistent that the music should be continuous, without gaps between the tiny barbed motifs which should jostle and jab one another. And there are the monolithic, implacable calls, such as the 'barking' cry of the herring gull, in which the pianist must resist adding a rallentando to the diminuendo which Messiaen marks.

These comments on the relative strictness or freedom of Messiaen's rhythms lead to a digression on the one or two aspects where I find his notation misleading. In his later music, Messiaen systematizes his verbal indications ('vif', 'modéré', etc) so that they align with metronome marks (vif = 138, 152, 160; très vif = 168, etc). Occasionally this gives a false impression of the musical character. The song of the mistle thrush, from 'La buse variable' (the buzzard), is anything but 'lively': it should be declamatory, somewhat obstinate ('courageous' is Messiaen's epithet). My other point concerns Messiaen's practice of writing out very long values in a way that measures them exactly, even down to the briefest added demisemiquaver. Messiaen possessed a super-fine ability to perceive gradations between long durations (Alexander Goehr testifies that in Messiaen's class in the 1950s composition pupils were trained to develop this faculty). Passages such as the 'night' from 'La chouette hulotte', or the procession of monsters in 'Le merle de roche', have to be calculated by the pianist from a common pulse, but are *experienced* as a series of pauses – albeit of very precise length – again an instance of Messiaen's breaking free from time measured rigidly in equal units.

The other way in which Messiaen subverts our sense of time is through tempos of extraordinary slowness. This question, a contentious one for performers, had been uppermost in my mind when preparing the *Vingt regards*; when I studied the work with Messiaen I made a point of asking his opinion on my playing of each of the great slow movements. Somewhat to my surprise he seemed entirely happy with all the tempos, commending especially my final six pages, which I had thought riskily spacious.

Messiaen was rightly proud of the accuracy of his scores, and any query had to be carefully phrased. He was not closed to suggestion, however; I remember in the call of the long-eared owl (from 'La chouette hulotte') substituting a glissando for his fingered scales, an effect which delighted him. I had been puzzled by many of the pedal marks in the *Catalogue* where phrases ending staccato had apparently a delay in the pedal's release. He confirmed that this was intentional, so that there is a contrast between calls which end abruptly and others which have a ringing semi-staccato. Messiaen was punctilious over pedalling, and he disliked any blurring of harmonies. The only exception was in the crashes of waves (in 'Le merle bleu' and 'Le courlis cendré') which were to be just tremendous effects. In the *Vingt regards* he explicitly contradicted the instruction 'brouillé de pédale' which occurs several times in the score (see Nos. 6, 10 and 20) in passages of great musical (and pianistic!) confusion; instead he insisted I pedal sufficiently lightly for every note to be distinct. Even in the exuberant flourish which ends No. 10 Messiaen wanted clarity: 'I must hear every note'; and even at the most tumultuous climax any muddying of the sound jarred him horribly – see for example p. 175 of the score, where the clearing of the harmonies towards the end of the penultimate system of the page takes precedence over sustaining the bass Bs (see Ex. 10.2).

This emphasis on purity of sound was typical of Messiaen's approach to the *Vingt regards*, which seemed markedly different to the birdsong pieces. Where in those his music is of gesture – of speech, of exclamation – he appeared to view the *Vingt regards* as symbolic or emblematic in their evocations. The music is no less vivid, however – I remember Messiaen's account of the 'Regard des anges': the ferocity of the angels was inspired, he said, by the 'angel with the trumpet' from Michelangelo's 'Last Judgement', and he mimicked the dismay of the angels (in the expanding phrases of the last page), his mouth gaping in correspondingly mounting astonishment. In general, however, his conception was 'classical', the expression powerful but simple, and above all entirely devoid of vulgarity or false heroics. The virtuosity – awesome as it is – is integral to the music, part of a huge spectrum the opposite end of which is an extreme simplicity.

The closing pages of the *Vingt regards* came at the end of my last rehearsal with Messiaen, and I remember playing them in a

EX. 10.2 *Vingt regards sur l'Enfant-Jésus* 20 'Regard de l'église d'amour'

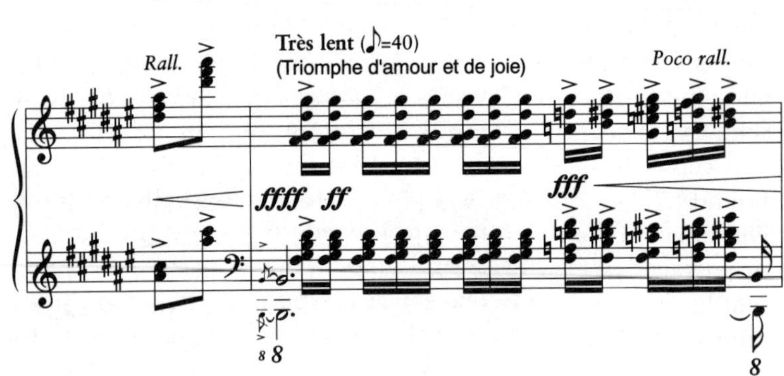

state of exhausted exaltation; our rehearsal had lasted twelve hours, until 10 o'clock in the evening, at which point we set to work checking through the tempos of the *Petites esquisses d'oiseaux*. The only break had been for an enormous lunch during which I was plied with extra helpings of sticky pudding (after lunch Messiaen took a short siesta, I a brisk walk up to Sacré Coeur). I was constantly struck by Messiaen's simplicity; he was entirely without affectation or desire to impress. His approach to our work was equally straightforward. Initially I found the directness with which he made criticisms disconcerting, but I came to value his frankness, and the high standards he expected were an inspiration.

When I accepted Messiaen's invitation to study with him I had already worked on his music over a number of years, and had taken the view that in order to make a contribution which was original I should avoid familiarizing myself with the solutions of other pianists. On first playing to Messiaen I wondered therefore whether my interpretations would sound to him very strange, if not wrong. In the event, however, he never showed the slightest inclination to impose an alien style on my playing; when I reflected on each of our sessions apparently disconnected details formed a pattern in which, I realized, Messiaen had been helping me to know my own mind. Indeed what astonished me most about Messiaen was that he was at least as interested in me and my view of his music as I was to learn his. I think he saw what qualities I had to offer, and exploited these, enriching rather than altering my ideas and insights.

Such selflessness was typical of Messiaen as a teacher of composition, but is nonetheless remarkable in teaching his own music. Certainly neither of us had in mind producing an 'authentic' performance, if by that one means the performer copying with exact fidelity a composer's own perceptions of his music; and certainly there were times when (after due thought) I felt bound to disagree with Messiaen's views.[6] Inevitably Messiaen was able to help in instances where I was completely off course, or passages where he felt the printed score inadequate to represent his intentions. But what influenced me most were the revelations which arose from Messiaen's frank discussions of his techniques and inspirations. Above all he emphasized that, despite their meticulous clarity, his scores are not an end in themselves. For Messiaen the 'music' was not in the notes, nor in the sounds they represent, but in the meaning which lies beyond and which through sound we hope to reveal.

Notes

1 This is a translation of Pierre Boulez's speech, 'La toute puissance de l'exemple', given at the Paris Opéra on 10 December 1978, following a performance of Messiaen's *Des canyons aux étoiles . . .* by Yvonne Loriod and the Ensemble InterContemporain, under the direction of Boulez, on the occasion of the composer's seventieth birthday. The speech was first published in *Points de repère* (Paris, 1980); this translation is from Martin Cooper's English version, *Orientations* (London, Faber and Faber, 1986), pp. 418–20.
2 This article first appeared in the *Guardian*, 13 March 1987.
3 See also Claude Samuel: *Entretiens avec Olivier Messiaen* (Paris, Belfond, 1967), p. 27.
4 On my second visit, I brought him a volume of *Birds of Great Britain* by the Victorian artist John Gould, and this so pleased him that a gift of this sort became a tradition of our meetings. (Indeed, I last heard from him, in a note from his wife, in the final week of his life, thanking me for a book which I had sent on learning of his illness.)
5 See the discussion on p. 339.
6 See the discussion of 'Regard du Fils sur le Fils' on p. 98.

Interview with Yvonne Loriod[1]

PH: The first time I visited this apartment I was struck by the silence, in the middle of Paris.

YL: Yes that's true. We live in an old mansion which was sold originally as small flats. This is where I used to live when I was young, before my marriage; later, when we were married, each time a room became available we had a door knocked through and added a room to our apartment. This is why all the rooms are so small. Of course, as we have many neighbours we have had to have our rooms sound-proofed. So in each room we've had to put layers of wood or plywood and material to make an additional 15 cm at least of insulation – essential when one is a composer who has need of peace and quiet, or when one is a pianist who must work at the piano without annoying the neighbours. As to the apartment itself, there's nothing in it of any great value. No valuable pictures or furniture. All the furniture is strictly functional, with large tables on which one can spread out manuscript paper. We have eight pianos spread around the various places in which we live but idiotically there are never two in the same room. That's eccentric! But given the size of the rooms there was nothing else we could do.

PH: It's been said that Messiaen, and you yourself also, had no liking for the life of the city, that you much preferred to go to the countryside at your home in the Dauphiné and to the house Messiaen built there.

YL: We disliked the city because it was a place where we had to work enormously hard. You appreciate Messiaen never took a single day of holiday. The religious feast days for him meant going to the church of La Trinité. At Christmas there was never any question of spending the day with the family. We were always very, very tired because he had played for three hours or so at La Trinité and then he had to play again at 9 o'clock the following morning. You must realize that Messiaen wrote an enormous amount of music, and then there were his pupils – in fact, I'm just at present in the process of editing his Treatise, which represents forty years of his teaching. My job is to sort it out according to the plan he outlined to me about a year ago. One problem is that several works are analysed more than once; there are, for example, three different analyses of *The Rite of Spring*. Then there are several of the *Vingt regards* and several of *Turangalîla*. Every year he would polish these chapters – this constant revision shows you that Messiaen was a person who never ceased to work. And while he was composing I was preparing my concerts, and I also used to proof-read all the orchestral scores. You can imagine what a huge task it was to correct all the material of *Saint François*. Messiaen himself spent eight years writing the opera; I was involved in making the vocal score and this took me more than two years, in addition to correcting all the orchestral parts. So I don't need to tell you that there was never time to take any holiday.

PH: Would you tell us more about the Treatise?

YL: The full title is *Traité de rythme, de couleur et d'ornithologie*. This represents all his teaching at the Conservatoire, 40-odd years. The first volume includes everything to do with time: that is to say, tempo and rhythm. The second volume is concerned with non-retrogradable rhythms; augmentation and diminution; rhythmic pedals and canons; *personnages rythmiques*; the analyses of *The Rite of Spring*; the analyses of *Turangalîla*, of the *Livre d'orgue* and of the *Vingt regards*. The third volume includes consideration of specific technical matters in Messiaen's music since 1983, and these I've added to myself; it also contains analyses of the *Quatre études de rythme*, the *Livre d'orgue* and *Chronochromie*. The fourth volume includes plainchant; accentuation in Mozart and analyses of all Mozart's concertos for piano. The fifth volume discusses birdsong and the ways in which it is used in the works of Messiaen, and includes an analysis of the *Sept haïkaï*. The sixth volume is concerned with Debussy, only Debussy: there is an analysis of the *Prélude à l'après-midi d'un faune*, the *Préludes* and some of the *Images*, and of important passages from *La mer* and *Pelléas et Mélisande*. The seventh volume deals with modes and colours. There is an analysis of colour chords and there are tables of modes and of the various harmonies used by Messiaen. There's a brief analysis of the *Trois petites liturgies* and a little on *Couleurs de la cité céleste* and *La Transfiguration*. Each volume will run to more than 300 pages. At the moment we're working very hard and a secretary from Leduc, Messiaen's publisher, arrives at 8 o'clock every morning and works in the office.

PH: Would you tell us something about the way in which Messiaen worked? Did he, for example, work at the piano?

YL: He worked at the piano and also at the table. All the harmonies were devised at the piano, but the rhythms were worked out at the table. He had his desk and the piano side by side.

PH: Did he make a lot of sketches for each work?

YL: An enormous number. He filled thousands of notebooks. For the last work I went through all his manuscript paper. To begin with there were large sheets on which particular rhythms or orchestrations were noted. Later he took another sheet in order to enlarge on these. Usually there were five more sketches before he arrived at the final version. After that came a rough draft of the orchestration – he only very rarely wrote directly into the score.

PH: Did he make sketches throughout the winter and then gather these together during the summer in the Dauphiné?

YL: Yes. Of course, he composed while he was in Paris, especially after he'd given up his class at the Conservatoire. He had a studio on another floor where there was no telephone, so that he wouldn't be disturbed.

PH: Are you able to tell us the whereabouts of any of Messiaen's unpublished music? I'm thinking particularly of early works.

YL: In 1943, when Messiaen wrote his *Technique de mon langage musical*, he'd written only a few works, and the publisher wanted to list more at the back of the volume. Messiaen told him: 'There are other works but they are student compositions and for the most part they have been destroyed.' So the answer is very simple: Messiaen suppressed from the catalogue of his works certain pieces which he felt to be merely student exercises in composition – they were not worth publishing. And, so far as I know, they no longer exist.

PH: Messiaen more than once apologized to me for the fact that his piano music was so difficult to play, but he said that no matter how difficult a passage was that he placed in front of you, you always seemed to master it immediately and without any problem, and that he'd therefore never had to worry about the difficulty of his music for piano.

YL: Messiaen was an excellent pianist and an excellent organist, and everyone agrees that whatever he wrote, for whatever instrument, was always well written. If you ask clarinettists their opinion they will say, 'Did Messiaen himself play the clarinet because this is so well written?' If you ask pianists they will say, 'It's difficult but it is playable.' In the piano music, which you yourself play so well, there are difficulties but they are difficulties which (as you yourself understand marvellously) can be overcome. It's the same for organists. At the beginning they may tear their hair out when reading through the music, but after a few days' work the music is so well written that it becomes almost easy – and it all fits into place. I believe that Messiaen never wrote anything which was against the nature of the instrument, even for the voice. Recently in the performances of the opera *Saint François* which were given here in Paris, all the singers were saying, 'This music is so well written for the voice that we are never drowned by the orchestra'. I remember also that when I played the *Vingt regards* in 1945 for their first performance it was clear that the work seemed extremely difficult to my generation, but to young people today – and you are a lot younger than I! – it's quite different, and now I have pupils who are only fourteen years old who can learn to play the great fugue 'Par Lui tout a été fait' in a fortnight.

PH: In your opinion what errors are most frequently made in performing Messiaen's music?

YL: That is difficult to answer because all the aspects of the music are so important. I would say that complete fidelity to Messiaen's text is vital. And I would especially emphasize the importance of rhythm, which is perhaps the aspect of Messiaen's music that is most difficult for the performer. Also the balance of chords is very important because if this is wrong the whole colour will change. So the pianist must have very even fingers.

PH: And what about the extremely slow tempos which can cause problems to performers?

YL: Messiaen always marked the tempos in his scores only after the work had been performed. It may be that in the *Vingt regards* the first piece, 'Regard du Père', is marked too slow – it's quite possible. In fact, I am hoping to make new editions of certain of Messiaen's works in order to incorporate the tempos Messiaen wanted. One has to bear in mind that the technique of performers has advanced and now everyone plays the 'Regard de L'Esprit de joie' more quickly than it is marked. One should remember, however, that different tempos suit different performers. Some people are lively and energetic, others relaxed and calm – so it's partly a personal matter.

PH: Now may we talk about you yourself? First of all would you tell us a little about your childhood, where you were born and what age you began to study the piano?

YL: Well, I'll keep it short because it's not very interesting. I was born in the outskirts of Paris and it was discovered that I had a good musical ear because, at a few months old, I would sing while my father accompanied me on the piano. My father was very musical and had a great gift for improvising. He would say, 'Now I will play something like Mussorgsky or like Chopin', and then he would improvise in that style. I began the piano, I think, at about six years old, and at the age of eleven it was discovered that I was very gifted, and my godmother, who herself was a gifted musician, gave me piano lessons and then arranged for me to have further lessons because my parents hadn't enough money to pay for piano lessons. She also arranged for me to have a course in harmony in which I was prepared for entrance to the Conservatoire. At the Conservatoire I had the chance to study with some marvellous teachers. For harmony I studied with Messiaen himself. Later when Messiaen was appointed Professor of Analysis I returned to the Conservatoire to study composition with Darius Milhaud. So I had some great names among my teachers. How did I first meet Messiaen? This was after he'd returned from being a prisoner of war. I was in André Bloch's class. At that time, in the middle of the war, all the Jewish teachers in France were persecuted so I was sent to Olivier Messiaen, who had just returned from captivity, to join his class in harmony. At the first class the pupils were absolutely astonished, because here was a man who was quite young and whose fingers were swollen on account of the privations which he had suffered during his time in captivity in Silesia. He brought out the miniature score of Debussy's *Prélude à l'après-midi d'un faune*, placed this on the piano and played it to us. We were absolutely astonished to discover that one could read and play from an orchestral score – we were very young! – and there he was, playing the piano with such beautiful sounds in spite of the deformity of his hands. We were absolutely captivated; the whole class adored him straight away. There you are, that was the first class and my first meeting with Messiaen.

PH: Did he hear you play the piano at that time?

YL: At about that time my piano teacher Lazare Lévy said to me, 'The publisher Durand had sent me the *Préludes* for piano by a certain Olivier Messiaen. Unfortunately, as you know, I'm very short sighted and I wonder if you would play them to me?' Subsequently my godmother said to me, 'As you're in Messiaen's class why don't you play him his *Préludes*?' So because of that I asked Messiaen to hear me, and my godmother, who had a salon where she got me to give a recital once a month, said to me, 'Now you will also be playing to a friend of Messiaen, called Jolivet'. So at the first concert I gave at which Messiaen was present I played a partita by Bach, Messiaen's *Préludes* and, after the interval, another Bach partita and finally *Mana* by Jolivet. That was quite a programme for someone who was still a young girl.

PH: I wonder if you ever considered yourself as a composer?

YL: Yes, I studied composition and I studied with teachers who were very gifted, Milhaud and Messiaen of course. But at that time my career as pianist was beginning, and I was advised by Claude Delvincourt, the Director of the Conservatoire, that I had to choose between being a pianist and being a composer; so unfortunately I had to give up my classes of composition with Milhaud, but over the years I still continued to write a number of works and indeed, Messiaen positively insisted that I go on composing.

PH: Tell us about your contemporaries who were also pupils of Messiaen.

YL: The first year in which Messiaen held a class in analysis his pupils included Marius Constant, who became a conductor, and Pia Sebastiani, who became a celebrated pianist in America. There was also Jehan Alain's brother Olivier, who became Director of the Conservatoire, and there were other personalities: Françoise Aubut, a very great Canadian organist who died recently. Altogether we were a group of gifted young people who'd jumped at the opportunity of taking part in the class.

PH: Messiaen spoke of his 'flèches', didn't he?

YL: Yes – but to explain that, I need to begin with Messiaen's experiences in the war. Messiaen had been taken prisoner in France (I think near the Maginot Line) and he was transported to Germany with thousands of French soldiers, all in cattle trucks. They suffered for several days without water or food until finally they arrived at a place where water was distributed. And then there was an extraordinary scene in which thousands of soldiers literally fought each other in order to get a drink of water. Messiaen was seated in a little courtyard and he began to take out of his pocket a score, some music, which he began to read. There was one other man, also seated, also reading, who'd refused to join in this struggle for water and his name was Guy-Bernard Delapierre (he was an Egyptologist).[2] Well, the two men got talking and they said to each other, 'Look, we are brothers, because we have placed the finer things of life above this struggle for earthly food', and they asked each other what they were reading. Later the two men were separated, but Messiaen found that Delapierre had left him a note giving him his name and his address in Paris. Eventually when both men had been repatriated to France they both set out to look for each other and became very good friends. As Delapierre had a very fine piano he made his drawing-room available to the young people who at that time were anxious to hear contemporary music, which was completely forbidden at the Conservatoire – that is to say music by Stravinsky or Berg – all that was completely banned. This group included Pierre Boulez, Serge Nigg, Françoise Aubut and me, and there were many other young people also who came after us to the courses in analysis which Messiaen gave here. We had resolved to undertake the analysis of many new works: among the first of these was the *Quatuor pour la fin du temps* by Messiaen (which he had written while in captivity), and then there was the *Trois petites liturgies* which he'd just composed and, among his other works, the *Visions de l'Amen* and the *Vingt regards*. I was always the one called upon to play the various works analysed by Messiaen, on that superb Bechstein. To answer your question, we were known as the 'flèches' because, like all young people, we imagined that we were going to revolutionize the world and we were shooting these arrows in every sense; and then we also thought that the arrows represented the letter M, M for Messiaen, and that the O of Olivier Messiaen represented the circle of his disciples.

PH: Did Messiaen work with you when he was in the process of writing *Visions de l'Amen* and *Vingt regards*?

YL: Absolutely not. Messiaen always worked completely alone and, out of discretion, I never wanted to ask what he was doing. No one, not a soul ever saw what he was writing. He only presented his works to the public once they were completely finished, orchestrated, fingered, with the pedalling written in; until that moment he never showed them to anyone.

PH: And did you never try over a few passages for him?

YL: Never, never, never! He tried them himself – he played the piano as well as he played the organ and even when he wrote for the voice he sang the vocal line himself. (You know he didn't have a beautiful voice but it was very expressive and he used to sing the whole of Wagner or Debussy or Berg's *Wozzeck* with his class.) I have to emphasize to you that I always respected the secrecy of Messiaen's composing. Even after we were married I never, never questioned him about his work – just imagine: I was so dense that I didn't even realize he was writing the opera *Saint François*.

PH: Even that was a secret?

YL: No one knew about the project – except Rolf Liebermann, who knew that Messiaen was writing an opera.

PH: In the scores of the works for piano, are the fingerings also by Messiaen?

YL: Entirely by Messiaen.

PH: Often the fingering is somewhat unorthodox.

YL: Messiaen had a very good feeling for piano sound. He used to play to the class, he played everything that we discussed, even very difficult works, and as a result his sense of fingering was very, very good. But of course there are differences between one person's hand and another's, and between a man's hand and a woman's. Some of his fingerings didn't suit me and so, before the work in question went to the printers, I would point these passages out to him and he would try over my fingering many many times, sometimes twenty times, and sometimes he would say, 'Your fingering is better, let's put your fingering in the printed edition'.

PH: I once showed him a fingering in one of the pieces from the *Catalogue d'oiseaux* – 'La chouette hulotte' – where I did a glissando with the thumb instead of a fingered scale and he was very pleased, or very tolerant, and said, 'That's good'.

YL: What you describe is the opposite of what happens in Ravel's 'Ondine' where some people play the black note glissandos with the fingers. I find that sometimes one discovers a wonderful fingering almost by accident; this happened to me once when I was actually playing the E flat Concerto by Mozart K482 in a concert in Liège, and I tried out the fingering for the first time then and there – in public that is a little dangerous!

Messiaen would not only write the fingering in his music for piano or for organ but he would also organize the 'stick work' of percussion instruments like the xylophone, xylorimba and the marimba – imagine doing that throughout the score of *Saint François*!

PH: I'd like now to go back to the years of the 1940s. Doubtless there was at that time a great sadness for Messiaen on account of his wife's illness.

YL: I didn't know Messiaen at the beginning of the 1940s because at that time he was a prisoner. He was a man who had suffered a great deal. You have to remember that he had lost his mother, whom he adored, when he was still young, eighteen years old. He'd been brought up during the First World War by his mother and his grandmother because all the men in the family were involved in the war. Messiaen's mother died of tuberculosis and at that time Messiaen himself also became very ill, probably with the same symptoms. He was nursed back to health by his aunts on his father's side, who farmed in the Aube near Rheims. These women were very kind to Messiaen, and they understood his talent and allowed him to use a large room with a piano in it where he could work. And they fed him as well as they could – they gave him milk, eggs and good food – and they compelled him to eat. It was probably on account of them that Messiaen survived at all. Not long afterwards Messiaen was appointed to the church of La Trinité, which was a great honour for him, but unfortunately the appointment was not well paid. To reach the church Messiaen had to travel from where he was living in the 19th *arrondissement* to the 9th, and he had to choose whether to take the Metro or go on foot. As he had so little money he would say to himself, 'Either I buy a Metro ticket or a loaf of bread. I must take a loaf back to my wife and so I'll walk to church.'

Well, in due course his wife gave birth to their son Pascal, who is now fifty-five and a teacher of Russian. He was always very gifted at languages and had no talent at all for music – the complete opposite of his father! Messiaen's wife became ill – she had to have an operation and following that she lost her memory. She had to be put into a home where everything was done for her. From that time Messiaen brought up his son by himself. He did all the housework and all the cooking and he would get up at 5 o'clock in the morning to make the coffee and get breakfast for his son before he went to school. Eventually, in 1959, his wife died.

Messiaen was a man who suffered greatly, not only the misfortunes of his personal life but those of a contemporary composer. He would sometimes win the admiration of the public, but the critics were very, very spiteful.

PH: I'd like to ask whether events in the outside world, whether politics or the war, for example, or events in Messiaen's personal life ever influenced his music?

YL: Messiaen had an extremely strong faith. He always said, 'No, I have no wish to waste my time on harrowing subjects. I am a musician of joy. I have composed various works on the subject of grief, but these are concerned with the grief of Christ – 'Jésus accepte la souffrance', for example, from *La Nativité*.' When he was asked to compose a work to commemorate the twenty-fifth anniversary of the outbreak of the war, a work in memory of the dead, Messiaen said, 'Death? That exists, but I myself emphasize the Resurrection.' For this reason Messiaen refused to write a Requiem and wrote instead *Et exspecto resurrectionem mortuorum*.

Messiaen had an absolute horror of hatred, of war, and of wickedness. But I think he had enough strength not to use these subjects in his works, in an opera for example. He was above that – even though he himself suffered. Think how much he did suffer. He spent more than a year as a prisoner in Silesia with very little to eat, only a bowl of soup once a day. He still had enough courage to say, 'I will get up at five o'clock in the morning in the cold in order to keep watch'. That was how he came to see the aurora borealis, something he was very proud of. Because he was a pacifist the German soldiers had no animosity towards him, and on one occasion a German officer said, 'As you are a musician I will lock you up in the wash-house with a piece of bread and some manuscript paper and you can continue to write music'. An incredible story!

PH: I want to turn now to the music for piano. Alexander Goehr, who was a pupil of Messiaen during the 1950s, has told how Messiaen played the class Beethoven's 'Hammerklavier' Sonata, a performance which he remembers as having been absolutely marvellous, and indeed Messiaen used to play a number of his own works. I am thinking of *Harawi*, of which he gave the first performance; and there is a recording he made of the *Quatre études de rythme* in 1951, under the auspices of UNESCO, which is also very fine. I wonder why Messiaen himself rather than you made that recording?

YL: Sandy Goehr: I had the honour of being his teacher! He

came to see me on the floor of this building where I used to have my studio when I was very young and I gave him lessons in harmony and in fugue. He was very, very nice and of course we had been great friends with his father, the conductor Walter Goehr. Going back to the class, Messiaen would analyse everything that he played and he played marvellously. He did indeed play the 'Hammerklavier'. I remember when Messiaen and I gave the first performance of the *Visions de l'Amen* and I wore a very pretty 'little girlish' green velvet dress. Later on, Messiaen had a great desire to hear contemporary music abroad, and in order to finance these trips, he and I played the *Visions de l'Amen* together in many countries on the Continent, and in England. And since we were not well known – at least, I wasn't known at all – the fees were absolutely tiny. Messiaen had to be able to pay his travelling expenses, so each time we went on a concert tour he kept the *Quatre études de rythme* for himself, to earn an extra fee to pay for the travel. That's the reason. When Messiaen came to make the recording it was still in the era of 78s, when one played four minutes at a time, and Messiaen used to tell the story of recording *Ile de feu* 2, which as you know is very tiring to play. Messiaen performed it eighteen times on end until he could play no more, and he had cramp afterwards for several weeks.

PH: There's one curious thing about the recording, and that is that in *Mode de valeurs et d'intensités* Messiaen uses the sustaining pedal rather than the middle one.

YL: You must understand that there simply weren't any Steinways to be played in France at that time and we did all our performances on Erards or Pleyels. Of course Messiaen knew how to use the third pedal, and he used it in his own music, in the *Catalogue d'oiseaux* for instance. And he recommended that I use it in other music, in the 'Hammerklavier', for example, and in Schumann's eighth

Novelette, but when he recorded the *Quatre études de rythme* it simply wasn't available.

PH: Many people, myself included, consider that the *Quatre études de rythme* and *Cantéyodjayâ* are very important works, and works which are remarkable in Messiaen's output because they are neither religious nor concerned with birdsong.

YL: Yes, it is true they stand apart. At the time they were written Messiaen was giving a course at Darmstadt and he was doing a lot of research. He was surrounded by young people like Stockhausen and Boulez, all of whom were very hot-headed. Well, Messiaen found that he had had enough of serial systems: he said that people were too concerned with pitch and not enough with rhythm. And that is how he came to have the idea of a *mode de valeurs et d'intensités* and this in turn gave birth to the idea of *Cantéyodjayâ*. It's an unpretentious virtuoso piece and Messiaen didn't like it much. However it's certainly fun to play.

PH: What are your recollections of Messiaen as an ornithologist?

YL: There's a story he used to tell. He was eighteen months old, and being pushed in a pram by his mother, when a bird began to sing, and he immediately threw down his bottle and raised his hand to tell his mother to be quiet and listen to the bird. He always loved birds and all his life he would note down their song. For *Saint François* he even travelled as far as New Caledonia. I never understood why he couldn't just go to Assisi. In the end I said to him, 'New Caledonia is a very long way away and it's going to be very expensive to get there; couldn't you make do with the birds of Europe?' But yes, yes, yes, he had to go. I found he was very stubborn about this, but I myself never understood why he needed the gerygone for his Angel.

PH: In the first works by Messiaen in which we find birdsong – for example the *Quatuor pour la fin du temps* – one feels that it's somewhat stylized compared with the later music (from the 1950s onwards), where it seems very real. Did Messiaen always intend to represent birdsong as precisely as possible in his music?

YL: At first Messiaen noted down the songs with a musician's ear. In due course, however, he realized that he needed to take lessons 'in the field' with real ornithologists in order to know exactly which bird was singing or making a particular cry. That was how he got to know M. Jacques Delamain, who invited him to his estate in the Charente on numerous occasions; indeed, one of these visits gave rise to *Réveil des oiseaux*, which contains nothing but birdsong. Messiaen travelled all over France collecting birdsong – which is how he came to write the *Catalogue d'oiseaux*. It was before we were married; I used to drive him into the countryside in my little car, and he would spend nights in haystacks or barns in order to hear the dawn chorus.

PH: One consequence of this fidelity to nature is that in the *Catalogue d'oiseaux*, for example, very few of the songs or cries of birds are ever repeated exactly, except for the very simple ones, like the call of the bittern.

YL: I have a story which dates from 1953, I think, when Messiaen was preparing to write the *Catalogue d'oiseaux*. He had been to the Isle of Ushant, off the coast of Brittany, in order to note down the call of the curlew. Because I get seasick, I hadn't been able to go with him, so I'd never heard a curlew. As you know, it's a seabird, and one day a few years later we were in the Auvergne, in the centre of France, Messiaen with his notebook, I with a small tape recorder, when I suddenly said to him, 'I can hear a curlew', and he said, 'No, that wouldn't be possible here.' And I said, 'But I'm sure I can, it's absolutely the same as the curlew in the *Catalogue d'oiseaux*.' 'No, no, that's simply impossible.' And then, suddenly, I saw Messiaen look upwards, and he cried out, 'Yes, you're right!' So I had been able to recognize a curlew simply from having played the music.

Wherever we travelled around the world together – the USA, Australia – we used to ask for a few days on each trip for collecting birdsongs. I remember particularly in Australia noting down the song of the celebrated lyre bird which is found in *Eclairs sur l'au-delà*, where it has a whole piece to itself. When we went to New Caledonia we had to have two tape recorders, one for recording and the other to trick the gerygone into believing that he had a rival on his territory. This persuaded him to sing all the better!

PH: To move on to *Saint François*. How was it that Messiaen was finally persuaded to write a work for the theatre?

YL: From when he first arrived at the Opéra de Paris, Rolf Liebermann had repeatedly asked Messiaen to write an opera, but each time Messiaen had replied that he had no gift for opera. Eventually Messiaen was invited to the Elysée Palace, where President Pompidou said to Messiaen, 'Mon cher maître, I have heard all your works and I adore your music and I believe that you now have a musical language which is ready to write an opera.' And again Messiaen replied, 'I'll think about it but I can assure you that I have no gift for opera.' I don't know exactly when Messiaen decided to compose *Saint François*, nor whether he had the idea in mind for a long time. As you know, in the preface to the opera Messiaen wrote that St Francis was his favourite saint, first because he received the stigmata, and second because Messiaen regarded him as a sort of soulmate because he too loved birds.

Well, in the end Messiaen decided that St Francis was the right subject for him, although I can't tell you exactly how Messiaen reached this conclusion because I never pried into his business.

PH: Are the instructions which Messiaen gave for the production of the opera mandatory or are they purely suggestions? I am thinking for example of the Angel – is it essential that the Angel resembles the Angel by Fra Angelico?

YL: Seeing that Messiaen had waited more than sixty years before writing an opera, he wanted it to be a total experience over which he had complete control – the music, the text, the orchestration, and also the production, even the scenery and costumes. The Angel haunted him – and it was the particular Angel of Fra Angelico's 'Annunciation' which he visualized and which had occupied his thoughts for nine years. And at the first performance his intentions were marvellously realized.

I have great respect for the director, Peter Sellars, who produced *Saint François* at Salzburg in 1992 and later in Paris. But what made me very angry was that he invented a second Angel, one that doesn't exist in the score, an Angel who danced and mimed. Messiaen would have categorically forbidden that. I tried my utmost to dissuade him, with tears in my eyes, and I am convinced that Messiaen wouldn't have approved of what he did because it is *false*. But I could do nothing, and when it came to it there were enormous miscalculations in the production, although there were also many good things, because the producer does actually love the work. I should mention here the producer for the performance of *Saint François* at the Royal Festival Hall in 1988, Michael Rennison. He was a man of great talent and took a lot of trouble to respect Messiaen's intentions, and the result was a great success.

PH: One of Messiaen's most difficult pieces for the piano, *La fauvette des jardins*, actually describes the scenery around your house in the Dauphiné.

YL: Yes, Messiaen kept the exact location of this house a secret because he didn't want to be disturbed, and it was there that he wrote all his works. It's to the south of Grenoble where there are several lakes. He'd bought the property in 1936 when it was simply a field, and he had a small house built. We went there only in summer because in winter it is extremely cold and the house is cut off by snow. This is where Messiaen's funeral took place and where he is at rest. I had a sculpture of a bird made as the headstone for his grave.

PH: I've just been playing another work, the *Petites esquisses d'oiseaux*, which seems to me unusual for Messiaen. These sketches contain birdsong, of course, but no descriptions of landscape; and the pieces are very short, whereas for the most part Messiaen's music is on an enormous scale.

YL: Messiaen spent eight years writing *Saint François*, and for the last four years, while he was doing the orchestration, he worked standing up with the score stretched out on the table in front of him. He became exhausted, and after the work was finished he became very depressed – he was unable to eat or walk or indeed do anything. And he told everyone that he'd finished with composing. But a year later he wrote the *Livre du Saint Sacrement* and then, after that, he wrote a series of four short works, beginning with the *Petites esquisses*, as a kind of relaxation. He was very doubtful about the *esquisses* and said, 'I'm tired, I can no longer write, the pieces are not very good'. Well, I worked at them and I told him 'They're marvellous, absolutely marvellous'. They're short but very difficult, and especially difficult to memorize.

PH: Messiaen's last work – *Eclairs sur l'au-delà . . .* – is again on a huge scale.

YL: Messiaen greatly loved this work. He was inspired by the Book of Revelation, with its description of the heavenly Jerusalem. As you know, the piece was commissioned by the New York Philharmonic, and only a fortnight before he died, between two stays in hospital, I said to him: 'I'm in the process of correcting the orchestral material for *Eclairs* but I'd like to know what tempo markings you have in mind, because nothing is indicated.' Well, he sang the themes to me and it was I who wrote down the metronome marks. So the work was actually finished only a fortnight before he died.

PH: He must have had extreme courage to have had the strength of will to finish the work.

YL: He was always a man of tremendous courage. He had had great misfortunes in his life, but also great joys – at the church of La Trinité, and when he heard his music well played.

PH: I remember the last time I visited you here you surreptitiously showed me the pages of the score of *Eclairs*, and Messiaen said to me, 'I'm like Richard Strauss – each day I have to complete a page of the orchestration before I'm allowed to have my supper.'

YL: Messiaen was in a great hurry to finish the music and to make a fair copy. He had suffered a great deal. After seven or eight operations his back became very painful and one of his vertebrae had to be pinned. From January to April he suffered a martyrdom – he would cry out in pain – it was terrible.

PH: We've spoken of religious music, of the music of birds, of the music of colour. I wonder what Messiaen's music says to those people who are neither religious nor ornithologists?

YL: Messiaen was not concerned with that. Many of the people who have seen *Saint François* know nothing of the saint – and yet the opera is a triumph. Atheists in the audience find the music wonderful and the subject matter touches them. Indeed they may know nothing about musical technicalities or about religion or ornithology. Yet they

1 Messiaen, 1931

2 Messiaen, 1952

3a & b Messiaen with Yvonne Loriod, 1952

4 With Yvonne Loriod outside Beauvais Cathedral, 1982

5 With Jean Leduc outside La Trinité, Paris, 1982

6 With George Banjamin and Yvonne Loriod, Bath, 1986

7 With students of the Royal Academy of Music during rehearsals for the Messiaen Festival, 1987

8 *St François d'Assise* at the Royal Festival Hall, London, 1988

9 With George Benjamin and Pierre Boulez, 1988

10 Messiaen

receive something and I believe that it's because Messiaen himself was completely sincere that his music communicates so strongly.

PH: Messiaen was a man of the twentieth century and yet he himself said, 'I am a composer of the Middle Ages'. Indeed his music has been compared to the great buildings of the Middle Ages, the cathedrals – very strong in architecture but also full of colour and truth and faith. There seems to be an enormous difference – even a gulf – between Messiaen and most of the artists of the twentieth century, for very few artists believe that there's a simple answer to the question 'Does human life have any meaning?', and yet for Messiaen his faith was absolute.

YL: Messiaen always used to say, 'I was born a believer', and never at any point in his life did he have a shadow of doubt. And birds were for him master musicians who sang to the glory of God, and he himself wanted to sing as they do. The whole of his life was an unbroken sequence. He celebrated all the mysteries of Christ and now his music speaks to those who, without knowing it, have need of faith. In this terrible century in which we live they cling to Messiaen's music because he had faith and because his music is full of colour and has a marvellous language, a language which gives joy, because all his life Messiaen believed in joy.

Notes

1 9 January 1993.
2 The dedicatee of *Technique de mon langage musical* (1944).

PART II

Piano Music II

PETER HILL

Messiaen seems to have possessed the rare ability to instruct and inspire composers, without expecting (or receiving) their uncritical loyalty. Indeed it is striking how little trace of Messiaen's idiom one finds in the music of his pupils. In part, this is a consequence of Messiaen's spiritual philosophy, which colours his music at every level. To those who studied with him in the 1940s, this side of Messiaen was uncongenial, even repellent, and Boulez is not the only one to have viewed Messiaen ambivalently, his comments veering between admiration and a tone which is almost offensively derogatory. (Incidentally, Messiaen was well aware – as he remarked to Samuel[1] – that his passion for birdsong was open to ridicule; his reaction to slights to his religious beliefs is not recorded.) It was always more likely, therefore, that Messiaen's influence would be indirect, arising from technical innovations, from his pioneering study of modern scores, and from his fascination with music of non-European cultures.

All these come sharply into focus in Messiaen's own work in the remarkable pieces with which he made a return to the piano (*Cantéyodjayâ* and the *Quatre études de rythme*) in the late 1940s. These stand in total contrast to the musical inflation of *Turangalîla*: the conciseness of utterance is without precedent in Messiaen's music to this date, and is matched by a brittle, percussive use of the piano, an exhilarating dryness of sonority from which the sensuous and contemplative side of Messiaen's music is almost completely excluded. Stripped of the usual descriptive and symbolic meanings, the radical and purely musical concerns of the works drew Messiaen into a musical mainstream, for the first and only time in his life; their cult status (of the *études* in particular, which became known through a pair of 78s made by Messiaen himself) was to confirm Messiaen, at least temporarily, as a father-figure to the post-war avant garde.

In *Cantéyodjayâ*, the music's high spirits reflect the stimulating circumstances of its composition, at intervals snatched between teaching at Tanglewood. As a non-descriptive piece, *Cantéyodjayâ* is a Messiaen rarity (the first since the *Rondeau* of 1943); but although there is no programme, the music hints at meanings beyond itself, as suggested by the titles sprinkled through the score. Those in a sort of pseudo-Sanskrit have been decoded by Paul Griffiths,[2] to reveal sly references to *Turangalîla*: 'statoua' for a phrase suggestive of *Turangalîlâ*'s 'statue' music, 'doubléafloréalîla' for the flower theme. In part, then, Messiaen's private game was a glance backwards. It would be wrong, however, to read too much into this: Messiaen was working at speed, quarrying ideas from his own music (as he always had done) simply because they were lying to hand.

Moreover the strong element of spoof should not disguise the fact that *Cantéyodjayâ* is the start of something decisively new, as Messiaen was surely aware; indeed the (at times) fanatical panache with which he worked through compositional schemes suggests a convulsive effort, consciously made, to slough off those parts of his language which for the time being had served their purpose. (Also indicative is the speed with which Messiaen continued *Cantéyodjayâ*'s experiments, beginning work on *Mode de valeurs et d'intensités* – according to his own account – only weeks later.)[3] Despite this, there is little on the technical side (with one important exception) that cannot be found in Messiaen's earlier music. What is new are the extremes to which these techniques are pushed, together with the force and brevity of the ideas and, especially in the later stages, a blistering turnover of events with (most unusually for Messiaen) little or no repetition.

The contradictory nature of *Cantéyodjayâ* means that while the ideas themselves are taut and compressed, their organization seems to be a matter of inspired impulse; indeed, no other work by Messiaen shows so little calculation or forethought in its design. In the early part of the piece the music's progress resembles an improvisation, with a series of self-contained episodes joined only by tiny flashbacks to the *Cantéyodjayâ* motif itself (with which the piece opens). The longest of these episodes is interesting as the nearest one gets to the 'old' Messiaen (the subtitle, 'Alba', the dawn song of the troubadours, is suggestive of the Tristan works, as is the marking 'avec une nostalgie passionée'). Even here, however, the richly ornamented melody is firmly pinned, with a thudding bass ostinato, whose rhythm (in units of seventeen semiquavers) runs out of phase with the 6/8 metre of the right hand, thus enabling a literal repeat of the tune to sound as though varied.

This counterpoint of fantasy with unyielding precision is typical of the ideas in *Cantéyodjayâ*. Typical also is the juxtaposition of this episode, with its strongly emotional colouring, with the succeeding section which is Messiaen at his most speculative and startlingly abstract. In this famous passage, Messiaen for the first time makes a thoroughgoing application of the idea of *mode* not only to pitch but to other elements, here dynamic and note values (duration). In effect each sound is a unique interaction of the three modes, retaining its identity throughout the passage (so that for example the D♮ (see Ex. 12.1) in the top stave is always *pp* and always has the value of one demisemiquaver). Messiaen's technique, often mistakenly referred to as 'serial', is in fact the antithesis of Schoenberg's

EX. 12.1 *Cantéyodjayâ*

Modéré (mode de durées, de hauteurs et d'intensités)

pp *ff* *p* *mf* *f* *ff* *ff*

method, since the *ordering* of sounds is entirely free. Paradoxically it is this freedom which allows Messiaen to produce occasional fleeting connections; apart from these, an extreme of organization gives an effect (as so often in his music) of randomness.

Another paradox is that the more the music teems with tiny sound-events, the more the global impression is entirely static. In the event, this is to be the last of *Cantéyodjayâ*'s culs-de-sac. At this point Messiaen alters course: the move is signalled decisively as the music feints to resume the 'Alba' episode, abruptly discarded in mid-phrase in favour of a beautiful arching melody (the 'doubléafloréalîla' mentioned earlier, Ex. 12.2e) which floats between resonances at the extremes of the keyboard. This moment of stillness proves to be a gathering-point: first, it distils the melodic core of so many of *Cantéyodjayâ*'s melodies (see Ex. 12.2), a knot of intervals, freely varied, which explore the semitones either side of the octave, balanced by a division of the octave at the fourth, fifth or tritone. In a more important sense it acts as a springboard, being the first of three refrains, each associated with a longer paragraph, or 'couplet', of music. The first couplet, for example, amplifies its parent refrain, catching its reflective tone in quiet winding melodies, and then (by contrast) inflating its soft bass resonances into the drummed syncopations of a savage dance.

Here, for the first time, the music gives some sense of ideas stated and developed; but it should be emphasized that the gathering momentum comes much more from the ways in which Messiaen gauges and exploits the potential energy in each block of material. The sections become increasingly compact, so that the music forms a mosaic of hard-edged fragments which jostle and strike sparks from one another. Again, many contrive to be both static and propulsive: so, for example, the criss-crossing 'scales of durations' which end the first couplet act as a 'machine', and hence are self-contained; yet, equally, as the left hand 'accelerates' towards the shortest value the music is catapulted into the next event. Similarly a snippet of this idea is reused at the end of the second couplet as an escape from the vast symmetrical rhythm in which the music has become embedded.

EX. 12.2 *Cantéyodjayâ*

(a)

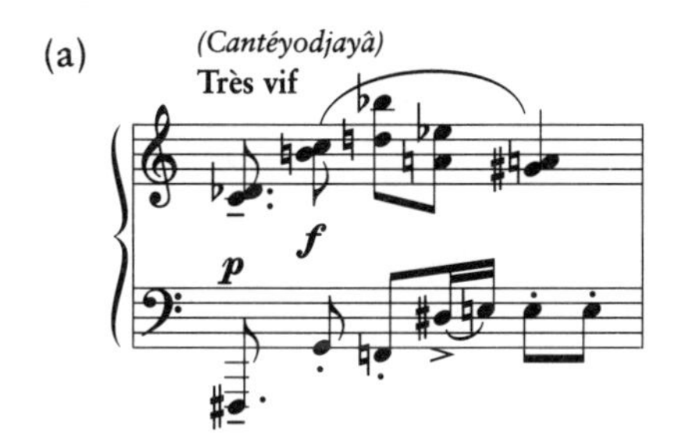

(b)

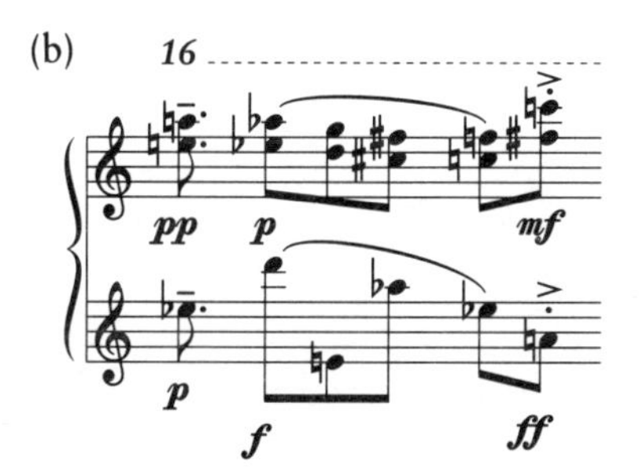

(c)

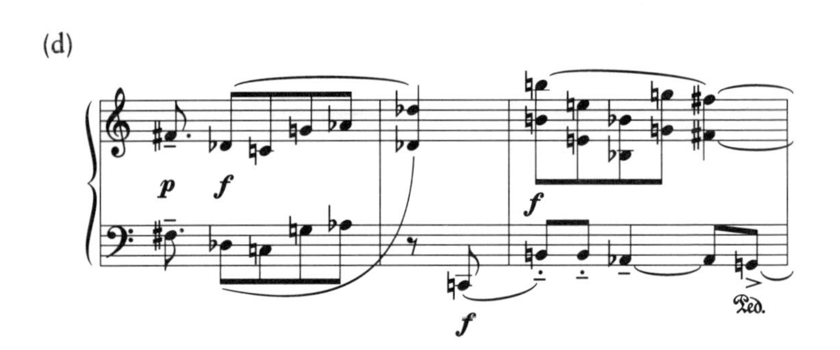
(d)

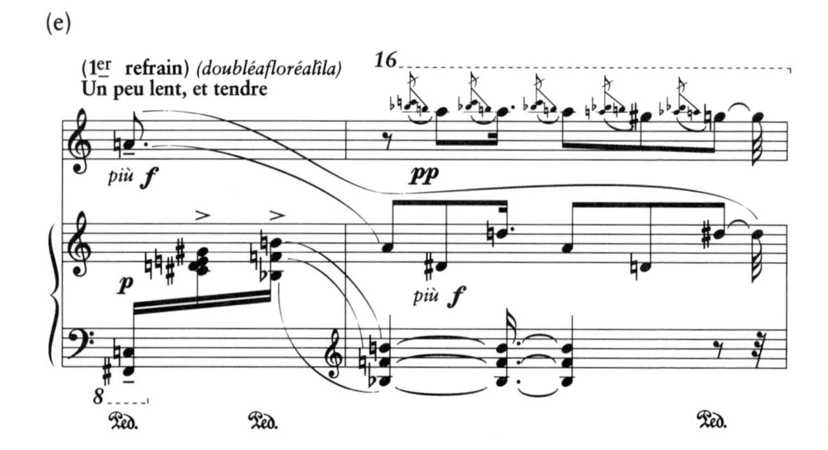
(e)
(1er refrain) (doubléafloréalîla)
Un peu lent, et tendre
16
più f
pp
più f

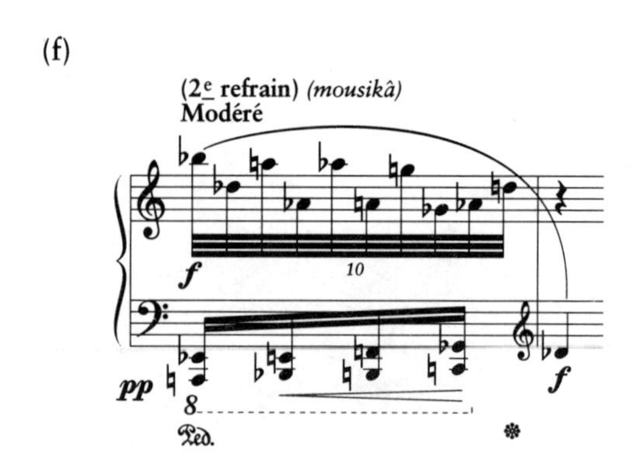
(f)
(2e refrain) (mousikâ)
Modéré
10

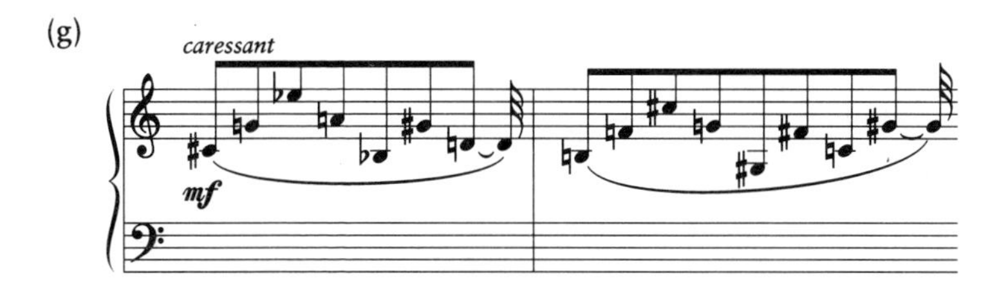

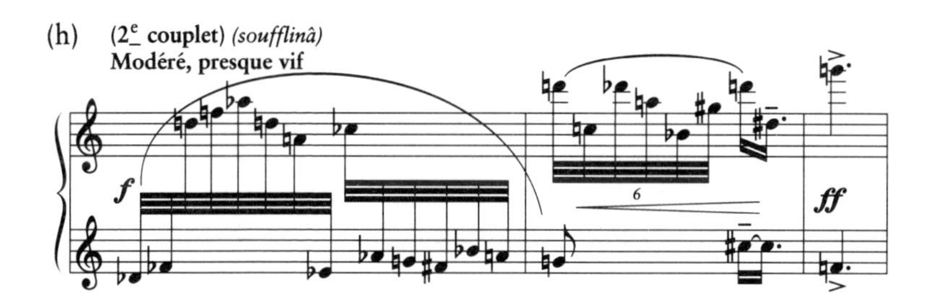

The third (and longest) couplet intensifies this contest. Of the obstacles which check the music's momentum, the most complex is a whirlwind six-part canon, and the couplet climaxes in a huge 'pyramid' amplified three times from its centre. From this impasse the most brilliant of the cadenzas springs free, and spills over, finally unresisted, into a *fortissimo* peroration on the first refrain, with sufficient energy to extend this treatment to a chordal idea heard only once before (but familiar from *Turangalîla* as the 'theme of chords'). After these great cliffs of sound, the resumption of the *Cantéyodjayâ* motif sounds comically trivial, and the perfunctory nature of this recapitulation is further pointed by another false start on the 'Alba', interrupted again, this time by a horribly knotty last line – Messiaen's final joke is at the expense of the pianist – as the hands cross and tangle before bouncing emphatically to the extremes of the keyboard.

Though owing more, as I have suggested, to inspired improvisation than to conscious design, the patchwork of *Cantéyodjayâ* was in the event Messiaen's first full-blooded foray into a 'collage' type of structure. As such its significance to Messiaen's future cannot be overstated. In particular it was a necessary preliminary, as a compositional sketch (Messiaen referred to it as a 'study in rhythm'), to the realizing of his aim, cherished since childhood, of bringing birdsong to the centre of his music. If birdsong was to be more than decoration, as it had been up to now, its incantatory qualities, together with its sheer variety, demanded a new way of ordering ideas. Put simply, without *Cantéyodjayâ* and the subsequent *Quatre études de rythme*, the *Catalogue d'oiseaux* would not have been possible.

In many ways the *Quatre études de rythme* represent a coming-to-terms with the territories charted with such spontaneity in *Cantéyodjayâ*, but in a more rigorous, concentrated way. In *Neumes rythmiques* one connection is the use of refrains. Here Messiaen employs two contrasting ideas in alternation, an important difference from *Cantéyodjayâ* being that the refrains themselves are subject to a consistent (if very simple) variation, by expanding their values (see Ex. 12.3). That this is progress-

EX. 12.3 *Neumes rythmiques*

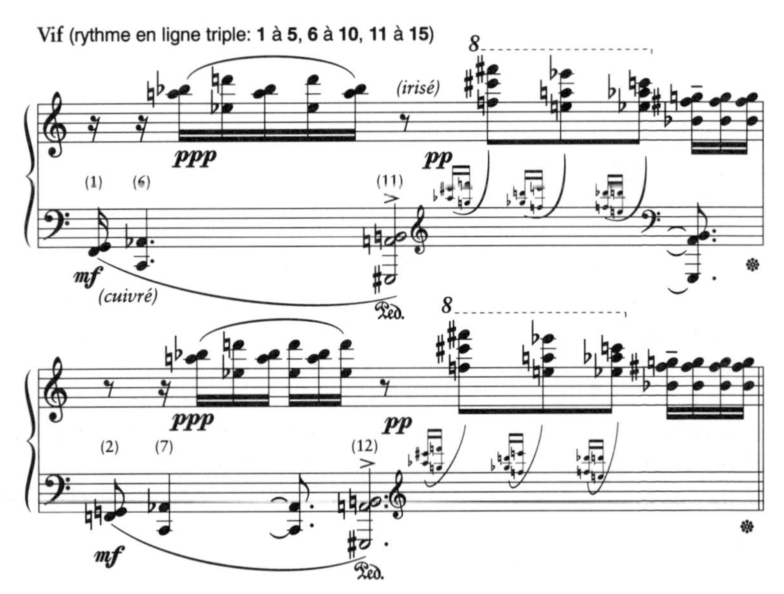

ive is clearly audible in the first refrain, less so in the strident second, partly because its accumulation is through higher prime numbers (41, 43, 47 etc) and partly because the pattern of clusters and inner tritone is varied each time, with the sense of pushing forward disguised by the symmetry of its rhythm. The refrains punctuate seven verses, each of which is a series of fragments, or 'neumes' (a term derived from the clustered noteheads of plainchant). In linking these disparate gestures, Messiaen again follows the example of *Cantéyodjayâ*, but again in a way that is more systematic. The 'neumes' are subject to two types of development. The first of these – hinted at within the first verse itself – is further illustrated by comparing the three parts of Ex. 12.4, where the pitches of the melody (on the inner stave) remain constant, though realigned with the *rhythmic* formulae. The second, and commoner, form of development preserves the 'neumes' in their original form but orders them into new groups.

It would be wrong, however, to think of this as simply a kind of kaleidoscope of interchangeable patterns. For one thing, we hear a steady influx of new material, introduced in a way that is far from aimless. There is, for example, the motif featuring C♮–C♯ – the notes missing from the melody in verse 1 (see Ex. 12.4a) – heard once quietly in verse 2 then emphatically developed at the end of verse 4; the little turn (see Ex. 12.4a, last bar) from which spring sweeping demisemiquavers, and the exquisite variant of this cadence which progressively anticipates the beautiful receding sonorities that end the final verse (see Ex. 12.4c). Moreover, the verses, though distinct in character, suggest a curve of impetus from the fourth, which is the most static and has least new material, the fifth, which is framed dramatically by the demisemiquaver gestures, and the sixth, the shortest and most incisively contrasted. The final verse draws together and develops all the material, and this sense of pushing forwards is underlined by Messiaen's rubato markings, suggesting a looser, more impetuous style of performance as the music moves to a crisis, and the extended dissolving cadence (see Ex. 12.4c).

In a sense, then, *Neumes rythmiques* confronts the same prob-

EX. 12.4 *Neumes rythmiques*

(a)

(b)

lem as *Cantéyodjayâ* – that of ordering fragmentary ideas – but advances a more sophisticated solution. In place of the grouping of material into the rigorous and the fantastic, we have two streams of process running in parallel, the one regular and predictable (the refrains) the other fluid, deceptive and imaginative. In *Mode de valeurs et d'intensités* the 'molecules' of *Neumes rythmiques* are further compressed, into single sounds. Again the point of departure is *Cantéyodjayâ*, with the technique of this extraordinary piece exactly as in Messiaen's first 'mode de valeurs' episode, with the additional refinement (highly artificial, it has to be said) of a mode which organizes 'attack' (accent, legato, and so on). As in *Cantéyodjayâ* the conjunction of the different modes generates three composite modes, each

EX. 12.5 *Mode de valeurs et d'intensités* (Preface)

made up of twelve points of sound (see Ex. 12.5, from Messiaen's preface to the score).

For all that it steps bravely, and without compromise, into an utterly new sound-world, considered as a musical experience the piece is a puzzle, not least in the discrepancy between what the technique promises and the effect produced. If one is expected to hear a counterpoint between the lines, the piece is a failure: for in reality, because of the spread of dynamic and the overlap of pitches between lines, what one experiences is simply a synthesis of all three. Another questionable consequence of the technique is that each note is so loaded with instructions that one might suppose that the pianist is merely a punctilious technician – were it not that the results of such 'pointillisme' are as arid as the blips of a computerized game. Far better, in my view, to respond to those shapes that Messiaen does manage to conjure (and it should be remembered that, as in *Cantéyodjayâ*, the order of sounds is freely chosen); for what fun there is in the piece comes from a feeling of a high-wire aerial ballet, with the flickering motifs in the treble dancing in opposition to the sostenuto gong-strokes in the lower registers (the final page is a particularly impressive instance), with momentary oases of stillness coloured by harmonies of surprising eloquence. Seen in this light, the piece is an 'étude' in the sense of a challenge from theorist to composer: how far is it possible to generate music from (or despite) a fantastically detailed set of *a priori* rules?

As a study in piano playing, the piece involves not only precision of nuance, but a virtuoso technique with the third pedal (and even on occasion some discreet cheating) if the lines are to be kept going without inappropriate blurring. Ex. 12.6 is an example of the contortions required, with the third pedal jammed down a fraction of a second after releasing the *sff* G but still in time to catch the low A♭. (There is every reason, therefore, not to play the piece too quickly.) None of these solutions is marked in the score, and indeed the piece is virtually unique in Messiaen's *œuvre* in that the practicalities of its performance are not fully worked out. Perhaps this is significant: certainly Messiaen's attitude to the piece seems to have been ambivalent, and to me he expressed exasperation with the work's notoriety, which was never intended nor, he felt, merited.

EX. 12.6 *Mode de valeurs et d'intensités*

The following year (1950) Messiaen gave these two pieces a performing context by adding a further pair of *études* entitled *Ile de feu* (they are dedicated to Papua, New Guinea), both as fiercely charged as the original studies are abstract and speculative. (Messiaen's preferred order for the set as a whole was: *Ile de feu 1*, *Mode de valeurs*, *Neumes rythmiques*, *Ile de feu 2*.) The brutal power of *Ile de feu 1* recalls 'La parole toute puissante' from the *Vingt regards*, the difference being again in the brevity of ideas. The piece revolves around a refrain, which remains unchanged but is heard in different guises, first hammered in the bass of the piano against deep percussive syncopations, subsequently with a birdsong descant. Between the refrains come virtuoso episodes, which gather in complexity, reaching their zenith just before the music grinds virtually to a halt in the grandest and final version of the refrain. The obstacle is smartly sidestepped by upward glissandos on black and white keys, a sort of exasperated simplification of the keyboard style of the earlier episodes. This then triggers the coda, with drumming semiquavers in the right hand circling out-of-phase with the left-hand tune, which is a loose extension of the original refrain (see Ex. 12.7).

If the first *Ile de feu* is the shortest and simplest of the *études* its companion builds on elements from each of the other three. Like *Ile de feu 1*, it too has a trenchant refrain, but this has a more complex construction with small motifs twisted in rhythm after the manner of *Neumes rythmiques* (see Ex. 12.8). The most significant innovation comes in the episodes. These use the 'mode de valeurs' technique, with the difference that disorder is brought under control by systematically permutating the sounds (twelve in number) through a scheme of ten 'interversions'.[4] With the episodes following a preordained course, any evolution takes place with the refrain, which with each recurrence is progressively enriched by accompaniments and descants. Matters come to a head as Messiaen abolishes the division between refrain and episode, bringing about a colossal collision between the theme (in octaves) and the final pair of interversions. Again, the climax is marked by a simplification: the upper line (the ninth interversion) is the twelve-note series in a pattern of

EX. 12.7 *Ile de feu 1*

descending and ascending whole tones, while the regular rising semitones (which form the tenth interversion) pick up from the chromatic scale in the previous bar, itself the culmination of a breathless sequence of twelve-note rows juggled between the hands (see Ex. 12.9). The refrain is abruptly torn off short of its conclusion, and the music is re-energized (just as in *Ile de feu 1*) by fierce, condensed fragments. Again this is a prelude to a coda of drumming, but this time technique and effect are infinitely more complex. While the right hand is freely melodic (derived from Hindu 'jâtis'), the left hand concertinas back and forth in twelve-note palindromes (making twenty-three notes in each phrase) before devouring itself by reversing the whole passage after the tenth such phrase. If this sounds complicated on paper, the reality is exacerbated (for listeners as well as pianist) by the

EX. 12.8 *Ile de feu 2*

maverick 'jâtis' which plunge on collision course below and among the left hand permutations. In terms both of the mental clarity and pianistic agility required this is one of the toughest tests for the pianist in all Messiaen; and as a summary of Messiaen's experiments with freedom and rigour it makes a fittingly ruthless climax.

As a footnote to the above, a fascinating curiosity is Messiaen's own performance of the *Quatre études*, recorded for Columbia in 1951 on a pair of 78s.[5] So far as I know, this is the only record in existence of Messiaen as a solo pianist (as distinct from his recordings of *Quatuor pour la fin du temps* and *Visions de*

EX. 12.9 *Ile de feu 2*

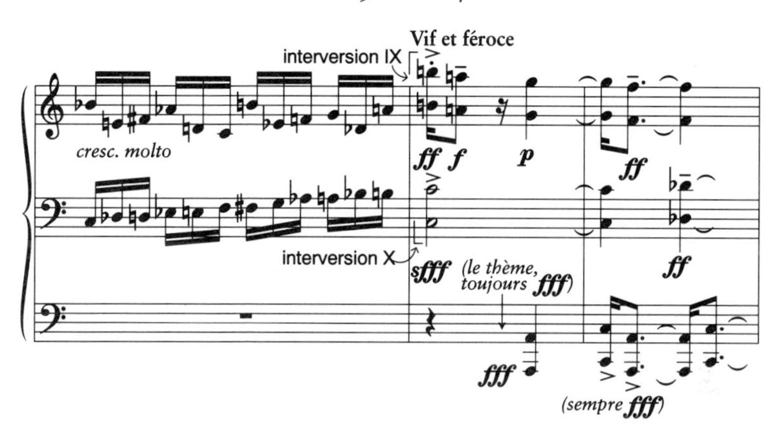

l'Amen). As often with such historic recordings there are moments when it is difficult to judge whether the playing is a matter of the composer's authentic view or arises from technical shortcomings (the turgid 'drumming' at the end of *Ile de feu 2* is a case in point). Some of the most instructive ideas come in *Neumes rythmiques*, in which the structure is meticulously delineated: the episodes are relentlessly hard-edged, with superb drive through the accumulations of the penultimate page. Remarkably (and entirely differently from how this is usually played) the refrains have a strange, shadowy intensity, very restrained in both tempo and dynamic (checking with the score, one notes that the clusters at the extremes of the keyboard never exceed a single '*f*', even at the end of the piece). *Mode de valeurs et d'intensités* is equally revelatory. Here, by contrast, Messiaen frankly ignores much of the meticulous detail of the score. Throughout, he uses pedal to sustain the low pitches, the result being a wash of sound in the upper registers apparently at odds with the precisely calculated durations.[6] Equally, his 'melodic' style of playing takes little account of the terraced dynamics. Though 'wrong', the effect is oddly enchanting – not a word normally applied to this piece – with a lyricism and sense of fantasy which makes this for once the centrepiece of the set; at the same time Messiaen's performance confirms the suspicion that a mere two years after the work's composition he had little conviction in the music's technical manifesto.

Catalogue d'oiseaux

I suggested in Chapter 3 that the *Vingt regards* demand to be experienced as a whole; with Messiaen's other great contribution to the piano's repertoire, *Catalogue d'oiseaux* (1956–8), complete performances are scarcely feasible, given both its superhuman pianistic demands and the fact that it is by some way the longest (at around 2 hours 45 minutes) of all Messiaen's works, with the exception of *Saint François d'Assise*. Nonetheless it *is* a single work, and much more than just a collection of like-minded pieces, as the care with which Messiaen constructs an overall design makes clear:

Book 1	
Le chocard des alpes (Alpine chough)	The Alps of the Dauphiné between Grenoble and Briançon
Le loriot (golden oriole)	Charente and Loir et Cher
Le merle bleu (blue rock thrush)	Roussillon: the Mediterranean coast near the border with Spain
Book 2	
Le traquet stapazin (black-eared wheatear)	Roussillon
Book 3	
La chouette hulotte (tawny owl)	Western outskirts of Paris, and between Petichet and Cholonge (south of Grenoble)
L'alouette lulu (woodlark)	Near St Sauveur-en-Rue, south of St Etienne
Book 4	
La rousserolle effarvatte (reed warbler)	The Sologne district, south of Orléans
Book 5	
L'alouette calandrelle (short-toed lark)	Near Les Baux, Provence
La bouscarle (Cetti's warbler)	On the River Charente just east of Cognac

Book 6	
Le merle de roche (rock thrush)	The 'cirque de Mourèze' in mountains west of Montpellier
Book 7	
La buse variable (buzzard)	At the southern end of Lake Laffrey, Dauphiné (south of Grenoble)
Le traquet rieur (black wheatear)	Roussillon
Le courlis cendré (curlew)	Ushant (Finistère)

At the most obvious level, the thirteen pieces, each accompanied by a preface outlining the interaction between birds and habitat which the music follows, are arranged in groups or 'books' containing one, two, or three pieces and making a palindrome: 3 1 2 1 2 1 3. Numerous other symmetries are also suggested. The *Catalogue* pivots around its central piece – 'La rousserolle effarvatte' – which is itself circular in that it describes the events of a twenty-four-hour period. Successive pieces in the *Catalogue* are always highly contrasted, and so 'La rousserolle effarvatte' – the longest piece – is followed by the shortest, and descriptively the most laconic. This is 'L'alouette calandrelle', set in the glare and heat of southern France, and thus a foil to the subtler light and shade of its companion in Book 5, 'La bouscarle', the nearest Messiaen comes in the *Catalogue* to an 'impressionist' landscape. Together both pieces balance the pair of nocturnes which make up Book 3, themselves a contrast between the peacefulness of 'L'alouette lulu' and the nightmarish 'La chouette hulotte', in which the darkness is a cloak for hunting predators. Symmetry is also apparent at the outer edges of the *Catalogue*: Book 7 is both a recapitulation, returning to two of the habitats found in Book 1, and the end of a geographical curve which takes us from the eastern extremity of France (the Alpine setting of the opening piece) to complete the journey in the mists and darkness of the Brittany coast.

The sheer detail of Messiaen's observations of nature makes his birdsongs seem sharply real. Nonetheless the claim which Messiaen made in interview for their accuracy could be misleading. These are not in any sense note-by-note transcriptions, nor could they be, given the velocity, range and micro-intervals of birdsong. Rather what Messiaen achieves is a sort of creative reconstruction, or *translation*, in terms of the piano. The important point to stress is that throughout his life (from his boyhood in the Dauphiné region of south-east France)[7] Messiaen heard birdsong as *music*. Hence it was the desire for verisimilitude that governed his earliest attempts (made at the age of fourteen)[8] to write birdsong in musical notation. He relied always on observations made 'in the wild';[9] for this reason the *place* is important to Messiaen's music – and the pieces of the *Catalogue* are as much about the landscapes of France as about the birds that inhabit them. Thus Messiaen's birdsong always reflects his own very personal response. Moreover, despite an encyclopedic knowledge of ornithology, Messiaen was unashamedly unscientific. As he himself conceded, his view of birds was anthropomorphic – that is, the way *he* experiences their song is then projected as *their* character. The robins and blackbirds of the dawn chorus are 'gentle' and 'lyrical', while at the other extreme are nature's villains, the harsh 'sniggering' gulls or crows, and most terrifying of all, the tawny owl, whose climactic call sears the memory, so we are told, like 'the shriek of a murdered child'. It was the character of birds – and of the places in which he discovered their calls – that Messiaen stressed most when I studied the *Catalogue* with him. Brilliant though much of it is, almost all the birdsong is lyrical, supple in rhythm and colour and rarely impersonal or mechanical.

Not surprisingly, for people who prefer unprogrammatic, 'pure' music, the *Catalogue* is the most difficult to approach of Messiaen's works. The sheer scale of its experience, contained within the hands of a single performer, gives it the quality of an intimate diary, an ornithologist's notebook, with every note, every gesture an observation from nature. How, the sceptic might ask, can these be made musical? And, still more to the point, how can they be arranged into a musical whole – especially given that each event (the songs of dawn, midday and evening, the rising and setting sun) must remain true to the rhythm of nature?

Take, as a very simple example, one of the least musically

EX. 12.10 *Catalogue d'oiseaux* 5 'La chouette hulotte'

promising of the birdcalls in the *Catalogue*, that of the tawny owl ('La chouette hulotte'), with its monotonous falling third (here C–A; see Ex. 12.10). Ornithologists might be puzzled, in Messiaen's version, by the huge chords which surround these pitches. These can be explained as Messiaen's analogy, in pianistic terms, to the changing timbre of the call, whether 'hollow' or screeching. Another aspect needs some ingenuity in writing for the piano: this is the owl's glissando, which Messiaen manages to create in illusion by a careful judgement of pedalling allied to fading dynamics. From all this it seems that Messiaen is seeking not so much to imitate the bird's call as to analyse it – and then the musician takes over, sensing in these fragments the germ of a structural idea. The music begins to acquire a sense of movement, first in a series of tiny variations in which the C–A is the common factor, varied in harmonization, then in a primitive development, which is simply a diminuendo (the owl fading into the distance). Lastly, as a codetta to the passage, there is the sinister thrumming, which Messiaen adds as an afterthought, by way of suggesting the shuddering or trembling which sometimes curdles the owl's call.

Of course, much of the *Catalogue* is concerned not just with things heard, the birdsong, but things seen; imagine Messiaen's task in reverse, a painter trying to render sound in visual terms. In addition to the landscapes, along with the colours which change with the time of day, a recurring image is that of night, found in varying musical guises throughout the *Catalogue*. A

EX. 12.11 *Catalogue d'oiseaux* 7 'La rousserolle effarvatte'

complex example is found at the opening to 'La rousserolle effarvatte' (Ex. 12.11) which follows the birdlife of the marshes through a complete cycle from deepest night to deepest night. Although the effect is intended to be mysterious, there is nothing vague about the music, which is precise, a rigorously organized 'machine'; so, again, a *metaphor* not an impression. The passage is extraordinarily difficult to catch in performance, partly, I think, because so many layers of meaning are interwoven. Not only is there the counterpoint between brittle sounds in the right hand and the gliding, circling harmonies in the left, but there is the mechanistic quality of the whole passage, with the cycle of repetitions bringing the hands back into alignment, rather like a clock at midnight. Too much rigour in performance and one loses the atmosphere; too much freedom and one loses the sense that the passage is a tiny microcosm of the whole, designed to set up a perspective for the vast and exuberantly varied piece which follows.

In total contrast with this hypnotic image, in 'La chouette hulotte' the violence of the calls inspires a turbulent, disordered metaphor for darkness. It is interesting that the musical technique, here so vivid and emotive, is descended directly from the most abstract of the *Quatre études de rythme*. As in *Mode de valeurs et d'intensités*, each note is a unique combination of pitch, duration and loudness (though here there is no attempt to organize 'attack'), giving the effect of isolated jolts of sound. Unlike the *étude*, however, the technique is refined with a view to musical effect: the durations are arranged in a descending 'chromatic' scale, with the result that lower pitches form slow-moving 'pools' into which the higher sounds inject menacing bursts of rapid activity. As before, the effect is paradoxical, the tension arising from a sense of energy unconnected to any feeling of forward propulsion. This characteristic is then exploited by Messiaen on a structural level, so that the passage as a *whole* (and a later variant) contrast with, and so underline, the sense of movement in the music of the birds – the owls heard, but not seen, as they approach and recede through the darkness.

This balancing of ideas which are static with others which change is a cornerstone of the *Catalogue*, as indeed it is of all Messiaen's designs, from his very earliest compositions. As a principle it is simple, but even in the shorter pieces from the *Catalogue*, it may be deployed with marvellous subtlety. 'L'alouette calandrelle' is both the briefest piece and represents Messiaen descriptive writing at its most astringent and economical. In this respect he reflects the setting, the arid landscape near Les Baux, in Provence, in high summer. The heat and thorny terrain are sketched with rigorous understatement: simply a pair of chords reiterated, with (equally telling) regular silences. Complementing them is a trio of monotonous sounds: whirring cicadas, and the mechanical, deadpan calls of kestrel and quail. These ingredients form the frame to the one mobile element, the soloist's song. In this each phrase departs from its predecessor, creating a tiny musical form, on the lines of 'statement–development–coda'. The song contains the seeds of the subsequent development, in effect a series of variations: first the lark's song is enriched by fluttering harmonies, then paired in a two-part 'invention' with the more nimble crested lark, from which it extricates itself for a final resounding statement. The momentum has taken the music as far as it will go: abruptly the piece alters course, from movement to stasis, with a view to a symmetrical return to the music of the opening lines. However, in order to regain the stillness of the beginning, an interlude is needed, and this Messiaen again fills with the music of cicadas, kestrel and quail, now considerably extended. With the return of the lark, the music appears to recede towards a peaceful conclusion, but Messiaen has a surprise in store – the explosive song of the skylark which rockets heavenwards in a torrent of virtuosity. Though shocking, this is not arbitrary: for its frenzy has the effect of throwing into relief the previously very deliberate release of energy.

Standing back from this, one can see that whereas 'La chouette hulotte' is comparatively primitive, the dynamic and static simply being juxtaposed, here they are folded together to create a shape that blends development with symmetry. What is remarkable is that this design is not merely effective as music, but is itself a supremely imaginative response to the observations of nature which inspired the piece. As such the form itself acts as another kind of metaphor, remarkably detailed and exact, for the spirit of the place: the stricken landscape irrigated only by the thin trickle of energy which is the lark's song.

Indeed, one of the marvels of the *Catalogue* is that its structures are so resourceful, with Messiaen avoiding any sense of formula; each piece creates a unique solution to the same task: nature into music. Messiaen's problem is one of continuity, posed most acutely where the music is most primitive or naive in its descriptiveness, as for example in the piece that opens the *Catalogue*, 'Le chocard des alpes'. Here it is exacerbated by the expressive character of the music: Messiaen describes this world of peaks and chasms in music that exists always on an extreme level – in the splintering harmonic and rhythmic dissonance of the mountains, the monolithic, insistent cries of raven or chough. Moreover, he takes the appalling risk of virtually abolishing all feeling of line, separating each block of music, without exception, with long silences. The voids, terrible and splendid in themselves, also ensure that we do *not* readily hear the music consecutively. Individual blocks connect up with the piece as a whole not by referring to their immediate neighbours but by cross-referencing with some more distant part of the design. The music of the mountains forms a symmetrical curve (A B and A[1]) and hence frames the piece. The events of the two intervening verses correspond to one another. And complexity is added to this design by the pairing of complementary opposites: the eagle, depicted only in flight, the raven only through its cries; whereas the chough (as soloist) is both heard and 'seen'.

It is very characteristic of Messiaen's thinking in the *Catalogue* that this piece could be experienced as a series of scenes which are then spliced together, like a film, so that they counterpoint with one another. Alternatively one might compare it to a fabric woven out of many independent threads; these surface and are visible at certain points, but even when out of view one senses that they are still present and functioning. All this recalls the example of *Cantéyodjayâ*, with the difference that here Messiaen interleaves his material so as to minimize any feeling of forward momentum. Even the ending of the piece conforms to this non-dynamic design by rigorously avoiding any feeling of reached goal or cadence. In effect the music just stops, with no sense of finality. And of course this is all part of Messiaen's musical metaphor: for the mountains are eternal, they exist outside time.

Where 'Le chocard des alpes' shows Messiaen's strategy at its most defiantly unyielding, the next three pieces in the *Catalogue* are determined efforts to generate a sense of forward flow, and to create musical points of contact between disparate materials. In 'Le loriot' the central device is to represent the passing of time, as experienced in a chorale of harmonies which, as they develop, represent the sun rising to its zenith at midday. These originate in the pair of quiet chords, used at the outset (Ex. 12.12a) to offset the boldly etched first solo of the oriole (the device is similar to the opening of 'L'alouette calandrelle'). The difference between the two strands is not just a matter of character and dynamic, but of harmony and mode: for where the chords step up a whole tone, the predominant line of the

EX. 12.12 *Catalogue d'oiseaux* 2 'Le loriot'

(a)

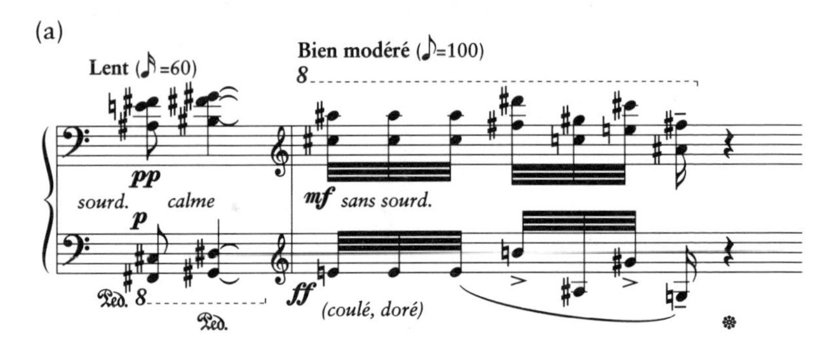

(b)

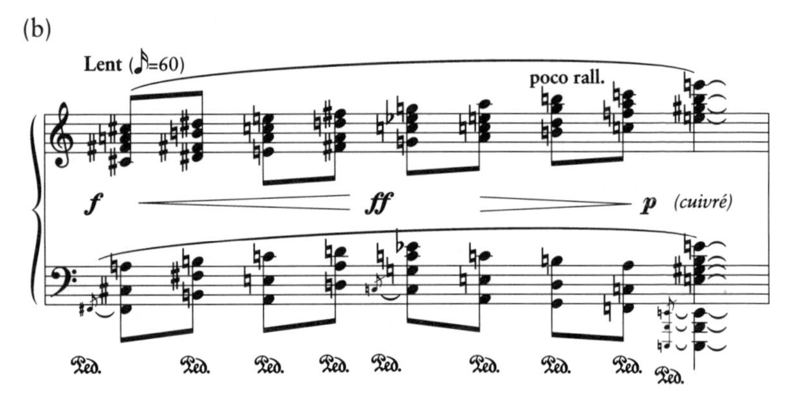

birdsong (in the left hand) is in Messiaen's mode 2, strongly coloured by E major (the notes foreign to the major triad, A♯ and G♮, are displaced down an octave). What follows is an extended 'modulation', in which the harmony of the low-lying chords moves by degrees into the orbit of the birdsong. Their first move – another whole-tone step – is down to E (a moment which Messiaen asked me to emphasize by gently bringing out the G♯ of the E major chord: see p. 277. By settling on E the underlying harmony, of course, becomes a reflection of the oriole's song. Also signalled is a change of texture. The birds which follow are from the dawn chorus and, for the most part, of the type Messiaen uses as musical descants. They sing in the upper registers while E major lingers on below. Quietly but unmistakably the chords move from background to foreground, a new independence confirmed as the F♯–E progression swells into a lovely Debussian phrase. This in turn forms the basis for another decisive change of texture as the chords become a line of pure triads which fan outwards along whole-tone steps: F♯, E (again), then D, C, F♯, so that the final step, to A minor, feels like a modulation. The phrases which follow continue, unhurried by the excited duetting in the upper registers of two garden warblers. Meanwhile the harmonic goal is the E major chord at the centre of the piece, on which the music finally comes to rest (see Ex. 12.12b). Looking at this last phrase we can see that the E major chord is a fulfilment in three senses. First, melodically, it completes a curve, the ascending triad of A minor formed by the last note of each phrase of the sunrise (one notices also that it is the A minor chord which breaks the sequence in this last phrase, initiating the quietening descent to E). Second, the phrase swings in a pendulum arc from F♯ to E, thus amplifying and fulfilling the prophetic F♯ to E at the end of the oriole's first solo. Finally, the cadence acquires a wonderful significance through the final step from F♮ – the note missing, it will be noticed, from mode 2 in the first statement of the oriole's song. By quietly replacing F♯ with F♮ Messiaen 'harmonizes' the chords with the oriole's song, and the music's strands merge and dissolve as they settle on E major. Thus, in purely musical terms, Messiaen parallels his preface – 'the gold of the sun becomes the visual manifestation of the gold of the oriole's song'.

All this is simply a preparation which makes possible the central purpose of the piece. We hear the song of the oriole again, as at the beginning, followed immediately by a slow passage which, especially in view of all that has gone before, we understand as an ecstatic contemplation on the bird's colouring. Up to this point the music has paid tribute to Yvonne Loriod, both in the pun of the title and in a dazzling virtuosity which testifies to her skill. Now the step from 'reality' to inner reflection is underlined by a quotation from *Cinq rechants* (the harmonies in the left hand come from the music to the line 'tous les philtres sont bus ce soir'),[10] and with this the piece enters a world of secret symbolism, as a homage on a much deeper level.

In 'Le merle bleu' the integration of birdsong and environment is again astonishingly detailed. The basic metaphor arises from an impression of the habitat (on the Mediterranean coast near the border with Spain) which exploits the natural resonance of the piano; in the bass reverberate huge dissonances (these represent the cliffs or the boom of the surf) while in the treble are the strident birdcalls: swifts, Thekla larks, and harsh, 'barking' gulls. In another kind of reflection, this teeming disorder is given perspective by the horizon, the calm 'blue sea', whose colour, Messiaen emphasizes, complements the different blues of the soloist's plumage (these are listed as 'purple-blue, slate, satin, blue-black': see Ex. 12.13a). This magical passage makes an oasis of stillness so exceptional and so riveting that it is used to define the sections of the piece; it concludes the first solo for the blue rock thrush (and later introduces its recapitulation), and divides the long central section. To these groups of material the thrush acts as a sort of reflective sounding-board, while even within its own solo (Ex. 12.13b) resonance is the vital ingredient, with the pianist's left hand crossing over the right to play the shadowing lines that produce its complex, rather acid colouring. At the same time the various chameleon-like appearances of the soloist point up the web of cross-references which give the piece as a whole its extraordinary fluidity, and which lead ultimately to the moment of most intense revelation. In the central development, for example, the soloist picks up the excitable quality of the Thekla larks, in a wild dance whose 'Balinese' inspiration mirrors the pentatonic flavour of the first solo. In addition, the thudding bass chords of the dance recall both the harmonies of the waves, above which the lark sings its winding song, but more particularly the quiet, deliberate bass resonance which colours the cadence of the 'blue sea'.

In the final section of the development the soloist's song is at its most introverted: indeed Messiaen's programme tells us that what we hear is not the thrush itself but its echo. This is a crucial moment, for not only does it distil the idea of the whole piece – the song floating, almost as if in illusion, above the crash of the waves – but it creates a stepping stone between the blue rock

EX. 12.13 *Catalogue d'oiseaux* 3 'Le merle bleu'

(a)

(b)

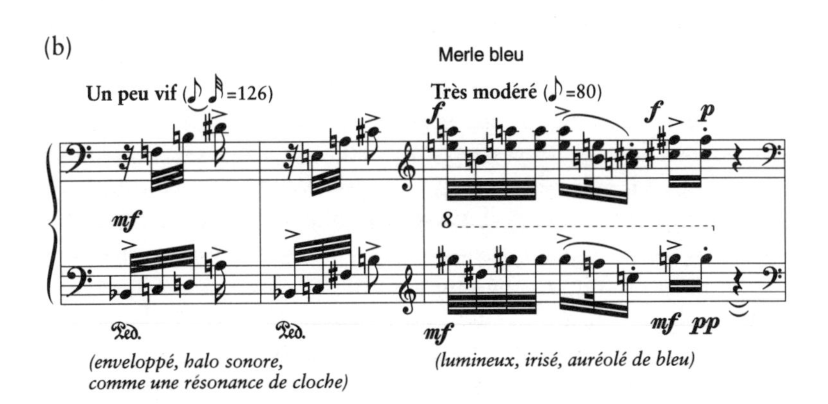

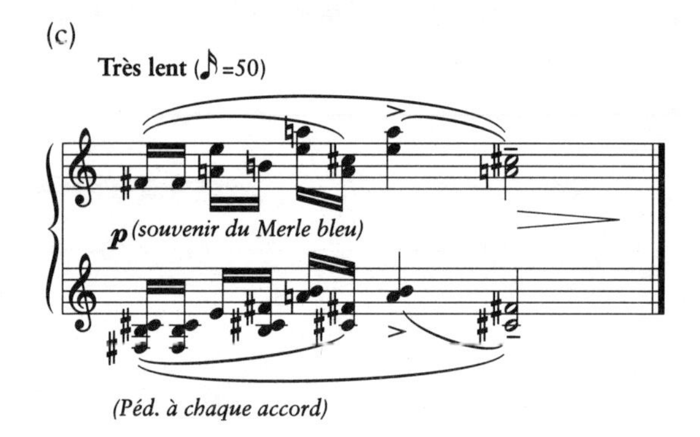

thrush in all its manifestations and the dream world in which the piece ends. For the coda (Ex. 12.13c) is far more than a nostalgic afterthought: it is the moment when the confrontation between the birds and scenery is stilled, symbolized as the contrasting hues of the sea and the blue rock thrush become one. In harmonic terms this is done by merging the A major of the bird with the strong F# colouring of the 'blue sea', in such a way that major/minor sonorities are held in a balance of marvellous purity.

The third in this trilogy, 'Le traquet stapazin', is also set on the so-called 'vermilion coast', but now the birds observed are for the most part on the landward side. The hero of the piece is not the soloist – its curt phrases are used only as interjections or brusque refrains – but the spectacled warbler, whose song, in Messiaen's interpretation, is saturated by the colours of E major (with added C#). Ex 12.14 shows its first appearance, an instance of the subtlety of Messiaen's imagination, with the fifth (C–G) in the bass of the introductory chord giving a lovely chromatic 'charge' to the major third (G#) of the ortolan bunting, with its uncannily 'flute-like' sonority, and to the C# of the spectacled warbler. The music of these two birds sets the prevailing lyrical tone, making the piece the most 'human' and immediately attractive of the *Catalogue* (it was also Messiaen's favourite). As with 'Le loriot', passing time is indicated by the progress of the sun, but here extended to the cycle of sunrise to

EX. 12.14 *Catalogue d'oiseaux* 4 'Le traquet stapazin'

sunset. At the same time the shape of the piece is a double-structure of the kind already described in 'L'alouette calandrelle'; the progressive element (the sun) is framed by the repetitive verses. A series of birdsongs begins the piece, headed always by the stepped harmonies of the 'terraced vines'. From the outset E major is used as the home chord, or tonic, on to which the music repeatedly cadences; so that, for example, when the goldfinch embarks on a wild excursion (pp. 3–4), its song can be absorbed into the measured underlying flow by resolving on to the E major of the spectacled warbler. Moreover, nothing in the *Catalogue* is merely decorative. The chords underlying the goldfinch belong to the rich category of harmonies which Messiaen called 'renversements transposés': their function is to anticipate exactly the piece's central harmonic move, whereby the sequences of chords through which the sun rises attain their ultimate resolution. These chords ascend through a regular sequence, on C♯–E–G–B♭, energized the while by the refrains of the black-eared wheatear and the rock bunting. Finally they reach a sunlit plateau, an expansive interlude for the songs of midday.

The closing pages are remarkable for the way Messiaen interleaves his two structures – the return of the verse forms of the opening with the descent of the sun – and, as in 'Le merle bleu', carefully prepares the moment of musical integration. First the laconic 'vines' resume, ushering in the stanzas of birdsongs, but significantly minus the spectacled warbler. A necessary spurt comes from a further fantastic development of the goldfinch's song, and this spills over into the first great climax, the resumption of the music of the sun, whose first chord completes the rising sequence abandoned several pages earlier. From this zenith, the sun sinks rapidly, paralleled by the birdcalls receding into the twilight. Its next step is to E, but now heard in the second inversion, the sonority of the spectacled warbler. Harmonically, this is Messiaen's moment of revelation: we are 'home', but enriched by the sense that the curve of time (represented in the colours of sunset) has met and merged with the colours of birdsong. In a halo of chiming resonances (on E^6) the music swells into a fervent hymn, against fragments of the spectacled warbler's song. The brusque chords disappear into the darkness, and we are left with the most serene of Messiaen's 'souvenirs', the spectacled warbler at a tenth of normal speed, a vibration hanging in the air, distilling the elements of the day into a single colour.[11]

The integration through colour, so striking in 'Le loriot', 'Le merle bleu', and 'Le traquet stapazin', recurs in only two of the remaining pieces, 'La bouscarle' and 'Le traquet rieur'. Colour, of course, plays no part in the nocturnal interlude (Book 3). Where there night is alternately terrible ('La chouette hulotte') or peaceful ('L'alouette lulu'), in 'La rousserolle effarvatte' Messiaen has in mind 'solemnity', represented by the timbres of 'cymbals, gongs, and trombones'. Indeed it is timbre, rather than harmonic colour, which throughout 'La rousserolle effarvatte' brings focus to what might otherwise be a sprawling series of descriptions. The orchestration of night applies equally to the creatures which stir or sing in the darkness (the heaving tremolos of the frogs, the boom of the bittern) – an instance of Messiaen harmonizing the sounds of nature with their surroundings which is increasingly a feature of the later stages of the *Catalogue*. The purpose of this passage is to set into the sharpest relief the first of the three solos for the reed warbler. The bird's timbre, spikey and abrasive, has been anticipated in the brittle ticking of the introductory 'music of the lakes' (see p. 328). This tiny overture is heard also at the end of the piece, with the difference that it becomes increasingly fragmented (the silences, Messiaen told me, represent mist creeping across the water). Both form part of a frame, the preliminary sections being repeated in reverse order at the opposite end of the piece. The frame's inner edge is the last and most gorgeous of the *Catalogue*'s depictions of passing time. As the sun rises, its hymn-like chords are garlanded with the songs of blackbird, redbacked shrike, and redstart. Sunset, lacking the dawn chorus, coalesces into a substantial slow movement, at the end of which Messiaen frankly abandons truth-to-nature, allowing the music to swell into a peroration, illogically *after* the sun has set. Thereby he emphasizes that this is one of those isolated moments, which occur once in almost every piece from the *Catalogue*, when the music moves from reality – from what is experienced – to what is felt.

From this it will be apparent that 'La rousserolle effarvatte' makes a climax to the *Catalogue* not only in scale and virtuosity, but in the intensity of its descriptions. Even tiny details are noted: the flowers at the margins of the lake (in music derived from *Turangalîla*'s 'Jardin du sommeil' by way of *Cantéyodjayâ*), and the trillings of the grasshopper warbler which graphically symbolize the stillness of midday, at the same time distilling into a single effect the sharp or grating cries of the water birds. The piece is a climax also in terms of birdsong, for the music of the reed warbler itself is of unparalleled virtuosity. The central solo is in particular a miracle of sustained energy. This develops in complexity as a duet, which produces a counterpoint of metre, accent and articulation, and a fantastic

EX. 12.15 *Catalogue d'oiseaux* 7 'La rousserolle effarvatte'

interplay of mood, from extremes of coarse slapstick to diamond-sharp lightness and intricacy. Ex. 12.15 shows a concentration of these ingredients – the rhythms, accents, the hocketing, the jagged broken chords – so breathlessly jumbled that in due course they necessarily dissolve into simpler trills and glissandos.

As noted earlier, the piece which follows, 'L'alouette calandrelle' is both the briefest and the least forthcoming in its descriptions; its effect depends entirely on pacing, the interlocking rhythm of stasis and movement. In 'La bouscarle', the companion piece in Book 5, Messiaen uses similar principles but, in accordance with the setting – an April day of dappled light and shade on a river bank – in a much more complex kaleidoscope of shapes. In one way the piece has a cyclic form of refrains and verses. The initiator of the refrains is the solo bird. It appears at regular intervals, beginning and ending the piece on its own, and on other occasions leading a medley of similarly 'brusque and violent' birdcalls (corncrake, wren and so on). It is also used to interrupt the first two verses, which represent the river. At the other extreme of character are the birds Messiaen characterizes as 'gentle', such as blackbirds and robins. These are followers (unlike the decisive Cetti's warbler) and appear always as descants or afterthoughts.

The five main appearances of the soloist act as refrains, spaced regularly throughout the piece. Within these refrains the symmetry of the piece is emphasized by the music of the willows and poplars, described in two passages occurring near to either end of the piece – one of the very rare instances in the *Catalogue* where Messiaen requires the performer to adopt an 'impressionistic' style of performance, with a hazy blending of half-lights and subtle use of pedal and half-pedal. His metaphor for the grey-green of the water, and of the reflections which form and dissolve, is interesting. The indeterminate colour is represented by the twelve-note mode, normally reserved for black or white, as in darkness, rocks or snow and ice; moreover, he uses the mode in a way which he described to me as 'not savage', allowing familiar musical objects (such as dominant-seventh chords) to swim in and out of the texture. This idea of musical objects forming and dissolving is extended in the closing pages, which recapitulate the music of the first three pages but in reverse order. Here the way in which the music is fragmented by silence could be taken to suggest that we are moving from the outward expression of reality to its inner contemplation – although the final tirade of Cetti's warbler is enough to bring us abruptly down to earth.

The other depiction of water, that of the flowing river, is quite different, having a purposeful, unfolding role. At its first appearance (placed tellingly immediately after the willows and poplars) the river forms four phrases which link into a whole: statement–variant–development–coda. The shape of this verse is then reflected in the subsequent music for the river. Its second verse is identical to the first, though there is a sense of variation because the intervening cadenzas and interruptions (for Cetti's warbler and kingfisher) are modified. The third verse parallels the third phrase of the original verse: a lengthy development, it incorporates the most important structural move in the piece, a large-scale modulation to the dominant. The fourth and final verse matches the 'coda', and indeed uses only the last of the four original phrases, with the cadence extended for quiet additional emphasis. The river, then, is a piece within a piece, flowing gently forwards through the symmetries and refrains which I outlined earlier. Within this triple structure a fascinating maverick role is played (with transcendent virtuosity) by the kingfisher. Of its five appearances the outer two are identical, and are identically positioned, just within the opening and closing tirades of the solo bird. In this sense the kingfisher belongs to the static and decisive world of Cetti's warbler. But it is also associated with the river because of its colouring – blue-green – which reflects the colour of the water. Musically Messiaen makes this reflection exact, since the opening chords of the kingfisher use the identical mode (and transposition of the mode) of much of the music of the river. And like the river its remaining three appearances form a cumulative piece within a piece: these three nuptial flights, as Messiaen calls them, are interleaved with the music of the river, and again reflect its colours with harmonies of A, E^7 and mode 3.

From 'La bouscarle' we move, abruptly again, to the starkest piece in the *Catalogue*, 'Le merle de roche'. Again there is an economy of purpose, with the passing of time marked not by the sun but by the birds themselves: the eagle owl for night, the onset of dawn through the cackle of jackdaws. Midday is reserved for the glorious solos of the rock thrush itself, at first voluble, then concentrated into pairs of fan-like cadences, and finally into a slow-motion 'souvenir', or, as Messiaen calls it here, the song 'idealized'. The huge contrasting frame is unrelievedly grim, though there is perhaps a black humour in Messiaen's depiction of the fingers of a magic 'stone hand' in the five black keys of the piano, or the silhouettes of the rocks as a procession of dinosaurs – in harmonies so monstrous that I could not resist asking Messiaen if he was satirizing his avant-garde contemporaries (he denied it). The musical analogy to this procession is appropriately one of Messiaen's most obscure techniques, an arrangement of a chromatic scale of durations, which calls to mind the 'Soixante-quatre durées' of the *Livre d'orgue*.

Another abstraction from the beginning of the 1950s is found in 'La buse variable', where the bird's flight is caught in a sort of freeze-frame, its spirals denoted by a series of twelve-note interversions. Again one senses the economy, for the scale of the mountain scenery is evoked solely by the vast extent of the bird's orbits. The return to old haunts, the Alps of the Dauphiné, makes a link with 'Le traquet rieur', which revisits the sunlit Mediterranean coastline beyond Perpignan. Another factor in common is that both pieces develop musically through a favourite device of Messiaen, a trio of musical 'personalities': action–reaction–commentary. In this case a flock of scavenging carrion crows initiates events by attacking the soloist, who responds, but only with agonizing slowness as the warning 'commentary' of a red-backed shrike becomes increasingly frantic.

In 'Le traquet rieur' the members of the trio other than the soloist are the blue rock thrush and (confusingly in English) the black-eared wheatear – so emphasizing the sense that this final book of the *Catalogue* is in part a recapitulation. The mercurial song of the black wheatear is (as its French name implies) relentlessly cheerful. The blue rock thrush responds at first quietly, a cadence in A major inflected by a minor third. Its song is a still voice; undeterred by its hyperactive surroundings – teeming refrains for herring gulls and swifts and the resounding 'joy of the blue sea' (A major again) – it progresses by a sort of musical response to the black wheatear, but with its mimicry always expressed poetically. Ex. 12.16 shows the climax of this development, the gentle arabesques in the right hand underpinned by a perfect cadence in A, which after some exquisite vacillations settles on the minor version. In the final stages of the piece the pendulum swings back from minor to major, the modulation articulated by the spectacled warbler (another old

EX. 12.16 *Catalogue d'oiseaux* 12 'Le traquet rieur'

friend from Book 2) whose volubility spurts the music into a triumphant dénouement.

From the Mediterranean to the Atlantic and from light to darkness, the final move takes us to perhaps the supreme achievement of the *Catalogue*, and certainly its most striking. The setting is the extremity of France, the western tip of Brittany, with the desolation of the shoreline and seascape conveyed as much as anything by the gaunt yet eloquent solo of the curlew. This is in three parts: first, oscillations over wide-spaced minor triads, then upward chromatic runs which culminate in fierce trills. As these dissolve, the final utterance brings a synthesis of the first two, with repeated ascending glissandos swelling and fading over another minor harmony. This tendency of ideas towards concentrating or simplifying governs the rest of the piece. A wild tumult ensues with the cries of seabirds, piercing or melancholy, hovering in the resonance of the surf.

These give way to the eddying of the water, a twelve-note passage which itself begins to condense (as its pitches become more repetitious), ultimately forming huge chords (the descent of fog). Finally the entire passage is encapsulated in a single gesture, the monstrous blast of the fog horn. In the almost palpable darkness, the music seems to step beyond reality, in fragments of birdsong which end with a tiny 'souvenir', the redshank – 'flute-like' – in slow motion. In the void the music recalls the curlew, but only in its final simplified version, and as we pass beyond the end of France (Finistère) Messiaen's beloved birds fall silent and we are left only with the muted splash of surf.

In many ways Messiaen's return to birdsong in 1970 appears like a conscious attempt to cap his achievement in the *Catalogue*. In *La fauvette des jardins*, no fewer than seventeen of the species from the *Catalogue* are heard again, and the soloist (whose stunning contribution to 'Le loriot' had been part of a musical act of homage to Yvonne Loriod – see p. 333) is the most virtuoso of these. (This piece, while another supreme tribute to her powers, is personal in another sense, being a return not only to Messiaen's spiritual home in the Dauphiné, but to the very scene – Lake Laffrey and the 'bald-headed' mountain, the Grand Serre – overlooked by the house which Messiaen built in the 1930s and to which he returned each summer to compose.)

Nonetheless, despite these similarities, *La fauvette des jardins* has a personality which makes it quite distinct. Whereas in the *Catalogue* Messiaen's perceptions of nature are pushed to extremes, made vivid by being dramatized, here the descriptions – though no less spectacular – are more relaxed, even genial. This is true particularly of the soloist. In the *Catalogue*, the garden warbler's song was frenetic, and so rapid as to be just an effect; here Messiaen's tempo is appreciably steadier, the playing to be 'bien prononcé, clair et melodique', an instruction repeated throughout the score. Certainly it should be fast enough to dazzle, but not so fast as to defeat the ear's ability to follow its contours. It must be heard as phrases, moods, and above all as *colours*, since it is the cadences (based on rich harmonies of the 'renversements transposés' category) which link the bird musically with its setting, and specifically with the colours of the lake.

Another indication is that there are none of the rigorous, abstract metaphors found in the *Catalogue*. Night, with which the piece opens and closes, is represented in a winding motif, whose calm rhythm suggests the sleep of some great beast. The motif is linked with the undulations first of water, then of the more richly harmonized music of the trees. Against this peaceful movement the dissonant syncopations of the mountain and violent declamations of the nightingale project starkly. This introduction is a prelude to the first of many punctuations or refrains. Their purpose is to indicate the passing of time, not by the progress of the sun but (as if Messiaen were Monet in old age) by painting the varied reflections of the evolving day in the colours of the lake (whose sequences of 'renversements transposés' also mirror the harmonies of the soloist).

The first solos of the garden warbler combine with the emerging of colour, as night turns to day, and the foliage of the alders and willows comes to life. In the long central section, heralded by the most intense version of the lake, now *fortissimo*, the soloist is increasingly assimilated within intense developments; these are crowned by the ecstatic fanfares of the golden oriole, a symbol of midday, after which the garden warbler reasserts itself with the longest, climactic solo. From these peaks, the music begins to parallel the cyclic pieces from the *Catalogue*, moving to complete the symmetry, with the return, ultimately, to the depths of night. It does so by way of two spectacular further developments, in which Messiaen contrasts *movement* with *repose*. First the undulations of the water are extended, energized by the skylark beating frantically against its upper note, and the tumbling rhythm of the mountain. From this grows the music of the black kite, whose unhurried spirals are a direct response to the earlier music of the alders, and complete this particular web of motifs.

The curve of the black kite forms another kind of musical bridge, as its final harmonies sink imperceptibly into those of the lake, reaching a climax of colour development, the lake at its most gorgeous in late afternoon ('every shade of blue: peacock, azure, sapphire . . .'). In this superb page Messiaen reveals the serenity of the landscape most familiar to him, and as the torrents of birdsong are resolved into an infinitely poetic meditation, he brings a chapter in his life to a close. The last fragments of song, and the onset of night, are held within a vast plagal cadence – the harmony of D (with chiming upper resonances in modes 2 and 3, which for Messiaen stand for the gold and green of the mountain) left suspended, reaching A only several pages later as the bottom note of the piano resounds through the last line of the piece.

The paradox of *La fauvette des jardin* is that, despite its glowing lyricism, the flood of stamina-sapping dexterity makes it the most demanding to play of all Messiaen's music for piano: in Himalayan terms a virtually unclimbable K2 to set beside the Everest of the *Vingt regards*. To these peaks, the *Petites esquisses d'oiseaux* (1985) make a deceptive codetta. Apparently slight, better acquaintance makes one appreciate the uniqueness of their qualities, a surface simplicity masking a subtle, intricate elegance which at times is coolly understated. They arose from a request by Messiaen's wife for a musical depiction of the robin; in the event Messiaen composed six portraits, arranging them in a pattern in which the first, third and fifth (devoted to the robin) form an evolving continuity of great finesse, interleaved with more robust evocations of the blackbird and song thrush, and followed by a fierce concluding toccata for the skylark. The music is exclusively concerned with song,[12] punctuated only by colour chords.

In the robin pieces Messiaen marks each phase of the music with chords of the 'renversements transposés' type; normally deployed over a fixed pedal-note (as, for example, in the 'music of the lake' in *La fauvette des jardins*), here they float with apparent freedom, gently guiding the music into fresh tonal areas, each of which opens up a new phase of development. A second harmonic idea acts as a counterweight, chords of 'resonance contractée' which crunch together in a curt gesture of punctuation. Similarly the shimmering descending arpeggio – so rapid as to be almost a glissando – is later matched by an equally

EX. 12.17 *Petites esquisses d'oiseaux* I 'Le rouge-gorge'

impressionistic sonority, high trilling clusters reminiscent of the whirring grasshopper warbler portrayed in 'La rousserolle effarvatte'. The arpeggio is the quickest of the robin's four tempos (see Ex. 12.17); the remainder intertwine in a balletic *pas de trois*, with the phrases of the medium tempo commuting ambivalently between energy and reflectiveness. From these minimal formulae Messiaen conjures a kaleidoscope of seemingly limitless variety, an interplay of grace and wit, its high spirits given poise by finely calculated pauses and silences. The third and fifth pieces continue in this vein, but with sufficient changes in emphasis to give each a defined character. Indeed they seem increasingly reflective, whereas the sturdier even-numbered pieces gain in energy. The work's air of mastery and confident wit is capped in the giddy acrobatics of the closing toccata; at the very end the skylark loses its grip on the insistent top note, just manages to regain its balance, then tumbles out of the sky, the final plunge ending in a muffled, laconic gesture.

Faced with the radical works from the late 1940s and early 1950s, Messiaen's artistic courage in remaking his language seems all the more remarkable when one remembers that at the time he was prone to doubts and depressions, on musical matters as well as personal. Against this background, the human and creative partnership with Yvonne Loriod was an enduring inspiration, and the extraordinary second flowering of Messiaen's keyboard style would not have been possible without her virtuosity. Messiaen used to apologize jokingly for the technical difficulties of his piano music which, because of Loriod's skill, he had never had to reconsider.

Given this, the truism that composers use the piano for their most personal music is particularly apt for Messiaen. In one sense, the piano was the medium for experiment, for the renewing of resources which Messiaen felt necessary after *Turangalîla*. The *Quatre études de rythme*, despite their pianistic challenges, are primarily studies in composition, a glimpse of Messiaen testing out ideas and techniques, struggling, at times, with the intractable tasks he set himself. No less fascinating, from the same point of view, is *Cantéyodjayâ*, the roughest, least polished, but most brilliant of Messiaen's diamonds.

Then in the *Catalogue* we find the first complete fulfilment of Messiaen's most personal vision, nature into music. It would be invidious to select highlights (although 'Le merle bleu', 'Le traquet stapazin', 'La rousserolle effarvatte' and 'Le courlis cendré' are incontestable masterpieces), for Messiaen's inspiration runs at a consistently exalted level; there is a freedom born of confidence and mastery (and perhaps the *Catalogue*'s long gestation) far removed from the repetitions of his early works, and unfettered by their sometimes dogged working-out of formulae. Above all, I have tried to show something of Messiaen as strategist – in the interleaving of architectural layers, the counterpoint of levels of musical time, and in the pacing of moments of climax and revelation which leave us moved as well as dazzled.

The musical achievement of these and the remaining bird pieces is such that even the most sceptical listener cannot fail to be touched by the source of Messiaen's inspiration. To those of us accustomed to birdsong as no more than a vague background twitter, the immediacy of Messiaen's birds may be startling. But part of his achievement in the *Catalogue* is to make us feel as though we are part of the world of birds, even as if in some degree we understand their language. We should realize that Messiaen does not use nature as a picturesque adornment to our man-made world, nor does he approach the countryside in any spirit of nostalgia. For Messiaen the world of nature *is* the real world, whose unending daily rhythm is symbolized by the cyclic form of many of the pieces in the *Catalogue*. For Messiaen also there was a profound unity in the twin inspirations of his art: his religious faith and his love of nature. There is no doubt that for him birds held a spiritual significance. Through their songs they are God's musicians and their flight symbolizes escape from earthly existence. As Messiaen so eloquently explained:

> In my hours of gloom, when I am suddenly aware of my own futility, when every musical idiom . . . appears to me as no more than admirable, painstaking experimentation, without any ultimate justification, what is left to me but to seek out the true, lost face of music somewhere off in the forest, in the fields, in the mountains or on the seashore, among the birds?[13]

Notes

1 Claude Samuel: *Entretiens avec Olivier Messiaen* (Paris, Belfond, 1967), p. 118.
2 Paul Griffiths: *Olivier Messiaen and the Music of Time* (London, Faber and Faber, 1985), p. 147.
3 Sleevenote to Adès ADE 650. This gives the date of composition of *Cantéyodjayâ* as 1948; according to Yvonne Loriod this should be 1949.
4 For a fuller discussion of 'interversions', see Griffiths, op. cit., p. 155.
5 LFX 998/9. My thanks to Timothy Day, of the National Sound Archive, London, for enabling me to hear the discs and for background information.
6 The piano used by Messiaen evidently lacked a third pedal (see remarks by Yvonne Loriod on pp. 296–7).
7 Samuel, op. cit., p. 27.
8 Ibid., p. 24.
9 Ibid., p. 29.
10 Griffiths, op. cit., p. 183.
11 This last phrase has a beautiful pianistic effect. The melody, though legato,

is very precisely marked to be played *without* pedal, this being added only after the final harmony has been reached, to give a just perceptible bloom.

12 The absence of landscape links back to Messiaen's first 'independent' bird composition, *Le merle noir*, for flute and piano (1951).

13 *Le guide du concert* (3 April 1959), quoted in Robert Sherlaw Johnson: *Messiaen* (London, Dent, 1975); p. 117; and Griffiths, op. cit., p. 188.

Organ Music II

GILLIAN WEIR

When I was young and fired by the thrill of devouring new works daily, I found great exhilaration in throwing myself into the music and 'bonding' with its essence. Later, however, I discovered another pleasure: the infinite satisfaction of playing a work one had lived with for twenty years, that fitted like a kid glove, that lay contentedly in its warm familiarity deep within the consciousness.

With the satisfaction came other perspectives. Instinctive response remains valid; but the later viewpoint is able to give a more conscious understanding of the music's nature. I saw then what had been felt but not yet articulated: that the essence of all Messiaen's earlier music was joy. And what is this joy? Not just a naive immersion in a warm bath of religiosity, but a driving energy that is the wellspring of creativity, and creation. At times in Olivier Messiaen's long career this did not pulse so strongly, and may even have been dimmed by his own attitude towards what he felt to be its source, but it is the force that gives so much of his output its hypnotic power.

This strength has not always been hailed as a primary characteristic. During the sixties and seventies attention centred on the long slow movements and the biblical quotations, and while devotees rejoiced in the sound-world, critics were apt to mutter darkly about 'sugary harmonies' and to shy away from the theological rainbows. Messiaen himself, however, had spoken of the 'horrific imagery' in his music, and said to me (when asked if he did not admire the sensitivity of a good mechanical-action organ) that the *power* of the Romantic organ was what mattered most to him.

A nascent power can be heard even in his first published

piece, *Le banquet céleste*. Infinitely slow-moving, it challenged accepted ideas by seeming hardly to move at all. But Messiaen was developing a quite new concept of rhythm, music's moving force, and this brief but perfectly formed piece is impelled by a formidable sense of movement that comes from the harmony. Bach, Beethoven are two prime exemplars of the art of rhythming (as the Greeks would say) by means of harmonic progression, but here Messiaen sustains movement even while holding a single chord. Throbbing gently on the prescribed undulating registration (Voix Célestes) the chord's component notes aspire to resolve. Their intensity of purpose compels the listener's attention. At last they move, amoeba-like, and form another shape (see Ex. 13.1). This process continues, raising the emotional temperature and constructing a line made of the unceasing search for a resolution. Eventually a peak is reached and Messiaen allows his agents to float to rest on a concord, after which the process will be set in motion again. This was at first heard as meandering, until the ears of the composer's listeners adjusted to the pace of the world-in-microcosm and began to feel the irresistible strength of the technique. It is seen in expanded form and the most expansive of moods in the eighty-minute *Méditations sur le mystère de la Sainte Trinité*, where the emotional pull *is* the form, every bit as much as is the grammatical structure.

The ability of the organ to sustain a sound indefinitely made it especially suitable for such a technique. However after the

EX. 13.1 *Le banquet céleste*

brilliant young Yvonne Loriod appeared in his classes in the early 1940s the piano dominated Messiaen's writing. When he returned to the organ in 1950, after an eleven-year gap, it was to provide a liturgical work for the first time. In this, the *Messe de la Pentecôte*, a new world swam into view.

The *Messe* is in five movements that supply the Mass with an instrumental counterpart. It is not of disproportionate length, as are many concert Masses, and was intended to be used in the service. For two decades Messiaen had been honing his techniques through improvising; he spoke[1] of using a different style for each Sunday Mass. For the 10 o'clock High Mass he played only plainsong, for the 11 o'clock service the repertoire, such as Bach or Romantic music, at noon his own music, and at the 5 p.m. Vespers he improvised, often in pastiche but always developing his own techniques. In the 1950s he said: 'One day I realized [these improvisations] tired me out and that I was emptying all my substance into them. I then wrote the *Messe de la Pentecôte*, which is a résumé of all my collected improvisations. Since writing this piece I've never improvised.'[2] (Happily, he soon began again.) The work is indeed a collage of his techniques and obsessions, with birdsong, waterdrops, plainsong, imaginative registrations, serialization in various forms and Greek and Hindu rhythms treated in new ways. The effect is to reinforce the idea of Messiaen as neither neo-Romantic nor modernist but impressionist, even though for a long time the piece was regarded as impenetrably 'modern'.

'Entrée', the first movement, comments on the tongues of fire that came upon the Apostles at Pentecost. The pedals have the melody on a pungent 4′ Clairon (a forceful trumpet sound, pitched an octave above unison); three manual-combinations juxtapose a high Mixture and the 16′ Bourdon with other combinations that stress the harmonics inherent in their sound. This registration creates an uncertainty of pitch that heightens the bizarre, eerie nature of the timbres. The manual parts repeat patterns whose angularity vividly suggests forked flames, darting, flickering and surging (see Ex. 13.2). The effect is of immense energy and brilliant colour, with simultaneously a kind of lofty remoteness that is far removed from the tender caresses

EX. 13.2 *Messe de la Pentecôte* 1 'Entrée'

of *La Nativité*. It is the work of a painter, splashing paint on to his canvas with the exuberant confidence of one sure of his vision. The rhythms are highly organized but do not rule the structure (as they are to do in his next work); they propel the action in bursts by pulses of energy that alternate weak with strong.

For Messiaen, rhythm meant the opposite of our common understanding of the term. For him it was the antithesis of metre and its strict regulation of the beat, its precise divisions. All the devices, from the early 'added-note value' on, were designed to allow him to express freedom, always his overriding philosophical aim. He said: 'Rhythmic music is music that scorns repetition, straightforwardness and equal divisions . . . it is music inspired by the movements of nature, movements of free and unequal durations.'[3] Thus a Sousa march or Vivaldi Allegro would be totally unrhythmical. At first the complication of the rhythmic techniques seem to constrict rather than set free, but in performance the effect is to liberate the music from earthbound patterns and set it bounding into life. Stravinsky has said, 'all order demands restraint. But one would be wrong to regard that as any impediment to liberty.'[4] The self-imposed disciplines act as a spur, much as the fugal form did to Bach. At first Messiaen had used groups of prime numbers ('Les anges', 'Dieu parmi nous') and begun to explore Hindu ideas (*Les corps glorieux*) to emancipate the living force from metre's prison, but in the *Turangalîla-symphonie* (1946–8) he had taken a step forward, systematizing rhythm and to some extent separating it from the harmony, in the manner of Stravinsky. A year later his *Quatre études de rythme* for piano became even more abstract. Techniques from these two seminal works appear in the *Messe*. One is a formula in which three rhythmic figures are used simultaneously: one repeats unchanged, one methodically increases the value of each of its notes, and the third diminishes in the same way. Poetically, Messiaen likens them to actors in a play: one is a neutral onlooker, passive; one is moving the action forward, becoming stronger; the third is being dominated, weakening.

They come on stage in the 'Offertoire', the second movement, where the music of the first bar, in the Hindu *tritîya* rhythm, never changes, that of the second (*caturthaka*) augments by three demisemiquavers each time it repeats, and that of the third diminishes by one demisemiquaver. Soon a related technique arrives, the *durées chromatiques*. Here the three parts (right hand, left hand and pedal) are serialized by duration. In the top part the first note lasts one semiquaver, the next two, the third three and so on, up to five; the pattern then repeats. In the left hand the first note lasts five semiquavers, the second four, the third one, the fourth two, the fifth three, and then the pattern repeats as 5, 4, 1, 3, 2, and further permutations. The pedal line is similarly organized (see Ex. 13.3). Messiaen calls this technique *interversions sur durées chromatiques*; they appear in their simpler direct form in the astonishing heart of the 'Sortie'. This is the last movement, a breathtaking toccata where the 'rushing mighty wind' of the Holy Spirit is created by great sweeps of the brush. Then an ecstatic chorus of larks, chosen because they fly higher than any other bird and so symbolize the greatest freedom, celebrate the message that liberates the Apostles, singing over two lines that respectively diminish and augment by one unit at a time: i.e. in the left hand the first note lasts twenty-three semiquavers, the next twenty-two and so on down to one, with in the pedal the reverse, from four to twenty-five (see Ex. 13.4). As always with Messiaen there is both a technical and a philosophical element in play; he compares this process to kinematics – the science of moving bodies – and to two streams of time, flowing in different directions at different speeds. John Cage's criticism of Messiaen is incomprehensible: 'Messiaen's rhythm is rigid, since Messiaen knows no accelerando and rallentando; he knows no bending of time, he always just patches one thing to another.'[5] On the contrary, the proper realization of the rhythmic elements employed here (if, possibly, not in every later work) creates an impetus that contains within itself great flexibility.

The *valeurs irrationelles*, apparently most rigid of all, are designed to create just that flexibility. To open the work Messiaen uses classical Greek rhythms (iambic, trochaic etc) but treated, he says, in 'irrational values'. The term is forbidding

EX. 13.3 *Messe de la Pentecôte* 2 'Offertoire'

EX. 13.4 *Messe de la Pentecôte* 5 'Sortie'

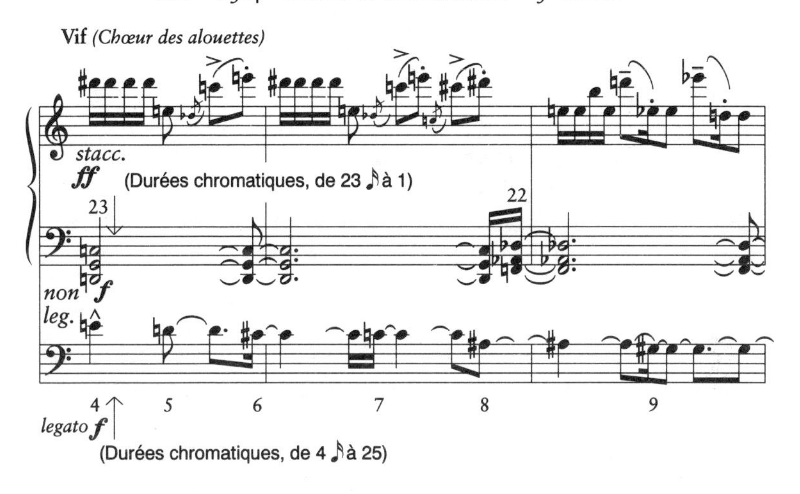

but implies the compression and expansion of traditional groupings of weak and strong so as to produce a feeling of changing tempos – a quick triplet followed by one more expansive, perhaps. To project the freedom that remains the *raison d'être* of these rhythms, as with all the others, it is essential that the performer find a way to view them entire and complete. They look so complex that a student will often determinedly set out to master them by counting in the smallest possible unit, hoping to produce a computer-like exactitude. The result is to remove all the character of their individuality, both as personalities (a triplet, a quintuplet) and within the context. Rather, their sound-shape must be comprehended and absorbed, and then set against the rudder of a larger, unchanging unit (such as the quaver, in this first movement). And then, although the various figures and/or voices will of course be played at the same time, each must maintain its freedom – achieved by an aural perception that remains aware of the activity within each part but recognizes that they may not of themselves be interacting. The question is often asked: is rubato possible in such a strictly notated score? The answer is certainly yes; it is subtle but always present, to enliven and to personalize the music as in any other score. The difference between this music and, say, Widor's is that in the essentially homophonic Widor the rubato will be on a bigger scale and across the stave; that is, the parts will support one another's fluctuations. It is like looking at a vast painting describing a scene filled with activity; the gaze shifts from one detail to another, but without one's losing awareness of others or of the whole. So there is neither anarchy nor tyranny, but a democracy that respects the freedom of the individual while perceiving the relationships that link him with all that goes on about him.

With this realization the conventional idea of development in music becomes unnecessary and Messiaen's conception of time is clarified. We are trapped in a linear concept of time in which event follows event, note follows note. But now that scientists are questioning time's immutability by postulating its flowing backwards, or the possibility of time travel, we can consider its essential unreality and give the idea, like a hanging prism, a half-turn to reveal another side. If one is present everywhere at once then time ceases to exist, and just as the painter's eye sees the whole and the part simultaneously so the musician can assimilate the relationships and throw off time's fetters without forfeiting its energy: stasis without stagnation. Undoubtedly Messiaen named his *Quatuor pour la fin du temps* with something like this in mind, and not as a reference to the end of the world.

The teeming images of the Mass's second movement, the 'Offertoire', make up a kaleidoscopic picture that illustrates this well. The composer quotes from the Nicene Creed, 'things visible and invisible', and writes:

> Things visible and invisible! There is everything in these words! Dimensions known and unknown: from the possible diameter of the universe to that of a proton, durations known and unknown: from the age of galaxies to that of the wave associated with the proton, the spiritual world and the material world, grace and sin, angels and men, the powers of light and the powers of darkness, the vibrations of the atmosphere, plainsong, birdsong, the melody of waterdrops and the growling of the monstrous Beast of the Apocalypse – finally, all that is clear and tangible, and all that is obscure, mysterious and supernatural, all that goes beyond science

and reasoning, all that we cannot uncover, all that we will never understand . . .[6]

The Beast growls on a powerful Basson; its low C recurrently emerges from the sea of images. There is birdsong and plainsong (the grace-notes of the latter also suggesting the former), shimmering modal colours, ominous throbbings and the splashing of waterdrops. In an especially imaginative passage Messiaen portrays waterdrops (on Flute 4′, 1′ and Tierce) falling onto the same notes – but played legato – in the pedal; apart from being strikingly evocative it gives the impression that the droplet has spread along the cool line drawn by the pedal (see Ex. 13.5). The diversity is unified by the connections made subconsciously which are enhanced by the timbres and their subtle references. The fourth movement is for the 'Communion (les oiseaux et les sources)'. It opens with a bird calling as from the depths of a wood – its song ends in a flurry like the rustle of wings when it is startled from a tree. Fountains sigh and the cuckoo and nightingale call, and then there is a rapturous cantilena for the birds, whirling against a background of waterdrops falling from different heights (and therefore of constantly shifting lengths). The justification for all these sounds of nature is that it is customary after the Communion to recite the canticle of the Three Young Men who were thrown into a burning fiery furnace but not

EX. 13.5 *Messe de la Pentecôte* 2 'Offertoire'

consumed and sang there a hymn of praise from all creation: 'O all ye works of the Lord, bless ye the Lord! O all ye fowls of the air, bless ye the Lord!' The piece ends with the drops ascending in pitch to the highest note possible on the organ, played on a 1′ stop, while the pedal supports them on the lowest note, a C on the 32′; the symbolism is the all-embracing nature of the love of God.

The central movement, for the consecration, celebrates the gift of wisdom, one of the seven gifts of the Holy Spirit. It consists of a plainsong theme (almost exactly the second alleluia of the Whitsun Mass) in alternation with two chordal passages. These remain the same each time, but the plainsong changes and grows. The pedal has an angular melody on a strident 4′ Clarion in one of the repeated motifs, and each of its notes is coloured by the shifting harmonies and timbres of the chord accompanying it, so that the linear melody has a ghostly partner, what Messiaen calls a 'melody of resonance' and a 'melody of timbres' (see Ex. 13.6).

In its austerity, this movement presaged Messiaen's next work, the *Livre d'orgue*. The title is a classical French term, used often to describe a collection of suites or smaller pieces by Messiaen's eighteenth-century predecessors. Never one to reject the past, but rather to possess and store all that it has to offer, to be poured out eventually in a new form, Messiaen gave the

EX. 13.6 *Messe de la Pentecôte* 3 'Consécration'

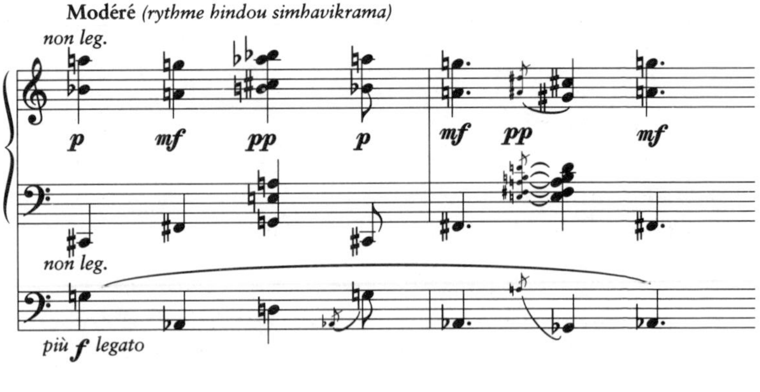
Modéré (rythme hindou simhavikrama)
non leg.
p
mf
pp
p
mf
pp
mf
non leg.
più f legato

name to a collection of seven pieces summing up all his rhythmic techniques in a magnificent synthesis. He gave the premiere in Stuttgart in 1953, inaugurating the organ at the Villa Berg; the second performance was at his own church of La Trinité for one of Pierre Boulez's Marigny concerts, to an audience of some 2000 people. (The composer was almost lost in the crush; he had to protest that there would be no performance unless he could gain entry, effected eventually by a side door, and the performance began forty minutes late. Messiaen lost two buttons from his overcoat and the chief of police, attending privately as an enthusiast, was crushed in the crowd.) The work is worlds away from the *Livres d'orgue* of Dumage and Raison, or the *Orgelbüchlein* of Bach. Working within stringent formal strictures Messiaen engages in a kind of musical isometrics – a strengthening of the muscles by pushing them against an unbending framework. But Messiaen's test of strength is made against more than superficial musical structure; taking up the ideas he had probed in the *Messe* he carries them to their ultimate conclusion, affirming that intensities, timbres and note-lengths have an importance equal to sounds.

Organization reaches its apogee in the first piece, 'Reprises par interversion'. Three Hindu rhythms become rhythmic personages, but in music that is entirely monodic. This music is then repeated but in the form, Messiaen says, of a 'closed fan' (*éventail fermé*): that is, the first note of this material is followed by the last, then comes the second note and the penultimate, and so on until we reach the middle note. Part 3 reverses this process – the fan opens: we go from the middle to the outer (so it is Part 2 backwards), and Part 4 is a palindrome of Part 1. The pitches, durations and timbres remain the same throughout; it is worth noting however that sometimes a pair or more of notes are used together rather than its being a literal note-by-note transference. The idea of the fan breathes a hint of the poetic over an alarmingly bleak landscape. Messiaen explains:

> in ancient art, gothic and romanesque cathedrals and even in modern art, the decorative figures ornamenting the pediments of the portals are nearly always two symmetrically inverse figures

> framing a neutral central motif. Ancient magical formulae included words which had, it appears, an occult power. It was impossible to read these words from left to right, then from right to left, without meeting exactly the same sound and the same order of letters. In nature we have an exquisite example: the wings of a butterfly. When butterflies are enclosed in their chrysalis, their wings are folded and stuck one against the other; the pattern on one is thus reproduced in the opposite direction on the other. Later, when the wings unfold, there will be a pattern with colours on the right wing which mirror those on the left, and the body of the butterfly, the thorax and the antennae placed between the two wings constitute the central value.[7]

He points out that this formula (called by him in certain contexts a non-retrogradable rhythm, since the pattern is the same when reversed) can be seen in ourselves – the symmetry of eyes, ears, nose, etc; and in the ultimate: the eternity that lies on either side of our every movement.

The last movement of the seven is even more complex. Called simply 'Soixante-quatre durées', it is described in the score by the composer as 'sixty-four chromatic durations, from one to sixty-four demisemiquavers – inverted in groups of four, from the extremes to the centre, forwards and backwards alternately – treated as a retrograde canon. The whole peopled with birdsong.' The rhythmic series consists of sixteen groups of four note-values each, augmenting and diminishing in sequence, alternately. The manuals begin the series as (in demisemiquaver values) 61, 62, 63, 64; 4, 3, 2, 1; 57, 58, 59, 60; 8, 7, 6, 5 – and so on. On the pedals two voices are presenting the pattern in retrograde. Some licence is taken, as when a cadenza whose note-values total the necessary thirty-eight takes over from the note itself (see Ex. 13.7). It strains credulity to believe that the listener is meant to hear the minute differences in duration as the piece unfolds. Indeed Messiaen said that in this piece he had 'pushed to the extreme limits of human perception very long and very short durations. And, something even more difficult, the perception of very small differences between very long durations.'[8] However he also said that he deplored the weakness of human perception in this respect and, concerning the sixty-four

EX. 13.7 *Livre d'orgue* 7 'Soixante-quatre durées'

durations: 'If I can think them, read them, play them, and hear them, all sixty-four, with their differences, others should be able to.'[9]

An intimidating, though fascinating, exercise in mathematical ingenuity. But the birdsongs scattered through the piece transform it into a landscape again, albeit lonely and cold. The unbroken succession of chords creates slowly shifting patterns of light that form a stark backdrop for the strange and remote calls of birds; there are two extended flurries as they are disturbed and beat their wings in agitation, while the accompaniment flows gravely on, dispassionate, detached. The absence of a recognizable form of development in either its Classical or Romantic meaning or, alternatively, of a programme (as in a *Sorcerer's Apprentice* or even a *Rite of Spring*), made this music eminently resistible to many, especially when familiar rhythmic attributes seemed also to be missing. But Messiaen is not concerned to present an argument, or explain, or even describe; he evokes, and when the listener has learned in what manner to respond, the pull is infinitely compelling. While the analyst focuses on the intricacy of the rhythmic devices, the real fascination lies in the way a sense of movement as gentle as the forming and reforming of clouds but as inexorable as the pull of the tides is driving the music. To experience this it is not necessary to be able to deconstruct its elements but only to capitulate and allow the music to refine the ear to its subtleties.

That said, I confess it is difficult to respond to the first piece, in which the leaps in the line and the nature of the stipulated sounds combine to defeat the ear, however willing it may be to follow. Monody is not necessarily melody. And is it still composition, when, given the initial material and the formula, the player could write it himself? Pierre Boulez has spoken in puzzlement of Messiaen's separation in his mind of technique and the music.[10] Here the technique does seem to have replaced the music rather than to be serving it. It may be that Boulez himself had a role in pushing Messiaen in the direction of such extremes. Messiaen's greatness as a teacher is legendary and he exerted a decisive influence on such younger composers as Barraqué, Stockhausen and Boulez; as the fruits of his own teaching ripened, especially in the works of Boulez, so he must have been newly stimulated himself to test his theories to the limit. In the fifties he said that the questions and the attitude of such as these 'compels me to new researches of which I might not have dreamt without them'.[11] Much has been said of Messiaen's endearing humility; this could on occasions amount almost to a curious insecurity – perhaps the less curious when one remembers the violence of the criticism he endured at the start of his career. Fortunately, insecurity can be a powerful spur to achievement.

Of the other five movements four are also strictly organized, but Messiaen supplies ideas to fuel the imagination. There are two trios, both dedicated to the Trinity. The first, which illustrates St Paul's familiar 'For now we see through a glass darkly', superposes a succession of Hindu rhythms. The composer's comment is intriguing: 'Here I utilized the different moving lines not only melodically but rhythmically, which permitted me, like the hero of Wells's time machine, to remount the stream of time and also to detach myself from it.'[12] It is the quality of detachment that alienates, especially the listener used to riding the leaping rhythms of Vivaldi or coasting on the soaring emotions of the Romantics. But I can attest that this piece does become a living entity, with a deeply satisfying sense of movement; and that the mood perfectly conveys the mystery of the text. Referring to the virtues of Asiatic thought, the philosopher Romain Rolland said that from it Europeans could 'learn the virtues of tranquillity, patience, manly hope, unruffled joy; as the *Bhagavad-Gita* says, it is "like a lamp in a windless place, that does not flicker" '. This last image is exactly right for Messiaen's music when it appears static in that there is no overt movement but is in fact alive, vital, *breathing*.

During the summer of 1950 Messiaen had retreated as usual to his favourite refuge in the mountains of the Dauphiné. He used to proclaim, 'I am a man of the mountains, like Berlioz',[13] and said of the *Livre d'orgue*: 'The whole work is under the sign of the mountains of the Dauphiné.'[14] This is most obvious in 'Les mains de l'abîme', for the time of Penitence, which is prefaced by the words: 'the deep uttered his voice, and lifted up his

EX. 13.8 *Livre d'orgue* 3 'Les mains de l'abîme'

R: voix humaine (avec trémolo), nazard $2\frac{2}{3}$, bourdon 16
Pos: tierce $1\frac{3}{5}$ et piccolo 1 (tout seuls)

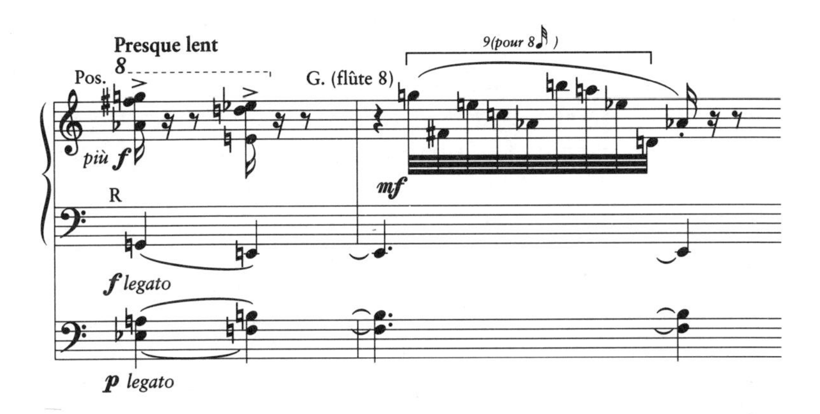

hands on high'. The full organ howls in anguish, hands stretch up from the gorges in the Romanche valley, imploring deliverance from terror. In between, slow-moving counterpoint in bizarre tone-colours powerfully conveys the coldness of ice, the desolation of great spaces, the cracking of crevasses (see Ex. 13.8). For Messiaen this was musically the best piece, but he accorded the second trio (No. 5) the accolade 'my greatest rhythmic triumph'.[15] It was composed in sight of the Meije, Râteau and Tabuchet glaciers, and the Hindu rhythms that shape the symbolic three voices undergo complicated permutations. As with the *Reprises* it is hard to perceive the piece as music, but given the three voices its failure to project an identity is more problematic. With three lines there is harmony, harmony gives emotion, from emotion comes meaning and thus – in that a message, or at least a mood, ensues – should come music. If the failure is the composer's and not mine, perhaps Furtwängler has supplied a pointer: 'Rhythmic complexities . . . must be kept within natural limits, if they are to play their full and vital functions side by side with the elements of melody and harmony.'[16] Of course this presupposes a subservient role for rhythm with which Messiaen may not have agreed.

The sixth movement is a tumultuous toccata of great difficulty to play. Called 'Les yeux dans les roues' it is for Whitsun. Analysis reveals its six sections (a note-row is thoroughly exploited and the durations in the pedal serialized) but it is heard as a spectacular evocation of the flashing eyes in the wheels of Ezekiel's prophecy and an explosive Wind of the Holy Spirit.

The stark 'Abîmes' and abstruse second trio are separated by the only movement in free rhythm. For Easter, it is called simply 'Chants d'oiseaux' and consists almost entirely of an aviary of birdcalls. Messiaen names both the birds and the places where he heard them. Even before his teacher Paul Dukas had adjured him, 'Study the birds. They are great masters', Messiaen had been obsessed with birdsong, and after the *Oiseaux exotiques* he announced that he would devote the rest of his life to collecting birdsong and writing music on it. Asked to describe himself he would say, 'I am an ornithologist and a rhythmist',[17] and would compare his study of the science of birdsong with landscape painters going into the woods and beside the rivers to take lessons in design, colour and lighting; punning on *les corps glorieux* he called the birds *les corps enseignant* – the teaching profession. But although birds had winged their way through the *Messe de la Pentecôte* they were still being used there as just one of the sounds of nature. In the 'Chants d'oiseaux' they become the whole composition, as they had comprised most of the great piano works of the fifties. It is interesting to note that the nature of the birdcalls can change radically on transfer from one instrument to another. Who would have thought that the gentle nightingale, marked *ppp* much of the time here and given to a haunting combination of flutes, would become loud and fierce in the piano music?

One of the factors is the context. Until I made a study of birdsong I belonged to the category on which Messiaen threw scorn: 'Most people think birds just go pi-pi-pi!'[18] Revelation lies in the discovery that the songs are highly elaborate, with choruses and sequences that change according to the season or time of day or mood; that there are love-songs, frightened calls and many others, that the young ones are taught their calls, even that some specialize in faking other birds' calls. He used them all, 'in counterpoint or solo, in duos, trios, semi-choruses, grand tuttis – just as they are in nature, in fact'.[19]

It is of course impossible to translate the extremely high

pitches and the infinitesimal intervals exactly. Instead Messiaen gives the shape of the call, transposing its pitch, rationalizing the microtones, transmitting its essence. For years he tramped miles to begin notating songs at 4 a.m.; in later years he would be taken by his wife who supplemented his 'artistic' notation with the precision of a tape recording. He then mixed the two, always staying faithful to the scale of the relationships. Every year he went off for two weeks with an ornithologist to collect songs from all over the world – Chinese birds, New Zealand birds, Persian – he had thirty-eight varieties from South America alone. When he arrived in Australia to launch the mammoth Messiaen Festival with which the Australian Broadcasting Corporation celebrated his eightieth year, when I was honoured to be playing the organ works, his first action was to vanish into the woods in pursuit of the bellbird.

But as always there were two levels of involvement. The complex songs provided a vast supply of rhythmic and melodic material to use as building-blocks, but the birds were also for him the symbol of liberty and epitomized his philosophy of freedom. 'We walk, he flies; we make war, he sings', he said, calling them 'servants of immaterial joy'.[20] He found the calls full of emotion; of the grey curlew's song he said: 'Slow, sad tremolos, chromatic scales, savage trills, and a glissando call tragically repeated express all the desolation of the marine locations.'[21]

He found much that was similar in plainsong and birdsong, and in his next organ work, the *Verset pour la fête de la Dédicace*, they combine. The piece was commissioned by the Paris Conservatoire for its organ *concours* and was written in December 1960 – again a lengthy gap had intervened. It is based on the alleluia and its jubilus with a part of the alleluia versicle, from the Proper of the Mass for the dedication of a church. The music of the church and the forest, nature's cathedral, alternate; after the 'Adorabo' of the versicle the song thrush bursts forth at its most rhapsodic, in a passage marked 'avec une joie étrange'. The two forces intertwine in a central cry of supplication, reaching an ecstatic peak before the grave plainsong returns and an echo of the birdsong recalls also the plainchant Strophicus.

The *Verset* was the first (and only) piece Messiaen wrote for an organ other than his beloved Cavaillé-Coll, and would have needed some adjustment when played there as it exceeded that organ's manual compass. The 1868–71 organ at La Trinité was added to in 1934 and in the mid–1960s was rebuilt by the firm Beuchet-Debierre; eight new stops were added and the action was electrified. A combination system was also added. For Messiaen the most important attribute of an organ was that it should have rich and powerful reeds and well-rounded foundation stops, and be capable of a big *fortissimo*. When I asked him whether he did not admire the subtleties possible with a sensitive mechanical action he said he did, but felt that the tendency at that time to build neo-Baroque organs prevented the playing of 'more powerful' works on new instruments designed to give clarity and brightness to the music of Bach and his contemporaries. He felt that it should be possible to play everything on one instrument (now felt to be contentious) and said: 'My love for the powerful, overwhelming organ (Berlioz called it 'the Pope of instruments') prevents me from preferring the classical type of instrument.'[22]

Controversy abounds concerning the registration of the music when played on other types of organ. Messiaen worked a great deal with the German organist Almut Rössler (whose book[23] is interesting on the subject), in particular at her Beckerath organ in Düsseldorf. This organ is large, but neo-classic, without the sub- and super-octave couplers Messiaen calls for; and although colourful it lacks the enormously forceful French reeds favoured by Messiaen – although French training inclined Beckerath to a style more Gallic than his German colleagues. It has, however, a multiplicity of mutation stops (those giving a pitch other than the unison or its octaves) and Messiaen spent a great deal of time exploring their possibilities. (When he had given the Berlin première of the *Livre d'orgue* in the Hochschule's Konzertsaal he had spoken admiringly of the organ's unusual mutations, the $1\frac{1}{7}'$ and the $\frac{8}{9}'$,[24] and shortly before his death had been discussing the possibility of acquiring a septième for his Cavaillé-Coll.) It emerged that he could be happy to change a direction of 16′, 4′, 2′ (in *Chants d'oiseaux*) to Flute 4′, $1\frac{3}{5}'$, $1\frac{1}{7}'$ and $\frac{8}{9}'$ – a radical translation of pitch as well as of the resulting timbre. When playing *L'Ascension* for him before a festival performance in the seventies I was surprised when he added a Larigot to the 8′ Bourdon for the last section of 'Alléluias sereins' – again a big change. What this last point emphasized was his wish for clarity. Although much of the music brings the acoustic into play as a colour effect and for harmonic complexity as well as for continuity through the rests (for example, in the first and third movements of *L'Ascension*), he certainly did not want the echo-drenched confusion from which some recordings of his music have (barely) emerged. There can be no hard and fast rule for transferring the registrations, but it is essential that the player fully understands the characteristics of the Cavaillé-Coll tradition, and knows those specific features of his own organ that especially delighted him. One of these was the Positif 16′ Basson, very powerful and with an extraordinary timbre in the bass, exploited fully in the 'Offertoire' of the *Messe* and in the later *Méditations*. It is a hollow sound, whose rich harmonies give an ambiguity of pitch in this range that poetically diffuses the sound in a way entirely in accord with his longing for the rainbow-coloured, or for seeing as through a prism. So to substitute a blatant and opaque 16' reed such as a Trombone – too often heard – is absolutely wrong.

The Positif division is partly enclosed; a swell-box houses the Clarinet and the five ranks of the Cornet composé. The foundation stops have intensity and the reeds are ringing and loud. He was very fond of the Positif 16′ Quintaton and used it repeatedly; gentle but with the piquancy of its strong harmonic, its elusive timbre perfectly evoked his sound-world. Playing his organ I was struck by the effectiveness of the Récit swell-box, especially with the combination of 16′ Bourdon and 2′ Flute that supplies the waterdrops in the 'Communion' of the *Messe*. The effect of the many mutation stops increasingly employed was to create a 'phantom' fundamental pitch resulting from the harmonics; it is important to remember that the aim is to build a new colour from the mixing of the pitches, so it is not enough simply to draw any stops giving those pitches. The English and American organ usually scales its mutations much too thinly for this to work; the French tradition is for wide-scale (Flute) mutations which cohere and are transformed in combination.

During its rebuilding in the mid-sixties Messiaen was without the use of his organ for more than two years, and it was not until 1969 that he wrote again for the medium. When at last he was persuaded to return to it he responded with an eighty-minute cycle of nine pieces that took him just a year to complete. He gave the premiere on 20 March 1972 at the basilica of the National Shrine in Washington DC, to an audience several thousand strong.

In the course of a lecture series in Spain in the late sixties he said: 'I fear nothing, not even the common chord',[25] and with the huge *Et exspecto resurrectionem mortuorum*, marked by basic harmonies and hammered, straightforward rhythms, he seemed to have reached the end of his intense rhythmic and harmonic experimentation; his later works project an overall grandiose simplicity even when their texture proves on inspection to be as intricately knit as ever. Apart from one striking innovation, the general impression in the *Méditations sur le mystère de la Sainte Trinité* (his organ, interestingly, is dedicated to the Holy Trinity) is that the swirling ideas and questing of almost half a century had crystallized into a compositional technique so natural that by using it as a language the composer could communicate from heart to heart. Indeed, the idea of music as a language seems so to have caught Messiaen's imagination as to have led him into an attempt to capture its very grammar. As both game and discipline (when I asked him about it he laughed and said, 'C'est un jeu'), Messiaen invented (and used here for the first time) a 'communicable language', for which he gave to each letter of the alphabet a fixed musical note – fixed in pitch and duration as well as musical name. Furthermore, he devised a musical motif for important verbs such as *to be* and *to have*, and another used in different forms for each member of the Trinity – Father, Son and Holy Spirit. For further clarity he applied the Latin system of cases; a set musical formula placed before each noun indicates its case. Using this precise language he is able to spell out explicitly the passages from St Thomas Aquinas which in this form make up the whole of the third movement and large parts of the first and seventh. (Messiaen's 'communicable language' is also discussed in Richard Steinitz's chapter in this book, pp. 466–8.)

Are we expected, as listeners, to translate this? Effectively, Messiaen says 'Yes', and implies that even without knowing its title or composer future listeners will be able to deduce his basic beliefs from the music. The idea was born when he read how the Egyptian hieroglyphics on the Rosetta Stone were deciphered by Champollion, the scholar and linguist who lived in Messiaen's home town of Grenoble in the time of Napoleon I. Rings around four words on the Stone gave the clue: they must be the names of kings; and by using Coptic to read these Champollion was able to decode the rest. The feat greatly impressed Messiaen, already fascinated by numbers and patterns and mysteries of all kinds, and he chose to honour in his own language the name of the *divine* king. He was entranced by the notion that one could send down the centuries a message that could be received with perfect clarity even when the original code was lost. He argued that languages could be based on movements, images, colours, even on fragrance, and pointed to the Braille alphabet, based on touch. He cited Wagner and his leitmotifs, and spoke of the angels, and their power to communicate without consideration of time or place but simply through thought.

Certainly such instantaneous perception leaves words – clumsy, imprecise and inadequate vehicles for our ideas – far behind. Might one not argue however that it is a step backwards to resort to this form of words; words moreover not in poetic form, which does manage to carry the profundities of thought a little farther on their journey, but words at their most prosaic, spelt out, dismantled machines. Words are the visible shapes of thought, struggling to express sensations and emotions and ideas by compressing them into fixed, preconceived patterns, the spoken word able to add only one dimension to the written by its addition of cadences and emphasis. But music has no such restrictions and can side-step the whole process, at a stroke reaching below the surface to the original untrammelled thought and triumphantly winging it directly into the mind or heart of the listener – almost like the speech of angels.

But perhaps the composer seeks to transmit only passionless equations, such as the one spelt out in the new language in *Méditation III*: 'True relationship in God is really identical with essential being.' This brief movement is the only one in which the communicable language is heard right through. An angular right-hand line traces the statement; in Indian rhythms the other two voices ponder it, producing a remarkable example of sustained polyphonic writing. Let him have his game: the musical effect is what matters. Of the nine meditations this is the only one posing problems of comprehension, but finally it is convincing, its inner tension sweeping the stark, majestic lines along in an unbroken curve, even if it is hard to say whether it succeeds because of the 'communicable language' or in spite of it.

It has a relatively small part in the cycle as a whole. In this masterly work all the familiar hallmarks are present: the modes of limited transposition, Hindu and Greek rhythms, plainsong, birdsong, waterdrops, notes of added value, colour combinations, and symbolism in various forms including the frequent use of groups of three or 3 × 3 (nine meditations, nine-note figure of God, ternary rhythms). An important difference emerges, however, with his use of plainsong: for the first time the Gregorian melodies are virtually unaltered. In the earlier works, the *Verset* for example, curiously distorted forms of the chant – 'as though seen through a prism or stained glass' – have given an impressionistic effect. Just as Messiaen had said that in homage to Debussy he would never use the pentatonic scale except hidden or in disguise, so it had seemed previously that these sacred melodies would appear only covertly. Each of the nine movements celebrates some attribute of the persons of the Trinity, and the jubilant shout in octaves of the 'Alléluia de la dédicace' launching the second meditation does full honour to its theme, 'God is holy!' Plainsong plays a vital role in the consummate manipulation of ebb and flow, tension and release, by which Messiaen magnificently unifies the complete work, giving the concept of form a new dimension. He uses emotions, colours and tempos as well as rhythms, harmonies and melodies as an integral part of the whole, to propel the music forward or to suspend all sense of time at will.

EX. 13.9 *Méditations sur le mystère de la Sainte Trinité*
I 'Le Père des étoiles'

The first movement shows Messiaen's power to create musical patterns that vividly suggest visual shapes. The theme is 'the Father of the stars', and on full organ Messiaen sets them revolving (see Ex. 13.9). This skill had earlier conjured up angels whirling from the sky to drop gently to earth before the infant Christ in 'Les anges' (*La Nativité*). Variations follow the first bold statement and a passage from Aquinas's *Summa Theologica* is quoted in the communicable language before the stars wheel and a spectacular burst of sound spells out the final word, '*inengendré*'. The second meditation concerns the holiness of God, and is in two 'panels' with a coda; after the radiant plainsong comes much birdsong and subtly coloured chords. The ending is magical: a yellow-hammer's song floats from the distance, holding the music in suspense, poised in eternity. It will return after the tumult of the fifth movement and again after the eighth, acting as a leitmotif and each time restoring the work's serene equilibrium.

After the asceticism of the third movement the fourth blazes with colour. Its theme is God as I AM, He whose name cannot be known. Messiaen writes: 'All that we can know of God is summarized in these words so complex and yet so simple: HE IS. These are words we can understand only in flashes . . . dazzling glimpses, instants of comprehension.'[26] Birds take centre stage again, but this is no gentle twittering; they flash past like brilliantly coloured tropical birds startled from their hiding-place, portrayed on the tutti or with bizarre combinations of Clarion and Mixture. These are interspersed with soft trillings from the shadows and a glittering motif, marked 'like silk tearing'. The climax is ecstatic: on full organ comes 'the vision of Moses: and I AM passed before him proclaiming I AM, I AM!' After a long silence the owl of Tengmalm calls from the distance and fades into the darkness, evoking the vastness of space and symbolizing the smallness of man before the mystery of the great 'I AM', 'overpowered by the flashing light of the sacred'.

Until now there has been a sense of immense power contained. First, three themes depict the attributes for meditation: God is immense, eternal, immutable; and then the breath of the Holy Spirit explodes in an electrifying toccata. It burns out, giving way to the sighing cadences of 'God is love', and the movement ends with, again, the benediction of the yellowhammer. The form can be seen as an inverted V, as can the entire work; despite an apparent lack of structure and the fragmentary nature of much of the material the emotional tension increases inexorably until the blaze of virtuosity at the centre of this movement lifts the work to a brilliant peak, before gradually subsiding to merge once more with the quiet sea of sound whence it came.

The sixth movement celebrates the Son as 'Life and Light of men'; rhapsodic plainsong themes in 'white-gold' harmonies leap into life. In the luminous seventh meditation, on the Holy Spirit as the medium of love, Messiaen's 'oiseau de Persépolis'

EX. 13.10 *Méditations sur le mystère de la Sainte Trinité*
8 'Dieu est simple'

makes its début, its artless song a touching contrast to the formalism of the communicable language it is set against. The bare, unadorned plainchant of the alleluia for All Saints opens the eighth: 'God is One'. Of the myriad effects that follow, one in particular enchants: chords coming towards each other from opposite parts of the keyboard 'like a fan closing' (see Ex. 13.10).

The final movement, 'I AM THAT I AM', is a riot of colour and movement and song, held together by affirmations of the opening 'theme of God'. Birdsong has been *primus inter pares* throughout, and as the work comes slowly to rest the innocent call of the garden warbler, fresh and sweet, emerges out of the passion and tumult and the work ends in peaceful simplicity with a last call from the yellow-hammer.

During the seventies Messiaen seemed to have forsaken the organ. Once unwilling to travel he had become an intrepid voyager, giving much pleasure by his readiness to oversee detailed rehearsals of his orchestral works and to be present at the increasing number of festivals of his music. It was to approach the mystery at the heart of the church, the sacrament of Communion, that he took up his pen again for the organ. He wrote the eighteen-movement *Livre du Saint Sacrement* in 1984 in response to a commission from the American Guild of Organists for their biennial National Convention, held this time in Detroit, and the world premiere was given there by Almut Rössler (at Messiaen's request) on 1 July 1986. The venue had been chosen by the composer from a description of the organ's specification, but the (Methodist) church was acoustically dead, the organ ciphered, and the reception was mixed as the audience sweltered in Michigan's stifling summer heat through re-starts caused by the organ's problems. The work struggled against an inadequate organ and arid acoustics again when Rössler gave the French premiere at the Radio France studio the following May, but came into its own when she repeated the performance at La Trinité two days later, where the church's visual and acoustical beauty embraced and enhanced the work. The piece's great length was, however, questioned as it became more widely known. (Indeed, very curiously, the composer himself was twice[27] reported as being 'somewhat apologetic' about the piece, though this was probably simply his customary modesty.) Some *longueurs* are perhaps to be expected in nearly two hours of music; the solution may lie in the title. As in 1951, Messiaen used the word *Livre*, with its connotations of a collection, and half-way through he indicates the place for an interval should a complete performance be given. His choice of words makes it clear that such is not mandatory; it is the only time that he made such a comment in a score. Although there is an overall theological plan for the work its sections are not related thematically as are those of, say, *Les corps glorieux*, and there is not the inexorable progression of tension and release in a readily identifiable shape that unifies the *Méditations*.

Individual movements however are magnificent. There is a theological plan: the first four movements are acts of adoration before Christ who, though unseen, is present in the sacrament. The next seven describe chronologically events in the life of Christ, each one representing one of the mysteries that are given through the sacrament. The last seven bring us to the present and concern the transubstantiation, and make other allusions to the moment of Communion. There is a touching simplicity in the opening two pieces and a warm familiarity in the tone-colours.

EX. 13.11 *Livre du Saint Sacrement* 2 'La Source de Vie'

The favourite combination of 16′ Quintaton with Nazard flows serenely above an unbroken curtain of sound provided by chords in left hand and (double) pedal; their harmonies shift only slightly, drifting from one to the next like light floating down dustbeams from a stained-glass window, an exquisite device (used effectively also in the second of the *Méditations*; see Ex. 13.11). New birds, from the Holy Land, appear in No. 3; the coolly impersonal Tristram's grackle (notated between Messada and the Dead Sea) and the olivaceous warbler (from Lod, near Tel Aviv) are interspersed with tenderly harmonized, sighing chords and plainsong, providing a study in contrasts. The fourth movement, 'Act of Faith', strides confidently into being. Messiaen has used exuberantly repeated staccato chords before to project power, in 'Force et agilité des corps glorieux'; here again the music is bursting with vitality.

The first of the narrative sections, No. 5, speaks of the Nativity, 'A child is born to us', and the first three notes of the plainsong 'Puer natus est' form a figure used throughout, rather like a birdcall itself, to punctuate murmuring cascades of semiquavers interspersed with the horn-like motif familiar from the *Méditations*. But Messiaen still has surprises to spring: No. 6 sets a scene of desolation on a Cymbale used alone – strikingly effective. The theme is the Bread of Life, the music seeking to depict the desert where manna fell from heaven. Desert birds call plaintively and the persistent wind nags the ear on extended multiple trills, swelling and receding (see Ex. 13.12).

Jesus's sermon on the Bread of Life foretold the Resurrection, and the seventh piece begins by proclaiming it *ffff* in communicable language, 'RESURRECTION!' The movement has a stark strength and directness that is almost brutal; it is much more than energy, and has a flavour subtly different from any of the earlier works. One might have expected a softening from the older composer, but the opposite seems to have occurred. But all is sweetness in the eighth movement, recalling Christ's institution of the Eucharist, an interlude for reflection before No. 9, 'the shadows'. Three forms of darkness are depicted in chilling style, ending with the eeriness of a chord containing all thirteen notes of the octave held low on the keyboard and dissolving into nothingness (see Ex. 13.13). The tenth pictures the Resurrection itself in rainbow-coloured chords that surge up the keyboard. A major scena is created with the next movement, a lengthy piece of programme music describing the appearance of the risen Christ to Mary Magdalene. A sense of wonder and gathering joy is projected as light dawns both literally and figuratively and Mary recognizes the identity of 'the gardener'; it is genuinely moving. For those armed with an explanation of the events being illustrated it remains affecting to the end, though it is perhaps arguable that, purely as music, the rest of the movement is somewhat fragmented, despite its many individual beauties and undoubted sincerity. It is underpinned by passages in 'communicable language', including the three interrelated themes for the Persons of the Trinity first encountered in the *Méditations*. The vision fades away with the consoling consonance of a C major chord low on the keyboard. With the last group of pieces we are in the church today, with the seven movements centring on the act of Communion. 'The Transubstantiation' (No. 12) recalls the second trio of the *Livre d'orgue* in its angularities and rhythms, although it is less complex, but here it vies with harmonized birdsong. The movement ends with a memory of the Christmas plainchant. The dramatic

EX. 13.12 *Livre du Saint Sacrement* 'La manne et le Pain de Vie'

EX. 13.13 *Livre du Saint Sacrement* 9 'Les ténèbres'

EX. 13.14 *Livre du Saint Sacrement* 13 'Les deux murailles d'eau'

heart of the cycle comes in the virtuoso thirteenth movement, 'The two walls of water'. Messiaen links philosophically the presence of God in the walls of water that parted the Red Sea with the actual presence of Christ in the broken Host and the two ideas alternate, expressed by tumultuous cascades of sound on full organ and the song of the melodious warbler. In the middle comes an immensely effective device: violent arpeggios in contrary motion seem to tear the keyboard apart, a quaver rest between each allowing the sound to swirl and mount. In the *Vingt regards* he had used this technique after noting it on the harp; it is even more savage on the organ (see Ex. 13.14).

'Prayer before Communion' (No. 14) alternates innocent plainchant with richly harmonized chords softly reflecting – the humility of 'I am not worthy' with the trust in forgiveness; the joy of the act itself is given entirely to the rapturous birdsong that makes up the fifteenth movement, and the contemplation afterwards (No. 16) harks back to No. 2 with its hovering melody and the gauze curtain of sound supplied by the left hand chord that gently shifts its harmonies a note or two at a time, like soft colours advancing and receding in the light, or indeed like the wafting of sweet perfumes, as in the quotation from St Bonaventure. The penultimate movement has a steely brilliance again, with an angular melody in double canon thrusting between *fff* chords cast in a throbbing rhythm; the theme is Christ's simultaneous presence in all the consecrated Hosts on earth. The final piece has won greatest popularity; called

EX. 13.15 *Livre du Saint Sacrement* 18 'Offrande et alléluia final'

'Offrande et alléluia final' it recalls ideas and figuration from the end of the *Méditations* but has an even more extrovert sense of assurance. Tossing themes into the air in ecstatic abandon it brings the cycle to a dazzling conclusion, spelling out 'LA JOIE' (see Ex. 13.15).

And so he spelt out his secret. I had first encountered Olivier Messiaen in Washington just after his premiere of the *Méditations*; unable to be at the performance because I was myself committed to playing elsewhere I was very pleased to be given the opportunity of meeting him there soon afterwards. We had arranged brunch, that admirable American institution, and I was relieved when he and Yvonne Loriod finally appeared, as they were an hour late. It was the day on which the time changed, and what more appropriate than that he should be blissfully unaware of it? No problem – except that they were due to fly to Bryce Canyon that day. (He was anxious to know whether there might be donkeys to ride.) I wrestled with my dilemma and resolved it cravenly by staying silent on the matter of the clock but praying fervently they would catch the plane. He was kind enough to offer me the score for a British premiere, and some weeks later it arrived with a generous letter. It was intensely interesting to work from a copy of the manuscript; evident was his attention to detail (such as fingering) and his concern for clarity – the complex chords were spread out in a kind of hill-slope so that every note was easily identifiable. While preparing the work for the Royal Festival Hall premiere. I received from him a recording of his own performance; again fascinating, with its magisterial control and commanding presence, while disconcerting as it often differed in details from the text. In discussion it became clear that the text was what mattered, not any deviations from it that might have appeared when he played it. Not that this meant he wanted a dry, machine-like reproduction of the score; rather that he did not expect his own interpretations to be copied blindly either. Furthermore, a great artist's performances are always different, responsive to the moment. Like any other and despite its precise notation this music must be shaped and moulded by the performer after having been deeply comprehended. His own performances have remained more compelling than any other at present on record because of their sense of authority that comes not simply from his being the composer but from his ability to express the greater freedom that is in the soul of the music.

He checked his scores meticulously; one wrong note escaped into the last organ work and a few into those from the thirties, but on the whole he was extraordinarily exact. The small deviations were chiefly in the tempos. I am frequently asked whether his tempo indications can be assigned a precise marking, as from a metronome, and whether rubato can be permissible in music so intricately rhythmed. As a pedantic child I can remember going with pencil and paper to an adult and demanding literal quantification of *some, a few, many, rather* etc. To effect a like straitjacketing of Messiaen's indications would be equally impossible, and undoubtedly the reason he did not, initially at least, attempt to allot metronome marks. Apart from the obvious consideration of the acoustics (not, in fact, as important as organists traditionally think) the issues are the inner movement provided by the harmonic tension, Messiaen's philosophy of the essential unreality of definitions of time and space, the quality of the tone-colour being used, the nature of the rhythmic figuration (is it intended to be heard as an ebullient triplet or quintuplet, or is it operating at a deeper level), what the relationship of the given passage is with others around it, and a host of others whose conscious identification becomes unnecessary or even undesirable after a lengthy immersion in the style.

What is seriously misleading, however, is the equation of tempo with religious fervour. Naturally the wealth of information and explanation given by the composer himself over his long life concerning his thought processes and the motivation for his music is extraordinarily interesting. As an aid to comprehension and even more as a stimulus actually to enter his perfumed and rainbow-coloured world it is invaluable. He would, however, have been the first to say that one need not be 'a believer' to experience his music, even though that might heighten the appreciation in one direction. It would be doing the music a disservice to suggest that it could not be understood, enjoyed or fully experienced on musical terms alone. One can go further: so personal is the nature of belief that reference to religious terminology can even distort the meaning. There is an apparent paradox here, in that Messiaen sought always to clarify, and he used the dogma of the church on which to hang his musical expositions of the faith. He has often been reverently called a mystic, by those unfamiliar with mysticism, but he himself eschewed that name, and the theology was his text. It is significant that in the *Méditations* he spelt out quotations from St Thomas Aquinas, the great theologian of the church, not from St Thomas à Kempis, her mystic.

But at the end of his life, Aquinas himself said: 'It was all as straw'. In the end the ineffable is the inexpressible, and spiritual communication is made at a level deeper than words can penetrate. Because of this, everyone's understanding of it is different, and an attempt to use what may be a severely limited religious perception as the basis for artistic decisions can confuse and confound (just as a producer eager to reinterpret an oft-performed opera or play in new terms *may* succeed only in diminishing the universality of the myth at its heart to a narrow particularity). In music based on an overtly religious text this often takes the form of proposing a slow tempo for performance; a feeling of devotion has led to one of humility, debasement; and this becomes the mood projected. (For years this was a factor in the performance of parts of *Messiah*, for example, and remains so with much of Bach's music.) But another view, equally widely held and worthy of validation, is that the source of spirituality is joy. Such a view externalizes musically in springing rhythms, exhilarating (though not driven) tempos, and powerful projection. I believe that even though it is arguable that Messiaen himself, in later life, became to some extent dominated by the more structured form of his beliefs (at least when attempting to explain them), the essence of his music at its extraordinary best nevertheless remains the explosive power of its sense of joy, synonymous here with creative energy. This must be (and is) discernible on terms separate from sectarian considerations; on musical terms. Thus to suggest that the principal section of 'Les bergers' (*La Nativité*) should be dragged out solemnly is, I believe, totally to destroy the uncomplicated serenity with which the music jogs happily along, propelled by Messiaen's device of the added rhythmic value.

Speaking in 1977 he said of plainsong that its effectiveness 'is manifested only with animation and joy. If plainchant were sung with the gladness and the rapidity it needs it would be so much loved that we could not live without it.'[28] That does not mean that when it appears in his music it should be played quickly, since it is there used in many different ways; but it is a notable comment, as is the way he makes the important point, 'All music that reverently approaches the divine, the sacred, the ineffable, is truly religious music in the fullest sense of the term', and mentions Mozart's *Die Zauberflöte*, the Japanese 'Gagaku', the great horns of Tibet. It was this view that first precipitated clashes with many critics early in his career. In response to their scandalized cries when his religious texts appeared to have been expressed with sensuous abandon, he spoke of the divine provenance of all love:

> I have the unhappy impression that my enemies know no more about human love than about the sacred texts. They have a petty view of human love . . . I prefer Liszt's attitude, replying to a bore who asked him what he thought of Mme d'Agoult:

'What do I think? But I would throw myself out of the window for her!'[29]

With such extravagance of emotion did the saints hurl themselves into a life of sacrifice. Perhaps the emotion of Messiaen's music is most forcefully paralleled in the metaphysical poets, as Stuart Waumsley has suggested; think of John Donne: 'Batter my heart!', or 'Death, be not proud . . . Death, thou shalt die!'

In his address in Notre Dame in 1977 on sacred music Messiaen ended by quoting St John: ' "Eternal life is to know Thee, the only true God" . . . This knowledge will be a perpetual ecstasy, an eternal music of colours, an eternal colour of musics.'[30] What better epitaph for this inimitable painter in sound.

Notes

1 Claude Samuel: *Entretiens avec Olivier Messiaen* (Paris, Belfond, 1967); translated by Felix Aprahamian as *Conversations with Olivier Messiaen* (London, Stainer & Bell, 1976), p. 5.
2 Ibid., p. 6.
3 Ibid., p. 33.
4 Igor Stravinsky: *Chroniques de ma vie* (Paris, 1935–6); translated as *Chronicle of My Life* (London, Gollancz, 1936), p. 215.
5 Remark by John Cage quoted in Karin Ernst: *Der Beitrag Olivier Messiaens zur Orgelmusik des 20. Jahrhunderts* (Freiburg, 1980), p. 341; translated by Timothy Tikker and quoted in Almut Rössler: *Contributions to the Spiritual World of Olivier Messiaen* (Duisburg, Gilles und Francke, 1986; English translation by Barbara Dagg and Nancy Poland), p. 170.
6 Programme note by Olivier Messiaen, translated by Felix Aprahamian, for a concert at Blenheim Palace in July 1967.
7 Samuel, op. cit., p. 44.
8 Antoine Goléa: *Rencontres avec Olivier Messiaen* (Paris, Julliard, 1960), p. 212.
9 Lecture in Brussels, 1958; quoted in Stuart Waumsley: *The Organ Music of Olivier Messiaen* (Paris, Leduc, 1968, R/1975), p. 49.
10 'Boulez on Messiaen': Roger Nichols in conversation with Pierre Boulez, *Organists' Review*, lxxi/283 (August 1986/3), p. 168.
11 Samuel, op. cit., p. 105.
12 Goléa, op. cit., p. 213.
13 Ibid., p. 19.
14 Ibid., p. 209.
15 Ibid., p. 211.

16 Wilhelm Furtwängler (with Walter Abendroth): *Gespräche über Musik* (Zurich, 1948); English translation (1953) as *Concerning Music.*
17 Samuel, op. cit., p. 33.
18 'Messiaen at 70: Interview with Roger Nichols', *Music and Musicians* (December 1978), pp. 20–2.
19 Goléa, op. cit., p. 227.
20 Goléa, op. cit., p. 234.
21 Ibid., p. 230.
22 Samuel, op. cit., p. 80.
23 Rössler, op. cit.
24 Paul Jordan: 'Karl Schuke: Organbuilder in the 20th Century', *Diapason* (July 1992), p. 14.
25 Nichols: 'Boulez on Messiaen', p. 168.
26 Programme notes by Messiaen, translated by Conrad Bernier, for the premiere of *Méditations sur le mystère de la Sainte Trinité* in Washington DC, March 1972.
27 *Music and Musicians* (December 1987), p. 45; private source.
28 Messiaen: *Conférence de Notre Dame* (Paris, Leduc, 1978)
29 Goléa, op. cit., p. 42.
30 Messiaen, op. cit.

Orchestral Music of the 1950s and 1960s

MALCOLM TROUP

Technique rythmique, inspiration retrouvée pour les chants d'oiseaux, c'est mon histoire.

Messiaen

Messiaen's life and music were all of a piece. The arch-like curve ('anacrouse–accent–désinence') to be found in each page of his music, and which forms the macro-design of entire movements and works, also informs his whole life and production. If one can speak of the first period 1928–39 as the anacrusis and 1964–92 as the terminal period when gigantism, which marks the end of so many epochs, had already set in, that leaves 1941–9 and 1949–63 as the twin high points when Messiaen was at his most influential. The second of these was to be the climactic period in Messiaen's career when he foreswore his box of tricks – his modes of limited transposition and deçî-tâlas – to set forth with only his acute musical ear, of which he was so rightly proud, as guide.

This period is not only marked by his revelling in birdsong for its own sake, and the increasing exploration of synaesthesia within his music but, towards its end, his return to religion in the form of plainchant adaptations, which had marked so much of his beginnings as an organist–improviser. Undoubtedly these have been his three guiding lights, but they should not blind us to the other contributory factors in his make-up: his transcriptive genius, without which his birdsong could not have prospered; his revindication of the keyboard as a fully contemporary instrument; his capacity for recycling ancient compositional techniques in modern dress; and his power to explain all he did patiently and lucidly.

Despite this last point, Messiaen was not able to disarm criticism on the part of those bred up in a tradition of specialization who look aghast at his wanton blurring of the musical margins. Shiva may crop up in the company of Jehovah and we may find ourselves being resurrected to the rhythm of a Hindu *simhavikrama* which itself is interpreted as containing within it a Cretic rhythm! Cultural, historic and stylistic promiscuity was Messiaen's hallmark long before post-modernism had proclaimed its creed. Without even trying, his particular idiosyncrasies have kept him as much in the vanguard now as his *Mode de valeurs et d'intensités* did in launching a new school of total serialism back in the Darmstadt of the 1950s.

In the previous decade, however, he was concerned to match his wits against the younger generation, who flocked to his unorthodox and eclectic classes in music analysis. One of these students was Yvonne Loriod: finding a role for her talents meant equally discovering a new one for the piano and it was here, thanks to the instrument's range, its brittle and chameleon-like nature – as capable of ersatz gamelan as twittering birdsong – that the die was cast. Speaking of the first orchestral work written with Loriod in mind, Messiaen gives an unequivocal description of this new role:

> In my *Trois petites liturgies*, what concerns the piano is as important as the chorus, the vibraphone, the ondes or the strings . . . it is treated to great soloistic prominence but with a diamond-studded role ('rôle de diamentation') which has nothing in common with the style of the Classical concerto.[1]

An influence on his music of the 1950s was from the experimental manipulation of sound. Messiaen had always been fascinated – both as composer and patriot – by *musique concrète* which had (since 1948) been developed in Paris. Twenty years later we still find him paying tribute to the developments which produced his own *Timbres-durées* (1952): 'if you think about it, it isn't the composers who've brought the most renewal to the musical language of the twentieth century but rather electronic music'.[2] One only need listen to the early products of Pierre

Schaeffer's 'school' to realize the new importance of sound itself – particularly ambient sound such as frogs croaking, locomotives at full steam or, however incongruous it may seem in such company, notes on the piano. What Messiaen did from 1950 on was to put some of these same components together after his own fashion – 'I chose the birds – others, the synthesizer.'[3]

Only gradually did the tape recorder take over the laborious manipulation of 78 rpm discs in the domestication of environmental sounds and by that time Messiaen had already found his own way to lower the often unmanageable range of birdsong, to approximate its micro-intervals by a process of proportionate augmentation with the semitone as his basic unit, and to transpose its time-scale along with its pitches to something more graspable by human ears. The British composer Jonathan Harvey still marvels at 'the extraordinary empathy with birds that Messiaen exhibits in those late pieces where something of the intensity, the higher body temperature, the quicker movements, the higher frequency range of utterance and hearing, the shorter lifespan is understood and transferred into the breathtakingly fast, complex and dense bird choruses'.[4]

Réveil des oiseaux

Birdsong has yet another justification in Messiaen's *œuvre*. Before all else and by his own confession, Messiaen is concerned with *time*. Not content simply to 'pass' time he consciously sets out to hypostasize it – to stop time as it were in its tracks, to turn it back upon itself, by a variety of artful dodges known as non-retrogradable rhythms, cancrizans canons and palindromic structures. With such an obsessive preoccupation with time, it is no wonder that Messiaen should devote so much of it to the birds who, long before sundials or astronomical calculations were even dreamt of, acted as our timepieces not only for the divisions of the day but for the seasonal round as well. Their other attributes, in so far as religions go, are too well known to require enumeration: think only of the white dove which is pictured in Christian iconography as whispering the secrets of plainchant into the ear of an attentive St Gregory – the same plainchant which provided Messiaen with much of his melodic inspiration.

At first the intoxication was total and seemed, in a work like *Réveil des oiseaux* (1953), to represent a wilful burning of bridges. Not a trace here of Greek or Hindu rhythms, of modes of limited transposition, of melodic templates – no reliance on outworn props and mainstays, only pure unadulterated bird-song (so far as his tonal system would allow) which in Messiaen's book of emblems stood for freedom. The modes had become something of a liability – limiting rather than limited – and it was not only a relief but a necessity to escape into a freer world of pure chromaticism.

Indeed birdsong provided a way forward, for in the early 1950s the truth is that Messiaen's life, both private and professional, had reached something of an impasse. 'In the face of so many opposed schools, of outmoded styles, of contradictory languages, there is no human music capable of restoring confidence to the despairing one. It is at this point that the voices of Nature intervene.'[5] Such thoroughgoing substitution of nature-worship for religious devotion may indeed have had something to do with Messiaen's inability to undergo a church wedding with Yvonne Loriod (the only sort to which in Catholic conscience he could lend himself) until the death of his first wife in 1959. However that may be, *Réveil des oiseaux* certainly represented a fresh springtime of the spirit – the piece was originally to have been entitled *Le printemps* – as well as an artistic consummation of their partnership when, in 1953, she gave the first performance in the Donaueschingen Festival, where subsequently both *Chronochromie* and *Couleurs de la cité céleste* were to receive their premieres.

It was as much what was absent as what was present in this score that testified to the courage of our composer in wilfully divesting himself of what had become almost an *ars inveniendi* – Hindu rhythms, modes of limited transposition *et al.* Like his great predecessor Rameau, he tried to perform what today we might call an act of phenomenological reduction – 'to put himself in the place of a child who tries to sing for the first time'[6] –

and begin all over again. In *Réveil* for the first time we have the Circadian time-scale which Messiaen was to make so much his own, stretching on this occasion from midnight to noon and making it programme music in the purest sense (as opposed to *Oiseaux exotiques* with its 'musical' structure). Messiaen himself called *Réveil* 'a completely truthful work'[7]; the names of the thirty-eight species meticulously notated in the score along with, in many cases, the onomatopoeic sounds with which ornithologists identify these calls and which were the closest one could come to an accurate notation before the advent of Messiaen's darting piano and woodwinds. Was this hair-splitting concern with authenticity, as Alain Perier implies,[8] born of the desire to confer scientific respectability on this latest obsession, or was it simply a further fruit of his thoroughness and desire to proselytize, as in the case of those endless Darmstadt afternoons where he used to propound his Hindu deçî-tâlas for literally hours on end?

All the public had to hang on to in this avian pot-pourri was its traditional concerto-style presentation by piano and orchestra in a rather relentless alternation of cadenza and ensemble. It was the same combination of piano, strings and 'gamelan' to be found in the *Trois petites liturgies* and *Turangalîla*. Indeed the strings undergo the same treatment as in the *Trois petites liturgies*, where each stringed instrument is frequently soloist. From now on, Messiaen's whole handling of the orchestra, possibly inspired by the dawn chorus, is increasingly that of a collection of individuals. Gone were the lush harmonies, the modes, the rhythmic canons; in their place an uncompromising linear polyphony.

From the very first note of his opening cadenza, Messiaen throws down the gauntlet to tradition by choosing the nightingale, the very songbird (already cultivated by the likes of Couperin, Beethoven and Granados) which had led the way in his own *Quatuor.* Immediately we are launched into a highly astringent series of augmented octaves, major sevenths and tritones (to be played with a pinched, harpsichord-like tone) although not before Messiaen has hammered home a strong point of departure – pitch centre, pivot note, drone, call it what

EX. 14.1a *Réveil des oiseaux*

you will – on F#, thus permitting us to keep our bearings amidst all the far-ranging swoops and scoops which follow (Ex. 14.1a). The birds provided him with exactly the justification he needed for almost unlimited repetition, whether of individual pitches, of melodic figures or of sections. Moreover, the fact that many birds have an extensive but easily recognizable vocabulary meant that he was able to retain the unifying character of their song without outright recapitulation. Most of the time, Messiaen is content for the piano simply to double in octaves or to counterpoint one nightingale in the right hand against another in the left as happens at figure 1 (ex. 14.1b) or as in the trio of

EX. 14.1b *Réveil des oiseaux*

blackbirds between celesta and piano at figure 5 – a style of writing carried over from *Trois petites liturgies*. In one or two cases, however, the composer is already trying his hand at fleshing out the bare bones of birdsong with their timbral (harmonic) implications. Although this generally remains in the primitive stage of parallel chord formations, as with the song thrush (Ex. 14.1c) and golden oriole, the enrichment of the hoopoe's cry (Ex. 14.1d) points the way ahead.

The spontaneous outpouring of this piece forbids any heavy-handed attempt to impose on it our human concern for groupings in twos (binary form) or threes (sonata form), unlike the subsequent *Oiseaux exotiques* where Messiaen's organizing genius was already beginning to subjugate this new-found world

EX. 14.1C *Réveil des oiseaux*

EX. 14.1d *Réveil des oiseaux*

to his innate sense of order. Taking as read the obvious arch-form of alternating cadenzas and ensembles leading up to and away from the grand centrepiece of the dawn chorus, here is Messiaen's own programmatic way of dividing up the work:

Midnight
Four o'clock in the morning
Dawn Chorus
Morning songs
Noon

The profound silences after the dawn chorus and before noon are more programmatic than structural ('With the sunrise, the tutti comes to an abrupt halt'; 'Noon: a great silence'[9]) although there is no denying that the organization of such silences was soon to take over a predominantly structural role in the articulation of such kaleidoscopic images.

The dawn chorus, the first of several of its kind in works by Messiaen, forms the cornerstone of *Réveil*. Beginning with a robin redbreast cadenza on piano, joined later by the blackbird on first violin, the texture gradually thickens until we finish with a total of twenty-one songs distributed among twenty-eight parts including redstart, cuckoo, chaffinch, hoopoe and magpie, some already heard, some new. The section is held together for the listener, on the one hand, by the song of the golden oriole on horns and cellos with an aureole of string sound and, on the other, by the threefold call of the song thrush on trumpet, woodwind and strings (Ex. 14.2). Indeed, this latter song serves to unify the work as a whole, cropping up from figures 15 to 16, 20 to 28, just before 34, and from 37 to 38, the first and last of which share the same ending.

It is this babel of calls which constitutes one of Messiaen's chief claims to originality in his treatment of birdsong, and the only one impossible to realize on the piano, where Messiaen is constrained to lay out his species horizontally rather than vertically, as in the final piano cadenza where the songs of fifteen birds are strung end to end. The first listeners to *Réveil* did not take kindly to what appeared a veritable free-for-all in which the

EX. 14.2 *Réveil des oiseaux*

composer seemed to have abandoned any regulatory function and simply engaged in a mass 'dictée musicale'. Yet an examination of Ex. 14.2 will show how carefully Messiaen calculated the effect, through the painstaking grading of dynamics. If by bringing the sounds of the environment into music he seems to have drawn near the ideas of Cage, Messiaen's birds are nonetheless anything but aleatoric: they are frozen on manuscript once and for all, denied their freedom of movement. It is this which has led so many fellow-composers to denounce Messiaen as having put his birds into cages.[10] Even Halbreich, arch-apologist that he is, finds its metric regularity 'peu naturelle'.[11] This becomes all too evident in the foursquare readings, with their ponderous downbeats, that we often get from conductors attempting to hold this treacherous section together come what may.

Much of the excitement in the works of this period, however can be attributed to the palpable tension between old-fashioned goal-direction and Messiaen's love for symmetry, as evinced by structural palindromes and non-retrogradable rhythms. A good example is provided by *Réveil* where everything breaks off in full spate just before figure 28, which could thus be interpreted as such a midway point. After a generous silence, a piano cadenza leads off the morning songs with that of the blackcap. It is as if we were being treated to an abbreviated replay of what had gone before. Not that the duet of whitethroats on celesta and glockenspiel does more than dwell on the same intervals of the piano's whitethroat cadenza at figure 6 or that the events from figure 32 do more than follow the same sequence of wryneck, little owl, Cetti's warbler, wood lark, song thrush and nightjar without any slavish duplication of material. What makes this hint of recapitulation more significant is that it is conjoined with the same cumulative *procedure* as before – until we reach a total of thirteen voices after figure 33, heralding the return of the golden oriole and wood thrush which had dominated the thick of the dawn chorus (see figures 20 to 28).

Oiseaux exotiques

By the appearance of *Oiseaux exotiques*, composed in the winter of 1955–6 at the behest of Pierre Boulez for his Domaine Musical series, with Yvonne Loriod as soloist, Messiaen's baggage-train had already caught up with his advance guard to the extent that he was now ready to bring into action his Greek and Hindu rhythms, his modes of limited transposition, and his first tentative explorations of *timbres-couleurs*. (At first glance, Messiaen's French expression seems to border on tautology since the accepted meaning of timbre *is* tone-colour. However, Messiaen uses it both in the metaphoric sense – of imparting the appropriate tone-colour to each note of his birdsong by treating it as the fundamental which he then combines with selected upper partials, brought within range, in lieu of chords – *and* in the literal sense of the *colour* of such a tone-complex which he ascribes to it synaesthetically and subjectively.)

With growing confidence his catchment area now extends to India, China, Malaysia and South America, although it is from North America that the bulk of his forty-eight songsters, many of whom we will meet again in *Des canyons aux étoiles . . .* , are drawn. No longer is he limited by Aristotelian unities of geographical proximity or Circadian time-scale. Not only are his individual pitches newly enriched vertically by chords of upper and lower resonance: even in the opening minah call the crisp sonorities of the piano are integrated into the whoosh of the horns' glissandos, one example of the way that purely musical considerations can be seen to play an important shaping role in the argument (Ex. 14.3). No longer are instruments or parts as stratified as before – the olive-backed thrush appearing first on piano and later taken over by clarinets and bass clarinet being only one example of this new confidence to interact instrumentally – while individual birdsongs co-operate as never before to project an overall textural or melodic shape. As Mari remarks,[12] no longer is one quite sure if it is Messiaen singing like a bird or the birds singing like Messiaen! Granted the orchestral resources are modest compared with *Réveil*: strings are conspicuous by their absence and only nineteen players in

EX. 14.3 *Oiseaux exotiques*

all are distributed among woodwind, brass and percussion. However, not a note goes to waste among this 'company of peers'. The same contradistinction in terms of keyboard attack which his teacher Dupré obtained with his Concerto for organ and piano Messiaen now obtains by lining up grand piano and xylophone in percussive propinquity in the front line, not forgetting the two clarinets, which are also given pride of place.

As to the form of the work there is reason enough for seeking to construe the thirteen sections, with their five punctuating piano cadenzas, in terms of those palindromic structures so dear to Messiaen (see Table 1). Certainly the central and closing sections would seem to support such an arch-wise interpretation but there is enough asymmetry to leave room for doubt, and there can be no question of the escalating brilliance and sense of climax towards the close. Within only the first three pages of score, we already have a foretaste of the richness of textures and timbres to come, with no fewer than six contrasting instrumental/motivic cellules, five of which portray the Indian minah and the last of which constitutes the Himalayan laughing thrush's gamelan tutti with which the work is to finish. In this tutti alone not a single instance of orchestral doubling occurs in any of the ten instruments taking part.

The first piano cadenza which follows at figure 3 expands further on the music of the minah, using the constant changes of register which Messiaen subsequently exploited extensively but which were often lacking in the treble-dominated *Réveil*. Gone are the days when left hand slavishly doubled right hand – now although they play synchronously, the octave relationship is the last to occur, the intervals between more likely to be augmented octaves or major ninths, etc, when not laced with timbral harmonizations opening out the whole range of the keyboard. Lessons in the structural utilization of repetition begin to appear with the American wood thrush's oft-repeated exclamation, which serves as the cadenza's climax just as the same call returns, in company with that of the cardinal, to herald the conclusion of the work. In the first ensemble at figure 4, Messiaen calls on a high-pitched homorhythmic woodwind quartet to convey the joyous timbres of the Baltimore oriole complemented by the Malaysian lesser green leafbird on piccolo, the friendly counterpoint of the Californian thrush on xylophone and the Chinese mesia on glockenspiel, all caught up in a repetitive round of calls. This is interrupted by a piano cadenza made up entirely of the brilliantly insistent cries of the Virginian cardinal in groups of two, five and seven which in turn breaks off with the return of the previous ensemble at figure 6 in repeats and extensions of what had been presented previously. Back comes the piano at figure 7 in an exact isorhythmic repeat of the former cardinal cadenza but transposed up. These abrupt but recurrent changes of timbre are not only form-creating but anticipate developments in timbral composition by at least a score of years.

The inner core of the composition is a grand tutti stretching from figures 10 to 22, introduced from 8 to 10 and concluded from 22 to 24 by the sound of thunder in the Amazonian rainforest (a mighty crescendo on the tam-tam) and the prairie chicken taking in air and expelling it in an almighty squawk. Within this central tutti, we have a framework provided by four rhythmic strophes each of which has the same fourfold succession of long-absent Greek metres and rhythms together with Hindu tâlas on unpitched percussion, each in turn identified for those with ears to hear by its own dynamic level and instrument (e.g. Asclepiad on side drum *pp*, Sapphic on woodblocks *p*, *nihçankalîla* on gongs and tam-tam), fleshed out by a variety of birdsongs. These rhythms behave as rhythmic personages, the Greek remaining unchanged while three of the Indian are subject to diminution.

The rhythmic strophes are only one of several homogenizing factors, others being the consistent use of two of the clarinets to convey the unmistakable call of the American robin and the prominence given to the Virginian cardinal, both in the piano part and later in the glockenspiel. Two mockingbirds on horns and trumpets play a key role in this central section from figures 15 to 19 where the partnership of glockenspiel and xylophone has, if anything, the edge on the piano soloistically. However, from figure 17 the piano takes on a more authoritative role, identifying itself with the Indian shama and grounding its mode of limited transposition firmly on E.

The consistent association of certain birds with certain instrumental combinations not only helps towards ease of identification but also gives a distinctly 'terraced' twist to Messiaen's orchestration. An earlier example of this can be found in *Réveil des oiseaux*: 'in order to make the listener's recognition of the bird easier . . . each time the golden oriole appears, it's played by horns and cellos in unison which are surmounted by tone complexes, the colour of which is constantly changing; there the solo horn parts, although not distinctly audible, lend another colour to the combined sound of the horns and cellos.'[13] For Messiaen, 'every bird is a living leitmotif'.[14] Also noteworthy is the fact that he seems in *Oiseaux exotiques* to be phasing out the trills of *Réveil*, which were once the common coin of birdsong transcriptions, in favour of tremolos of major and minor sevenths and ninths on piano, xylophone and even glockenspiel.

Suddenly at figure 24, Messiaen becomes alive to the possibilities of superimposition of birdsong whereas previously juxtaposition – at least in the piano cadenzas – had been the order of the day: a virtuoso piano cadenza in two matching halves superimposes the meow of the catbird with the bobolink – newcomers to the aviary – in ever more climactic passagework and manual competitiveness. At figure 25 the shama returns in a triumphal triadic tutti in rondo form which, for all its points of resemblance with what went before, is considerably shortened. The piano caps the shimmering glissandos on xylophone and piccolo with its distinctive version of the call, the whole underwritten by a further extended series of Greek and Carnatic rhythms beginning late with the recurrent dhenkî-tâla. The characteristic intervals, B, G# and C, firmly grounded on E and usually given extra bite by the synchronized temple blocks, appear in a multitude of guises at figure 27, twice before figure 28 and four times after figure 30 – vertically, horizontally and in textural diminution – as well as in the figuration (glockenspiel, etc). As with the golden oriole's motif on horns and strings in the *Réveil* tutti, here Messiaen applies the same *Hauptstimme* treatment to the shama. This jubilant flow is momentarily checked by a brief telescoped reminiscence of the first, second and third piano cadenzas in which the American wood thrush's call, repeated note for note, is rounded off by a variant of the cardinal's closing flourish. The ending follows after a moment's silence with an enormous minah upbeat, a bar's wait and then the 'implacable vociferation'[15] – tutti, *fff* – of the Himalayan laughing thrush – insistently hammering home the same twelve-note chord.

Oiseaux exotiques represents the first systematic attempt on the part of Messiaen to capture the timbre of birdsong instead of, as in *Réveil*, contenting himself with outline alone. As a result, he achieves a whole new conception of 'harmonization' – a harmony whose 'function' it is to realize the upper partials of the fundamental note of a song, like so many earlier instances in his piano music (eg 'Noël' in the *Vingt regards*) where he uses clusters to capture the complex spectrum of a bell or a gong. Tone-colour, and self-confessedly the tone-colour of birdsong, was what led Messiaen to a fascination with colour *per se*. As so often in his career as a composer, what began as one more ingredient in the common pot eventually gets distilled off into a heady concentrate to be valued and enjoyed for its own sake. The wonder is that with so many affinities between sound and colour – one need think only of râga (= colour); *color* (which in the Ars Nova meant melos); coloration (which for sixteenth-century German organists meant melodic figuration); *Augenmusik* and the very derivation of *chroma*ticism – it had occurred to so few composers before to follow them up. *Oiseaux exotiques* is thus the first work in which we find Messiaen heightening the songs themselves; this he does not so much with the environmental evocations of the *Catalogue d'oiseaux* – apart from the Amazonian rainstorm – but with approximations of the brilliant plumage of each soloist. In fact, such colour considerations, whether conscious or not, may well have determined the motley grouping in *Oiseaux exotiques* of specimens from disparate parts of the globe. As the composer admonishes his readers in the First Preface, 'they should not forget that this work is highly coloured, it contains all the colours of the rainbow, including

Table 1 *Oiseaux exotiques*

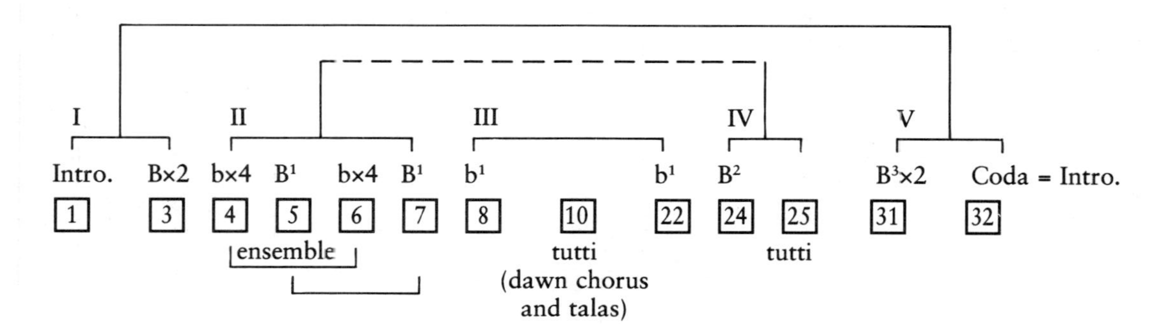

B mynah (India); red-billed mesia (China); wood thrush and veery (N. America)
B^1 cardinal (N. America)
b lesser green leafbird (Malaysia); Baltimore oriole; red-billed mesia; California thrasher
b^1 prairie chicken
central tutti: songs of 32 birds
B^2 catbird and bobolink
closing tutti (in order of appearance):
shama (India), Western tanager, Carolina wren, red-eyed viveo, horned lark, brown thrasher, purple finch, warbling vireo, yellow-throated vireo, lazuli bunting, blue-headed vireo (all of N. America)
B^3 ($B + B^1$) wood thrush and cardinal
*B = piano cadenza; b = ensemble

red, that colour especially associated with hot countries – the colour of the American bird known as the "cardinal" '. Elsewhere, he speaks of the 'orange mixed with gold and some red' of the horn parts of the second tutti, and of the 'green and gold' in the first and last piano cadenzas. 'The central tutti mixes blues, reds, oranges, greens, violets, and purples in coloured spirals, in gyrations of fused rainbows'.[16]

Chronochromie

In Messiaen's music, we can trace the continuing inroads of his birdsong studies. Beginning with the mere aural identification of each songster, under the guidance of his friend, the ornithologist Jacques Delamain – to whom *Réveil* is dedicated – this began to take into account their distinctive colours as well (as when he says of the rock thrush in *Catalogue d'oiseaux*: 'its song is bright orange like its plumage'). Such colour considerations break through to an overtly conscious level in the very next orchestral work, *Chronochromie* (1959–60), commissioned by Heinrich Ströbel and performed in 1960 by Hans Rosbaud in the Donaueschingen Festival, although they had already undergone a lengthy gestation in his *Catalogue d'oiseaux*. Ondes martenot and piano were pointedly excluded; in their place we have a wealth of tuned percussion including marimba and a fully chromatic set of twenty-five tubular bells, besides a copious array of woodwind, brass and strings. Like *Oiseaux exotiques*, *Chronochromie* unites birds from countries as far apart as France, Sweden, Mexico and Japan but, unlike *Réveil* and *Oiseaux exotiques* (and following in the footsteps of the *Catalogue*) it depicts other sounds of nature – wind, rocks and mountain torrents of the French Alps – notated as meticulously and methodically as any robin redbreast.

Colour implies much more than 'colourful' orchestration or harmony, being at once more literal and more figurative. It takes in the melos of birdsong, used as figuration to 'colour in' – to make perceptible – the durational schemes of the 'Introduction', two strophes and 'Coda' (the two antistrophes are unaffected). Consequently the birdsong is subordinated to the articulation of the symmetrical series of chromatic durations or, in the composer's own words, 'submitted to all kinds of manipulation in the manner of composers of electronic music and *musique concrète*'.[17] In fact birdsong is being called on here to yield some of its hitherto hegemony, an act 'dishonest towards nature but perhaps more befitting the work of the composer',[18] as Messiaen is the first to confess.

Instead of Greek and Hindu rhythms Messiaen here avails himself of the Greek poetic triad of strophe, antistrophe and epode derived from a somewhat wayward adaptation of the Greek originals where both strophe and antistrophe enjoy the same structure while a contrasting note is introduced by the epode. The form first occurs in the opening number of the *Catalogue d'oiseaux* and will crop up again in *Des canyons aux étoiles . . .* , where it adheres more to the Greek sense of the term. (Robert Sherlaw Johnson even makes out a case for discovering its roots as far back as the fourth of Messiaen's early *Préludes*.[19]) But in *Chronochromie* Messiaen opts for two conjunct strophe/antistrophe pairs where the only structural correspondence is between strophes or antistrophes respectively. Other ways in which he marks the various sections of this work are through the use of brief silences, just as he did in *Réveil* (except that this time nothing is left to chance and rests are scrupulously notated).

What are these ubiquitous 'interversions' which appear to invade every movement but the 'Epode' and thus help bind *Chronochromie* together? Episodic they well may be in the outer movements and in the antistrophes but they become the exclusive scaffolding of the two strophes and, as such, go far to justify the title of the work as a whole. Why Messiaen should need such a rhythmic *cantus firmus* is a moot point but the fact is that the central tutti of *Oiseaux exotiques* had owed at least some of its cohesion to the use of a similar if less far-reaching framework of rhythmic strophes. The genotype or series of chromatic durations, with which we are dealing here, consists of thirty-two durational values, from the demisemiquaver to the semibreve (hence the term chromatic – extrapolated by Messiaen from a scale of pitches to a scale of durations). The very act of writing down all the permutations of such a series would take years. Consequently, Messiaen hit upon a means of reducing these permutations to a manageable cross-section which would at the same time conform to a consistent procedure for generating them symmetrically. He proceeded to contrive a 'mode of limited permutation', analogous to his existing modes of limited transposition and possessed of the same 'charm of impossibilities' – impossible, that is, to go beyond a certain number of positions before returning to one's point of departure. Always the born teacher, Messiaen has vouchsafed us his own much simplified example of four such chromatic durations. He chooses the semiquaver, rather than the demisemiquaver, as his minimum durational unit and orders his values as follows: 𝅘𝅥𝅯 ♪ ♪. ♩. Next he chooses an arbitrary algorithm, say, 3 1 2 4. This he now numbers from 1 to 4 and reads in the same order 3 1 2 4 which produces 2 3 1 4. Continuing, we obtain 1 2 3 4 and finally 3 1 2 4, thus completing the permutational cycle. For those who wish to work out for themselves the thirty-six permutations of the series of thirty-two durations based on the demisemiquaver, we give the original series (interversion 1):

> 3𝅘𝅥𝅯. 28𝅗𝅥.‿♪ 5♪‿𝅘𝅥𝅰 30𝅗𝅥.‿♪. 7♪‿𝅘𝅥𝅯. 32 𝅝 26 2 25 1 8 24 9 23 16 17 18
> 22 21 19 20 4 31 6 29 10 27 11 15 14 12 13.

A glance at the score shows us some of the means – melodic, chordal or timbral – by which he hopes to 'colour' these durations, to turn them from mere number games into our lived experience. Both 'Introduction' and 'Coda' provide as good examples as any of how such durational series are to be made manifest. The first 'interversion' we hear by itself is No. 35 at figure 4 (Ex. 14.4), and its durations are articulated by the Japanese paradise flycatcher and grey thrush, which obligingly adopt the demisemiquaver as their minimal durational value by which we must set our mental clocks. Messiaen calls this process 'monnayant', or minting, referring to the way he subdivides longer durations into rapid figuration, just as in the market-place an object may be held to have 'value', but can only be 'transacted' by building up the stipulated price from the lowest

EX. 14.4 *Chronochomie* 2 'Strophe I'

pic
fls
obs
cor a
cl (E♭)
cls
b cl
bns
xylo
mar
bells
gongs
susp. cym
Chinese cym
vns 1 (divisi)
vns 2 (divisi)
vas (divisi)
vcs (divisi)
dbs (divisi)

Merle Japonais
Gobe-mouches de Paradis (du Japon)
Modéré (♪=120)
(interversion 35)

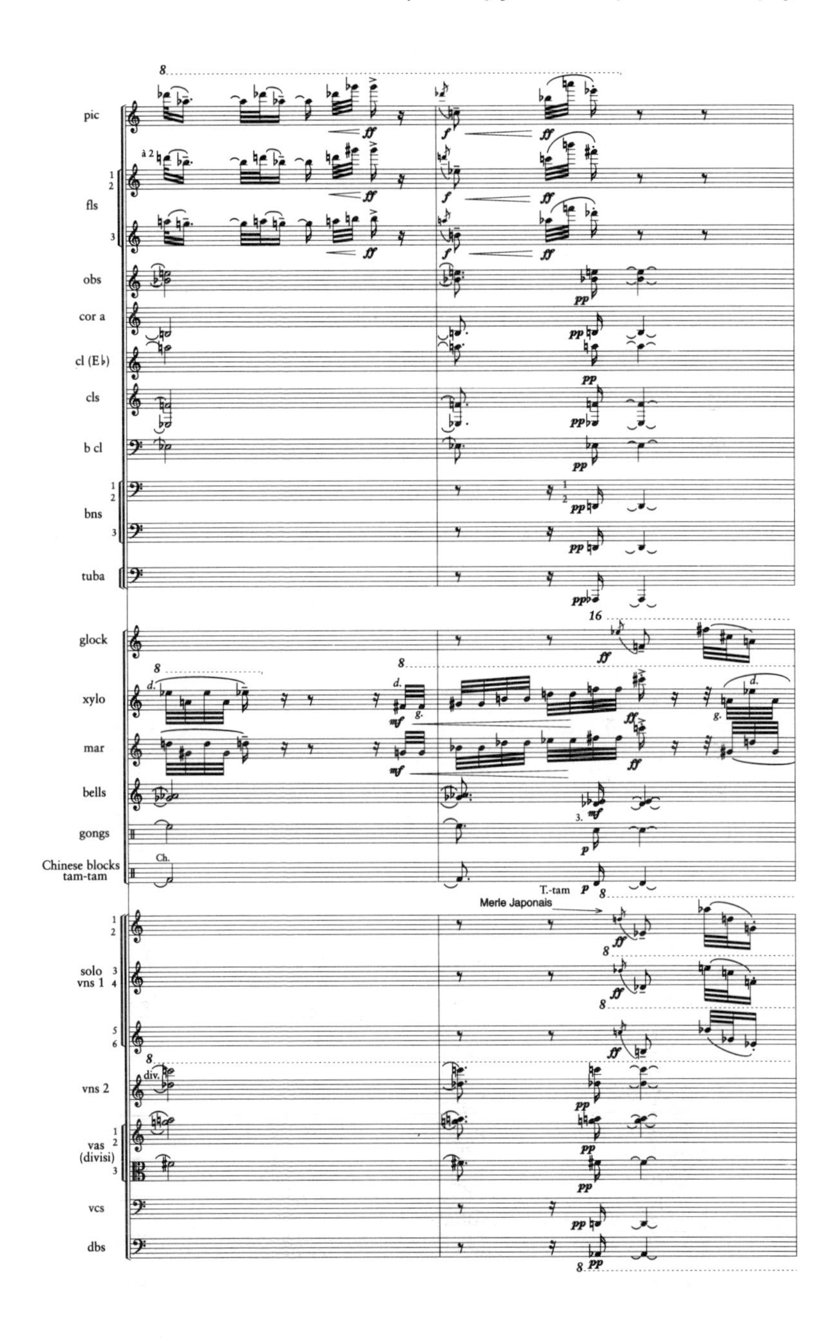
pic
fls
à 2
obs
cor a
cl (E♭)
cls
b cl
bns
tuba
glock
xylo
mar
bells
gongs
Chinese blocks
tam-tam
Ch.
T.-tam
Merle Japonais
solo
vns 1
vns 2
div.
vas
(divisi)
vcs
dbs

common denominator of the coinage of the realm – which in musical terms becomes the demisemiquaver.

Nothing could better illustrate Levi-Strauss's contention that the aesthetic enjoyment of a work arises 'from the contradictory feeling it arouses that the tests it is subjecting us to are impossible' (i.e. the perception of such elongated durations), 'at the same time as it prepares to provide us with the marvellously unpredictable means of coping with them' (i.e. the birdsong figuration never twice the same, which serves us as a measuring unit in demisemiquavers). In other words, structures are manifested by an ever-changing turnover of contents.

Ever since *Ile de feu 2* of 1950, closely followed by the 'Soixante-quatre durées' of the *Livre d'orgue* (in which each duration was likewise coloured by birdsong, timbre or chords), these interversions or permutations, as you care to call them, have kept cropping up in Messiaen's music – 'Le merle de roche' and 'Le courlis cendré' from the *Catalogue d'oiseaux* being only two examples – but never so exhaustively as in these two strophes of *Chronochromie*. They repay our special attention because vestiges from the selfsame series live on in the *Sept haïkaï* and even in *La Transfiguration*. By means of them, Messiaen thought to put himself on a par with the hero of H. G. Wells's *The Time Machine*, who could 'go back in time and change its course, alternately progressing or regressing'.[20]

It is this harmonic tagging of the interversions on which Messiaen sets greatest store: interversion 1 in 'circling chords' ('accords tournoyants'), interversion 2 in chords on the dominant, interversion 3 in chords of 'contracted resonance', and all in conformity to the principle of the colour of time.

> One note-value will be linked to a red sonority flecked with blue – another will be linked to a milky-white sonorous complex embellished with orange and hemmed with gold – another will use green, orange, and violet in parallel bands – another will be pale grey with green and violet reflections – another will be frankly violet or frankly red. Juxtaposed or superimposed, all will be made prominent by colorations . . .[21]

There is a sense of greater freedom here. Whereas *Réveil* was exclusively birdsong and *Oiseaux exotiques* birdsong underpinned by Greek and Hindu rhythms, *Chronochromie* builds on the experience of *Catalogue d'oiseaux* and *Messe de la Pentecôte* (1949–50) in its palette of impressionistic tone-painting:

> Complex noises of water in the cascades and torrents of the Alps. The sonority of water is conveyed by several circling movements (which pivot on themselves with various changes and different rhythms), confided to solo violas and cellos: this is the moving mass which unfolds and flows. The little supplementary rustling noises of the spume and the sheaves of droplets are given by figures on the bass clarinet, by dives on the bassoon, pizzicatos on double basses. A trilled chord, unchanging on the violas and changing on the double basses, expresses the colour of the resonance against the rocky walls. Sometimes this resonance generates a powerful and deep 'hum': it is the bassoon and tuba in their lowest notes.[22]

However much Messiaen may strive for verisimilitude in his transcriptions of birdsong, nature provides a less focused sound in the case of a swirling mountain torrent, represented by ostinato demisemiquavers on violas and cellos with lapping sounds from the bass woodwind, while violin and double bass trills create what the composer terms a 'vaporous confusion'; or of the increasing gusts of wind blowing through the movement, the rocks ranged in a succession of jagged *fff* twelve-note chords throughout the orchestra. Particularly in the case of rocks, such descriptive devices are bound to become increasingly subjective and symbolical in nature (as when Messiaen uses the same strict dodecaphonic note-rows in 'Le courlis cendré', either horizontally in regular semiquavers or stood on end in quaver chords to convey the obscurity and amorphousness of night, and water, and fog descending). Even in his scoring of wind effects, one finds the same symmetrical working-out from centre, in this case vertically, from the quaver triplets of the first violins 7 and second violins 1 to the demisemiquaver ninths of first violins 1 and second violins 7 (the miracle being that such self-conscious means achieve exactly the end he was aiming at! – see Ex. 14.5).

EX. 14.5 *Chronochromie* I 'Introduction'

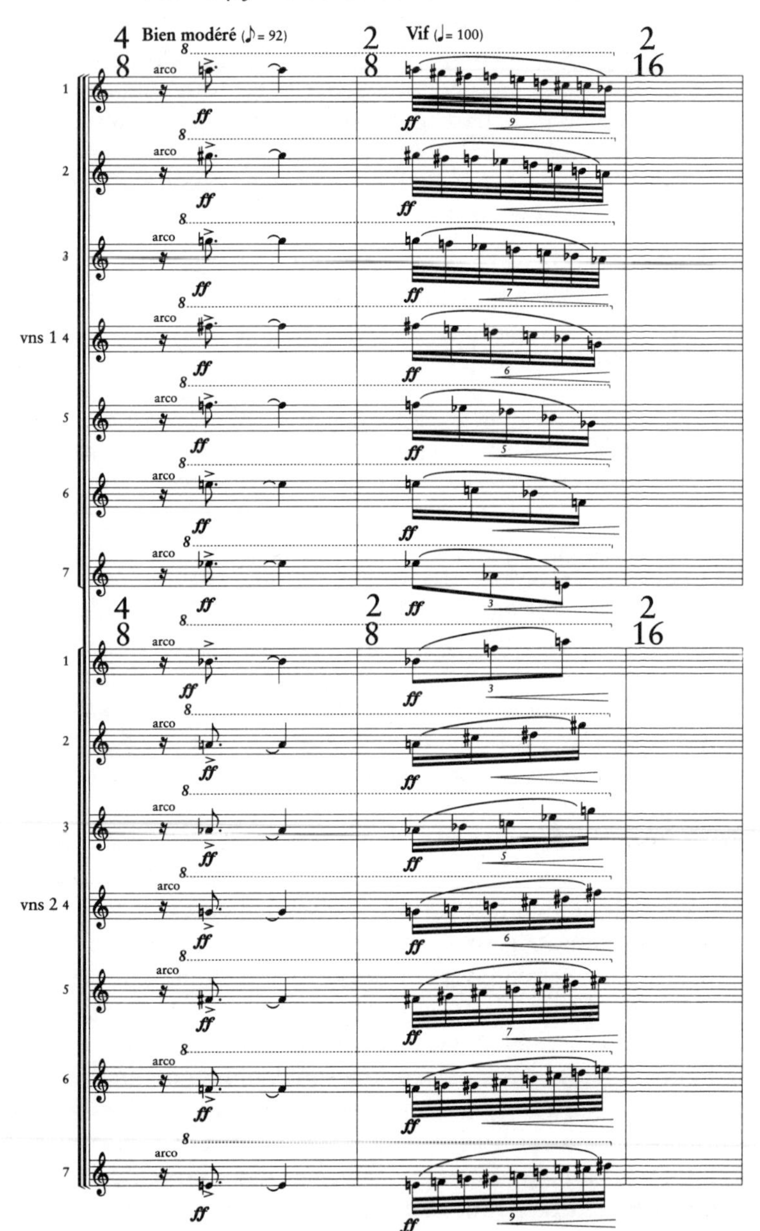

To say that the 'Epode', which follows the two pairs of strophe and antistrophe, lives up to its ancient Greek function by contrasting with them, would be a masterpiece of understatement. When this four-minute-long outpouring of birdsong was first performed in Donaueschingen it set off howls of protest and the composer himself fully accepted its power to provoke scandal. Not only does it run without a break but it is set apart instrumentally by its exclusive use of solo strings. Here Messiaen uncages his birds, rather than constricting them to any extrinsic rhythmic or harmonic framework – or at any rate that is the effect that performance should succeed in conveying. (Too often, frantic attempts to keep the eighteen independent violin, viola and cello parts under control result in a slavish adherence to the 4/8 time-signature assigned by Messiaen only as a visual aid to the conductor. No wonder the composer preferred the comparative freedom offered him on solo piano!) Entries are staggered and in descending order: six blackbirds bear the brunt of the action in the opening pages with two to three voices of the eighteen predominating at a time until the full ensemble suddenly breaks off with the arrival of a linnet accompanied by a trio of two garden warblers and a whitethroat on violins 2, 3 and 4, along with two chaffinches from the previous tutti, thus dividing the 'Epode' almost exactly in half. Almost immediately, the blackbirds and nightingale resume their staggered entries and, but for the second solo first violin, we are back to full capacity. Part of the overall kaleidoscopic effect arises from the fact that individual melodic cells and intervals recur albeit irregularly as in the case of the second blackbird's opening motif which, thanks to its typically tritonal make-up, can be recognized all of seven times.

Sept haïkaï

Nowhere has Messiaen enjoyed greater success than in Japan, whence many of his most devoted disciples have originated and where composers, like Takemitsu, have espoused his particular brand of nature-worship. This is hardly surprising in a land where no cultural 'shame' is attached to the realistic copying of natural phenomena. The sounds of nature have traditionally inspired blind shakuhachi players so that lifelike transcriptions of, say, the mating cry of the hart, had become a commonplace centuries before Messiaen's music was first performed in Tokyo.

The stage was therefore more than set for Messiaen's visit in 1962 – made even more propitious in that it doubled as a working honeymoon following the composer's long-awaited marriage to Yvonne Loriod. This was a period when Western composers, writers and cinematographers were quick to appreciate this archaic culture in the period of Mishima and Kurosawa. It was the year that Messiaen's pupil Stockhausen brought the Noh theatre to Darmstadt for the first time – a theatre which had already taught Varèse, Benjamin Britten and Harry Partch the importance of sound for its own sake, a point not lost on Messiaen (as witness his later *Et exspecto resurrectionem mortuorum*, where the tam-tam's reverberations are left to dissipate themselves in their own time). Indeed, Messiaen makes the claim that his opera *Saint François d'Assise* was directly 'inspired by the Noh drama – the most beautiful form of theatre I know'[23] and dwells on the points in common: 'Whenever the angel appears, a melody is heard, then a big glissando on the ondes martenot, then very high notes on the oboe, just as for the entrance in the Noh drama' where the appearance of the actor is greeted by a 'high, shrill, narrow-sounding flute'. Then 'the very slow gait of the angel, step by step like an actor in the Noh drama, who appears with a particular foot position before very slowly stepping on to the ground.'[24] As Messiaen freely acknowledges: 'there is, if you like, something oriental in my music; the use of unusually slow tempos as in Noh.'[25] On a more personal note, Messiaen's lifelong aesthetic principle of anacrusis, emphasis and decay – so fundamental to his own compositional processes – found its exact counterpart in the Noh concept of *jo*, *ha*, *kyu*, where the 'melody moves from beat to beat in a rhythm more akin to that of a breath taken in deeply, held for an instant, and then expelled'.[26]

Whereas for Stockhausen, in his *Telemusik* of 1966, all this represented a new alien aesthetic on which to draw, for Messiaen it proved to be a timely convergence of many previous lines of development. Japanese music gave him the courage not to seek to reconcile these lines so much as to allow them to coexist. Having broken the thrall of harmonic rootedness in the name of tone-colour as regards his chord formation he was now emboldened to do the same for counterpoint, returning to the sort of stratification associated with the 'successive' school of composition before the latter was ousted by the 'simultaneous' school as long ago as the late fifteenth century. Instead of sustaining one linear argument, to which all others must defer – as in Schoenberg's *Haupstimme* or in traditional voice-leading – the *togaku* and *komagaku* taught him the rarefied delights of a true heterophony. As William Malm tells us, 'individual instrumental lines are designed to be heard separately, rather than merged as they are in the Western orchestra',[27] another point in common which could not have been lost on Messiaen. The palaeo-magical chords of the *sho*, built up in fourths over a *cantus firmus* without regard to European harmonic functions, seemed to vindicate Messiaen's own approach to questions of superior and inferior resonance and to revive a lost pre-Renaissance art of combining tones, while the actual sound of the gagaku ensemble is evoked so consummately on European instruments in the fourth movement of *Sept haïkaï*.

The consequence of this spiritual homecoming can be experienced in the superimposed recto- and retrograde traceries of the work's 'Introduction' and 'Coda' which open out their rhythmic canons at either end in a display of symmetry calling to mind the art of the fan, that centuries-old accessory of the Japanese Noh theatre which had, even before his visit, assumed such an important role in Messiaen's creative processes. Messiaen himself compares the 'Introduction' and 'Coda' to 'the two guardian kings who frame the entrance to Buddhist temples'.[28] Instead of stringing things out laterally, as in the final piano cadenza of *Oiseaux exotiques*, he piles them high – their vertical trope and the miniature nature of the haiku (consisting in poetry of three lines of five, seven and five syllables respectively) serving to curtail his former prolixity. Of the two elements which were always fighting for precedence in his piecemeal style of working, superimposition has here decisively trumped juxtaposition and a higher-order heterophony is born – of the kind that Messiaen's student Boulez was quick to identify as consisting of polyphonies of homophonies rather than of single melodic lines as before. One glance at the 'Introduction' will show what this involves: reading from top down, the woodwind play the piano's same concatenation of six Hindu rhythms – *sama*, *vijaya*, *simhavikrama*, etc – backwards, with the *sama* ♪ ♪ 𝅘𝅥𝅯. 𝅘𝅥𝅯. ushering in each series in turn. As for pitches, one 'talea' (one must indeed go back to the Ars Nova for an appropriate terminology) on the piano equals two 'colors' of sixty-two chords each, the piano repeating from two bars before figure 5. Meanwhile trumpet and trombone reinforce the metallic percussion which offers the so-called 'rhythms of the three Shakti' – the female forms of Brahma, Shiva and Vishnu respectively. The first occurs in pairs of ever decreasing durational values from eight to two semiquavers, thus giving rise to the same effect as the gradually accelerating stroke which announces the arrival of the *shite* in the Noh theatre or, closer to home, Messiaen's own use of an accelerating motif in the first movement ('Introduction') of the *Turangalîla symphonie*. The second is the same as the *simhavikrama* deçî-tâla which is also the third tâla to appear undotted in the piano part. The third 𝅘𝅥𝅯 𝅘𝅥𝅯. ♪ ♩ (around figure 2) corresponds to a *lakskmîça* rhythm destined to undergo irregular augmentation. The eight violins play the first strophe of the only melody worthy of the name (the second strophe based on the first is not heard until the 'Coda') but insouciantly marked 'of little importance' by the composer, for whom melodic continuity in the narrative sense – whether birdsong or otherwise – begins for a time to lose something of its age-old pre-eminence, making this work – if not this whole period – one of the most difficult for Western ears to grasp. While all this is going on, xylophone and marimba set about transforming a *miçra varna* rhythm into the *simhavikrama* – a lengthy process which can be better studied with score in hand.

The sound-world of *Sept haïkaï* is a comparatively modest one: solo piano, xylophone and marimba, eight violins, woodwind, trumpet and trombone – apart from the ubiquitous metallic percussion. Bells in Eastern Europe are omnipresent just as they are in the Orient, as much in the art music as in the liturgy, the music of Arvo Pärt being the latest example to spring to mind. Only in Europe have we kept the spheres of sacred and secular so rigidly apart: that is, up until the advent of Messiaen, whose writing for percussion, as indeed for piano, abounds (glories, even) in bell-like sonorities with their rich sound spectra. Even his love of wood and temple blocks could be linked to the use of 'holy boards' in lieu of bells during the Holy Week in monasteries such as Solesmes and in Eastern Orthodox churches throughout the year. All the same, it is doubtful whether Messiaen, who made a special and for the time atypical study of percussion in his student days, would have gone so far in indulging this partiality had it not been for the aid of the *Batteurs de Strasbourg* – as potent an inspiration in their way as Yvonne Loriod had been in terms of the piano.

In many ways *Sept haïkaï* serves as an exotic sequel to *Chronochromie*, with which it shares its sevenfold groundplan (equally a feature of *Les corps glorieux* and *Visions de l'Amen*), together with its intimate relationship of first and last movements, and its use in second and fourth movements of permutations of the chromatic series of durations (a device first broached in *Chronochromie*). Unlike the latter, however, its 'epodic' section occurs in the dead-centre of the work. The orchestra, too, is deployed in a similar manner, with tuttis being saved up for the outer movements (with the exception of the fifth), while instrumental combinations are as stylized as they were in *Oiseaux exotiques*. Some of the Japanese birds which proliferate in its twenty-five pages have already made their debut in *Chronochromie*. To some extent, though, *Sept haïkaï* represents a separation of two strands previously at one in both *Catalogue* and *Chronochromie*: impressionistic tone-painting and birdsong.

'Le parc de Nara et les lanternes de pierre' gives us a foretaste of the *sho*, soon to appear in the fourth movement, 'Gagaku', with its eight eerie violin soloists playing interversion 5 in *sul tasto* and non-vibrato chords in a style which has come to be associated with Messiaen. First to appear is a marimba solo recalling the dry timbre of the Chinese panku; only the clarinet family, entering in order of ascending pitch, is left from the previous woodwind ensemble to provide an independent stratum of irrational values, seven in the time of eight, eleven in the time of ten, which ratios can also be calculated as a simple change of metronome marking. Unlike his pupil Stockhausen, Messiaen had previously expressed reluctance to use such irrational values out of sympathy for the all-too-human performers, but given the fact that we are here as elsewhere increasingly dealing with the *primus inter pares* instrumentalists of the increasingly soloistic Messiaenesque orchestra, one can understand his being stung sufficiently by snide remarks about his 'caged' birds to wish to release them from the foursquare time-signature 4/8 which, sure enough, applies here throughout. For all that, the Cretic rhythms recall similar woodwind passages in *Chronochromie*; here they are superimposed rather than juxtaposed in a movement which uses the 'Japanese' tone-colours of the eight violins (*sho*) and marimba to evoke a sound-world of the composer's very own.

In the third movement, 'Yamanaka-cadenza', the birds are once again in full swing on woodwind, trumpet, xylophone and marimba, in a triptych of bird choruses followed by individual piano cadenzas – representing kibitaki, hôaka and kuro-tsugumi respectively – some of the few opportunities for the solo piano to unhitch itself from the troika it usually forms with the xylophone and marimba. The first two choruses have the identical birds but not the identical songs, while the same thrice-repeated signature-theme of the kibitaki recurs at the start of the kibitaki piano cadenza. Only in the third chorus do the birds change over, with the exception of the kibitaki, now on both second clarinet and marimba, to be joined soon by the first clarinet. The uguisu's 'victorious turn' on trumpet is heard once in the first tutti, twice in the second and a full three times in the extended third. A subtle rhythmic continuum is supplied throughout, *pianissimo*, by the metal percussion, with embroidery from the bassoons and bass clarinet.

Practically the same birds accost us in the sixth movement, 'Les oiseaux de Karuizawa', again in the form of three tuttis, the second on the great reed warbler, and the first divided in two by the cadential cry of the kibitaki (on piano) which also rounds off the third tutti with its wealth of new birdsong. But it is the tireless uguisu (Japanese bush warbler) on trumpet and woodwind which most commands our attention in both third and sixth movements with its two songs – 'a long whistled note followed by a victorious turn' and a rapid descent followed by a 'broken third oft-repeated with a progressive rallentando'.[29] The latter of these is reserved for the close at figure 27, when all the birds converge as if by common agreement on a spread-out trill followed by the uguisu's 'progressive rallentando', like some mighty machine running down till only the bells, cymbals, gongs and tam-tams remain (Ex. 14.6).

The slow fourth movement, 'Gagaku', provides a triumphant affirmation of the composer's transcriptive genius, too long bewitched by birdsong. The movement takes its place among his other empathetic transcriptions of India, Tibetan and Balinese ensembles in terms of our Western instruments.

Here Messiaen captures the noble yet nasal court music of the seventh-century Mikados, heterophonic like so much of Messiaen – by way of a solo trumpet doubled by oboes and cor in lieu of the 'shrill and acid'[30] hichiriki; a piccolo and E♭ clarinet in lieu of the ryoteki; and the eight violins divisi taking the part of the *sho*, non vibrato, *sul ponticello* and with the bow grating mercilessly against the strings so as to produce the 'vinegarish, almost disagreeable' sonority which the composer prescribes.[31] The characteristic chords of the *sho*, built up in fourths over its tenor melody, are here replaced by Messiaen's own thirteen colour-chords, transposed so as always to have the same bass note in common, a procedure which he had already used in both the *Trois petites liturgies* and in the 'Introduction' of *Turangalîla*. Meanwhile, cencerros, crotales and bells provide an additional rhythmic underlay based on interversions 19, 20 and 21. The melodic sequence could not be simpler – ABCBA′B – or in Messiaen's terminology a 'ternary structure' (theme and its consequent; commentary on theme; repeat of theme and consequent) with a straightforward repeat in all parts from figure 6 but for the interversions on metallic percussion and an irregularly augmented ostinato figure in gongs and tam-tam.

EX. 14.6 *Sept haïkaï* 6 'Les oiseaux de Karuizawa'

The fifth movement represents an important turning-point in Messiaen's development since it establishes his first attempt to evolve an 'exact science' of pitch-colour correspondences from what had previously been part and parcel of his modes of limited transposition: 'each mode has a precise definable colour which changes every time it's transposed' with mode 2 turning 'through certain violets, certain blues and violet-tinged purple' while mode 3 'corresponds to an orange with pigmentations of red and green, touches of gold and also a milky white with iridescent reflections like those of opal'.[32] Ex. 14.7 shows the three ostinato colour-chords of the eight violins vibrato outlined by tubular bells. To them the piano adds chords of upper resonance – likewise limited to three in number and of which two are linked to colours – which sound in continually shifting rhythmic presentations accompanied by triangles, crotales and cencerros, whenever the violins pause in their leisurely gyrations. In fact, we can trace the immediately preceding stage of this evolution by glancing at the following movement, 'Les oiseaux de Karuizawa', where 'coloré', 'très coloré' and finally 'fulgurant' seem to indicate a crescendo of colour-consciousness which was bound to explode, in the hands of so organized an intellect as Messiaen's, into overt systemization. 'The piece is really green, red, gold and blue, and I've even added some other colours – violet, lilac, purple (my favourite colours) by combining different sounds and different instrumental timbres.'[33]

Whereas previously all eight Japanese birds listed for this movement in the composer's preface would have been described in terms of their songs alone, now a good half are described only in terms of their plumage. Just as birdsong first appeared in his pages without further comment and only reached the disclosure stage with *Réveil*, so now do colour associations, long subliminal in his style or subject to durational concerns, come editorially to the fore in 'Miyajima et le torii dans la mer', scored for full orchestra, which the composer describes as a rich, violent and complex superimposition of colours. Consequently both form and melodic movement are kept as simple as possible, with only a modicum of birdlike figuration in piccolo and flute, xylophone and marimba. Over these colour-chords there rides

EX. 14.7 *Sept haïkaï* 5 'Miyajima et le torii dans la mer'

an angular seven-note theme, *fortissimo* on trumpet and trombone in two parts, which the composer has marked 'red, lilac and purple' and to which the continuing other parts of violins, keyboards and metallic percussion serve as prelude, interlude and postlude.

Couleurs de la cité céleste

Only a year separates the *Sept haïkaï* from *Couleurs de la cité céleste* (composed in 1963 and performed in 1964 at the Donaueschingen Festival), which now confidently proclaims the new faith in its very title, offering the first fruits of Messiaen's *style couleur* on the altar of the Almighty. Other familiar figures at this feast of consecration are Gregorian plainchant, which had scarcely been heard of since 1951; Apocalyptic symbolism of the seven angels with seven trumpets, and of the abyss; birdsong; Greek and Hindu rhythms; interversions; and the same small orchestra of high-pitched solo piano, wind and percussion which had served our composer so many times before, only now it is the brass, from little D trumpet to bass trombone, which comes into its own, foreshadowing the world of *Et exspecto*. 'The work does not end, having never really begun: it turns on itself, interlacing its temporal blocks, like the rose-window of a cathedral with its vivid invisible colours.'[34] This turning on itself suggests that Messiaen's rose-windows in sound have become for him a Christian version of the Buddhist *mandala* (Sanskrit for circle) – a sacred art-form or spiritual exercise, an example of which, entitled 'The Wheel of Time', was on display at the Royal Academy's 1992 Tibetan Exhibition; this was made of precious stones and coloured sand, in a design working always outwards from the centre.

If birdsong was Messiaen's way of smuggling melody back into his music, then colour served the same purpose as far as harmony was concerned. By now, Messiaen had worked out something of a systematic symbolism in which he was aided by the fact that the precious and semi-precious stones which constitute the celestial city of the Apocalypse, to which he turned once again for inspiration, are exactly twelve in number, and that crystalline jasper ('the light of the city was like crystalline jasper'[35]) contains them all just as white light contains the full colour spectrum. From this it follows that by reducing the full 'chromatic' range he must perforce produce colours: 'when one hears all tones simultaneously . . . one hears nothing. Only when a tone fails does a colour begin to emerge. A cluster must therefore be prepared, one must take away tones from it in order to give it a colour.'[36] Nonetheless even full twelve-note chords, of which he had used a variety in *Chronochromie*, arc by their spacing and voicing capable of giving off as many sparkling hues as a well-cut diamond (Ex. 14.8). Messiaen

EX. 14.8 *Couleurs de la cité céleste*

escapes all concerns with consonance and dissonance to inhabit a world of hues and intensities which for him at the same time reflects his beloved 'rainbow around the throne of the Almighty'. This at once carries us back to Messiaen's teacher, Paul Dukas (whose influence in this respect Messiaen freely admits) and the latter's *Ariane et Barbe-bleue*, where all the precious colours of rubies, emeralds, ameythysts, sapphires and pearls are foresworn by Ariana in favour of the all-embracing white light of the diamond.

Even more immediately arresting that the colour-coding, which is after all only sparingly applied, is the way this work passes in review so many other elements indigenous to Messiaen's style – birdsong as enunciated by the three clarinets, xylophone and marimba; plainchant in the brass; Hindu rhythms in the metallic percussion – all combined together according to the free-wheeling principles of the *Catalogue d'oiseaux*. One can only admire the spirit of a composer who is eager to come into the presence of the Almighty from such a new and unexpected quarter, yet with all his other baggage intact.

In the introduction the songs of birds not normally found together are again subordinated to musical considerations, while retaining their homophonic single-mindedness of motion, as when the opening motif passes from clarinets to piano, keyed percussion and back while the last upward flourish of the parson bird anticipates that of the great kiskadee. After the stripe-backed wren's piano cadenza, which returns in a much-expanded version at figure 80 just before the grand climax, the kiskadee's cry is developed briefly before the arrival of the yellowhead – always on the same alternating group of instruments. This returns us to a decisive statement of the original parson bird capped by an expansion of its four-note motif which has been with us from the start – a miniature example of economy and cogency to which the metal percussion imparts a shimmering radiance on each subdivision.

After this briefest of preambles, we are presented with the Ariadne's thread which is to guide us through all this rich tapestry of sound in the shape of the alleluia of the eighth Sunday after Pentecost in mode 6, the first of four such alleluias of which the second (b: i) and fourth (d: i) are left in their original Gregorian state (Ex. 14.9). It is played on the D trumpet and cencerros over the rest of the brass (which symbolizes the seven trumpets of the seven angels of the Apocalypse). Although transcribed into Messiaen's modal language with much emphasis on the opening tritone – symbolic of purity and disembodiment – the whole-tone profile is such as to be immediately recognizable even when it returns to divide the work into two parts (or three depending on preference) at figure 33 and during the numerous other instances (at figures 12, 17, 19, 25, 68, 69, 70, 71, 72, 76, 77 and 81) when it is announced by the keyed percussion supported by cencerros and bells. This whole-tone element on the bells is present to guide us through even the penultimate birdsong cadenza at figure 81, when Messiaen in a polyphonic *tour de force* (the only instance of its kind) superimposes birdsong, plainchant and tâlas alike.

As if these were not milestones enough, we have the two principal sections of this sevenfold work clearly demarcated by the Corpus Christi alleluia (Ex. 14.9b) in mode 2 on the same brass ensemble as delivered the trumpet fanfare with which the exposition began. Not only is this repeated, but the two immediately preceding subsections – 'the star with the key to the abyss' and the meadowlark – are as well. Indeed, repetition becomes something of an organizing principle in what one might call the 'development section' of this work – development in the rhythmic if not melodic sense. From figures 47 to 67, we have an extended repetition of figures 33 to 47, and so alike are the alternations of birdsong, plainchant and colour-chords generally, if one discounts which birds or which chants are in question, that one might well imagine some form of double cursus at work. At all events, one must fight back any tendency to see in the eight sections of this work an exposition, development (figure 33) and recapitulation (figure 67), interrupted before the closing tutti by a final cadenza at figure 81, reminiscent of the Classical concerto, with elements of the Baroque concerto grosso, with its ritornello, thrown in for good measure. The two anomalies in such an interpretation would be the repeated development section and the double recapitulation of tutti and

EX. 14.9a *Couleurs de la cité céleste*

(i)

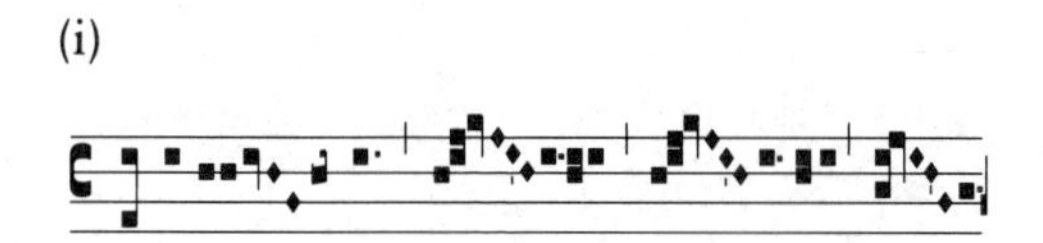

(ii)

Alleluia du 8e dim.
après Pentecôte

8

Modéré (♪=108)

tpt

ff

les 7 Anges aux
7 trompettes

1

tpts 2

3

f

5 (p.4 ♯)

1

hns

2

à 3

trbns

b trbn

2/8

4/8

Alleluia du 8e dim.
après Pentecôte

8

cenc

gongs

1er mf 2e 3e 4^e

EX. 14.9b *Couleurs de la cité céleste*

(i)

(ii)

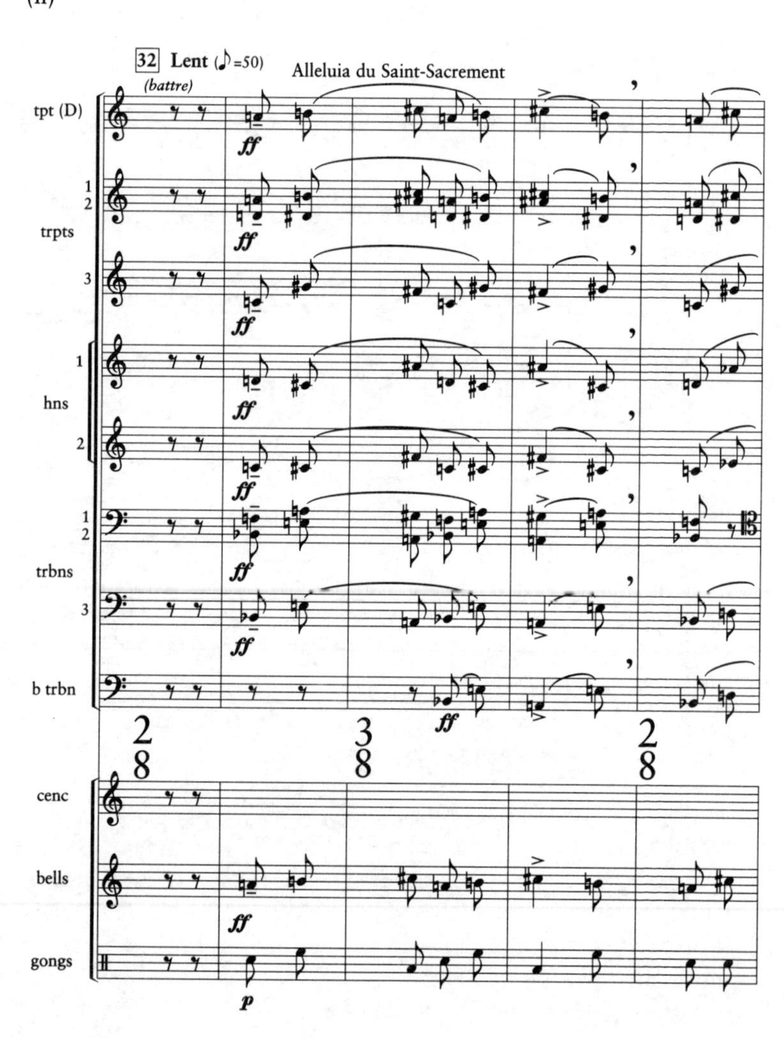

EX. 14.9c *Couleurs de la cité céleste*

piano instead of the more normal double exposition. Whether or not this reconstruction of the events is unduly anachronistic, it shows what an unassailable infrastructure *Couleurs* presents to the listener – even one who is rash enough to forget the composer's own injunction which stands squarely at the top of the score: '*the form of this work depends entirely on colours*'.

Et exspecto resurrectionem mortuorum

The return to a lofty music of religious affirmation was still further strengthened the following year (1964) when Messiaen received the commission from André Malraux, then Minister of Culture, for an official Requiem to celebrate the dead of two World Wars – a requiem which must have called to Messiaen's mind the *Symphonie funèbre et triomphale* of Berlioz, a com-

EX. 14.9d *Couleurs de la cité céleste*

(i)

(ii)

poser who stood high in his estimation. Ironically, unlike *Et exspecto resurrectionem mortuorum*, which – if Messiaen had had his way – would have been destined for 'vast spaces and mountain heights', Berlioz's was actually first peformed out of doors. Indeed, if *Et exspecto* had successfully captured the rugged grandeur of the Hautes-Alpes, among which Messiaen spent so many inspirational summers, it might have held a higher place in his output. As it was, monumentality, which had before been only an infrequent feature of his style in works such as *L'Ascension*, now became something of an occupational disease. Messiaen began a succession of works which were as vertically conceived and with as little forward movement as any mountain range. *Et exspecto* – 'I await the resurrection of the dead' taken from the Catholic Creed – received its first performance in Sainte Chapelle (1965) and subsequently in Chartres Cathedral, both edifices possessed of the rose-windows on which Messiaen had already modelled the cyclical form of *Couleurs*. His life's mission – or at least one to which he attached major importance – 'to accomplish a liturgical act, that is to say, to transfer a kind of divine office . . . to the concert hall', as begun in the *Trois petites liturgies*, had now come full circle to its point of sacred origin. After all, churches and cathedrals were but architectural metaphors for the original magic mountain of stone. No greater apotheosis of his life's work could possibly be imagined by a composer who, for all his modesty, had always had a hankering after officialdom and honours, and whose years of experience as organist of La Trinité made him keenly aware of the acoustical changes to be rung. It was only natural, in such a setting, that spacious chant-like periods should replace the short-term twittering of birds – surprising that only two actual chants are acknowledged – while carefully notated silences which articulated each of the sections of *Couleurs* now become minute-long to allow for reverberation time. Amid such organ-like sonorities, there was no place for piano nor keyed percussion, only large-scale woodwind, brass and massive metallic percussion instruments, with brass – a D trumpet counterbalancing tuba and saxhorn – in the ascendancy. It was as if Messiaen had been groomed for his task by the conscious simplification of *Couleurs* – on that occasion to throw into heightened relief his absorption in colour, but now for its own sake: for instance, in the whole of the first five pages there are only two note values – quavers and crotchets – grouped in twos and threes to resemble plainchant.

The first movement, 'Des profondeurs de l'abîme, je crie vers toi, Seigneur: Seigneur, écoute ma voix!', divides the orchestra into two antiphonal choirs, beginning unison in the extreme bass with the 'theme of the depths' on brass reinforced by tam-tams – a return to the stark monody of *Les corps glorieux* (which in *La Transfiguration* will carry all before it). These angular phrases, whether plainspoken or harmonically enriched by woodwind and horns, alternately rise in register and slip back into the depths with the close of the first phrase returning to lock us in. There follows the 'cry from the abyss', a favourite subject of Messiaen, more vociferously if less subtly handled than in *Couleurs*, in a treatment which would become standard for later works, with piccolos, flutes and oboes added for the first time to the upper woodwind to provide delayed-entry chords of resonance to the eight *fff* minim chords of mode 3 on brass and lower woodwind, gongs and tam-tams. Each such chordal pairing constitutes for Messiaen the painterly principle of 'simultaneous contrasts' which, whether 'played by other instruments or in another register, be it in a high register like a bell-resonance, or in a low register like the "hum" of a bell',[37] adds up to the full twelve-note complement.

The second movement, 'Le Christ, ressuscité des morts . . .', relies for much of the time on Lisztian thematic transformation (Ex. 14.10): a lightning flash on the woodwind, representing the descent of Christ into human form, reveals itself to be the same melodic outline then spelt out on oboes, flutes and horns, by what Messiaen likes to call 'melody by default' – that is to say, the notes of the theme sounded simultaneously and then successively dropping out in the order in which they appeared in the melody, symbolizing the death of Christ. Its characteristic drop of a whole tone, perfect fourth and tritone is the retrograde of the first four notes of the 'theme of the depths'. Finally we hear the reconstituted melody stretched out on end in pastoral

EX. 14.10 *Et exspecto resurrectionem mortuorum* 2 'Le Christ, ressuscité des morts, ne meurt plus . . .'

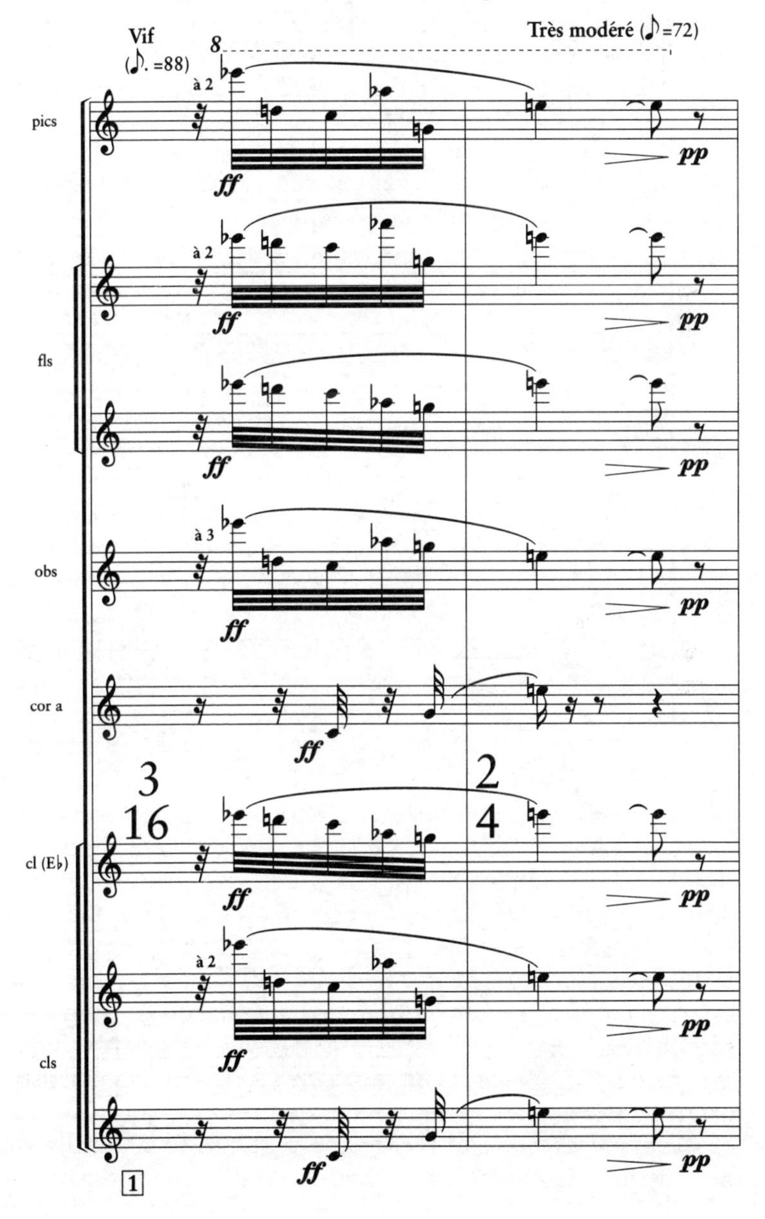

Très lent (♪=72)
fls
obs
cor a
cls
bns
hns
mf
pp
ppp
p
2
Presque lent (♪=52)
long
3

fashion as a predominantly woodwind duet. If for all their brevity we call these transformations A, B and C, there now follows a more extensive section D in which we have a typically tritonal trumpet tune, symbolizing the risen Christ, accompanied by the 'rainbow-radiance' of the woodwind and a generous patchwork of ostinatos on metallic percussion in the *simhavikrama* tâla, symbolizing the power of the 'lion' and recalling the 'Alléluia sur la trompette, alléluia sur la cymbale' of *L' Ascension*, where equally Christ 'rises to the sound of the trumpet'. Transformation C now returns unaltered but for the mysterious 'minting' of the gongs. The latter are then added to the *simhavikrama* when D in turn comes back with trumpet and woodwind permutating their previous material. The movement ends as it began with lightning flash, melody by default and pastoral duet, the final tally being ABCDCDABC.

In the third movement the voice of Jesus calling on the dead to rise in 'L'heure vient où les morts entendront la voix du Fils de Dieu' is that of the Amazonian uirapuru (a bird featured by Villa-Lobos) on combined woodwind, traditionally heard in the hour of one's death and here representing the hour of Resurrection. The movement is made up of two halves, each of which divides into three constituent elements: (1) three similar outbursts of the uirapura's song hedged about by prolonged silences; (2) a peal of tubular bells of which the four pitches are permutated twice at each appearance, followed by an earth-shaking tutti crescendo, literally enough to wake the dead, on a chord with individual pitches highlighted in ascending order by horns, trumpets and bass trombone – another but much abbreviated member of that family of 'granite-like' crescendos typified by *Apparition de l'église éternelle*; after which (3) the four-note figure of the bells reveals itself on low winds in unison as the last two bars of our pastoral theme from the second movement, hence the 'voice of Christ', and is overlapped by a prolonged roll on gongs and tam-tams from *pp* to *ffff*, with slow decay. The first and third of these are extended the second time round, by which stage we begin to hear the tutti crescendo as an orchestral equivalent of that on gongs and tam-tams.

An equally drastic limitation of ingredients, despite its being the longest, is also to be found in the fourth movement, 'Ils ressusciteront, glorieux, avec un nom nouveau – dans le concert joyeux des étoiles et les acclamations des fils du ciel', in which three long successively descending strokes of the tam-tams recall Messiaen's use of the instrument at the end of the eighth movement of *Turangalîla* where it speaks in the 'langages de l'au-delà'. They begin *pp* and subsequently punctuate each of the six sections of this movement until by their fifth recurrence they have reached a *fff* level. On the sixth and last, they are joined by the six gongs in two final repetitions, the one *piano* and the other *forte*. In between these mysterious episodes, symbolizing between them the Trinity, the Resurrection and the music of the spheres, we have three alternating homorhythmic rounds of plainchant and birdsong, abruptly broken off in each case except for the last by the return of the tam-tams. The birdsong is exclusively that of the short-toed lark, the second of only two birds to gain admittance to this work. Messiaen has chosen her not only for her 'great rhythmic variety and rapid tempo'[38] as compared to the moderate pace of the plainchant, with its even semiquavers and quavers grouped in twos and threes, but also for her 'alleluiatic and twittering virtuosity'[39] as conveying the gift of joy and agility which characterizes the resurrected.

The plainchant comprises the Easter introit on tubular bells coloured by cencerros, and alleluia on trumpets and woodwind, but fitted on to the Procrustean bed of Messiaen's modes, the introit in the hexachordal mode 2 and the alleluia in the ten-note mode 7, with both modes sharing two major triads in common. This means that the 'Resurrexi' starts off uncharacteristically in major thirds and minor seconds (the reverse of its Gregorian guise) while the incipit of the alleluia is intoned by the first trumpet and repeated by the second and third trumpets responsorially before engaging in parallel organum with the woodwind and being superimposed on the ongoing introit of the three cencerros and tubular bells. The latter gets as far as the first incise of the second Gregorian period on its first presentation and, on the second, like the alleluia, recapitulates from the beginning of the period where it left off previously. On its third and last appearance, the introit recommences just before the start of the third period, finishes the response and begins again one bar after figure 31 getting as far as 'facta est'. Similarly, the alleluia repeats the response three times without ever embarking on the verse. There is only one point where the melodic profile departs radically from the Gregorian template so as to introduce a succession of tritones and at the same time to prepare for the 'theme of the depths' when it returns at figure 29 on horns and trombones. Each time the alleluia puts in an appearance it is earlier than the time before, first with ten bars of anticipation in the introit, then five bars and finally only one. In the second and third plainchant episodes we have the six gongs entering last with the *simhavikrama* rhythm from the second movement to add yet a further dimension to this *fin-de-siècle*-style superimposition of introit, alleluia and, eventually, 'theme of the depths'. As Messiaen puts it, 'angels and stars unite to acclaim the resurrected in their glory, in superimposing four musics, four corruscations of colour, four sound-complexes'.[40] After the last double episode of the *musica celestis*, in the form of chords on gongs and tam-tams, has died away, we hear a mighty chorale of the entire orchestra, resembling the end of the first movement, of which each of the eight semibreve chords is marked *ff* with fermata.

The fifth movement, 'Et j'entendis la voix d'une foule immense', begins like a dead march in stark unison on six horns, low brass and metallic percussion with undamped gongs throughout in evenly pulsed semiquavers. The theme is drawn from the same melodic reservoir, ending as it began on a falling tritone. This is then echoed exactly by woodwinds and trumpets playing *fortissimo* with cencerros trills in rich harmonies. Twice more we hear these giant strides with minor changes, the third time much extended, but always with this remorseless alternation of unison and harmonization. Finally, a huge crescendo (in pitch as well as dynamics) to *fffff* on four heaven-storming chords indicates that the promised resurrection is at hand. As Roger Nichols points out, having begun in the depths – *de profundis* – on A♭, our spiritual journey has taken us all of six octaves to finish on an exalted height of G♯ *in altissimi*![41] Of it, one could say, as Messiaen did of his 'tombeau' for Paul Dukas:

'static, solemn and unadorned, like an enormous block of stone'.[42]

When one stands back from all the triumphalism and transcendence of Messiaen's later works to view the phenomenon dispassionately one can only catch one's breath at the thought of a man who out of a few Hindu citations in Lavignac's Dictionary, out of a few exotic scales culled from Liszt, Debussy and Rimsky-Korsakov could construct a whole universe of sound. Descartes, another Frenchman, who is famous for saying 'Give me motion and extension and I will make you a world', would have been proud of him. Like the marsh warbler, which migrates to Africa and comes back with an enhanced repertoire of the birdsong of many nations, Messiaen's music has indeed grown wings and helped towards that universal language, a 'world music'.

It would be all too easy to round off the chapter with praise-songs extolling Messiaen as defender of the faith, be it Catholicism or the Western tradition in which the components of music are melody, harmony and rhythm. But this would be to cleave unduly to the conservative side of his legacy.

Better to remember him as taking up the cudgels on behalf of yet another movement in contemporary music, which has become known as timbral composition and which, partly thanks to Messiaen's Midas touch, has subsequently become the gold standard of his younger contemporaries. For this is what all these works, from *Chronochromie* on, best convey, albeit couched in a metaphoric language of colours which serves as well as any at a time when there is still no accepted standard vocabulary for such timbral concerns.

What else might have conspired to awaken this interest in Messiaen? The question brings us around full circle to the beginnings of our chapter where we spoke of his fascination with *musique concrète*. Fortunately the means lay literally at his elbow. The organ may have stamped its imprint on generations of organist–composers, among them Franck and Bruckner, with their partiality for banked wind and brass, for pregnant silences under cover of which to alter the registration – all mannerisms of style and orchestration to which Messiaen himself fell heir. But only for Messiaen did the organ with its sine wave flutes, square wave diapasons and sawtooth reeds, provide a heaven-sent vehicle to new levels of sonic experience and an escape from the impasse into which postserial music had fallen.

> As I grew old, I drew increasingly nearer to timbre – my last works such as *Des canyons aux étoiles* . . . contain far more tone-colour effects than my earlier works. At least in this respect, I followed the trend of my era. Young people who use synthesizers are undoubtedly right; it'll compel them to discover new effects and renew their way of thinking.[43]

Throughout his compositional life, Messiaen has time and again shown the rewards of a step-by-step approach, buttressed by tradition – to a century all too apt to kick over the traces and lurch from one extreme to the other. Here again we have him taking up what began as yet another Schoenbergian 'futuristic fantasy'. In his *Harmonielehre* of 1911, Schoenberg foresaw 'progressions of tone-colours between which one would be able to perceive relationships akin to those whose logic satisfies us in the melody of pitches' – a process immensely speeded up by the infusions of 'local colour' which, beginning as a trickle with Debussy and Ravel, grew to floodtide with the development of the 'world village' mentality of the 1950s and 60s, in the musical aspects of which Messiaen played a leading role. But while his pupil Stockhausen and younger contemporaries preferred to concentrate on the infinitesimal changes in static blocks of sound, as in *Stimmung*, he remained of the opinion voiced by Lerdahl in 1985 that 'timbral hierarchies are likely to be of greater aesthetic interest if combined with pitch hierarchies in an interactive fashion'. It is through this hybrid approach, of which we have had so many dazzling proofs in the course of this chapter, that Messiaen reasserted his position as one of this century's greatest innovators.

Notes

1 Claude Samuel: *Entretiens avec Olivier Messiaen* (Paris, Belfond, 1967); translated by Felix Aprahamian as *Conversations with Olivier Messiaen* (London, Stainer & Bell, 1976), p. 135.
2 Almut Rössler: *Contributions to the Spiritual World of Olivier Messiaen*, translated by Barbara Dagg and Nancy Poland (Duisburg, Gilles und Franke, 1986), p. 107.
3 Ibid., p. 109.
4 Jonathan Harvey: *The Music of Stockhausen* (London, Faber and Faber, 1975), p. 105.
5 Messiaen: World Exhibition, Brussels, 1958 (Paris, Leduc, 1960); and in Metzger and Riehn (eds), *Musik-Konzepte: Die Reihe über Komponisten*, Heft 28 (1982).
6 Jean-Philippe Rameau: *Démonstration du principe de l'harmonie* (1750).
7 Samuel, op. cit., p. 86.
8 Alain Perier: *Messiaen* (Paris, Edition du Seuil, 1979), p. 122.
9 Messiaen: Composer's Preface to *Réveil des oiseaux*.
10 Trevor Hold: 'Messiaen's Birds', *Music and Letters* (April 1971); reprinted in *Guildhall School of Music and Drama Review* (1974), p. 27.
11 Harry Halbreich: *Olivier Messiaen* (Paris, Fayard/SACEM, 1980), p. 393.
12 Pierrette Mari: *Olivier Messiaen: l'homme et son œuvre* (Paris, Seghers, 1965), p. 163.
13 Rössler, op. cit., p. 33
14 Ibid., p. 109.
15 Messiaen: Composer's Note in orchestral score of *Oiseaux exotiques* (London, Universal, 1959), p. 85.
16 Halbreich, op. cit., p. 400.
17 Samuel, op. cit., p. 63.
18 loc. cit.
19 Robert Sherlaw Johnson: *Messiaen* (London, Dent, 1975, R/1989), p. 27.
20 Antoine Goléa: *Rencontres avec Olivier Messiaen* (Paris, Julliard, 1960), p. 113.
21 Samuel, op. cit., p. 91.
22 Messiaen: *Traité de rythme, de couleur et d'ornithologie* (Paris, Leduc, forthcoming); quoted in Halbreich, op. cit., p. 403.
23 Rössler, op. cit., p. 128.
24 Ibid., p. 127.
25 Ibid., p. 99.
26 William P. Malm: *Music Cultures of the Pacific, the Near East and Asia* (Englewood Cliffs, NJ, Prentice-Hall, 1967), p. 141.
27 loc. cit.
28 Messiaen: composer's footnote to p. 1 of orchestral score of *Sept haïkaï* (Paris, Leduc, 1966).
29 Halbreich, op. cit., p. 413.
30 Messiaen: *Sept haïkaï*, footnote to p. 46.
31 loc. cit.

32 Samuel, op. cit., p. 42.
33 Ibid., p. 93
34 Messiaen: First Composer's Note to orchestral score of *Couleurs de la cité céleste* (Paris, Leduc, 1966).
35 Ibid., Second Composer's Note.
36 Messiaen: 'Gespräch mit O. Messiaen', in Karin Ernst: *Der Beitrag Olivier Messiaens zur Orgelmusik des 20. Jahrhunderts* (Freiburg, 1980), p. 323.
37 Messiaen, quoted in Halbreich, op. cit., p. 389.
38 Messiaen: Composer's Note to orchestral score of *Et exspecto resurrectionem mortuorum* (Paris, Leduc, 196), p. 2.
39 Messiaen, quoted in Halbreich, op. cit., p. 427.
40 Messiaen: Composer's Note to *Et exspecto*, p. 2.
41 Roger Nichols: *Messiaen* (Oxford University Press, 1975, 2/1986), p. 71.
42 Messiaen, quoted in Halbreich, op. cit., p. 209.
43 Messiaen, quoted in Rössler, op. cit., p. 108.
44 Fred Lerdahl: 'Timbral Hierarchies', in *Contemporary Music Review*, vol. 2, Part 1 (1987), pp. 135–60.

La Transfiguration de Notre-Seigneur Jésus-Christ

WILFRID MELLERS

Except for the mystery-opera *Saint François d'Assise*, *La Transfiguration* is its composer's largest orchestral work, both in its length (at least an hour and a half) and the huge forces for which it is scored (a very big choir, with seven instrumental soloists, and a 'très grande orchestre'). Yet in a characteristically Messiaenic sense it is an extraordinarily simple work – as perhaps it had to be, if it were to deal with so sublime a subject as 'God's Presence in Himself'. It embraces vast numbers of notes, in astonishingly varied sonorities, while its rhythms and metres are of mind-boggling complexity. Even so, a considerable proportion of the work is conceived monophonically or at most heterophonically, as befits the oneness of God; the densely sensuous harmonies, however incidentally dissonant, gravitate around and return to clearly defined tonal points; and even the elaborate rhythms tend to be simple in effect – in so far as they are affirmatory, in being either pre-ordained, or intentionally chaotic. 'Difficult' music, in European tradition, is so because it is concerned with growth through conflict, within the mind, as Beethoven's music surpremely demonstrates. Messiaen's music is never difficult in this inward, psychological sense, since it is preoccupied with elementals and eternities. It may of course be inapprehensible by people for whom such concepts seem untrustworthy; but that is a different story.

The work was commissioned by the Gulbenkian Foundation for their thirteenth festival at Lisbon, where it was performed in the Coliseum, on 7 June 1969, before an audience of 9000; Loriod and Rostropovich were among the seven instrumental soloists. The numbers involved, on both sides of the podium, inevitably imparted a ritualistic grandeur to the occasion; this was no mere concert, but an act of praise and hopefully of incarnation and transcendence, performed not in an orthodox church or temple, but before a world-gathering of 'all sorts and conditions of men'. The Christian liturgy, as Messiaen envisages it, is indeed a global phenomenon and – as was noted in the general article on Messiaen's mysticism and theology – the techniques he employs are not restricted to European precedents. Moreover, the polyethnicity of the notion is reinforced by the geographical locations of the innumerable birds that warble, chirrup, squeak and squawk throughout the score. Not only their names but also their geographical habitats are scrupulously specified.

The literary and dramatic form of the work is a cross between Christian Passion music with Gospel narration, and a celebratory oratorio, like an extended liturgical Eucharist. Messiaen tells us that he has evoked the mystery of Christ's Transfiguration through a 'mosaic' of Latin texts, chosen to promote meditation and potential transcendence. They are taken from St Matthew's Gospel (for the narrative sections), and from Genesis, the Psalms, the Wisdom of Solomon, the Epistles of St Paul, the Roman Missal, and the *Summa Theologica* of St Thomas Aquinas. The structure falls into two 'septénaires' – seven (magic) movements; each half comprises a percussive prelude leading to a 'Récit évangélique' followed by two meditations, this sequence being capped by another 'Récit' and another two meditations, rounded off by a final *choral*. The disposition of these many sections is elaborately planned, with multiple recurrences; but – as one would expect from Messiaen's previous music – the musical structure, like the verbal, is essentially mosaic-like. There is no 'development', for the at once patent yet profound reason that the Divine Presence is 'as it was in the beginning, is now, and ever shall be, world without end'.

We begin with preludial percussion, at first inarticulate and unpitched. Suspended cymbals, gongs and tam-tam reverberate in aweful solemnity, punctuated by temple blocks pinging in complex, pre-ordained metrical proportions. From a gradual crescendo pitched percussion emerges in the form of bells, clanging in the tritone (literally at the pitch of the medieval 'si contra fa') that had had so significant a function in *Cinq rechants* and *Chronochromie*. This tritone introduces the first 'Récit évangélique', sung by tenors in unison. The words, from Matthew 17: 1–2, tell of how Jesus went with Peter, James and John into 'an high mountain apart', and was 'transfigured before them. His face did shine as the sun and his raiment was white as the light.' The rhythms follow the natural declamation of the words, changing the time-signatures frequently, at a basic word-measure of semiquaver equals 112. Yet the narration is always lyrical, intermingling repeated notes with figures derived from Messiaen's invented 'second mode', consisting of alternating tones and semitones. Much of the melodic and harmonic material of the entire work will be generated from these two motifs (see Ex. 15.1 and Ex. 15.2).

The second of them appears when the tenors have been joined

EX. 15.1 *La Transfiguration de Notre-Seigneur Jésus-Christ*
1 'Récit évangélique'

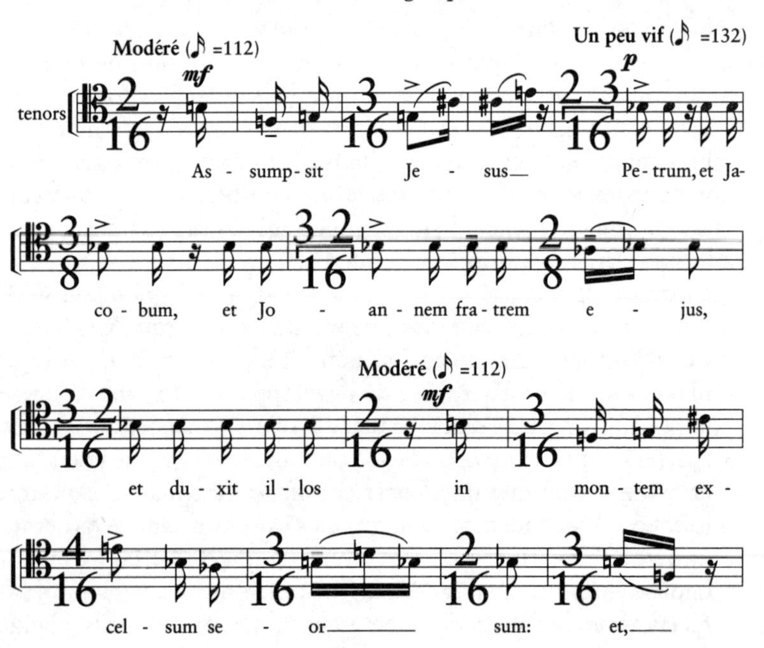

EX. 15.2 *La Transfiguration de Notre-Seigneur Jésus Christ*
1 'Récit évangélique'

by sopranos in a cadential tritone, B to F. Sopranos and tenors wing together in a seraphic cantillation pivoting on both tritones and major thirds. The voices are now doubled by bells; altos and basses join in unison octaves as the transfigured Jesus 'shines' in glory.

The words of the first meditation are from St Paul's Epistle to the Philippians, prophesying how Christ may, if we let him, make our 'vile body' shine, too. Nature, God's earthly manifestation, has a share in this, for woodwind and strings, interspersed with barks on brass, emulate an exotic African bird, at whose savage, rather than seraphic, summons the chorus is encouraged to extol eternal light. Appropriately, this bird is known as the great indicator: its function here seems to be analogous to that of the angel of the Apocalypse in *Quatuor pour la fin du temps*. Many other wild birds join in the hubbub, personified by piano and the other 'gamelan' instruments, with help from strings and woodwind. The chorus, still in octave unisons, expands the lyrically flowing, tritone-oscillating theme as they chant another text (from the Wisdom of Solomon 7: 26) about 'the brightness of the everlasting light'. This fades again into a tritone and appears to be dismissed by the raucous great indicator, whose squawk is identically repeated. At the recitation of Christ's name, however, a complementary theme riddled with euphonious major thirds renders the visionary excitation more stable; and although the meditation alternates in 'mosaic' between these undeveloping blocks of material, consummation is hinted at when the choir, doubled by woodwind and strings, sways in slow, level crotchets, gradually defining the tonality of E major. Throughout the work, E major is to be the key of paradise: as for that matter it had traditionally been in European music, at least since the Baroque era, probably because it was the sharpest, ('highest') major key in common use. Although nature's discordant chaos is by no means silenced, E major has the last word (chord), if garlanded with multiple added notes.

The second meditation is constructed on the same principle, and is heralded by an even savager bird, the chuck-will's widow. The savagery is appropriate, for the light here celebrated invokes terror as well as glory. The words, from Psalm 77, relate how 'the lightnings lightened the world; the earth trembled and shook'; but they are rendered affirmative by a postscript from Hebrews, aligning the brightness of the Son (and sun) to that of the Father. All the birds audibly rampant here come from harsher northern climes in the mountains; they exhort the choir (mankind, and us) to a ferociously dissonant climax on the word 'illuxerunt', although climax – as usual with Messiaen – does not imply progression. Indeed the squawky 'illuxerunt' leads into a richly harmonized, more relaxed chorale-like section, again gravitating towards E major; and the rest of the movement consists of a mosaic of all the non-developing facets. Awe accrues from the contrast between the hectic bird-chitterings on marimba and xylorimba and the bellow of contrabass tuba, which threatens to open fissures in the turning earth. At the end, the 'brightness of the Father's glory' wins through, abetted by a hooting of barred owls on horns. We are told that Messiaen notated all his bird-calls 'in the field', catching them, as it were, in the act; we do not know, however, on what principles he allocates one creature rather than another to a given situation – unless there is an allegorical dimension, as in the case of the great indicator. Maybe it matters in this present context that owls are traditionally associated with wisdom.

Another interlude, repeating the hierarchical percussion-motif of the work's opening, ends once more with the pitched tritone on bells. This introduces the next Gospel narration from Matthew, recounting the meeting of Jesus and Peter with the prophets Moses and Elias, and their decision to build three tabernacles in the holy mountain, one for Christ, and one each for the prophets. This recitative is again sung by tenors in unison, soon joined by sopranos and bells, and then by altos and basses. Basically, the theme is unchanged: though on repetition we are perhaps more responsive to a curious – one might almost say *marvellous* – quality of Messiaen's recitative', which is that although the line embraces intervals (such as tritones, sevenths and ninths) that might be expected to generate stress, it sounds ineffably calm, floating in time and space.

The sequent meditation on the Three Tabernacles finds its texts in Psalm 84 and the Wisdom of Solomon, 'for wisdom is the brightness of the everlasting light'. This is really a slow movement, though the birds are as spasmodically violent as usual, with corybantic flutterings, mostly in parallel seconds, from a white-cheeked honeyeater. The lyrical nature of the movement is established by a solo cello, flowing in aspiring arches, in dialogue with the chorus and with prickly commentaries from the birds. The form is again sectionally non-progressive; but not even the jittery antics of an Australian Willie wagtail (on piano solo) can dampen the ardour of the chorus, let alone the cello's soulful ecstasy. Chorus and divided strings close on a long sustained second inversion of an E major triad, with chromatic added notes. The only bird surviving, in the silence of the night, is the dulcetly amorous nightingale.

The sixth movement – the second meditation of this group –

depicts 'For she is the brightness of the everlasting light, the unspotted mirror of the power of God, and the image of his goodness', the words again being from the Wisdom of Solomon. Women's voices declaim the text in unison, haloed by a veritable babel of birds of many sorts and sizes, insouciantly unconcerned to accommodate themselves to the human voices, or to anything else. Their unconcern is their innocence, or what seems like innocence to Messiaen: they assert not nature's contrariety, but her necessary coexistence; that their chaos is an affirmation of independent life and lives. This must be why the lovesick solo cello remains audible throughout the hubbub, and is why the whirligig textures sound lucently beautiful. Allied to this miracle is the fact that although Messiaen's sundry 'devices' recur again and again throughout the long work, they do not stale. If they do not grow *more* exciting, and are not intended to, they retain their pristine vernality: for they are, again, 'as it was in the beginning'. The musical manifestation of this lies in the fact that the textures, however densely exacerbated, are controlled metrically by age-old Indian deçî-tâla patterns involving successive augmentation and diminution; and harmonically by Messiaen's personally codified 'modal harmonic colours', which are systematic if without scientific backing. Of course one does not 'register' this consciously, while it is happening; and the hurly-burly simply stops, *in medias res*. It finds an approach to consummation, however, in the *choral* that ends the first *septénaire*: an extravagantly slow piece (quaver equals 30), scored in massive homophony for ten part chorus, the voices doubled by full orchestra. But the dynamics are fairly soft, and the quaver pulse inexorable: so that the psalmist's words, praising God 'in the mountain of His Holiness', evoke awe and wonder. Despite the chromatic added notes, E major is unambiguously established; and the first *septénaire* fades out on a protracted E major triad, without even the radiant adulteration of an added sixth!

La Transfiguration is already, in its first *septénaire*, a substantial work. That Messiaen should add a second *septénaire*, even more massive and constructed on exactly the same plan, might seem supernumenary, were it not that cyclical recurrence is the heart of the divine mystery. We get the point when the second part begins with the familiar rhythm-prelude for percussion, leading to another 'Récit évangélique'. Once more, the prelude ends with the pitched tritone, B–F, on bells. This gives the pitch to the tenors who proclaim the Gospel words 'out of the cloud', announcing that 'This is my beloved Son, in whom I am well pleased'. The tenor theme is unchanged, but this time its clauses are separated by chains of glissandos on multiply-divided strings, magically incarnating the luminous cloud. As before, sopranos join the tenors in the final falling tritone, after which the cloud quivers in multiply-divided trills and harmonics on strings, tingled by triangle and cymbals. The cloud-music is sustained through an immense crescendo while the full chorus rounds off the recitative, ending a further tone lower on unison Cs.

The first meditation of the second *septénaire* has the longest and most theologically abstract text thus far, taken from Question 45, Article 4, of Aquinas's *Summa Theologica*. This 'question' concerns the conformity of image between God the Father and God the Son, achieved by the imperfect conformity of Christ as 'wayfarer' and pilgrim, capped by the perfect conformity of the Father's glory. For us, imperfect conformity is attained through baptism, while the glory to come is foreshadowed in the Transfiguration. Unsurprisingly, the music of this movement is the most awesome so far, giving utterance to what Messiaen calls 'the heights and depths of the Mystery'. The metrical proportions are rigid; the harmonies are harshly percussive; cavernous gongs and tam-tam reverberate; the choric basses pretend to be superhuman Tibetan priests. Indeed the 'mountain' becomes a Tibetan temple, in and out of which flock raucously exotic birds in full pelt. But the harsh, statically tritonal chords of the movement's opening recur at regular intervals, always unchanged, like God himself. The penetrating Tibetan basses are answered by terrifying deep pedal notes on trombones, saxhorn, tuba and contrabass tuba: extravagant orchestral demands justified by extravagent effect. Against this holy horror, a lyrical theme for unisonal chorus flowers from the second-mode figurations; and once more leaping tritones and ninths do not disturb devotional serenity. Tonality wavers around G rather than E major: an effect that may, in the context of the horrendous saxhorns and tubas, be described as benedictory, as 'European' G major traditionally was. Even so, there is throughout this vast movement no development or modulation in the orthodox sense. The violently contrarious episodes recur in their mosaic-patterns, flowing through harmonies that are, according to Messiaen, 'blue striped with green to black spotted with red and gold, by way of a diamond, emerald, purplish-blue, with a dominant pool of orange studied with milky white'. We know this only because Messiaen tells us so, though his colour symbolism is not a frivolous game but an (admittedly non-scientific) attempt to relate nature's colour spectrum to the acoustical prism of the harmonic series. All Messiaen's technical–symbolic devices are called on: cadenzas for a tipsy posse of Mexican birds; three percussion rhythms using various Greek metres superimposed on the already 'pre-ordained' rhythms of the chorus; and Indian deçî-tâla patterns in retrograde movement. At intervals, a baritone solo, helpfully given his pitch by pizzicato cello, continues St Thomas's narration, chanted on a single note that slowly droops. After the lyrical refrain has recurred, it cadences from its G majorish root on to a second inversion of the 'paradisal' E major triad. A cello solo, still active in this movement, sings no human love-song but the more ravaged cries of a Mexican saltator grisâtre, who nonetheless presumably stands as surrogate for us. It sweeps the immense movement into unisons or heterophonies for the entire choral and orchestral forces on – as Messiaen puts it – 'the terrible words; *perfectae generationis*'. The ultimate unisons are on C.

The meditation paired with this shattering movement takes its text from a prayer for the Feast of the Transfiguration, appealing to God to make us co-heirs with Him who is King of Glory, and concluding in ceremonial alleluias. The solo cello returns to its human role as an agent of love and harbinger of the peaceable kingdom, seemingly carrying man closer to God, as he contemplates the visible, aural and tactile beauties of the world. But the movement, if less scarifying, is no less complex than the previous one, as a multiplicity of birds (widely ranging from France, Spain and Greece, to Africa and North America) yell a paean of created nature through the choral invocations and the iridescently coloured chord-clusters. Again, the wildly varied 'material' rotates sequentially, going nowhere, like nature itself. But the solo cello, singing in wide-ranging arabesques, provides a thread through the labyrinth, until the ripe E majorish harmonies of the final alleluias attain a momentary triumph, if not a final resolution. The babbling birds, non- if not exactly a-tonal, manage, however, to have the last non-word.

Messiaen's church is identified with the solitudinous mountain, so that his Christian theology and his pantheistic mysticism are one. The divine vision awaits us, as the percussive prelude to the final 'Récit évangélique' returns unchanged, as is the beginning of the tenors' declamation. The line is, however, extended, for the Gospel narrative is longer, describing the disciples' awe at the spectacle of the transfigured Christ, who warns them to 'tell the vision to no man, until the Son of Man be risen again from the dead'. Sopranos, and then the other choric voices, join the tenors as before, doubled by bells and haloed by unpitched percussion.

The ensuing meditation has a multiple text from Psalm 104, Aquinas, St Luke, the Ordinary of the Mass, the Wisdom of Solomon, and Genesis. These fragmentary verses revolve around identity between the inner and outer light; and Messiaen offers an autobiographical gloss in telling us that, while looking at Mont Blanc and at Alpine glaciers in bright clear weather, he was 'suddenly struck by the difference between the small splendour of snow and the great splendour of the sun – that is where I could also imagine the extent to which the site of the Transfiguration was awesome'. As so often in Messiaen's music, 'naive' physical depiction becomes visionary: trills and clusters grumbling and groaning on bottom strings fuse with sepulchral pedal notes on the deepest brass instruments, evoking awe, while majestically fearsome birds like eagles and falcons screech in abandon. Stratospheric strings in trills and harmonics combine with a gamelan of bells, crotales and piano to quiver in the white light of snow and sun: through which the chorus, always in octave unisons, swells ecstatically from the original 'second mode' recitatives. The identification in this movement of metaphysical qualities with pictorial physicality bears on the fact that its structure is even more episodic than that of the previous movements: the vision is glimpsed in flashes, 'even in the twinkling of an eye'. The acceptance of nature's abundance seems, however, to bring rewards, for the movement ends with a thrilling passage of choral vocalise, whirling in twenty real parts, with an extra one for the solo cello, making twenty-one (the magic three times seven) in all. The lines rock between the familiar perfect and imperfect fourths and fifths, while divided string harmonics, trills and glissandos auralize the sheen of snow and sun. The last word, 'terribilis', is set to a diminished fourth followed by rising tritone, the voices reinforced by brass and punctuated by tolling bells and gongs.

Purely aural sublimity – as distinct from any presumptive psychological 'content' – could hardly be carried beyond this scalp-prickling moment. But Messiaen, never scared of excess, manages to make the second meditation – the penultimate movement of the whole work – consummatory, at least in size and scope. It is cast in three chorally liturgical sections, framed by a massive orchestral prelude, interlude and postlude. In the orchestral prelude real bells and gongs are interspersed with normal orchestral instruments that simulate them, to awe-inspiring effect. The first choral episode combines resplendent alleluias with an invocation of light from Psalm 43. Other texts come from the Vespers of the Transfiguration and from St Thomas Aquinas, recounting the miracle of the Trinity as the Father, Son and Holy Ghost are simultaneously manifest in the 'bright cloud'. The quasi-liturgical vocal sections are again in octave unisons, in the mysterious second mode whereby tritonal melodic–harmonic tension is transmuted into timeless radiance. The instrumental ritornellos involve a stupendous descent through fourths perfect and imperfect: a passage that freezes nerves and sinews. If this movement approaches an epiphany, it may be because the mosaic sections tend to be more sustained than in previous movements, while the chaotic birds excite themselves to orgiastic frenzy only at a comparatively late stage in the divine–human ritual. Then, however, they are the more enraptured: nature seems no less multifarious, but more directed towards a (humanly apprehensible?) goal of praise and glory. Slightly more conventional musical behaviour operates during the passage from Aquinas that names in sequence the three persons of the Trinity, in massive chords that, still stemming from the ambiguous second mode, move inexorably towards an unambiguous E major. Each monolithic chord, resonating on full orchestra and festooned with pulsating added notes, echoes through the mountains, obliterating the distance between earth and heaven.

This is really the End: except that an end to atemporal experience is a paradox. So Messiaen appends a *choral* dedicated to the glory of light in words, from Psalm 26, that equate the Divine Presence with the mountain and tabernacle wherein 'thine honour dwelleth'. The music adds nothing to the end of the previous movement since there is nothing to add; but it reinforces glory by returning to the *choral* that had ended the first *septénaire*, moving in immensely slow, solemn procession at quaver equals 30, but now in very loud homophony for chorus in eight or ten parts, all massively doubled by full orchestra. The whole edifice rests on the bellowing bass of those trombones, saxhorns and tubas; and the tonality, for all its coruscating chromatics, restores the E major blaze of the end of the previous movement. Occasional silences allow the 'transcendent' sonorities to echo through the mountain; but the very last chord, in ten choric parts with first sopranos on high B, is unsullied E major. If there is a paradox in Messiaen's equating ultimate metaphysical bliss with such obstreperous physicality, one recognizes that such has been the burden of his art from his early years. The message is here writ (very) large, and one has to admit that the unabashed nature of the utterance is part of its potency. Some people find it foolhardy, even to the point of embarrassment; others find it genuinely Apocalyptic and epiphanic. Even those who, like this writer, cannot share its convictions may be dazzled by its bravery, which may make us simultaneously laugh and cry. One might risk saying that to Messiaen's music no one can be indifferent. There are not many artists of whom as much can be said.

Des canyons aux étoiles . . .

RICHARD STEINITZ

Throughout his life, Messiaen offered musical praise to the miracle of creation at its grandest, dedicating his art to the dual but related purposes of celebrating religious faith and expressing his intense devotion to nature. *L'Ascension* is outdoor music. *Catalogue d'oiseaux* shows off birds in their natural habitat. *Et exspecto resurrectionem mortuorum*, says Messiaen, ideally should be experienced among high mountains. In *Chronochromie* huge, stone-hard chords depict rocks and splashy figurations the sound of water cascading in the Alps; while its sixth movement, 'Epode', an incredible polyphony of eighteen solo strings, represents the dawn chorus. In the *Quatuor pour la fin du temps* and *Turangalîla-symphonie* flowers, gardens, birds and rainbows are drawn into a fantasy of religious and sensual passion. Messiaen relates, in the preface to the *Quatuor*, how

> in my dreams I hear and see classified chords and melodies, known colours and forms; then, after this transitional stage, I pass into the unreal and submit in an ecstasy to a wheeling, a gyrating interpenetration of superhuman colours. These swords of fire, these blue and orange lava flows, these sudden stars: here is the jumble, here the rainbows!

Given such visionary obsessions, it is hardly surprising that Messiaen's imagination should have been captivated by the canyons of the American West, with their vibrant colours by day and brilliant panoply of stars by night.

When Messiaen accepted the commission from the patroness, Alice Tully, to compose a work for large chamber orchestra in honour of the American Bicentennial, he turned for inspiration to his huge library of geography books, particularly to a favourite series of volumes called *Les merveilles du monde*. Here he found confirmation of his impression of the Utah canyons as 'the grandest and most beautiful marvels of the world' and of Bryce Canyon as supreme. After much deliberation, and toying briefly with an alternative subject suggested by the mountains of Hawaii, Messiaen decided that Bryce Canyon, 'the most beautiful thing in the United States', would be central to his theme. And so, in the spring of 1972 (too early in the year to meet many other tourists but an ideal season for notating birdsongs) he set off with his wife to visit Utah, staying for eight days in a 'little inn' at the entrance to Bryce Canyon which enabled them to explore at their leisure.

Images of the American canyons must be etched on every mind, although, to comprehend their enormous scale and extraordinary rock formations, you must physically go there, wandering, perhaps for several days, along the upper rims and trekking down, with amazed incredulity, into their deep inner valleys. Although less well known, Bryce Canyon is as astonishing, and its geology as apparently preposterous as that of the Grand Canyon. Compared with the latter's rugged magnificence, Bryce Canyon has a breathtaking elegance and beauty all its own. Any visitor to Bryce Canyon comes upon a unique world in the middle of an already spectacular country; its pinnacles and spires have an almost Gothic delicacy; it is weird and other-worldly and at the same time an elemental, sculptural part of the Earth. Messiaen realized at once that its natural beauty far surpassed any photograph, 'so big, immense, a landscape of nothing but cliffs and boulders in fantastic shapes. There are castles, towers, dungeons, there are turrets, bridges, windows, and then, even more beautiful, there are the colours. Everything is red, all sorts of reds'.[1]

Des canyons aux étoiles . . . conveys through every gesture the unforgettable impact of seeing the Utah canyons. Although limited to an orchestra less than half the size of that required for the *Turangalîla-symphonie*, Messiaen's imagination takes off in astonishing flights of instrumentation, his ardour is infectious, the grandeur of the music's design is immensely impressive. *Des canyons* is a tribute to the magnificence of all creation and expresses the contemplation of a unity between heaven and earth. And, since Messiaen sees creation as a manifestation of God, it is a deeply religious work. Few pieces of nature-poetry have attempted to embrace so dazzling and momentous a subject; and even Messiaen, despite a lifelong absorption in nature and birdsong, is not, in his human frailty, entirely equal to the immeasurable scale of the task. His music conveys the magnificence of the scene, the exuberant colours and fantastic shapes, but also risks, at times, the accusation of being too naively symbolic, over-orderly in its symmetries and, perhaps, a shade too routine and medium-scale. Yet *Des canyons* has great splendours and is one of Messiaen's most poetic and accessible scores. Being conceived soloistically for an ensemble of forty-four players, a number falling in between the normal resources of chamber and symphony orchestra, it is, unfortunately, only infrequently performed. The size of the ensemble was presumably governed by the capacity of the Alice Tully Hall in New York where the work was premiered on 20 November 1974. However, by including quadruple woodwind, nine brass instruments and a generous helping of percussion, although only thirteen strings, Messiaen was able to re-create at least something of the powerful tuttis he had composed in *Chronochromie*, and yet imbue the whole work with the intimacy and clarity of chamber music; while the choice of instruments, which includes such curiosities as an eolophone (wind machine) and geophone (sand machine), encouraged him to invent many novel and ingenious timbral combinations.

Most of Messiaen's music contains specific extra-musical ideas: virtually all of it, indeed, had for him unashamedly programmatic origins. *Des canyons aux étoiles . . .* is no exception, being arranged as a sequence of twelve vivid and momentous pictures (listed on p. 543). In its different way, each is intriguing. Heard as a whole, the presence of so many different musical portraits raises structural problems – problems not wholly absent, of course, from his other music in which we may also observe Messiaen's painterly delight in catalogue exhibitions, notably in the keyboard works. From his first published work,

Le banquet céleste of 1928, he had spread his music out spaciously. One came to expect from him the slowest tempos, huge and richly coloured tableaux, an expansive vision of humanity, God, nature and eternity. *Des canyons*, even for Messiaen, is exceptional and is one of only a handful of orchestral works by any Western composer whose performance takes up a whole concert. Messiaen's longer works, particularly those for organ and piano, require sustained attentiveness from his listeners who, for the most part, are handsomely rewarded. But the great canvas of *Des canyons* stretches tolerance even of Messiaen's extended time-scale. Can this monumental cycle of meditations on the majesty of God's creation really hold our interest over twelve movements and one-and-a-half hours of playing time? What structural coherence does that require, what kind of musical language and resources? Its idiom is not so far removed from that of the *Turangalîla-symphonie*, but that work is shorter and is spectacularly scored for a huge orchestra whereas *Des canyons* has, as we have seen, an ensemble less than half that size.

Of similar length to *Des canyons* is Messiaen's *La Transfiguration de Notre-Seigneur Jésus-Christ* for large orchestra with the additional dimension of chorus and seven instrumental soloists. *La Transfiguration* may be regarded, perhaps, as the protracted ritual of some vast, imaginary religious ceremony. *Des canyons*, however, purports to be more of a concert piece.[2] Putting aside music involving words, which, in opera and oratorio, usually means narrative, *Des canyons* has almost no counterpart. Terry Riley's *In C* and Steve Reich's *Drumming*, both of whose durations may be varied in performance, approach it. Stockhausen's *Sternklang*, which uses voices but in an essentially instrumental manner, lasts for some three hours depending on the area of its (ideally, outdoor) performance space. Significantly, the musical processes in these pieces are homogeneous and intentionally elongated, absorbing the listener in the minutiae of extremely gradual change. Messiaen, on the other hand, does not eschew traditional rhetoric, with its implied dramatic contrasts and expectations of variable pacing – here accelerated, there retarded, always eventful.

Our perception of how time passes is inevitably subjective.

What transports one listener into a state of entrancement, to another may seem intolerably tedious. Our own mental state as listeners affects our attention-span, and that which the composer contrives to induce in his audience will also influence attitudes to time-scale; whether, for instance, we appear to be hurled along in cloak-and-dagger drama, or soothed into thoughtful contemplation. Messiaen's manner of handling such long pieces is to juxtapose different states and, thus, to proceed through a series of contrasts. Nevertheless, in *Des canyons* as in his other music, one has to accept that the nature of his faith reduces the possibilities of dramatic tension. This great hymn to heaven and earth has no darker side. There is no hint, for instance, of the pain of Gerontius's blinding encounter with the absolute perfection of God, no shadow of concern that the deity should allow agony as well as joy in his creation. Quoting, in the third movement, the prophecy of Daniel, 'MENE TEKEL UPHARSIN', Messiaen disregards its awesome promise of divine justice, retaining only ideas of quantity, weight and measurement. He has prefaced the score of 'Cedar Breaks', the fifth movement, with a quotation from Ernest Hello's *Paroles de Dieu*: 'To replace fear by awe opens a window for adoration', and added the comment that 'in the scale of feelings, the fear of punishment ranks rather low – Awe, which is the reverence of the sacred, of the divine presence, is more noble, and leads to adoration which stands at the very top'. *Des canyons*, therefore, is a work of ascension, of celebration for the resurrected, of breathtaking adoration rather than of disquieting mystery. Pascal's eternal silence of infinite space has no terror here.

This is a view of creation and eternity without evil or sin. Inspired by his visits to Utah, Messiaen's preoccupation, as one might expect, is with its astonishing physical splendour, as if a symphony of earth, rocks and sky were extolling the wonders of geology and astronomy. To keep vivid the detail of all that he found in Bryce Canyon throughout the subsequent months of composition, Messiaen wrote down copious descriptive notes, his wife took over 200 photographs and, of course, he transcribed birdsong. Birds, which for Messiaen represent ideal behaviour, are the only living dramatis personae to take the stage in *Des canyons*. Flawed humans are wholly absent. Indeed, apart from the Tristanesque love celebrated in the *Turangalîla-Symphonie*, *Harawi* and *Cinq rechants*, Messiaen's entire *œuvre* passes over problems of suffering humanity. Through the externalization of religious faith, his art rises above the subjective and is utterly without self-centredness or nostalgia. It is an essentially childlike delight in the wonder of creation that leads him to derive every note from extra-musical observation and objective symbolism. Indeed, one could claim that illustration, *per se*, is Messiaen's main and most essential structural principal, a lifelong dependence upon programmatic guidelines which could hardly have been less fashionable in the mid-twentieth century and was only temporally diverted by the prevailing intellectualism of the post-war years in pioneering experiments like the *Quatre études de rythme*. If representative symbolism is the music's primary stimulus, Messiaen's skill is in the clothing of these pictorial intentions in a systematic technique of exceptional orderliness. And, as with Bach, the paradox of emotional ardour and deep spirituality combined with rigorous discipline is fundamental to the music's stature. From this arises its radiance, passion and conviction.

Des canyons aux étoiles . . . has visual, philosophic and emotional sensibility in abundance; but architecturally it is less convincing. Perhaps the methods detailed so precisely in Messiaen's treatise of 1944, and still the basis of his technique much later, prove less than adequate to serve these bold aspirations? To answer this question, we must examine the structural principles of *Des canyons* in more detail. After which, to conclude, I want to consider further Messiaen's role among nature poets.

Symbolism and structure

Messiaen has chosen to divide *Des canyons aux étoiles . . .* into three parts, there being five movements in each of Parts 1 and 3, two only in Part 2. As Messiaen says in his Preface, the music begins with an evocation of the desert, 'symbol for that emptiness of the soul which allows it to perceive the inner conversation of the Spirit', whose disjointed, astringent character immediately creates a sense of unearthly majesty. Each of the three parts ends with a picture of one of the wonders of Utah, their associations for Messiaen indicated in the titles: 'Cedar Breaks et le don de crainte', 'Brice Canyon et les rochers rouge-orange', 'Zion Park et la cité céleste'. The radiant A$^{\#}$ major tonality of 'Zion Park', the twelfth movement, symbolizes paradise, joyful destination of the whole work. In between are five movements based on birdsongs and three devoted to the stars. Why the stars? Because, as Messiaen observed, from the depths of the canyons one inevitably looks up, 'one progresses from the deepest bowels of the earth and ascends towards the stars'. In the first part we hear 'Ce qui est écrit sur les étoiles'. The second begins with an 'Appel interstellaire' for solo horn, and the third with 'Les ressuscités et le chant de l'étoile Aldebaran'. Attracted by its 'charming' name which, in arabic, means the follower, Messiaen chose Aldebaran to represent himself (as Stockhausen had already identified himself with Sirius, the brightest star in the heavens) because Aldebaran 'has great velocity, a great light, and because it follows the Pleiades. I found that to be an admirable function of the follower.'[3] It is the most blissful movement in *Des canyons*, a long harmonized melody for strings reminiscent of 'Jardin du sommeil d'amour' in the *Turangalîla-symphonie*.

A passing curiosity in two of the movements is Messiaen's representation of the 'alphabet' by specific pitches and durations, using a system he had developed for the organ *Méditations* in 1969 (see p. 374–6). For that work, pondering the inability of music to communicate precise ideas, and inspired by St Thomas Aquinas's remarks in the *Summa* about the language of angels, Messiaen had devised for himself 'a kind of communicable language' partly as a game, partly to re-stimulate his own musical thoughts. Beginning with the familiar musical letter names used in German:

EX. 16.1

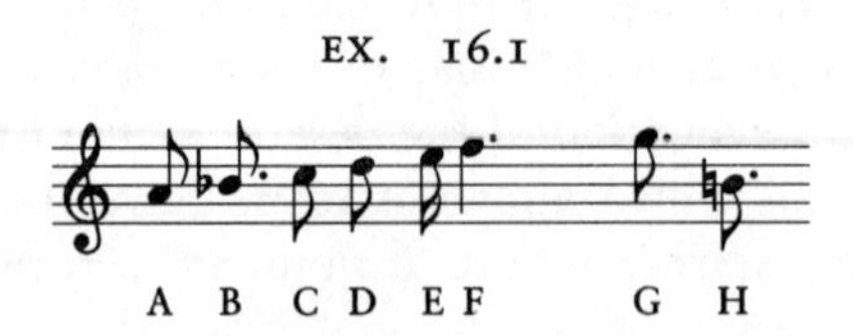

he extended this sequence to include the five vowels:

EX. 16.2

and, by further subgroups, to take in palatals, dentals, labials, sibilants etc, until he had invented a complete series providing each letter of the alphabet with its own pitch and duration:

EX. 16.3

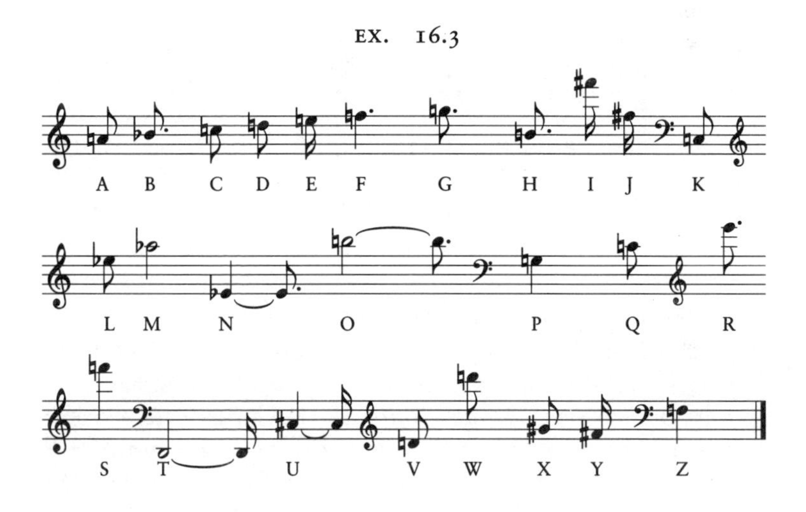

In *Des canyons* this 'communicable language' occurs in movements 2 and 4. In 'Cedar Breaks et le don de crainte' it articulates three Greek invocations: 'Agios o Theos' (Saint, o God!), 'Agios ischyros' (Saint and powerful!), and 'Agios athanatos' (immortal Saint!) But its most impressive use is to spell out the awful words of the writing on the wall at Belshazzar's Feast (in French 'MENÉ, TEQÉL, PARSIN') which open and end the third movement. For this monumental passage Messiaen gives each letter not only matching pitch and duration but its own chord and instrumentation, what one might perhaps call *Klangfarbenharmonie* (See Ex. 16.4).

EX. 16.4 *Des canyons aux étoiles . . .* 3 'Ce qui est ecrit sur les étoiles' (opening): pitches representing letters in Messiaen's musical alphabet are arrowed, and emphasized by his orchestration

These passages of musical alphabet are but brief moments in a mosaic of numerous components. Particularly important, therefore, is Messiaen's management of such extended montage. With its vast dimensions, *Des canyons* puts his large-scale architecture to a considerable test. Not only do its twelve movements follow each other as a succession of contrasting blocks, their internal structures are also highly episodic. Of course, most of Messiaen's music is sectional, which is not to say that it lacks driving forces. His skilful juxtaposition of varied 'characters' (*personnages*, one might say) enables elaborate sectional structures, like that of the *Turangalîla-symphonie*, to build a cumulative intensity. In *Des canyons* the faster tempos in 'Bryce Canyon', for example, which accelerate the music towards the joyful conclusion of Part 2, are supported by orchestration at its most ebullient and by the arrival on E major, the first definitive and resolutory tonality of the whole work. Here the pacing is admirable. Yet, on the whole, *Des canyons* has less dynamic thrust than *Turangalîla* and, because of its length, the cohesion of its sectional edifice is subjected to greater strain. Up to a point its twelve movements proceed progressively, but equally one could argue that their order is as potentially variable as the ways in which a painter might hang pictures of similar subject matter at an exhibition (notwithstanding the palindromic sequence of tutti and solo piano movements by means of which Parts 1 and 3 reflect each other).

To counter this view, one can observe how the cyclic repetitions and verse–refrain formulas of Messiaen's mature music are animated by many other energy-generating devices. Pitch material may be progressively stretched, so that what began in a restricted register ends with dazzling athletic leaps (as in No. 3, 'L'échange' and the last page of No. 14, 'Regard des anges' in *Vingt regards*). His music grows by accretion. Phrases are added, like new tableaux in a pageant, to make the picture more vivid and brilliant. Sections are successively transposed, or elongated so that each reaches a new point of harmonic arrival. A passage may come back spectacularly superimposed upon others or doubled-back on itself, like the impressive return of the orange-red rocks theme in retrograde canon in the second antistrophe of 'Bryce Canyon'. Particularly thrilling in the orchestral scores, with their huge resources, is the return of those sections in which the composer gradually piles on more and more independent layers in a mesmeric display of asymmetric polyphony. In *Des canyons* it is the eleventh movement, 'Omao, leiothrix, elepaio, shama' (a delightfully animated and vivacious party for Hawaiian birds and friends!) which best demonstrates this exciting process of accumulation. Its structure alternates four refrains and four verses, concluding with a piano cadenza and coda. The simple horn and bassoon melody of the first refrain, on both its second and third returns, gains intriguing new polymetric counterpoints (see Ex. 16.5); while each of the verses is thrillingly elaborated and extended by the arrival of new visitors to the aviary.

Architecture, intuition and routine

What is crucial, to make such large-scale architecture convincing, is the spontaneity of the ongoing sequence as well as the proportional balance between sections and movements (which are but collections of sections), and the nature of the timbral and temporal contrasts between them. Messiaen thrives on extreme contrasts of mood, colour and tempo. Even within movements of consistent character, whose cyclic repetitions must eventually surrender to the onward thrust of the music, the change of direction, when it comes, is usually masterful; the expressive role of new material is made immediately clear. Concluding sections are given a grandeur or extravagance that makes their finality indisputable. Messiaen seems to have judged such things intuitively; so that, despite his schematic and orderly approach to musical material, the broader disposition of movements in his large-scale works is as much sensed as calculated. At first sight there may seem to be a contrived order, like the palindromic symmetry of the thirteen pieces which make up the *Catalogue d'oiseaux*, or his adoption, in several works including *Des canyons*, of the archetypical forms of strophe, antistrophe and epode, borrowed from the choral odes of ancient Greek drama. Such titles have a certain resonance, but their structural implications are only skin deep, since, into the vessels which bear

EX. 16.5 *Des canyons aux étoiles . . .* 11 'Omao, leithrix, elepaio, shama'

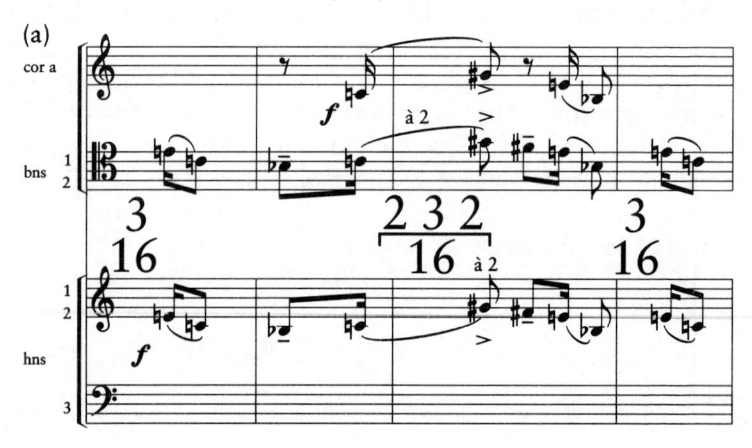

(b)

pic
fls
obs
cor a
cl (E♭)
cls
bns
à2
(original horn and bassoon melody unchanged)
hns
à2
3
16
2 3 2
16
3
16
glock
xylor
1
2
vns
3
4
5
6
II crot
I bells
III tpl bl

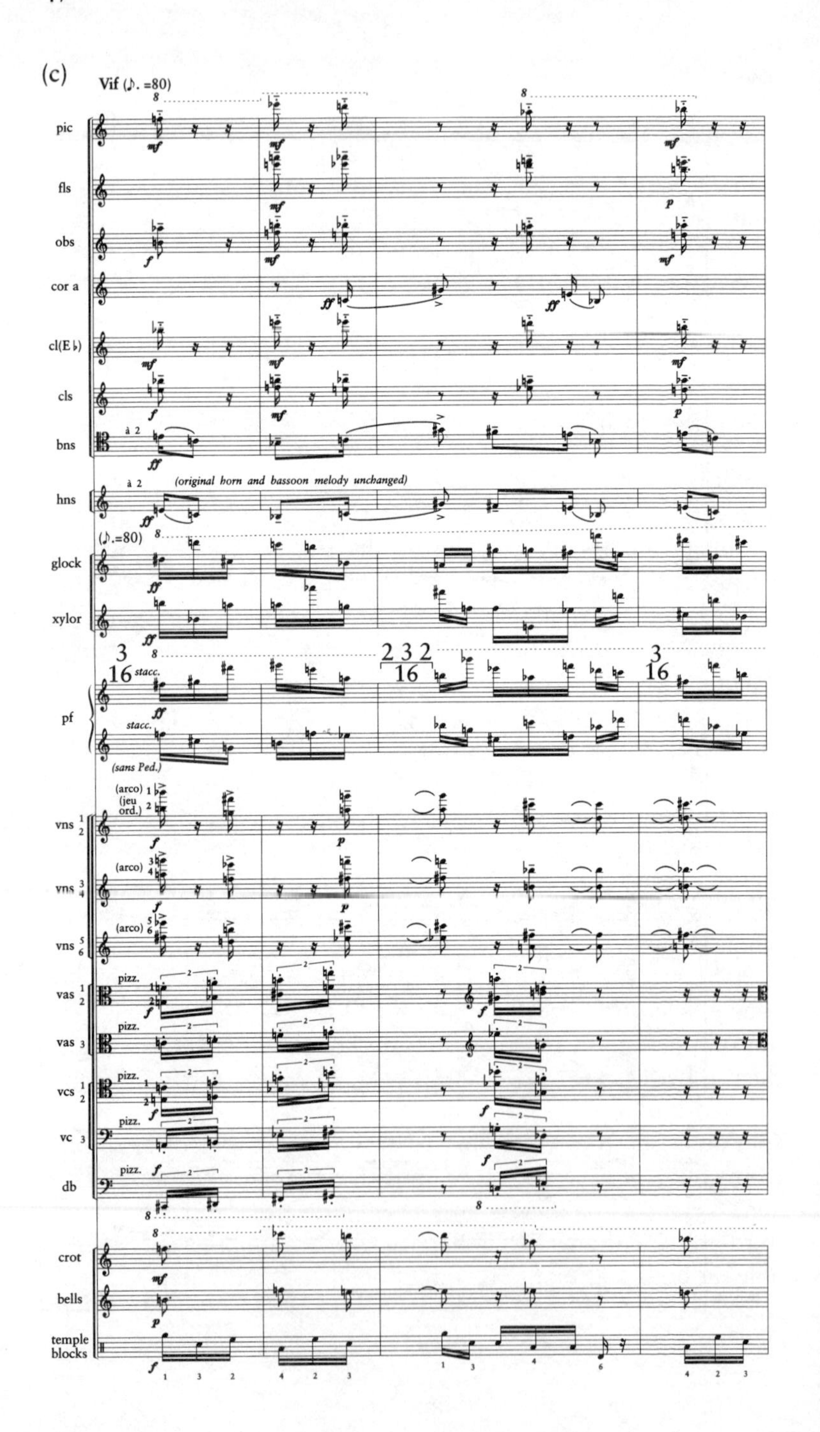
(c)
Vif (♪. =80)
pic
fls
obs
cor a
cl(E♭)
cls
bns
à 2
hns
à 2
(original horn and bassoon melody unchanged)
(♪.=80)
glock
xylor
pf
stacc.
(sans Ped.)
(arco)
(jeu ord.)
vns
vas
pizz.
vcs
vc
db
crot
bells
temple blocks

these names, Messiaen poured whatever music he wanted. Whereas he organized the harmonic, rhythmic and melodic processes *within* his music with, at times, elaborate rigour, its broader formal outlines are dictated mostly by instinct.

In *Des canyons* one feels that Messiaen's instinct was not infallible. Within individual movements, some sections are arranged very symmetrically. Would not the riotous irregularity of creation have been better represented by less orderly and predictable geometry? The inclusion of three solo pieces among the twelve movements of *Des canyons* allows tension to sag, and the grandeur and vivid scene-painting of the surrounding orchestral movements momentarily to contract and grow monochrome. Two of these solo movements are for piano and another, the sixth, is for horn. The horn writing is technically spectacular and its character, as always in Messiaen, symbolic: this unaccompanied melody, punctuated by pauses as if seeking a reply, evokes the vastness and emptiness of space in which the horn's lonely calls go unanswered. The image is certainly poetic. But the very presence of a display by the solo horn, however splendidly executed, at the heart of an orchestral-ensemble work of the grandest aspirations, is curiously unconvincing. Its position here seriously dissipates the energies gathered together in the previous movement at a time when they needed to be held in readiness, as it were, for the seventh – the last of Part 2 and the climactic movement before the interval (if it is taken) – whose subject, Bryce Canyon itself, 'the greatest wonder of Utah' as Messiaen observes, is central to the grand vision of the whole work.

Piano solos, in the midst of orchestral compositions, are, of course, what we have come to expect from Messiaen. They were not only set pieces for his wife to perform, but also represented the pirouettes, *pas de deux* and choreographed ensembles of his beloved birds. The fourth movement of *Des canyons*, a piano solo depicting the white-browed robin, 'a wonderful songbird' from south-east Africa, makes an effective contribution. Messiaen's keyboard writing is no longer innovatory, but he uses his 'bird-piano' colourfully enough to complement the very remarkable timbral spectrum of the other orchestral movements. Moreover, his representation of this one bird's song, albeit a compilation of different routines, creates a more homogeneous impression than the often fragmented character of the first three movements and so restores, rather than intrudes upon our sense of continuity. The considerably longer piano solo of the ninth movement is more problematic. Here the mockingbird (for whom, as the most famous bird of the United States, Messiaen perhaps felt obliged to provide a part) shares the stage with other feathered accomplices from Australia. The style of the piano writing is flamboyant and contains some novelties, like the clusters played with the palm of the hand and with both arms. But its general character is disturbingly familiar, and it is difficult to see what it adds to our sense of the awesome splendour of the natural world which *Des canyons* generally conveys. Intimacy, Messiaen might have argued, is as important as immensity in what is as much a work of religious meditation as of praise. Yet the fragmented, seemingly directionless phrases of the mockingbird do somewhat undermine the broader architecture and pacing of the whole work.

Even the division of *Des canyons* into three parts appears arbitrary, particularly since a division into two would have better suited normal concert conditions. Each part ends with its most brilliant and spectacular movement. And, on the face of it, the two outer groups, each of five movements, balance each other around the central pair. In performance, one is hardly aware of such equivalence since the sequence of movements sounds more random. On the other hand, while the ordering of the twelve movements is, to a degree, arbitrary, their internal structures, as I have observed, are often elaborately symmetrical.

A harmonious equilibrium – the music of the spheres – has long been regarded as a facet of creation. And verses are the stuff of hymnody, which is basic to much of Messiaen's work. Yet, cumulatively, one is nagged by the feeling that the frequent alternation and repetition of sections and phrases becomes too orderly and inevitable. After all, neither the amazing rock formations of Utah nor the constellations of the night sky are so regular. Messiaen's more intricate rhythmic material, particularly of course that derived from birdsong, is always internally elastic, but he is inclined to repeat what in themselves are asymmetric phrases in predictable cycles of insistent regularity, the music for 'Bryce Canyon' being a case in point. Much earlier in his life, Messiaen had espoused rhythmic music as a 'music which eschews repetition, bar-lines, and equal divisions, which ultimately takes its inspiration from the movements of nature, movements which are free and unequal in length'.[4] So it is curious that he often does not apply this credo to the very music which purports to represent nature at its most extraordinary and fantastic.

Not that classic principals of proportion are to be wholly despised. For Messiaen, such perfection is symbolic. Among the stars he finds an exquisite symmetry. The Book of Job, he reminds us in his introduction to the eighth movement, 'Les ressuscités et le chant de l'étoile Aldebaran', talks about the 'happy concert of morning stars'. Certainly these well-drilled choristers perform faultlessly,[5] so that this movement has as poised and perfect a structure as any. The strings play twenty-four phrases grouped in four stanzas, the third and fourth being varied recapitulations or extensions of the first and second. Matched dynamics reinforce the impression of orderly behaviour which the presence of several birds in counterpoint above the strings, dutifully following regular cues, does nothing to dispel. But Messiaen avoids too frequent multiples of four beats in the lengths of phrases and the total effect is most graciously choreographed.

The fourth stanza's extended phrases, and their increased number, are characteristic of Messiaen's technique. By adding weight to the final section of the movement the expressive vision is intensified. Luminous and serene, the homogeneity of this movement is affectingly beautiful. The glissando harmonics of the violins, high-pitched indeterminate *col legno* of the solo double bass and rustling wind chimes of the percussion, which trail silken wisps through each of the four cadences ending each stanza, are moments of delicate and charming coloration. This is a beatific vision of the resurrected among the stars. Not for Messiaen the unfathomable mysteries of Gustav Holst's *Planets* or the icy impersonality of the star Betelgeuse (Aldebaran's near neighbour[6]) which Holst evokes so numbingly in the haunting last song of his Humbert Wolfe cycle.

Symmetry is also the hallmark of the third movement 'Ce qui est écrit sur les étoiles', with its carefully balanced ternary grouping of fifteen alternating sections. Sections 1 to 4 (up to fig. 8) and 12 to 15 (from fig. 28) on the outsides mirror each other palindromically and are strongly contrasted. Sections 5 to 11 (figs 8–28) are also symmetrically arranged; although Messiaen's ever-inventive treatment of the birdsong delivers continuously new variants, giving this central group a more volatile and developmental character and more forward energy. If a harmonious symmetry is written in the stars, what of the earthly scenes? In that 'Cedar Breaks' and 'Bryce Canyon' both use the same formula of strophe, antistrophe I, antistrophe II, epode and coda, they exhibit similar disciplines. Their threefold cyclic repetitions, comprising each movement's strophes and its two antistrophes, would seem to derive more from liturgical convention (the threefold Kyrie?) than from natural spontaneity. But the bizarre and strange musical ideas they contain complement this structural routine with material that sounds more mercurial. One thinks of Birtwistle's advocacy of both order and capriciousness as essential simultaneous attributes of great music.

I have already instanced the multilayered ternary form of 'Les orioles' as an example of cyclic structure that is more passive and statuesque, and, in general, the many sectional repetitions in *Des canyons* are subjected to less creative renewal than in Messiaen's earlier works. The cumulative effect of so many episodic and cyclic structures inevitably impedes the development of a broader directional energy sufficient to sustain dynamic impetus across the whole work. The listener gets disorientated, as he might equally lose his sense of direction in the bewildering inner labyrinth of Bryce Canyon itself.

Subtleties of coloration

The absence of dramatic opposition and the multisectional geometry of *Des canyons* means that, overall, the work lacks focus and thrust. Its totality is less than the sum of its parts. Its formulas are routine. What repeatedly saves *Des canyons* from sounding predictable is their extraordinary variety of musical character, and the inspired ingenuity with which Messiaen employs his medium-sized orchestra. As we have seen, not all sections repeat exactly. For instance, in the verse–refrain exchanges of the eleventh movement, Messiaen adds always sparkling new contrapuntal layers to each successive appearance of the refrain. This and the previous movement, 'La grive des bois', with their eerie string effects produced by playing both sides of the bridge, are among the most colourful pieces in *Des canyons*, and there are many other examples throughout the work of strange and lovely subtleties of orchestration, inspired, perhaps, by the widespread pursuit of extended playing techniques which characterized the decade of the 1960s just before *Des canyons* was written. For instance, avant-garde practices may have encouraged Messiaen to employ such 'experimental' techniques as that in No. 6 where the horn is directed to play high oscillations with valves pressed only half-way down (see Ex. 16.6).

EX. 16.6 *Des canyons aux étoiles . . .* 6 'Appel interstellaire'

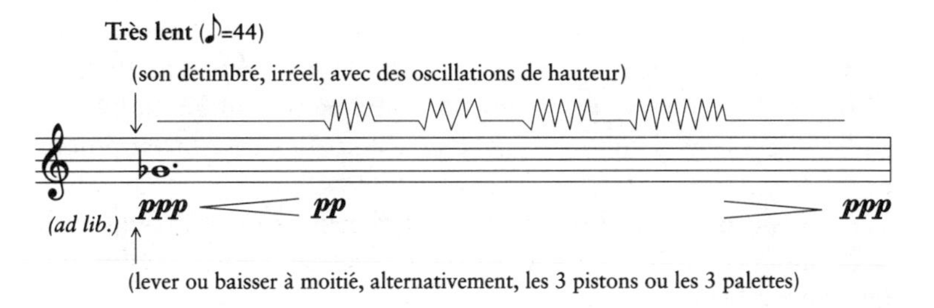

EX. 16.7 *Des canyons aux étoiles . . .* 11 'Omao, leiothrix, elepaio, shama'

The indeterminate pitches in the piccolo part in No. 11 are another currently fashionable device employed for convincingly expressive ends (Ex. 16.7).

One could find many such instances: the strangely disembodied melody shared between bowed crotales, piccolo and solo violin harmonics, to the accompaniment of high double bass tremolos played with the metal nut of the bow while damping the lower pitches with the left hand, plus flutes playing 'quasi pizzicato' in the first movement can be cited as one of the most ingenious (see Ex. 16.8).

Perhaps the most memorable aspect of *Des canyons* is the degree to which Messiaen's refined technique of overtone and timbral coloration, combined with a lifelong desire to turn natural into notated sounds, leads him into these extraordinary sound combinations. It is not only in the use of the wind machine, and the somewhat naive whistling produced by blowing through a trumpet mouthpiece detached from its instrument, that the border between musical sounds and noise are blurred, an artificial distinction in any case already rendered obsolete by John Cage. 'Cedar Breaks', for example, contains quite remarkable aural images. Its ingenuities of orchestration and unconventional instrumental techniques are exceptional, even for Messiaen. In this movement, Messiaen comes closest to discovering in nature a wild anarchy, an Ivesian unity in diversity. Daring both technically and expressively, the piece is unique in Messiaen's *œuvre*. Here birdsong is metamorphosed into an abstract power, primeval, hallucinatory and cataclysmic: witness the monumental treatment accorded the red-shifted flicker and blue grouse in the opening tutti. In such passages Messiaen's music becomes less harmonic than sculpted, hewn from elemental sonic matter like the music of Varèse.

Dissonance and resolution

As to the broader harmonic structure of *Des canyons*, basically it may be heard as a prolonged resolution of multifarious harmonic and intervallic colours into the secure and serene radiance of major triads. In the course of its twelve movements, Messiaen

EX. 16.8 *Des canyons aux étoiles . . .* I 'Le désert'

EX. 16.9

runs the gamut from extreme chromatic ambiguity to lustrous diatonic stability. But even when, as in the first movement, the harmony is consistently ambiguous and astringent, there is a tendency towards triadic resolution, here from D major down to D♭ major, both as second inversion chords contained within a more complex chromatic bitonality (see Ex. 16.9). The 'stress–release' characteristic of this semitonal slide is significant. It is typical of Messiaen's music that the ends of phrases sink, subsiding into chords of resolution, as in the second movement with its arched melodies and piano birdcalls that repeatedly cadence through an octave drop on to a reposeful G major added-sixth chord (see Ex. 16.10).

EX. 16.10 *Des canyons aux étoiles . . .* 2 'Les orioles'

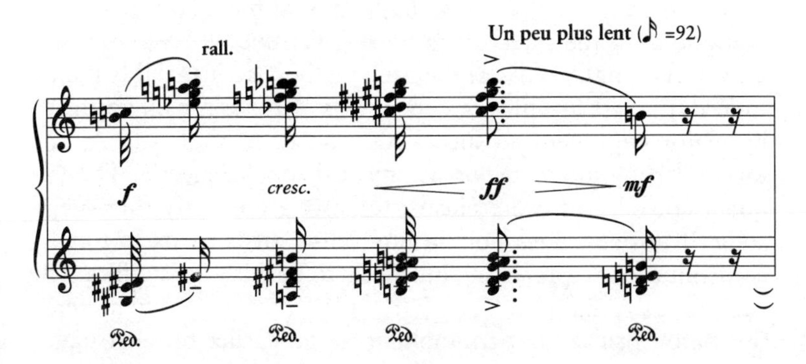

Messiaen's association of harmony with visible colour is well known, so one might reasonably expect the extravagant hues which are part of the splendour of the Utah canyons to have inspired from him a matching exuberance of coloured harmony no less fantastic. In the notes he made while visiting the canyons, Messiaen lists 'red-violet, a red-orange, rose, dark red carmine, scarlet red, all possible varieties of red, an extraordinary beauty'.[7] To represent these predominant shades of red, should not also the harmonic character of *Des canyons* have a unique pigmentation among Messiaen's works? Alas, despite the wonders of orchestration in *Des canyons*, the listener will probably conclude, with some disappointment, that the composer's harmonic palette here is indistinguishable from that of his other music. Nevertheless, there are some striking, if familiar, juxtapositions. One such contrast occurs between the glowing E major tonality of the seventh movement, representing the flamboyant oranges and reds of Bryce Canyon, and the bitter-sweet of the clusterous chords which paint the prevailing 'blue sky' A major, already alluded to, of No. 8, 'Les ressuscités et le chant de l'étoile Aldebaran'.

The unique sonic fantasy of 'Cedar Breaks' and the extent to which, despite its typically symmetrical sectional structure, it sounds erratic makes it, for me, the most interesting movement in *Des canyons*. After it, the following movements tend towards more conventional chordal harmony and structural formulas. Indeed, overall, the harmonic language of *Des canyons* harks back to the period of *Turangalîla*, and is far more consonant and diatonic than the intervening works, *Chronochromie* and *Sept haïkaï*. As tonalities assert themselves, they are invariably major. Indeed, the last five movements of *Des canyons* are all governed by major keys, centred successively on E, A, C, E and A, and unassailed by modulations or any real tonal dialectic. The frequent episodes of more elusive tonality are exactly that – episodic. Messiaen does not, in any sense, treat them as tonally confrontational, preferring his music to be without conflict. The sumptuous A major of 'Zion Park et la cité céleste' is in no sense the victor, bruised but triumphant, of an earlier tonal struggle. Only in that A major arrives like the high priest or celebrant in a colourful procession, does the music of this final movement achieve its glorious conclusion. Such is the composer's right. Fancifully, we might have wished that the wandering, nineteenth-century American pioneers, the Mormons (who, when they 'discovered the pink, white, mauve, red, black walls, the green trees and the limpid river of Zion Park, looked at it as a symbol of Paradise',[8] had been assigned parts in *Des canyons* as care-laden pilgrims, who could have trudged through the pages of the score like Childe Harold through Berlioz's Italian landscape, or crossed over the river of death, like Mr Valiant-for-Truth, to be greeted by a hard-won A major as 'all the trumpets sounded for him on the other side'. Nothing could have been further from Messiaen's creative mind. A narrative of human drama would have interfered distractingly in this theocentric song of praise.

A lineage of nature-poets

If the human dimension of Romanticism is generally absent from Messiaen's music, nevertheless, his leading position among nature-poets interestingly associates him with earlier composers, not only with Debussy and Ravel but, more closely perhaps, with Wagner, Berlioz, Schumann and Bach. Like Bach, Messiaen indulges in naive, almost childish illustration; yet more significant in the music of both composers is their spiritual response to the natural world as a manifestation of the divine. Bach's tone-painting appeals to the conceptual imagination; the cantatas abound in musical portraits of landscape (for example, the rolling waves of a lake, swaying ears of corn and distant church bells) as much as they convey feeling (for example, the emotional state of Christ's disciples).

Theories, albeit unproven, of the affinity between music and colour also go back a long way. The great nineteenth-century French painter Delacroix, himself a keen amateur musician, associated colour closely with mood, ranking colour above draughtsmanship for its ability to convey a purely abstract or 'musical' quality independent of the subject depicted.[9] Baudelaire, Kandinsky and Skryabin held similar views, the poet in his turn constantly haunted by E. T. A. Hoffmann's vision in his *Kreisleriana* of the relationship between colours, sounds and perfumes. In this novel Hoffmann presents his hero, Johannes Kreisler, as 'the little man in a coat the colour of C sharp minor with an E major coloured collar' – an eccentric metaphor maybe, but are Messiaen's colour associations any less fanciful? The continued absence of any demonstrable scientific correspondence between sound and light waves has evidently failed to kill the aspirations for such union which emerged out of the artistic idealism of the Romantic era.

Although Messiaen shares with Bach a liking for representative illustration and colourful religious imagery, he is aesthetically closer to the *Naturphilosophen* of the early nineteenth century, to those nature-worshipping German Romantics who strove for a new synthesis of art, religion and the whole of creation. Novalis, the leading poet of early German Romanticism, developed an intense belief in the mystical unity of all things. Others, like Wilhelm Wackenroder, Jean Paul, Friedrich von Schelling and Friedrich Hölderlin, immersed themselves in an idealized transfiguration of the natural world in communion with the divine. However, their quest was bound up with an intolerable ecstasy and yearning intensified through the act of creation, which, for some, resulted in an agonizing sense of inadequacy, and for others, like Hölderlin and Schumann, led to isolation and madness. Messiaen, on the other hand, seems to have been blessedly endowed, even as a child, with a serene confidence in his God-given vocation, and to have achieved what the Romantics sought less successfully, an escape from 'self' to espouse the whole of creation.

Messiaen was, after all, no pantheist but a devout Roman Catholic. Nevertheless, his creed is close to that of Schelling, the leading aesthetician of *Naturphilosophen*, who said 'nature is visible spirit, and spirit is invisible nature'. 'I'm not ashamed of being a Romantic', Messiaen remarked to Claude Samuel.[10] And although Messiaen's music may be devoid of nostalgia, his love of orientalism and birdsong has its counterpart in the Romantics' escape into medievalism from the withering rationalism of the Enlightenment. His taste for the exotic has its parallel in their readiness to embrace everything fantastic. And by rejecting the sardonic detachment and intellectual excesses of his own immediate predecessors – the post-war French composers of the 1920s – and co-founding with Yves Baudrier, Daniel-Lesur and André Jolivet the group La Jeune France, Messiaen allied himself emphatically with a Romantic concept of music.

The magical forest, home to many of Messiaen's birds, with its teeming life, dappled light and quiet mystery, has been a recurrent source of musical inspiration especially for Germanic composers. It wove its spell around Schumann and Weber, divulged new insights to Siegfried and enfolded Hänsel and Gretel in sleep. Mahler built his composing retreat high in the forest, the love of Pelléas and Mélisande is enveloped in its shadows. The sun rises above Arcadian groves in *Daphnis et Chloé*; the numbing grey of *Tapiola* extends across bleak Scandinavian forests. In Tippett's *Midsummer Marriage* an English woodland glade witnesses both the charming courtship of Jack and Bella and the ritual dances of hunters and hunted, birds among them. If, in Messiaen's music, the woods and forests so meaningful to Romantic experience have been replaced by a fascination with mountains, glaciers and desert canyons, this is but a natural imaginative progression. Indeed, looking back over the twentieth century, it would now appear that composers have turned no less for inspiration to the natural world than in the nineteenth, despite the structural emphasis of many of its artistic movements, neoclassicism, modernism and minimalism being but three of the most abstract. Latterly, mankind's imagination has been caught up in a greater vastness of time and space, conjuring images like the ancient megaliths of Maxwell Davies's *Stone Litany* and Birtwistle's *Silbury Air*, the impenetrable distances of Ligeti's *Lontano*, the prehistoric supercontinent of Murail's *Gondwana*, the imagined psychological landscapes of Berio, or the natural wonders and technological vistas over which glide the cameras in the Philip Glass/Godfery Reggio film *Koyaanisqatsi*, with its striking time-lapse photography. Narrative music[11] may have declined in the twentieth century, but extra-musical associations continue. In the wake of Monet's gradual transformation of pictorial definition, throughout his late series of waterlily paintings, into an abstract yet lyrical form of energy in which colour and atmosphere function like music, composers likewise have generally moved away from narrative and naturalism towards a lyrical symbolism, exploring the inner depths and intangible far horizons of matter and the mind.

The Romantics, too, were perpetually groping at the frontiers of the mysterious, wondering at the nature of God and time, questioning the place of man in the universe and delving into every branch of science. The German painter, Philipp Otto Runge, in a letter to his brother dated 9 March 1802, encapsulates a philosophy of Romantic art to which, one suspects, Messiaen could have subscribed:

> When the sky above me teems with countless stars, when the wind whistles through endless space . . . when the sun lights up the universe and mists rise from the valley, then I throw myself down on the grass among the rose-sparkling dewdrops, and each blade of grass quivers with life, the earth beneath me writhes with life, and everything is in tune with everything – then my soul cries aloud with joy and hovers around me in immeasurable space; there is no longer any above or below, no longer any beginning or end; time is stilled, and I feel the living breath of God which drives the world through space and is the motive force and life of all.[12]

Nearly two centuries later, the infinity of space has become vaster, time more enigmatic, and the known world more extraordinary and wonderful. Messiaen's adoration is for the creator of an even more astonishing universe, but his Romantic sentiments, tempered like Bach's by the organ loft, submit to an unshakeable religious conviction rare among twentieth-century composers. Untroubled by doubt, his vision of creation is as theologically correct as it is devout.

Notes

1 This passage and the quotations in the previous paragraph are taken from 'Canyons, Colours and Birds – an Interview with Olivier Messiaen' by Harriet Watts, *Tempo*, 128 (1979), pp. 2–8.

2 Not that the presence or absence of text makes much difference to the character of Messiaen's music. Virtually all his music is programmatic, and

some of it even embodies implied texts represented symbolically, like the 'alphabetic' pitch and duration series devised for the organ *Méditations* of 1969 and used in the third and fifth movements of *Des canyons*, in which letters are assigned precise pitch and duration equivalents. When Messiaen uses voices, their role is on a par with birdsong. The latter may be more interesting rhythmically and melodically; but human voices, moving in serene chordal homophony, suggest that unity of the communion of angels and of the resurrected which is an essential part of Messiaen's vision. To this end, he invariably prefers texts which are contemplative and non-dynamic. Where, in *La Transfiguration*, we meet fragments of biblical *narrative*, these serve only to define a context; their musical setting has the impersonal neutrality of quasi-plainsong through which the composer distances himself from any hint of developing drama. But if word-setting has no effect upon Messiaen's penchant for episodic structure and does little to increase dramatic tension, undoubtedly voices add lustre to what are already splendid scenes of musical pageantry.

3 Watts, op. cit., p. 6.

4 Claude Samuel: *Entretiens avec Olivier Messiaen* (Paris, Belfond, 1967); quoted in Roger Nichols: *Messiaen* (Oxford University Press, 1975, 2/ 1986), p. 21.

5 Messiaen composed this movement in the belief that the stars *do* sing, since one can record their vibrations, each star having its own frequency and 'pitch'. More recently Gérard Grisey has employed the periodic radio transmissions from pulsars, received directly in the concert hall via a radio telescope, in his multidimensional piece, *Le noir de l'étoile*.

6 Incidentally, both Aldebaran and Betelgeuse are orange-red stars, but Messiaen overlooks this fact, as their colour is harmonically inconvenient. Orange-red is, of course, also the colour of Bryce Canyon, and its introduction into 'Les ressuscités et le chant de l'étoile Aldebaran' would only confuse the prevailing 'blue' sonority which the composer had planned to be the prevailing colour of this movement.

7 Watts, op. cit., p. 4.

8 From Messiaen's programme notes on *Des canyons aux étoiles*. . . .

9 See Edward Lockspeiser's extensive study of this fascinating subject in *Music and Painting* (Cassell, London, 1973).

10 'Je n'est pas honte d'être romantique' (Samuels, op. cit., p. 141).

11 There is no narrative in *Koyaanisqatsi* and the Glass operas are also conceptually non-narrative.

12 I am indebted to Marcel Brion's book, *Schumann and the Romantic Age*, translated by Geoffrey Sainsbury (Collins, London, 1956) both for this extract and for his illuminating discussion of the aesthetics of the *Naturphilosophen*.

Saint François d'Assise

PAUL GRIFFITHS

A Messiaen opera? When the prospect came into view, around 1980, it was unimaginable. The only vocal work the composer had produced during the previous thirty years had been a concert-hall liturgy, *La Transfiguration*. More generally, his music had never come near the narrative continuity that had made opera an open possibility during the diatonic period, and there was nothing in his output to suggest a potential for human (as opposed to avian) characterization. Perhaps most baffling of all was the idea of Messiaen's music – with the powerful suggestions he had himself endorsed of imaginary visual experience, of colour beyond what the earthly eye can see – being tied to singers and scenery on a stage, of the immaterial being dragged through the all too material mill of the theatre.

The bewilderment was there despite the fact that Messiaen's introduction to his art had been partly, and importantly, through the medium of opera. As a young child, between the ages of seven and ten, he had asked for operatic vocal scores as Christmas presents: *Don Giovanni* and *Die Zauberflöte*, Gluck's *Alceste* and *Orfeo*, Berlioz's *Faust*, and *Die Walküre* and *Siegfried*.[1] During this same period he had recited the whole of Shakespeare, with his brother as participant or audience, and made a toy theatre for his shows.[2] Then, as a climax to this apprenticeship in dramatic sorcery, there had been the gift, when he was ten, of the score of *Pelléas et Mélisande* – 'probably the most decisive influence on me'.[3] However, that influence, like the earlier enthusiasm, had its place at the piano, not in the theatre: almost never, in his published conversations, did he talk about attending opera performances. Opera came to him as music conveying a story in the imagination – or perhaps rather as music conveying particular moments in a story, since a boy at the piano is free to jump around the score, to play favourite bits over and over. So, however distant he may have remained from the practices of traditional opera, there could after all have been some continuity between his childhood musical preferences and the fragmented expositions of sacred stories he produced in works from *La Nativité du Seigneur* to *La Transfiguration*.

His adult experience of opera, too, would seem to have been largely through scores played and examined at the piano in his Conservatoire classes, which were often devoted to musical drama – to a choice selection that overstepped his childhood repertory only to include *Tristan*, *Boris* and *Wozzeck*. As he was later to avow, in the whole history of opera 'there are hardly more than ten indisputable masterpieces'.[4] (His teacher's *Ariane et Barbe-bleue*, the subject of one of his very few essays,[5] he would perhaps have placed in his category of works 'which are musically very fine but whose stumbling block is their dramatic inadequacy'; the alternative lesser class, of works 'which make good theatre but are musically very poor', would have to include a great deal in general circulation.)

Only for an inferior composer would the infrequency of success have been a real reason for avoiding the genre. More central to the unlikelihood of a Messiaen opera was the nature of his music, and it was an unlikelihood he felt himself. 'I didn't think I had the gift, and that's what I said in reply to Rolf Liebermann, general administrator of the Paris Opéra, when he wanted to give me a commission.'[6] (This must have been between 1973, when Liebermann took up his Paris appointment, and 1975, when Messiaen began work on the opera.) The reason for his change of mind was not, surely, any discovery that he had 'the gift', but rather his realization that no special aptitude was necessary, that he could write an opera – as he had written a symphony – sublimely aside from the traditions of the form.

What also gave him confidence, so it would seem from his conversation with Claude Samuel, was his discovery of an appropriate subject – or rather, his acceptance of a subject which had been in his mind for thirty years.[7] 'I tell you, my dream was to write a Passion or a Resurrection of Christ. But I thought that

I was unworthy of it and, most importantly, that such a thing wasn't stageable, except in the case of works conceived in faith and naivety, like the Oberammergau folk performances.' Hence the choice of St Francis: 'someone who wasn't a god but only a man, and yet who resembled Christ because he was chaste, because he was humble, because he was poor, and because he suffered'.[8]

From that choice followed a necessary literary preparation:

> In my opinion the major books are first of all the saint's own writings: the different rules he prepared for the Franciscan community, the prayers he composed, the famous poem entitled *Cantico delle creature* or *Cantico del sole* – a poem which I used almost in its entirety in my opera, and of which Saint François sings a strophe in each scene. I also drew on the *Fioretti* and the *Considerations on the Stigmata*, where various anonymous Franciscans relate the saint's daily existence . . . I read the lives of the saint . . . St Bonaventure wrote two excellent Lives of St Francis, which demand to be read . . . Some modern books are quite successful, but romanticised . . . Only one of them did I quote from: an admirable book called *Lire François d'Assise*, whose author, Father Louis Antoine, is a Capuchin. It's a masterpiece which, curiously, talks a great deal about beauty, and which relates to the ideas Urs von Balthazar put forward in *Glory and the Cross*.[9]

Then, in the summer of 1975,[10] Messiaen put together his text, including quotations not only from these sources but also from various places in the Bible. 'I made some borrowings from Holy Scripture, including this very important phrase which the Angel speaks to the Leper: "Your heart condemns you, but God is greater than your heart." That phrase, taken from the First Epistle of St John, is too beautiful to be mine.'[11] Even so, the French wording throughout is the composer's own, as it is in *La Transfiguration* and nearly all the vocal works of the 1930s and 1940s. The reason for that preference was, so he told Samuel, a practical one: to give him the freedom to adapt the words to his rhythms and to the needs of his singers ('I like singers, and have no wish to make them whistle or hiccough. Even *Sprechgesang* doesn't interest me.'[12]) But it is hard to imagine that a composer of such individual vision could ever have been able to voice his music through the words of someone else.

As to the content of the text, Messiaen began at a point where François is already the leader of a community:

> Some people have said to me: there's no sin in your work. But for myself, I find sin isn't interesting, filth isn't interesting. I prefer flowers. I omitted sin. I also omitted the disputes between father and son, for a particular reason. I've known several psychoanalysts, even within my family, but I have a horror of psychoanalysis. I thought such a scene would give them an opportunity to embroider on the theme of the Oedipus complex.[13]

Saint François was not to be a psychological opera. For a similar reason he left out St Clare: because the relationship between the saints could have been seen, through rudely secular modern eyes, as a love story. Then for fear of ridicule – for fear of the absurdity he saw in the dragon and rams of the *Ring* – he excluded the episode of the wolf which Francis persuaded not to terrorize the local population. And in order to concentrate the action – to avoid, so it seems, incidental characters in period costume – he eliminated a 'very beautiful scene from the end of the saint's life' in which the bishop of the place was reconciled with the civic leader.[14]

What he chose to show, in a sequence of eight scenes, was 'the progresses of grace in St Francis's soul'.[15] 'At the start he's Francis. Then, little by little he becomes St Francis, and even super-St Francis.'[16] This may be made clear by a synopsis: that which follows refers to the score (each published scene is in a separate volume, prefaced by the composer's outline of its events, themes and birdsongs),[17] and also includes further explicatory remarks from the conversations with Samuel.[18]

(ACT I) SCENE I: 'LA CROIX' ('THE CROSS')

Two monks are travelling: the young Frère Léon (baritone) and Saint François (baritone: this enormously long central role com-

EX. 17.1 Scene 1: La Croix

bines, Messiaen said, the 'vigour' of Golaud with the 'declamatory solemnity' of Boris[19]). François wears a brown habit and a light, reddish beard; he is to resemble Cimabue's portrait of the saint at Assisi, and to recall in his postures Giotto's frescos. He is also distinguished by a musical theme, introduced to punctuate his first reply to Léon, and played by all the violins, violas and cellos in octaves (Ex. 17.1). (The alternation of unaccompanied voice with orchestral ensemble is characteristic of the work. On the practical level, this makes it possible for the soloists to sing without strain in a context of immense instrumental forces. The interchanging further produces an effect of text and commentary – or perhaps, if one were to think in terms of a medieval manuscript, of text and illumination, as if the orchestra were providing great initials, pages of pattern, and images of the supernatural, while the plain black characters of the chant continue.) Léon, like each of the other monks, wears a black Franciscan habit. He speaks three times of his fear; François's responses are oblique, addressed not only to him but to the challenge of Christ. (In the middle of the stage, and at the back, there is a staircase, leading up to 'a great black Cross on the blue sky'.) François's responses are also negative, stating that the exercise of saintly virtue – of healing power, of prophesy, of discourse with the angels, of conversion – is not 'perfect joy'. Perfect joy consists, rather, in joyfully accepting misery, trouble and sacrifice for love of Christ. 'François knows what sanctity is, but for the moment he can reach no further than to know.' The scene ends with the chorus singing Christ's words to his would-be followers, that they must take up the Cross.

(ACT I) SCENE 2: 'LES LAUDES' ('LAUDS')

Bass voices, led by Frères Sylvestre, Rufin and Bernard, are singing the office in the Franciscan community's little church. Their monotone chant is framed by sepulchral instruments, and interleaved with François's first verses from the *Cantico delle creature*. Finally François prays for the capacity to love a leper. According to the composer: 'He knows that he has not yet accomplished the principal act of his life.'

(ACT I) SCENE 3: 'LE BAISER AU LÉPREUX' ('THE LEPER KISS')

In a leprosery, the Leper (tenor) rails against his fate. He 'must be horrible and repulsive. He is half-naked, dressed only in tattered rags. His arms and legs are covered in black spots and blood. He should look like the Leper depicted by Matthias Grünewald in the Issenheim altarpiece.' Saint François enters, and discourses with him fruitlessly on the merits of patience and penitence. Then the Angel (soprano) arrives in the street outside, seen by the audience through a window but unseen by the two men onstage. Messiaen's description of his appearance and costume is detailed:

> The Angel has long blond hair curling at the neck. On his head a halo: a narrow gold circle, raised above the crown of his head. His costume should reproduce that of one of Fra Angelico's Annunciations (in the Museo San Marco in Florence).[20] He wears a robe of mauve-pink (between lilac and salmon), with a gold pectoral, the top of the back also gold, and two gold ornaments halfway along the sleeves. The robe is long, trailing to the ground. At the same time, from his back and sides, four great yellow ribbons fall to the ground and prolong the robe. His wings, unfurled on his back, are quinticoloured and divided into vertical bands of different colours. For each wing, at the edge a first band, red and festooned, ends in a large, red, pointed feather – second band blue, third black, then five bands successively yellow, blue, yellow, green, yellow – at the centre of the wing an enormous blue roundel. The two wings are like two harps, or two sets of organ pipes.

The Leper's violence is stilled by the angelic voice, and he asks forgiveness. François summons the strength to embrace him, and does so, as the orchestra plays themes (Ex. 17.2) associated with 'decision' (a double-octave descent with harmonic heavying) and 'joy' (a rushing third-mode cadence).

The Leper is cured. Dressed now in a medieval nobleman's costume of yellow-orange and red, he dances wildly: his earlier theme (Ex. 17.3a) is reborn in a higher, brighter realm leaning towards A major (Ex. 17.3b; the key has long associations of joy, azure and clarity in Messiaen's music: see, for example, the *Visions de l'Amen* and *Le merle bleu*), and enhanced with jubilant repeated brass chords. Then, conscious of his earlier transgressions, he falls into tears of unworthiness, but François comforts him, saying that he too is unworthy of the healing he has received. 'In one instant a double miracle occurs: the Leper

EX. 17.2 Scene 3: Le baiser au lépreux

EX. 17.3 Scene 3: Le baiser au lépreux

(a)

(b)

is cured and Francis becomes St Francis. It's the decisive moment. And in my opera, it's the key scene.' Again there is a closing chorus on words of Christ: 'To those who have greatly loved, all is forgiven.'

(ACT II) SCENE 4: 'L'ANGE VOYAGEUR' ('THE ANGEL TRAVELLER')

This is the only scene from which Saint François is absent. It begins with a substantial orchestral introduction, based on birdsongs and on themes associated with the monks: a calm but strong melody for Frère Bernard, who is the doyen of the community, Frère Léon's song from the first scene, and ill-tempered glissandos of strings and trombones for Frère Elie, the community's businessman and intellectual. The scene is set at the monastery on La Verna, as Frère Léon goes off to work leaving Frère Massée to serve as porter. The Angel arrives again: this time he can be seen by those onstage, but only under the disguise of a young traveller. This time, too, he comes with a full array of musical signals, including a vociferous two-octave upward glis-

EX. 17.4 Scene 4: L'ange voyageur

(a)

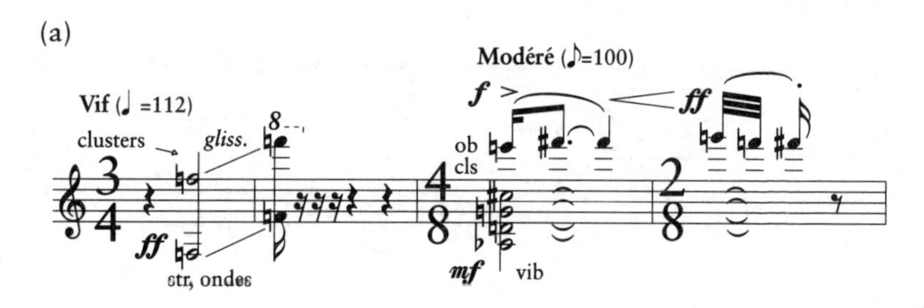

(b)

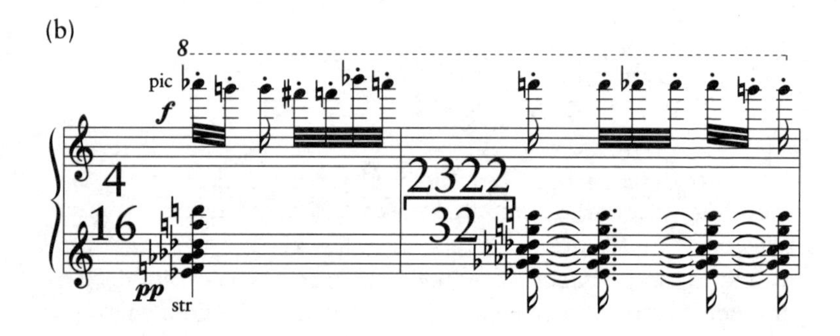

sando followed by what Messiaen described as a 'noh-style' call from high woodwind (Ex. 17.4a), and the song of the gerygone, one of the many New Caledonian species in this score,[21] represented in the extreme high register by piccolo (Ex. 17:4b; at other times the song is picked out by tuned percussion). The Angel knocks at the convent gate, but though his gesture is gentle, the sound we hear is formidable: the bass chord of the 'decision theme' repeated, emphatically *fortissimo*, by almost the whole orchestra in the dochmiac rhythm (short–long, long, short–long) of the Leper, though at less than half its speed in the earlier scene. Frère Massée (tenor) chides him for making such a noise, then goes at his request to fetch Frère Elie, whom he wants to question. Elie (tenor) duly arrives, with more of his violent musical material, angered that he has been interrupted in his labours. The Angel, who sings always in the radiant serenity of third-mode E♭ major with luminous orchestral support, asks him what he thinks of predestination; he furiously refuses to reply, and goes back inside. So the Angel knocks again, and this time asks Massée to summon Bernard, whose response is more patient, considered and spiritually developed. The Angel congratulates him, and he in turn asks the Angel a question: 'What is your name?' The Angel replies that he has come from far away to speak to François, and that he will now do so, but that he cannot be asked his name: 'It is marvellous!' (This is just one point at which Messiaen shows how he can, like Wagner, incorporate a characteristic fairy-tale motif with complete freshness and artistic certainty.) He goes, and Bernard and Massée are left wondering if this was an angel.

(ACT II) SCENE 5: 'L'ANGE MUSICIEN' ('THE ANGEL MUSICIAN')

Messiaen's analysis in the score begins by noting that this episode 'was more than tempting for a composer, which is why I selected it immediately'. Saint François is in contemplation, and in a long solo quotes from his *Cantico* and other texts, with accompaniment and punctuation provided by birdsongs (some which Messiaen notated on the site of St Francis's cell on La Verna, others from more distant places) and by themes from earlier in the opera (the sixth-mode theme from Ex. 17.1, which is repeatedly associated with the central character, and also the themes of 'decision' and 'joy'). He prays for a glimpse of heavenly existence, and the gerygone song, heard this time over the blue haze of an A major added-sixth chord hummed by chorus, announces the nearness of the Angel. François's companion falcon calls out, and the Angel arrives. He quotes from St Thomas Aquinas: 'God dazzles us by excess of Truth. Music carries us to God by want of Truth.' He then plays, on his viol, 'the music of the invisible', which the audience hears as a slow melody passed from one to another of the three ondes martenot in the auditorium (ondes 1 to the conductor's left, ondes 2 to the right, ondes 3 behind), a melody cushioned on C major chords from strings or humming chorus (see Ex. 17.5).

The forest resounds (an extraordinary deep resonance) and the Angel plays more exuberantly, before departing with a rep-

EX. 17.5 Scene 5: L'ange musicien

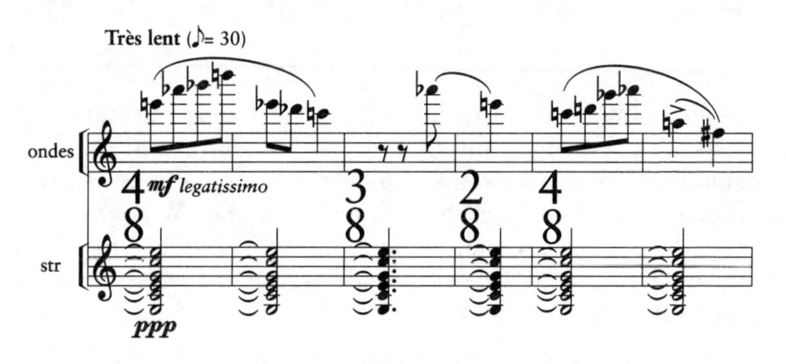

etition of his celestial melody. François passes into a faint, from which he is revived by Léon, Massée and Bernard when they find him. He tells them of angelic music, and says that it if it had gone on, his soul would have parted from his body; the 'decision' and 'joy' themes are again prominent in the surrounding orchestra.

(ACT II) SCENE 6: 'LE PRÊCHE AUX OISEAUX' ('THE SERMON TO THE BIRDS')

If the previous scene was an obvious occasion for music, this one is a natural for Messiaen's music in particular, and as he states in his analysis, the text is almost entirely his own invention, adding to Franciscan tradition a vignette of the saint as ornithologist–teacher. The scene also adds something to the composer's repertory of techniques, in that, right from the beginning, there are moments where solo instruments depart on flights of birdsong at their own tempos, independent of the conductor once they have been given the sign to start: the opening birdsong chorus is largely for high woodwind, tuned percussion, ondes and small string ensembles. Then, into a setting of green oaks and blue sky, comes Saint François with Frère Massée. In response to the latter's questions, François identifies the birds whose songs are projected by the orchestra: the turtle dove, the wren, the robin and the blackcap. Since these are all European species, the passage is, to that extent, realistic. But now François passes into recollection of a dream, a dream of 'an island like an exclamation mark', and the orchestra suddenly moves to the songs of New Caledonian birds, which the saint continues to recognize. There follows another birdsong concert: garden warblers, chaffinches and cuckoos with other species from Morocco and Sweden. Afterwards, at a moment marked by the 'decision–joy' signal, François sits down to reflect. A development of the 'decision' and 'joy' themes leads to an immense climb of tutti chords, and François advances towards the birds. His sermon, accompanied by blackcap music, is in praise of God's gifts to them: the gifts of flight, of nourishment, of plumage, of song. After yet another birdsong interlude, this time bringing together Japanese and European species, he gives the birds his blessing. There is a moment of silence, followed by a long cascade of birdsongs: skylarks, garden warblers, blackbirds, blackcaps, orioles and – a foreigner – the lyre bird of Australia. The birds fly off to the four points of the compass, making a great cross in the sky, and leaving the two monks alone, though still with occasional birdsongs in the orchestra. The scene ends with François clarifying the lesson, that all of creation points the way to the Cross.

(ACT III) SCENE 7: 'LES STIGMATES' ('THE STIGMATA')

It is night on La Verna: night expressed in an introduction of owl cries, hummed choral clusters and triple counterpoints in a chromatic mode where, as in works of the 1950s, each note is unchanging in duration and volume (see Ex. 17.6). (From the starting-point of treble-staff A as a demisemiquaver, rhythmic values increase by one unit with each semitone descent. The trumpet's falling minor second characteristically stands out as the only repeating melodic element.) François prays for two gifts of grace before he dies: that he may feel the marks of Christ's Passion in his body and the power of Christ's love in his heart. Weird timbres sound out –

> tremolo chords in two ondes, percussed breath in the third, arpeg-

EX. 17.6 Scene 7: Les stigmates

gios between the bridge and the tailpiece in the violins, cluster glissandos in the violas, rising clusters in the horns, dull blows on the bass drum, chords in superimposed ostinatos, pizzicatos, trilled chords in the strings, pedal sounds from the trombone, whistlings from the wind machine, a mountain of sand that collapses in the geophone

– and above this 'orchestra of anxiety' the chorus in block harmony sings as with the voice of Christ, but in words of Messiaen's own:

If you want . . . the Sacred Host to transform you more fully into Me, you must suffer in your body the five wounds of my Body on

> the Cross, accept your sacrifice, in union with my Sacrifice, and, going ever beyond yourself, like a higher music, become yourself a second host.

François exclaims his weakness and unworthiness, and, as a great black Cross again appears in the sky, the men of the chorus, with the orchestra, create a huge crescendo on the repeated words 'C'est moi!' Full chorus and orchestra continue in the solid *fortissimo* that has now been achieved: 'I am that afterwards that was before. I am that before that will be afterwards . . . It is I who thought the visible and the invisible, angels and men, every living creature . . . The Man-God! Who comes from beyond time, goes from future into past.' For a moment there is silence. Then four rays of light strike from the Cross to François's hands and feet, while the orchestra repeats the enormous dochmiac tutti of the angel's knock. A fifth ray strikes his side, with the chorus now joining the orchestra in the noise of eternity's arrival. After another silence, the whole atmosphere changes. The scene is lit by red-orange light; the Cross is glittering gold; and the choral Christ calls François by name on soft E major chords. François responds, and receives the message, to a ladder of chords reaching up to a high E major, that if he carries the Cross it will lead him to eternal life.

(ACT III) SCENE 8: 'LA MORT ET LA NOUVELLE VIE' ('DEATH AND NEW LIFE')

The final scene is set inside the little church of Porziuncola, where François is lying on the ground close to death. He makes a series of farewells: to the landscape, to the birds, to the city and its churches, to his brother monks. Then he sings the final verses of his *Cantico*, addressed to death, punctuated by bass voices chanting on C$^{\#}$ as in the second scene. The whole chorus cries out in distress, and the gerygone announces a last appearance of the Angel, who comes with the Leper – now dead and resurrected – to help François in his final hour. When this last blissful angelic solo has ended, François makes his ultimate prayer for salvation, his voice alternating with great clangs as of bells in the orchestra. He dies, and Frère Léon, like Arkel in *Pelléas*, remarks on the stillness of his going. Then the stage is flooded with blinding light as chorus and orchestra – interrupted by the dochmiacs and fanfares of the Leper's dance, and by the songs of skylarks – sing a C major chorale of Resurrection.

According to Messiaen's own account, the opera was composed during a period of four years, between 1975 and 1979, and then 'orchestrated' over a further four years:[22] since it is impossible to imagine the score's having been conceived without any thought for its instrumentation, this latter process presumably involved the writing out in full of some abbreviated draft. The composer began his task with the fourth scene, 'perhaps because the inn scene from *Boris* was in my mind', then proceeded to the second, 'which I absolutely had to write before the final tableau, because it's the same music – amplified, magnified – in the last scene'. After that came the third scene, the fifth ('the most difficult to achieve, because it's the moment where Heaven opens'), the seventh ('the scene most contrary to my nature'), the eighth, the first, and 'finally the sixth, which terrorized me, because I'm an ornithologist and was absolutely determined to make this my best birdsong music'.[23]

During the eight years of the work's composition, the directorship of the Opéra changed twice, so that it was Bernard Lefort who contracted the principal singers (notably José van Dam for the title role,[24] which he also sang in the 1992 Salzburg and Paris performances) and Massimo Bogianckino who placed the staging in the hands of the director Sandro Sequi and designer Giuseppe Crisolini-Malatesta. Messiaen had wanted to produce the work himself, but he expressed satisfaction with a *mise-en-scène* that was faithful to his requirements in respect of natural action, the Fra Angelico costume for the Angel, and scenery giving scale-model views of the Umbrian countryside. He was also pleased by Sequi's solution to the problem of accommodating an orchestra of over a hundred players (the score requires a hundred and twenty, but the strings were reduced in the original production) and a chorus of a hundred and fifty: there were platforms on either side of the stage for woodwind (to the left) and tuned percussion (to the right), and further stepped platforms at the rear for the chorus, so that most of the action was confined to a small square space in the middle of the stage.[25]

The world premiere, on 28 November 1983, was followed by a run of seven more performances, after which this production was never seen again. In March–April 1986 Seiji Ozawa conducted three scenes (nos. 3, 7 and 8) in concert performances in Tokyo, London, Berlin, Boston and New York. In September that year Kent Nagano, who had been Ozawa's assistant in Paris, conducted complete concert performances in Bonn, Ghent, Utrecht and Madrid.[26] Nagano also conducted a semi-staged performance of four scenes (nos. 3, 6, 7 and 8) in the Royal Festival Hall, London, on the composer's eightieth birthday, 10 December 1988, and in his presence.[27]

The work returned to full-scale production at the Salzburg Festival on 17 August 1992, in the Felsenreitschule, with Esa-Pekka Salonen conducting the Los Angeles Philharmonic Orchestra.[28] This time the staging, by Peter Sellars, was in a different mode. George Tsypin's set was a wooden structure, dominated by a cathedral-like skeleton of Gothic arches to the right and a lightly tilted square framework of fluorescent tubes to the left. This latter apparatus provided an almost continuous display of coloured light, either in the shape of the Cross, or more usually, in horizontal, vertical or diagonal stripes in different harmonies: yellow and green, orange and red, or blue, red and violet like the windows of Chartres. (Messiaen, in a note in the score, mentions the need for projections and, among several specific suggestions, proposes the use of lasers for the stigmatization – a proposal followed in both the 1983 and the 1992 productions.) François and his brother monks were dressed in habits as at the première, but the Angel was a woman in an ash-grey suit: a modest, unremarkable arrival, but remarkable in the hieratic gestures she used to invest the power of her announcing music (Ex. 17:4a) in her body. There was also a second angel – a slender girl in scarlet, with scarlet wings – to execute the Leper's dance in the third scene.[29]

With no Fra Angelico and no Umbria, but with a bevy of video monitors relaying images related to the text (a monk in solitary agonized contemplation, poinsettia bracts, birds), the 1992 production took a different approach to realism. Messiaen's own attitude may be glimpsed in one of his responses to Samuel, who was bold enough to suggest there might be an inconsistency in wanting a 'realistic spectacle' for a 'magic subject'. 'It's not a magic subject,' the composer rejoined:

> It's a religious subject in which Earth is marrying Heaven. But the Earth is present, St Francis's wounds are real. He's surrounded by real brothers and real birds, to whom he really talks. A stylized production would be contrary to the spirit of St Francis, who constantly praised all the things of the Earth.

One difficulty here is in knowing whether Messiaen is talking about the saint or the character, St Francis or Saint François. Most probably there was, for him, no difference, just as there was no difference between the birds that sing in the natural world and those that sing in his works. He habitually elided this latter difference in his descriptions of his music, writing, for example, of 'a long skylark solo entrusted to the three xylophones', or of 'a mistle thrush [which] strikes off on the solo clarinet', or of 'the second ondes which does the Japanese Uguisu', or of 'a chaffinch on three solo violins, reco-reco and three trumpets playing in the third mode with Harmon mutes'.[30] Indeed, one of the attractions of birdsong for Messiaen may have been that it allowed him to abolish or ignore the distinction between reality and representation. He spoke of 'trying to trace as exact as possible a musical portrait'[31] of a bird, but the portraits he produced are icons, doing duty for the real, and in the same way *Saint François* is an iconic opera.

The great paradox of Messiaen's music – and most spectacularly of his largest work – is that there is no conflict between the icon-maker's selfless transcription of what is given and the artist's assertion of an unmistakably individual world. His music is instantly recognizable as his, and yet it says nothing about him – beyond what it says by saying nothing. The goal of his creation is a transparency to the divine creation: to the natural world, and to the natural history, too, of heaven.

One can find explanations for his detachment from the personal in his detachment from the diatonic progression and metrical uniformity of post-Renaissance musical time – a double detachment shared with other composers who have addressed themselves to the sacred, including the growing throng who, around the time of *Saint François*, were beginning to make Messiaen's position as a twentieth-century religious composer less isolated. Yet he remained extraordinarily isolated in combining singleness of purpose wth vast multiplicity of means. *Saint François* is the testament of a man who found no musical event alien to him: neither the songs of a hundred different birds nor the smooth lines of modal chant, neither triads nor twelve-note chords, neither ebullient dancing in his 1930s style nor the kind of abstract note manipulation that had featured in works between the *Turangalîla-symphonie* and *Chronochromie*, neither block-harmony strings nor the myriad sounds of an enormous orchestra enriched by electronic instruments and constellations of percussion. There is no retreat here from contemporary experience: on the contrary, the score resumes the discoveries of half a century of creative adventure and, in the bizarre nocturne of the stigmata scene or the unco-ordinated birdsong ensembles of its predecessor, continues the progress.

Only in the vocal parts is there nothing new: no trespass beyond singing, no deviation from modal authority. This is the contrast with which and through which the opera lives – the contrast between archaic musical converse among the characters and continuous surprise from the orchestra (see Ex. 17.7). At this point in the bird-sermon scene, for instance, Frère Massée sings in the second mode, inside the interval of a sixth, and in free rhythm recognizing only two different values (the roles of Frère Elie and the Leper are similarly notated in the tenor clef, itself an archaism), whereas the robin orchestra of flutes, clarinets, ondes and crotales enjoys far wider freedom. Both, though, deny the boundary between image and reality (real monk, real bird).

EX. 17.7 Scene 6: Le prêche aux oiseaux

The reason for the simplicity of the vocal lines may be found in Messiaen's doctrine of transcription, in his attempt 'to trace as exact as possible a musical portrait' of each of his medieval characters as well as of his birds. The effect, again, is to dissolve the alterity of the image, but also to place at the centre of *Saint François* just the kind of enactment 'conceived in faith and naivety' he had found in the Oberammergau play, or might equally have found in the miracle plays and liturgical dramas of the Middle Ages: an enactment by means of chant and modality, albeit modality of a special kind. That, however, could not be enough – not for a composer who had grown through and contributed to musical history from the time of Debussy to that of Tristan Murail. The further paradox of *Saint François* – and one might even say the miracle – is to have the whole panoply of late twentieth-century musical sound not only illuminating the chanted sacred history but bending close to it, participating, without a moment of contradiction.

Notes

1 Claude Samuel: *Entretiens avec Olivier Messiaen* (Paris, Belfond, 1967), pp. 121–2.
2 Ibid., p. 39.
3 Ibid., p. 124.
4 Olivier Messiaen: *Musique et couleur: nouveaux entretiens avec Claude Samuel* (Paris, Belfond, 1986), p. 228.
5 '*Ariane et Barbe-bleue* de Paul Dukas', *Revue musical*, 166 (1936), pp. 79–86.
6 *Musique et couleur*, p. 227.
7 *Ibid.*, p. 237.
8 *Ibid.*, pp. 229–30.
9 *Ibid.*, pp. 230–1.
10 According to Harry Halbreich on p. 42 of the special number of *L'Avant-scène Opéra* (Paris) issued to coincide with the 1992 Salzburg production. This bilingual French-German publication also includes the libretto, a co-extensive musical description by Halbreich, an interview with Messiaen, and other material relating to the opera and its subject matter.
11 *Musique et couleur*, p. 237. The reference is to 1 John 3: 20: 'For if our heart condemn us, God is greater than our heart, and knoweth all things' (Authorized Version).
12 *Musique et couleur*, p. 236.
13 Ibid., p. 233.
14 Ibid., pp. 235–6.
15 *L'Avant-scène Opéra*, 1992 special number, p. 36.
16 *Musique et couleur*, p. 234.
17 The prefaces may also be found in the Opéra de Paris Bastille programme for the December 1992 revival of the Salzburg production. This publication also includes the libretto, monochrome reproductions of the source paintings (by Cimabue, Giotto and Fra Angelico), photographs of places in the action and of pages from Messiaen's sketchbook recording Umbrian birds, and two essays by theologians on the composer's Franciscanism and spirituality.
18 *Musique et couleur*, pp. 234–5.
19 Philippe Godefroid: 'Entretien avec Olivier Messiaen', *Opéra de Paris*, 12 (1983), pp. 8–13.

20 For a colour reproduction of Fra Angelico's angel see the cover of the 1992 special number of *L'Avant-scène Opéra*.
21 See interview with Yvonne Loriod, p. 297.
22 Opéra de Paris Bastille programme, p. 18.
23 *Musique et couleur*, p. 237.
24 The other leading members of the cast were Christiane Eda-Pierre (Angel), Kenneth Riegel (Leper), Philippe Duminy (Léon), Georges Gauthier (Massée), Michel Sénéchal (Elie) and Jean-Philippe Courtis (Bernard), with Seiji Ozawa conducting.
25 For Messiaen's remarks on the first production see *Musique et couleur*, pp. 271 and 243. For photographs of that production see the 1992 special number of *L'Avant-scène Opéra*, pp. 122–3, and also Paul Griffiths: *Olivier Messiaen and the Music of Time* (London, Faber and Faber, 1985), plates 5–6. The production was recorded by French television; a compact-disc sound recording was issued on Cybélia CY 833–836.
26 A second compact-disc recording, on KRO Hilversum, was associated with these performances.
27 For a complete list of performances to 1992 (there are not so many more than are mentioned here) see the special number of *L'Avant-scène Opéra*, p. 123.
28 Apart from Van Dam, the cast included Dawn Upshaw (Angel), Ronald Hamilton (Leper), Urban Malmberg (Léon), John Aler (Massée), Thomas Young (Elie) and Tom Krause (Bernard). When the production was revived at the Bastille in December the same year, it was with Sylvain Cambreling conducting the house orchestra and with Robin Leggate in the role of Elie.
29 For further discussion of this production see Paul Griffiths: 'Master and Pupil', *The New Yorker* (14 September 1992), pp. 85–9.
30 All these examples are from his preface to the sixth scene of *Saint François*, and concern the scene's introduction.
31 *Musique et couleur*, p. 101.

Eclairs sur l'au-delà . . .

PAUL GRIFFITHS

Any of the major works in the sequence from *La Transfiguration* to the *Livre du Saint Sacrement* could have been a fitting conclusion to Messiaen's creative life, and that is partly how those works were successively greeted, as grand summations. In many respects *Eclairs sur l'au-delà . . .* might be seen as another, as a sequence of 'lightning visions' not only 'into the beyond' promised in the title but into the past, the past of the composer's entire output. Life after death had been his greatest subject since the 1930s, and this final work revisits much of the musical imagery he had found for it: the dazzling woodwind and percussion jewels of *Couleurs de la cité céleste*, the string adagio song of *Les offrandes oubliées* and *L'Ascension*, the wind-orchestra chanting of *L'Ascension* and *Et exspecto resurrectionem mortuorum*, the birdsongs as harbingers of the brilliance and agility of the angels, the potentially endless rhythmic mechanisms as fragments of eternity. Above all, the contrasts from movement to movement – and the depictions of scenes from Revelation, and the presence of two slow movements for strings – point back towards the *Quatuor pour la fin du temps*.

And yet the sense is less one of culmination than of continuing, as if everything Messiaen had ever created were still permanently attainable. The ending of time is conveyed not only inside each piece, but across the output as a whole, in that Messiaen was able, in his eighties, to achieve again what he had achieved as a young man, without any dimming, and certainly without any nostalgia. The only signs of age in this last piece are in its orchestral virtuosity, its breadth of reference, and perhaps also its audacity, not least in bringing together an ensemble of a hundred and twenty-eight players only to leave many of them silent for long periods (the ten double basses, for instance, play nothing until the eighth of the eleven movements, a piece whose coda provides the single tutti in a composition otherwise for smaller, if majestic, groupings). But even this audacity – accompanied as it is by the supreme and serene confidence that had always shone from this composer's scores – is the sign of an ageless spirit. The gift that Messiaen took from his fame was the liberty to disregard professional decorum.

Eclairs sur l'au-delà . . . was commissioned by the New York Philharmonic Orchestra for their 1992–3 sesquicentenary season, and first performed by them under Zubin Mehta in Avery Fisher Hall, New York, on 5 November 1992, a little over six months after the composer's death. When writing to Mehta to accept the commission, in August 1987, Messiaen had remarked that he still had two orchestral pieces to complete (presumably *La ville d'En-haut* and *Un sourire*) and that he could not yet predict the size or the scoring of the work he would write for New York. It might then have seemed, even to the composer himself, that his output was to end in miniatures, for since the completion of the *Livre du Saint Sacrement*, in 1984, he had written only small pieces having the aspect of postscripts to earlier achievements: the *Petites esquisses d'oiseaux* (1985) as a pendant to the *Catalogue*, *Un vitrail et des oiseaux* (1986) as a reminiscence of the 1950s and 1960s pieces for piano and small orchestra, and the presumably in-progress *La ville d'En-haut* (1967) as another such memory, though with a wind–percussion ensemble more on the scale of *Et exspecto*. *Un sourire* (1989) was again to be a brief monument, and the *Pièce* for piano and string quartet (1991) a greetings telegram for the ninetieth birthday of Alfred Schlee, who, as director of Universal Edition, had published *Oiseaux exotiques* as well as much of the music of Berio, Boulez and Stockhausen.

This sequence of short pieces, out of which *Eclairs sur l'au-delà . . .* so astonishingly grew, may conveniently be considered before the major work. The little birdsong sketches, described elsewhere by Peter Hill (p. 347), portray birds which had sung in Messiaen's music before, and the manner of transcription is familiar, with avian neumes (appeals and quick downward scales from the generally quiet robin, loud swirling gestures from the blackbird, a variety of crashing repeated motifs from the songthrush, jubilant repetitions in crescendo from the skylark), and short chordal interludes in the robin and blackbird pieces. The chief novelty is that, though Messiaen's introduction describes the piano writing as 'highly worked', the relatively light textures and gentle speeds make this one of his few compositions that amateur players can approach – at least until they come to the exuberantly fast skylark finale.

The next piece, *Un vitrail et des oiseaux* ('A stained-glass window and birds'), is an eight-minute movement in simple block form, as follows:

A. Nightingale music, played by the xylophone trio of *Couleurs de la cité céleste* with metal percussion.
B. Trumpet and bells, with changing harmonies in the symphonic woodwind ensemble, and with cymbal and tam tam, announcing the first phrase of a chorale.
C. Chaffinch (xylophones) answered by blackcap (woodwind and trilling triangle).
D. Birdsong cadenzas for piano, flute and clarinet, all independent of each other and not conducted.
B′. Second phrase of the chorale.
C′. Chaffinch again, with more of the blackcap.
D′. Birdsong cadenzas for piano, two flutes and two clarinets, as before.
B″. Third phrase of the chorale.
C″. Chaffinch again, with still more of the blackcap.
D″. Longer birdsong cadenzas for piano, three flutes and three clarinets, as before.
A′. Return of the wooden nightingale.
B‴. Concluding chorale, now complete in four phrases, and with the piano dabbing complementary chords on to each harmony.

In its title the piece acknowledges two of Messiaen's favourite images, which the music itself makes intersect one another. For while the chorale is most obviously concerned with conveying colour through harmony, it is also a song, and while the other sections are, as usual, marked in the score with their birdsong models, their chords are also brilliantly coloured. This is music of flying glass. As such it may seem only a memento of the far more elaborate *Couleurs*, though with the new device of ad libitum heterophonies (the D sections) following the precedent of the sermon to the birds in *Saint François*, which is also recalled by the prominent blackcap music. Messiaen's introduction notes the difficulty created by the superimposed tempos. 'But the birds are more important than the tempos, and the colours more important than the birds. More important than everything else is the aspect of the invisible.'

La ville d'En-haut ('The city above') is another visit to the invisible, again shaped as an unpretentious antiphony:

A. Monumental chorale-summons for the full symphonic wind with cymbal and tam-tams, and with complementary decoration of sustained chords from piano, glockenspiel and, again, xylophone trio.
B. First phrase of a more flowing chorale, like the corresponding section in *Un vitrail*, but the ensemble is larger and there is a high-treble counterpoint from piano and glockenspiel.
C. Song of the melodious warbler, given by the xylophones with trilling cymbal.
A. Exact repeat.
B′. First and second phrases of the chorale.
C′. Longer song of the melodious warbler.
D. Alternation between blackcap (for almost exactly the same woodwind–triangle grouping as in *Un vitrail*) and garden warbler (piano solo), each heard five times.
A. Exact repeat.
B″. Chorale, considerably extended beyond its first two phrases.

Connections of form, substance and ornithology with *Un vitrail* mirror a connection of metaphor. As Messiaen put it at the end of his preface to the score:

> The brass chorale [he had used this term only for the A sections] represents the glory of the Heavenly City. The birds of the xylophones, of the woodwinds, of the piano solo, symbolize the joy of the resurrected, assured of being always near to Christ. The chords' colours change almost constantly, and symbolize in their turn the colours of the light Above.

The third and last of these short orchestral pictures, *Un sourire* ('A smile'), was Messiaen's contribution to the Mozart bicentenary. It contains no musical quotation: imagination boggles at the thought, despite the admiration Messiaen repeatedly expressed for *Don Giovanni*, for Mozartian rhythm and for the piano concertos. Instead the tribute is personal, to Mozart's cheerfulness through a life of adversity. The orchestra is now full, yet light and luminous, providing a first glimpse of the new radiant world of *Eclairs sur l'au-delà . . .*, which by 1989 was in progress: the levitated sound of a large string orchestra without double basses is common to both works, and in *Un sourire* there is also a complex exclusion of the heavier brass, the trombones and tubas. In other respects the piece looks back to its immediate predecessors. Messiaen makes a select choice from the percussion instruments favoured in those scores: tubular bells, xylophones (just two this time, clipping off the bass member of the team, the marimba), and the trilling cymbal that accompanies these last. And again the form is a simple litany:

A. The strings, with wind highlighting, sing a phrase which presents Messiaen's modality in elemental form (see Ex. 18.1).

   The opening motif is a variation on his favourite interval, the tritone, harmonized in the second mode; the continuation is a close variant, in a different form of the second mode, coming to rest on a favourite chord: A major with added sixth. The second, longer part of the melody moves through two successive forms of the third mode.

B. Birdsong music from wind (1), percussion (2) and both groups together (3). Most unusually, the species are not named in the score.

EX. 18.1 *Un sourire*

3 fls
3 obs
cor a
3 cls
3 bns
hns
vns 1
vns 2
vas
vcs
1ère
pp
ppp
3/16
2/16
3/8
4/8
4/8

A′. Repeat, with varied second section.
B′. Extension of (3) alone.
A″. Further variation of second section alone.
B″. Repeat of (1) and (2), with further extensions of (3) introducing new material and adding final crescendo climb.
A‴. Further, much prolonged variation of second section, eventually reaching the goal of A major.

Like *La ville d'En-haut*, *Un sourire* contrives the prolongation of a musical thought through episodes separated by other music. In both works the process has – of necessity in earthly time – to come to an end, but the sense is of widening windows into a celestial endlessness. Each time when the lengthening music begins – chorale in the earlier work, song in the later – it is as a recommencement; the interludes between the recommencements function as frames and preparations (the end of the last interlude in *Un sourire* has a marked introductory force), setting the stage for new beginnings; and each recommencement initiates a longer unfolding, one not so much developed as stretched, presented in a slower time. *Un sourire* is thus music of eternity as much as homage to Mozart, and stands close to *Eclairs sur l'au-delà* . . . in points of style and form as well as orchestration.

The little sketch for piano and strings has much less to do with its great companion. As an occasional piece, and as a chamber composition, it has a doubly marginal place in Messiaen's output; its form is a simple palindromic ABA of generally antiphonal patches around a toccata which similarly – and, for the performers, challengingly – uses the keyboard and the quartet in alternation. It could easily have been written at the time of the *Préludes*, and to that extent it makes a small, acutely direct statement of the permanence of musical thought displayed so much more vastly by *Eclairs sur l'au-delà*. . . .

That work's eleven movements – surely intended to be played continuously, and as the sole event of a concert – extend for about seventy minutes, and the orchestra includes whole suborchestras of flutes and clarinets (ten of each), and of percussion, with a dozen or so players on xylophones (the full trio), crotales, glockenspiel, tubular bells, gongs, triangles, wood-blocks, bass drum, wind machine, cymbals, whip and reco-reco. The only other conspicuous inflation is of the brass section, made up of five trumpets, six horns, three trombones and three tubas.

The first movement, 'Apparition du Christ glorieux', is scored for a large symphonic wind ensemble of thirty-five players, similar to those used for parallel movements in *L'Ascension* and *Et exspecto resurrectionem mortuorum*. This is a new place, a new time, but we could be back thirty or sixty years in Messiaen's output. Alternatively we could be back in the age of the ziggurats, temples and pyramids that provided some of the inspirations for *Et exspecto*. The vision, as in Stravinsky's *Zvezdoliki*, is that of Christ across the heavens: 'I saw the Son of Man, clothed with a long robe and with a golden girdle around his breast; his eyes were like a flame of fire, his face shone like the sun. In his right hand he held seven stars.' (Each movement is headed with at least one inscription, most of them taken, as in this case, from the Book of Revelation.) The wordless hymn has a broad ternary form, with the central section rising to recall – according to the programme notes provided in Messiaen's scrupulously descriptive manner by his widow, Yvonne Loriod – the alleluia of the Feast of Christ the King. Characteristically, the chords are monumental and smoothly fused, except the tubas, equally characteristically, bulge out a dissonant bass line, so that these huge blown sounds have the thrumming inharmonicity of bell resonances, and the achievement of a primitive immensity depends on a twentieth-century understanding of harmony and instrumentation.

After this strongly unified piece, the second movement breaks into a pattern of small ensembles to represent 'La constellation du Sagittaire' (Messiaen's birth-sign, and the centre of our galaxy). Wind and bells sound a robust melody on two of the deçî-tâlas (Ex. 18.2). A more assuaging fragment of tune, but again in the second mode, is played – against flute birdsongs and rhythmic canons in percussion – by strings (Ex. 18.3). First violins play natural-harmonic glissandos (marked as a nebula

EX. 18.2 *Eclairs sur l'au-delà . . .* 2 'La constellation du Sagittaire'

EX. 18.3 *Eclairs sur l'au-delà . . .* 2 'La constellation du Sagittaire'

image in the score, whose three volumes are bound with photographs of galaxies and nebulae as frontispieces) against an accelerating upward rush from seconds and violas. Six flutes play six different birdsongs from around the world, each in its own tempo, the whole sounding like a sextet of stars, as if cosmic distances were rushed down into the throats of birds. Each of these four kinds of music is then repeated in turn, though the material is different, and a third arrival of the first kind is followed by a coda of string chords with waterdrop staccatos from piccolo, flutes and glockenspiel. The modal phrases in this movement (such as Ex. 18.2 and Ex. 18.3) are as instantly recognizable as, to an ornithologist, the songs of particular birds, and the laying down of human and avian musics together, side by side or simultaneously, is a gentle statement of the composer's artlessness. Stars, birds and man are all singing to the same purpose.

Then, in the third movement, comes a whole cascade of music from just one creature: the superb lyrebird, which Messiaen heard and saw as it put on its show in a sunlit eucalyptus forest. (The Australian birdsongs throughout the score are souvenirs of the composer's eightieth birthday tour – just as other travels are documented in earlier pieces – though at the same time the southern-hemisphere birds are emblems of another world, as they were in *Saint François*.) Lyrebird motifs leap around the entire ensemble in 'la Ville-Fiancée' – the image of the bird's plumage display as the Heavenly City's dressing of herself for espousal to Christ. But, quite unusually for Messiaen, there is a registering of the absurdity of the moment; the absurdity of the high metaphor, and of the bird's irrepressible song. Different as it is from the calm singing of *Un sourire*, this music also smiles. That gift of serene good humour was the most remarkable last gain Messiaen's music could have made, and it is not restricted to this movement.

The fourth movement folds back into abstraction. Like sections of *Chronochromie*, which was Messiaen's only other major orchestral piece without a solo piano part for Loriod, the music marks out three simultaneous interversions of number sequences in rhythmic durations tolled by bells, gongs and strings, while woodwinds and xylophone infiltrate birdsongs into the arithmetic. The title, 'Les élus marqués de sceau', refers to the passage in Revelation where an angel places a seal on the foreheads of the elect, but the music seems to be remembering a particular feature of this episode: the holding back of the four winds by four other angels, 'that no wind might blow or harm the earth'. Abstruse and quiet, the piece suggests withdrawal and waiting.

What is awaited is the works' interior conclusion: the fifth movement, 'Demeurer dans l'Amour', which is the first of the two slow movements for strings, a long adagio for violins, violas and cellos, as the final movement also will be. The melody is carried by all the first violins, playing with mutes, over changing harmonies that keep middle C as bass note (see Ex. 18.4). We

EX. 18.4 *Eclairs sur l'au-delà* . . . 5 'Demeurer dans l'Amour

are back in the 'Jardin du sommeil d'amour' of *Turangalîla* as well as in the praises of the *Quatuor*, though with an extra chromatic urgency and flexibility in the line, and a searing, glistening colour that arrives when the muted violins are taken up to an extreme high register. The harmony suggests stasis and quiescence; the melody has an extraordinary slow respiration too, as it unfolds in four long sections. But while 'abiding in love', it is still going in search. Loriod tells us that the sketches carry a quotation from Psalm 49: 'As a hart longs for flowing streams, so longs my soul for thee, my God.'

Up to this point the movements have succeeded each other as distinct and separate blocks, but the sixth, which seems to open a longer second phase in the work, begins with a shock. The strings die away, and are replaced by a loud thwack on the bass drum, initiating a drama of rhythmic characters that again has a precedent in the *Turangalîla-symphonie*. Three quaver drumbeats start each cycle in the same way, and each cycle also ends similarly with a crack on the whip, or slapstick, but between these elements the rhythm of low gongs and tam-tams progressively lengthens and shortens from three dotted quavers to three crotchets and so on up to three double-dotted crotchets, then back again. The septuplenesses here (values of from one to seven semiquavers; a total of seven semiquavers measured out by the drums and whip) are apparently intended in cryptic homage to the fanfaring angels of the title: 'Les sept anges avec les sept trompettes'. At the same time – echoing on from Messiaen's treatment of the same subject in the *Quatuor* – a rugged theme is repeated in its own cycles, independent of the percussion mechanics, by a fused ensemble of horns, trombones and bassoons (Ex. 18.5).

EX. 18.5 *Eclairs sur l'au-delà . . .* 6 'Les sept anges avec les sept trompettes'

After this comes the gentlest movement, and the one least like anything else in Messiaen's music: 'Et Dieu essuiera tout larme de leurs yeux . . .' ('And God will wipe away every tear from their eyes . . .': again the quotation is from Revelation). The tone of consolation, of cherishing, of God stooping to man, is unusual for an artist whose spiritual gaze normally went the other way, towards the grandeur, the mightiness, the bewilderment; and for anything like the tenderness of this movement one has to look back as far as the *Vingt regards*. Violins set up a high trill (the trill, not a common feature in Messiaen until this late period, is the musical signature especially of *Eclairs*: there was a trill of triangle tintinnabulation behind the six flute-stars of the Sagittarius movement, and there will be another such image of high white light behind and above the finale), preparing for a condescension of woodwind chords, marked 'like a caress' in the sketches (Ex. 18.6). What cannot be illustrated on paper is how the idea is made to fall through various colours from flute clarity to bassoon warmth: just this single phrase could provide an object lesson in orchestration. After it comes a rising horn summons; a tiny echo of Siegfried's call, echoed in turn by flutes and cellos taking over the harmony, and completed by a welcome from a xylophone's birdsong. After a blackbird solo on the flute – an extraordinary moment where the entire orchestra rests and listens to just one player – and then a little more of the xylophone, the whole first part is repeated. And that is all.

This is the point where the double basses come in, with the contrabass clarinet. The previous movement was all in the

EX. 18.6 *Eclairs sur l'au-delà . . .* 7 'Et Dieu essuiera tout larme de leurs yeux . . .'

middle-high register; suddenly here is this plummetting into the previously unheard far bass, for the loud introduction of a four-note motif in ascending tritones (B–F–E–B), a motif whose subsequent speeding-up and lifting through the orchestra will generate the power to justify the title: 'Les étoiles et la Gloire'. This is the biggest and boldest of the movements, setting its assertive main theme against and among birdsongs and nimbuses of nebulae, the latter pictured this time by murmurings from cellos. There are birds here from around the world: birds from Australia and from Papua New Guinea, together with the shama of *Oiseaux exotiques* and one of Messiaen's home favourites, the garden warbler, associated with the flute. Once again the birds seem to be standing in for the stars, the stars who give voice in the quotations from the Apocryphal book of Baruch ('God called the stars, and they answered: "Here we are!" ') and from Job ('. . . when the morning stars sang together, and all the sons of God shouted for joy . . .') Finally comes the climactic enlargement of the principal motif, and then a pause before the colossal chorale-coda, also just based on the motif (Ex. 18.7). Just for this moment the whole orchestra comes together, joining in the angels' chorus to the shepherds: 'Glory to God in the highest!'

EX. 18.7 *Eclairs sur l'au-delà . . .* 8 'Les étoiles et la Gloire'

Once more the work breathes back into itself, for the ninth movement is scored only for eighteen woodwinds, all playing different birdsongs: this is why there have to be ten flautists in the orchestra, mingled here with eight clarinettists. The eighteen lines flicker and fade in luminous confusion, at least for mortal ears: in the eternal time of paradise, where the successive can be simultaneous and the simultaneous successive, each of the birds has honour. Uniquely for this movement, Messiaen takes his inscription not from the Bible but from a French mystic, Dom J. de Monléon, who imagines the souls of the redeemed as birds in the branches of the tree of life, gathering its fruits and singing. There is an obvious similarity with the 'Epode' of *Chronochromie*, but 'Plusieurs oiseaux des arbres de Vie' is an enhanced realization of the image, with the airy lustre of wind tone, and with the lines now released from conducted tempo (as in earlier birdsong ensembles, in this work, in its immediate predecessors, and in *Saint François*), so that they can move and flex their wings of decoration.

The penultimate movement, 'Le chemin de l'Invisible', swivels back from paradise to review the difficulties of the approach. The mood is restless and punishing: only one bird sings in this movement, and the principal theme is a strenuous appeal in the sixth mode, an appeal presented as a pair of phrases (Ex. 18.8). Usually these phrases are carried by six horns in the face of hammerings from strings. Messiaen relives this angularity and the anxiety that came before the bliss in *Les offrandes oubliées*, and the piece ends as it had begun, with a wrenching chord and a slump to a low C, as if it had not got anywhere.

However, the work goes on to arrive at its destination in heaven – though this is not properly an arrival when heaven has already been glimpsed so much along the way, and when the music's time has always been the eternal time of repetition,

EX. 18.8 *Eclairs sur l'au-delà . . .* 10 'Le chemin de l'Invisible'

(a)

(b)

EX. 18.9 *Eclairs sur l'au-delà . . .* 11 'Le Christ, lumière du Paradis'

reversal and endless protraction rather than the earthly time of progress and development. The final movement, 'Le Christ, Lumière du Paradis', is the second extreme lento of muted violin melody couched on chords from other strings (Ex. 18.9). One difference from the fifth movement is that now there is the achieved light of the three high-trilling triangles. And though, as in that earlier adagio, there are places where the melody comes to rest, these are not now partitionings of a form: instead they are pauses for breath along an endless path, around an endless circuit. Nor is there any more striving into the uppermost register: the echo of the far treble – the light of Christ, perhaps – is always there in the metal shimmer of the triangles. The melody unfolds only because it is being played and heard by people still on earth: it is the extension on to our time scale of an instant. And similarly the triangles are projecting a reverberation which does not stop until time itself has stopped.

Appendix: The Organ at La Sainte Trinité, Paris

JEAN-LOUIS COIGNET

Concerning the organ it was in 1927, Raugel gives the following specification:

Grand-Orgue

16 Montre
16 Bourdon
8 Montre
8 Bourdon
8 Flûte Harmonique
8 Gambe
4 Prestant
$2\frac{2}{3}$ Quinte
V Cornet
III–VI Plein Jeu
16 Bombarde
8 Trompette
4 Clairon

Positif

16 Quintaton
8 Flûte Harmonique
8 Salicional
8 Unda Maris
4 Prestant
4 Flûte Octaviante
2 Doublette
1 Piccolo
II–V Cornet
16 Basson
8 Clarinette
8 Trompette

Récit expressif

8 Bourdon
8 Flûte Traversière
8 Voile de gambe
8 Voix Céleste
4 Flûte Octaviante
2 Octavin
6 Trompette
8 Basson-Hautbois
8 Voix Humaine
4 Clairon

Pédale

32 Soubasse
16 Contrebasse
16 Soubasse
8 Flûte
8 Bourdon
8 Violoncelle
4 Flûte
16 Bombarde
8 Trompette
4 Clairon

Combination Pedals

- Tirasses
  - Grand-Orgue
  - Positif
  - Récit
- Appel Grand-Orgue, Appel Pédale
- Octaves Graves Grand-Orgue
- Anches
  - Pédale
  - Grand-Orgue
  - Positif
  - Récit
- Copula
  - Positif/Grand-Orgue; Récit/Positif
  - Récit/Grand-Orgue; Trémolo du Récit

According to other authors there was a Flûte Octaviante 4 on the Grand-Orgue; I think this quite likely; there are often such discrepancies between various sources.

In 1934, on Olivier Messiaen's request, seven new stops were added to the organ as well as a Barker lever for the Positif. (Messiaen told me the Récit/Positif was quite unplayable before this addition!)

Grand-Orgue		*Positif*		*Récit expressif*	
16	Montre	16	Quintation	16	Bourdon
16	Bourdon	8	Principal	8	Gambe
8	Montre	8	Salicional	8	Voix Céleste
8	Gambe	8	Unda Maris	8	Flûte
8	Flûte harmonique	8	Flûte Harmonique	8	Bourdon
8	Bourdon	8	Cor de Nuit	4	Flûte
4	Prestant	4	Prestant	2⅔	Nasard
4	Flûte	4	Flûte	2	Octavin
2⅔	Quinte	2⅔	Nasard	III	Cymbale
III–VI	Plein Jeu	2	Doublette	8	Trompette
V	Cornet	1⅜	Tierce	4	Clairon
16	Bombarde	1	Piccolo	8	Basson-Hautbois
8	Trompette	II–V	Cornet	8	Voix Humaine
4	Clairon	16	Basson		Tremolo
		8	Trompette		
		8	Clarinette		

Pédale	
32	Bourdon
16	Contrebasse
16	Soubasse
8	Violoncelle
8	Flûte
8	Bourdon
4	Octave
16	Bombarde
8	Trompette
4	Clairon

From 1962 to 1965 both stop and note actions were electrified by Beuchet-Debierre and eight new stops were added to the organ together with a new Positif box to enclose seven Positif stops, a new console and a combination system:

Grand-Orgue

16	Montre
16	Bourdon
8	Montre
8	Gambe
8	Flûte Harmonique
8	Bourdon
4	Prestant
4	Flûte
$2\frac{2}{3}$	Quinte
2	Doublette
V	Plein Jeu (recomposition)
IV	Cymbale
V	Cornet
16	Bombarde
8	Trompette
4	Clairon

Positif non expressif

16	Quintaton
8	Principal
8	Flûte Harmonique
8	Salicional
8	Unda Maris
4	Prestant
2	Doublette
II–V	Cornet
IV	Fourniture
16	Basson
8	Trompette
4	Clairon

Positif expressif

8	Cor de Nuit
4	Flûte Douce
$2\frac{2}{2}$	Nasard
2	Flageolet
$1\frac{3}{5}$	Tierce
1	Piccolo
8	Clarinette

Récit expressif

16	Bourdon
8	Flûte Traversière
8	Bourdon
8	Gambe
8	Voix Céleste
4	Flûte Octaviante
$2\frac{2}{3}$	Nasard
2	Octavin
$1\frac{3}{5}$	Tierce
III	Cymbale
16	Bombarde
8	Trompette
4	Clairon
8	Basson-Hautbois
8	Voix Humaine

Pédale

32	Soubasse
16	Contrebasse
16	Soubasse
8	Flûte
8	Bourdon
4	Flûte
IV	Plein Jeu
16	Bombarde
8	Trompette
4	Clairon

+ Tremolo du Récit

After the extensive cleaning and renovation of the church's interior, the organ is being cleaned and overhauled (there were many leaks in the wind-trunks). Olivier Messiaen would have liked two new mutations on the Récit: a Septième $1\frac{1}{7}$ and a Neuvième $\frac{8}{9}$, a 32′ Bombarde on the Pédale and an 8′ Trompette en Chamade (not overwhelming, he said). At the present time I do not know whether these additions will be done or not; I should be inclined to keep the organ exactly as Messiaen played it.

Chronology of Messiaen's Life and Works

YEAR	LIFE	WORKS
1908	Olivier Eugène Prosper Charles Messiaen born (10 December) at Avignon, elder son of Pierre Messiaen and Cécile Sauvage	
1914	Pierre Messiaen joins the army; Cécile moves to her mother's house in Grenoble with Olivier and his younger brother Alain	
1917	Olivier receives his earliest piano lessons	*La dame de Shalott**
1918	Jehan de Gibon, his harmony teacher, gives him score of Debussy's *Pelléas et Mélisande*. Pierre Messiaen returns from the war and takes his family to Nantes	
1919	They move to Paris, and Olivier enters the Conservatoire	
1921		*Deux ballades de Villon**
1924	Gains second prize in harmony with Jean Gallon	
1925		*La tristesse d'un grand ciel blanc**
1926	First prize in counterpoint and fugue with Georges Caussade	
1927	First prize in piano accompaniment with C. A. Estyle. Mother dies (26 August)	*Esquisse modale**
1928	First prize for history of music	*Le banquet*

* unpublished

	with Maurice Emmanuel. Begins *Préludes*	*eucharistique**; Fugue in D minor*; *Variations écossaises**; *L'hôte aimable des âmes**; *Le banquet céleste*
1929	First prize in organ playing and improvisation with Marcel Dupré; unsuccessful attempt at Prix de Rome Completes *Préludes*	
1930	First prize in composition with Paul Dukas. Again fails to win Prix de Rome. Leaves the Conservatoire	*Diptyque*; *La mort du nombre*; *Les offrandes oubliés*; *Trois mélodies*; *Simple chant d'une âme**
1931	Takes up appointment as organist of La Trinité in Paris, a post he will occupy for more than 60 years. Public debut (19 February) with a performance of *Les offrandes oubliées* under Walter Straram. At the Exposition Coloniale, hears Balinese gamelan	*Le tombeau resplendissant*
1932	Marries Claire Delbos. *Le tombeau resplendissant* conducted by Pierre Monteux	*Apparition de l'église éternelle*; *Hymne au Saint Sacrement*; *Fantaisie burlesque*; *Thème et variations*
1933	*Hymne au Saint Sacrement* conducted by Straram (19 March)	*L'Ascension* (orchestra); Mass*; *Fantaisie**;
1934		*L'Ascension* (organ)
1935	Premiere of *L'Ascension* conducted by Robert Siohan (Paris, February)	*La Nativité du Seigneur*; *Pièce pour le tombeau de Paul Dukas*; *Vocalise*
1936	With André Jolivet, Daniel-Lesur and Yves Baudrier, founds 'La jeune France'. Begins teaching at the Schola Cantorum and the Ecole Normale de Musique	*Poèmes pour Mi* (voice and piano)
1937	Birth of son Pascal (14 July). Premiere of *Poèmes pour Mi* sung by Marcelle Bunlet, Messiaen accompanying (28 April)	*Poèmes pour Mi* (voice and orchestra); *Fêtes des belles eaux**; *O sacrum convivium!*

1938	Visits London, where he plays two pieces from *La Nativité* at the ISCM Festival in June	*Chants de terre et de ciel*; *Deux monodies en quarts de ton**
1939	Called up for military service as a medical auxiliary	*Les corps glorieux*
1940	Taken prisoner of war and interned at Görlitz in Silesia. Begins *Quatuor pour la fin du temps*	
1941	*Quatuor* performed to an audience of 5000 prisoners of war (15 January). Later that year he is released and becomes professor of harmony at the Paris Conservatoire	*Chœurs pour une Jeanne d'Arc**
1942	Begins *Technique de mon langage musical*	*Musique de scène pour un Œdipe**
1943	Gives private composition classes to a group of young composer-musicians that includes Pierre Boulez, Yvonne Loriod, Maurice Le Roux, Yvette Grimaud and others. Premiere of *Les corps glorieux* given by Messiaen at La Trinité (15 November)	*Rondeau*; *Visions de l'Amen*
1944	*Technique de mon langage musical*	*Trois petites liturgies de la Présence Divine*; *Vingt regards sur l'Enfant-Jésus*
1945	Premiere of *Vingt regards* (26 March) and *Trois petites liturgies* (21 April)	*Harawi*
1946	Begins *Turangalîla-symphonie*	*Chant des deportés**
1947	Appointed to analysis class at the Paris Conservatoire. Visits Budapest, where he teaches, and the US, where Leopold Stokowski conducts *Hymne au Saint Sacrement* and Serge Koussevitsky *L'Ascension*	
1948	Completes *Turangalîla*. Teaches at Tanglewood	*Cinq rechants*

1949	Teaches at the Darmstadt Summer school. Premiere of *Turangalîla* conducted by Leonard Bernstein in Boston (2 December)	*Cantéyodjayâ*; *Mode de valeurs et d'intensités*; *Neumes rhythmiques*
1950	Teaches at Darmstadt	*Ile de feu 1*; *Ile de feu 2*; *Messe de la Pentecôte*
1951	Records *Quatre études de rythme*. Teaches at Darmstadt and meets Stockhausen, who is impressed by *Mode de valeurs et d'intensités*	*Livre d'orgue*; *Le merle noir*
1952		*Timbres-durées**
1953	Premieres of *Livre d'orgue* (Stuttgart, 23 April) and *Revéil des oiseaux* (Donaueschingen, 11 October)	
1955	At Domaine Musical, plays *Livre d'orgue* (21 March). Begins *Oiseaux exotiques*	
1956	Premiere of *Oiseaux exotiques* by Domaine Musical in Paris (10 March). Begins *Catalogue d'oiseaux*	
1958	Completes *Catalogue d'oiseaux*	
1959	Premiere of *Catalogue d'oiseaux* in Paris (15 April). Death of Claire Delbos, his first wife. Begins *Chronochromie*	
1960	Premiere of *Chronochromie* in Donaueschingen (16 October)	*Verset pour la fête de la Dédicace*
1961	Marries the pianist and composer Yvonne Loriod	
1962	Visits Japan	*Sept haïkaï*
1963	Premiere of *Sept haïkaï* by Domaine Musical under Boulez (Paris, 17 October)	*Couleurs de la cité céleste*
1964	Premiere of *Couleurs de la cité céleste* by Domaine Musical under Boulez (Donaueschingen, 17 October)	*Et exspecto resurrectionem mortuorum*

1965	Premiere of *Et exspecto* in Ste Chapelle (7 May). Begins *La Transfiguration de Notre-Seigneur Jésus-Christ*	
1966	Appointed professor of composition at the Paris Conservatoire	
1967	Elected a member of the Institut de France	
1969	Premiere of *La Transfiguration* in Lisbon (7 June)	*Méditations sur le mystère de la Sainte Trinité*
1970		*La fauvette des jardins*
1971	Awarded Erasmus Prize. Begins *Des canyons aux étoiles . . .*	
1972	Premieres of *Méditations* (Washington, 20 March) and *La fauvette* (Paris, 7 November)	
1974	Premiere of *Des canyons aux étoiles . . .* in New York (20 November)	
1975	Begins *Saint François d'Assise*	
1978	Retires from Conservatoire. Messiaen Festival in Paris (November–December)	
1983	Premiere of *Saint François d'Assise*, Paris Opéra under Seiji Ozawa (28 November)	
1984		*Livre du Saint Sacrement*
1985		*Petites esquisses d'oiseaux*
1986	Premiere of *Livre du Saint Sacrement* in Detroit (1 July)	*Un vitrail et des oiseaux*
1987	Premiere of *Petites esquisses* in Paris (26 January)	*La ville d'En-haut*
1988	Premiere of *Un vitrail* in Paris (28 November)	
1989	Premiere of *La ville d'En-haut* in Paris (17 November)	*Un sourire*
1991	Premieres of *Pièce pour piano et quatuor à cordes* by Harald Ossberger and the Arditti Quartet (18 November), and of	

	Un sourire (5 December), both in Paris
1992	Messiaen dies (28 April)
	Premiere of *Eclairs sur l'au-delà* in New York (5 November)

List of Works and Discography

CHRISTOPHER DINGLE

The list provides information in the following order: title (and subtitle); forces; individual movements and/or section titles; date and place of composition (and orchestration); publisher. Unless otherwise stated, texts are by Messiaen himself. The works have been arranged into the following categories:

I OPERA
II ORCHESTRAL
III VOCAL
IV CHAMBER AND INSTRUMENTAL
V ORGAN
VI PIANO
VII ELECTRONIC

Discography

The recordings chosen are either currently available[1] or of particular historical interest, and they are listed in alphabetical order of conductor/principal performer. In some cases there is also a short paragraph intended to aid the collector in the task of building a Messiaen library. I have listed all available catalogue numbers for each recording; those which currently apply appear in **bold type**. Unless stated otherwise, current catalogue numbers refer to the compact disc format and present couplings are given in square brackets. The recordings listed at the end of each entry as BBC sound archive or NSA are of particular historical value and can be listened to at the National Sound Archive in London.[2] I should mention at this point the boxed set of seventeen CDs issued by Erato to commemorate the composer's eightieth birthday and

1 At time of writing.
2 These form only a small fraction of the recordings available at the National Sound Archive. NB Listening time should be booked at least one week in advance.

again after his death (ECD 71580; 2292–45505–2). Although currently deleted,[3] the set can still be found in enough record stores to warrant inclusion. It is by no means a 'complete edition' (works such as *La dame de Shallot* and *Fêtes des belles eaux* have been omitted despite their existence in Erato's back catalogue), but it nevertheless includes a number of valuable recordings, together with an interview with Messiaen by Claude Samuel.[4] I have marked the recordings contained in this set with an asterisk. I should like to thank Timothy Day at the National Sound Archive for his generous help in compiling the discographical information.

I Opera

Saint François d'Assise (scènes françiscaines)

SOLO ROLES: Saint François (Bar), Frère Léon (Bar), L'Ange (S), Le Lépreux (T), Frère Massée (T), Frère Elie (T), Frère Bernard (B), Frère Sylvestre (B), Frère Rufin (B)

CHOIR: s.s.m-s.a.a.t.t.bar.b.b (15 voices to each part)

ORCHESTRA: 7.4.8.4; 6.4.3.3; xylophone, xylorimba, marimba, glockenspiel, vibraphone, 5 percussion, 3 ondes martenot; 16.16.14.12.10

Act I Scene 1: La Croix Scene 2: Les laudes Scene 3: Le baiser au lépreux
Act II Scene 4: L'ange voyageur Scene 5: L'ange musicien
Scene 6: Le prêche aux oiseaux
Act III Scene 7: Les stigmates Scene 8: La mort et la nouvelle vie

COMPOSED: 1975–9
ORCHESTRATED: 1979–83
PUBLISHER: Leduc: full score, libretto
RECORDINGS:

1) Philippe Rouillon (Saint François), Phil Frohnmayer (Frère Léon), Maria Oràn (L'Ange), John Gilmore (Le Lépreux), Groot Omroepkoor; Nederlands Kamerkoor, Radio Symfonie Orkest, Radio Kamer Orkest, conducted by Kent Nagano.
   KRO (Live recording from concert performance at Utrecht on 28 September 1986) **KK 8802** (4 discs)
2) José van Dam (Saint François), Michel Philippe (Frère Léon),

3 Erato have now begun to issue the discs separately.
4 Translated in the booklet.

Christiane Eda-Pierre (L'Ange), Kenneth Riegel (Le Lépreux); Chorus and Orchestra of the Paris Opéra, conducted by Seiji Ozawa
Cybella (live recording from original production) **CY833/6** (4 discs)

II Orchestral

Fugue in D minor

COMPOSED: Paris, 1928

Le banquet eucharistique

COMPOSED: Fuligny, 1928

Simple chant d'une âme

COMPOSED: Paris, 1930

Les offrandes oubliées (méditation symphonique)

ORCHESTRA: 3.3.3.3; 4.3.3.1; timpani, percussion; strings
COMPOSED: Fuligny, 1930
PUBLISHER: Durand: study score, piano reduction
RECORDINGS:
1) Orchestre de Paris, conducted by Serge Baudo
EMI (Rouge et Noir) **CZS 7 626692** (2 discs)
[with various French orchestral works]
*2) Orchestre Philharmonique de l'ORTF, conducted by Marius Constant
Erato STU 70673; ECD 71588; 2292–45505–2/IV; **4509–91707–2**
[with *Hymne au Saint Sacrement*, *Visions de l'Amen*]

Le tombeau resplendissant

ORCHESTRA: 3.3.3.3; 4.3.3.1; timpani, percussion; strings
COMPOSED: Fuligny, 1931
PUBLISHER: Durand [NB no material available for sale]

Hymne au Saint Sacrement

ORCHESTRA: 3.3.3.3 4.3.3.0; timpani, percussion; strings
COMPOSED: Paris, 1932
PUBLISHER: Broude Bros: study score (reconstructed by Messiaen from memory) for a performance by Leopold Stokowski, the original score having been lost during the war.
RECORDINGS:
*1) Orchestre Philharmonique de l'ORTF, conducted by Marius Constant
Erato STU 70763; ECD 71588; 2292–45505–2/IV; **4509–91707–2**

[with *Les offrandes oubliées*, *Visions de l'Amen*]

L'Ascension (méditations symphoniques)

1 Majesté du Christ demandant sa gloire à son Père 2 Alléluias sereins d'une âme qui désire le ciel 3 Alléluia sur la trompette, alléluia sur la cymbale 4 Prière du Christ montant vers son Père

ORCHESTRA: 3.3.3.3; 4.3.3.1; timpani, percussion; 16.16.14.12.10
COMPOSED: Paris/Neussargues, May–July 1932
ORCHESTRATED: Monaco, May–July 1933
PUBLISHER: Leduc: study score (NB arranged for organ, 1933–4)
RECORDINGS:
*1) Orchestre Philharmonique de l'ORTF, conducted by Marius Constant
Erato STU 70673; ECD 71587; 2292–45505–2/III; 4509–91706–2
[with *Et exspecto resurrectionem mortuorum*, *Couleurs de la cité céleste*]
2) Orchestre de l'Opéra Bastille, conducted by Myung-Whun Chung
DG 435–854–2 GH (CD); 435–854–5 GH (DCC[5])
[with Saint-Saëns: Symphony No. 3]

Turangalîla-symphonie

1 Introduction 2 Chant d'amour I 3 Turangalîla I 4 Chant d'amour II 5 Joie du sang des étoiles 6 Jardin du sommeil d'amour 7 Turangalîla II 8 Développement de l'amour 9 Turangalîla III 10 Final

ORCHESTRA: 3.3.3.3 4.5.3.1; piano solo, ondes martenot solo, glockenspiel, celesta, vibraphone, 5 percussion; 16.16.14.12.10
COMPOSED: 17 July 1946–29 November 1948
PUBLISHER: Durand: study score, solo piano part, solo ondes martenot part
RECORDINGS:

Of the seven commercial recordings of *Turangalîla* listed below there are two which deserve particular attention. Chung's version (DG) uses a revised version of the score and has the composer's imprimatur, although it is the timbre of a true French woodwind sound that makes this recording particularly desirable. With the transfer to compact disc of the first recording of *Turangalîla* conducted by Hans Rosbaud we now have a valuable insight into the difficulties the work originally provided for performers. The technical strain on the orchestra creates a tension and an excitement which is lacking in too many current performances.

5 Digital Compact Cassette.

1) J.-Y. Thibaudet (pf), T. Harada (ondes) Royal Concertgebouw Orchestra, conducted by Riccardo Chailly
Decca **436 626–2DH** (CD); **436626–5** (DCC)
2) Y. Loriod (pf), J. Loriod (ondes), Orchestre de la Bastille, conducted by Myung-Whun Chung
DG **431 781–2**
3) Y. Loriod (pf), J. Loriod (ondes), Orchestre Symphonique de Radio-Tele-Luxembourg, conducted by Louis de Froment
Forlane
UCD 16504/05 (2 discs)
[with *Trois petites liturgies*]
4) P. Donohoe (pf), T. Murail (ondes), CBSO, conducted by Simon Rattle
EMI EX 270 468–3; EX 270 468–5; **CDS 747463–8** (2 discs)
[with *Quatuor pour la fin du temps*]
5) Y. Loriod (pf), G. Martenot (ondes), Sinfonieorchester des Südwestfunks Baden-Baden, conducted by Hans Rosbaud
Wergo **WER 6401–2**
6) P. Crossley (pf), T. Murail (ondes), Philharmonia, conducted by Esa-Pekka Salonen
CBS/SONY **M2K 42271** (2 discs)
[with Lutosławski: Symphony No. 3, etc]
7) R. Muraro (pf), V. Hartmann-Slaverie (ondes), French Radio Philharmonic Orchestra, conducted by M. Janowski
RCS/BMG **09026 61520–2**
[with *Un sourire*; Lutosławski: Concerto for Orchestra]

Réveil des oiseaux

ORCHESTRA: 4.3.4.3; 2.2.0.0; piano solo, celesta, xylophone, glockenspiel, 2 percussion; 8.8.8.8.6
COMPOSED: 1953
PUBLISHER: Durand: study score, solo piano part
RECORDINGS:
1) Y. Loriod (pf), Czech Philharmonic Orchestra, conducted by Vaclav Neumann
Supraphon SUA ST 50749 (record)
[with *Oiseaux exotiques*]

Oiseaux exotiques

ORCHESTRA: 2.1.3.1; 2.1.0.0; piano solo, glockenspiel, xylophone, 5 percussion
COMPOSED: 5 October 1955 – 23 January 1956
PUBLISHER: Universal: study score, solo piano part

RECORDINGS:
1) Y. Loriod (pf), Ensemble InterContemporain, conducted by Pierre Boulez
Disques Montaignes **XXIIII**
(live performance from composer's 80th birthday concert)
[with *Un vitrail et des oiseaux*, *Sept haïkaï*, *Couleurs de la cité céleste*]
2) Y. Loriod (pf), Czech Philharmonic Orchestra, conducted by Vaclav Neumann
Supraphon SUA ST 50749 (record)
3) P. Crossley (pf), London Sinfonietta, conducted by Esa-Pekka Salonen
CBS/SONY 40–44762 (2 tapes); **CD 44762** (2 discs)
[with *Des canyons aux étoiles . . .*, *Couleurs de la cité céleste*]
4) Y. Loriod (pf), Domaine Musical, conducted by Rudolf Albert
Vega (1st performance) C30 A65 (record)
5) Y. Loriod (pf), BBCSO
BBC sound archive tape (1st English performance, 1 June 1961) T27366
6) Y. Loriod (pf) Südwestfunk Symphony Orchestra, conducted by Pierre Boulez
NSA Tape (BBC broadcast, 20 September 1967) M 1080 W

Chronochromie

1 Introduction 2 Strophe I 3 Antistrophe I 4 Strophe II
5 Antistrophe II 6 Epode 7 Coda

ORCHESTRA: 4.3.4.3; 4.4.3.1; glockenspiel, xylophone, marimba, 3 percussion; 16.16.14.12.10
COMPOSED: 1959–60
PUBLISHER: Leduc: study score
RECORDINGS:
1) BBCSO, conducted by Antal Dorati
EMI (HMV) ALP 2092; ASD 639; ZRG 756; **CDM 7 63948 2**
[with *Et exspecto resurrectionem mortuorum*; Koechlin: *Les Bandar-Log*; Boulez: *Le soleil des eaux*]

Sept haïkaï (esquisses japonaises)

1 Introduction 2 Le parc de Nara et les lanternes de pierre
3 Yamanaka cadenza 4 Gagaku 5 Miyajima et le torii dans la mer 6 Les oiseaux de Karuizawa 7 Coda

ORCHESTRA: 2.3.4.2; 0.1.1.0; piano solo, xylophone, marimba, 4 percussion 8.0.0.0.0
COMPOSED: 1962

PUBLISHER: Leduc: study score, solo piano part
RECORDINGS:
1) Y. Loriod (pf), Ensemble InterContemporain, conducted by Pierre Boulez
Disques Montaignes **XXIIII**
[with *Couleurs de la cité céleste*, *Un vitrail et des oiseaux*, *Oiseaux exotiques*]
*2) Y. Loriod (pf), Ensemble Ars Nova – conducted by Marius Constant
Erato STU 70796; ECD 71584; 2292–45505–2/II
[with *Des canyons aux étoiles . . .*]

Couleurs de la cité céleste

ORCHESTRA: 0.0.3.0; 2.4.4.0; piano solo, xylophone, xylorimba, marimba, 3 percussion
COMPOSED: 1963
PUBLISHER: Leduc: study score, solo piano part
RECORDINGS:
1) Y. Loriod (pf), Ensemble InterContemporain, conducted by Pierre Boulez
Disques Montaignes **XXIIII**
[with *Oiseaux exotiques*, *Un vitrail et des oiseaux*, *Sept haïkaï*]
*2) Y. Loriod (pf), Groupe Instrumentale à Percussion de Strasbourg, Orchestre du Domaine Musical, conducted by Pierre Boulez
Erato SBRG 72471; STU 70302; ECD 71587; 2292–45505–2/III; **4509–91706–2**
[with *Et exspecto resurrectionem mortuorum*, *L'Ascension*]
3) P. Crossley (pf), London Sinfonietta, conducted by Esa-Pekka Salonen
CBS/SONY 40–44762 (2 tapes); **CD 44762** (2 discs)
[with *Des canyons aux étoiles . . .*, *Oiseaux exotiques*]

Et exspecto resurrectionem mortuorum

1 Des profondeurs de l'abîme, je cris vers toi, Seigneur: Seigneur, écoute ma voix! 2 Le Christ, ressuscité des morts, ne meurt plus; la mort n'a plus sur lui d'empire 3 L'heure vient où les mort entendront la voix du Fils de Dieu 4 Ils ressusciteront, glorieux, avec un nom nouveau – dans le concert joyeux des étoiles et les acclamations des fils du ciel 5 Et j'entendis la voix d'une foule immense

ORCHESTRA: 5.4.5.4; 6.4.4.2; 6 percussion
COMPOSED: Petichet, 1964
PUBLISHER: Leduc: study score

RECORDINGS:

1) Ensemble de Percussion de l'Orchestre de Paris, Orchestre de Paris, conducted by Serge Baudo
EMI ASD 2467; **CDM 7 63948 2**
[with *Chronochromie*; Boulez: *Le soleil des eaux*, Koechlin: *Les Bandar-Log*]

*2) Groupe Instrumentale à Percussion de Strasbourg, Orchestre du Domaine Musical, conducted by Pierre Boulez
Erato SBRG 72471; STU 70302; ECD 71587; 2292–45505–2/III; **4509–91706 2**
[with *Couleurs de la cité céleste*, *L'Ascension*]

3) Bamberger Symphoniker, conducted by Ingo Metzmacher
EMI **CDC 7 549162**
[with Hartmann: Symphony No. 4]

4) Orchestre du Domaine Musical, conducted by Pierre Boulez
NSA tape M 410W (from BBC broadcast on 11 June 1965)

5) Members of the Group Instrumentale à Percussion de Strasbourg, brass players of the Brussels ensemble, conducted by Pierre Boulez
NSA tape M 566 R (from BBC broadcast on 12 November 1965)

Des canyons aux étoiles . . .

1 Le désert 2 Les orioles 3 Ce qui écrit sur les étoiles 4 Le cossyphe d'Heuglin 5 Cedar Breaks et le don de crainte 6 Appel interstellaire 7 Bryce Canyon et les rochers rouge-orange 8 Les ressuscités et le chant de l'étoile Aldebaran 9 Le moquer polyglotte 10 La grive des bois 11 Omao, leiothrix, elepaio, shama 12 Zion Park et la cité céleste

ORCHESTRA: 4.3.4.3; 3.3.3.0; piano solo, glockenspiel, xylorimba, 5 percussion; 6.0.3.3.1

COMPOSED: 1971–4

PUBLISHER: Leduc: full score, solo piano part

RECORDINGS:

*1) Y. Loriod (pf), Ensemble Ars Nova, conducted by Marius Constant
Erato STU 70974/5; ECD71584; 2292-45505-2/II
[with *Sept haïkaï*]

2) P. Crossley (pf), London Sinfonietta, conducted by Esa-Pekka Salonen
CBS/SONY 40-44762 (2 tapes); **CD 44762** (2 discs)
[with *Oiseaux exotiques*, *Couleurs de la cité céleste*]

3) Y. Loriod (pf), A. Civil (hn), J. Holland (xyba), T. Emery (glock), BBCSO, conducted by Pierre Boulez
NSA tapes T1052BW/T1053BW and T 2066BW/T 1067BW (BBC

broadcast of UK premiere on 12 November 1975, repeated on 11 December 1978 for the composer's 70th birthday)

Un vitrail et des oiseaux

ORCHESTRA: 4.4.5.3; 0.1.0.0; piano solo, xylophone, xylorimba, marimba, 5 percussion
COMPOSED: 1986
PUBLISHER: Leduc: full score
RECORDINGS:
1) Y. Loriod (pf), Ensemble InterContemporain, conducted by Pierre Boulez
Disques Montaignes XXIIII
[with *Couleurs de la cité céleste*, *Sept haïkaï*, *Oiseaux exotiques*]

La ville d'En-haut

ORCHESTRA: 5.4.5.3; 6.4.3.1; piano solo, glockenspiel, xylophone, xylorimba, marimba, 4 percussion
COMPOSED: 1987
PUBLISHER: Leduc: full score
RECORDINGS:
1) Y. Loriod (pf), BBCSO, conducted by Pierre Boulez
NSA tape NSA B 5646 (live performance, UK premiere 23 November 1989; broadcast by BBC, 12 March 1990)
2) Y. Loriod (pf), BBCSO, conducted by Pierre Boulez
NSA tape NSA B 5381 (live performance from Huddersfield festival: 26 November 1989; broadcast by BBC 9 January 1990)

Un sourire

ORCHESTRA: 4.4.3.3; 4.1.0.0; xylophone, xylorimba, 2 percussion; 16.16.14.12.0
COMPOSED: 1989
PUBLISHER: Leduc: full score (in preparation)
[NB composed for the Mozart bicentenary]
RECORDINGS:
1) French Radio Philharmonic Orchestra; conducted by M. Janowski
RCA/BMG 09026 61520–2
[with *Turangalîla*; Lutosławski: Concerto for Orchestra]

Eclairs sur l'au-delà . . .

1 Apparition du Christ glorieux 2 La constellation du Sagittaire 3 L'oiseau-lyre et la Ville-Fiancée 4 Les élus marqués de sceau 5 Demeurer dans l'Amour 6 Les sept anges aux septs trompettes 7 Et Dieu essuiera toute larme de leurs yeux . . . 8 Les étoiles et la Gloire 9 Plusieurs oiseaux des

arbres de Vie 10 Le chemin de l'Invisible 11 Le Christ, lumière du Paradis

ORCHESTRA: 10.4.10.4; 6.5.3.3; crotales, glockenspiel, xylophone, xylorimba, marimba, 10 percussion; 16.16.14.12.10
COMPOSED: 1988–92
PUBLISHER: Leduc: full score (in preparation)
RECORDINGS:
1) Orchestre de la Bastille, conducted by Myung-Whun Chung
DG **439 929 2GH**
2) Orchestre National de la Radio Polonaise Katowice, conducted by Antoni Wit
Jade **JAD K 099** (tape); **JADE C 099** (CD) (live performance from 'Autumn in Warsaw' festival, 23 September 1993)
3) NSA tape H2498 (live performance, UK premiere, 21 November 1993; broadcast by BBC, 17 December 1993)

Concert à quatre

The *Concert à quatre* (duration 20–25 minutes) is scored for four soloists (flute, oboe, cello and piano) and large orchestra. The work was commissioned by Myung-Whun Chung and Heinz Holliger and was composed during the last months of Messiaen's life. Of the four movements, three were complete at the time of Messiaen's death; the remaining movement was left partially orchestrated and this was completed by Yvonne Loriod with the advice of George Benjamin. One movement of the *Concert* is an arrangement (for oboe and small orchestra) of the *Vocalise*.

Premiere scheduled for 26 Sept 1994 at the Opéra-Bastille, Paris, with the Orchestre de la Bastille, conducted by Myung-Whun Chung and including Heinz Holliger (oboe) and Yvonne Loriod (piano) among the soloists. The work will be recorded by DG with the same forces.

III Vocal

Jane Manning's performances, a leader in this field, are currently deleted, but a re-release at mid-price is envisaged. There is at present a gap in the catalogue as far as the orchestral version of *Poèmes pour Mi* is concerned, with the long-deleted version by Jill Gomez and Pierre Boulez well overdue for transfer to compact disc.

Deux ballades de Villon

1 Epître à ses amis 2 Ballade des pendus

SCORING: voice and piano
COMPOSED: 1921

Trois mélodies

1 Pourquoi? 2 Le sourire (Cécile Sauvage) 3 La fiancée perdue

SCORING: voice and piano
COMPOSED: Paris, 1930
PUBLISHER: Durand
RECORDING:
1) Michèle Command, Marie-Madeleine Petit
EMI (L'Esprit français) 2C 167 1626–8; CMS 7 64092 2 (2 discs)
[with *Poèmes pour Mi*, *Chants de terre et de ciel*, *Harawi*]

La mort du nombre

SCORING: soprano, tenor, violin and piano
COMPOSED: Paris, 1930
PUBLISHER: Durand
RECORDING:
1) A. Murray, P. Langridge, A. Watkinson (vn), R. Vignoles (pf)
Virgin VC 7 91179–2
[with French songs and duets]

Mass

SCORING: 8 sopranos and 4 violins
COMPOSED: Neussargues, 1933

Vocalise

SCORING: soprano and piano
COMPOSED: Paris, 1935
PUBLISHER: Leduc

Poèmes pour Mi

1 Action de grâces 2 Paysage 3 La maison 4 Epouvante
5 L'épouse 6 Ta voix 7 Les deux guerriers 8 Le collier
9 Prière exaucée

SCORING: soprano and piano
COMPOSED: Petichet, 1936
PUBLISHER: Durand
ORCHESTRATED: Paris, 1937
SCORING: soprano; 3.3.2.3; 4.3.3.1; 3 percussion; strings
PUBLISHER: Durand: study score
RECORDINGS:
Original version:
1) Michèle Command, Marie-Madeleine Petit
EMI (L'Esprit français) 2C 167 16226–8; CMS 7 64092 2 (2 discs)
[with *Chants de terre et de ciel*, *Harawi*, *Trois mélodies*]

2) Jane Manning, David Mason
Unicorn Kanchana DKP 9043; DKPC9043; DKPCD9094
[with *Chants de terre et de ciel*]
*3) Maria Oràn, Yvonne Loriod
Erato ECD 75502; 2292–45505–2/X

Orchestral version:
1) Felicity Palmer, BBCSO, conducted by Pierre Boulez
Decca (Argo) ZRG 703

O sacrum convivium!

SCORING: SATB choir or soprano and organ
COMPOSED: Paris, 1937
PUBLISHER: Durand
RECORDINGS:
1) Groupe Vocale de France
ARION **ARN 68084**
[with *Cinq rechants*; Xenakis: *Nuits*]
2) London Sinfonietta Chorus, conducted by Terry Edwards
Virgin VC 7 91472–2
[with *Trois petites liturgies*, *Cinq rechants*]

Chants de terre et de ciel

1 Bail avec Mi (pour ma femme) 2 Antienne du silence (pour le jour des Anges gardiens) 3 Danse du bébé-Pilule (pour mon petit Pascal) 4 Arc-en-ciel d'innocence (pour mon petit Pascal) 5 Minuit pile et face (pour la mort) 6 Résurrection (pour la jour de Pâques)

SCORING: soprano and piano
COMPOSED: Petichet, 1938
PUBLISHER: Durand
RECORDINGS:
1) Michèle Command, Marie-Madeleine Petit
EMI (L'Esprit français) 2C 167 16226–8; **CMS 7 64092 2** (2 discs)
[with *Poèmes pour Mi*, *Harawi*, *Trois mélodies*]
2) Jane Manning, David Mason
Unicorn Kanchana DKP 9043; DKPC9043; DKPCD9094
[with *Poèmes pour Mi*]
3*) Maria Oràn, Yvonne Loriod
Erato ECD 75502; 2292–45505–2/X
[with *Poèmes pour Mi*]

Trois petites liturgies de la Présence Divine

1 Antienne de la conversation intérieure (Dieu présent en nous . . .) 2 Séquence du Verbe, cantique divin (Dieu présent en lui-même . . .) 3 Psalmodie de l'ubiquité par amour (Dieu présent en toutes choses . . .)

SCORING: 36 women's voices; piano solo, ondes martenot solo, celesta, vibraphone, 3 percussion; 8.8.6.6.4

COMPOSED: Paris, 15 November 1943–15 March 1944

PUBLISHER: Durand: study score, chorus part

RECORDINGS:

*1) Y. Loriod (pf), J. Loriod (ondes), Maîtrise et Orchestre de Chambre de la RTF, conducted by Marcel Couraud
Erato STU 70.200; ECD 71594; 2292–45505–2/VII; **4509–92007–2**
[with *Méditations sur le mystère de la Sainte Trinité*]

2) London Sinfonietta, London Sinfonietta Chorus, conducted by Terry Edwards
Virgin **VC 7 91472–2**
[with *Cinq rechants*, *O sacrum convivium!*]

3) Y. Loriod (pf), J. Loriod (ondes), Ensemble Vocal à Cœur Joie, Ensemble Instrumental de Grenoble, conducted by Stéphane Cardon
Forlane **UCD 16504/05** (2 discs)
[with *Turangalîla*]

4) Y. Loriod, G. Martenot, Chorus and Orchestra of the Paris Conservatoire, conducted by Roger Désormière
Pathé PDT 190/4S (78s – 9 sides)

PDT 190	Side 1)	SOFX 1008–1
	Side 2)	SOFX 1009–1
PDT 191	Side 3)	SOFX 1006–1
	Side 4)	SOFX 1007–1
PDT 192	Side 5)	SOFX 1001–2
	Side 6)	SOFX 1002–1
PDT 193	Side 7)	SOFX 1003–2
	Side 8)	SOFX 1004–2
PDT 194	Side 9)	SOFX 1005–1

Harawi (chant d'amour et de mort)

1 La ville qui dormait, toi 2 Bonjour toi, colombe verte
3 Montagnes 4 Doundou tchil 5 L'amour de Piroutcha
6 Répétition planétaire 7 Adieu 8 Syllabes 9 L'escalier redit, gestes du soleil 10 Amour oiseau d'étoile 11 Katchikatchi les étoiles 12 Dans le noir

SCORING: dramatic soprano and piano

COMPOSED: Petichet, 15 June – 15 September 1945
PUBLISHER: Leduc
RECORDINGS:
1) Michèle Command, Marie-Madeleine Petit
EMI (L'Esprit français) 2C 167 16226–8; **CMS 7 64092 2** (2 discs)
[with *Poèmes pour Mi*, *Chants de terre et de ciel*, *Trois mélodies*]
2) Jane Manning, David Miller
Unicorn-Kanchana DKP9034; DKPC9034; **DKPCD9034**
*3) Rachel Yakar, Yvonne Loriod
Erato ECD 75501; 2292–45505–2/IX

Chant des déportés

SCORING: choir and large orchestra
COMPOSED: 1946

Cinq rechants

SCORING: 3 sopranos, 3 altos, 3 tenors, 3 basses
COMPOSED: Paris, December 1948
PUBLISHER: Salabert
RECORDINGS:
1) Groupe Vocale de France
ARION **ARN 68084**
[with O *sacrum convivium!*; Xenakis: *Nuits*]
2) London Sinfonietta Chorus, conducted by Terry Edwards
Virgin **VC 7 91472–2**
[with *Trois petites liturgies*, O *sacrum convivium!*]
*3) Solistes des Chœurs de l'ORTF
Erato STU 70.457; ECD 71597; 2292–45505–2/VIII;
4509–91708–2

La Transfiguration de Notre-Seigneur Jésus-Christ

Premier septénaire: 1 Recit évangélique 2 Configuration corpori claritatis suae 3 Christus Jesus, splendor Patris 4 Récit évangélique 5 Quam dilecta tabernacula tua 6 Candor est lucis aeternae 7 Choral de la sainte montagne
Deuxième septénaire: 8 Récit évangélique 9 Perfecte conscius perfectae generationis 10 Adoptionem filiorum perfectam 11 Récit évangélique 12 Terribilis est locus iste 13 Tota Trinitas apparuit 14 Choral de la lumière de gloire

CHOIR: s.s.m-s.a.t.t.bar.b.b. (10 voices to each part)
ORCHESTRA: 7 soloists: piano, cello, flute, clarinet, xylorimba, vibraphone, marimba; 5.4.5.4; 6.4.4.2; 6 percussion; 16.16.14.12.12
COMPOSED: 28 June 1965–20 February 1969

PUBLISHER: Leduc: full score
RECORDINGS:
1) Y. Loriod (pf), J. Starker (vc), W. Mann (fl), L. Kitt (cl), F. A. Ames (mar), J. A. C.Cane (xyba), R. Barnett (vib), Westminster Symphonic Choir, National Symphony Orchestra, conducted by Antal Dorati
Decca HEAD 1–2; **425161–2 DM2** (2 discs)
[with *La Nativité*]
2) Y. Loriod (pf), M. Gendron (vc) D. Whittaker (fl), C. Bradbury (cl), J. Delécluse (vib), F. Brana (mar), A. Jacquet (xyba), BBC Choral Society, BBCSO, conducted by Serge Baudo
NSA tapes P 535 W, 1570 R, P 536 W (UK premiere; opening concert of 76th Promenade season, 17 July 1970)

IV Chamber and Instrumental

Thème et variations

SCORING: violin and piano
COMPOSED: Paris, 1932
PUBLISHER: Leduc
RECORDINGS:
1) Gidon Kremer, Martha Argerich
DG **427 351–2 GH**
[with Bartók, Janáček: sonatas]
2) Christoph Poppen, Yvonne Loriod
[with *Quatuor pour la fin du temps*]
EMI CDC 7 54395 2
3) Lorraine McAslan, Nigel Clayton
Collins **11732**
[with 20th-century recital]

Fantaisie

SCORING: violin and piano
COMPOSED: Paris, 1933

Quatuor pour la fin du temps

1 Liturgie de cristal 2 Vocalise pour l'ange qui annonce la fin du temps 3 Abîme des oiseaux 4 Intermède 5 Louange à l'éternité de Jésus 6 Danse de la fureur, pour les sept trompettes 7 Fouillis d'arcs-en-ciel, pour l'ange qui annonce la fin du temps 8 Louange à l'immortalité de Jésus

SCORING: violin, clarinet, cello and piano
COMPOSED: Stalag 8A, Görlitz, Silesia, 1940–1

PUBLISHER: Durand: score and parts, study score
RECORDINGS:
1) Luben Yordanoff (vn), Claude Desumont (cl), Albert Tétard (vc), Daniel Barenboim (pf)
DG 2 531 093; **423 247–2 GC**
2) Erich Gruenberg (vn), Gervase de Peyer (cl), William Pleeth (vc), Michel Béroff (pf)
EMI (L'Esprit français) ASD 2470; **CDM 7 63947 2**
[with *Le merle noir*]
3) Chamber Music NW
Delos **DE 3043**
[with Bartók: *Contrasts*]
4) Ensemble Walter Boeynkens
Harmonia Mundi **HMC 90 1348**
5) Eduard Brunner (cl), Trio Fontenay
Teldec **9031–73239–2**
6) Saschko Gawriloff (vn), Heinz Deinzer (cl), Siegfried Palm (vc), Aloys Kontarsky (pf)
EMI 1C065 99711; EX 270468–3; EX 270468–5; **CDS 7 47463 8** (2 discs)
[with *Turangalîla*]
7) G. Pieterson (vn), V. Beths (cl), A. Bylsma (vc), R. de Leeuw (pf)
Philips 9500 725; 422 834–4 PO; **422 834–2 PO**
8) Christoph Poppen (vn), Wolfgang Meyer (cl), Manuel Fischer-Dieskau (vc), Yvonne Loriod (pf)
EMI **CDC 7 54395 2**
[with *Thème et variations*]
9) Madeleine Mitchell (vn), David Campbell (cl), Christopher van Kampen (vc), Joanna MacGregor (pf)
Collins **13932**
10) Jean Pasquier (vn), André Vacellier (cl), Etienne Pasquier (vc), Olivier Messiaen (pf)
Musidisc RC 719 (record)
*11) Huguette Fernandez (vn), Guy Deplus (cl), Jacques Neilz (vc), Marie-Madeleine Petit (pf)
Erato STU 70.156; ECD 71597; 2292–45505–2/VIII; **4509–91708–2**
[with *Cinq rechants*]

Le merle noir

SCORING: flute and piano
COMPOSED: Paris, 1951
PUBLISHER: Leduc

RECORDINGS:
1) Jonathan Snowden (fl), Andrew Litton (pf)
Virgin VC 790846 4; **VC 7 90846 2**
[with French flute music]
2) Karlheinz Zöller (fl), Aloys Kontarsky (pf)
EMI (L'Esprit français) **CDM 7 63947 2**
[with *Quatuor pour la fin du temps*]

Pièce pour piano et quatuor à cordes

SCORING: string quartet and piano
COMPOSED: 1991 (as gift for Alfred Schlee's 90th birthday)
PUBLISHER: Universal Edition: full score
1) Claude Helffer (pf), Arditti String Quartet
NSA Alfred Schlee's 90th birthday Compact Disc

V Organ

There are currently two readily available complete recordings of Messiaen's organ works, with a third due to appear during 1994. Jennifer Bate's series on Unicorn-Kanchana was recorded at Beauvais, with the exception of the *Livre du Saint Sacrement* which was recorded at La Trinité, and the command of the repertoire is often breathtaking, helped along by the voluptuous French reed and mixture stops. Hans-Ola Ericsson's marvellous set on BIS is pervaded by the awe-inspiring sound of the organ at Lule Cathedral in Sweden, and there is a bonus of birdsong recordings as a coupling to the *Livre du Saint Sacrement*. Gillian Weir has just recorded the complete set for Collins which should become an essential part of any collection. Lastly, Messiaen himself recorded all but two of his organ works. The first set is on EMI and includes everything up to, and including, the *Livre d'orgue*, while for Erato he recorded the *Méditations sur le mystère de la Sainte Trinité*. Despite poor sound quality in the EMI set, these are compelling performances which should be heard by any lover of organ works. Interpretations range from mildly enlightening to the outrageous, usually, though not always, conveying the music in renditions that most protagonists would not dare even to consider. These recordings should be avoided by anyone who believes in definitive performances!

Esquisse modale

COMPOSED: 1927

Le banquet céleste

COMPOSED: Fuligny, 1928

PUBLISHER: Leduc
RECORDINGS:
*1) Marie-Claire Alain
Erato ECD 75503; 2292–45505–2/XI; 2292–45470–2
[with *La Nativité*, *Apparition de l'église éternelle*]
2) Jennifer Bate
Unicorn-Kanchana DKPC 9005; **DKPCD 9005**
[with *La Nativité*]
3) Hans-Ola Ericsson
BIS **BIS-CD 409**
[with *Dyptique*, *Apparition de l'église éternelle*, *L'Ascension*]
4) Susan Landale
Adda **58 1039**
[with *La Nativité*, *Apparition de l'église éternelle*]
5) Olivier Messiaen
EMI DUC 260 C 074; 2C 153 16291/6; **CZS 7 67400 2** (4 discs)
6) Olivier Messiaen
EMI 'Composers in person' DUC 260 C 074; 2C 15316291/6; **CDC 5 55037 2**
[with *L'Ascension*; organ works by Widor, Vierne and Dupré]
7) Gillian Weir
Collins 70312 (7 discs)
[complete organ works]

L'hôte aimable des âmes

COMPOSED: Fuligny, 1928

Variations écossaises

COMPOSED: Paris, 1928

Diptyque (essai sur la vie terrestre et l'éternité bienheureux)

COMPOSED: Paris, 1930
PUBLISHER: Durand
RECORDINGS:
1) Jennifer Bate
Unicorn-Kanchana **DKPC 9004** (tape); **DKPCD 9004**
[with *Les corps glorieux*]
2) Hans-Ola Ericsson
BIS **BIS-CD 409**
[with *Le banquet céleste*, *Apparition de l'église éternelle*, *L'Ascension*]
3) Olivier Messiaen
EMI DUC 260 C 075/6; 2C 153 16291/6; **CZS 7 67400 2** (4 discs)

4) Thomas Trotter
Decca 436 400–2 DH
[with *Messe de la Pentecôte*, *L'Ascension*, *Apparition de l'église éternelle*]
5) Gillian Weir
Collins 70312 (7 discs)
[complete organ works]

Apparition de l'église éternelle

COMPOSED: Paris, 1932
PUBLISHER: Durand
RECORDINGS:
*1) Marie-Claire Alain
Erato ECD 75503; 2292–45505–2/XI; 2292–45470–2
[with *La Nativité*, *Le banquet céleste*]
2) Jennifer Bate
Unicorn-Kanchana DKPC 9028; **DKPCD 9028**
[with *Livre d'orgue*, *Verset pour la fête de la Dédicace*]
3) Hans-Ola Ericsson
BIS BIS-CD 409
[with *L'Ascension*, *Le banquet céleste*, *Diptyque*]
4) Susan Landale
Adda **58 1039**
[with *La Nativité*, *Le banquet céleste*]
5) Olivier Messiaen
EMI DUC 260 C 074–81; 2C 153 16291/6; **CZS 7 67400 2** (4 discs)
6) Thomas Trotter
Decca 436 400–2 DH
[*Diptyque*, *L'Ascension*, *Messe de la Pentecôte*]
7) Gillian Weir
Collins **70312** (7 discs)
[complete organ works]

L'Ascension

1 Majesté du Christ demandant sa gloire à son Père 2 Alléluias sereins d'une âme qui désire le ciel 3 Transports de joie d'une âme devant la gloire du Christ qui est la sienne 4 Prière du Christ montant vers son Père

COMPOSED: 1933–4
PUBLISHER: Leduc
RECORDINGS:
1) Jennifer Bate
Unicorn-Kanchana **DKPC 9025** (tape); **DKPCD 9024/25** (2 discs)

[with *Messe de la Pentecôte*, *Méditations sur le mystère de la Sainte Trinité*]
2) Hans-Ola Ericsson
BIS **BIS-CD 409**
[with *Le banquet céleste*, *Diptyque*, *Apparition de l'église éternelle*]
3) Susan Landale
Adda **58 1059**
[with *Les corps glorieux*]
4) Olivier Messiaen
EMI DUC 260 C 074; 2C 153 16291/6; **CZS 7 67400 2** (4 discs)
5) Olivier Messiaen
EMI 'Composers in person' DUC 260 C 074; 2C 153 16291/6; **CDC 5 550372**
[with *Le banquet céleste*; organ works by Widor, Vierne and Dupré]
6) Thomas Trotter
Decca **436 400–2 DH**
[with *Apparition de l'église éternelle*, *Diptyque*, *Messe de la Pentecôte*]
7) Gillian Weir
Collins **70312** (7 discs)]
[complete organ works]

La Nativité du Seigneur (neuf méditations)

1 La Vierge et l'Enfant 2 Les bergers 3 Desseins éternels 4 Le Verbe 5 Les enfants de Dieu 6 Les anges 7 Jésus accepte la souffrance 8 Les mages 9 Dieu parmi nous

COMPOSED: Grenoble, 1935
PUBLISHER: Leduc
RECORDINGS:
*1) Marie-Claire Alain
Erato ECD 75503; 2292–45505–2/XI; 2292–454470–2
[with *Le banquet céleste*, *Apparition de l'église éternelle*]
2) Jennifer Bate
Unicorn-Kanchana **DKPCD 9005**
[with *Le banquet céleste*]
3) Hans-Ola Ericsson
BIS **BIS-CD 410**
4) Susan Landale
Adda **58 1039**
[with *Le banquet céleste*, *Apparition de l'église éternelle*]
5) Olivier Messiaen
EMI DUC 260 C 075/6; 2C 153 16291/6; **CZS 7 67400 2** (4 discs)
6) Simon Preston

Decca ZRG 5447; 414 436–1LE; **425 161–2 DM 2** (2 discs)
[with *La Transfiguration*]

7) Gillian Weir
Collins **70312** (7 discs)
[complete organ works]

Les corps glorieux (sept visions brèves de la vie des ressuscités)

1 Subtilité des corps glorieux 2 Les eaux de la grâce 3 L'ange aux parfums 4 Combat de la mort et de la vie 5 Force et agilité des corps glorieux 6 Joie et clarté des corps glorieux 7 Le mystère de la Sainte Trinité

COMPOSED: Petichet, 1939 (completed 25 August)
PUBLISHER: Leduc
RECORDINGS:

1) Jennifer Bate
Unicorn-Kanchana **DKPC 9004; DKPCD 9004**
[with *Diptyque*]
2) Hans-Ola Ericsson
BIS **BIS-CD 442**
[with *Verset pour la fête de la Dédicace*]
3) Susan Landale
Adda **58 1059**
[with *L'Ascension*]
4) Olivier Messiaen
EMI DUC 260 C 077/8; 2C 153 16291/6; **CZS 7 67400 2** (4 discs)
5) Gillian Weir
Collins **70312** (7 discs)
[complete organ works]

Messe de la Pentecôte

1 Entrée (Les langues de feu) 2 Offertoire (Les choses visibles et invisibles) 3 Consécration (Le don de sagesse) 4 Communion (Les oiseaux et les sources) 5 Sortie (Le vent de l'Esprit)

COMPOSED: Tanglewood, 1949 – Paris, 1950
PUBLISHER: Leduc
RECORDINGS:

1) Jennifer Bate
Unicorn-Kanchana **DKPC 9025** (tape); **DKPCD 9024/25**
[with *Méditations sur le mystère de la Sainte Trinité*, *L'Ascension*]
2) Hans-Ola Ericsson
BIS **BIS-CD 441**
[with *Livre d'orgue*]
3) Olivier Messiaen

EMI DUC 260 C 079; 2C 153 16291/6; **CZS 7 67400 2** (4 discs)
4) Louis Thiry
Calliope **CAL 9927**
[with *Livre d'orgue*]
5) Thomas Trotter
Decca **436400–2 DH**
[with *Apparition de l'église éternelle*, *L'Ascension*, *Diptyque*]
6) Gillian Weir
Collins **70312** (7 discs)
[complete organ works]

Livre d'orgue

1 Reprises par interversion 2 Pièce en trio I 3 Les mains de l'abîme 4 Chants d'oiseaux 5 Pièce en trio II 6 Les yeux dans les roues 7 Soixante-quatre durées

COMPOSED: 1951
PUBLISHER: Leduc
RECORDINGS:
1) Jennifer Bate
Unicorn-Kanchana DKPC 9028; **DKPCD 9028**
[with *Apparition de l'église éternelle*, *Verset pour la fête de la Dédicace*]
2) Hans-Ola Ericsson
BIS **BIS-CD 441**
[with *Messe de la Pentecôte*]
3) Olivier Messiaen
EMI DUC 260 C 080/1; 2C 153 16291/6; **CZS 7 67400 2** (4 discs)
4) Louis Thiry
Calliope **CAL 9927**
[with *Messe de la Pentecôte*]
5) Gillian Weir
Collins **70312** (7 discs)
[complete organ works]

Verset pour la fête de la Dédicace

COMPOSED: Paris, December 1960
PUBLISHER: Leduc
RECORDINGS:
1) Jennifer Bate
Unicorn-Kanchana DKPC 9028; **DKPCD 9028**
[with *Livre d'orgue*, *Apparition de l'église éternelle*]
2) Hans-Ola Ericsson
BIS **BIS-CD 442**

[with *Les corps glorieux*]
3) Gillian Weir
Collins **70312** (7 discs)
[complete organ works]

Méditations sur le mystère de la Sainte Trinité

1–9 (untitled)

COMPOSED: 1969
PUBLISHER: Leduc
RECORDINGS:
1) Jennifer Bate
Unicorn-Kanchana **DKPC 9024** (tape) **DKPCD 9024/25** (2 discs)
[with *L'Ascension*, *Messe de la Pentecôte*]
2) Hans-Ola Ericsson
BIS **BIS-CD 464**
*3) Olivier Messiaen
Erato STU 70750–1; ECD 71594; 2292–45505–2/VII;
4509–92007–2 (2 discs)
[with *Trois petites liturgies*]
4) Gillian Weir
Collins **70312** (7 discs)
[complete organ works]

Livre du Saint Sacrement

1 Adoro te 2 La source de Vie 3 Le Dieu caché 4 Acte de Foi 5 Puer natus est nobis 6 La manne et le Pain de Vie 7 Les ressusicités et la Lumière de Vie 8 Institution de l'Eucharistе 9 Les ténèbres 10 La Résurrection du Christ 11 L'apparition du Christ ressucité à Marie-Madeleine 12 La Transsubstantiation 13 Les deux murailles d'eau 14 Prière avant la Communion 15 La joie de la grâce 16 Prière après la Communion 17 La Presence multipliée 18 Offrande et alléluia final

COMPOSED: 1984
PUBLISHER: Leduc
RECORDINGS:
1) Jennifer Bate
Unicorn-Kanchana DKPC 9067/8; **DKPCD 9067/8** (2 discs)
2) Hans-Ola Ericsson
BIS **BIS-CD 491/492**
[with European and Israeli birdsongs]
3) Almut Rössler
Motette **DCD 1106 1**

4) Gillian Weir
Collins 70312 (7 discs)
[complete organ works]

VI Piano

Yvonne Loriod and Peter Hill provide complementing interpretations of the composer's entire published output for piano. Peter Hill's cycle is undeniably superior in the quality of recorded sound, and this should form the basis of any collection of this repertoire. The commemorative Messiaen boxed set mentioned above is as much celebration of the talents of Yvonne Loriod as it is of Messiaen's music but Erato unaccountably neglected to transfer the 'minor' works, leaving the set incomplete.

La dame de Shalott

COMPOSED: Grenoble, 1917
RECORDINGS:
1) Yvonne Loriod
Erato OME 1 (8 records)
[with 'complete' piano music]

La tristesse d'un grand ciel blanc

COMPOSED: Paris, 1925

Préludes

1 La colombe 2 Chant d'extase dans un paysage triste 3 Le nombre léger 4 Instants défunts 5 Les sons impalpables du rêve 6 Cloches d'angoisse et larmes d'adieu 7 Plainte calme 8 Un reflet dans le vent . . .

COMPOSED: Fuligny, 1928–9
PUBLISHER: Durand
RECORDINGS:
1) Michel Béroff
EMI (Rouge et Noir) C 065–10.676/8; C 181–11.117/18; **CZS 7 69161 2** (2 discs)
[with *Vingt regards*]
2) Peter Hill
Unicorn-Kanchana DKP 9037; **DKPCD 9078**
[with *Quatre études*, *Cantéyodjayâ*]
*3) Yvonne Loriod
Erato STU 70433; OME 1; STU 70875; ECD 71589; 2292–45505–2/V

[with *Petites esquisses d'oiseaux*, *Quatre études*]

4) Yvonne Loriod
   Pathé Nos. 5, 1 and 3 PDT 132 (78, 2 sides)
      Side 1) CPTX 635–1
      Side 2) CPTX 636–2

Fantaisie burlesque

COMPOSED: 1932
PUBLISHER: Durand
RECORDINGS:

1) Peter Hill
   Unicorn-Kanchana DKP 9051; DKPCD 9144
   [with *Visions de l'Amen*, *Petites esquisses d'oiseaux*, *Pièce pour le tombeau de Paul Dukas*, *Rondeau*]
2) Yvonne Loriod
   Erato OME 1 (8 records)
   [with 'complete' piano music]

Pièce pour le tombeau de Paul Dukas

COMPOSED: Grenoble, 1935
PUBLISHED IN: Revue musicale, 166 (1936)
RECORDINGS:

1) Peter Hill
   Unicorn-Kanchana DKP 9037; DKPCD 9144
   [with *Visions de l'Amen*, *Petite esquisses d'oiseaux*, *Fantaisie burlesque*, *Rondeau*]
2) Yvonne Loriod
   Erato OME 1 (8 records)
   [with 'complete' piano music]

Rondeau

COMPOSED: Paris, 1943
PUBLISHER: Leduc
RECORDINGS:

1) Peter Hill
   Unicorn-Kanchana DKP 9051; DKPCD 9144
   [with *Visions de l'Amen*, *Petites esquisses d'oiseaux*, *Pièce pour le tombeau de Paul Dukas*, *Fantaisie burlesque*]
2) Yvonne Loriod
   Erato OME 1 (8 records)
   [with 'complete' piano music]

Visions de l'Amen

2 pianos

1 Amen de la création 2 Amen des étoiles, de la planète à l'anneau 3 Amen de l'agonie de Jésus 4 Amen du désir
5 Amen des anges, des saints, du chant des oiseaux 6 Amen du jugement 7 Amen de la consommation

COMPOSED: Paris, 1943
PUBLISHER: Durand
RECORDINGS:
1) Martha Argerich, Alexandre Rabinovitch
EMI **CDC 7 54040 2**
2) Peter Hill, Benjamin Frith
Unicorn-Kanchana **DKPCD 9144**
[with *Petites esquisses d'oiseaux*, *Fantaisie burlesque*, *Pièce pour le tombeau de Paul Dukas*, *Rondeau*]
*3) Katia Labèque, Marielle Labèque
Erato STU 70.567; MUS 1 9048; ECD 71588; 2292–45505–2/IV; **4509–91707–2**
[with *Les offrandes oubliées*, *Hymne au Sainte Sacrement*]
4) Yvonne Loriod, Olivier Messiaen
Adès 8.509; **AD 13 233–2**
[with *Cantéyodjayâ*]
5) Yvonne Loriod, Olivier Messiaen
NSA tape P 557 R (from BBC broadcast on 2 February 1970, with introduction in French by Messiaen)
6) Yvonne Loriod, Olivier Messiaen
NSA tape T949BW (from BBC broadcast on 24 March 1975)

Vingt regards sur l'Enfant-Jésus

1 Regard du Père 2 Regard de l'étoile 3 L'échange 4 Regard de la Vierge 5 Regard du Fils sur le Fils 6 Par lui tout a été fait 7 Regard de la Croix 8 Regard des hauteurs 9 Regards du temps 10 Regard de l'Esprit de joie 11 Première communion de la Vierge 12 La parole toute puissante 13 Nöel
14 Regard des anges 15 Le baiser de l'Enfant-Jésus
16 Regard des prophètes, des bergers et des mages 17 Regard du silence 18 Regard de l'onction terrible 19 Je dors, mais mon cœur veille 20 Regard de l'église d'amour

COMPOSED: Paris, 23 March – 8 September 1944
PUBLISHER: Durand
RECORDINGS:
1) Michel Béroff

EMI (Rouge et Noir) C 065–10.676/8; C 181–11.117/18; **CZS 7 69161 2** (2 discs)
[with *Préludes*]
2) Peter Hill
Unicorn-Kanchana **DKPCD 9122/23** (2 discs)
3) Yvonne Loriod
Erato OME 1; ECD 71581; 2292–45505–2/I (2 discs)
4) John Ogdon
Decca (Argo) ZRG 650/1; **430 343–2DM2** (2 discs)
5) Malcolm Troup
Continuum **CCD 1004/5** (2 discs)
6) Yvonne Loriod
Pathé No. 10 PDT 170 (78)
Side 1) CPTX 748–1
Side 2) CPTX 749–1
7) Yvonne Loriod
Pathé No. 15 PDT 113 (78)
Side 1) CPTX 633–1
Side 2) CPTX 634–1

Cantéyodjayâ

COMPOSED: 1949
PUBLISHER: Universal
RECORDINGS:
1) Peter Hill
Unicorn-Kanchana DKP 9037; **DKPCD 9078**
[with *Quatre études*, *Préludes*]
2) Yvonne Loriod
Adès 8.509; **AD 13 233–2**
[with *Visions de l'Amen*]
3) Yvonne Loriod
Erato OME 1 (8 records)
[with 'complete' piano music]
4) Yvonne Loriod
NSA tape (from BBC broadcast on 21 August 1977) P1192BW

Quatre études de rythme

1 *Ile de feu 1* 2 *Mode de valeurs et d'intensités* 3 *Neumes rythmiques* 4 *Ile de feu 2*

COMPOSED: (No. 1) Paris, 1950; (No. 2) Darmstadt, 1949; (No. 3) Tanglewood, 1949; (No. 4) Paris, 1950
PUBLISHER: Durand

RECORDINGS:

1) Peter Hill
   Unicorn-Kanchana DKP 9051; **DKPCD 9078**
   [with *Cantéyodjayâ*, *Préludes*]

*2) Yvonne Loriod
   Erato OME 1; STU 70.433; ECD 71589; 2292–45505–2V
   [with *Petites esquisses d'oiseaux*, *Préludes*]

3) Yuji Takahashi
   Denon **33CO–1052**
   [with Xenakis: *Evryali*, *Herma*]

4) Olivier Messiaen
   Pathé (sponsored by UNESCO) LFX 998/999 (78s)

LFX 998 Side 1) CLX 2843–21
Side 2) CLX 2844–21
LFX 999 Side 3) CLX 2845–21
Side 4) CLX 2846–21

Catalogue d'oiseaux

Book 1: 1 Le chocard des alpes 2 Le loriot 3 Le merle bleu
Book 2: 4 Le traquet stapazin
Book 3: 5 La chouette hulotte 6 L'alouette lulu
Book 4: 7 La rousserolle effarvatte
Book 5: 8 L'alouette calandrelle 9 La bouscarle
Book 6: 10 Le merle de roche
Book 7: 11 La buse variable 12 Le traquet rieur 13 Le courlis cendré

COMPOSED: October 1956 – 1 September 1958
PUBLISHER: Leduc
RECORDINGS:

1) Peter Hill
   Unicorn-Kanchana Books 1–3 DKPC 9062; **DKPCD 9062**
   Books 4–6 DKPC 9075; **DKPCD 9075**
   Book 7 DKPC 9090; **DKPCD 9090**
   [with *La fauvette des jardins*]

*2) Yvonne Loriod
   Erato OME 1; STU 70595–8; ECD 71590; 2292–45505–2/VI (3 discs)
   [with *La fauvette des jardins*]

3) Anatol Ugorski
   DG **439 214–2 GH 3** (3 discs)
   [with *La fauvette des jardins*]

La fauvette des jardins

COMPOSED: Petichet, 1970
PUBLISHER: Leduc
RECORDINGS:

1) Peter Hill
   Unicorn-Kanchana DKPC 9090; **DKPCD 9090**
   [with *Catalogue d'oiseaux*, Book 7]

*2) Yvonne Loriod
   Erato OME 1; STU 70796; ECD 71590; 2292–45505–2/VI (3 discs)
   [with *Catalogue d'oiseaux*]

3) Yvonne Loriod
   NSA tape P 951 Y (from BBC broadcast on 28 June 1973, with an introduction by Messiaen)

4) Anatol Ugorski
   DG **439 214–2 GH3** (3 discs)
   [*Catalogue d'oiseaux*]

Petites esquisses d'oiseaux

1 Le rouge-gorge 2 Le merle noir 3 Le rouge-gorge 4 La grive musicien 5 Le rouge-gorge 6 L'alouette des champs

COMPOSED: 1985
PUBLISHER: Leduc
RECORDINGS:

1) Peter Hill
   Unicorn-Kanchana **DKPCD 9144**
   [with *Visions de l'Amen*, *Fantaisie burlesque*, *Pièce pour le tombeau de Paul Dukas*, *Rondeau*

*2) Yvonne Loriod
   Erato OME 1; STU 70.433; ECD 71589; 2292–45505–2/V
   [with *Quatre études de rythme*, *Préludes*]

VII Electronic

Fêtes des belles eaux

SCORING: 6 ondes martenot
COMPOSED: Paris, 1937
RECORDINGS:

1) Ondes martenot ensemble, soloist Jeanne Loriod
   Erato STU 70.102
   [with works by Milhaud and J. Charpentier]

2) Sextuor Jeanne Loriod
   Adès 21.007 (2 records)
   [with works by Milhaud, Jolivet, Tessier]

Deux monodies en quarts de ton

SCORING: ondes martenot
COMPOSED: Paris, 1938

Musique de scène pour un Œdipe

SCORING: ondes martenot
COMPOSED: Paris, 1942

Timbres-durées

SCORING: tape
COMPOSED: 1952
REALIZED BY: Pierre Henry
[NB withdrawn]

Bibliography

Messiaen's Publications

With others: *Vingt leçons de solfège moderne* (Paris, Lemoine, 1933)
'Ariane et Barbe-bleue de Paul Dukas': *Revue musicale*, 166 (1936), pp. 79–86
'Le rythme chez Igor Strawinsky': *Revue musicale*, 191 (1939), pp. 91–2
Vingt leçons d'harmonie (Paris, Leduc, 1944; English translation, Leduc, 1957)
Technique de mon langage musical (Paris, Leduc, 1944; English translation, Leduc, 1956)
Preface to André Jolivet: *Mana* (Paris, Costallat, 1946)
'Maurice Emmanuel: ses "trente chansons bourguignonnes': *Revue musicale*, 206 (1947), p. 108
Conférence de Bruxelles (Paris, Leduc, 1958)
With Bernard Gavoty: 'Who are you, Olivier Messiaen?' *Tempo*, 58 (1961), pp. 33–6
Conférence de Notre-Dame (Paris, Leduc, 1978)
With Claude Samuel: *Musique et couleur: nouveaux entretiens* (Paris, Belfond, 1986)
Traité de rythme, de couleur et d'ornithologie (Paris, Leduc, in preparation)

Books on Messiaen

Ahrens, Sieglinde, Möller, Hans-Dieter, and Rössler, Almut: *Das Orgelwerk Messiaens* (Duisburg, Gilles und Francke, 1976)
Bell, Carla: *Olivier Messiaen* (Boston, Twayne, 1984)
Borum, Paul, and Christensen, Erik: *Messiaen: en handbog* (Copenhagen, Egtved, 1977)
Goléa, Antoine: *Rencontres avec Olivier Messiaen* (Paris, Julliard, 1960)

Griffiths, Paul: *Olivier Messiaen and the Music of Time* (London/Boston, Faber and Faber, 1985)
Halbreich, Harry: *Olivier Messiaen* (Paris, Fayard/SACEM, 1980)
Hirsbrunner, Theo: *Olivier Messiaen: Leben und Werk* (Laaber, Laaber-Verlag, 1988)
Hohlfeld-Ufer, Ingrid: *Die musikalische Sprache Olivier Messiaens, dargestellt an dem Orgelzyklus 'Die Pfingstmesse'*; with Almut Rössler: *Zur Interpretation der Orgelwerke Messiaens* (Duisburg, Gilles und Francke, 1978)
Johnson, Robert Sherlaw: *Messiaen* (London, Dent, 1976, R/1989)
Mari, Pierrette: *Olivier Messiaen: L'homme et son œuvre* (Paris, Seghers, 1965)
Massin, Brigitte, *Olivier Messiaen: une poetique de merveilleux* (Aix-en-Provence, Alinéa, 1989)
Metzger, Heinz-Klaus, and Riehn, Rainer (eds): *Olivier Messiaen* (Munich, Text + Kritik, 1982)
Morris, David: *Messiaen: A Comparative Bibliography* (Belfast, University of Ulster, 1991)
Nichols, Roger: *Messiaen* (London, Oxford University Press, 1975, 2/1986)
Perier, Alain: *Messiaen* (Paris, Seuil, 1979)
Reverdy, Michèle: *L'œuvre pour piano d'Olivier Messiaen* (Paris, Leduc, 1978)
Reverdy, Michèle: *L'œuvre pour orchestre d'Olivier Messiaen* (Paris, Leduc, 1988)
Rössler, Almut: *Contributions to the Spiritual World of Olivier Messiaen* (Duisburg, Gilles und Francke, 1986)
Rostand, Claude: *Olivier Messiaen* (Paris, Ventadour, 1958)
Samuel, Claude: *Entretiens avec Olivier Messiaen* (Paris, Belfond, 1967; English translation, London, 1976)
Samuel, Claude: *Musique et couleur: nouveaux entretiens* (Paris, Belfond, 1986)
Waumsley, Stuart: *The Organ Music of Olivier Messiaen* (Paris, Leduc, 1968)

Other Literature

Armfelt, Nicolas: 'Emotion in the Music of Messiaen', *Musical Times*, cvi (1965), pp. 856–8
Barraqué, Jean: 'Rythme et dévéloppement', *Polyphonie*, 9–10 (1954), pp. 47–73
Bernard, Jonathan W.: 'Messiaen's Synaesthesia: the Correspondence

Between Color and Sound Structure in His Music', *Music Perception*, iv (1986) pp. 41–68

Boulez, Pierre: 'Olivier Messiaen', *Anhaltspunkte* (Stuttgart and Zurich, Belser, 1975), pp. 154–62

Burkat, Leonard: '*Turangalîla-symphonie*', *Musical Quarterly*, xxxvi (1950), pp. 259–68

Demuth, Norman: 'Messiaen's Early Birds', *Musical Times*, ci (1960), pp. 627–9

Drew, David: 'Messiaen: a Provisional Study', *The Score*, 10 (1954), pp. 33–49; 13 (1955), pp. 59–73; 14 (1955), pp. 41–61

Evans, Adrian: 'Olivier Messiaen in the Surrealist Context: a Bibliography', *Brio*, xi (1975) pp. 25–35

Gardiner, Bennett: 'Dialogues with Messiaen', *Musical Events*, xxii (1967), pp. 6–9

Heiss, Hellmut: 'Struktur und Symbolik in "Reprises par interversion" und "Les mains de l'abîme" aus Olivier Messiaens *Livre d'orgue*', *Zeitschrift für Musiktheorie*, i/2 (1970) pp. 32–8

Hold, Trevor: 'Messiaen's Birds', *Music and Letters*, lii (1971) pp. 113–22

Melos, xxv/12 (1958), Messiaen issue

Messiaen Festival Programme Book (Paris, La recherche artistique, 1978)

Morris, David, 'A semiotic investigation of Messiaen's "Abîme des oiseaux" ', *Music Analysis*, viii (1989) pp. 125–58

Musik-Konzepte, 28 (1982), Messiaen issue

Nichols, Roger, 'Boulez on Messiaen', *Organists' Review*, lxxi/283 (August 1986/3), pp. 167–70

Nichols, Roger: 'Messiaen's "Le merle noir": the Case of a Blackbird in a Historical Pie', *Musical Times*, cxxix (1988), pp. 648–50

Samuel, Claude, 'Discographie complète', *Diapason-Harmonie*, 344 (December, 1988), pp. 78–9

Smalley, Roger, 'Debussy and Messiaen', *Musical Times*, cix (1968), pp. 128–31

Walker, Rosemary, 'Modes and pitch-class sets in Messiaen: a Brief Discussion of "Première communion de la Vierge" ', *Music Analysis*, viii (1989), pp. 159–68

Watts, Harriet: 'Canyons, Colours and Birds: an Interview with Olivier Messiaen', *Tempo*, 128 (1979), pp. 2–8

Contributors

PETER HILL, the editor of *The Messiaen Companion*, is a leading interpreter of the music of Messiaen. He has recorded all Messiaen's music for solo piano and two pianos, and studied with the composer during the last years of his life. Noted for his writings and broadcasts on twentieth-century music, he holds a Personal Chair in music at the University of Sheffield.

JONATHAN BERNARD earned his bachelor's degree at Harvard College and his doctorate at Yale University. Since 1987 he has taught at the School of Music, University of Washington (Seattle), where he is now Professor of Theory and Associate Director for Academic Affairs. He is the author of *The Music of Edgard Varèse*, published by Yale University Press in 1987, and of numerous articles on a wide range of topics including eighteenth-century theory, minimalism, and the music of Varèse, Messiaen, Carter, Ligeti and Bartók. He is currently at work on a book about the music of Ligeti.

PAUL GRIFFITHS has written several books on music, including *Olivier Messiaen and the Music of Time* (1985). He was music critic of *The Times* from 1982 to 1992, then he moved to *The New Yorker.*

MALCOLM HAYES studied music at St Andrews and Edinburgh Universities, lived for seven years in the Outer Hebrides working mainly in the weaving industry, and now lives in London. Formerly music critic of the *Sunday Telegraph* from 1986 to 1989, he is now a music critic with *The Daily Telegraph* and also writes regularly for *Opera Now* magazine. He is currently working on a biographical study of Webern for Phaidon Press.

ROBERT SHERLAW JOHNSON is a Fellow of Worcester College, Oxford. He is also a composer and a pianist, specializing in the piano works of Messiaen. He has made recordings of his own works as well as those of Messiaen and Liszt and he gave the first complete performance in England of *Catalogue d'oiseaux* at Coventry Cathedral in

1973. His book, *Messiaen*, was published by J. M. Dent in 1975 and was reissued in an enlarged edition in 1989.

JANE MANNING is recognized internationally as a leading exponent of contemporary vocal music, and has given more than 300 world premieres. She made her professional debut in 1964 and maintains an active performing career; her recordings include all Messiaen's major song cycles and Schoenberg's *Pierrot lunaire*. In 1988 she formed her own ensemble of young musicians, *Jane's Minstrels*. She has been Visiting Professor at Mills College, California, and artist-in-residence at universities all over North America and Australasia, and frequently gives master classes and seminars for singers and composers at academic centres and festivals around the world. Her book *New Vocal Repertory*, published in 1985, will be issued in a new edition in 1994. She was awarded an honorary doctorate by the University of York in 1988, and received the OBE in 1990.

IAIN MATHESON was born near Stirling in 1956, and grew up in Glasgow. At school he became fascinated by the music of Ives and Ligeti, and went on to gain a B.Mus from Glasgow University. After work with a (very) small theatre group and as a piano teacher, he returned to Glasgow University to study theology. He is now a minister of the Church of Scotland, and is particularly interested in the relationship between the arts and Christian theology.

WILFRID MELLERS is Emeritus Professor of Music, University of York, having been the founding professor of the department in 1963. He has written many books, including *François Couperin and the French Classical Tradition* (1950, revised edition 1987); *Music in a New Found Land: Themes and Developments in American Music* (1964); *Man and His Music* (1957, with several later editions); *Bach and the Dance of God* (1981); *Beethoven and the Choice of God* (1983); *Vaughan Williams and the Vision of Albion* (1989); *Percy Grainger* (1992); *Francis Poulenc* (1993). He has also written extensively about pop and folk musics (the Beatles, and Bob Dylan), and on music education. A pupil of Edmund Rubbra and of Egon Wellesz, he was active as a composer during the fifties, sixties and seventies. He has made many academic visits to the United States and to Australia; and still lectures itinerantly at summer schools.

JOHN MILSOM is a lecturer in music at Christ Church, Oxford. He studied composition at the University of Surrey, and took his doctorate at Oxford University with a study of Tallis. Best known for his work on early music, he retains a keen interest in the twentieth century, and regularly reviews new recordings of contemporary music for *Gramophone*.

ANTONY POPLE is head of the Music Department at Lancaster University. He has published widely on twentieth-century music, and his books include *Skryabin and Stravinsky: 1908–1914* and *Berg: Violin Concerto*. A member of the editorial board of the journal *Music Analysis*, he is also the producer of Peter Hill's acclaimed series of Messiaen recordings for Unicorn-Kanchana.

RICHARD STEINITZ is a Professor of Music at the University of Huddersfield and Artistic Director of Huddersfield Contemporary Music Festival, one of the world's leading new music festivals, which he founded in 1978. He was a music scholar at King's College, Cambridge and studied composition with Goffredo Petrassi. Several of his works have been broadcast, and he writes regularly for the BBC and music journals. Recently he has contributed a number of essays to *Contemporary Composers* published by St James Press in 1992.

MALCOLM TROUP had devoted much of his career to the study and advocacy of Messiaen's music. A noted pianist, he has recorded excerpts from the *Catalogue d'oiseaux* for RCA, and a much admired version of the *Vingt regards* (Continuum). A former Director of Music at the Guildhall School of Music and Drama, he founded the Department of Music at City University where he holds a personal chair.

GILLIAN WEIR. The concert organist Gillian Weir CBE is known internationally for her advocacy of the music of Messiaen. She gave the British premiere of the *Méditations sur le mystère de la Sainte Trinité*, from the composer's manuscript, and among her many performances of the complete cycle of the organ works are those for the BBC, Epo '88, and at the Royal Festival Hall for the European Festival celebrating his eightieth birthday. In 1988 she was artist-in-residence with the composer for the Australian Broadcasting Corporation's major Messiaen Festival. She has written and lectured widely on the organ works and is regarded as a leading interpreter and authority.

Index of Messiaen's Works

General Index

Note: Works by Messiaen will be found in the Index of Messiaen's Works; works by other composers are listed at the end of the composer's entry.